TEACHING ABOUT SCIENCE AND SOCIETY:

Activities for Elementary and Junior High School

Rodger Bybee
Carleton College

Rita Peterson
University of California — Irvine

Jane Bowyer
Mills College

David Butts
The University of Georgia

Charles E. Merrill Publishing Company
A *Bell & Howell Company*
Columbus Toronto London Sydney

Published by
Charles E. Merrill Publishing Co.
A Bell & Howell Company
Columbus, Ohio 43216

This book was set in Helvetica
Production Coordinator: Jan Hall
Text Design: Cynthia Brunk
Cover Design: Tony Faiola
Cover image courtesy of: Jean Greenwald

Library of Congress Catalog Card Number: 83–43231
International Standard Book Number 0–675–20059–8

1 2 3 4 5 6 7 8 9—89 88 87 86 85 84
Printed in the United States of America

PREFACE

American education is under review. In the early 1980's several national commissions have evaluated the status and needs of education. The findings indicate that a period of change and reform is required. While recent educational history has witnessed a "back to basics" movement, the national commissions have been unanimous in suggesting that science and technology education should be updated and included among the basics.

There are inevitable comparisons of American priorities with those of other countries. Whether the comparison is with the Soviet Union's military or with Japan's economy, the discussions show the central position of science to society.

Two challenges for science and technology education are evident. One challenge is the need for more scientists and engineers. A second is the development of scientifically and technologically literate citizens. Teachers in elementary and middle schools can help meet both of these challenges. The first way to meet the challenges is to teach more science. This is up to the individual teacher since he or she decides the emphasis given to different subjects. The second way to meet the challenge is through a curriculum and activities that maintain and enhance student interest in science and technology. Finally, there is a need to introduce scientific and technological concepts in a social context. You must make the decision to meet the first challenge and increase the time spent teaching science. In order to help you meet the second and third challenges we have developed the activities for this book.

Teaching About Science and Society can be used as a companion volume to *Science and Society* or it can be used independently. Although some activities are found in both texts, the overlap is marginal, only ten activities out of eighty-two. We felt the need for continuity, completeness, and balance justified the inclusion of those ten activities in the two books.

Teaching About Science and Society begins with an introduction by Rodger Bybee. Activities are organized into four major sections: Environmental Biology, written by Rita Peterson, Health and Nutrition, written by Jane Bowyer, Physical

Science, written by Rodger Bybee and David Butts, and Earth and Environmental Science, written by Rodger Bybee. The activities are divided into grade levels: kindergarten through second grade (K-2), third grade through fifth grade (3-5) and sixth grade through eighth grade (6-8). Each grade level section is preceded by a planning chart that provides an overview of the activities. Each major group of activities concludes with an annotated listing of resources for that discipline.

The individual activities are designed to meet the needs of new and practicing elementary and middle school teachers. Activities begin with an *overview* that provides a summary of the lesson. Next there is a section on *science background* in which the major concepts are presented in a short "in depth" discussion for the teacher. This discussion is intended to provide an understanding of the scientific content of the lesson. A section on *societal implications* follows. Here the scientific content is extended to the social context. The next sections are basic to most lessons: *major concepts, objectives, materials, vocabulary* and *procedures*. We hope *Teaching About Science and Society* will help you meet the challenges confronting education in the 1980's. We have tried to design a book to assist you in your efforts.

We would like to conclude by expressing our appreciation to all who assisted in any way with this project. We realize that the recognition for this book extends to many, and we thank you.

RB
RP
JB
DB

CONTENTS

II   HEALTH AND NUTRITION ACTIVITIES

TEACHING ABOUT SCIENCE AND SOCIETY:

Activities for Elementary and Junior High School

Teaching about Science and Society: An Introduction and Rationale

Rodger W. Bybee
Carleton College

Many citizens are deeply concerned about economic trends, employment opportunities, social welfare and their quality of life. Issues underlying these concerns are related to the broad theme of science and society. On one side of the ledger there are scientific discoveries, technological innovations and medical advances that promise to make life better. On the other side there are resource shortages, environmental mismanagement, population problems and a nuclear armaments race that threaten the quality of life, or life itself.

While most individuals share a vision of a better future, projections of global trends, particularly those related to population growth, resources use and environmental deterioration, are not encouraging. The effects of these trends are going to concern citizens for the next decades. The effects of these trends are particularly relevant to the theme of this essay and book. I will summarize some projections from *The Global 2000 Report to the President* (U.S. Government Printing Office, Washington, D.C. 1980). This study was a major attempt to identify and evaluate long-term changes in the world's population, natural resources, and environment. Completed under government sponsorship, the report was the most comprehensive study to date, and its findings were generally consistent with other global studies. Some of the major projections for the year 2000 were:

☐ The world population will be 6.35 billion. This represents a 50 percent increase between 1975, when the population was 4.1 billion, and the year 2000. Most of this growth will occur in less developed countries.

☐ World food production will increase at a higher statistical rate than the population between 1970 and 2000. This increase will be in developed countries. Per capita food consumption in less developed countries will improve only slightly, or it will decline. In developed countries real food prices will probably rise because the cost of production will increase due to substantial use of fertilizers and pesticides.

1

- ☐ Agricultural areas will increase only slightly. Present agricultural lands will continue to deteriorate through erosion, loss of organic matter, and desertification.
- ☐ Fuels will continue to become scarce and prices will rise as production costs increase.
- ☐ Water resources will decline due to depletion of groundwater supplies, deforestation, and contamination. The population growth will, on the other hand, double the present requirements for water.
- ☐ Extinction of plant and animal species will increase significantly, primarily because of reduction of tropical forests.
- ☐ Atmospheric pollution will increase because of the processing and use of fossil fuels. Damage to freshwater lakes, aquatic flora and fauna, soils, forest resources, buildings, and human health due to acid rain are predictable results.
- ☐ All of these conditions — population growth, resource use, and environmental damage — will result in price increases in basic necessities such as food, fuel, clothing, and housing. There will also be demands for investment in environmental protection and restoration and public health.

My intention in presenting this summary is not to outline a doomsday scenario. It is the opposite. All of these statistics are only *projections based on present trends*. The point is simple. Trends can change. And educators are in a central position to facilitate the change.

Nations, communities and individuals can develop new policies and practices that will bring about trends with favorable results by the year 2000. Without question, there are many possibilities that may change these projections: technological innovations, adjustments due to market mechanisms, governmental interventions, and changes in social and personal values are only a few examples. We need not debate the merits of these means for changing the trends described earlier. Advocating only one approach misses the point. In all likelihood, many means will be used to alter present trends and to achieve the kind of world all people desire. Many of the improvements will be based on knowledgeable foresight and intelligent action by citizens. Here is where the role of education, and particularly science education, will play a valuable part.

The role of education has been obscured in debates about science-related social issues. Now it is time to give full recognition to the important role of education. I hope that the introduction has established the need for a theme of science and society in educational programs.

SCIENCE, EDUCATION AND SOCIETY

Let me briefly summarize my theme and then establish the educational connection. Our society is in the midst of a period of significant change. The signals for this transformation are abundant: economic problems, the energy crisis, environmental deterioration, resource depletion, and worker alienation. Weaving through discussions of these issues, as both hero and villain, is the recurrent theme of science and technology. The present social situation requires a rethinking of science education goals, programs, and practices. The historical moment makes clear the necessity of teaching citizens about science and society.

Science education exists within society. It is also closely related to the enterprise of science. These associations help define the purposes, policies, and practices of science teaching. The association also creates a source of conflict among those who formulate policies. This conflict often occurs among those primarily concerned with the enterprise of science, with science education, or with education in general. The interaction among these different factions usually brings the conflict to constructive resolution. There is a delicate balance that must be achieved in formulating policies for science education. The appropriate scientific and educational aims for the society must be achieved. Science educators must be mindful of changes in science, education, and society, especially as they focus attention on science education for the citizen.

Once formed, curriculum and instruction procedures in science education tend to remain in use for a long period of time. While there is some change through textbook revisions, teacher education and other methods, with time science programs become outdated. A variety of current problems such as budgets, enrollments, obsolete materials, and uninterested students all indicate the need for change. This seems to be the present situation of science programs, especially in the United States. Several national commissions have supported the thrust of my argument. The need to establish new programs and practices becomes apparent when either the general social situation or the situation in the schools is examined.

A BRIEF HISTORICAL REVIEW OF CHANGES IN SCIENCE EDUCATION

Historically, it is possible to identify different policy orientations in science education. The policy orientations resulted from the interaction among scientific, educational, and societal forces. At the beginning of science education in America, in the mid-eighteenth century, the dominant method of science instruction was teaching factual information that supported theological ideas. As the nineteenth century approached, religious indoctrination decreased and utilitarian objectives increased. The goal of science instruction was to contribute to the development of a new nation.

In the 1860's, an educational innovation called object lessons became a part of science education policies. The object lesson movement was based on the ideas of Johan Pestalozzi. The aim of object lessons was to align science curriculum and instruction with the child's natural development.

In the 1880's, both science and society influenced science education policies. The social pressure was a response to the post-Civil War depression of 1873. Pressure was exerted by the scientific and technological community because of their importance in the industrialization process.

About the turn of the century the nature study movement emerged from the object lesson movement. The nature study movement was an educational means for achieving the social end of slowing population migration from rural settings to urban centers. The migration had been catalyzed by the need for industrial workers and a decline in the need for agricultural laborers. As the role of science and technology became central to industrial development, science education policies reflecting this orientation became dominant. In time, the nature study movement waned.

In the early twentieth century, the progressive model of education, with its social and democratic aims, became influential in science education programs. The policies of the Progressive Education Association and John Dewey did not have the same emphasis as the "scientific" model of science education.

The final reformulation of science education policies was the curriculum reform movement of the late 1950's and 1960's. The primary purpose for developing new science education programs was social. There was a shortage of trained scientists, which was symbolized by America's falling behind in the space race with the Soviet Union. New science programs were almost exclusively scientific in orientation, reflecting the "structure of a discipline." The new policies and programs were intended to increase the quantity and quality of scientists and engineers. The orientation toward "the structure of a discipline" was reinforced by the fact that scientists were primarily responsible for the design of educational programs. This orientation was appropriate for the stated social and scientific needs.

In this brief historical survey I have tried to show that science education policies are formed through the interaction of science, education and society. In the introduction I made a case for including science and society topics because of population, resource, and environmental problems. Calls for update and modification of science programs may also be based on other social needs. There are two immediate examples. American education is inevitably cited in economic comparisons with Japan and in military comparisons with the Soviet Union. In both cases there are demands for more scientists and engineers. A third example centers on scientific advances and computer technology and discussions of an "information society." Here there is a broader need for scientific and technological literacy. So, we again return to the theme of this essay. The present social, scientific and educational situation suggests that science education policies should emphasize teaching citizens about science and society.

EDUCATING CITIZENS ABOUT SCIENCE AND SOCIETY

Before continuing with the science and society theme, a subtheme of citizenship should be mentioned. In *The Revival of Civic Learning* by R. Freeman Butts (Phi Delta Kappa Educational Foundation, 1980), the author presents the thesis that the idea of citizenship was developed in two major periods. The first period was the establishment of Greek city-states and occurred from the seventh to the fourth centuries B.C. Citizenship based on membership in a political community rather than family, clan, or tribe was a significant change. Secondly, citizenship meant that laws were set, administered, and judged by free citizens. Both of these ideas remain important today.

The second period in which citizenship was both revived and redefined was the late eighteenth century. In *The Age of Democratic Revolutions: A Political History of Europe and America, 1760-1800* (Princeton University Press, 1959) Robert Palmer outlines the thesis that the idea of citizenship was reformulated through revolutions such as those that occurred in America and France. The revolutions had separate origins, but according to Palmer, they were initiated by citizens in order to maintain their freedom. A nation-state concept of citizenship resulted from the new social orders created by these revolutions.

4

We are now in the process of reformulating the idea of citizenship for the third time. The nation-state concept is evolving into a nation-globe concept. All nations are realizing the fact of global interdependence. Earlier discussions of population, environment, and resources underscored the interdependence theme. World interdependence is not without its problems. Still, it seems to be a dominant social trend, and one that educators can ill afford to ignore. As in the past, this shift to global citizenship does not eliminate the fact that one is still a citizen owing allegiance to a particular nation, state, city, or family.

The discussion in this section is intended to help determine what kind of society we should be teaching citizens about. The answer is a global society. I now turn to more specific questions of science education.

SCIENTIFIC AND TECHNOLOGICAL LITERACY

"What should the scientifically and technologically literate person know, do, and value as a citizen?" I would answer this question by outlining a policy for science education. The policy can in turn be translated into practices, through lessons such as those included in this book.

Science education programs should help citizens: (1) fulfill basic human needs and facilitate personal development; (2) maintain and improve the physical and human environment; (3) conserve natural resources; and (4) develop greater social harmony at the local, regional, national and global levels.

The first aspect of scientific and technological literacy has to do with the *practical use of science and technology* by individuals. Physiological needs such as food, air, and water are basic for all in society. So, too, are needs associated with safety, security, sense of self and relation to others. While science and technology cannot solve all practical problems, they can help resolve some of them. By focusing on the basic needs of individuals, it is easy to show that all individuals have needs, even though the needs may differ in developing and developed countries. Examples of the practical use of knowledge and skills are plentiful: appropriate diet, energy efficiency in homes, the effects of inappropriate food, air, and water, and the long-term detrimental effects of personal habits such as smoking.

Related to the practical uses of scientific and technological literacy are the need to maintain and improve environments, and the need to conserve resources. These are probably the areas where most citizens confront the need for scientific and technological knowledge. Participation in the democratic process requires some knowledge of scientific concepts and processes, as well as an understanding of the limits and possibilities of science and technology. Citizens should either understand enough about science and technology to make their decisions known, or they should know how to acquire and use the information sources to which they have access. Understanding *science and technology in social issues* is the second major component of literacy. Many examples of this type of scientific and technological literacy have already been presented, such as an understanding of population, pollution, energy, and acid rain.

Finally, there is a need to stress the humanistic side of science and technology. This is an appeal to teach *about science and technology in society* — its assets and liabilities, its products and processes. This type of literacy includes

5

knowledge, and attitudes about science and technology as an important human endeavor and social force. Some of the essential goals for citizens in this area of literacy include understanding the relationship between research and development and social progress, understanding the connection between technological innovation and employment, and recognizing problems associated with science and technology. Literacy in this area also includes some understanding of the history, philosophy, sociology, and psychology of science and technology. Teaching can demonstrate the fact that science and technology as an enterprise is able to transcend a particular culture and contribute to global welfare. Students should also see that science and technology exist in their own society at personal, local and national levels.

TEACHING ABOUT SCIENCE AND TECHNOLOGY IN SOCIETY

The ideas in this section represent some ways in which science curriculum and instruction could be modified to meet the policies stated. I should point out that these ideas do not represent a curriculum and are not intended to prevent new ideas, topics or approaches from being used.

In the next decades it will be important for science teachers to address many scientific, technological and social problems. Some important problems include armaments, population, natural resources, renewable and non-renewable energy, food, environment, and climate. To understand these topics, it will be necessary for students to apply concepts such as systems, synergy and symbiosis, information, communication and feedback, producer and consumer competition and cooperation, interaction, interrelationship and interdependence, and cost, benefit, and risk.

Students should be encouraged to use holistic, as well as reductive, thinking as they resolve problems. A holistic perspective is an essential complement to the reductive approach that is prevalent in science programs. Science teachers can help students develop holistic concepts of problems by starting with simple concepts, such as a system and subsystem, and applying this concept to increasingly larger domains.

Today's problems do not lend themselves to the neat compartments of academic disciplines. Energy, for example, has to do with physics, chemistry, biology and the host of earth sciences. In addition, it has to do with sociology, economics and politics. It is a disservice to students and future citizens to fail to introduce them to the interdisciplinary nature of contemporary problems.

Science programs should extend the student's perceptual orientation from the present to the future, from self to society to humanity, and from isolated phenomena to interacting systems.

These are a few of the ideas that should guide the selection, organization and teaching of lessons about science and technology in society.

Science and Society: A Bibliography

This bibliography is for elementary and middle school teachers who are interested in the general theme of science and technology in society and in more specific topics related to population, resources, and the environment.

GENERAL

Ian G. Barbour. *Technology, Environment, and Human Values.* New York: Praeger, 1980.

Gerald O. Barney (Director). *The Global 2000 Report to the President.* Washington, D.C.: U.S. Government Printing Office, 1980.

Lester R. Brown. *Building a Sustainable Society.* New York: W. W. Norton, 1981.

———. *The Twenty-Ninth Day.* New York: W. W. Norton, 1978.

Harrison Brown. *The Human Future Revisited.* New York: W. W. Norton, 1978.

Rachel Carson. *Silent Spring.* Greenwich, Ct.: Fawcett Books, 1964.

Barry Commoner. *The Closing Circle.* New York: Bantam, 1974.

Council on Environment Quality. *Global Future: Time to Act.* Washington, D.C.: U.S. Government Printing Office, 1981.

René Dubos. *The Wooing of Earth.* New York: Charles Scribners' Sons, 1980.

William Faunce. *Problems of an Industrial Society.* New York: McGraw-Hill, 1981.

Gerald Feinberg. *Consequences of Growth.* New York: Seabury Press, 1977.

Albert Fritsch. *Environmental Ethics.* New York: Anchor Books, 1980.

Willis Harman. *An Incomplete Guide to the Future.* New York: W. W. Norton, 1979.

Erwin Laszlo, ed. *Goals for Mankind.* New York: E. P. Dutton, 1977.

William McNeill. *The Human Condition.* Princeton: Princeton University Press, 1980.

Donella Meadows, Dennis Meadows, Jorgen Runders, and William Behrens, III. *The Limits to Growth.* New York: New American Library, 1974.

John Naisbitt. *Megatrends.* New York: Warner Books, 1982.

The National Research Council. *Science and Technology: A Five Year Outlook.* San Francisco: W. H. Freeman, 1979.

Colin Norman. *The God That Limps: Science and Technology in the Eighties.* New York: W. W. Norton, 1981.

William Ophuls. *Ecology and the Politics of Scarcity.* San Francisco: W. H. Freeman, 1977.

Dennis Pirages. *The Sustainable Society.* New York: Praeger, 1977.

E. F. Schumacher. *Small is Beautiful.* New York: Harper and Row, 1973.
Maurice Strong, ed. *Who Speaks for Earth?* New York: W. W. Norton, 1973.
Jan Tinbergen. *Reshaping the International Order.* New York: E. P. Dutton, 1976.
Barbara Ward. *Progress for a Small Planet.* New York: W. W. Norton, 1979.
Barbara Ward and René Dubos. *Only One Earth.* New York: W. W. Norton, 1972.
Glen E. Watts, chair. *Science and Technology: Promises and Dangers in The Eighties.*
New York: W. W. Norton, 1981.

INTERRELATION OF POPULATION, RESOURCES, AND ENVIRONMENT

Daniel Botkin and Edward Keller. *Environmental Studies: The Earth As a Living Planet.*
Columbus, Oh.: C. E. Merrill, 1982.
Paul Ehrlich, Anne Ehrlich and John Holdren. *Ecoscience: Population, Resources and
Environment.* San Francisco: W. H. Freeman, 1977.
G. Tyler Miller. *Living in the Environment.* Belmont: Wadsworth, 1982.
Joseph M. Moran, Michael D. Morgan, and James H. Wiersma. *Introduction to Environ-
mental Science.* San Francisco: W. H. Freeman, 1980.
P. Walton Purdom and Stanley Anderson. *Environmental Science: Managing the Environ-
ment.* 2d ed. Columbus, Oh.: C. E. Merrill, 1983.

POPULATION

Kathryn M. Fowler. *Population Growth: The Human Dilemma.* Washington, D.C.: National
Science Teachers Association, 1977.
Phillip Hauser. *World Population and Development: Challenges and Prospects.* Syracuse,
N.Y.: Syracuse University Press, 1979.
Priscilla Reining and Irene Tinker, eds. *Population: Dynamics, Ethics and Policy.* Washing-
ton, D.C.: American Association for the Advancement of Science, 1975.
Zero Population Growth. 1346 Connecticut Ave, N.W., Washington, D.C., 20036. Numerous
publications available free if you include a self-addressed stamped envelope.

FOOD AND AGRICULTURE

Phillip Abelson, ed. *Food: Politics, Economics, Nutrition and Research.* Washington, D.C.:
American Association for the Advancement of Science, 1975.
Lester R. Brown. *By Bread Alone.* New York: Praeger, 1974.
Erik Eckholm. *Losing Ground: Environmental Stress and World Food Prospects.* New
York: W. W. Norton, 1976.
Frances Moore Lappé and Joseph Collins. *Food First.* Boston: Houghton Mifflin, 1977.
Scientific American. "Special Issue on Food and Agriculture." Vol. 235, No. 3. September,
1976.

ENERGY

Phillip Abelson, ed. *Energy: Use, Conservation, Supply.* Washington, D.C.: American
Association for the Advancement of Science, 1974.
Denis Hayes. *Rays of Hope: The Transition to a Post Petroleum World.* New York:
W. W. Norton, 1977.
Amory Lovins. *Soft Energy Paths.* Cambridge, Ma.: Ballinger, 1977.
———. *World Energy Strategies.* Cambridge, Ma.: Ballinger, 1975.
Scientific American. *Energy and Power.* San Francisco: W. N. Freeman, 1971.

Robert Stobaugh and Daniel Yergin, eds. *Energy Future.* New York: Random House, 1983.

Daniel Yergin and Martin Hillenbrand, eds. *Global Insecurity: A Strategy for Energy and Economic Renewal.* Boston: Houghton Mifflin, 1982.

RESOURCES

American Association for the Advancement of Science. *Materials: Renewable and NonRenewable Resources.* Washington, D.C.: American Association for the Advancement of Science, 1976.

Committee on Mineral Resources and the Environment, National Research Council. *Mineral Resources and the Environment.* Washington, D.C.: National Academy of Science, 1975.

Conservation Foundation. *Water Resources. State of the Environment, 1982.* Washington, D.C.: Conservation Foundation, 1982.

BIOLOGICAL DIVERSITY

Erik Eckholm. *Down to Earth: Environment and Human Needs.* New York: W. W. Norton, 1982.

Paul Ehrlich and Anne Ehrlich. *Extinction: The Causes and Consequences of the Disappearance of Species.* New York: Random House, 1981.

Norman Myers. *A Wealth of Wild Species: Storehouse for Human Welfare.* Boulder, Colo.: Westview Press, 1983.

ACID RAIN

Robert Boyle and Alexander Boyle. *Acid Rain.* New York: Schocken, 1983.

Rodger Bybee, ed. "Special Focus Issue on Acid Rain." *The American Biology Teacher.* Volume 45, Number 4, April-May, 1983.

Robert Ostmann. *Acid Rain.* Minneapolis, Mn.: Dillion Press, 1982.

Howard Ross and Michael Perley. *Acid Rain.* New York: McGraw-Hill, 1982.

AIR POLLUTION

Conservation Foundation. *Air Quality. State of the Environment, 1982.* Washington, D.C.: Conservation Foundation, 1982.

William Kellogg and Margaret Mead, eds. *The Atmosphere: Endangered and Endangering.* Bethesda, Md.: The National Institute of Health, 1977.

A Curriculum for Teaching About Science and Society

The lessons in this book can be used as a year-long program. The teacher simply begins with the first activity in environmental biology in his or her grade level and proceeds through biology to health, physical science, and the earth and environmental science. Note that the activities within a discipline are also organized.

There may be some elementary and middle school teachers who, through interest or necessity, would like to organize the lessons of this book into a year's program that represents the theme of science and society more than the disciplinary orientation that provides the present structure. There is a sequence of activities at K–2, 3–5 and 6–8 that presents the theme of science and society. The classroom teacher will have to modify the activities for his or her situation and supplement the activities with films, film strips, readings, and other lessons. There are approximately thirty-five additional activities in the textbook *Science and Society* by the authors and publisher of this book. In addition, we refer you to the resources guides in this book.

The following tables list a suggested sequence of activities for the grade levels K–2, 3–5 and 6–8. Refer to the planning charts for each discipline and to the lessons themselves for further details about the lessons. The sequence of activities at each grade level provides students with an initial background, represents a developmental progression from concrete to abstract and, very importantly, presents basic scientific knowledge, processes and skills in a social context.

A Science and Society Program for Grades K–2

A Science and Society Program for Grades 3–5

A Science and Society Program for Grades 6–8

1

Environmental Biology Activities

Children are curious naturalists. Their interest in the environment, and particularly the living world, makes biology an essential part of any science program for elementary and middle schools.

Biology is the science of life and living. Let us examine this definition. Science is a systematized body of knowledge formed by the process of continuous inquiry. The empirical processes of observation, measurement, experimentation, and organization of knowledge into theories all serve to further differentiate science from other realms of knowing such as religion and art. Science requires curiosity, creativity and persistence. These qualities create a natural connection between science and children.

The words life and living were used to define biology. The words are not synonymous. Life is a set of characteristics and capacities given to an organism when it comes into existence. Living is the process by which these capacities are used. Each organism has a unique capacity for living that is based on a genetic endowment and on its interactions with other organisms and the environment. To summarize the idea of life and living in the simplest terms: life is what an organism gets, living is what is done with what it gets.

We have used the term environmental to describe the biology activities. This is in keeping with our theme of science and society and with our understanding of the natural interests and developmental capacities of children. They learn best those things about which they are curious. These activities are also an excellent introduction to science in a social context.

You should refer to the planning charts for each grade level, K–2, 3–5, or 6–8. The planning charts summarize the activities, objectives (knowledge, processes, skills, attitudes and decision-making skills), teaching methods, and related curriculum areas. These are quick references that should assist in the organizing and sequencing of lessons.

PLANNING CHART FOR ENVIRONMENTAL BIOLOGY ACTIVITIES: GRADES K–2

ACTIVITY	OBJECTIVES					TEACHING METHODS	RELATED CURRICULUM
	Conceptual Knowledge	Learning Processes	Psychomotor Skills	Attitudes and Values	Decision-making Skills		
1. Comparing Familiar Animals	Living things have identities based on their characteristics.	Observe, compare.	Handle animals under supervision.	Accept guidance in caring for animals.	Discuss consequences of alternative actions.	Field trip.	Language Arts.
2. Comparing Familiar Plants	Living things have identities based on their characteristics.	Observe, compare.	Handle plants under supervision.	Accept guidance in caring for plants.	Discuss consequences of alternative actions.	Field trip.	Language Arts.
3. How are Living Things Alike yet Different?	Living things have identities based on their characteristics.	Compare, classify.	—	Value the uniqueness of one's identity.		Inquiry. Evaluation. Review.	Language Arts.
4. Describing Changes in Familiar Animals	Living things change when they interact with other things (living/non-living matter) in the environment.	Observe, compare, measure.	Handle and care for animals under supervision. Handle non-toxic substances.	Value the health and welfare of animals.	Select alternative actions and accept consequences.	Laboratory. Learning Center.	Math. Art. Language Arts.
5. Changes in Organisms	Living things can change and still keep (conserve) their identities.	Observe, compare, classify.	Use and care for simple tools.	Actively explore environment, combine materials in new ways.	—	Discussion. projects. Learning Center.	Language Arts. Art.
6. Recognizing Limits of Change and Identity: Death	There are limits to how much living things can change and survive (conserve their identities).	Observe, compare.	Handle plants and animals under supervision.	Accept guidance in caring for plants and animals.	Recognize personal decisions that involve self and others. Discuss consequences of alternative actions. Select alternatives.	Projects.	
7. Watching Things Decompose	When living things are changed beyond their limits they lose their identity, but the stuff they are made of (matter and energy) is still there (conserved).	Observe, compare.	Handle plants and animals under supervision.	Actively explore the environment, ask questions, listen to alternative points of view.	Recognize personal decisions that involve self and others. Discuss consequences of alternative actions. Select alternatives.	Nature Walk. Experiments.	Social Studies.
8. Recycling Matter and Energy	When living things are changed beyond their limits they lose their identity, but the stuff they are made of (matter and energy) is still there (conserved).	Observe, compare, measure.	—	—	Recognize personal decisions that involve self and others. Select alternatives and accept consequences.	Projects.	Social Studies.

15

Comparing Familiar Animals
Grades K-2

ACTIVITY OVERVIEW

In this activity, students develop the concept of identity and consider the identity of individual animals at a pet store. They learn to recognize and describe individual differences within familiar species of animals.

SCIENCE BACKGROUND

Today scientists use several systems for classifying organisms. These systems vary according to the number of divisions and may divide or combine classes in somewhat different ways, but there is general agreement among biologists on the classification of the animals that you would be likely to see at a pet store and that are described here.

There are about 44,000 species of animals with backbones in the world; they are called Vertebrates. This group includes about 20,000 species of bony fishes, 8,000 species of reptiles such as turtles, lizards,and snakes, 8,600 species of birds, and 4,500 species of mammals. Among the mammals are many subgroups or orders such as Carnivores (including dogs and cats), Lagomorphs (including rabbits), Rodents (including rats, mice and squirrels),and Primates (including monkeys and apes). Scientists further divide these orders into families, genera (the singular is called a genus), and species. Understanding this organization of one group of animals to another is important to scientists.

Dogs are a species, then, because they can interbreed. Yet, there are numerous kinds of dogs. Examples of these subspecies are spaniels, collies, beagles, and shepherds. And within any subspecies such as collies, there are clear differences that make each dog unique. Color, hair texture and length, size in relation to other litter mates,and behavior combine to give every puppy within a litter an identity that is unique. Recognizing these individual differences helps scientists and children communicate about animals.

SOCIETAL IMPLICATIONS

Animals are one of the earth's natural resources. Responsibility for conserving this natural resource belongs to everyone. Students who value the variety of species they see, and value the uniqueness of individuals within familiar species may also learn to value and protect less familiar species of animals in the environment.

MAJOR CONCEPT
     Living things have identities based on their characteristics.

OBJECTIVES--By the end of this activity the student should be able to:
     -Describe an animal in such a way that its identity is recognized
by others.
     -Observe and compare animals.
     -Handle animals under supervision and accept guidance in caring
for animals.
     -Discuss consequences of alternative actions with animals.

MATERIALS
     Pet store within walking distance of the school, or a litter of
puppies or kittens brought to the class for the occasion.

VOCABULARY
     -Color or pattern words for puppies.
     -Texture word for fur.
     -Feature words for tails, ears, etc.
     -Size words for puppies.
     -Descriptions of behavior.

PROCEDURES
     A. Make arrangements with the manager of the pet store to bring
the class to see a litter of young puppies or kittens. Find out if
the children will be permitted to touch or hold the animals with
supervision; and tell the children in advance whether or not they will
be able to touch or hold the animals.
     When children first arrive, take them on a tour of the pet store
as they can see the variety of animals living there. Encourage the
children to closely observe and carefully describe the characteristics
of each different kind of animal: fish, reptiles (such as turtles,
lizards,or snakes), birds,and mammals.
     Then focus children's attention on the puppies (or kittens,
rabbits,or some other mammals). Allow them to watch the puppies for
a while without interruption. Then ask them:

          "HOW CAN YOU TELL THE PUPPIES APART?"

Encourage all of the children to answer this question, as their
observations and comparisons continue.
     When it is about time to leave the pet store, ask the students
to look carefully at the puppies so that they can draw a picture of
all of the puppies when they return to school.
     Have the students draw pictures of their observations when they
return to school.

Comparing Familiar Plants
Grades K-2

ACTIVITY OVERVIEW

Students extend the concept of identity and the identity of familiar animals to consider the uniqueness of individual plants in their surroundings.

SCIENCE BACKGROUND

When most of us hear the word PLANTS, what comes to mind are trees or forests, shrubs, wild flowers, or horticultural flowers and perhaps weeds. Soon after, we recall that a large percentage of the foods we eat consists of parts of plants. Beans, peas, and all the other canned, fresh, or frozen vegetables; apples, oranges, and the entire variety of fruits, rice, wheat, and a host of other grains or grain products all are, strictly speaking, parts of what scientists call Flowering Plants. That is, the berries, apples, and rice that we eat are only a small part of the entire plant which reproduces by developing flowers that produce seeds.

There are about 250,000 species of Flowering Plants known. This group includes most of the trees, shrubs, and smaller flowering plants that have leaves, stems, and roots. Of course, there are other groups of plants that produce seeds but that have no flowers: the Conifers (pines, firs, spruces) produce seeds in their cones for example. There are about 550 species of Conifers in the world. And there are other groups of plants which produce no seeds at all: ferns and club mosses are two such groups.

All of these plants, the flowering plants, called Angiosperms because they literally have a "seed borne in a vessel", the Conifers, which produce seeds but no flowers, and the ferns and club mosses which have no seeds or flowers, all have one thing in common: they are terrestrial or land plants with stems, leaves, and roots that anchor them in the ground, and they have a well-developed and efficient system for transporting water, minerals, and food (the products of photosynthesis). Yet even knowing this much is not the whole story: since the surface of the earth is nearly two-thirds water, there is a vast array of plant species that are not terrestrial but aquatic and live in the oceans and fresh water. Understanding the organization of these and other groups of plants and the IDENTITY of plants within these groups, is important to scientists because it allows them to communicate with each other about plants and build on each others' knowledge.

SOCIETAL IMPLICATIONS

Plants are the link between mankind and the sun. They capture the sun's energy in their leaves and convert it, through the process of photosynthesis, into food that sustains all animal life on earth. Therefore, plants are one of the earth's natural resources; they are solar collectors for the nearly 200 million square miles that comprise the earth's land and water surface.

Most organisms carefully regulate the amount of energy they use. They are not able to survive very long without renewing energy they expend. Since civilized people now spend about 10 calories in energy for every calorie of food they eat, they cannot afford to ignore the role plants play in their own survival.

In a technological society where many of the foods we eat are processed, teachers need to reestablish the importance of plants as a link between humans and the sun for their students.

MAJOR CONCEPT

Living things have identities based on their characteristics.

OBJECTIVES

At the completion of this activity students should be able to:

-Describe a plant (fruit or vegetable in the produce section of the supermarket) in such a way that its identity is recognized by others.

-Observe and compare different plants.

-Handle plants under supervision; accept guidance in handling plants.

-Discuss consequences of alternative actions on plants.

MATERIALS

-Supermarket within walking distance of the school; or a walk through the school yard if it has a variety of plants and trees.

-Alternatively, different fruits, vegetables, and plants may be used in the classroom.

VOCABULARY

-Color words for fruit, vegetables, flowers, shrubs, or trees.

-Size words for these same plants.

-Texture words and shape words for these plants.

-Taste words for plants at the supermarket.

PROCEDURES

A. At the supermarket, begin by encouraging children to describe the differences among various fruits such as apples, oranges, and bananas. Then hold up two pieces of fruit of the same kind and ask children how they can tell the two apart. Help them focus on differences between the two. Repeat this question each time holding another set of two or three pieces of fruit or vegetables.

B. Comparing plants is an activity that can be done in many places; the school yard, on a neighborhood walk, in a park, or among plants grown in a garden that the children plant. Not only does this activity improve the children's power of observation, it also increases their vocabulary.

How Are Living Things Alike Yet Different?
Grades K-2 first

ACTIVITY OVERVIEW
     Students bring together their experiences from earlier activities
and look at living things in a new way: as groups, related to each
other.

SCIENCE BACKGROUND
     You are surrounded by living things. Some of these can be
seen, like the people around you and the plants and animals you
encounter on the way to school or the store. Others like the
bacteria and fungi that live on your skin or the spores that are
carried by the wind, cannot be seen. Yet there are over 1,500,000
species of plants and animals that populate the earth's surface from
the Arctic to the Tropics and from high mountain peaks to the depths
of the oceans.
     Scientists who catalog nature for us are called SYSTEMATISTS.
They have organized the 1,200,000 species of animals and 400,000
species of plants into a taxonomy with five kingdoms, making the
IDENTITY of individuals and the ORGANIZATION of individuals into
groups easier for anyone wishing to add to--or learn from--the
knowledge scientists have accumulated about living things.
     The MONERA kingdom includes bacteria, the oldest and most
abundant group of organisms on earth, and also includes blue-green
algae and viruses. In the PROTISTA kingdom, the best known examples
are seaweeds (red, brown, and green algae) that are found in the
oceans, near shores, rich in minerals. The FUNGI kingdom contains
well-known organisms as mushrooms, toadstools,and the minute fungi
species that are so important in the processing of beer, wine,and
cheeses such as Camembert and blue cheese. The PLANT kingdom includes
mosses and ferns as well as all of the seed-bearing plants. And
finally, the ANIMAL kingdom with animals ranging in complexity from
the "simple" sponges to Homo sapiens.

SOCIETAL IMPLICATIONS
     As the world population increases, natural resources are consumed
at an increasing rate. This fact has led to the general recognition
that the survival of some of the world's 1-1/2 million species of
living things is endangered.
     This diversity of life, and the variability of individuals
within any single interbreeding group called a SPECIES, all but
escapes our attention because we become accustomed to seeing the
same life forms on a more or less regular basis and we grow to ignore

them. Often it is only when these individuals behave in ways that we don't expect that we notice their diversity and variability at all.

Thus, it becomes important to awaken students' interest in the diversity of living things and to sharpen their abilities to perceive and describe these differences. At the same time, students need to recognize and value the uniqueness of the individual with groups of living things.

MAJOR CONCEPT
Living things have identities based on their characteristics.

OBJECTIVES
Upon completion of this activity the student should be able to:

-Describe characteristics of groups and individual living things which contribute to their identity.

-Differentiate between similar living things so that others can recognize the objects described.

-Observe and compare different organisms.

-Value the uniqueness of individuals.

MATERIALS
-Pictures that children have drawn of puppies at the pet store, plants at the supermarket, school yard or elsewhere, and pictures of themselves and each other, should be arranged around the room.

VOCABULARY
-Use all of the words introduced in earlier activities.

PROCEDURES
A. Have children sit in a circle or in some other arrangement that is conducive to discussion. Begin the discussion by holding up two pictures of different individuals and ask:

HOW ARE THE (PUPPIES, PEOPLE, OR PLANTS) IN THESE PICTURES ALIKE? HOW ARE THEY DIFFERENT? HOW CAN YOU TELL THEM APART?

B. Repeat the question using another set of pictures. Then invite children to take turns holding up pairs of pictures and asking the same questions above.

C. Guide the discussion so that children recognize that all individual living things have identities which are based on differences in their appearance and behavior, and that every living thing is unique in its identity. Also lead children to discover that their similarities lead us to organize living things into groups that are related; groups such as plants, vegetables, fruits, animals, cats, dogs, and so forth.

D. You might want to use pictures from a variety of sources, including pictures the children bring, and invite the children to play the game just before or on their return from recess, lunch or the beginning and end of the day.

Describing Changes in Familiar Animals
Grades K-2

ACTIVITY OVERVIEW
Students enlarge the concept of change by considering change in individual animals. They learn to recognize and describe changes in the appearance and behavior of familiar animals.

SCIENCE BACKGROUND
All living things change throughout their life spans as a result of interacting with the environment, that is, individuals exchange forms of energy and matter within their immediate environment. Land animals, for example, breathe air (non-living matter), eat plants or some form of animal life (living matter), which in turn gives them energy to move and food necessary for normal growth and development, allowing them to reproduce identical offspring when they reach adulthood. Having reared their young, or a series of broods, litters, or individuals, adult land animals reach old age and die of some disease unless they fall prey to some predator before old age.

Changes in the development and behavior of animals is of special interest to ZOOLOGISTS, who study all aspects of animal life, to ECOLOGISTS who study animal life in relation to plant life and the physical environment of animals, and to ETHOLOGISTS, people who study animal behavior.

Zoologists have described the life cycles (the series of stages an organism passes through from egg to adult) for all of the animals you and your students are likely to encounter. Life cycles vary greatly among animals. Some animals change forms dramatically, such as caterpillars, which change from an egg to a worm-like animal, go through a resting stage in a cocoon or crysalis, and emerge as a moth or butterfly. Other animals change forms only slightly; rabbits, dogs, and cats are examples of mammals which change in size and texture of hair but change very little in shape or color.

Ethologists or animal behaviorists have contributed to our understanding of some of the origins or causes of animal behavior. For example, certain kinds of learning in animals occur only within limited time spans called periods of IMPRINTING. Baby chicks or ducks, soon after they are hatched, (usually within 12-16 hours) will follow the first moving object they see. In nature this is generally their mother; but in unusual circumstances--such as when the mother hen or duck has died and the young have been adopted by a different species of bird or by people, the new hatching ducks or chicks will adopt the surrogate as mother. Attempts to induce this following of a mother or surrogate mother are largely unsuccessful after 30 hours. The effects of imprinting often last into adulthood.

24

Ducks and geese for example, who are IMPRINTED to follow a human being may reject members of their own species as sexual mates when they are adults in preference for their adopted parent or a similar individual.

SOCIETAL IMPLICATIONS

Observing the growth, development, and behavior of animals has satisfied the natural curiosity of scientists and non-scientists alike. There is an intrinsic satisfaction that comes from watching living things change. But in addition, knowledge about the life cycles, functioning processes, and behavior of animals has allowed scientists to protect endangered species of animals and to use other species for experimental purposes in laboratories which has led to the development of disease control, treatment and prevention, and to a better understanding of ourselves.

MAJOR CONCEPT

Living things change when they interact with other living things and the environment.

OBJECTIVES

Upon completion of this activity the student should be able to:
-Describe changes in animals' appearance and behavior.
-Observe, compare, and measure different organisms.
-Handle and care for animals.
-Handle non-toxic substances.
-Value the health and welfare of animals.
-Select alternative actions for their own behavior and accept the consequences.

MATERIALS

-Chart paper (4' x 6') and felt-tip pen; chalkboard.
-A young animal that can be cared for in the classroom.
Sources: a pet store for animals such as guinea pigs, baby chicks, or ducklings that might be raised in class for a few weeks and later adopted by a children's zoo, individual student, or farmer. Someone in the class may have a young kitten or puppy that could be a day visitor in the class for several days and taken home in the evenings. Some children's zoos have animal-lending programs with various animals that can be borrowed for 1 or 2 weeks at a time.

PREPARATION

-A plan for the animal's basic needs, and who will take the animal at the end of its visit in the school.
-Approval from the principal of the school to bring an animal to the classroom.

PROCEDURES

A. Talk with the students about bringing the animal into the classroom, once you have followed the preparation steps above. Describe the animal and its basic needs and ask the students what they would need to do to prepare an adequate and safe environment for the animal, if it were to be a temporary visitor in their classroom. List their ideas on the chalkboard and add to their ideas until the list includes a procedure that will assure the animal's well-being and allow instruction in all areas of the curriculum to proceed. Later put these on a chart so children and you may refer to them often. A sample is suggested below.

GUIDELINES FOR PET CARE

1. Make sure the animal has the right kind and amount of food.
2. Provide fresh water daily.
3. Clean its home/nest daily.
4. Allow the animal to sleep as much as it wants.
5. Pick up the animal only when the teacher is with you. (This rule can be changed later to "with permission").
6. Do our regular work in the classroom when asked.

B. Once the animal arrives, find a place for its box, cage, nest, or home so that it will be free from drafts, foot traffic, and excessive noise. Explain that the animal needs this special place for its own health; but add that part of every day will be devoted to watching the animal and enjoying it.

Sit the students in a circle on the floor and place the animal in the circle (probably in its home). Allow the students to talk freely as they observe. Later, ask several questions to promote closer observation:

HOW WOULD YOU DESCRIBE HIS/HER/ITS...(SIZE, SHAPE, COLOR, TEXTURE, BEHAVIOR)?

Repeat the question several times so that several students have an opportunity to respond.

Toward the end of the first observation period, ask students how they might keep a record of how the animal changes while it is on its visit in their class. List their ideas on the chalkboard. Add to their ideas so that the procedure will reflect your objectives.

A sample might be:

DESCRIBING CHANGES IN OUR ANIMAL

1. Draw pictures of it now and later.
2. Take a picture of it with a camera, now and later.
3. Write down how much it eats, drinks, and sleeps.
4. Weigh it now and later to see how much it grows.
5. Measure it with a tape measure to see how much it grows.
6. Watch how he/she acts, and describe how his/her behavior changes.

Implement as many of the ideas as seem worthwhile. Hold daily observation and discussion periods to assess students' learning.

C. Place a container of wild bird seed near the window of the classroom. After several days a few species of birds may begin to feed if they find periods during the day when they feel safe to approach. When a bird is first sighted at the container, ask students to remain in their seats and watch—gradually, more birds may come. If they do, it provides an excellent opportunity for students to observe an enormous variety of changes in animals' behavior.

Changes in Organisms
Grades K-2

ACTIVITY OVERVIEW
     Students extend their understanding of reversibility, the limits
of change, and the conservation of identity in organisms by identifying permanent changes in living things.

SCIENCE BACKGROUND
     While many changes in living things appear to be reversible,
there is nevertheless within every organism a genetically coded life
cycle which results in irreversible changes in the organism. Children
become adolescents, then young adults, middle-aged adults,and ultimately old adults. The life cycle of Homo sapiens is never reversed,
in spite of the efforts of many people to "return to their youth".
     The life span for some species of living things is longer than
that of humans, a fact that makes it difficult for people to visualize
changes in these species. For example, some of the Coast Redwood
trees in California (Sequoia sempervirens) are more than 2000 years
old. Nevertheless the tallest of these trees (360 ft.) never reverse
their height or their life cycle.

SOCIETAL IMPLICATIONS
     Permanent changes in living things have been accepted more or
less routinely in the past because changes associated with life
cycles were viewed as "natural", change in living and non-living
matter is recognized as perpetual.
     However, with our growing capacity to "control" nature by
changing the weather, the course of rivers, the variety and rate of
plant growth and decay, and so forth, scientists have discovered that
some technological changes have changed environments in ways that may
be harmful to human health or the survival of the species. For
example, insecticides like DDT and other persistent hydrocarbons
that kill insects are also passed on to other animals along the food
chain, and ultimately can affect the groups that were to receive the
greatest protection or benefit.
     In the 1950's, no one imagined that the vast oceans or atmosphere
could be polluted but when DDT was found in the bones of penguins in
the Antarctic, presumably carried by currents from continents in the
northern hemisphere,and when the volume of lumber harvested in the
Sierra Nevada range of California was reduced due to a 65-85cm reduction
in the diameter of Ponderosa Pine, Sugar Pine,and Incense Cedar due
to air pollution, it became obvious that human intervention in natural
environments and cycles was much more complex than anyone had imagined.

MAJOR CONCEPT

Living things change and still keep (conserve) their identities.

OBJECTIVES

Upon completion of this activity students should be able to:
-Describe living things that change permanently.
-Observe; compare living things.
-Use and care for simple tools.
-Assemble simple projects with guidance.
-Actively explore the environment.
-Combine materials in new ways.

MATERIALS

-Old magazines with pictures of people, food, plants, or animals
-Comic sections of newspapers
-Scissors, tape
-Long strip of Butcher paper (about 5' long) posted for a mural

VOCABULARY

-Change, permanent, different

PROCEDURES

A. Introduce the topic of PERMANENT CHANGE by showing students photographs of yourself taken from childhood to adulthood. Or you may prefer to use pictures of a pet, taken during different stages of its developments or a series of pictures of animals like puppies--dogs, kittens--cats, calves--cows, etc.

Explain that many changes in nature are permanent: for example, when things grow up they don't change back to babies again. Cite several other examples.

```
EXAMPLES OF PERMANENT CHANGES

Children grow up and don't get small again
Pencils get sharpened and don't get whole again
Eggs get cooked and don't become raw again
Matches burn and don't get unburned
Food gets eaten and doesn't get uneaten
Animals die and don't come alive again
```

Compare these permanent changes with the temporary changes discussed in Activity 11.

B. Invite children to find pictures of permanent changes. The pictures they find will be cut out and shared with the class. Open a magazine and turn pages, showing children as you turn and saying:

IS THIS PICTURE OF SOMETHING THAT (HAS/CAN/WILL) CHANGE(D) PERMANENTLY?

Find 2 pictures that will illustrate permanent change, for example a puppy and an adult dog. Cut them out of the magazine and tape them onto the mural (butcher paper). Draw an arrow in the direction of the change: from the puppy to the dog, and explain why this is an example of permanent change. (See illustration).

Place a supply of magazines or comics in a Learning Center. Provide guidelines for students using the Learning Center. As each student chooses cut-out pictures of permanent change, ask him/her to tell you how the examples illustrate permanent change. If the student understands the concept, have him/her paste or tape the two pictures on the mural, and draw the arrow in the direction of the permanent change. On the other hand, if the student can't explain how his/her pictures show permanent change, help the student find an appropriate picture. In other words, teach the concept on an individual basis.

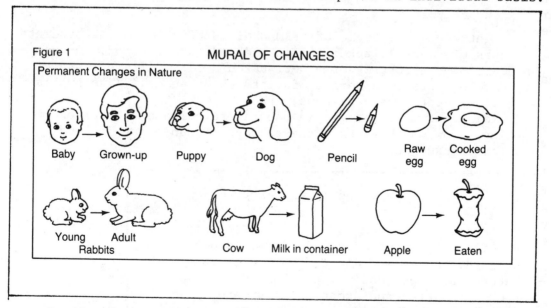

Figure 1   MURAL OF CHANGES

Permanent Changes in Nature

Baby   Grown-up   Puppy   Dog   Pencil   Raw egg   Cooked egg

Young   Adult
Rabbits   Cow   Milk in container   Apple   Eaten

C. Go outside and have the students identify changes that are temporary and changes that are permanent.

Recognizing Limits to Change and Identity: Death
Grades K-2

ACTIVITY OVERVIEW

Students are introduced to the idea that plants--whether in nature or in containers on window sills of the classroom, continuously adapt to changes in their environment and die when the limits of their adaptability are exceeded.

SCIENCE BACKGROUND

All living things are composed of one or more cells which take in food and combine food with oxygen to obtain energy to carry out functions associated with being alive. In human beings those functions include breathing, digesting food, pumping food throughout the body, removing wastes that are by-products of other processes, and reproducing ourselves.

Through highly developed medical technology, doctors are able to artificially support some organs when organs can no longer carry out their natural functions; for example kidney machines can take over the process of waste removal, heart transplants have replaced poorly functioning ones, and iron lungs support the breathing of persons with partially paralyzed lungs. Nevertheless the majority of animals die when some organ ceases to function. Their cells can no longer be nourished or combine oxygen to produce energy.

Plants and animals engage in a continuous struggle to acquire what they need to survive. If they are largely successful, they grow to maturity, reproduce themselves and finally die. Their life cycle is genetically coded. However, when the environment fails to provide these basic needs, living things cannot survive if they remain in that environment.

Thus, death is regulated both by: (1) the limits of an individual's life cycles which are in turn determined by genetically coded information in cells; and (2) by an individual's ability to acquire his/her/its basic needs, which is determined in part by what the environment has to offer and by the individual's capacity to adapt or seek a more suitable environment.

SOCIETAL IMPLICATIONS

Death is a topic that is avoided by a large percentage of the American people. Parents often try to shield their children from facts about death. It is even difficult to find the term "death" listed in the index of many of the most popular college textbooks in Biology, a fact that is surprising since biology is the study of living things and death is a natural process for living things.

In spite of the reluctance of many adults to deal with the topic, children demonstrate curiosity and interest in this natural process.

MAJOR CONCEPT
There are limits to how much living things can adopt or change and survive (conserve their identity).

OBJECTIVES
After completion of this activity the student should be able to:
-Recognize limits of change in a plant or animal.
-Observe; compare, and measure change in plants and animals.
-Handle plants and animals under supervision.
-Accept guidance in caring for plants and animals.
-Recognize personal decisions that involve self and others.
-Discuss consequences of various alternatives and select alternatives.

MATERIALS
-Plants (a variety of common household plants).
Note: You may wish to have the students grow the plants from seeds. Use simple containers and radish, bean, and pea seeds.

VOCABULARY
-Change, limits, identity, basic requirements, death, environment.

PROCEDURES
A. As a teacher you will be guiding students to provide the basic needs of plants in the classroom. Yet, in spite of your attention and students' efforts, some classroom plants may die, just as they would in nature. Help students understand that the death of organisms is part of nature; also help them try to understand the cause(s) of their plants' death as an example of living things that could not adapt to their environment.

If some students' plants die, talk with them individually or in a small group and examine their plants. Have students tell you about the care they gave them. You may be able to relate the plants' death to some condition such as too much water or heat or seeds planted too deep.

Speculate with students about the cause(s) for some plants' or animal's dying. Then use an analogy to help them understand the many factors that limit survival. Compare the problems that plants and animals have when they live outside the classroom in nature. They must depend on the rain for water, since no one brings it to them. They must make their own food (plants) or find it (animals) since no one provides it. They must protect themselves from enemies

that might eat them, but they cannot always. And they must survive
all kinds of weather.

Of all the plants and animals that are sprouted, hatched, or born
in nature, only a very few survive to become adults because so many
things can go wrong.

Explain that plants and animals in nature have a difficult time
finding everything they need to grow into adults and have offspring.
They try to adapt to fit their environment, but there are limits to
how much they can change. For example, if a plant in a forest doesn't
get enough light to make its own food, it will grow tall and thin,
trying to reach the sunlight. But if a tree blocks the sunlight, the
plant can never grow tall enough to reach the sunlight, and it dies.
Yet, other seeds like it, a few feet away, may survive because they
aren't under the shade of the tree.

Every plant and animal changes, trying to fit its environment, even
if the environment doesn't provide what it needs. The care students
provide for plants in the classroom may be better than what nature
offers or it may lack some essential requirement one of them needs
to survive. Living things try to adapt to their environment in
nature and classrooms, but each one has limits to its capacity to
change and survive. When it can no longer survive, it loses its
identity.

B. Ask students what will happen to these plants when they die.

Watching Things Decompose
Grades K-2

ACTIVITY OVERVIEW
Students observe the natural process of decay of leaves, bark, twigs, insects, and other bits of living things that have died. They are introduced to the idea that change continues even after the death of organisms, and that although identity ceases, matter and energy are conserved.

SCIENCE BACKGROUND
When living things die, they continue to change just as they changed continuously while they were alive. Their organic material is broken down through the digestive processes of microorganisms such as yeast, bacteria, and molds and small animals such as sawbugs or pillbugs which feed on dead plant and animal material. This process of breaking down organic material into raw materials that can be used again is called DECOMPOSITION, and the organisms that aid in this process are called DECOMPOSERS. As dead leaves, twigs and roots, animal feces, carcasses, and exoskeletons are left to decay, and are converted to inorganic substances that are returned to the soil or water, they once more enter the bodies of other plants and begin their cycle again.

SOCIETAL IMPLICATIONS
The decomposition of organic matter is essential to the continuation of all living species. However, decay and decomposition are not always welcomed processes. Food producers, packagers, and retailers wage a continuous battle against this natural process, and keep the Federal Food and Drug Administration busy.

MAJOR CONCEPT
When living things are changed beyond their limits they lose their identity, but the stuff (matter) they are made of is still there (conserved).

OBJECTIVES
After completion of this activity the student should be able to:
-Describe living things in the process of decomposition.
-Observe; compare decomposition of living things.
-Explore the environment and ask questions.
-Recognize situations which require personal decisions, select alternatives and accept consequences.
-Listen to alternative points of view.

MATERIALS
-A natural area with a few trees or shrubs and small plants, possibly on the school grounds, and a spade or trowel.

-OR 2 trays (glass or aluminum) or bake pans deep enough to hold a 5cm-8cm layer of soil or water.

VOCABULARY
-Decompose, disappear, die, crumble, break apart, organisms, microorganisms

PROCEDURES
A. After the rain, take children on a walk to see what has happened to the plants and animals that have lived in the neighborhood.

Encourage children to look for leaves, needles, cones or seeds, bark, branches, or flowers that have fallen from trees, shrubs, or small plants. Also look for insects such as butterflies, flies, and bees that have died and are on the ground. They may still be wet or water-logged if you find them soon after the rain.

Point out to the children that all of these plants or parts of plants and animals will continue to change even after they have died. Some will be eaten soon by animals looking for them. For example, birds will be looking for seeds washed from plants after a rain. Others will get wet with many more rains, be walked on perhaps by people and animals, and finally covered up by newer leaves falling and by soil, dust, or sand blown over them. There they will be eaten by small animals that live in the soil like pillbugs--and other organisms so small they can't be seen without a microscope.

B. Ask students if they would like to see what happens to plants or parts of them and animals when they die. For those who are interested, invite them to come back with you in several months and see what happened. Then use the spade or trowel and dig up a small plot of soil (about 5cm x 5cm) and bury the leaves, twigs, seeds, flowers, or insects. Cover them with soil and mark the place they are buried. In about 3 months, or sooner if the school year is ending, return to the site and dig up the plot. Along with the decomposition of the plant and animal material, children will be able to see many of the small soil animals that depend on dead organic matter.

C. Students can also observe what happens to plants and animals that die by burying them in containers (glass or aluminum bake pans) of soil or water in the classroom.

Place a small amount of needles or leaves, small twigs, flowers, bark, or seeds from trees and shrubs in a container, filled with soil from a nearby outdoor area. Sawbugs or pillbugs and small micro-organisms from the soil will begin the process of decomposition.

Students can keep track of the length of time it takes for changes to take place. Keep the material moist and serated (frequently turned over) to speed up the process.

Students who live near creeks, rivers, ponds, lakes, or the ocean may wonder if dead plants and animals decompose faster in water than soil. Set up an experiment to find out.

Later, place the containers outside in an undisturbed area if unpleasant gases are given off by decomposition.

Figure 2   DECOMPOSITION OF MATERIAL

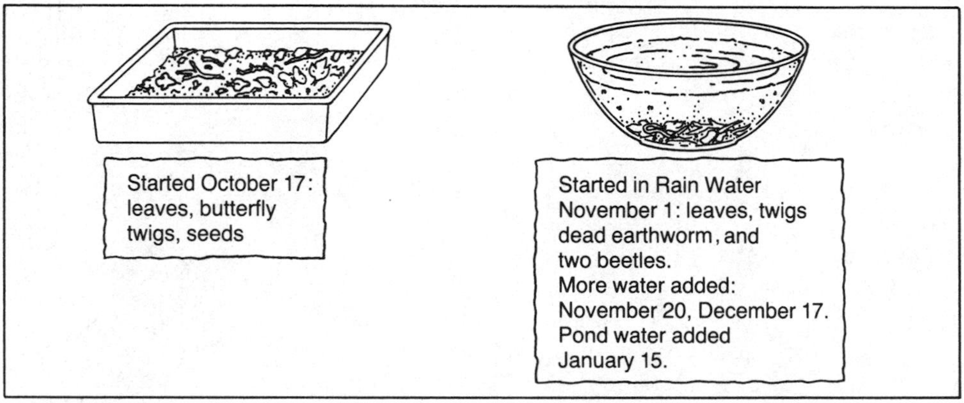

Started October 17:
leaves, butterfly
twigs, seeds

Started in Rain Water
November 1: leaves, twigs
dead earthworm, and
two beetles.
More water added:
November 20, December 17.
Pond water added
January 15.

D. As the materials in Activity B or C begin to decompose, ask students if they still recognize the leaves, etc. Have their identities changed? When they are no longer leaves or insects or other recognizable organisms their identities are gone, but the materials they are made of have been used by other plants or animals that live in soil or water.

Recycling Matter and Energy
Grades K-2

ACTIVITY OVERVIEW
    Students use compost to start a new garden (outdoors or in a pot)
and observe the effect of recycled matter and energy.

SCIENCE BACKGROUND
    The sun is the source of energy for all organisms. Our earth
receives an average of 2 calories of radiant energy per minute from
the sun for every square centimeter of the earth's surface. Roughly
half of this energy is absorbed into the ground and radiated back in
the form of heat; the rest never reaches the earth's surface but is
reflected from clouds and dust in the earth's atmosphere, causing
the earth to appear as a shining planet when viewed from outer space.
    When this amount of the sun's energy reaches the earth and is
combined with carbon, oxygen, water, and a few minerals, about 90
billion metric tons of organic matter are produced each year on a
world-wide basis. Plants and algae make up about 99% of this organic
matter, while all other life--the organisms that eat plants and
animals--combine to make up the remaining 1%. If it were not for the
DECOMPOSERS, imagine the effect when carbon, oxygen, water, and minerals
could not be recycled.

SOCIETAL IMPLICATIONS
    The practice of COMPOSTING (converting organic wastes into
fertilizer) appears to have originated along with agriculture about
11,000 years ago. Today, many home gardeners use composting as a
means of disposing of leaves, straw, manure, and garbage, and as a
means of conditioning soil or cutting down on the cost of commercial
fertilizers. A large pile of leaves can be reduced to one-fifth their
original volume, for example, through composting and studies with large
municipal compost piles at Berkeley, California, showed that compost
piles which were kept moist and aerated took between 2 weeks to 3
months to completely compost.
    Compost is generally less rich in minerals than commercial
fertilizers: a fairly rich compost has about 1.5% to 3.5% Nitrogen,
0.5% to 1.0% Phosphorus, and 1.0% to 2.0% Potassium. Interestingly,
if compost is worked into the soil before it has decomposed it can
actually take nitrogen from the soil.

MAJOR CONCEPT
    When living things are changed beyond their limits, they lose
their identity, but the stuff (matter and energy) they are made of is
still there (conserved).

OBJECTIVES

After completion of this activity the student should be able to:
-Describe the recycling of matter and energy in a classroom project.
-Observe; compare, and measure the decomposition of material.
-Handle and care for plants.
-Value the wise use of natural resources.
-Recognize personal decisions that involve self and others.
-Select alternatives and accept consequences.

MATERIALS

-Shovel, grass. Seed or wildflower seeds. Compost material from earlier activities either in the soil outdoors or in the glass/aluminum bake pans in the classroom

VOCABULARY

-Compost, decomposed, recycled, broke up, changed, gases, liquid, solid, reuse

PROCEDURES

A. After the compost in the last activity has begun to decompose mix it with soil. This can be done by chopping it with a shovel or trowel and working it into the ground outdoors. At the same time, spade up an area of equal size near the area which received the compost. Mark these two miniature gardens so that they are protected from foot traffic.

Flower pots can be used for this project if the class made an indoor compost in a bake pan, or if a suitable area outside is not available.

B. Sprinkle grass seed or the seeds from wildflowers over the two miniature gardens, and sprinkle them with water. Finally sprinkle a fine layer (about 1cm) of soil over the seeds. When students have finished planting, they have two miniature gardens--one planted with compost and the other without. After young plants begin to appear, students will be able to compare the two gardens.

Remember that compost which is added to the soil before the decomposition process is complete actually takes nitrogen from the soil. Also recall that a rich decomposed compost adds small amounts of nitrogen, phosphorus, and potassium to the soil. When the children compare their two gardens they will be able to see which contains the greater amount of these minerals--the garden with the more luxurious plant growth.

PLANNING CHART FOR ENVIRONMENTAL BIOLOGY ACTIVITIES: GRADES 3–5

ACTIVITY	OBJECTIVES					TEACHING METHODS	RELATED CURRICULUM
	Conceptual Knowledge	Learning Processes	Psychomotor Skills	Attitudes and Values	Decision-making Skills		
9. Making a Key for a Nature Collection: Classification	Individuals and groups of living things have identities based on their characteristics.	Observe, compare, classify.	———	Actively explore and ask questions. Combine objects/materials in new ways. Compare alternative views.	———	Guided Discovery; Learning Center; Problem-Solving.	Language Arts, Math.
10. Describing Changes in Groups of People	All groups of living things change. Members of the groups interact with each other, with other groups and with the environment.	Observe, compare, infer.	———	Value changes in growth and development.	———	Discussion; Pantomime; Individual Projects.	Art, Language Arts, Social Studies.
11. Collecting and Caring for Small Animals	All groups of living things change. Members of the groups interact with each other, with other groups and with the environment.	Observe, compare, infer.	Handle small animals and construct small projects without supervision.	Actively explore the environment and ask questions. Assume responsibility for wise use of natural resources and provide basic needs for wildlife.	Describe consequences of various alternatives to self and others.	Field trip; individual projects.	Social Studies.
12. Observing Changes in Small Animals	All groups of living things change. Members of the groups interact with each other, with other groups and with the environment.	Observe, compare, gather and organize information, infer, predict.	Handle and care for small animals; conduct simple experiments.	Actively explore the environment and ask questions. Assume responsibility for wise use of natural resources and provide basic needs for wildlife.	Describe consequences of various alternatives to self and others.	Guided discovery, "hands-on" lab, lab report.	Language Arts, Art.
13. Exploring the Limits of Change in Animals	When groups of animals are forced to change beyond their limits, the group loses its identity (does not survive) even though matter and energy are conserved.	Gather and organize information, infer, predict.	———	Value responsibility for the natural environment; Compare alternative views.	Describe the decisions that involve self and others. Discriminate between facts and attitudes/values. Describe consequences of various alternatives to self and others.	Research projects, oral projects.	Art, Social Studies, Language Arts.
14. Reaching the Limits of Change and Identity	When groups of living things are forced to change beyond their limits, the group loses its identity (does not survive) even though matter and energy are conserved.	Observe, compare, infer, predict.	———	Actively explore the environment and ask questions.	Recognize decisions that involve self and others. Describe consequences of various alternatives to self and others.	Field trip.	———
15. Conserving Plants and Animals	When groups of living things are forced to change beyond their limits, the group loses its identity (does not survive) even though matter and energy are conserved.	Compare, gather, and organize information.	———	Combine ideas in new ways. Assume responsibility for wise use of natural resources in the environment, and for health and welfare of self and others.	Differentiate between facts, attitudes and values. Formulate alternatives which reflect facts, attitudes and values of self and others.	Brainstorming.	Social Studies.

Making a Key for a Nature Collection: Classification
Grades 3-5

ACTIVITY OVERVIEW

Students explore various ways to group or classify the objects in a nature collection, and finally settle on a chart that illustrates the final arrangements of the contents of their collection.

SCIENCE BACKGROUND

You probably have some background about how scientists group living things. They use taxonomies that differentiate different types of organisms. The taxonomies begin with big differences such as plants and animals and progressively differentiate organisms from kingdoms to phyla, family, genus and species. (See activity for further discussion).

SOCIETAL IMPLICATIONS

Human beings are interesting and complex living things. We have an aesthetic nature which leads us to create and value beauty and organization. We also have an analytic nature which leads us to ask religious or philosophic questions about our origins, a deity, life after death, or the origin of all ideas. And, of course, we also have a biological nature which links us to all other living things as we take food and water, oxygen, and sunlight from the environment.

Because of the complexity of humans, there are disagreements about the "true" nature of being human. Such disagreements are inevitable when individuals or groups focus on a single aspect of human nature and ignore or reject others. Just as scientists, philosophers, theologians, and aestheticians have sometimes disagreed about the nature of humanity, students may find themselves in disagreement about ways to group or classify the objects in their nature collection. You will find suggestions here for helping students see other points of view.

MAJOR CONCEPT

Groups of living things have identities based on their characteristics (structure/appearance) and behavior.

OBJECTIVES

After completion of this activity the student should be able to:
—Describe differences between groups of natural objects.
—Observe; compare, and classify living things.
—Actively explore and ask questions; combine objects and materials in new ways.
—Attempt to compare alternative points of view.

MATERIALS

-A collection of natural objects (rocks, twigs, pine cones, insects, and flowers, for example) brought in by students.

Note: Be sure to have the students bring in the objects and organisms the day before you plan to complete the activity.

VOCABULARY

-Key, identification key, groups

PROCEDURE

A. Introduce the idea of making a key for a nature collection by asking if someone can describe the way large supermarkets help people find what they want in the store. Department stores use a similar system. Both post signs in conspicuous places to guide people to the things they need. The yellow pages of a telephone book help in the same way by leading people to information they want.

The purpose of a key in doors is to unlock them--to let people enter. The purpose of a nature key is to help people find the names of things in nature that they care about or want to know more about.

Explain that there are many ways to make nature keys. Scientists agree, more or less, on a key that helps them classify nature; but scientists have to make changes in their keys from time to time because they discover a new species or decide to regroup when a new discovery is made about the structure that many things have in common. Generally, scientists have made relatively few changes in their keys to nature in the past 100 years.

Demonstrate to students how a nature key works. Use the analogy of a key to a door; once you unlock the door, you can go into any room in the house; the living room, kitchen, bedroom, or bathroom. In every room, certain kinds of furniture and smaller objects are kept. These things are grouped in rooms because certain kinds of activity happen there; eating, sleeping, and so forth. At this point you might sketch a four-roomed house on the chalkboard showing a front door, living room, kitchen, bedroom, and bath.

Imagine that friends gave you the key and invited you to live in their house while they were gone. You would be able to find a place to cook and eat because you would recognize the kitchen by its appearance. And you would expect to find a bed in the bedroom, a toilet in the bathroom, and chairs or other comfortable things to sit on in the living room. The same thing is true for a nature key.

Draw another house like the one below, and ask how students might find "rooms" for everything in their nature collection.

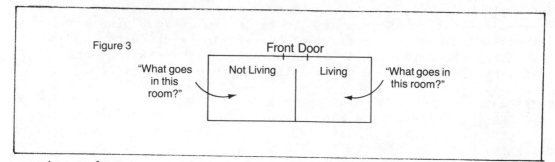

Figure 3

As students name things that go into one side of the house or the other, list them on the chalkboard until the house is full. Where there are disagreements among students, suggest that someone check in the field guide, or that together the class will check several references to see how scientists have most often decided to group the object. In the meanwhile, list that object outside the house until students decide where it belongs.

When it has become apparent that (a) the house isn't big enough to list everything in the nature collection, or (b) that things have to be further grouped within their "side of the house", agree with this conclusion and suggest that more "rooms" or groups are needed within each "side of the house". Continue enlarging the chalkboard house, adding "rooms", and helping students make smaller and smaller groups until they have "rooms" or groups for everything of a similar nature.

Figure 4

Living		
Plants	Animals	
Trees	Birds	Bugs
Shrubs	Mammals	
Grass		

This process may take two or three sessions before everyone is content with the arrangement. Since you will need the chalkboard for other activities, have 2 or 3 students copy the first "house" on chart paper so that the class can return to the activity. It is important that students go slowly enough in the process of classifying the things in their own collection to understand each other's point of view for grouping. This process should not be shortened for convenience; learning is taking place so long as students are trying to understand one another's point of views for grouping.

To avoid conflicts of a verbal nature, conduct this activity in smaller groups. To avoid conflicts about physically grouping objects, set up a learning center where one or two students at a time can go to try their hand at improving the grouping. Your role as a teacher in this instance--is to help individual students grow in their capacity to classify. Once students understand classification as a system for subgrouping within groups with the acceptability of using any of a number of criteria for grouping, they can usually come to agreement as a class on a classification of any number of objects. Reinforce the idea that there are many ways to classify groups of objects, and that the class is to develop a key (system of grouping the nature collection) that will be easy for everyone to understand who uses or wants to enjoy the nature collection that will be given to the school. If some of your students have not learned to classify things, see (b) of this activity.

Once the class has agreed more or less on a final system for grouping the nature collection, put the final arrangement--called a Nature Key--on a chart large enough to include all of the information. See the example of a Nature Key developed by one teacher and her students. The key includes some decisions made by the students and others made by the teacher. For example, the students wanted to list in the nature key every object (like pine cones, snake skins, etc.) and every picture that was a substitute for an animal (pictures of lions, horses, etc.). They also decided which objects and pictures went in which groups--with a few exceptions where the teacher pointed out new ways of looking at objects. The teacher guided students to accept some terms for groupings made by scientists because she thought that would help everyone learn some important new ideas as well as express their own.

When the nature key is completed, put it in a visible place on the wall and display the nature collection on table tops in approximately the same spatial arrangement as depicted in the key. A school hallway or library is an excellent place to display or exhibit a class nature collection.

Figure 5

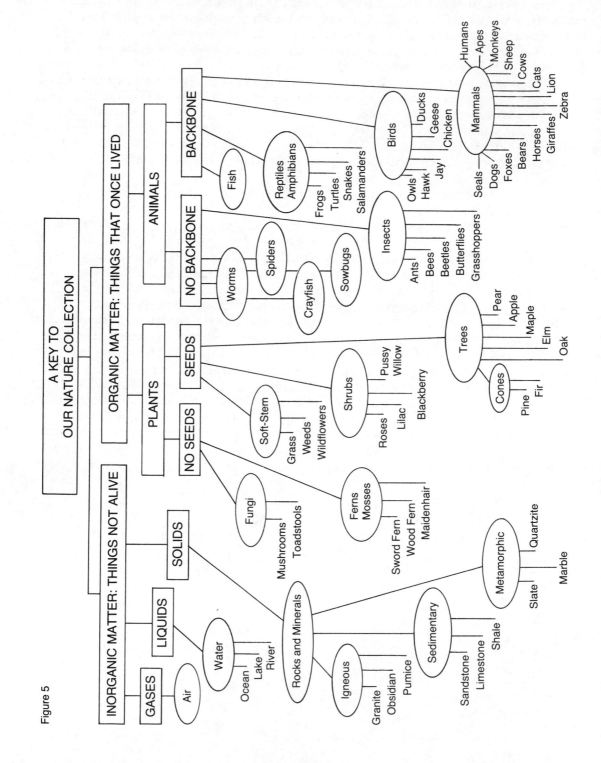

B. Most students learn to classify objects during the intermediate grades. If you have some students who have not developed
this important and basic skill, you should teach them to classify.
To find out if a student, or your class, can classify, conduct the
following activity.

Invite students to consider various ways to sort or group objects
in their nature collection. List their ideas on the chalkboard. An
example might be:

WAYS TO GROUP THINGS

By color   Where an object was
                      found (on what field trip)

By size
                      The way scientists group
                      things in nature
By texture

Permit students to explore all of the containers of objects
holding the nature collection. Some students will actually need to
handle the objects and try sorting 10 or 15 objects by color, then by
size, and still later by texture to recognize that things can be
grouped in many ways.

To classify, students need to be able to group all of the objects
by a single quality (like LIVING/NOT LIVING or WARM COLORS/COOL COLORS),
and then subdivide those two groups by a new quality (like PLANTS/
ANIMALS/ROCKS) and still more subgroupings if they choose.

Describing Changes in Groups of People
Grades 3-5

ACTIVITY OVERVIEW
     Students examine changes in human populations they know about.
They talk about the growth development and aging process, see it
illustrated and apply it to their own lives. They also explore changes
in the social behavior of populations of people.

SCIENCE BACKGROUND
     A group of people living in the same place at the same time is
called a POPULATION. The human population in Prudhoe Bay, Alaska is
about 3,000 people, in Berkeley, California about 125,000,and in
Washington, D.C. about 1 million people. Because populations of
people generally engage in organized cooperative behavior, biologists
also refer to them as SOCIAL GROUPS. For example, people voluntarily
govern themselves through law enforcement and a democratic process
and care for the members through various social agencies. Social
groups are often formed in one place because of favorable environmental factors such as temperature, humidity,or the beauty of the
land forms or water.
     Social groups of people change in at least three ways. First,
membership in the group may change: people come and go. And the size
of the population may change; Honolulu's population is still increasing;
in the tiny river village of Ambler, Alaska, it is decreasing.
     A second way that populations of people change is through gradual
change in the physical status of the majority of the members. When
fluorine was introduced into the drinking water in various cities during
the 1960's and 1970's, their rate of tooth decay through cavities
declined. Historically, immigrants such as explorers and missionaries
have introduced diseases into native populations that had never
experienced the disease. Without resistance, the effect was sudden:
many individuals died. Gradually immunity to the disease developed
within the population through the survivors.
     A third noticeable change in human populations is found in social
behavior. In response to pleasant experiences,such as attending a
funny movie or stimulating musical event, being at a vacation resort,
or with others who enjoy the wilderness, populations of people may
simultaneously smile, laugh, play,or move in similar ways. And in
response to sudden natural disasters such as hurricanes, volcanoes,
floods,or earthquakes, most of the population affected behaves in
similar ways.
     All of the above examples of change in the social behavior of
people are immediate and situational. However, there are also
examples of gradual change in social behavior; snow mobiles replacing

46

sled dogs in Alaska, and television sets in American homes are just two instances which affected a large percentage of the population within a decade.

SOCIETAL IMPLICATIONS

Some of these changes, like changes to population of all organisms, originate from the environment while others are genetic in origin.

Because of the age of the students in your class, some will need to focus on changes in individuals within population. However, you can guide students to look at themselves as part of a specific human population, and as such begin to observe changes within the population. Through awareness of what is happening to the population, people can alter their behavior to benefit the population in some cases.

MAJOR CONCEPT

All groups of living things change: members of the group interact with each other, with other groups, and with the environment.

OBJECTIVES

After completion of this activity the student should be able to:
-Describe changes in groups of people.
-Observe, compare, and infer changes in groups of people.

MATERIALS

-Paper, students' photographs from childhood (optional)

VOCABULARY

-Change, families, human beings

PROCEDURES

The four activities described here (A-D) are designed to focus on the fact that human beings change in predictable ways as they go through life.

A. First ask students to think about the way people change with age. What do babies look like; how are they different from young children, older children (like intermediate grade school children), adolescents, young adults, middle aged adults, and old people?

Invite students to portray these changes by:

1. Drawing pictures of people of all stages of their lives from babies to old age; or

2. Cutting out pictures from magazines and newspapers, showing people of all nationalities and ages; and then seriating them (putting the pictures in order from youngest to oldest); or

3. By simulating the actions of people at all ages, showing how walking and other movement differs between infancy, childhood, adolescence, adulthood, and old age.

When students have finished preparing their representations, ask them to share them with the class.

B. Conduct a discussion with students on the topic: WHAT CAN CHANGE and HOW FAST PEOPLE CHANGE FROM BABIES, TO CHILDREN, TO ADULTS, TO OLD AGE? Do all people change at the same rate? Do some people get old faster than others? In this discussion, encourage students to express their ideas. Examine the ideas as a group. Establish an atmosphere of acceptance of all ideas, with a desire to search for facts backed up by evidence.

Attempt to clarify misconceptions and to reinforce accurate understanding of the process of human growth and development.

C. Have students describe how they have changed in their lives by writing autobiographies. Ask them to describe things they recall about how they have changed, what they could do (ride a bike, skate) at cer'ain ages, and what foods, hobbies, and toys they liked or changed liking, and how their appearance has changed.

Encourage students to illustrate their autobiographies with drawings (for example, losing baby teeth in first grade, learning to ride a tricycle, etc.) or photographs from home.

Invite students to share their autobiographies with the class, but do not insist.

D. Introduce the idea that there are several kinds of change that take place in people. They have been learning about slow changes in activities (A-C) above. This activity focuses on fast temporary changes in people: changes that are visible in their faces because of emotions and the way they feel.

Ask several students to pantomime various emotions: anger, happiness, surprise, fear, sadness, suspicion, and boredom.

Talk about the causes of these changes in emotional states. Do they occur because people interact with other people? Are these changes permanent? How can they control these changes?

Encourage students to watch for these changes in facial expression or behavior of each other, in an effort to learn more about actions that contribute to the happiness and well-being of their classmates.

Collecting and Caring for Small Animals
Grades 3-5

ACTIVITY OVERVIEW
    Students go on a neighborhood walk to observe ants and spiders
in their HABITATS (the particular "home" of each organism) and collect small animals such as Pillbugs or Sowbugs, Snails and Caterpillars
to bring back to the classroom for observation.

SCIENCE BACKGROUND
    Almost any neighborhood walk offers a variety of small animals
to watch if, like Alice in Wonderland, observers are willing to "get
down to the level" where these small animals live and work. A close
look at their world reveals lots of scurrying around, hard work,
hiding from enemies and some life-and-death struggles.
    Who are these animals, where do they live, and what do they do
all day? Joint-legged animals without backbones, known as ARTHROPODS,
are likely to be the most abundant. They can be found all around you;
flying about you or knee-high, perched on or hanging from leaves,
branches, or fences, in their private leaf litter world or under rocks
and underground. Insects are Arthropods; so are spiders, centipedes,
millipedes and crustaceans such as the familiar Pillbug that rolls up
into a ball. What insects lack in size they make up for in numbers.
There are more species of insects (700,000+) than there are among all
of the other animals combined. In addition to the Arthropods, at
least one other resident is likely to be found; the familiar representative of the Mollusks, the land snail.
    Among this group of Arthropods and Mullusks some will be eating
plant materials and are called HERBIVORES, while others may be seen
eating one of their neighbors--usually other small Arthropods--and
are called CARNIVORES. Snails and the Pillbugs are herbivores,
spiders are carnivores, and the insects sort themselves into one of
the other of these options. Grasshoppers and caterpillars (the worm-
like stage of moths and butterflies) are herbivorous; some beetles
are carnivorous.
    Because of their unusual EXOSKELETONS (their hard outer body
covering instead of a backbone), the Arthropods have developed some
interesting ways of getting around. To move in their segmented armor-
like suits, some, like crickets and grasshoppers, have powerful hind
legs. Others have many pairs of legs, like the centipedes, millipedes,
and sowbugs which are great scurriers when disturbed from a dark humid
habitat under rocks or leaf litter. Even the slow moving snail has a
load to carry with its hard calcium-like shell, but manages to get
around when the head-foot of its soft body glides across the smooth
surface of plants.

There are many more unusual features. The compound eyes of insects cannot change focus but they can see things only 1 millimeter away. And the small holes (SPIRACLES) in the exoskeleton of insects and some spiders provides a form of air conditioning combined with respiration. Complex nervous systems of arthropods allow some to perform such feats as mating and building webs in mid-air.

SOCIETAL IMPLICATIONS

The Arthropods and Mollusks of the world greatly affect human survival. Insects are major pollinators of flowering plants; bees' pollination of orchards is just one example. Relatives of the pill-bug are other crustaceans such as crabs and lobsters, that are favorite and important food sources for much of the world; and aquatic relatives of the land snail are other Mollusks such as clams and oysters, also important as food.

Among the Arthropods are several known for their bite or sting; bees, yellow-jackets, hornets, and wasps are all related and their sting causes an allergic reaction in some individuals. Mosquitoes are carriers of malaria, a serious disease in some parts of the world. The bite of some spiders (the Black Widow, Brown Recluse, and Tarantula) can be painful and serious although they are not in the majority.

MAJOR CONCEPT

All groups of living things change: members of the group interact with each other, with other groups, and with the environment.

OBJECTIVES

After completion of this activity the student should be able to:
-Observe, compare, infer differences in organisms.
-Construct small projects with supervision.
-Handle animals with supervision.
-Actively explore the environment and ask questions.
-Assume responsibility for the wise use of natural resources.
-Assume responsibility for providing basic needs of small animals.
-Describe consequences of various alternatives to self and others.

MATERIALS

-Paper bags (4 or 5), crumbled cookie, small pocket knife, and from students' homes: 4 or 5 jars, an old nylon stocking, or other optional materials (see "Instructions" at end of this activity)

VOCABULARY

-Environment, communication, immediate response, ants, insects, spiders, arachnids, pillbugs/sowbugs, crustaceans, caterpillars, metamorphosis, snails, mollusks.

PROCEDURES

    A. Plan a short walk around the school premises or neighborhood surrounding the school in search of small live animals. Ask students what animals they might expect to see and where they might look. Take along 4-5 paper bags, a crumbled cookie, and a pocket knife and explain that you will be looking for some small animals to bring back to the classroom for observation in the coming week. Remind students of their discussion about ways animals change and suggest that perhaps students will be able to look more closely at changes in animals if they are able to take back a few for observation. Also point out that students are likely to see some animals change today during the field trip.

What to look for along the way

    1. <u>Ant hills</u> - Ant hills can be found in cracks between sidewalks, along margins of walks or asphalt next to lawns, playing fields, and buildings. Once you and the students have located an ant hill, observe it for a while. Where are the ants going? What are they carrying? Then place some crumbled cookie near the ant hill. Watch the ants until they discover the new food source. How long does it take? Notice how the ants communicate with one another as they approach or leave the new food source. Was this a slow or fast change in animal behavior?

    Invite any students who wish to learn more about ants by reading about them or adopting an ant hill near their home and making regular observations. Like bees, ants always have a queen ant that lays eggs for the colony, and worker ants. Because they have 6 jointed legs, have segmented bodies, and no backbone, ants are insects.

    2. <u>Spiders</u> - Look for spiders (or spider webs) on branches of trees or shrubs, or fences. Students can see an example of immediate response to change by touching a spider's web with a slender twig, branch, or grass stem. Some spiders will quickly move to the corner of the web, others will run to the web's center when it is touched, still others will stay where they are and pull into a small ball. How long does it take a spider to respond to a change in his/her environment when something touches the web?

    Spiders have jointed legs and soft bodies like insects, but they have eight legs and are therefore called arachnids.

What to take back to the classroom for observation

    3. <u>Pillbugs</u> - Pillbugs and sowbugs are related to shrimp and crabs and are Crustaceans, have segmented bodies and legs, and hatch from eggs. But as land animals, pillbugs and sowbugs can usually be found in dark, damp places near the surface of the soil. Generally, they hide under leaf litter, boards, or rocks.

    Lift up leaf litter, rocks, or boards carefully with a stick since other animals, like spiders or centipedes, may be hiding there as well.

When you locate several pillbugs in a single location, observe them for a few minutes to see what their response to being disturbed and to bright light is. Do they scurry off? Does the pillbug roll up into a ball or "pill"? Sowbugs do not roll up as pillbugs do.

Ask students to gather up 8-10 pillbugs, or sowbugs if pillbugs aren't available. Have them put the bugs into one paper bag and drop some leaf litter on top of them before closing the bag to provide a dark damp environment and food supply for them.

4. <u>Snails</u> - Snails are Mollusks and related to other animals which have hard shells covering their soft bodies, like clams, oysters, and mussels. They can usually be found in garden-like areas where there are several kinds of plants. Snails are easiest to find in early morning or evening as they feed openly on leaves of plants; in midday they often hide beneath leaves and on the stems of plants. When students find a snail or several of them, ask the students to observe closely what snails do when they are picked up. Have students gather 4-6 snails, put them into a paper bag and, using the small pocket knife, cut some 4-5" stems with leaves from plants where the snails were found; this will insure a food supply for the snails while they are in the classroom.

5. <u>Caterpillars</u> - Because caterpillars eat plants, they are often found on the branches of shrubs or trees. Caterpillars make especially interesting classroom pets because they illustrate complete metamorphosis, that is, they are insects which change forms several times as they grow from (1) eggs to (2) larve (called caterpillars) to (3) pupa in a cacoon or chrysalized to (4) adult moths or butterflies.

If students find caterpillars, they need to collect the caterpillars and the leafy branch they are on at the same time, using a pocket knife to cut the branch, since caterpillars will die without the specific kind of leaves they depend on for food. Put the branch with leaves and caterpillar into a paper bag.

B. Take all the animals back to the classroom. They may be kept in the paper bags (held closed with a paper clip) overnight but should be placed in small containers the next day. Several are illustrated next and can be made by students without difficulty. You may want to duplicate and give copies of the instructions to students.

Figure 6

INSTANT HOMES

Jar with piece of nylon stocking and rubber band for lid. Suitable for most small insects, and spiders, and snails.

Two 6.5 oz. tuna cans hold a 8.5″ × 11″ roll of screen in place without staples or stitching. Suitable for small insects (crickets, grasshoppers, caterpillars), pill bugs, spiders. Double the size for butterflies or moths.

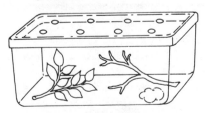

Clear plastic shoebox from drug/variety store with ventilation holes punched with hot ice pick. Suitable for snails, caterpillars, spiders, pill bugs, small turtles and salamanders.

INSTRUCTIONS
FOR
CARE OF SMALL ANIMALS

SPIDERS

Food: *live insects:* flies, gnats for small spiders, mealworms and grasshoppers for large spiders. Spiders also eat other spiders, so separate them unless you intend them for food.
Water: on a small wad of cotton in the jar.
Other: branch for climbing is important.

PILL BUGS AND SOWBUGS

Food: soft, moist leaves and decaying woodland material found in leaf litter, also chunk of raw potato.
Water: sprinkled on soil twice a week or enough to keep soil damp, not wet.
Other: put small amount of soil, then leaf litter in bottom of container with ample ventilation.

SNAILS

Food: leaves of various kinds, especially those where snails were collected.
Water: sprinkle leaves with water.
Other: handful of soil in bottom of container that is ventilated, need smooth surface (glass/plastic) container for locomotion.

CATERPILLARS

Food: eat only one kind of plant, the one they were on when they were found; need fresh leaves *daily.*
Water: sprinkled lightly on the leaves.
Other: shed their skins several times during their larval stage (caterpillars are larva); need a small twig or branch to climb on when they pupate (form their cocoon or crysalid).

Observing Changes in Small Animals
Grades 3-5

ACTIVITY OVERVIEW

Students explore slow and fast changes in animals' appearance and behavior as they observe small animals' (such as insects, pillbugs, and snails) reactions to each other and to changes in light, heat, or moisture.

SCIENCE BACKGROUND

What causes groups of animals to respond to each other and to the environment as they do? The study of animal behavior (ETHOLOGY) is a relatively new branch of biology and questions about the origins of animal behavior are just beginning to be announced.

Animals respond to members of their own species in very predictable ways: either with responses of COOPERATION--such as when adults provide food, care, and protection for members of their family, or with responses of COMPETITION--for food, mates, nests, or sleeping sites. Generally, animals do not kill or eat members of their own species, although spiders are an exception. Instead, most live in large social groups--like bees and ants, or as small groups of families that are TERRITORIAL to prevent over-crowding and competition for food, mates, and a place to sleep. The males of the population "stake out" their territory and take one or more mates who will share their territory, produce offspring, and be protected. Territoriality is often challenged and defended but rarely do males kill or seriously injure each other over territorial fights. Rather, displays of aggression are the rule. Birds announce their territories with songs and display stereotypic postures or flight patterns to ward off intruders. Male fish may change color or puff up to display aggression and primates such as apes, chimpanzees, and baboons may shriek, stamp, or rush at intruders.

Animals respond to different species in predictable ways too: either by engaging in a life-death struggle, cooperating with other species, or ignoring them altogether. Within any COMMUNITY (place where several populations of organisms co-exist), only animals who eat or are eaten by their neighbors engage in attack/flee behavior. PREDATORS (animals who eat another species) such as lions, leopards, and tigers, and their PREY (those eaten by the predator) zebras, wildebeasts, and antelope, are well known examples. In any community, animals which do not have a predator-prey relationship usually co-exist peacefully and ignore one another. For example, the wildebeast, zebra, and antelope mingle on the Serengeti without conflict. But there are also species that have learned to cooperate and live together (SYMBIOSIS): birds that feed on the bugs on backs of impala and rhinoceros are familiar examples.

As animals interact with each other and the environment, they change. Through quick actions, they seek food, defend themselves and territories, mate, and rear offspring. Rapid changes in small animals such as Arthropods and Mollusks include moving in response to changes in heat, light, or moisture.

SOCIETAL IMPLICATIONS
Through television programs such as NOVA and Wild Kingdom, and through personal appearances or popular publications on the work of animal behaviorists such as Jane Goodall, the study of animal behavior has become popularized. The impact of these experiences may result in greater protection of wildlife in general or in specific areas.

MAJOR CONCEPT
All groups of living things change; members of the group interact with each other, with other groups, and the environment.

OBJECTIVES
After completion of this activity the student should be able to:
-Describe changes and infer causes of change in small animals.
-Actively explore and ask questions about animal behavior.
-Combine materials in new ways.
-Compare alternative points of view.
-Assume responsibility for basic needs of small animals.
-Handle and care for tools and equipment, non-toxic substances, plants, and animals.
-Conduct simple experiments without guidance.
-Observe, compare, gather, and organize information.
-Infer, predict.

MATERIALS
-Chart paper (2 pieces about 1 meter x 1 meter each); Felt-tip pen
-Animals collected from Activity 2; snails, pillbugs or sowbugs; if these are not available, purchase mealworms from a pet store (enough for each student to have one mealworm). Or students might bring animal pets (lizard, rat, puppy, rabbit, kitten, or hamster) from home for these same observations.

VOCABULARY
-Change, environment, adapt, responses (slow, fast, sudden, immediate, small, large, gradual) metamorphosis, shedding, migration

PROCEDURES

A. Introduce the concept of change in groups of animals with a discussion. Ask the students:

WHO CAN DESCRIBE CHANGES THEY HAVE
OBSERVED IN ANIMALS?

After several students have described changes they have seen, read about, or watched on TV, put up the chart paper and as you list students' ideas, put them in columns like those below, but without the headings. As you have several examples for each column, stop and ask students how all of these changes are alike and how they differ from those in the other column. See the example below:

WAYS ANIMALS CHANGE

add later: SLOW   FAST

ask: ("How are all of these   (Are these changes different from
changes alike?)   the others in the other column?)

Babies grow up	They change color (chameleon)
They get horns, etc.	They puff up (snakes)
They get larger	They roll up (pillbugs)
They learn new things like	Skunks squirt stuff
flying, swimming	Turtles tuck in their heads and legs
They change color (molting)	So do snails

If students don't guess, suggest that those on the right are very fast changes that animals make. In fact, they are the kinds of changes that animals make in response to changes in their environment or others by meeting other animals. The changes in the left column are changes that are slow, gradual, and sometimes seasonal (like animals shedding a winter coat or a skin that is too tight). Growing up for animals is slow compared with other changes they make like skunks sending out a spray to ward off enemies.

Next, place headings on the chalkboard SLOW-FAST for these two columns and ask students to see how many other examples of these kinds of change they can think of for animals.

B. Invite students to help plan and conduct a careful study of the ways small animals change, linking this idea with the way people change in response to each other and the environment. Refer to the small animals you have brought (mealworms) or the small animals collected on the field trip (snails, pillbugs, or sowbugs) and pose the following questions:

56

WHAT KINDS OF CHANGES CAN WE OBSERVE IN THESE SMALL ANIMALS?
HOW CAN WE FIND OUT WHAT CAUSES THESE CHANGES?

If you have the chart from A (WAYS ANIMALS CHANGE), put it up and encourage students to decide if the chart helps them think of ways they might expect to see these animals change.

Put up a new piece of chart paper and write the questions you have first asked (See underlined example in Chart below). Encourage students to express their ideas about ways to observe animals change. Listen and let students build upon one another's ideas. List on the chart paper their suggestions for what they want to find out and how they would like to proceed.

If you prefer to guide students' discovery rather than follow students' spontaneous suggestions, the chart below illustrates how you might proceed.

WE WANT TO FIND OUT:

1. What changes we can observe
2. What causes the changes

How can we find out? By observing:

A. How animals change when they interact with others like them. (Do they fight, hide, ignore each other?)
B. How animals change when they interact with animals unlike themselves. (Do they fight, hide, ignore each other?)
C. How animals change in response to their enviornment or changes in it. (What do they do when it's too light/dark, warm, cool, wet/dry? How much do they eat, sleep, rest or play?)

Prepare students to assume responsibility for the care and well being of the animals they will observe. Talk about the need to provide every animal with options for safety and survival. For example, if students wanted to see what would happen if they put two animals together, they first need to know what each animal does to protect itself from sudden exposure to bright light or being touched with a twig; both are things that might cause it to hide. Provide a safe hiding place (a stone or leaf litter to hide under of a branch to climb) for both animals if they are to be put in the same container.

Another example is useful to illustrate the student's responsibility for the care and well-being of animals. If students wanted to see how an animal would respond to having its environment warmer or cooler, wetter or drier, lighter or darker, they need to provide options for the animal: a place to get warmer (nearer the sunshine

or a lamp) or cooler (by hiding under a rock or leaf litter); a place
to get wetter (by crawling into damp soil) or drier (by climbing
onto a branch or up the side of the container); a place to get more
light (by moving toward the lightest end of the container) or more
darkness (by hiding under leaf litter).

Talk with students to be sure they understand this need to provide
for animals' safety and well-being, and to prevent the unnecessary
loss of an animal's life or an unexpected result. If animals do not
eat the food provided within 4-5 days, they should be returned to the
place where they were found.

Finally, prepare students to make careful observations and to
organize the information they gather. Prepare a ditto which will help
them with their task. Several examples are offered in Figure 7. Allow
each team to pursue questions of interest to them. You may wish to
have the students pursue questions you have suggested. In the end,
have all teams share the results of their observations.

Figure 7

EXAMPLES FOR DITTOS FOR ACTIVITY

Animal:_____

```
┌─────────────────────────────┐
│                             │
│                             │
│                             │
│                             │
└─────────────────────────────┘
```
          Picture of Animal

The change I observed was
_____
_____
_____
_____

I think the reason for the change was
_____
_____
_____
_____

For students who want to observe
but make no changes.

Animal(s)_____

```
┌─────────────────────────────┐
│                             │
│         (optional)          │
│                             │
│                             │
└─────────────────────────────┘
```
          Picture of the animal

The change we made was
_____
_____
_____

The animal(s)' response was
_____
_____
_____
_____

For students who want to see what
happens when they make a change:
*putting two alike animals together, or
*putting two different animals together, or
*changing the animals' environment.

Comparing Animals' Response to _____ *temperature*

	warm	*cool*
snail / animal 1		X X X
pill bug / animal 2	X X X	
animal 3		
animal 4		
animal 5		

change in (choose only one):

Temperature

warm/cool   or

Moisture

wet/dry   or

Light

bright/dark

Put an (X) to show what
each animal preferred.
Many X's means many
students made separate
observations.

Exploring the Limits of Change in Animals
Grades 3-5

ACTIVITY OVERVIEW

Students choose research topics to learn about the limits of change in animals. Some read about extinct animals, others write for information about endangered species, still others talk with local experts about nearby animals that need protection, or read about migratory animals.

SCIENCE BACKGROUND

Change in animal species is slow, if we consider the animal species that are around us today. For example, the cave art throughout France and Spain in the central Pyrenees depicts bison, deer, horses, and owls that look very much like species living today. Yet these paintings and drawings are estimated to be 10,000 years old.

Because change is slow, there are limits to animal species' capacity to adapt to environments, as we see from fossils of trilobites that once lived. Even the great wooly mammoth that roamed in Siberia also disappeared about 10,000 years ago as glaciers receded and forests replaced once cold grasslands.

The disappearance of a species, called EXTINCTION, has always gone on in nature. It has been estimated that the species alive today--including plants and animals and smaller organisms, represent between 1/10 and 1/1000 of 1 percent of all the species that ever lived. Major changes in climate have been associated with the extinction of many species.

ENDANGERED SPECIES of animals are those whose survival has been threatened, usually by human activity. The sea otters which were once killed off California's coasts for their pelts are now protected, as are Bengal tigers, brown pelicans, and a growing list of animal and plant species. Unlike those species which faced extinction due to natural causes like the Ice Age, endangered species are often threatened by human activities like hunting, encroachment into wilderness habitats which prevents wary animals from mating or building nests, and by the release of toxic chemicals into the environment. When toxins we release enter natural cycles, such as fossil fuel emissions entering the water cycle in the form of acid rain, or--like DDT--enter food chains and become cumulative as they move up the chain with each consumer, human intervention begins to pose a major test of animals' and plants' capacity to adapt or survive.

SOCIETAL IMPLICATIONS

Human survival depends upon protection of the natural environment. Yet through various kinds of activity, especially associated with

highly industrialized and technologically advanced societies such as
ours, we have begun to threaten our survival and the survival of other
species by making major changes in the physical and biological environment.

By learning about the limits of change in other species, scientists
hope to prevent further unintentional destruction of life. Endangered
species, like the canary that coal miners once kept below ground with
them to detect gases,may be the telltale sign that we are in danger.

MAJOR CONCEPT
When groups of animals are forced to change beyond their limits,
the group loses its identity (does not survive) even though matter
and energy are conserved.

OBJECTIVES
After completion of this activity the student should be able to:
-Describe the limits of change or adaptability in groups of
animals.
-Gather and organize information; infer, predict.
-Value responsibility for the natural environment.
-Attempt to compare alternative points of view.
-Describe decisions that involve self and others.
-Discriminate between facts, attitudes and values.
-Describe consequences of various actions or decisions.

MATERIALS
-Books about extinct species of animals (dinosaur, wooly mammoth,
saber-toothed tiger, homing pigeon) about endangered species (certain
whales, herons, fish,and orangutans), and about migratory species of
animals

VOCABULARY
-Extinct species, endangered species, hazards, adapt

PROCEDURES
A. Help students to discover the limits of animals' capacity to
change and still survive or conserve their identities. Have students
work in teams or individually to explore the causes for animals like
the homing pigeon and dinosaur disappearance from the earth.

Four kinds of research projects are described below. Following
them, plan to have a presentation of students research projects and
a discussion of their ideas about the impact on people when species
of animals disappear from the world or when they are endangered.

EXTINCT SPECIES OF ANIMALS

Research
Project 1

Read several books about an animal species such as dinosaurs, wooly mammoths, mastodons, and saber-toothed tiger. Try to find out:
    –How long ago they lived, what their environment was like, what they ate;
    –Their actual size and appearance (in comparison to your size);
    –Who or what were their enemies;
    –Why they died as an animal (species group).

Draw a picture of the animal or make a clay or plastisine model of it, and show its size in relation to people.
Present your findings to the class in an oral report.

ENDANGERED SPECIES OF ANIMALS

Research
Project 2

Write to several sources to find out about endangered species; or read about them in sources listed below. Write to the National Audubon Society, or the American Nature Study Society, or the Sierra Club. Read Natural History magazine, the Curious Naturalist or similar magazines. (for children, The Conversationist). Find out:
    –What species are endangered;
    –Where they live, what they eat, who or what their enemies are;
    –Why they are endangered; and
    –What people can do to protect these animals

Find pictures of these animals.
Present your findings to the class in an oral report.
Addresses: The National Audubon Society, 1130 Fifth Ave., New York, N.Y. 10028. American Nature Study Society, John Gustafson, R.I., Homer, N.Y. 13077.
References: Natural History
Curious Naturalist, Massachusetts Audubon Society, Lincoln, MA.
The Conversationist, (has a regular feature: Youth and the Environment), New York State Department of Environmental Conservation, 50 Wolf Road, Albany, N.Y. 12201

PROTECTING LOCAL ANIMALS

Research
Project 3

Talk with an expert on local wildlife (someone from the parks
and recreation department, the farm advisors office, the forestry
department, the fish and game department, or a science department of
a local college or university, and find out:
1. What groups of animals in the area are most in need of
protection;
2. What suggestions they have for improving the situation;
3. What you can do to help.

Try to find pictures of the animals. Give an oral report to
the class.

RESEARCH ON MIGRATORY ANIMALS

Research
Project 4

Read about species of animals that migrate long distances
in order to be in environments that meet their needs. Salmon migrate
from fresh water to salt water and back again to lay their eggs;
geese and ducks fly from Canada to southern United States and back
each year. Try to find out:
1. What the two environments that the animals migrate to are
like;
2. How far the animals migrate; and,
3. What will happen if the animals didn't migrate.

Try to find pictures of the animals to show the class. Give
an oral report to the class.

B. Presentation of students' research projects should be given
careful preparation. Arrange with each team or person when and how
they will make their presentation. Go over their plans before the
actual presentation to be sure their information is accurate and
clearly organized, and that students see the relationship of animals
interacting with other animals and plants, and with the physical
environment.

C. Following the presentations, have a general discussion which (a) allows students to express their own ideas about the topic, and (b) draws students' attention to the fact that extinct species became transformed into other natural products when they died. Their bodies were changed. Where skeletons remained as fossils, we were able to piece together something about their history. Yet other parts of their bodies were converted to matter and energy; matter and energy were conserved. Invite students to speculate about what happened to the bodies of extinct species plants and animals, and finally to describe why it is important to protect endangered species.

Reaching the Limits of Change and Identity
Grades 3-5

ACTIVITY OVERVIEW
Students take an informal walk through the neighborhood to look for plants and animals that seem unable to adjust to changes in the environment or appear to be dying. Students look for evidence of environmental change.

SCIENCE BACKGROUND
All living things respond to changes in their environment: to changes in temperature, rainfall, or the amount of sunlight, and to changes in the presence or absence of other living things. Everywhere you look you can see evidence that living things respond or react to environmental factors; thus, we say that the origin of some behavior is EXOGENOUS, meaning it originates outside the organism.

But there are limits to the repertoire of responses any organism has. Forget-me-not wildflowers cannot grow infinitely tall in order to gather more sunlight if they happen to grow in a dense forest. There are physiological limits to the height of wildflowers; their nonwoody stems prevent them from growing as tall as trees. The harbor seal found along the shores of northwestern Europe, the Atlantic coast, and the Pacific Ocean often can be seen on rocks and sand bars, proof that they are air-breathing mammals; yet they cannot survive long without an aquatic habitat. Such limits to the growth, development, and behavior of living things are ENDOGENOUS, that is their origins come from within the organism.

The genetic code within every species of organism regulates the limits of its growth, development, and behavior. Genetic codes change very slowly through MUTATIONS, that is, the random occurrence of a new characteristic which, unless lethal, is passed on to succeeding generations. Mutations may be harmful or beneficial.

SOCIETAL IMPLICATIONS
Scientists continue to search for the origins of various plant and animal behaviors and explore the limits of their growth, development, and behavior. They recognize that all living things change naturally as they interact with each other. Organisms change and are changed by their environment.

The goal of many scientists is to learn enough about the capacity of living things to change, before people change the environment so much that familiar organisms cannot survive. It is a race against time, in a way. On the one hand scientists are still learning about the limits of change among various species in the natural scheme of things including natural population explosions or declines, natural

65

disasters, and so forth. On the other hand, society is using its resources at an unparalleled rate, and through technological advances making subtle but major changes in the environment, while at the same time hoping scientists will be able to estimate the impact of these changes on the survival of organisms. Environmentalists are concerned that the risk is too great: the speed at which we are making changes outstrips our knowledge of the impact of changes.

MAJOR CONCEPT

When groups of living things are forced to change beyond their limits, the group loses its identity (does not survive) even though matter and energy are conserved.

OBJECTIVES

After completion of this activity the student should be able to:
-Recognize groups of living things that are reaching their limits of change and identity.
-Observe; compare, infer, predict.
-Actively explore the environment and ask questions.
-Recognize decisions that involve self and others.
-Describe consequences of various alternatives to self and others.

MATERIALS
-None

VOCABULARY
-Limits, change, identity, conserve, matter and energy

PROCEDURE

A. Plan an informal field trip or walk through the neighborhood to look for groups of plants and animals that appear to be dying or that seem unable to adjust to the environment they are in. Look for:

1. Vacant lots where weeds predominate. Within the lot, look for the remnants of a former yard, or plants that have escaped from nearby yards and grow among the weeds. Examples might be flowers or shrubs that are normally cultivated. Notice the quality of these plants that are unattended. Generally their form, color, and size is different from what would be found in someone's yard that is well cared for.

Also look for an area within the vacant lot where conditions are more favorable for plants and animals: weeds may be larger, more robust and greener; more insects and other small arthropods (small animals with jointed legs) may be found in this area. For contrast, look for an area where conditions are less favorable for plant and animal survival; it may be an area exposed to more foot traffic.

Ask students to observe this contrast carefully to see how the size, form, color,and number of plants and animals vary between more favorable and less favorable areas. Try to find examples of plant and animal groups that appear to be dying or are unable to adjust well to the harsher environment.

2. Yards where owners have watered and cared for the plants in their yards, yards where owners have neglected the plants. Without trespassing, note the differences in plants' abilities to adapt to the local environment. Have students describe differences in the plants' size, softness,and greenness, flowering,and fullness; ask them to infer what differences might be present in these two yards. Might there be differences in watering, fertilizing, mowing or pruning, foot traffic,or spading to loosen the soil?

3. A large tree that is in poor health as indicated by bark that has been injured or disfigured, leaves that are being eaten by insects or other small animals, or crown (the top portion of branches and leaves) that has broken,or rotted branches. Talk with students about the condition of the plant (tree) and possible causes for its condition. Could the environment be changed in any way to help the tree survive? Ask students what role the insects or other small animals (or plants such as mold) plays in the deterioriation or decay of the tree. What would happen to the tree when it dies? Get students to think about and discuss the question: AT WHAT POINT WILL THE TREE CEASE TO EXIST AS A TREE...WHEN WILL IT LOSE ITS IDENTITY AS A TREE?

Conserving Plants and Animals
Grades 3-5

ACTIVITY OVERVIEW
Students brainstorm to generate ideas for what can be done to conserve plants and animals in the environment.

SCIENCE BACKGROUND
Within any geographic area settled by people, there were species of plants and animals, called NATIVES, that once lived and thrived in the area before humans settled there. Native plants and animals survived because their basic requirements were met by the environment.

When people move into an area and change the environment, native plants and animals frequently disappear. Native animals may be killed as game, displaced because other animals introduced by people compete for the same food, or frightened off by the presence of people. And native plants may disappear because people cut down trees or replace natives with cultivated trees, shrubs, grasses, or flowers.

SOCIETAL IMPLICATIONS
In most urban areas, people choose not to have the native animals present--or at least not large mammals like deer, fox, and bear. Smaller natives such as squirrels and birds are generally accepted. Native plants on the other hand, have gained in approval because of greater public concern for the conservation of natural resources. People recognize that native plants require almost no watering or fertilizer since their former survival in the environment depended upon existing soil conditions, rainfall patterns, and temperature.

MAJOR CONCEPT
When groups of living things are forced to change beyond their limits, matter and energy are conserved, but individuals and groups lose their identities.

OBJECTIVES
After completion of this activity the student should be able to:
-Describe ways to conserve the identity of plant and animal groups.
-Compare; gather and organize information.
-Combine ideas in new ways.
-Assume responsibility for the wise use of natural resources in the environment.
-Assume responsibility for the health and welfare of self and others.
-Describe decisions that involve self and others.
-Differentiate between facts, attitudes and values.

-Form alternatives which reflect facts, attitudes and values of self and others.
-Describe consequences of various alternatives and rank them.

MATERIALS
-2 pieces of chart paper (3' x 5') and felt tip pen or chalkboard

VOCABULARY
-Conserve, change, limits, matter, energy, transition, identity

PROCEDURE
A. Introduce a brainstorming session to answer the question:

CHART 1

WHAT CAN BE DONE TO CONSERVE PLANT AND
ANIMAL LIFE IN NATURE?

Put up chart 1 and write the title posed by the question above. Ask the question and write all of the ideas students suggest. Fill chart and don't worry about order, form, or style.

When the first round of brainstorming tapers off, put up chart 2. Write the same title as on chart 1 and explain that you would like to consider the same question and see how many of their ideas can be translated into things they or others can do to conserve plants and animals (a) in the neighborhood/city, (b) in the United States, and (c) in the world. Put these as subheadings on Chart 2 (illustrated below), and ask students to sort their ideas into these areas of things to do. Some new ideas may be added during this stage.

CHART 2

WHAT CAN BE DONE TO CONSERVE PLANTS AND ANIMALS IN NATURE?

In our neighborhood/town, we can...
-Plant wildflowers around school and town
-Find out what plants and animals are endangered
-Make the public aware of native plants and animals
    -Put labels on trees on Main Street
    -Put displays in stores showing what plants and
     animals are endangered or to be protected
    -Plant some trees in places they are needed
    -Ask downtown merchants to support improvement plan
     to protect certain plants and animals
    -Write several articles for the newspaper about our
     plan
-Have a children's zoo that shows what animals to protect
-Find out how to use safe insecticides

In the United States, we can...
-Use less paper (save trees from other states)
-Use less energy
-Find out about endangered species
-Find out about fishing and hunting regulations
-Read newspaper articles about plants and animals
-Watch TV programs like NOVA about plants and animals
-Write to our governor, U.S. Senators, and Representatives
 about our concern for protecting specific plants/animals

In the world, we can...
-Invite someone like Mr. X to come to class and tell us about
 endangered species in the world
-Contribute some of our camping fund money to save the whales
-See if we can get a list of pen-pals in other countries to
 write to and share ideas about saving plants and animals

When chart 2 is finished, form action groups to begin putting some of these ideas into effect. Chart 2 indicates some ideas that might be appropriate for students in Grades 3-8.

PLANNING CHART FOR ENVIRONMENTAL BIOLOGY ACTIVITIES: GRADES 6–8

ACTIVITY	OBJECTIVES					TEACHING METHODS	RELATED CURRICULUM
	Conceptual Knowledge	Learning Processes	Psychomotor Skills	Attitudes and Values	Decision-making Skills		
16. What is an Environment?	Environments have identities based on physical and biological characteristics.	Observe, compare.	—	Explore and ask questions.	—	Discussion, film analysis	Social Studies.
17. Planning a Field Trip to Compare Two Ecosystems	Environments have identities based on physical and biological characteristics.	—	—	Compare alternative points of view. Assume responsibility for health and welfare of others.	Consider consequences of alternatives before making decisions. Make decisions based on consequences to self and others.	Chalkboard, discussion.	Social Studies.
18. Taking a Field Trip to Compare Ecosystems	Environments have identities based on physical and biological characteristics.	Observe, compare, measure, classify, gather and organize information.	Use tools that require fine adjustment and discrimination.	Assume responsibility for health and welfare of others. Assume responsibility for wise use of natural resources.	—	Field trip.	Social Studies.
19. Exploring the Limits of Environmental Change	An environment can change and still conserve its identity, but when its capacity to change is exceeded, it loses its identity.	Observe, compare, classify, form hypotheses, predict, infer.	Handle plants and animals. Use and care for tools and equipment.	Actively explore and ask questions.	—	Field trip.	
20. Improving the School Environment	Environments can change and still conserve their identities.	Gather and organize needed information, seek alternative points of view.	—	Assume responsibility for the wise use of natural resources, and for contributing to the health and welfare of others.	Describe decisions that involve self and others, differentiate between facts, attitudes and values, formulate alternatives which reflect facts, attitudes and values.	Brainstorming, discussion.	—
21. Surveying World Environments	When the environment's capacity to change is exceeded, it loses its identity, even though matter and energy are conserved.	Gather and organize information, describe relations among variables.	—	Seek alternative points of view and multiple sources of evidence.	Describe immediate and long-range consequences of various alternatives in changing the environment.	Team learning, oral reports, simulation.	—
22. Understanding the Consequences of Changing World Environments	When the environment's capacity to change is exceeded, it loses its identity, even though matter and energy are conserved.	Gather and organize information, describe relations among variables.	—	Demonstrate the need to use natural resources wisely, and contribute to the health and welfare of society.	Describe immediate and long-range consequences of various alternatives in changing the environment.	Debate, discussion.	—

What Is an Environment?
Grades 6-8

ACTIVITY OVERVIEW
Students view pictures of different environments and describe their defining characteristics.

SCIENCE BACKGROUND
What is an ENVIRONMENT? It is easiest to understand by visualizing a specific place like a lake, a mountainside, or sand dunes, devoid of living things. The environment in each of these places is the part that is non-living. It includes the landform (the bedrock) and water and minerals found in it, the sunlight that falls on it, and the climate that surrounds it.

As you look around you though, the environment that you see is not devoid of life. There are plants and animals and other organisms too small to see--like bacteria and viruses. These living things and the physical environment interact with each other; that is, they exchange matter and energy and therefore, they change one another. Together they form what is called an ECOSYSTEM because they work together as a unit.

Ecosystems vary in size. The aquarium which contains fish, snails, sand and water, and a few plants make up an ecosystem. So is the pond, a forest, or a lake an ecosystem. Some scientists view the entire BIOSPHERE as one continuous ecosystem where the layer of land, water, air, and all living things on the surface of the earth circulate matter and energy on a global basis.

Consider the ecosystem you live in. If you live in a city, the urban ecosystem consists of people, their pet animals, some wildlife (perhaps birds, squirrels, etc.), insects and smaller organisms, as well as a mixture of native and cultivated plants. The landforms may have been altered somewhat to build transportation systems, housing, and industrial or commercial structures; but the climate and amount of light are and have been relatively stable throughout the city's history.

SOCIETAL IMPLICATIONS
The recognition of environments and ecosystems helps to focus attention on the interrelatedness of living things and the earth. As we make decisions about changing the environment, we need to "see" the ecosystem, not just the physical environment. Many ecosystems such as swamps, salt marshes, or deserts are thought of as wastelands by some people, land that should be improved for public use. Many of these changes make valuable contributions to the welfare of people; and occasionally some "improvement" backfires. By increasing

public awareness of the impact of environmental changes on ecosystems, we may be able to make more informed decisions.

MAJOR CONCEPT

Environments have identities based on physical factors (such as climate and landforms) and living forms (the specific plants and animals that live there).

OBJECTIVES

After completion of this activity the student should be able to:
-Explore and ask questions.
-Describe environments that are different from the local one.
-Observe, compare.

MATERIALS

-Set of 3" x 5" color slides (provided by film library, teacher, students,or parents) or film which shows one or more natural environments (travel films are excellent for this purpose)

Note: Pictures from magazines, such as National Geographic, can also be used in this activity.

VOCABULARY

-Environment, climate, landforms, fauna (animal life), flora (plant life)

PROCEDURES

A. Have a slide show which shows as many different environments as possible. Use your own slide collection or invite students to bring in 3" x 5" slides from their travel. Clearly label each person's slides to make returning them easy. Then assemble all of the students, slides in a single container and show them at one time. Ask each student to tell about the characteristics of the environment he or she has visited.

Environments that show great contrast are best. Examples are: snowcapped mountains, forests, rushing rivers, quiet ponds or lakes, deserts, grasslands, agricultural areas, cities,and rural areas.

B. If no slides are available (or for students who did not bring slides), invite two or three students to briefly tell about a contrasting environment they have experienced. Write these terms on the chalkboard: climate, landforms, flora (plants) and fauna (animals), and ask students to describe the environment in terms of the general climate, the land form itself (flat, hilly, mountainous, etc.), the abundance of plants (tree, shrubs,and flowers) and animals (mammals, birds, other).

C. Arrange for a film which depicts a foreign environment. You might select one from your school's catalog of film rentals, or scan the television guide and recommend one for students to watch. After students have seen the film, ask them to describe the environment in as much detail as they can: the climate, the landforms, the plants, and animals (that were seen or could live there).

D. Bring in travel posters which depict foreign environments (can be obtained from travel bureaus and posted on the walls) and books with colorful illustrations of environments.

E. Close this introductory session by describing some of the activities that will be taking place in the coming weeks as the class begins to learn about environments in nearby sites, the changes that occur in environments, and how they (students) can change the environment at school.
A list of coming activities might include:
a. Field Trip to 3 different environments
b. Mapping the environment
c. Find out what this (local environment was like 100 and 200 years ago.

F. Ask students to contrast two environments they know about (from television, reading, movies, or travel).

Planning a Field Trip to Compare Two Ecosystems
Grades 6-8

ACTIVITY OVERVIEW

In this activity, students select two neighboring ecosystems to visit and plan a field trip to compare and contrast them.

SCIENCE BACKGROUND

When two or three ecosystems are compared, the parts or building blocks of each ecosystem become apparent, and the way the parts are interdependent becomes clear. What are these parts and how are they related? Consider "who" lives there.

The presence or absence of any organism in an ecosystem is determined by the range of tolerance the organism has for the various environmental conditions. If any single factor such as amount of rainfall, high or low winter or summer temperature, or mineral content of the soil is lower than the amount the organism requires, it cannot survive. Thus, any minimum requirement which limits whether or not an organism survives in an environment is called a LIMITING FACTOR.

Therefore, all organisms that live in the ecosystem are having their basic needs filled. Every organism in the ecosystem also has an ECOLOGICAL NICHE, a role it plays in the whole scheme of things. For example, there are usually several species of birds in any terrestrial ecosystem: some birds have short beaks for cracking seeds while others have longer beaks for probing for insects and still others have beaks specialized for tearing meat. By specializing in their food selection, the birds avoid competition; each fills a unique role or niche.

Scientists draw a diagram called a FOOD CHAIN or FOOD WEB which depicts the relationship of organisms to each other--a sort of "who eats whom" flow chart.

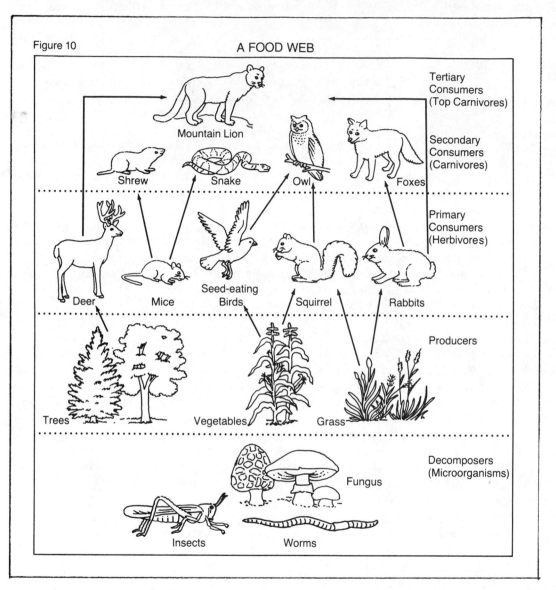

Figure 10 — A FOOD WEB

The purpose of diagramming food chains and food webs is to illustrate how energy passes from one species to another. For example, energy is transferred from the sun to the green plants; the field mice who eat the grass in turn transfer the energy to the hawk who eats the field mice. Scientists call this transfer of energy from one species to another a transfer between TROPHIC LEVELS.

In a food chain then, the green plants are referred to as PRODUCERS (producing food), the mice are HERBIVORES (eating herbs) and hawk are CARNIVORES (eating meat). Together they represent three trophic levels. Ultimately the green plants, field mice,and hawk die, and become food for the DECOMPOSERS, microorganisms that break down living things into raw materials.

SOCIETAL IMPLICATIONS

There is a delicate balance among the parts of every ecosystem. When changes occur to any one part, this delicate balance is upset. For example, without sufficient rain, the grass would die, leaving nothing for the mice to eat, which in turn leaves the hawk hungry. If the hawk were shot by someone, more mice would stay alive, eating more of the grass seed than usual, leaving insufficient grass seed to germinate for next years' crop. In a grassland ecosystem, that may not seem like a serious loss, especially if one lives in an urban area. But by comparing two or three ecosystems, it becomes obvious that the balance in an ecosystem is important. Recognizing this fact has led many people to become concerned about protecting the balance within ecosystems: their own and even those where there are few people, areas called wilderness.

MAJOR CONCEPT

Environments have identities which are based on the specific climate, landforms, plants,and animals that occur in one place.

OBJECTIVES

After completion of this activity the student should be able to:
-Assume responsibility for the health and welfare of ecosystems.
-Describe alternatives for making decisions about natural habitats.
-Consider consequences of various alternatives to self, others, and the environment.
-Make decision based on consequences of all alternatives.

MATERIALS

-Chalkboard or chart paper (4' x 6')
-Map showing the local area and the location of the nearest contrasting environments

PREPARATION

-Knowledge that the school district or students can afford transportation for the field trip.
-Knowledge that transportation is available to the sites.
-Knowledge of the appropriateness of the environments to be visited.

VOCABULARY

-Environment, climate, landforms, limiting factor, ecological niche, food chain, food web, trophic levels, producers, consumers, decomposers, herbivores, carnivores, ecosystem

PROCEDURES

A. Set the stage for planning a field trip to compare two contrasting ecosystems. Begin with a discussion of the environment where students live. On the chalkboard, write:

Figure 11

```
OUR ENVIRONMENT:
climate    (seasons)
landforms  (Geology)
fauna      (animal life)
flora      (plant life)
```

Ask several students to describe the environment. List actual names of plants and animals if students know them; if not, begin with terms such as forests, scattered trees, etc.

After the description is more or less complete, ask what word best describes the environment--in other words, WHAT IS THE IDENTITY OF THE ENVIRONMENT? Suggest the identity of several environments and have students try to recognize their own environment by name: "Rural, urban, desert, tropical island, Arctic, forest, alpine, grasslands, ocean, marsh..." Then write the name of their own environment on the chalkboard.

Next, continue the discussion by having students describe two contrasting environments that are adjacent to their own. Post the map in a conspicuous place. Name several towns, suburbs or familiar landmarks that are located in these contrasting environments. Ask if anyone has ever flown over these regions; and if so, have the students describe the appearance of the environment from the airplane. When the students finish the description, ask how many students have visited these regions or locations by car or bus. Invite several students to describe the regions again, from the ground. Try to have them describe the climate, landforms, and any characteristic animals or plants they observed. Then give names to the two adjacent environments; write their names on the chalkboard.

B. Ask if the class would like to learn more about these two environments first-hand. If there is general enthusiasm, begin planning the field trip.

Put on the chalkboard the following outline and invite students to help you fill in tentative details.

Field Trip to _____ and _____
Transportation:
<u>What we will see</u>: (here list several alternative sites to visit within each environment; imply that the class will decide which ones to see.)
<u>What to wear</u>: (such as boots for hiking, rain gear, etc.)
<u>What to take</u>: (such as cameras, clipboards, lunches, daypacks)
<u>Expected Behavior</u>: (encourage students to name these, and the consequence of various rules)

Discuss as many options and alternatives as possible, if they are consistent with the purpose of the field trip: to compare 2 environments that are different than the immediate environment. Encourage discussion of the various options, for a brief period. Than ask students to help finalize the plan. After the reasons for various choices have been summarized, and the consequences of various alternatives have been described, ask students to help you rank the choices.

Explain that you will have a ditto sheet prepared which summarized the final plan; and will hand it out for them to take home for parental permission to go on the field trip.

Have a student copy the information from the chalkboard for you, after you have erased the items of lowest priority. You can make any final revisions when you put the information on the ditto, along with two additions: 1. <u>the purpose of the field trip</u>.
2. <u>place for parental consent</u>.

C. Ask students to see how much they can learn about each environment before the field trip. Encourage individuals to look in the library, at county or municipal offices (Highway Dept., Parks and Recreation,) and talk with acquaintances who might know about the areas and their history.

D. If you are unfamiliar with the key features of the environments, consider asking an expert in the area to come along on the field trip. Or plan to spend an hour or so talking with the person to help fill in your background. An expert might be a science teacher at the local high school, community college or university, a farm advisor or person from the Parks and Recreation or Forestry Departments, a scout leader or simply someone who has lived in the area for a long time.

If no expert is available, use field guides to enrich your general background, and explore these new environments along with the students, without being overly concerned about identifying specific plants and animals. In other words, learn as you go.

Taking a Field Trip to Compare Ecosystems
Grades 6-8

ACTIVITY OVERVIEW
Students take a field trip to compare and contrast two ecosystems. They follow a transect across two ecosystems and describe the characteristic features of each.

SCIENCE BACKGROUND
One way that ECOLOGISTS, people who study the interaction of organisms with each other and the environment, study an ecosystem is to plot a route that falls along a more-or-less straight line across the ecosystem. They call this line a TRANSECT, and follow it sampling all of the plants and animals along the line.

The transect, like any cross-section, reveals the variety and density of living things in the ecosystem. Ecologists then look for the dominant species in the ecosystem--the key plants or producers, and the key animals (herbivores and carnivores together are called CONSUMERS) in the food chain or web. And they study how these organisms interact with the environment, how they have adapted to the landforms, the climate, minerals, and water, and how matter and energy are recycled within the ecosystem.

Typically, ecologists look for the following groups of organisms in a terrestrial ecosystem: the dominant (1) Trees, (2) Shrubs, (3) Soft-stemmed plants, (4) Mammals, (5) Birds, (6) Reptiles and Amphibians, and (7) Arthropods. They also describe the environment in terms of: (8) the Landform, (9) Elevation above sea level, (10) Annual rainfall, and (11) high and low temperatures for winter and summer. These last three are usually obtained from records if available.

SOCIETAL IMPLICATIONS
A part of most any ecosystem your class will explore will probably have people living in it or at least visiting it. It will be interesting to observe how human activity has influenced the ecosystem, and whether their activity is different in one ecosystem than the other.

MAJOR CONCEPT
Environments have identities based on their specific climate, landforms, plants, and animals.

OBJECTIVES

After completion of this activity the student should be able to:

-Actively explore the environment.

-Observe, compare, measure, classify, gather, and use organized information in the study on ecosystems.

-Use tools and equipment that require fine adjustment and discrimination.

-Assume responsibility for contributing to the health and welfare of self, others, and the environment.

-Assume responsibility for wise use of natural resources in the environment.

MATERIALS

-The following materials may be useful, if they fit your objectives: field guides (describing landforms, plants, or animals in the area); camera; note pad/paper or 3" x 5" cards for notes; day pack for carrying things; plastic bags w/wet paper towel inside, plant collecting is planned and permitted; battery-powered microphone, if the teacher's voice is soft; binoculars.

VOCABULARY

-Environment; cross-section or transect; names of landforms seen; indicator species or names of plants and animals seen (these may be named in general terms such as Ponderosa Pine and Swallowtail Butterfly, if field guides are used to identify them). Also names of tools or equipment used.

PROCEDURES

A. Before the field trip, take the planned route and decide where to stop along the way, how long to stop at each place, and where suitable places are for lunch, rest stops, or refueling. If the field trip is to be an overnight trip, see the campsite that has been reserved and find out about rules or regulations restricting use of any of the sites to be visited.

B. Make a CROSS-SECTION map of the route to be taken. The field trip to compare contrasting environments is a form of transect which cuts across the environments. It will be helpful to sketch this cross-section on a ditto master and provide copies for the students to help them see the larger picture. Students may also want to take notes on the cross-section map during the field trip.

An example of such a cross-section map or transect is illustrated on the following page.

Figure 12

CROSS-SECTION OR TRANSECT SHOWING SEVERAL ENVIRONMENTS

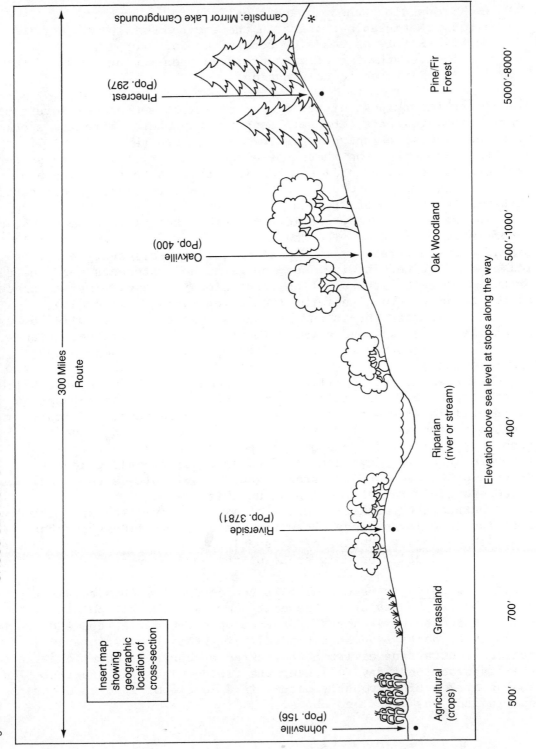

300 Miles

Route

Insert map showing geographic location of cross-section

Campsite: Mirror Lake Campgrounds

*

Pinecrest (Pop. 297)

Oakville (Pop. 400)

Riverside (Pop. 3781)

Johnsville (Pop. 156)

Agricultural (crops)

Grassland

Riparian (river or stream)

Oak Woodland

Pine/Fir Forest

Elevation above sea level at stops along the way

500'   700'   400'   500'-1000'   5000'-8000'

C. Stops along the way are usually determined by:
1. Noticeable changes in the environment.
2. Safety of roadside conditions for stopping.
3. Length of time students have been riding.
4. Distance to destination.

Since the purpose of the field trip is to see and explore contrasting environments, choose places to stop where there are special
features such as abrupt changes in landform and vegetation. If it
is not possible to stop where these occur, point them out to students
on the bus, and wait until you get into an area that is safe and
characterizes the new change in terrain and vegetation. Then permit
students to get out of the bus and explore these areas.

To explore an area, consider either of two teaching methods, or
a combination of them: The teacher/leader as expert who points out
significant features; or students' exploratory-discovery activity
followed by guided inquiry. Or you might have students work in pairs
or teams of 3-4, with each team responsible for exploring one aspect
of the environment: landforms (including rocks or minerals),
vegetation (trees, shrubs and herbaceous plants such as wildflowers,
weeds, ferns, etc.), and animals (mammals or signs of their tracks,
fur, or homes; birds or sounds of them; reptile or amphibians;
insects; etc.).

The team method is effective if students know in advance which
aspect they are responsible for studying. They may photograph or
may use field guides to anticipate what will be seen, or simply
explore at the site. In any case, the teacher brings students
together after a brief exploratory period and asks each team to
report on their exploration and findings, using field guides to
provide pictures of things present but not visible - such as animals,
or to provide more information about things seen.

Whether the teacher-directed or exploratory-discovery method of
teaching is used to study the environment, it is important that
students recognize the indicator species of each environment as the
key to the identity or uniqueness of the environment.

D. Wrap-Up is essential. It can occur at each site visited
along the way by having the teacher summarize the key points of
contrast in the environment. Or wrap-up can occur at the end of the
day when students have seen the full extent of the differences
between contrasting environments. Wrap-up can also occur back in
the classroom on a day following the field trip. The greatest
amount of learning probably occurs if 3 levels of wrap-up occur,
one in each way described above.

Exploring the Limits of Environmental Change
Grades 6-8

ACTIVITY OVERVIEW
Students transplant two different "chunks" of soil and vegetation, each into the environment of the other. By "switching" environments for the two transplants, students will discover how environmental change affects living things.

SCIENCE BACKGROUND
The dandelion that grows in a 10 cm. strip of soil between the bank and the sidewalk on Third Street survives because its needs for temperature, sunlight, water, and minerals are being met. Botanists know that every species of plant has a genetic code which regulates its growth, development, and survival. This code "spells out" the range of conditions the plant can tolerate in terms of temperature, light, water, and minerals.

Some plants like the familiar dandelion can grow in a variety of environments because they have a wide range of tolerance for environmental changes while others like the bristlecone pine have a very limited range. These differences in tolerance account for the widespread or limited distribution of various species of plants and animals.

Environments change very slowly. But people have accelerated that natural process. Scientists now realize that the continued use of fossil fuel has a cumulative effect on environments which is beginning to show up in the quality of air in major cities throughout the world. Los Angeles, California is no longer unique in its radio weather forecasts which tell listeners "The quality of the air today is unhealthful."

Changes in the environment do not happen in isolation; as environments change so do plants and animals in the environment that depend on them. Thus, scientists watch very closely the health of plants and animals in the environment, because they are an index of the health of the environment.

SOCIETAL IMPLICATIONS
Twenty years ago conservationists were concerned about the depletion of natural resources; but the resources they spoke of were lumber, precious metals, coal and oil, water and soil. Soon another resource may be added: clean air. But naming any single factor in the environment that is in short supply should remind us that every species' survival depends upon the limiting factor, that factor which when is in short supply, makes it impossible for the species to survive. Thus, in this activity students will see how changing an

environment can rather quickly threaten the survival of some organisms while others seem to adapt to the change without great difficulty. It is a visual representation of the variability of adaptability.

MAJOR CONCEPT

Environments can change and still conserve their identities; but when their capacity to change is exceeded, environments lose their identities even though matter and energy are conserved.

OBJECTIVES

After completion of this activity the student should be able to:
-Observe, compare, classify, form hypotheses, predict, and infer about the natural environment.
-Handle plants and animals on field trips.
-Use and care for tools and equipment.

MATERIALS

-Spade or shovel, tape measure or ruler, 2 sheets of plastic (about 4' x 4'), 2 cardboard boxes (about 1 ½ cu. ft. or more), anti-shock liquid for transplanting plants.

VOCABULARY

-Transplant, environmental factors, interact.

PREPARATION

-Read earlier activities on ecosystems to understand background for this concept.

PROCEDURES

A. In a brief introductory lecture, explain that many environmental factors interact or work together to determine how well species of plants and animals will survive in any one environment.

List on the chalkboard and discuss the following terms and their relationship to each other:

ENVIRONMENTAL FACTORS

Climate: Amount and frequency of rainfall (da/mo/yr)
            Temperature range (daily, monthly, yearly) fog, humidity, wind
            Amount of sun and shade, day length

Landforms: Substate/rock
            Soil-amount (depth), mineral content, and porosity
            Slope of ground, elevation from sea level
            Orientation to light: SW, NE, etc.

Flora: Other plants that compete for same soil nutrients,
             sun, water.

Fauna: Animals which compete w/each other for food, shelter,
             etc. and depend on plants.

B. Propose an experiment the class can perform to demonstrate
the fact that plants in any one area are those which are best suited
to the combination of physical and biological factors in the environment. By the end of the experiment students will begin to see the
limits of plants to respond to change when a single factor or two in
an environment are changed.

Describe two microenvironments nearby that offer contrast in
vegetation. If possible, choose a place where most other factors
(elevation, slope, amount of rainfall, temperature) are the same.

Explain the experiment to dig up a plot of soil 20x20x20 cm.
with plants intact--from each environment, and to transplant the two
samples of soil/plants each in the other environment. The purpose
of this experiment is to find out how well the plants survive in
another environment. Students will find it exciting to wait and
watch day by day or week by week for changes that will occur.

Draw a diagram on the chalkboard like the one below and write
a brief description of each environment beneath each soil/plant
sample.

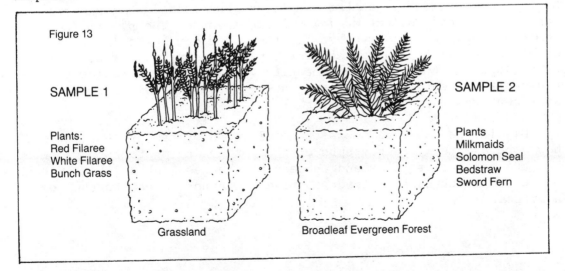

Figure 13

SAMPLE 1

Plants:
Red Filaree
White Filaree
Bunch Grass

Grassland

SAMPLE 2

Plants
Milkmaids
Solomon Seal
Bedstraw
Sword Fern

Broadleaf Evergreen Forest

Ask students to speculate: what will happen to the plants in
each area? List their guesses or predictions on the chalkboard.
After they have actually visited the two sites, the class can finalize
their hypotheses about changes in the transplants.

C. Take the students out to see the two environments, one after the other. Select the actual sites for the transplants in one environment. Find a place where the vegetation is typical of the environment, that is, has one or two of the most abundant ground cover plants. (These soil/plant transplants will not include trees or shrubs for obvious reasons). Ask 2 or 3 students to measure the spot for the sample: 20 cm x 20 cm. Then have other students water down the soil/plant sample before they dig it up. An anti-shock plant liquid should be added to the bucket of water before pouring it over the sample.

After a few minutes, have students dig up the sample and place it in the cardboard box which has been lined with the sheet of plastic. The plastic should be wrapped over the top of the sample to prevent loss of water while the first sample is being transported to the second environment.

Students carry the first sample to the second environment and repeat the process: finding a typical area of plants for the sample, measuring the 20 cm. x 20 cm. area, watering it down, digging up the sample, placing it in the second plastic lined box. Then students place the first soil/plant into the second hole. Once the transplant is safely in place, students can pour additional water with diluted anti-shock liquid into the transplant. The process is repeated, taking the second sample to the first environment, placing it in the hole, and watering it.

Finally, students make a record of their experiment, noting the time of day, date, weather conditions, and location of the transplants. They may collect additional specimens of the plants (not from their samples) to take back to the classroom to be identified so that more can be learned about the plants. Or some students may try to identify the plants at the site while others are doing the spade work. Identification is certainly not essential in this experiment however.

D. In the days and weeks that follow, a system of observations should be planned. Photographs of the changes help students remember what the original samples and subsequent changes looked like. Students should see which plants cannot survive or cannot adjust to the new environment.

Improving the School Environment
Grades 6-8

ACTIVITY OVERVIEW

Students consider the question of how they can improve their school environment and develop a plan that they discuss with others in the school environment.

SCIENCE BACKGROUND

In the spring of 1979, more than a dozen homes tumbled down the hillside into Bluebird Canyon in the small town of Laguna Beach, California. Geologists who were brought in to analyze the situation and prevent the loss of still more homes explained that the hillside, like many along the coast of Southern California, was unstable.

On another spring day more than a decade earlier, several blocks of houses were instantly destroyed as an earthquake, measuring 8.0 on the Richter scale, which originated in Prince William Sound shook Anchorage, Alaska. Both of these changes in the environment were caused by natural forces. They dramatically affected the lives of all who happened to be living there.

When environmentalists remind us of the changes we have made in the environment, it is sometimes easy to forget that nature also makes rather large, and sudden, changes in the environment.

But people do change the environment: they seed clouds to produce rain; they irrigate deserts to increase agricultural lands; and they alter hillsides and mountains, rivers and valleys to "improve" nature or the quality of life by building freeways, mining fossil fuels, and building high-rises.

SOCIETAL IMPLICATIONS

Environmental planning has become a part of our language and actions in the 1980's. For example, a quick glance at the Yellow Pages of the Berkeley-Oakland, California telephone directory in 1980 showed over 60 organizations, services, and consultancies that specialized in environmental protection and planning. Across the United States this increased concern for the environment has led to the formation of action groups, political initiatives, and regulations to protect the environment. Environmental "improvements" that replace human-made structures for natural habitats no longer go unquestioned.

MAJOR CONCEPT

Environments can change and still conserve their identities.

OBJECTIVES

After completion of this activity the student should be able to:
-Actively explore the environment.
-Assume responsibility for the wise use of natural resources in the environment.
-Assume responsibility for contributing to the health and welfare of others.
-Attempt to compare alternative points of view.
-Describe decisions that involve self and others.
-Gather information needed and become aware of differences between facts and attitudes or values.
-Form alternatives which reflect facts, attitudes, and values of self and others.
-Rank alternatives and select those with most benefits.

MATERIALS

-Chart paper (about 1 m. x 2 m), felt-tip or marking pens, (10-20)

VOCABULARY

-Improve, environment, native plants, native animals, brainstorm alternatives, attitudes, values, facts, opinions, benefit

PROCEDURES

A. Recall with students their earlier projects in which they learned about their present environment.

B. Then ask the students if they think it would be possible to improve the school environment. As students begin to consider the question, put up a large sheet of chart paper, get out the felt-tip pens, and tell them you would like to begin a brainstorming session. Describe the rules for brainstorming. Put the title on the chart: IDEAS FOR IMPROVING OUR SCHOOL ENVIRONMENT. List all of the students' ideas; remember that the goal is to generate as many ideas as possible-- not to evaluate the practicality or value of any ideas at this stage. Explain that you hope the class might be interested in trying to put some of these ideas into use. Then outline the next steps.

```
┌─────────────────────────────────────────────────────────────────┐
│          EXAMPLE OF A BRAINSTORMING CHART BY ONE CLASS            │
│                                                                   │
│             Ideas for Improving our School Environment            │
│                                                                   │
│   Pick up trash                 Put in a new play field and       │
│   Sweep up                         bleachers                      │
│   Paint the school              Put a safe place for the little   │
│   Fix the broken window            kids to play                   │
│   Plant flowers                                                   │
│   Plant trees and bushes        AFTER THOUGHTS:                   │
│   Put in a lawn                                                   │
│   Put in a lake                 Paint the trash cans and bike     │
│   Have animals                     rack                           │
│   Have a garden with flowers    Have music at recess and          │
│      and vegetables                lunchtime                      │
│   Make a miniature farm         Window boxes for those who        │
│   Make a little zoo                want them                       │
│   Separate the play area and    New rules for behavior at         │
│      the plant, animal stuff       school                         │
└─────────────────────────────────────────────────────────────────┘
```

C. Follow the brainstorming session with a walk around the school ground itself. Have one or two students take notes, recording ideas that students have while the class looks critically at the school environment. When this on-site field trip is over, ask students to add any ideas they have for improving the school environment to the brainstorming chart.

D. Finally, encourage students to think about improving the school environment for the remainder of the day and to add any ideas they have to the chart, so that next day the class can begin to develop a plan to put some of the ideas into practice.

E. Set the stage for a discussion of the ideas for improving the school environment; explain that you would like to help students develop a plan to put some of their ideas into action. Put up the brainstorming chart from (B) above, and ask:

HOW CAN WE DEVELOP A PLAN TO IMPROVE OUR SCHOOL ENVIRONMENT?

Explain that students should consider all of the ideas suggested and decide which ideas will contribute most to the health and welfare of others and to preserving or improving the environment. As students begin to discuss each of the ideas on the chart, guide them toward searching for those ideas which will benefit most students or balance the interests of various groups, gradually revising and ranking the ideas on the brainstorming chart. Avoid excessive criticism of any one idea by pointing out the positive values to it.

F. Once the class has agreed upon some ranking of the ideas on the brainstorming chart, begin the new chart by putting at the top of the title:

PLAN FOR IMPROVING OUR SCHOOL ENVIRONMENT

Then list in rank order the 4-6 ideas that students liked best. Leave 3-4 lines of space after each of the ideas you put on the new chart.

G. Next, direct students' attention to the fact that they will need more information about many of the ideas before they can make a final decision about which ideas to include in their plan for improving the school environment. Beside each idea, ask:

WHAT DO WE NEED TO KNOW BEFORE WE CAN PUT THIS IDEA INTO ACTION?

and list the students' questions or information that is needed.

EXAMPLE OF A PLAN CHART BY ONE SCHOOL

Plan for Improving Our School Environment

1. Plant native trees, shrubs, and flowers in one area for people who like nature.
   -Where do we get the trees and things?
   -Where will we put them?
   -How will we get them here?
   -Who will pay for them?
   -Will the principal let us do it?

2. Fix the play field with new lines and fill in the holes.
   -Will the custodian do it?
   -Who decides if it's OK if our parents want to help?
   -Whose parents will help?

3. Paint the trash cans and make new rules about clean-up and litter.
   -How much will it cost?
   -Can we do it (permission)?
   -Who will make the rules?
   -How will we enforce them?

H. To gather the information students need, invite the key people as guests to your classroom to hear about students' interest in improving the school environment. Begin with the school principal, since he or she has the final responsibility for decisions affecting the safety and welfare of students and staff, school budgets, codes and rules, and the school grounds. Explain to the principal in advance the purpose of his or her visit.

Others who might be invited on separate occasions include the custodian, someone from the Parent-Teachers Association, or persons who might contribute in some ways to implementing the students' plan to improve the school environment.

I. Help students revise their plan, discuss alternatives, and add new ideas until their plan becomes realistic.

J. Implement the plan for improving the school environment. The exact procedures will have been worked out by you, the students, and the administration.

Surveying World Environments
Grades 6-8

ACTIVITY OVERVIEW

Students pool their impressions of ways people have changed the environment throughout the world, and classify these changes as positive, negative or neutral.

SCIENCE BACKGROUND

Throughout the world, environments are in constant change. Some of these changes are natural--meaning caused by natural processes. For example, on a beautiful spring day in May of 1980, Mt. St. Helens in the state of Washington erupted. The volcanic activity that continued for months made major changes in the plant and animal communities that surrounded the region.

But human activity also accounts for many major changes in environments throughout the world. These changes may be beneficial or harmful to surrounding plant and animal communities, and may often have results that do not become visible for several decades. Consider two examples, one with beneficial effects and the other with serious consequences.

In the 1930's, President Roosevelt approved a plan to develop a major water reclamation project in the Tennessee Valley. By damming the water of the Tennessee River the plan was designed to provide inexpensive electrical power, flood control, improved navigation, and irrigation for the population in and around the Tennessee Valley. For nearly half a century, this TVA project has served the population in a beneficial way.

During the same decades, fish in pristine lakes of the Adirondack wilderness and Canada have died out completely due to acid rains. The problem is not limited to eastern United States however; lakes in the Rocky Mountains are beginning to show the same signs of acidification that were first found in the Adirondacks and concentrations of toxic materials are showing up in the ground water in Sweden. Acid rain forms when air pollutants from fossil fuel combustion combine with moisture in the atmosphere; it is the end product of a series of chemical reactions that result when industrial and automobile pollutants enter the air.

On November 16, 1979, the first world-wide steps were taken to curtail the international forecast for increased acid rain: In Geneva, 34 member countries of the U.N. Economic Commission for Europe signed the first broad international agreement dealing with acid rain. The resulting "Convention on Long Range Transboundary Air Pollution" provides for the sharing of information, cooperative research, and continued monitoring of pollutants and rainfall. It sets no numerical goals, limits, or time-tables and has no plan for abatement or enforcement of controls. According to Armin Rosencranz of the Environmental Law Institute, the prospects for the future look bleak. The problem with international or bilateral agreements is that the acid rain patterns do not coincide with the pollution-producing countries; where acid rain falls depends on how the winds blow and they usually carry the acid rain to areas away from the source of pollution. Thus, cooperation between countries is presently limited. Britain may be sending an estimated 60% of the sulfur compounds that Norway receives, yet the British are publicly skeptical about the urgency of the acid rain problem. A similar condition exists between the United States and Canada, with our country sending four times as much sulfur dioxide pollution to Canada as it receives from its northern neighbor.

SOCIETAL IMPLICATIONS

Many changes that people make in the environment have a delayed effect like the acid rain that is caused by pollution. If we look at the major environmental changes made by people, most were planned to improve the quality of life, but many result in detrimental consequences a decade or so later. We can learn from our mistakes before it's too late.

MAJOR CONCEPT

Environments can change and still conserve their identities. There are limits to the capacity of environments to change and still conserve their identities. When the capacity to change is exceeded, environments lose their identities even though matter and energy are conserved.

OBJECTIVES

After completion of this activity the student should be able to:
-Gather and organize information about world environments.
-Describe relation among variables influencing changes in environments.
-Seek alternative points of view and multiple sources of evidence.
-Demonstrate the need to use natural resources wisely.
-Demonstrate responsibility for contributing to the health and welfare of others in society.
-Describe immediate and long term consequences of various alternatives to society and the environment.

MATERIALS/RESOURCES

-Print Media: Newsweek, Time, U.S. News and World Report, Science, New York Times, Los Angeles Times, Washington Post, and similar periodicals

-Electronic Media: Television programs such as the Evening
News, NOVA and documentaries on special issues regarding the environ-
ment, and similar programs to these on radio.
-Ditto listing all of these and other sources available.
-Chart paper (1m x 2m)

VOCABULARY

-Contamination, change, limits of change, extinction, (other
terms determined by the resources selected and referred to in
materials above)

PROCEDURES

A. Introduce the topic by asking the question, HOW HAVE PEOPLE
CHANGED THE ENVIRONMENT ON A WORLD-WIDE BASIS? Refer to a stack of
magazines and newspapers, reading a few titles of articles in
magazines and headlines of newspapers which deal with the topic
question.

Invite students to describe ways that people have changed the
environment. List these ideas on the chalkboard. The list below
includes ideas that were suggested by one group of students. Notice
that the list was largely negative in its outlook at first until the

```
        WAYS PEOPLE HAVE CHANGED ENVIRONMENTS IN THE WORLD
     -Pollution-containers, smog, insecticides
     -Waste from factories, from garbage, and old cars people
        don't want
     -Cut down forests to make houses and paper
     -Use farm lands to make cities
     -Cut down forests to make farms
     -Lakes have been contaminated and poisoned fish
     -Endangered species (whales and some birds)
     -Lakes were made artificially (rivers were dammed)
     -Some endangered species have been saved and increased
     -Coal mines have destroyed mountains
     -Radioactive wastes are being dumped
     -Irrigation for farm lands
```

teacher asked if there might be any changes that were beneficial.
Also notice that the teacher made little attempt to organize the
ideas or ask for specifics; rather all assumptions were accepted,
and as students' ideas were offered, they were recorded, in order
of their occurrence.

B. After students have expressed most of their ideas, put up the chart paper with a title such as the one illustrated below and subtitle the categories POSITIVE, NEGATIVE, and NEUTRAL changes. Ask the class to help put their ideas from the chalkboard into sentences or statements that they believe about the changes people have made in the environment and to classify these changes as to the benefit or harm they might have on a long-term basis. The chart below illustrates how one set of ideas was organized:

HOW HAVE PEOPLE CHANGED THE WORLD'S ENVIRONMENTS?

Negative
Changes
  -Forests have been cut down.
  -Using too much fossil fuel makes air
      contaminated
  -Mining, drilling,or transporting fossil fuels
      have changed the surface of the earth and
      disrupted animals' habitats.
  -Radioactive materials in water and underground
  -DDT and other insecticides have contaminated
      water and fish

Positive
Changes
  -Hydroelectric needs have created dams, lakes,
      and reservoirs
  -Irrigation has made deserts into farms

Neutral
Changes
  -Cities have been built
  -Farms have been created

CHART SHOWS REORGANIZATION OF SOME OF STUDENTS' IDEAS INTO STATEMENTS THAT CAN SERVE AS RESEARCH TOPICS.

Understanding the Consequences of
Changing World Environments
Grades 6-8

ACTIVITY OVERVIEW
   Teams of students search for reliable and accurate information
about the consequences of changes in the environment and present
their findings to the class in one of three forms: oral report,
simulation,or debate.

SCIENCE BACKGROUND
   Changes in the environment can have delayed but profound effects
on the plant and animal communities of the region affected and that
sometimes, as in the case with acid rain, changes in one environment
can affect living things in another environment.
   Here we consider the value of long-term studies of the impact
of environmental change. Consider the first 10-year report of the
effect of the Alaskan Pipeline on wildlife. In 1968, the Atlantic
Richfield Co. (ARCO) discovered oil in Prudhoe Bay on the Alaskan
North Slope. In this frozen land above the Arctic Circle where winter
nights last 24 hours, ARCO, British Petroleum,and several other oil
companies developed a 250 square mile oil field and constructed
the first trans-Alaskan Pipeline that transported Prudhoe crude to
Valdez where it was loaded onto tankers.
   Envrionmentalists were concerned about the effects of the oil
fields and pipeline on native wildlife. Systematic surveys have
been conducted each year between 1969 and 1979, sponsored by ARCO.
Their first 10-year report acknowledged that there had been
disruptions and disturbances in wildlife habitats, but assumed there
would be no long-lasting effects. The Central Arctic Herd of caribou
around Prudhoe Bay has remained between 5000 and 7000 despite a decade
of activity in its range.
   One hopes the ARCO report looks at the whole picture and in
sufficient detail to prevent intentional changes with unintentional
consequences like that made in the Kaibab National Forest in Arizona
where deer herds were to be "protected" from coyote and other
predators. After 20 years, the herd of 4000 mule deer increased to
100,000 individuals. During the next 15 years, disease and starvation
brought the population down to 10,000 but not before they had destroyed
the ecosystem. In Alaska, where many plants put out only a few leaves
each year, the consequences of disrupting an ecosystem are much more
serious since the time-table is slower.

SOCIETAL IMPLICATIONS

In this activity students are guided toward objective analysis of information about environmental issues that affect their welfare and that of other living things and the environment. Human beings are curious, inventive, and acquisitive individually and as a species. Because of this fact, humans are likely to continue to change their environment. When the population of the world was smaller, these human traits and the changes we made did not have such serious consequences. But with a population of 4 ½ billion people, environmental changes have more profound effects. Thus, the goal of these activities for students has been to provide them with the tools to look closely at the individuals, populations, and environments around them and in the world at large; and to pay attention to changes, knowing that there are limits to change and survival in nature; and finally to openly question issues that involve change in the environment.

MAJOR CONCEPT

When the capacity of an environment to change is exceeded, it loses its identity even though matter and energy are conserved.

OBJECTIVES

After completion of this activity the student should be able to:
-Gather and organize information.
-Describe relation among variables.
-Identify alternative explanations for changes in environments.
-Demonstrate the need to use environments and resources wisely.
-Describe short, medium, and long term consequences of changing environments.

MATERIALS

-Various materials from libraries and agencies dealing with the environment

VOCABULARY

-Environment, detrimental, consequences, cost, risk, benefit, analysis (other terms will be unique to the projects selected by students)

PROCEDURES

A. After students identified environments which have changed suggest several ways they could find out more about whether or not these environments have really been changed "beyond their capacity to change"; in other words, whether the identities of the environments themselves (defined by the plants, animals, landforms, and climate) have been lost.

Cite as an example of permanent change species of animals that are extinct (the homing pigeon) or environments that have disappeared (the age of dinosaurs). Cite as an example of reversible change Lake Erie, which was once severely contaminated.

Encourage students to learn more about the controversies surrounding specific incidents and environments. Display the periodicals you have brought in. Distribute a list of these resources to the students. Ask students to organize themselves into teams of 4-6 members. Encourage each team to select a topic they would like to research. During this stage, allow teams to overlap in their interests rather than to insist any team take a topic they are not interested in. Later you can subdivide topics to avoid too much overlap.

Suggest how the teams might organize their research, and describe the various ways they might present their findings to the class. A list is suggested below; develop your own plan, put it on a second ditto and distribute copies to students.

PLAN FOR ORGANIZING RESEARCH TEAMS
AND PRESENTING FINDINGS
(sample ditto for students)

Once your team has chosen a topic to research, do (a) or (b) below.

(a) Have each person in your team search one or two kinds of resource.
Example: Charlie reads several issues of Science and Newsweek; Bill reads several issues of U.S. News and World Report; Jim reads several month's of the Washington Post; Irene watches the evening news on TV; Phyllis listens to news on radio.

(b) Have each person try to answer a single question (or two) within the topic, and use many resources.
Example: Charlie tries to find out how many nuclear power plants there are in the U.S. and where they are; Bill tries to find out how many risks or accidents like Three Mile Island's leak have occurred; Bill tries to find out what scientists think are safe procedures for dumping nuclear wastes, etc.

To present your team's findings, plan to do one of the following kinds of presentation:

(1) oral reports   (2) simulation   (3) debate.

SCHEDULE:
-Progress reports (discussion with teacher) due in
 one week (date)
-Sign-up for final presentation (date)
-Actual final presentation: (Dates) _____,_____,
_____,_____,

B.   When teams present their findings, help the entire class to
learn from each team's report or presentation. Prepare a ditto that
focuses attention on the <u>major concept</u>, and the thoroughness students
have demonstrated in their <u>search</u> of the topics. Following each
team's presentation, ask the class to engage in discussion of the topic
and consider whether the team has provided evidence to support their
conclusions. A sample GUIDELINES FOR PRESENTORS AND LISTENERS is
suggested below.

GUIDELINES FOR PRESENTORS AND LISTENERS

<u>Major Concepts relating Science and Society</u>
A.   Environments can change and still conserve their
     identities.
B.   Each environment has a limit in its capacity to change
     and still maintain its identity (survive as an
     environment).
C.   When an environment changes beyond its capacity for
     change, it loses its identity, even though matter
     and energy (within plants, animals,or landforms,
     for example) are conserved.

Q.1 Did the team's topic fit one of the concepts?
Q.2 Did the team state their conclusions?

<u>Research Methods</u>

Q.1 Did the team gather and organize information?
Q.2 Did they seek alternative points of view and more
     than one source of evidence?
Q.3 Did they describe immediate and long-term consequences
     of the change on society and the environment?
Q.4 Did they discuss the need to use natural resources
     wisely?
Q.5 Did they demonstrate responsibility for the health
     and welfare of all in society and the environment?

RESOURCES FOR TEACHING ENVIRONMENTAL AND BIOLOGICAL SCIENCES

More materials on environmental science will be found in the section on Environmental and Earth Sciences.

Brown, Vinson. Knowing the Outdoors in the Dark. New York: Macmillan, 1973. 175 pp. $2.95, paperback. Teacher Resource. Interesting and sometimes poetic suggestions for exploring nature, wilderness, or front porch at night.

Carson, Rachel. The Sense of Wonder. New York: Harper & Row, 1965. 90 pp. $12.95. Beautiful, evocative photographs by Charles Pratt convey a sense of wonder and a sense of places frequented and described by Rachel Carson before she died. Intended for adults, but should appeal to children.

Cornell, Joseph. Sharing Nature with Children. Nevada City: Ananda Publications, 1979. 143 pp. $4.95 + $1.00 postage. Teacher Resource. From 900 Alleghany Star Rt., Nevada City, CA 95959. A creative and sensitive collection of 42 nature games and activities suitable for children of all ages and city parks and backyards, as well as rural areas. Games are arranged by mood—calm/reflective, active/observational, and energetic/playful. All of these games have been field-tested with thousands of children through teachers, scout leaders, and camp groups.

Couchman, J. K., and others. Examining Your Environment Series. New York: Holt, Rinehart, and Winston. 13 vols. $4.26 each. Teacher's Guide, $1.95. Grades 4-6. An activity-oriented science series which uses free or inexpensive apparatus (some of which can be constructed by students) to explore local environments—city, suburb, or rural—through touching, seeing, hearing, observing. A flexible series, easily adapted to any classroom situation, with a fine teacher's guide. Individual titles include: Astronomy, Birds, Ecology in Your Community, Mapping Small Places, Mini-Climates, Pollution, Running Water, The Dandelion, Trees, Your Senses and others.

Hensel, Karen, and others. New York Aquarium Brown Bag/Education Kit. Brooklyn: New York Aquarium Education Department, 1979. Kit, $3.25. Grades 3-7. From New York Aquarium Education Department, Boardwalk and W. 8th Street, Brooklyn, NY 11224. Useful in helping teachers develop class investigations of various subjects in marine biology with suggested projects and bibliographies. Includes six curriculum infusion units: Fish, Sea Plants, Invertebrates, Realia, At the Aquarium, and Water. Other inexpensive materials are available from the same source, for example $.40 each will buy Puzzles and Games for ages 5 to 8 or 9 to 12, Whales for ages 9 to 12, Beaches for the same ages.

Hickman, Mae, and Guy, Maxine. Care of the Wild, Feathered, and Furred: A Guide to Wildlife Handling and Care. Santa Cruz: Unity Press, 1974. 197 pp. $4.95, paperback. Helps the reader look after wildlife that may be afflicted with broken bones, oil ingestion, or other disabilities; provides good advice on raising baby birds and animals. Highly recommended by such groups as the National Audubon Society and the Defenders of Wildlife.

Nickelsburg, Janet. Nature Activities for Early Childhood. Menlo Park: Addison-Wesley, 1976. 158 pp. $9.00. Pre-school and up. An attractive book by an author in her 80's still actively involved in nature study organizations and teaching science. This project book has sections dealing with outdoor groups, small animals, indoor projects, watching things, growing things, looking for things, keeping things alive, and caring for things. Each project has suggestions for materials, vocabulary, and activities, with book lists for children and adults.

Russell, Helen Ross. Ten Minute Field Trips: Using the School Grounds for Environmental Studies. Garden City: Doubleday, 1970. 173 pp. $7.95, paperback. Thousands of interesting activities and observations appropriate for any urban or suburban setting can be gleaned from this impressive book. Projects relate to plants, animals, earth science, and physical sciences--and the interrelationships of these.

Skelsky, Alice, and Hackaby, Gloria. Growing Up Green: Parents and Children Gardening Together. New York: Workman, 1973. 240 pp. $5.95. Grades 3 and up. Teacher Resource. Intended for parents, but excellent for teachers with unusual, creative suggestions such as repeating experiments of famous plant-scientists, studying sprigs of plants, harvesting and cooking, as well as planting and growing.

Children's Resources: Books, Games, Records, and Pictures

Arnowsky, Jim. Crinkleroot's Book of Animal Tracks and Wildlife Signs. New York: Putnams, 1979. Unpaged (about 47 pp.) $7.95. Grades 3-7. A charming, profusely illustrated book, which uses the character of Crinkleroot, a backwoodsman, to present a great deal of information on animals and their behavior through animal tracks. Covers eight animals in depth and 21 other mammals and birds in less detail.

Barchas, Sara. Everyone Has Feelings and Other Children Songs. Folkways Records, 1979. Record. $7.98. Grades K-3. From West 61st Street, New York, NY. A 33-1/3 record album including such songs as "Just by Watching," "What Happened to the Dinosaurs," "Walking in the Woods," and "Once I Had Two Rabbits."

Bester, Roger. Guess What? New York: Crown, 1980. 32 pp. $6.95. Grades K-1. A fun book with animal riddles (on horses, squirrels, ducks, cows, chickens, pigs, sea gulls, etc.) that use photographs and words to provide authentic clues. Pleasurable, yet quite informative.

Blough, Glen. Discovering Cycles. New York: McGraw-Hill, 1978. 48 pp. $5.72. Grades 3-7. Suggests activities to help youngsters discover for themselves some of the important cycles of nature and how they operate.

Brown, John Cuthbert, translator. The Way Things Work Book of Nature: An Illustrated Encyclopedia of Man and Nature. New York: Simon & Schuster, 1980. 525 pp. $17.50. Grades 6 and up. Teacher Resource. One of the Way-Things-Work series translated from the German, and highly popular with older children. This well-indexed, well-organized,and well-illustrated volume is concerned with the environment and environmental policies.

Cochrane, Jennifer, and Coleman, Jill. Animals and Their Homes. New York: Grosset & Dunlap, 1979. Unpaged. $5.99 Grades 1 and up. A wide variety of homes built by animals in many habitats is depicted in interesting colorful illustrations. No index.

Cole, Joanna, and Wexler, Jerome. Find the Hidden Insect. New York: Morrow, 1979. 40 pp. $6.95. Grades 4 and up. Black-and-white photographs illustrate how insects are able to blend into their environments for a safe place to live, or a place to find food.

Cook, Jan Leslie. The Mysterious Undersea World. Washington D.C.: National Geographic Society, 1980. 104 pp. $6.95. Grades 3 and up. A colorful pictorial album accompanied by a descriptive text suggests activities at the edge of and in the sea, as well as sections on sea pets and aquariums and a folder of classroom activities (puzzles, games, and books).

Dowden, Anne Ophelia. The Blossom on the Bough: A Book of Trees.
New York: T. Y. Crowell, 1975. 71 pp. $8.95. Grades 4 and up.
A beautiful art-science book with thirty magnificent full-color
paintings of tree-flowers. Text incorporates history and
botany, and includes a substantial chapter on tree regions of
the U.S.

Endangered Species Series. Washington, D.C.: U.S. Department of
the Interior, 1970's. Leaflets. Free. From Fish and Wildlife
Service, U.S. Department of the Interior, Washington D.C. 20240.
Separate leaflets with background information on and drawings of
such animals as the grizzly bear, timber wolf, alligator, and
ivory-billed woodpecker.

Extinction: The Game of Ecology. Burlington: Carolina Biological
Supply Company, 1978. Board Game. Price not given. Grades 5-7.
From Carolina Biological Supply Company, Burlington, NC 27215.
A three-hour board game for two, three, or four players that
illustrates principles and processes by which species evolve,
survive, or become extinct. In this game, make-believe animals
compete on the imaginary island of Darwinia. Each player starts
with 30 of a species and tries to survive until his/her species
is the sole or most abundant inhabitant. The board itself represents
a six-color map of Darwinia, where each color represents a distinct
habitat like woodland or marsh.

Farrar, Richard. The Bird's Woodland: What Lives There. Illus.
by William Downey. New York: Coward, McCann & Geoghehan, 1976.
Unpaged. $4.99. Grades 2-6. A bird's eye view of a forest,
and a people's eye view of the birds who live there--with
exceptionally attractive and clear illustrations.

Fisher, Aileen. Anybody Home? New York: T. Y. Crowell. 30 pp.
$6.95. Grades K-1. Aileen Fisher has a unique gift of using
poetic form to convey an understanding of nature. In this poem,
a small girl walks through the woods eager to explore the homes
of the animals she encounters.

Freedman, Russell. Animal Architects. New York: Holiday, 1971.
126 pp. $4.95. Grades 4-7. Describes an amazing variety of
homes built by animals (insects, spiders, fish, frogs, birds,
and mammals) telling how animals use particular construction skills
to build their structures.

Freedman, Russell. Getting Born. New York: Holiday House, 1978. Unpaged (about 40 pp.) $6.95. Grades 2-4. An introduction to animal reproduction with dramatic photographs and matter-of-fact, precise information. Animals covered include tadpoles turtles, snakes, dolphins, and horses with pictures depicting the developmental stages of all these species at birth.

Freedman, Russell. Growing Up Wild: How Young Animals Survive. New York: Holiday, 1975. 63 pp. $5.95. Grades 3 and up. Uses individual nature narratives (of beavers, tadpoles, lions, etc.) to discuss survival techniques of young animals.

George, Jean Craighead. All Upon a Sidewalk. New York: Dutton, 1974. 43 pp. $6.95. Grades 1-4. This ant's eye view of the world describes in eloquent detail the adventures of a common yellow ant. A valuable resource for a city child interested in ecology with excellent illustrations.

Godfrey, Michael A. A Closer Look. San Francisco: Sierra Club, 1975. 148 pp. $14.95. All grades. A group of natural history essays illustrated with exceptional biological photographs. Emphasis is on behavior, appearance, and habits of plants and animals associated with wilderness habitats close to home: a suburban backyard, a park, a vacant lot, a brook.

Hirsch, S. Carl. He and She: How Males and Females Behave. Philadelphia, J. B. Lippincott, 1975. 160 pp. $7.95. Grades 4 and up. Provides a great deal of interesting, factual information within the framework of investigations into the social life and sexual behavior patterns of animals. Describes the people, processes and results of several now-famous studies, including Fabre's spiders, Lorenz's geese, Goodall's apes, and Mead's New Guinea societies.

Hopf, Alice L. Misunderstood Animals. New York: McGraw-Hill, 1973. 128 pp. $6.95. Grades 3 and up. Accurate, well-written and well-illustrated, intended to provide accurate information rather than mythology for such animals as killer whales, porcupines, pigs, spotted hyenas, gorillas, and others.

Jacobson, Morris K., and Franz, David R. Wonders of Snails and Slugs. New York: Dodd, Mead, 1980. 96 pp. $5.95. Grades 4 and up. An interesting scientific treatment of one class of mollusks, divided into marine, freshwater, and land snails, and marine and land slugs. Includes clear, fascinating information on how snails reproduce, feed, move, and the like. Uses black-

and-white photographs; includes a glossary, bibliography, and an index.

Jaspersohn, William. How the Forest Grew. New York: Greenwillow (Morrow), 1980. 56 pp. $5.95. Read Alone Books. Grades 1-4. Covers the chronology of a forest's development with emphasis on forest ecology; suggests what to look for and how to look when studying a forest.

Johnson, Hannah Lyons. From Seed to Salad. New York: Lothrop, Lee, and Shepard, 1978. 48 pp. $6.95. Grades 3-6. "How to do it" book for children and a resource for teachers with suggestions on how to select seeds, how to decide on the garden's location, what kind of tools to use, how to protect crops from insects and bad weather, when to harvest and ways to enjoy produce, including salad dressing recipes.

Kavaler, Lucy. Life Battles Cold. New York: John Day, 1973. 160 pp. $7.95. Grades 6 and up. A lucid study of the ways in which animals (particularly humans) and plants deal with conditions of cold in their environments. Covers metabolism, temperature, human activities in cold climates, migration, hibernation, dormancy, and suspended animation.

Lowell, Marie. The Pollination Game. Oakland: Ampersand Press, 1976. Game with 72 cards. $6.50. Grades 6 and up. From 2603 Grove Street, Oakland, CA 94612. An attractive deck of 72 cards, with cards for pollinators (yucca moths, flies, bees, etc.) for pollinating and pollinated plants, and for spoilers. Can be adapted to rummy, fish, whist, and many other card games.

Lowell, Marie, designer. Predator. Oakland: Ampersand Press, 1974. Game with 40 cards and instructions. $5.00. Grades 3 and up. From 2603 Grove Street, Oakland, CA 94612. Forty easy-to-handle 3" x 4" cards based on predator-prey relationships in forest food habitats teach food chains and webs, the cyclical nature of matter, and the importance of plants in food energy. Each animal card takes what it eats and is taken by what eats it. Plant cards score higher since they are basic for all food. For two to eight players. Can be adapted to such standard card games as war and rummy. Also available in French or Spanish, where it can be used in language teaching and enrichment for bilingual classes or gifted kids.

National Wildlife Federation. _Wildlife in Your World (Animals of North America)_. Washington, D.C.: National Wildlife Federation, 1979. Picture series set of sixteen 8½" x 11" color photos. $8.95. Pre-school and up. From 1412 16th Street NW, Washington, D.C. 20036. This companion to _Your Big Back Yard_ includes color poster cards of each animal, a 40-page booklet of short stories, written on several skill levels, and a 20-page _Teacher's Guide_. This picture series stimulates respect and wonder about nature.

Oxford Scientific Films. _The Chicken and the Egg_. New York: Putnam's, 1979. Unpaged. $6.95. Grades 1 and up. Uses brief text and exceptional photographs to describe the behavior, daily activities, and development of chickens from eggs--especially good for vertebrate development at all levels.

Patent, Dorothy H. _Animal and Plant Mimicry_. New York: Holiday, 1980. 122 pp. $6.95. Grades 4 and up. Includes a glossary, index, and suggested readings for those who wish to explore further examples of mimicry.

Patent, Dorothy H. _How Insects Communicate_. New York: Holiday, 1975. 126 pp. $7.95. Grades 6 and up. Insects, who need to communicate for courtship, mutual protections and foraging, use chemistry, sound, touch, surface vibration, dance patterns, and even light production. Last two chapters deal with spiders and scorpions. The text is supplemented with excellent photographs.

Patent, Dorothy H. _Hunters and the Hunted: Surviving in the Animal World_. New York: Holiday, 1981. $7.95. Grades 4-7. Covers the fascinating and sometimes surprising methods animals use in their struggle for survival.

Patent, Dorothy H. _Shapes in Nature: What They Mean_. New York: Holiday, 1979. 160 pp. $7.95. Grades 4-9. Deals with factors which influence the enormous variety of sizes and shapes in plants and animals, as they interact with their environment. Provides clues to the meaning of plant and animal form. A fascinating subject, presented in a well-written, well-organized account. Includes glossary and suggested reading list.

Ploutz, Paul E. _110 Animals_. Athens: Educational Games, 1977. Card game. $6.00, plus postage and handling. Grades 3 and up. From Union Printing Co., 17 West Washington Street, Athens, OH 45701. A card game that pictures animals from five classes-- amphibians, birds, fish, mammals, and reptiles--with 45 of their major characteristics relating to habitats, habits, physical features, relationship to humans, and ecology. Several variations are available.

Pringle, Laurence. Natural Fire: Its Ecology in Forests. New York: Morrow, 1979. 63 pp. $5.95. Grades 3-7. Introduces the consequences--benign and destructive--of fire on the flora and fauna of forests. Has fine black-and-white photographs for illustration, as well as a glossary, bibliography, and index.

Rahn, Joan Elma. How Plants are Pollinated. New York: Atheneum, 1975. 136 pp. $5.95. Grades 4 and up. In-depth description of how plants are pollinated, with separate chapters on pollination by wind, animals, bees, wasps, butterflies, and moths. Includes an interesting summer project and a five-page glossary.

Rhodes, Frank H. T. Evolution: A Golden Guide. New York: Western Publishing Co., 1974. 160 pp. $9.95; $1.95, paperback. Grades 5 and up. A good resource with four essentially self-contained chapters dealing with "overview of life," "indications of evolution," "the process of evolution," and "the course of evolution." Book is logically developed and supplemented with color pictures, charts, and diagrams. Includes list of references and an index.

Ricciuti, Edward. Older than the Dinosaurs: The Origin and Rise of the Mammals. New York, T. Y. Crowell, 1980. 85 pp. $7.95. Grades 5 and up. Describes the evolution of mammals in the past 70 million years with a geological time scale, and explains the physiological differences and advantages of being reptile, amphibian, or mammal. Vivid descriptions of animals and their environments.

Ricciuti, Edward. Plants in Danger. New York: Harper and Row, 1979. 89 pp. $8.95. Grades 5-9. Samples and discusses some of the more than 20,000 plants that are endangered today, with accounts of steps being taken on the national and international levels. Clearly presented with detailed drawings.

Roberts, David. Animals and Their Babies. New York: Grosset & Dunlap, 1978. Unpaged. $10.15. K and up. Large pictures and easy-to-follow text show and describe characteristics of mammals, reptiles, birds, fish, and amphibians.

Ruggiero, Michael; Mitchell, Alan; and Burton, Philip. Spotter's Handbook: Flowers, Trees, and Birds of North America. New York: Mayflower, 1979. 192 pp. $5.95. $3.95, paperback. Grades 4 and up. One of a series of well-organized, simply written (but accurate) handbooks, with glossaries and indexes. Another one in this series is Philip Burton's Spotter's Guide to Birds of North America. (64 pp., $3.95; $1.95, paperback).

Schwartz, George L. and Bernice S. Food Chains and Ecosystems: Ecology for Young Experimenters. New York: Doubleday, 1974. 120 pp. $5.25. Grades 4 and up. Contains forty experiments (and suggests 27 others) using materials that can be simply made or easily acquired, to explore animal and plant communities such as forests, ponds, with suggestions for observations and experiments in school yards, vacant lots, etc., with a final chapter on nature study indoors. Activities are interesting and well thought out though tightly programmed.

Selsam, Millicent E. How Animals Live Together. Rev. ed. New York: Morrow, 1979. 79 pp. $6.67. Grades 3 and up. Detailed description of animal social organization (herds, flocks, troops, colonies, etc.) and the methods that scientists use to gather information on these animals. Interesting discussion of a number of animal societies, chickens, pigeons, ants, gorillas, seals, penguins, bees, etc., backed by black-and-white photos.

Selsam, Millicant E. How Animals Tell Time. New York: Morrow, 1967. 94 pp. $7.44. Grades 5-9. Discusses biological rhythms, determined by moon, tide, days,and seasons, with observations on humans and animals.

Selsam, Millicent E. How to Be a Nature Detective. New York: Harper & Row, 1966. 47 pp. $6.95. Grades 1-5. A classic introduction to science methods by one of the deans of nature writing. It uses tracks and other traces to sharpen young children's senses of observation and deduction.

Silverstein, Alvin and Virginia. Animal Invaders: The Story of Imported Animal Life. New York: Atheneum, 1974. 124 pp. $5.95. Grades 4 and up. Deals with the consequences (sometimes disastrous) of transferring animals from original environments into other countries and habitats. Interesting and well-written, with a wealth of examples. Chapters discuss the balance of nature and the effects of various imported birds, fish, mammals, insects, and plants, as well as the future of animal transplants. Includes an index and good black-and-white photos.

Simon, Seymour. Exploring Fields and Lots: Easy Science Projects.
Champaign: Carrard, 1978. 64 pp. $5.97. Grades 2-6. Short
book designed to encourage young children to explore fields and
lots using simple inexpensive equipment for simple investigations.

Simon, Seymour. Pets in a Jar: Collecting and Caring for Small
Wild Animals. New York: Viking Press, 1975. 91 pp. $7.95.
Grades 4-7. Each of the fifteen pets presented in this book can
live for a time comfortably within a gallon jar: hydras,
planarians, pond snails, water bugs, tadpoles, newts, toads,
earthworms, ants, crickets, praying mantises, butterflies and
moths, brine shrimp, hermit crabs, starfish. For each, Simon
discusses habitats and characteristics, how to care for the
pet--and how and when to let it go. This book has a fine
index and a brief,but helpful list for further reading.

Weber, William J. Wild Orphan Babies: Caring for Them and Setting
Them Free. New York: Holt, Rinehart,and Winston, 1975. 158 pp.
$5.95. Grades 4 and up. Practical guide to emergency care for
wild mammals and birds, for the amateur. Useful illustrations
and good index.

Woodbury, Marda. What is Man? Oakland: Cliche Press, 1975. 20 pp;
Teaching Suggestions, 12 pp. $1.50/set. From Research Ventures,
3050 College Avenue, Berkeley, CA 94705. A cartoon book in which
animals comment on humans, accompanied by teaching suggestions
and activities for using the book in teaching ecology, mythology,
literature, values education--essentially a well-rounded view of
animals and their roles.

Films and Filmstrips

Aquarium. Chicago: Coronet, 1978. 16 mm. Color film. 10 minutes.
$185.00. All Grades. A visual (not narrated) glance at some
unusual sea creatures, each accompanied by a vibrant musical score
that emphasizes its appearance, movements, or behavior. An
evocative introduction to diverse and intriguing adaptations in the
sea.

Animal Homes. Los Angeles: Churchill Films, 1980. 16 mm. Color
film. 10:30 minutes. $180.00. Grades K-8. A simple, direct
film that emphasizes the roles of homes for protection, shelter,
and nursery with close-up photographs of appropriate animals and
their homes.

Animals and Their Foods. Chicago: Coronet, 1978. 16 mm. Color film. 10 minutes. $171.00. Grades 2-6. Nature photography and close-up scenes show how both wild and domestic animals are specially adapted to gathering and eating different types of food. Includes beaver, deer, giraffes, elephants, chipmunks, lions, dogs, raccoons, birds, bees, and grasshoppers. A similar film (at the same level) deals with Animals and Their Homes.

Animals: Prehistoric and Present. Pompfret Center: Pompfret House, 1977. Four color filmstrips, four cassettes. Life in the Sea, 48 frames, 16:38 minutes. From Reptile to Birds, 52 frames, 17 minutes. Dinosaurs: The Terrible Lizards, 45 frames, 15 minutes. Came the Mammals, 57 frames, 21 minutes. $96.00/set. Grades 5-9. An excellent straightforward introduction to animal evolution, with emphasis on concepts. Good artwork, clear narration. Fine guide with scripts, comprehension questions, glossaries for each filmstrip, and an excellent bibliography.

Beaver Valley. Burbank: Walt Disney Education Media, 1953. 16 mm. Color film. 32 minutes. True Life Adventure Series. $545.00. All grades. One of a series of fine nature films. This one deals with the environment of a mountain stream, shows how beavers build dams to affect the environment and how other animals relate to each other and their watery environment.

Birds and Their Young. Chicago: International Film Bureau, 1980. 16 mm. Color film. 10 minutes. $175.00; $12.50, rental; $145.00 video. Grades K-6. Covers birds' annual cycle of courtship, procreation, nesting, feeding, and growth and a few species of familiar and appealing birds including the Canada goose, the pelican, and loon. Emphasis is on visual presentation rather than narration, with sensitive photography.

Color in Nature. Chicago: Encyclopedia Britannica Educational Corp., 1980. 16 mm. Color film. 12 minutes. $220.00; $14.00, rental. All grades. An outstanding use of color explores the diverse applications of color in nature, its interactions with the environment in such things as prey-predator relationships, sexual identification, camouflage, pollination, the importance of reflection, seasonal changes, etc. Suitable for any age group.

Developing Language Skills: The Seasons. Chicago: Encyclopedia Britannica, 1976. Four color filmstrips. What Can You Do and See in Spring?, 50 frames. What Can You Do and See in Summer?, 53 frames. What Can You Do and See in Autumn?, 42 frames. What Can You Do and See in Winter?, 46 frames. $32.90. Grades K-4.

Fine imaginative photographs serve as springboards for discussion and for children to compare information and impressions from the filmstrips with that gleaned from their own individual backgrounds and experiences. A very flexible, adaptable series which can be used to generate discussion and vocabulary development as well as observations and appreciation of natural phenomena. Guide includes summaries, objectives, and suggestions for activities. A similar series at the same price is Developing Language Skills: Nature Walks, which includes Watching at the Pond, Walking Along the Seashore, Visiting the Forest, and Exploring the Deserts.

Ecology of a Swamp. Oxford Films, 1971. 16 mm. Color film. 8 minutes. Ecology of the United States Series. $290.00 Grades 1-8. Explains, for children, the complex ecology of a swamp, kept in balance through plants, animals, and the climate cycle. Raises the question of what will happen if there is no more water. Other Oxford Films deal with the ecology of plateaus, forests, etc.

How Animals Live and Grow. Chicago: Encyclopedia Britannica Educational Corp., 1980. 6 color filmstrips 63-78 frames each; 6 cassettes 9-11 minutes each. $135.00; $25.00 each. Grades K-3. An elementary overview of the habitat and development of insects, fish, amphibians, reptiles, birds, and mammals with outstanding photography and clear narration.

I'm a Mammal and So Are You. National Film Board of Canada, 1980. 16 mm. Film or videocassette. 4 minutes. With Teacher's Guide. $120.00; $20.00, rental. Grades K-5. An enchanting quick view of mammals nursing their young, eating different foods, showing their fur, and adapting to different surroundings, accompanied by a catchy tune. Very appealing to children and teachers. Teachers suggest two viewings and a discussion period for the primary grades.

Life and Death of a Tree. Washington, D.C.: National Geographic Society, 1979. 16 mm. Color Film. 20 minutes. $290.00; $20.00, rental. Grades 3 and up. Shows the interactions of an oak tree with the other denizens of a forest ecosystem and shows how the oak eventually provides food for foraging animals and insects, fungi, mosses, and lichens until nothing is left but organic humus. Scientifically accurate with especially good close-up photography.

Looking at Birds. Chicago: Encyclopedia Britannica, 1963. 16 mm. Color Film. 10 minutes. World of Animals Series. $150.00. Grades 5 and up. Demonstrates how birds differ from other animals in appearance, body structure, functions, behavior, etc. Other comparable films in this series include Looking at Mammals, which groups animals according to specific characteristics.

Ways of Plants. Los Angeles: Bowmar, 1977. 10 color filmstrips with 10 seven-inch records or 10 cassettes. Plant Magic, 24/30 frames, 4/5 minutes. Mysteries in the Garden, 36/32 frames, 4/4 minutes. Swords and Daggers, 31/31 frames, 4/5 minutes. And a Sunflower Grew, 24/33 frames, 3/5 minutes. Petals Yellow and Petals Red, 36/29 frames, 6/5 minutes. Now That Spring Is Here, 25/40 frames, 3/5 minutes. As the Leaves Fall Down, 30/36 frames, 4/6 minutes. Prize Performance, 38/35 frames, 6/5 minutes. Three With a Thousand Uses, 29/32 frames, 4/4 minutes. Seeds on the Go, 27/31 frames, 4/4 minutes. $226.50/ set. Grades 1-3.

An appealing, visually beautiful, and scientifically accurate, combined language experience/basic life science program for primary children, based on 10 story poems of Aileen Fisher, each of which illustrates a different facet of plant life. The poem is presented in the first part of each filmstrip, while the science concepts are amplified and illustrated with photographs in the second part. The guide includes objectives, suggestions, science processes, summaries, pre- and post-questions, activities, a bibliography, and evaluation suggestions.

Pete and Penny's Pet Care. New York: ACI, 1975. Four color film-strips, four cassettes. Healthy Dogs and Happy Cats, 67 frames, 10 minutes. Bright Fish and Singing Birds, 58 frames, 9 minutes. Turtles, Rabbits,and Others, 65 frames, 10 minutes. Pets You Can Find, 70 frames, 9 minutes. $65.00/set. Grades K-6.

An interesting introduction to pet care that includes a filmstrip on the care of wild pets such as lizards and snakes. Stresses owner's responsibility, suitable habitats, how to handle each animal physically,and what to feed them. The guide includes objectives, summaries, activities, and a bibliography.

Places Where Plants and Animals Live. Washington, D.C.: National
    Geographic Society, 1975. Five color filmstrips, five records,
    five cassettes. The Woods, 42 frames, 11 minutes. The Meadow,
    41 frames, 11 minutes. The Stream, 44 frames, 12 minutes. The
    Seashore, 46 frames, 13 minutes. The City Park, 42 frames, 11
    minutes. $67.50/set. Grades K-4.

A very useful introduction for primary children, with beautiful
photographs (of insects, tide pool life, etc.) and information
presented clearly and understandably. Good for discussion with
a supportive guide.

Vanishing Animals of North America. Washington, D.C.: National
    Geographic Society, 1975. Five color filmstrips, five records,
    five cassettes. Tragedy of the Past, 49 frames, 13 minutes.
    Hunted Animals, 48 frames, 13 minutes. Damage to Ecosystems,
    50 frames, 13 minutes. Protected Animals, 46 frames, 13 minutes.
    Prospects for the Future, 50 frames, 13 minutes. $67.50/set.
    Grades 4-12.

An intelligent comprehensive presentation that covers extinct
animals, threatened animals, and the efforts of scientists to
preserve endangered species. Useful for classes or individual
students. Guides integrate social studies and science concepts
and include objectives, background information, summaries,
bibliographies, and scripts.

Health and Nutrition Activities

While it can be said that many science-related social problems have developed in the twentieth century, it can also be stated that public health and nutrition have improved during the same time. Advances in sanitation, food production, the practice and technology of medicine, and health care delivery systems have all contributed to progress in public health. The statistics on public health are impressive: mortality rates (excluding death in war) declined steadily during the first fifty years of the twentieth century. In 1900 the mortality rate was approximately 20/1000. In 1975 and 1976, it was 8.9/1000. Life expectancy rates have increased. In 1900, a woman could expect to live fifty-one years, a man forty-eight years. A girl born in 1975 could expect to live seventy-five years, a boy from the same year could expect to live to age sixty-six. These are just two indicators of improved public health.

One way of improving public health is through prevention. Awareness of personal health services, changes in individual behaviors, and living in healthy environments all contribute to health. All of these measures can be introduced early in a child's life. This is where health education activities become important.

Children should become aware of the health and nutrition services available in the community. For example, millions of Americans still are not immunized against diseases for which vaccines are available. Progress must be made in improving environmental detriments to health. The use of chemicals for food crops and the dumping of toxic wastes that eventually enter the water supply are two examples of environmental detriments.

Individual behavior has been recognized as a key to health. Shaping individual behavior is an essential part of promoting good health. It is also an important area for elementary and middle school teachers. Cigarette smoking is a major cause of many common illnesses, including lung cancer, coronary heart disease, and chronic respiratory disease. Yet, increasing numbers of adolescents, especially girls, are smoking. More women now die of lung cancer than any other form of that disease, except cancer of the breast. This fact underscores the need for health education.

Refer to the planning charts for each grade level. These charts should assist you in the selection and organization of health and nutrition activities.

PLANNING CHART FOR HEALTH AND NUTRITION ACTIVITIES: GRADES K–2

ACTIVITY	Conceptual Knowledge	Learning Processes	Psychomotor Skills	Attitudes and Values	Decision-making Skills	TEACHING METHODS	RELATED CURRICULUM
			OBJECTIVES				
23. Family Health Practices	Life styles, peer groups and individual families influence health choices.	Compare and contrast family practices that affect health. Construct histograms.	—	Recognize that daily health practices are influenced by the family.	Differentiate between facts, attitudes and values.	Teacher-directed.	Math.
24. Communicating Your Emotions	Emotional stability is influenced by an awareness of personal feelings and reactions.	Identify some common emotions experienced by primary-age children.	—	Recognize that emotions are universal.	Evaluate alternative points of view.	Simulation activity.	Language Arts.
25. Pedestrian Safety	Maintaining a safe and healthful environment is a shared responsibility of the individual, family and society.	Understand the rules for pedestrian safety in the school neighborhood environment.	Build a model of a street intersection.	Develop respect for traffic rules and safety helpers.	Consider consequences of alternatives before making decision. Make decisions based on consequences to self and others.	Guided experience.	Social Studies.
26. A Midnight Call to the Fire Department—A Pantomime	A variety of health resources are needed to promote and protect the health of people in the community.	Understand the role of the Fire Department in maintaining and promoting safety of the family and community.	—	Appreciate the helpfulness of the community in emergency situations.	Accept direction in caring for health and welfare of self and others.	Simulation.	Social Studies.
27. Caring for Minor Injuries	Primary responsibility for improving and maintaining the health of the community is a function of its members.	Describe evidence which constitutes a health emergency. To practice care for simple injuries.	Clean and bandage cuts and abrasions. Apply ice to burns or swelling.	Appreciate the part that children can play in caring for simple injuries.	Accept direction in caring for health and welfare of self and others.	Teacher demonstration, stations for practice.	—
28. Pollution and Your Environment	An interrelationship exists between human health and environmental quality.	Use the word pollutant to refer to any substance that is added to the environment in a quantity harmful to life.	—	Motivate students to participate in activity that fosters a positive human environment.	Discuss consequences of alternating actions.	Teacher-guided.	Language Arts.

Family Health Practices
Grades K-2

ACTIVITY OVERVIEW
    Children consider their families and family health practices.
The children: (1) make a collage illustrating activities that the
family does together, (2) participate in a class survey concerning
family health habits, and (3) collectively construct histograms and
compare and contrast family health practices.

SCIENCE BACKGROUND
    Habits established in childhood can lead to or prevent health
problems later in life. The family, particularly the parents, have
the most significant influence in developing the habits of children.
Practices tolerated or encouraged in the home, such as overeating,
poor hygiene, smoking; or eating a balanced diet, getting adequate
sleep, and exercising regularly become rooted patterns in a person's
lifestyle. Habits, knowledge, and attitudes learned early can have
a lasting effect. Children can be helped to understand their present
health patterns and learn the role their families play in developing
these habits.

SOCIETAL IMPLICATIONS
    A young child's first society is his family. It is here that he
first learns standards of living or behavior. Until a youngster
enters school, he may think of himself only as a member of a family.
School becomes the child's next society. Practices tolerated or
encouraged at school also influence the developing child. Many
habits he establishes now will follow him until adulthood where,
as a parent, he too will have a role in influencing the health and
development of his children.

MAJOR CONCEPT
    Life styles, peer groups, and individual families influence
health choices.

OBJECTIVES:
    By the end of this activity, the children should be able to:
    -Compare and contrast family practices that affect health.
    -Construct a simple histogram.

MATERIALS
     For survey: paper, pencils; Optional: ditto paper
     For collage: construction paper, scissors, paste, magazines,
crayons, or paint
     For histograms: chart paper or chalkboard

VOCABULARY
     custom, cultural/ethnic background, family, habit, health,
influence, leisure time, recreation, tradition

PROCEDURES
     1. Begin by inviting the children to make collages that tell
about their families. Ask the children to consider what the family
does together: eating meals, recreation, resting, leisure time
activities.
     2. Share the collages and discuss different family practices
concerning eating habits, dental practices, bedtime rituals, etc.
     3. Next, conduct a class survey of family health practices.
Invite each child to suggest one question to be answered by class
members. Sample questions include: Do you always eat breakfast?
Does your family make you eat vegetables at dinner? Do you ever
play outdoor games with your family? What time do you usually go to
bed?
     4. The survey can be typed in questionnaire form to be read
and answered by older students.
     5. Pool information gained from surveys and collectively
construct class histograms that illustrate similarities and differences among family practices. For example:

```
+---------------------------------------------------------------+
|            WHAT TIME DO YOU USUALLY GO TO BED?                |
|                                                               |
|    7:30     X    X                                            |
|    _____ |
|                                                               |
|    8:00     X    X    X    X                                  |
|    _____ |
|                                                               |
|    8:30     X    X    X    X    X    X                        |
|    _____ |
|                                                               |
|                   NUMBER OF CHILDREN                          |
+---------------------------------------------------------------+
```

     6. Compare and contrast family health practices as indicated
in surveys and histograms.

1. Why do you think it is so important to your parents that you eat your vegetables or brush your teeth after meals?
2. Could the habits your family helps you establish now stay with with you as you grow up?
3. Ask your parents to name health habits they practiced as children that they still practice today.
4. Ask them to name health practices that changed as they grew up.

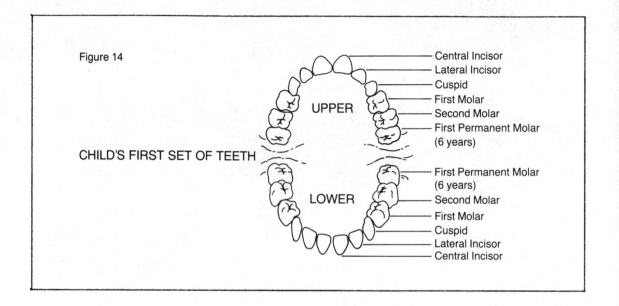

Figure 14

CHILD'S FIRST SET OF TEETH

UPPER
- Central Incisor
- Lateral Incisor
- Cuspid
- First Molar
- Second Molar
- First Permanent Molar (6 years)

LOWER
- First Permanent Molar (6 years)
- Second Molar
- First Molar
- Cuspid
- Lateral Incisor
- Central Incisor

Communicating Your Emotions
Grades K-2

ACTIVITY OVERVIEW

Children respond to a variety of suggested situations by demonstrating and describing their feelings. The students practice skills of identifying and communicating emotions.

SCIENCE BACKGROUND

Your feelings about yourself and your life start developing at a very early age. Although your body continually changes from birth to death, there are individual qualities that are retained and integrated with your identity. For example, your enthusiasm for life (or your despair over life) and the way you treat yourself are examples of those qualities that contribute to who you are. Whether you control the way you participate in life or are controlled by forces around you depends on your ability to recognize and evaluate knowledge and feelings in particular situations. How well you are able to distinguish between reality and unreality also depends on your skillfulness in integrating intellectual and emotional information.

Children can learn to recognize their feelings and those of others. They can also learn to discriminate between feelings and physical demonstrations of feelings. Initially, feelings and actions are fused in the minds of children. For example, although sadness and crying are related, they are not the same. Sadness is a feeling; crying is a behavior that sometimes gives evidence of sadness although it may also indicate pain. The ability to verbalize rather than "act out" feelings is a sign of mental health and developing maturity. We learn that it is better to say "This makes me mad," or "I'm frustrated" than to display anger through physical acts of violence. Emotional stability is influenced by awareness of personal feelings and reactions.

SOCIETAL IMPLICATIONS

Society has an enormous stake in maintaining a citizenry of healthy individuals. Health has been defined by the United Nations' World Health Organization as "a state of complete physical, mental, and social well-being, and not merely the absence of disease or infirmity." The inclusion of the mental and social health components suggests that it is extremely important for us to learn to mentally recognize our feelings and to be able to socially communicate them to others in acceptable, informative ways for optimum health.

Schooling accomplishes many things for our children, particularly in the areas of academic skills and learning about the nature of our universe. Unfortunately, behaviors that encourage mental health and emotional maturity are often left to "develop naturally." For children to recognize that emotions are universal and to learn to appropriately communicate their feelings to others is helpful not only to them as individuals but also to members of society.

MAJOR CONCEPT
Emotional stability is influenced by an awareness of personal feelings and reactions.

OBJECTIVES
By the end of this activity the student should be able to:
-Identify some common emotions experienced by primary age children.

VOCABULARY
Emotions (introduced in the lesson)

PROCEDURES

1. Ask the entire class to show how they really feel right now without using any words.
2. Ask for two or three volunteers to tell in words how they feel right now.
3. Ask the children to show you how they feel when they eat an ice cream cone.
4. Ask the children to tell you a word that describes how they feel when they eat an ice cream cone.
5. Write the children's descriptive words on the chalkboard and tell them that these words are called emotions.
6. Ask the children to show you how they feel when they have to stop playing with their favorite friend to go to bed in the evening.
7. Ask the children to tell you, using just one word, how they feel in the above situation, and again write the words on the chalkboard.
8. Ask the children what the words on the board are called.
9. Ask the children to show you how they feel when they listen to a very, very scary story in the dark.
10. Ask the children to tell you all the words they can think of that describe how they feel in the above situation.

Pedestrian Safety
Grades K-2

ACTIVITY OVERVIEW
Children observe rules for pedestrian safety. The pupils build a model intersection to simulate traffic situations and pedestrian practices.

SCIENCE BACKGROUND
Accidents account for 40% of all deaths among preschool and early school age children. Many of these accidents could be prevented; even children can help reduce the possibility of an accident by practicing safe behavior.

Traffic safety is of special importance for kindergarten and elementary school age children. Many students walk to and from school, and all must enter and leave school grounds by means of street entrances and exits. Communities--cities, town, and school communities as well--establish rules to insure the safety of all people. Basic guidelines for pedestrian safety include the following:
   -Obey all traffic signs.
   -Walk in designated areas, on sidewalks, or along the left
    side of the roadway.
   -Cross streets only at designated intersections or crosswalks.
   -Cross only when the light changes from red to green.
   -Look in all directions before crossing a street or railroad
    track. Be sure each way is clear.
   -Watch for turning cars.
   -Never enter or cross the roadway from behind a parked car.
   -If out at night, wear or carry something white.
   -Obey school safety patrol members, policemen, bus drivers,
    and crossing guards.
   -Do not accept rides from unknown persons.

SOCIETAL IMPLICATIONS
Each year, nearly everyone is involved in some type of accidental injury. Accidents imply carelessness, unconcern, or ignorance about the causes of injuries and methods for their prevention. Most accidents involving children occur as a result of unsafe behavior because the danger is unrecognized. Some accidents occur because of dangerous conditions surrounding the home, school, or neighborhood environment. To live and play safely in their environment, children must learn to identify hazards and deal with them appropriately, and to respect traffic rules and safety helpers. With guidance and safety training, children can develop attitudes and habits that accompany them into adult life and influence others in maintaining a safe community.

MAJOR CONCEPT
Maintaining a safe and healthful environment is a shared responsibility of the individual, family, and society.

OBJECTIVES:
By the end of this activity, the students should be able to:
-Describe the rules for pedestrian safety in the school and neighborhood environment.

MATERIALS
-Table or sand table, blocks, model cars, buses, trucks, small boxes and cardboard for making buildings, signs, roadways, people, etc., crayons, marking pens, paint, scissors

VOCABULARY:
crosswalk, danger, loading zone, one-way, pedestrian, rule, safety, slow, stop, yield

PROCEDURES

Part One
1. Begin by taking the class on a walk around the school grounds, surrounding neighborhood, and intersections. Discuss rules concerning pedestrian safety. Direct the children's attention to traffic signals or signs, loading zones, crosswalks, bus stops, traffic helpers, etc. Be sure to point out any hazardous situations, such as construction or repair sites, blind spots, or sharp corners.
2. After returning to class, invite the children to assist you in preparing a list of safety practices for pedestrians going to and from school.

Part Two
1. Have the students use the materials suggested above to build a model representing a street intersection that includes buildings, crosswalks, traffic signals, etc.
2. Ask the students to demonstrate safe and unsafe situations and pedestrian practices using model people, cars, and buses.

A Midnight Call to the Fire Department--A Pantomime
Grades K-2

ACTIVITY OVERVIEW

The children partake in a class pantomime that simulates a home fire. The children role play family members, community fire fighters, and neighbors. The students review emergency behavior, possible causes of the fire, and the role of the fire department.

SCIENCE BACKGROUND

Over 1,000 home fires occur in the United States daily. Of these fires, 37% begin in the living room, 22% in the kitchen, 14% in the basement, 13% in bedrooms, and 14% in other areas. The majority of home fires start between the hours of midnight and 6:00 a.m., when people are asleep and unprepared. With these facts in mind, one can quickly understand why practice in fire prevention and training for fire emergency preparedness through home fire drills are of vital concern to the community.

Some general home fire-safety precautions that can help prevent the most frequent causes of fire are:

- Don't smoke when sleepy or in bed.
- Use adequate, stable ashtrays, and never empty them into waste-paper baskets.
- Store matches in a safe place, such as a metal container, out of the reach of children. (Matches and smoking cause about 25% of all fires of known origin.)
- Never overload outlets or extension cords. Keep use of extension cords to a minimum; never place them under rugs.
- Give damaged cord insulation, plugs, fixtures, and appliances immediate attention.
- Don't let rubbish or unwanted combustibles pile up. Throw out oily dust cloths and paint rags.
- Use flammable liquids only in ventilated areas, away from ignition sources.
- Keep gasoline outdoors.
- Keep the stove, range hood, and filter clean to prevent grease fires.
- Keep combustibles away from room heaters, fans, and other heat-producing appliances.
- Install a smoke detector outside of the sleeping areas.

Family fire escape drills should emphasize the following practices:
- Sleep with bedroom and hall doors closed, as doors can keep out fire long enough to allow escape.
- Agree on a common family fire alarm (e.g. whistle, yell, etc.).
- Test doors before opening them.
- Arrange for two escape routes from each room.
- Have an outside meeting place for a quick safety check.
- Using a neighbor's phone, notify the fire department as soon as everyone is safe. At this point, one should speak slowly and plainly, saying "My name is _____. I want to report a fire at _____." Then wait to answer questions.

SOCIETAL IMPLICATIONS

Each year over 12,000 deaths and 300,000 injuries occur as a result of fire, explosions, and burns. As a point of comparison, one should note that in the peak year of the polio epidemic and panic during the early 1950's, there were 3,145 deaths due to polio, according to a government report. Clearly, statistics prove that burning is the greater danger. Unfortunately, scientific discovery cannot solve the entire fire problem as it solved the polio problem. Rather, human precautions can prevent many of the tragedies resulting from fire and burns. A variety of health resources also work to assist, promote, and protect the health of people in the community in this respect.

Children and the elderly are the most common victims of fire. They often lack the physical coordination or knowledge to react correctly in an emergency. Some of the most common fire-related accidents among school age children occur as a result of playing with matches, tending an outdoor grill or open fire, using flammable liquid near a hot water heater or open-flame applicance, and getting loose fitting sleepwear caught in an open space heater or ignited on a gas flame or electric burner of the stove. Children can be taught to recognize the dangers of matches, flammable liquids, and clothing near a heat source, and to practice both fire-safe and emergency behavior.

Fire protection and prevention agencies, as well as community fire departments, recognize the importance of teaching even the youngest children about fire safety and prevention. Knowledge and appreciation of the helpfulness and concern of the community can lead children to use these resources effectively before and during emergency situations and to contribute to the safety of others in time of need.

MAJOR CONCEPT
A variety of health resources are needed to promote and protect the health of people in the community.

OBJECTIVES
By the end of this activity, the students should be able to:
-Understand the role of the Fire Department in maintaining and promoting the safety of the family and the community.

MATERIALS
-Pantomime script to be read aloud by teacher (see page ___.)
-Scene cards for Scenes I, II, III, IV
-Banners with the names Mother, Father, Billy, Susie, Fire Chief, Fireman 1, Fireman 2, Mr. Neighbor, and Mrs. Neighbor
-Display cards marked Children's Bedroom, Parents' Bedroom, Kitchen, Living Room, Front Door, Back Door, Fire Station, Fire Hydrant, Neighbor's House
-Suggested Props: large shirts to wear as nightclothes; rain slickers, hats, and boots for firemen; jump rope for firehose, and play telephones

VOCABULARY
-community, emergency, extinguish, Fire Department, fire engine, fire hazard, fire hydrant, Police Department, smoke alarm

PANTOMIME SCRIPT: A MIDNIGHT CALL TO THE FIRE DEPARTMENT

Scene I: In the House, at Midnight
The children are asleep in their bedroom; the parents are asleep in theirs. Billy awakes, coughing. He smells smoke. Quickly he jumps to Susie's bed and awakens her. The two take hands and make their way to their parents' room. At the sound of their cries, Mother and Father jump out of bed. Father looks for the best way to lead the family out of the house--the back door in the kitchen? No, too much smoke! The windows? We can make it out the front door! The children and Mother gasp at the smoke on their way out.

Scene II: Outside Neighbor's House
Mr. and Mrs. Neighbor are asleep inside. While the children and Father are watching flames escape from one of the kitchen windows, Mother bangs on the Neighbor's door. Mr. and Mrs. Neighbor awaken and rush to the door. Mother points to their house across the street and asks to use their phone to call the Fire Department. Mrs. Neighbor takes Mother to the phone, while Mr. Neighbor joins Father and the children. Mother has no trouble finding the phone number because the Neighbors have a list of Emergency Phone Numbers stuck right on the phone. Mother dials the Fire Department.

Scene III: At the Fire Station

The fire fighters are asleep, while the Fire Chief sits on phone duty. He answers the phone. When he hears of the emergency, he asks Mother for her address, which he jots down on paper. He takes a quick look at a wall map, to locate the address of the burning house. The Firemen hop out of bed and put on their fire gear--hats, coats, and boots. They all climb on the Fire Engine, and off they go. (The children can hold each other at the waist to form a chain. Children around the circle simulate the loud fire siren.)

Scene IV: At the Scene of the Fire

The family and the Neighbors are out in the street watching the burning house. Fireman 1 directs them back across the street away from danger. Fireman 2 attaches the hose to the nearest fire hydrant. All the Firemen extend the hose and enter the house through the front door. They locate the fire in the kitchen. Using the hose, they extinguish the fire. Then the Firemen wind the hose and board the truck. The Fire Chief goes to the family and leads them back into their house, which has been saved from much damage. The Fire Chief suggests that the family install a smoke alarm to alert them in case of fire again. He makes a date to return to their home to conduct an inspection for dangerous fire hazards. The whole family thanks the Fire Chief. He gets aboard the fire engine. Family and Firemen wave good-bye to each other as the truck drives off.

PROCEDURES

1. Have the students sit in a circle.
2. Distribute the name banners to be worn by the volunteer cast.
3. Set the stage by placing display cards for the rooms and structures of the family house, the Neighbor's house, and the Fire Station. Scene cards may be given to four students to display prior to each scene.
4. Read each scene aloud, pausing frequently to allow the volunteer actors to pantomime the scene.

SUGGESTED QUESTIONS

1. What are all of the things that might have caused a fire in this house?
2. How would the story have been different if the community did not have a Fire Department?

Caring for Minor Injuries
Grades K-2

ACTIVITY OVERVIEW

The children visit six separate stations at which they practice basic first-aid measures on dolls, themselves, and/or each other. They follow illustrated instructions and proceed to clean, bandage, and apply cold compresses or pressure when directed to care for a bruise; a cut, a scrape, or an abrasion; minor bleeding; a small animal bite or burn; and a mild nosebleed.

SCIENCE BACKGROUND

The American Red Cross recognizes several first-aid procedures that youngsters can follow in caring for some minor injuries that children commonly face.

-A <u>bruise</u>, caused by a hit or bump, may swell up and turn color. To lessen the swelling, apply a cold wet cloth, or ice wrapped in cloth, to the bruise right away. Leave the cloth on for half an hour.

-Wash all small <u>cuts</u>, <u>scrapes</u>, or <u>abrasions</u> with soap and water. Bandage a cut to keep it clean. Because a deep hole or cut in the skin is a good place for a tetanus infection to start, a doctor should be seen to treat large or deep cuts and to administer a tetanus shot, if necessary.

-Stop or slow mild <u>bleeding</u> by holding a thick piece of cloth (shirt, sheet, or towel) over the bleeding area and pressing hard.

-In the case of an <u>animal bite</u>, wash the wound with soap and water. Stop the bleeding and bandage the bite. Try to remember what the animal looks like. A doctor, police officer, and veterinarian should be notified. An animal control officer will try to catch the animal to determine if it has rabies.

-With a small <u>burn</u>, place the burned part of the body in cold water, keeping it there for awhile. Cold water causes the burn to hurt less by keeping air off and cooling it. Cold wet cloths or ice wrapped in cloth can also help minor burns and sunburns. If cold water isn't available, cover a burn with a clean, dry bandage. Do not put a burn in water if the skin has burned away. Never break or open blisters. Gently bandage them.

-To stop a <u>nosebleed</u>, pinch your nose shut. If it continues to bleed after you stop pinching, pinch longer. If it bleeds very much or if bleeding lasts for more than fifteen minutes, call a doctor.

Even minor injuries have the possibility of becoming more serious. All injuries should be reported to a responsible adult.

SOCIETAL IMPLICATIONS

Most primary age children could not be expected to treat a victim of a serious accident without adult assistance. They can, however, be instructed to recognize evidence of a health emergency and to seek help effectively and independently. Practice in first-aid care for minor injuries and exposure to emergency behavior are active means by which children can partake in the health of their families and friends. Building confidence and awareness at this age encourages individuals, as adults, to take active roles in maintaining the health of their community.

MAJOR CONCEPT

Primary responsibility for improving and maintaining the health of the community is a function of its members.

OBJECTIVES

By the end of this activity, the student should be able to:
-Describe evidence that constitutes a health emergency.
-Provide care for minor injuries.

MATERIALS

-Six charts for illustrated instructions
-Six dolls (Children can be asked to supply these for temporary use.)
-Ice, clean cloths and towels, four pans or bowls for holding water, two bars of soap, bandages

VOCABULARY

-abrasions, address, animal bite, bandage, bleeding, bruise, burn, cuts, emergency, injury, minor injury, nosebleed, rabies, scrapes, swelling, tetanus

PROCEDURES

1. To prepare for this activity, set up six stations, each for dealing with a single minor injury: (a) bruise, (b) minor bleeding, (c) cut, scrape, or abrasion, (d) animal bite, (e) burn, and (f) nosebleed. Equip each station with a chart of illustrated directions for treating the injury, a doll on which to practice care, and necessary supplies suggested for use in caring for the injury (e.g. ice, water, soap, bandages, cloth, towels).

2. Introduce the activity with a class discussion on injuries. Help the students to distinguish between a minor injury and an emergency situation. An emergency can be defined simply as a situation in which a person cannot explain what is wrong with him. Discuss possible emergency situations and help the children identify sources of immediate help and how to notify help via the telephone.

130

3. Remind the children that although they will learn how to care for some common minor injuries, these too have the possibility of becoming more serious and should be reported to a responsible adult (parent, teacher, nurse, etc.).

4. Invite the children to proceed in pairs through the stations. At each station, the pupils follow the illustrated instructions and practice simple first-aid care on the doll, themselves, or each other. Make sure the children visit each station.

Pollution and Your Environment
Grades K-2

ACTIVITY OVERVIEW

The children learn the meaning of a pollutant by means of a simple simulation. After examining their local environment, the students identify and illustrate pollutants and their sources. The students then suggest and participate in activities that help improve their environment.

SCIENCE BACKGROUND

An environmental <u>pollutant</u> can be defined as any substance added to the environment in a quantity harmful to life. Today, many factors result in the pollution of our environment, threatening the natural growth, proper development, and sheer enjoyment of life within the environment.

Pollutants are added to the air through several sources. Transportation accounts for the greatest amount of air pollution. Nitrogen oxides are produced when fuel is burned at very high temperatures. Smog results when particulate matter and photo-chemical combustion are released at high temperatures by means of incinerators. Factories burning coal and oil produce sulfur dioxides which, when inhaled from the air, can cause serious damage to the respiratory tract. Forest fires and burning also contribute to air pollution. The incomplete burning of carbon and fuels releases carbon monoxide into the air.

Water pollutants come from many sources, both natural and artificial. Natural pollution may occur where dead leaves and animals (organisms) result in algae blooms in lakes and ponds. Communities, industries, and homes that dump waste materials or raw sewage into bodies of water can become major sources of water pollution. Nuclear power plants increase the temperature of water, which can kill fish. Agriculture that permits the runoff of silt, fertilizers, and accumulations on feed lots into streams pollutes these water sites.

Many types of noise pollution are also present in our environmental settings, both indoors and out. From excessively loud music with highly tuned amplifiers indoors, to jet aircraft, industry, traffic and construction sources outdoors, high noise levels can result in mental or physical distress (e.g., headaches and, in extreme cases, a ruptured eardrum or temporary, partial, or total hearing loss).

SOCIETAL IMPLICATIONS

If Earth is to remain our dwelling place, we, its dwellers, including children and youth, must become aware of our responsibilities regarding the well-being of our fellow humans. We must consider particularly the quality of other life and the environment. Today's society is witnessing a growing consciousness for environmental concerns and is responding, in many ways, to the problems of pollution. In major metropolises, air pollution is monitored daily for the purpose of informing the public of dangerous pollution levels. Motor vehicle designers work to create systems that cause fewer air pollutants. Environmental agencies have been created to examine industrial pollutants in the air and water. State boards of health or other agencies screen bodies of water for health safety and recreational use. Sewage treatment plants are established to create clean water from water that has previously been used. In agriculture, contour plowing--plowing against the normal flow of water--works to reduce the amount of silt and fertilizer that reaches bodies of water. In spite of this type of response, individual indifference and apathy to the earth's problems, overpopulation, and economic competition continue to threaten the balance that must exist among all living things--human, plant, and animal.

Encouraging children to respect their environment and to recognize the threats from pollution are the first steps in motivating them to take constructive actions that foster and safeguard a positive human environment.

MAJOR CONCEPT
An interrelationship exists between human health and environmental quality.

OBJECTIVES
By the end of this activity, the students should be able to:
-Use the word <u>pollutant</u> to refer to any substance that is added to the environment in a quantity harmful to life.

MATERIALS
-Bowl, clean water, liquid soap, crayons, paints, or marking pens

VOCABULARY
-air pollution, community, environment, factory, industry, natural pollution, noise pollution, pollutant, smog, water pollution

PROCEDURES
1. <u>Simulation</u>. Begin by showing the children a simple simulation of pollution. Take a bowl of clean water and add soap to it. Ask the children to tell what might have happened to animals if they had been living in or around this water.
2. <u>Definition</u>. Define <u>pollution</u> in simple terms for the children. Discuss the cause/effect relationship of a pollutant and its effect on health and life in the environment.

3. <u>Activity</u>. Take the students on a walk in the community--a nearby neighborhood recreational area, or park; and/or an urban center. Help the students identify environmental pollutants and their sources, such as motor vehicle exhaust, litter, smoke from industry or burning, or unpleasant loud noises. (This activity can be pursued during a field trip of any sort.)

4. <u>Follow-up Activity</u>. Upon returning from the field excursion, review the air, water, and noise pollution observed. Discuss the implications of pollution on the health, enjoyment, and life of people, animals, and plants. Ask questions such as the following:

    a.   How do you think flying in smog-filled air affects a bird?

    b.   How do you think a dirty pond or lake might change the life of a duck who lives there?

    c.   Can you play freely on a beach or playing field with trash, cans, and broken glass thrown about carelessly?

    d.   Who can think of a way people in our community might help correct the pollution we see?

5. Invite the children to illustrate ways in which the environment is polluted. Possibilities include before and after pictures that also show how the environment could look in a pollution concerned community. Encourage the children to add slogans that promote environmental protection. Illustrations can be bound together to form a class book or displayed as posters.

Figure 16   SAMPLE CARDS FOR COLLECTING POLLUTION DATA

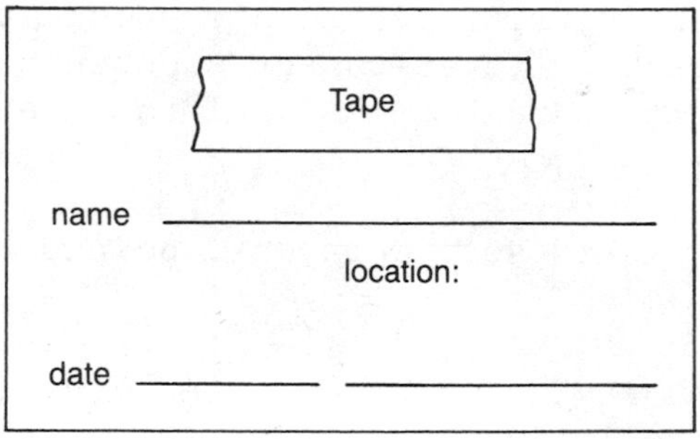

Tape

name _____

location:

date _____ _____

PLANNING CHART FOR HEALTH AND NUTRITION ACTIVITIES: GRADES 3–5

ACTIVITY	Conceptual Knowledge	Learning Processes	OBJECTIVES			TEACHING METHODS	RELATED CURRICULUM
			Psychomotor Skills	Attitudes and Values	Decision-making Skills		
29. You Are What You Eat	Individuals develop eating patterns which contribute to wellness.	Identify the recommended number of daily servings and the amounts of food in a single serving from each of the four food groups.	Measure food quantity.	Recognize that eating habits affect weight and health.	Recognize personal decisions that involve self and others.	Mastery learning.	Math.
30. Identifying and Using Community Resources	Obtaining and utilizing appropriate information and community services that promote personal health is a responsibility of the individual.	Plan and carry out an independent investigation to solve a given problem.	—	Appreciate the variety of forms in which community health protection and care can be provided.	Select alternative actions and accept consequences.	Problem solving.	Social Studies.
31. Basic First Aid in Emergency Situations	Primary responsibility for improving and maintaining the health of the community is a function of its members.	Evaluate an injury situation for the purpose of determining appropriate care. Utilize skills in basic first aid.	Measure body temperature.	Understand that preparedness in dealing with emergency situations contributes to community wellness.	Consider consequences of alternatives before making decision. Make decisions based on consequences to self and others.	Teacher demonstration, Competency-based instruction.	Social Studies, Math.
32. Bicycle Safety	Maintaining a safe and healthful environment is a shared responsibility of the individual, family and society.	Understand and use the rules for bicycle safety.	Coordinate bike and arm signals.	Accept responsibility for obeying traffic rules pertaining to bicycle safety.	Accept direction in caring for health and welfare of self and others.	—	Social Studies.
33. Food— Preservation and Packaging	In the consumer environment, knowledge of packing and processing procedures contributes to responsible decision-making concerning products that affect one's health.	Investigate the relationship between food preservation and packing.	—	Appreciate how food packaging procedures provide consumers with variety and quality food.	Discuss consequences of alternative actions.	Discovery, learning.	Social Studies.
34. World Health Problems	Because health of all people is fundamental to the attainment of world peace and security, world-wide health is a shared responsibility.	Compare some of the major causes of disease in the world today. Describe the activities of international health organizations.	Construct a class histogram.	Appreciate the accomplishments of groups that work to improve health throughout the world.	Accept direction in caring for health and welfare of self and others.	Guided discovery.	Math, Social Studies.

You Are What You Eat
Grades 3-5

ACTIVITY OVERVIEW
     The children use sculpture dough to construct a model meal of
foods, in appropriate serving sizes, from the four food groups.

SCIENCE BACKGROUND
     A calorie is a unit devised for measuring energy. The body uses
energy for heat, growth, maintenance, reproduction, motion, repair,
and resistance to disease. The National Research Council recommends
a daily intake of approximately 2,400 to 2,800 calories for children
between the ages of seven and fourteen years. However, a relationship
exists between food intake, activity, and body weight. If, day after
day, more calories are used than provided by the foods eaten, weight
loss occurs. On the other hand, if fewer calories are used than
consumed, the surplus energy is stored as fat, and weight gain occurs.
Both extremes contribute to stress on the body.
     To help evaluate the diet, food quantities have been established
in terms of number and size of servings from the four food groups.
From the Dairy Food Group, three or four 8-ounce servings of milk
are recommended for children. Equivalents for a cup of milk can be
1 ½ slices of cheddar cheese, 1 cup pudding, 1 3/4 cups ice cream,
or 2 cups of cottage cheese. Two or more servings from the meat
and protein group are recommended. A serving means 2 to 3 ounces
of lean, boneless, cooked meat, poultry, or fish; 1 cup of cooked
dry beans, peas or lentils; or 4 tablespoons of peanut butter.
Four or more servings each day are recommended from the fruit and
vegetable group. A serving of fruit, vegetable, or juice is equal
to 1/2 cup or a typical sized portion, such as a medium apple,
banana, potato, or 1/2 medium grapefruit. From the bread and cereal
group, four servings are recommended for a good diet. One serving is
the equivalent of one tortilla, pancake, slice of bread, small waffle,
hamburger bun half, 1 cup of ready-to-eat cereal; or 1/2 cup cooked
cereal, grits, pasta, rice, or noodles.

SOCIETAL IMPLICATIONS
     About 25 million or one out of eight Americans are obese or
seriously overweight. Obesity is considered a major health problem
because of its association with heart disease, high blood pressure,
hardening of the arteries, arthritis, diabetes, and numerous other
diseases. Many characteristics of contemporary society contribute to
this problem: a large and accessible food supply, available leisure
time, limited physical activity, and trends toward increased snacking.

The eating habits we develop affect our weight and, therefore, our health. Most experts on human behavior agree that many cases of adult obesity can be prevented by exposure, early in life, to the problems of being overweight. Understanding the relationship of food intake and physical activity to weight gain, in addition to awareness of reasonable food quantities, can effectively help children develop good eating habits.

MAJOR CONCEPT

Individuals develop eating patterns which contribute to wellness.

OBJECTIVES

By the end of this activity, the student should be able to:
-Identify the recommended number of daily servings and the amounts of food in single servings from each of the four food groups.

MATERIALS

-For each student: One paper plate, modeling dough: mix 1 cup salt to 2 cups flour; add 1 cup water a little at a time, kneading dough until smooth and puttylike.

-Acrylic paints or poster paints, paint brushes, varnish (optional), measuring cups, scale, utensils for modeling (e.g. forks, knives, garlic press--for making spaghetti)

-Optional: lifesize photographic food models (from National Dairy Council)

VOCABULARY

-arthritis, calorie, diabetes, four food groups, energy, hardening of the arteries, high blood pressure, obesity, overweight, underweight

PROCEDURES

1. Invite the students to construct a meal on a paper plate, using modeling dough. The students can make their own dough by following the simple instructions above. The meal must include representations of foods from each of the four food groups in appropriate serving sizes. Devices for measuring and weighing should be used. The students may need to examine food packages to determine serving sizes of some foods.

2. Allow food models to air dry for 48 hours, or bake them on a cookie sheet at 325° until light brown. When cool, they may be painted or varnished as desired.

Identifying and Using Community Resources
Grades 3-5

ACTIVITY OVERVIEW

Students learn to locate community resources that provide help in solving personal, family, or community health problems. By means of a field trip the students gain detailed information about a community agency.

SCIENCE BACKGROUND

Community health, protection, and care is available in a variety of forms. In most communities, health resources include many more people and organizations than just physicians and hospitals. Police and fire departments, poison control centers, county health departments, clergy, counseling professionals, exterminators, the Red Cross and American Heart Association are among numerous public, private, and volunteer health resources. These individuals and groups provide services and information dealing with both the physical and emotional health of community members.

The telephone directory is a comprehensive source for use in locating community health resources. Community directories, which are updated yearly, list all community resources that have a phone. In addition, the directories are easily available--they are found in most homes and public telephone booths.

SOCIETAL IMPLICATIONS

Obtaining and utilizing the appropriate information and community services that promote personal health is the responsibility of each individual. Acquainting young people with the scope of health resources available in their own community lets them know that trained help is available. With this knowledge, young people are more likely to seek out solutions to personal or family health problems. Practice in information-gathering skills--in particular, the use of the telephone directory--can give young people the confidence to take personal responsibility in achieving and maintaining the physical and mental health of themselves and their families.

MAJOR CONCEPT

Obtaining and utilizing appropriate intervention and community services that promote personal health is the responsibility of each individual.

<u>MATERIALS</u>
    -Box of problem task cards
    -Telephone directories

<u>VOCABULARY</u>
    -Alcoholics Anonymous, Cardiopulmonary Resuscitation (CPR), chemical dependency, family counseling, health resources, home care, optometrist, poison control center, prescription, public health depart-ment, social services, tetanus, visiting nurses

<u>PROCEDURES</u>
    1. Prepare problem task cards. Each card should contain a practical problem and directions that suggest ways of finding a solution.
    2. Place the task cards in a box accessible to students for independent investigation in groups of two.
    3. Suggested <u>problems</u> can include the following (one per card):
    -You can't read the chalkboard from your desk in the classroom.
    -A dog bites your friend on the way home from school.
    -You need help in getting rid of cockroaches in the school cafeteria.
    -You want to know what the weather is like so travel will be safe.
    -You have an elderly family member who needs special help with food, personal care and medicine.
    -A friend is very ill and must be taken to the hospital in an ambulance.
    -You want help for someone who drinks too much alcohol.
    -You are walking home and find a wire down from a telephone pole.
    -You have a question about a medical prescription.
    -You want to report a fire.
    -You want information about sickle-cell anemia.
    -You want accurate information about a new food product.
    -A neighbor child swallows some liquid detergent. You need to get help.
    -An older neighbor child is taking drugs.
    -You need help when members of your family are fighting.
    -You think there is a gas leak in your house.
    -You want to learn how to administer Cardiopulmonary Resuscitation (CPR).
    -You have a friend that has been abused by an adult.
    -You stepped on a rusty nail and need a tetanus shot.
    -There is a disabled person in your neighborhood who needs help.
    -Someone has stolen your bike.
    4. Suggested directions for finding solutions (include these questions on all cards):
    a. Who in your community can help you with your problem?
    b. Use the telephone directory or other community resource guides

139

to help you contact the appropriate community resource that can help you.

c. Contact the resource to learn information about the services they provide.

d. Present your information to the class in the form of an oral report.

5. Plan a field trip to one community agency. After the students have completed the preliminary identification and use of community resources, have them plan a field trip to visit one resource. This visit should not be to the usual police or fire station. Suggestions for this visit include:

-Social Services
-Community Mental Health
-Poison Control Center
-A Twenty-Four Hour "Hot Line"
-Visiting Nurses or Home Care

Basic First Aid in Emergency Situations
Grades 3-5

ACTIVITY OVERVIEW
Students practice and demonstrate skill in administering basic first-aid treatment for shock, bleeding, loss of breathing, and broken bones.

SCIENCE BACKGROUND
Skill in administering emergency first-aid care (while waiting for medical aid) can be learned by the intermediate student. While detailed first-aid instruction is available through the American National Red Cross, discussion follows for basic treatment of four serious or emergency conditions: shock, bleeding, loss of breathing, and broken bones.

Symptoms of shock include: pale, cold, clammy skin that is mottled in color; apathy; nausea; and weak, irregular breathing. Shock, however, is not always easily determined. A victim of any serious injury must be treated for shock. Early treatment can prevent an injured person from going into shock. Treatment for shock stipulates:

-To minimize any work for the body, have the victim lie down.

-If the victim can breathe sufficiently, elevate the legs about 18 to 30 centimeters, unless that causes pain. If the head is injured or the victim has trouble breathing, elevate the neck and shoulders.

-Cover the victim lightly with a blanket to keep her warm. If she is cold or damp, place a blanket under her. Be sure not to move a victim if a back or neck injury is suspected.

-If the weather is warm, shade the victim and keep her comfortable.

Immediate direct pressure and elevation of the injury are important for controlling bleeding. Instructions are as follows:

-Using a gauze pad, clean cloth, clothing, or your bare hand if necessary, press down with the heel of the hand directly over the wound.

-Elevate injured limbs higher than the heart unless you suspect a fracture.

-Continue to press until bleeding is controlled. Apply additional cloth pads over the initial pad if necessary.

-When bleeding is controlled, bandage or tie the pads on the wound firmly, but not too tightly.

-Check the pulse below the wound. If you cannot feel a pulse, loosen the bandage until a pulse returns.

-Treat victims of severe cuts for shock.

Mouth-to-mouth breathing is the best way to get air into the lungs and initiate breathing in someone who has stopped breathing. Preparation instructions include:

-Turn the victim's head to the side, and use two fingers to remove from the mouth anything that might obstruct air from passing through.

-Placing one hand on the victim's forehead and the other hand under his neck, tip the head far back and keep it tipped. This prevents the tongue from blocking the airway. In this position, victims sometimes resume breathing.

-Listen for breathing. If breathing does not resume, pinch the nose closed to prevent air leakage.

Breathing instructions include:

-Taking a deep breath, open your mouth wide and place it over the victim's mouth, making a tight seal.

-Blow hard to fill the victim's lungs and watch his chest rise.

-While watching for his chest to fall, listen for air to come out.

-Repeat the blow-and-listen steps once every five seconds, 12 per minute, until the victim breathes spontaneously or medical aid arrives.

-If air cannot be blown into the lungs, repeat preparation procedures and try again.

Sometimes it may be impossible to make a seal over a victim's mouth due to injury or size. In this case, mouth-to-nose breathing is necessary. Breathing instructions remain the same, except that the mouth is now placed over the victim's nose, and his mouth is held closed when breaths are given. The victim's mouth is then held open to expel air.

The recommended treatment for dealing with broken bones is to keep the victim immobile. The victim of a suspected fracture should lie still if a doctor is on the way. If the victim must be moved to get to a doctor, the broken bones must be kept stationary by immobilizing joints on both sides of the break. A splint can be made from wood with cloth padding when possible, from rolled magazines or newspapers, or from a tongue depressor or the like for broken fingers. The splint should be tied with cloth strips on either side of the break and at intervals along the splint. Another part of the body can also be used to immobilize a break. For example, a broken arm can be tied to the victim's side or, in the case of a fractured leg, padding can be placed between the legs, which can then be tied together. When it cannot be determined if a bone is broken, treat the victim as if it is, and immobilize the injured area as described.

SOCIETAL IMPLICATIONS

Preparedness in dealing with emergency situations contributes to community wellness. Even the younger members of the community can contribute help and safety to an injured person by evaluating the injury, contacting medical aid, and administering appropriate basic first-aid care.

MAJOR CONCEPT

Primary responsibility for improving and maintaining the health of the community is a function of its members.

OBJECTIVES

By the end of this activity the student should be able to:

-Evaluate an injury situation for the purpose of determining appropriate care.

-Utilize skills in basic first aid.

MATERIALS

-Blankets (2-3), clean gauze and clean cloths, wooden pieces and boards of various lengths, large dolls for mouth-to-mouth breathing, tongue depressors, magazines, newspapers, telephone directory

VOCABULARY

-Direct pressure, elevate, emergency, immobilize, injury, mouth-to-mouth breathing, mouth-to-nose breathing, shock, splint, wound

PROCEDURES

1. Prepare certificates of competency in First-Aid Emergency Care.
2. Prepare a First-Aid Learning Station. Include:
    a. Charts with printed instructions on first-aid treatment for shock, bleeding, loss of breathing, and broken bones.
    b. First-aid materials (i.e., blankets, cloths, etc.--See Materials list.)
    c. Large dolls for practicing. (You may want to ask the students to bring these.)
    d. A local telephone directory.
3. Invite the class or groups of students to join you at the First-Aid Station for an introduction. Define emergency injuries, their evidence, and symptom. The students may enjoy sharing personal experiences of injuries, broken bones, etc. Discuss community resources for emergency help and locate emergency phone numbers in the telephone directory. Demonstrate basic steps in first-aid care using the dolls and volunteer students. Invite the children to try the procedures with your help and supervision.

4. During free time or designated time in the next weeks, invite the students to practice in pairs the given first-aid procedures on dolls. You may want to assign a single procedure, such as controlling bleeding, to be practiced and mastered during a given week. Also ask the students to practice locating emergency phone numbers in the phone book.

5. During a demonstration or practice session, you might ask the students to consider the following questions.

1. Suppose you witness a friend being thrown from his bicycle when hit by a car. Your friend immediately gets to his feet, though trembling, and insists that he is all right. What would you advise your friend to do? What actions would you take?

2. Suppose you cut your foot badly on a broken bottle at the seashore. Your towel is up on the beach with your friends. Should you try and walk up from the shore to get your towel to use in stopping the bleeding? If not, what should you do first?

3. Which joints would you need to immobilize in the case of a broken forearm? How do you suppose you could immobilize a suspected broken foot? (Remove or cut away shoe. Immobilize with a padded splint, using a blanket, pillow, etc. Tie it snugly, but not too tightly.)

Bicycle Safety
Grades 3-5

ACTIVITY OVERVIEW

Students design, construct, and use a bicycle course on the playground. The students conduct a bicycle safety check, and they demonstrate their understanding of traffic rules and skill while riding a bicycle. Pupils receive a safety proficiency certificate upon completion of the bicycle course.

SCIENCE BACKGROUND

Each year, the careless operation of bicycles accounts for some 400 accidental deaths due to collisions with automobiles and about 25,000 disabling injuries. In four out of five cases, the bike rider violates one or more laws or safety rules. Some accidents also result from a bicycle's faulty operation: inadequate brakes, handlebars, or seat; or lack of reflectors or lights. Observing bicycle safety rules and maintaining safe operation of the bicycle are clearly imperative for safe bicycle riding.

It is no surprise that the first basic rule for bicycle safety is to keep a bike in good repair. Brakes should be adjusted or replaced if the rider cannot make the rear tire skid on dry, clean, level pavement. A rider who is used to foot brakes should become thoroughly comfortable with hand brakes before riding the bike in traffic. Every bicycle should be equipped with a glass reflector and/or reflecting tape on the rear, and with a working light on the front. Another safety rule emphasizes the proper use of arm signals and turning lanes. For turning right, the left arm (used for all arm signals) is extended out to the left with the elbow bent at a right angle, hand pointing upward. For turning left, the left arm is extended straight out to the left.

However, a bicyclist who wants to turn left should stay by the right curb, cross the perpendicular street on foot, and then turn the bicycle left and cross the street on which the approach was made. (See the diagram.) Except when making signals, both hands should be kept on the handle bars to assure better control of the bicycle.

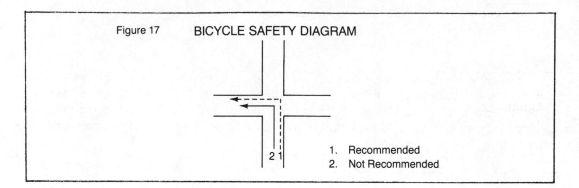

Figure 17   BICYCLE SAFETY DIAGRAM

1. Recommended
2. Not Recommended

Additional bicycle safety practices include the following:

-Obey all traffic lights and traffic signs, as these apply to bicycle riders.

-Keep to the right.

-Groups should ride in single-file formation.

-Walk across busy intersections.

-Do not carry riders.

-Never hitch a ride on a car or truck.

-Watch speed, it is a major factor in accidents.

Children of this age should avoid bike riding at night except on rare and necessary occasions. The chance of accident increases with darkness.

SOCIETAL IMPLICATIONS

Maintaining a safe and healthful environment is a shared responsibility of the individual, family, and society. The power and speed that a bicycle gives its young rider lends itself to the taking of unnecessary chances such as speeding, "showing off," cutting corners, disregarding traffic signals, etc. With this increased mobility also comes much responsibility in regards to the double role of a bicyclist in the street. The bicycle rider is considered "in between" a pedestrian and an automobile driver. In most respects, the bicycle and rider are regarded as a vehicle and should give the right of way to pedestrians. In relation to cars, trucks, and buses, the bicycle is less of a vehicle. Young riders in particular, and bicyclists at corners, are looked upon as pedestrians. Taking personal responsibility for both maintaining a bicycle and learning and obeying traffic and bicycle safety rules is a significant way for a child of this age to do his/her part in maintaining a safe environment.

MAJOR CONCEPT

Maintaining a safe and healthful environment is a shared responsibility of the individual, family, and society.

OBJECTIVES:

By the end of this activity, the student should be able to:

-Understand and follow the rules for bicycle safety.

MATERIALS

-Poster paint and marking pens, tagboard for posters, cardboard and/or tagboard for making traffic signs,and simple cones, used to designate roadways, intersections, lanes, etc., index cards, onion skin,or ditto paper for proficiency certificates

VOCABULARY

-bicycle lane, license, motor vehicle, pedestrian, reflector

PROCEDURES

1. Invite a traffic officer, highway patrolman, or police officer to discuss bicycle safety and licensing. Group discussion might also include a comparison of a bicycle in good condition with one in poor condition and student demonstrations of getting on and off a bicycle, applying brakes, parking, etc.

2. Divide the class into three committees and assign the committees their tasks.

    a. Committee #1: Draw up a simple plan for a bicycle course on the playground. Include intersections, traffic signs, bike lanes, single land roadways, etc. Using suggested materials, make simple cones and traffic signs.

    b. Committee #2: Develop a safety code for safe bicycle riding and prepare a large poster of the code for the classroom. Be prepared to judge safe bicycle riding proficiency.

    c. Committee #3: Develop a "Safe Bicycle Checklist" and be prepared to conduct safety checks on bicycles.

3. Collectively review the committee projects (bicycle course plan, safety code, checklist).

4. In advance, prepare a Safe Bicycle Rider proficiency certificate for each student.

5. Invite the students to bring their bicycles to school on a given day. Children without bikes can arrange to use a classmate's bike.

6. Committee #1 sets up the bicycle course in a designated area of the playground. Selected members of Committee #2 station themselves at strategic points along the course to evaluate bicyclists' practice of all safety rules. Members of Committee #3

---

*Bicycle safety materials are available through: Bicycle Institute of America, Inc., 122 East 42nd Street, New York, New York

take turns operating the safe bicycle check station at the entrance to the course.

7. Taking turns, all the students complete a bicycle check at the check station and proceed through the course, careful to observe all safety practices. Upon correct completion of the course, the students receive proficiency certificates.

Food Preservation and Packaging
Grades 3-5

ACTIVITY OVERVIEW

Students remove foods from their packages and leave the foods exposed to the air. Over a period of a week, the students observe, record, and compare the changes in the food, discovering what happens to foods when they are stored improperly.

SCIENCE BACKGROUND

In today's society, large segments of the population live far from the places where food is grown and produced. Since food must often travel far from source to table, methods of keeping food fresh are essential; foods lose nutritional and aesthetic value, as well as sometimes becoming poisonous, when improperly stored. Such simple environmental factors as oxygen, moisture, and temperature can contribute to the spoilage of food.

The two conditions that most often result in food spoilage are (a) chemical changes and (2) the growth of organisms. Chemical changes, such as rancidity, color and flavor that are "off," and loss of vitamin efficiency, develop from the interaction of such things as oxygen, moisture, and temperature on substances occurring naturally in the food (such as oils). Moisture particularly contributes to the growth of organisms (such as botulism). The growth of spoilage-causing organisms, if uncontrolled, can lead to food poisoning. Chemical changes do not result in food poisoning.

Several effective food processing methods have been developed to control food spoilage. Canning is one way of preserving food. Canned foods are sealed airtight and cooked at high temperatures to kill organisms. The airtight container prevents new organisms and/or oxygen from entering and causing spoilage. Freezing is another method of preserving food. Some foods can be frozen and stored at low temperatures to prevent the growth of organisms and to slow chemical changes. Refrigeration of foods functions similarly but for a shorter period of time. Since all organisms require water for growth, the removal of water from food (dehydration) also prevents food spoilage. Thus we can see how food packaging forms an integral part of food preservation by providing a barrier against organisms, oxygen, and moisture.

SOCIETAL IMPLICATIONS

In a world of limited resources, we cannot afford to waste food by allowing inadequate preservation and packaging to cause spoilage. Yet consumers are confronted daily by the media with conflicting claims about the benefits and hazards of processed foods. Appreciating the role of food processing and packaging in providing a variety of quality food the year around helps students, as present and future consumers, to understand the importance of proper food selection, storage, and preparation for healthy living.

MAJOR CONCEPT
In the consumer environment, knowledge of packaging and processing procedures contributes to responsible decision-making concerning products that affect one's health.

OBJECTIVES
By the end of this activity the student should be able to:
-Investigate the relationship between food preservation and packaging.

MATERIALS
-Five plastic sandwich bags, sample foods in their own packages: one canned food, such as tomatoes; one frozen food, such as spinach; one refrigerated food, such as cottage cheese; one dry food, such as cereal

VOCABULARY
-Canning, dehydration, freezing, organism, refrigeration

PROCEDURES
1. Have the students remove the food samples from their packages and place 1/2 cup of each food in a separate sandwich bag.
   a. Boxes of dry cereal can be divided into two plastic bags.
   b. Have the students add water to one cereal sample and seal the bag to prevent evaporation.
   c. All the other bags should be left loosely open to air exposure.
2. Invite the students to attach the samples to a bulletin board or chart in the classroom. Samples should be labeled and dated.
3. Over a period of a week, have the students observe the food samples daily and keep a journal of observed changes.

World Health Problems
Grades 3-5

ACTIVITY OVERVIEW
Students collect and compare data relating to the causes of
diseases and death in the Western and non-Western world. The students
learn about the role of international groups working to improve the
health status of people around the world.

SCIENCE BACKGROUND
Our most serious diseases in the United States are sometimes
called "diseases of civilization"; we are a nation of television watchers
and desk sitters and this passivity is detrimental to our health.
Our number-one killers are diseases of the heart and blood vessels:
heart attack, stroke, high blood pressure, and arteriosclerosis.
Other major causes of death include obesity, diabetes, cancer,
emphysema, drug side-effects, alcoholism, suicide, and automobile
accidents. The common factors related to death-causing disease in
the United States are (1) improper diet, (2) lack of serious physical
exercise, (3) smoking, and (4) stress.

The two major diseases in most of the non-Western world (outside
Europe and North America) are malaria (a blood disease carried by a
mosquito) and tuberculosis (a disease, usually of the lungs, which
is passed from an infected person to another by way of breath).
Other diseases that cause much illness, suffering, and death are:
smallpox, yaws, yellow fever, leprosy, influenza, typhus, typhoid
fever, trachoma, and cholera. Most sickness and death in the non-
Western world are related to: (1) poor sanitation in relation to
disposal of human excreta, (2) lack of personal cleanliness brought
about by insufficient clean water for use in washing and bathing,
(3) close contact with others having communicable diseases, (4) low
resistence to disease, and lack of medical care and drugs to cure
one disease before another strikes, and (5) inadequate food supply,
particularly protein foods, which build muscle, bone, body tissue,
and disease-fighting cells in the body.

The most significant wasters of human life in non-Western countries,
and historically in the United States, are infectious diseases.
Methods of control and eradication in this country have come about
through improved nutrition, sanitation, and housing and, more recently
through the development of immunizations and antibiotics. Good health
is a fundamental right of all people. International cooperation is
critically needed to help solve many world health problems.

SOCIETAL IMPLICATIONS

While health problems are not limited to any one country or continent, sickness and early death occur more frequently in the underdeveloped nations of the world. In most instances, health standards are higher in Europe and North America than in non-Western countries.

The international health organization that embodies a principle of cooperation by encouraging health personnel from developing nations to work with trained health experts is known as The World Health Organization (WHO). WHO was founded in the United States in 1945, a year after its parent body, the United Nations, was founded. There are now more than 100 nations that are members of WHO, headquartered in Geneva, Switzerland.

WHO is based on the belief that: (1) It is the fundamental right of each person in the world to be as healthy as possible; and (2) The health of all peoples is fundamental to the attainment of peace and security. Awareness of major world health problems and the impact of these problems on various countries helps students to appreciate the accomplishments made by groups that work to improve health throughout the world.

MAJOR CONCEPT

Because the health of all peoples is fundamental to the attainment of world peace and security, worldwide health is a shared responsibility.

OBJECTIVES

By the end of this activity the students should be able to:
-Compare some of the major causes of disease in the world today.
-Describe the activities of the World Health Organization.

MATERIALS

-Butcher paper for histogram, marking pens

VOCABULARY

-Malaria, malnutrition, sanitation, tuberculosis, World Health Organization (WHO)

PROCEDURES

1. Assign students the task of finding out from parents and/or neighbors the names of major diseases that caused death to family members or friends.

2. Ask the students to help you make a histogram that lists all the major death causing diseases they found during their surveys and the number of persons that suffered from each.

3. List the major causes of death in the non-Western world, and ask the students to compare the diseases with those listed on their histogram.

4. Discuss reasons for the differences in the two lists. Include in the discussion the major causes of diseases in the non-Western world.

5. Invite the children to think of ways of eliminating causes of major diseases in the United States and in the non-Western world.

6. Tell the students about the World Health Organization: its purpose, activities, and results.

7. Ask the students to discuss reasons why the health of persons in far-away countries might affect them.

PLANNING CHART FOR HEALTH AND NUTRITION ACTIVITIES: GRADES 6-8

ACTIVITY	OBJECTIVES					TEACHING METHODS	RELATED CURRICULUM
	Conceptual Knowledge	Learning Processes	Psychomotor Skills	Attitudes and Values	Decision-making Skills		
35. Evaluating Food Choices	Individuals develop eating patterns which contribute to wellness.	Analyze and evaluate food choices in terms of the Recommended Daily Allowance (RDA) of protein, energy and nutrients.	Collect and graph data.	Appreciate that a balanced diet helps produce good health, while an unbalanced diet can result in health problems.	Discuss consequences of alternating actions.	Individual investigation.	Math.
36. Hassles and Hangups	Building self-acceptance and reducing stress and anxiety contribute to mental health.	Identify causes and effects of stress experienced by young adolescents and describe healthy ways of coping.	—	Motivate active involvement in seeking solutions to stress related situations.	Select alternative actions and accept consequences.	Student-led discussions.	Language Arts.
37. Information Interviews with Community Resource Personnel	Obtaining and utilizing appropriate information and community services that promote personal health is a responsibility of the individual.	Identify major health issues facing today's teenage and adult population. Investigate specific treatment agencies in the community.	Develop interview techniques.	Appreciate the quality of concern and professionalism available to individuals in the community.	Accept direction in caring for health and welfare of self and others.	Individual inquiry.	Social Studies, Language Arts.
38. Analyzing Advertising	In the consumer environment, knowledge of packing and processing procedures contributes to responsible decision-making concerning products that affect one's health.	Identify major enticement themes used in advertising. Make inferences from student-collected advertisement data.	—	Develop discriminating attitudes toward advertisements.	Select alternative actions and accept consequences.	Discovery.	Language Arts, Art.
39. Smoking and Health	Maintaining a safe and healthful environment is a shared responsibility of the individual, family and society.	Plan and carry out independent investigations in order to understand effects of smoking on the body.	Graph data. Construct a smoking machine.	Recognize the effects of smoking on the immediate environment.	Evaluate alternative points of view.	Inquiry.	Math, Social Studies.
40. Vocations and avocations in Community Health	Primary responsibility for improving and maintaining the health of the community is a function of its members.	Investigate and evaluate the wide range of opportunities that exist for contributing to the health of individuals in the community.	Develop interview techniques.	Motivate students to take an active role in promoting health in the community.	Accept direction in caring for health and welfare of self and others.	Inquiry, Evaluation.	Social Studies, Language Arts.

Evaluating Food Choices
Grades 6-8

ACTIVITY OVERVIEW

Students keep a record of the food they eat for one day. By means of a graph, the students evaluate their food choices.

SCIENCE BACKGROUND

Nutrients can be defined as the different substances in foods that function specifically to keep the body healthy, active, and growing. Some of the major nutrients needed by the body include protein, fats, carbohydrates, vitamins, and minerals.

Protein is the body's building material. It contains nitrogen, which is necessary for all tissue building. Protein is essential for maintaining body structure, for providing substances that act as body regulators, and for producing compounds necessary for normal body functions. Milk products, meat, fish, poultry, eggs, legumes, and nuts are good sources of protein.

While protein can also provide energy for the body, fats and carbohydrates are the major food substances that provide the body with calories for heat and energy. If the body lacks sufficient amounts of fats and carbohydrates, or if there is an excess of protein in the diet, the body will use protein for heat and energy. Fats are normally consumed from margarine, butter, mayonnaise, salad dressings, and meat. Carbohydrates are found in grain products, fruit, and sugar-sweetened foods.

Although vitamins and minerals are needed in smaller quantities than are protein, fats, and carbohydrates, they remain essential to normal body functioning. Our discussion is limited to those often lacking in the diets of adolescents.

Vitamin A is important for vision. Night blindness, an inability of the eye to adjust to dim light, can result from a lack of vitamin A in the diet. Yellow, orange, and dark green vegetables, and fruits contain vitamin A (sweet potatoes, carrots, squash, spinach, broccoli, melon, apricots, and peaches).

Vitamin C contributes to the formation of a substance called collagen, which holds body tissue together and encourages healing. Vitamin C also strengthens blood vessel walls and helps the body utilize calcium in making bones and teeth. Scurvy, a disease characterized by swelling and tenderness of joints and gums, loosening of teeth, hemorrhaging and puffiness can result from severe lack of vitamin C. Citrus fruits, broccoli, spinach, greens, potatoes, tomatoes, melon, cabbage, and strawberries contain this vitamin.

Iron is a mineral that is essential to hemoglobin, the substance of the blood that carries oxygen. Oxygen is necessary for all cells.

155

PROCEDURES

1. Have the students keep a complete written record of all foods eaten for one day.

2. Using the "Comprehensive List of Foods," the students should then determine the nutritive values and graph the percent of RDA that chosen foods contained. (See sample graph below.)

3. Upon completion of the bar graphs, invite the students to answer the following questions:

Is the percentage of calories (energy) in your daily diet too low, about right, or too high?

Nutrients I need more of are: _____.

Which foods could provide these nutrients?

Foods I ate that had a lot of calories (energy) but not many other nutrients are: _____.

How can I improve my diet?

GRAPH OF FOOD CHOICES
FOR ONE DAY

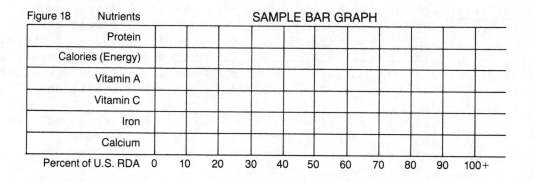

Figure 18   Nutrients   SAMPLE BAR GRAPH

Protein										
Calories (Energy)										
Vitamin A										
Vitamin C										
Iron										
Calcium										

Percent of U.S. RDA 0 10 20 30 40 50 60 70 80 90 100+

A diet that fails to supply a sufficient amount of iron may lead to anemia. This condition is characterized by a tired and listless feeling due to a lack of energy. Although liver is a major source of iron, greens, beans, beef, pork, prunes, and raisins are also good sources.

Calcium is the bone and tooth building mineral. It forms the structure of teeth and bones and helps keep them strong. Milk products are good sources for calcium.

SOCIETAL IMPLICATIONS

There is no perfect food, no single food that provides all of the nutrients needed for growth, maintenance, and regulation of body processes. Although we may have a fair understanding of food and nutrition facts, this understanding is not often apparent in our selection of daily meals and snacks. An appreciation of the varied components of a balanced diet and their effect on health, in addition to practice in evaluating and planning meals, can influence young people to make reasonable daily food choices for themselves and their families in the future.

MAJOR CONCEPT

Individuals should develop eating patterns that contribute to wellness.

OBJECTIVES

By the end of this activity, the students should be able to:

-Analyze and evaluate food choices in terms of the Recommended Daily Allowance (RDA) of protein, energy, and selected vitamins and minerals.

MATERIALS

-"Comprehensive List of Foods" booklet with nutritive values and percent of U.S. RDA for 139 foods, available from the National Dairy Council. Contact the office serving your area or write:

National Dairy Council
630 North River Road
Rosemont, IL 60018

VOCABULARY

-anemia, calories, carbohydrates, fats, minerals, night blindness, nutrient, proteins, Recommended Daily Allowance (RDA), scurvy, vitamins

Hassles and Hangups
Grades 6-8

ACTIVITY OVERVIEW

Students survey stressful situations and reactions experienced among themselves. They brainstorm behavioral suggestions to cope with stress in the cited situations. The students then keep a record of stressful situations, responses, efforts to relieve stress, and evaluations over a given period of time.

SCIENCE BACKGROUND

To some degree, sensitivity to stressful or arousing circumstances is common to each of us. In response to a strange noise in the house during the night, to a near accident, or to giving a presentation before a large group of people, our bodies react automatically and involuntarily in a variety of ways. A racing heart rate and pulse, varied breathing, increased perspiration and saliva flow, sweaty palms, contraction of the stomach muscles, and trembling are familiar bodily reactions experienced by all of us in certain situations. These measurable physiological responses are the body's alert system, functioning to help meet and cope with frightening, difficult, or intensely pleasurable situations.

In response to emotional stress, some people experience more unpleasant, residual reactions, such as a tension headache, skin rash, or sleep disturbance. A variety of techniques to deal with stress have been developed and have, in some cases, helped to reduce stress and tension. These efforts include physical exercise, relaxation techniques, hypnosis, biofeedback, tranquilizers, and psychological counseling that encourages self-acceptance, expectation reduction, and adopting a slower pace.

SOCIETAL IMPLICATIONS

Due to the complex tasks and transitions required of young people, adolescence is not an easy period of life. The adolescent is trying to define his or her identity, while at the same time struggling with the approach of economic, legal, and psychological independence. Determining future economic and vocational aspirations and assessing the educational goals needed to reach these aspirations, developing a personal,ethical,and moral framework by which to live, dealing with the contradictory values that exist in society, realizing their approaching and inevitable separation from home, and learning how to develop meaningful interpersonal relationships while dealing with their own sexuality are difficult, though necessary, facets of the maturation process through which adolescents pass.

That many teens turn to drugs and alcohol indicates, to some degree, the pressure of this period. Chronic alcoholism is now considered a common problem of adolescents, while surveys also show increases in marijuana usage with each year of teenhood. Figures on sufferers of migraine headaches show rises at the onset of puberty, and stress is a commonly cited factor in headaches for all people. Among adolescents, suicide is the third most common cause of death.

Building self-acceptance and reducing stress and anxiety contribute to sound mental health. By focusing on the causes and effects of stress experienced by young adolescents, the students may be motivated to actively seek solutions to stress related situations in their own lives.

MAJOR CONCEPT

Building self-acceptance and reducing stress and anxiety contribute to mental health.

OBJECTIVES

By the end of this activity, the students should be able to:
-Identify causes and effects of stress experienced by young adolescents, and
-Describe healthy ways of coping with this stress.

MATERIALS

-Chalkboard, small notebook or simple record book for each student

VOCABULARY

-Relaxation technique, stress, tension

PROCEDURES

Discussion

1. Initiate a class discussion by telling the students about a situation in which you experienced stress or tension, such as a public speaking assignment or a family argument. Explain how you responded to the incident and conclude with the question: "Have any of you ever felt this way?"

2. Select a student to direct a large group discussion in which students share stressful situations they experience (e.g. exams, grades) and explain how they respond to these circumstances (e.g. tears, headaches). List the stressful situations and reactions to stress on the chalkboard.

3. Invite the students to brainstorm techniques that can be used to reduce or cope with stress in their lives. Have the students divide into small groups and make lists of possible solutions or suggestions.

4. A representative from each small group can then summarize
the coping mechanisms used by members of the group.

Activity
    1. Invite the students to keep a Personal Stress Record for two
to four weeks. Included in the record should be dates and descriptions
of stressful situations, the students' experiences, their emotional
or physical responses to tension, the effort made to cope with or
solve the problem, and a brief evaluation of how the technique worked
to relieve the stress.
    2. Have a follow-up discussion of the different types of stresses
experienced by the students and the means of coping with stress.

Information Interviews with Community Resource Personnel
Grades 6-8

ACTIVITY OVERVIEW

Students focus on current major health issues facing them and adults. The students investigate their community for agencies and organizations that offer assistance or guidance regarding specific issues. Following interviews with agency or professional personnel, the students share information they have gathered on a selected issue or health problem and the services that are available for assistance with the problem.

SCIENCE BACKGROUND

Many of the health issues and problems facing adults today also make their way into the junior high and high school settings: prevalence of drugs, alcohol and smoking; availability of contraception and changing sexual morals; family physical, emotional and sexual abuse; and mental stress, to name just a few. Numerous agencies and organizations designed to help people deal with these issues and problems exist in most communities, such as Alcoholics Anonymous, Planned Parenthood, Parents Anonymous, crisis centers, and Suicide Alert. Such groups offer counseling and professional services to help solve a problem, in addition to providing free printed materials explaining the facts, trends, and effects of these problems or issues on society.

SOCIETAL IMPLICATIONS

The services of community agencies are only as useful as we allow them to be. Adolescents, and adults as well, frequently fail to recognize a dangerous or detrimental situation or to admit to its effects in their personal lives.

Identifying circumstances that threaten personal and public health, understanding the effects of these conditions, and knowing sources of help can lead to responsible decision-making, such as seeking guidance and solutions.

MAJOR CONCEPT

Obtaining and utilizing appropriate information and community services that promote personal health is the responsibility of the individual.

OBJECTIVES

By the end of this activity the students should be able to:
-Identify major health issues facing today's teenage/adult population.
-Investigate specific treatment agencies in the community.

MATERIALS
    -Chalkboard, telephone directories

VOCABULARY
    -Abortion, Alcoholics Anonymous, alcoholism, crisis centers, depression, obesity, Planned Parenthood, suicide, veneral disease

PROCEDURES
    1. Lead an open-ended discussion on serious problems that affect the health of some teenagers and adults.
    2. List the problems brought up during the discussion on the chalkboard. The list might include the following: depression or suicide, runaways, teenage pregnancy, abortion, birth control, unwed motherhood, drug abuse, alcoholism, obesity, venereal diseases.
    3. Present the question: "What resources does the community have to deal with these problems?
    4. List community agencies and organizations that might offer some help: crisis centers, Suicide Alert, Alcoholics Anonymous, Planned Parenthood, Parents Anonymous, and homes for runaways and unwed mothers.
    5. Divide the class into pairs and have each pair of students:
        a. Select a problem, contact the appropriate agency, and set up an appointment for an interview to find out what services the agency has to offer an individual with this problem.
        b. Using materials gained from the community resource, supplemented by information available from a community and/or school library, determine the effects of this problem on one's health.
        c. Report to the class the information obtained through the interview and research.

Analyzing Advertising
Grades 6-8

ACTIVITY OVERVIEW

Students survey a variety of television advertisements for health-related products. The students identify and evaluate techniques commonly used to induce consumers into buying these products. Pupils conclude the activity with recommendations for wise, informed, consumer decision-making.

SCIENCE BACKGROUND

The consumer environment is continually being supplied with new health products. Advertisements for these goods are typically designed to appeal to buyers or to motivate them on a variety of levels, from statistics to sex. Certain techniques for making products desirable to consumers can commonly be found in today's television advertisements. Some popular inducements include: A recommendation of a famous person; an appeal to youthful or youth-desiring individuals; statistical proof of the product's effectiveness; the use of humor to attract attention; a testimonial of another consumer who reports positive results from using the product; the enticement or promise of sex appeal to potential buyers; encouragement to be part of the "in" crowd that enjoys the product; an appeal to the consumer's concern for his or her health; making the consumer believe she will be part of an elite group if she uses the product and providing a competitive edge to the aspiring athlete.

SOCIETAL IMPLICATIONS

Adolescents constitute a large segment of the audience for commercial advertisements through the media, making them a primary target for advertisers. Examining common techniques used to motivate buyers can help young consumers develop discriminating attitudes towards the advertisements that confront them. Knowledge of and experience with commercial television practices, may aid young people in making informed decisions concerning health products.

MAJOR CONCEPT

Knowledge of advertising techniques contributes to responsible decision-making concerning products that affect one's health.

OBJECTIVES

By the end of this activity, the students should be able to:

-Identify major themes used in advertising to induce consumers to purchase a product.

<u>MATERIALS</u>
    None
<u>VOCABULARY</u>
    -Advertisement, bandwagon, commercial, consumer, elite, entice-
ment, fallacy, fame, humor, jingle, sex appeal, statistics, testimonial

<u>PROCEDURES</u>
    1. Have the students identify 5-6 television commercials for
health nutrition related products. Examples include: cereal, vitamins,
foods, beverages and milk products. (You may have them include any
product advertised as health related.) Ask them to consider the
following questions in categorizing their ads.
    a. How is the ad trying to induce the consumer to buy the
        product?
    b. To whom is the ad appealing? Men? Women? Young? Old?
    c. What characteristics does the person in each ad have? (For
        example, fame, wealth, medical authority, average person,
        etc.)
    d. What characteristics would you expect a person who likes
        each ad to have?
    e. Who might ignore each ad? Why?
    f. Which advertisements would you believe? Why or why not?
    g. What other questions would you ask about the advertising
        claims? (For example, how was the sample selected? How
        many people were surveyed? What effect does the product have
        on health?)
    2. Invite the students to discuss the advertisements in relation
to the above questions. Ask them to recall these and other ads they
have heard or seen on radio, billboards and magazines and to collectively compile a list of common advertising enticement techniques
(e.g. fame, sex appeal, humor, elitism, etc.)
    3. Have the students identify 5 different products in their
homes. Ask them to interview their parents concerning their (the
parents) motivations to purchase the products.
    4. This activity can be extended by having the students ask
their friends why they use a certain product. Have the class decide
on one product and survey 100 students in the school. Accumulate the
responses and compare them to the original list of advertising
inducements.
    5. After these investigations, have a class discussion that
centers on the following questions:
    -Are the health products that are most popular with your family
and friends the ones that are most heavily advertised?
    -From which media source did you find ads that mostly appeal to
children?

-To educated adults? To the elderly? To the elite? To teenagers like yourself? What type enticements are most used for each
group?

-From the ads that are aimed at your age group, what kinds of
things do you think the advertisers expect to be important to American
youth?

-What criteria do you think is important for evaluating health-
related claims in advertising?

Smoking and Health
Grades 6-8

ACTIVITY OVERVIEW
     Students complete a library research project on the effects of
smoking. The students discuss their findings in a Forum on Smoking.

SCIENCE BACKGROUND
     In 1964, a committee of ten distinguished scientists were appointed
by the Surgeon General, with the approval of President Kennedy and the
tobacco industry. The purpose of this committee was to conduct a
Public Health Service Report on smoking and health. The scientific
judgments and conclusions from The Report of the Advisory Committee
to the Surgeon General led to the requirement, by an Act of Congress,
that all cigarette packages manufactured in the United States state:
"Warning: The Surgeon General Has Determined That Cigarette Smoking
Is Dangerous to Your Health."
     The major facts, taken from this report and four subsequent
reports entitled "The Health Consequences of Smoking" (issued in 1967,
1968, 1969, and 1971), have been summarized by the Public Health Service
of the United States Department of Health, Education, and Welfare.
     Findings stress that among individuals age 35 and over, death
rates are higher for smokers than for nonsmokers. Among men between
the ages of 45 and 54, the death rate for smokers is almost three
times that of nonsmokers. Cigarette smokers have more disability and
illness than nonsmokers. One estimate is that 77 million work days
are lost each year in our country due to the higher frequency of chronic
respiratory conditions and sickness among smokers.
     Cigarette smoking is most closely associated with diseases of
the respiratory and circulatory systems: lung cancer (of which smoking
is the major cause), coronary heart disease, emphysema, and chronic
bronchitis. The more a person smokes, the greater the risk. If a
person smokes two packages a day, he or she has more than twice the
chance of dying of heart disease and twenty times the chance of dying
from lung cancer than the nonsmoker. Even smokers of average (one-
pack-a-day) and light amounts can be affected significantly. In
laboratory studies, tobacco smoke has been found to contain a number
of carcinogens: chemical compounds that can cause cancer. Additional
elements, called cocarcinogens, are also found in smoke. Combined,
these interact with other compounds to promote the development of
cancer.
     The delicate tissues of our air passages are protected by mil-
lions of tiny hairs called cilia. The cilia move constantly to propel
foreign substances, such as dust or pollen, into the throat where it
can be removed. Direct contact with cigarette smoke paralyzes the cilia

166

and inhibits the function of macrophages, cells that assist in cleaning the lungs. In this way, cancer-causing and cancer-promoting compounds accumulate on the lining of the bronchial tubes. The length of time an individual has smoked, the number of cigarettes smoked per day, the depth of inhalation, and the level of tar in the brand used all adversely affect the risk of developing lung cancer.

Chronic bronchitis and pulmonary emphysema are two common respiratory ailments of which smoking is also a major cause. Smoking promotes the development of chronic obstructive lung diseases. When the cilia's cleaning function is inhibited, foreign substances can penetrate the lungs. Irritation and increased mucus production result, clogging air passages. Symptoms of this type of damage to the respiratory system are excessive coughing and sputum production.

Cigarette smoking is also considered an important risk factor in the development of coronary heart disease--the Number One American killer disease. Nicotine and carbon monoxides, found in smoke, appear to be directly linked to the production of coronary heart disease. Nicotine increases the demand of the heart for oxygen and other nutrients, while carbon monoxide reduces the oxygen-carrying performance of the red blood cells.

Additional effects of cigarette smoking on the heart and circulatory system include an increased risk of cerebrovascular disease (stroke) and peripheral vascular disease, which affects the circulation of the arms, hands, feet, and legs.

In addition to major diseases of the heart and lungs; cigarette, pipe, and cigar smoking are also linked to many other illnesses and conditions. These include cancer of the larynx; the oral cavity, including the pharynx, mouth, and cheek; the esophagus; the lip; the pancreas; and the kidney. Smoking is associated with illness and higher death rates from peptic ulcers, particularly gastric ulcers, and with a greater incidence of "low birth weight" babies among women who smoke regularly during pregnancy.

Considering the harmful effects of tobacco smoke on the body, a case can be made against "involuntary smoking"--the inhalation by a nonsmoker of many of the same components of tobacco smoke that smokers ingest, as an unavoidable consequence of breathing in a smoke filled environment. Through smoke that is inhaled and then exhaled by a smoker, called mainstream smoke, and from the smoke that generates from a smoldering cigarette, sidestream smoke, nicotine and carbon monoxide, among other substances, enter the environment. In conditions of unusually heavy smoking and insufficient ventilation, CO levels have been found to exceed the maximum permissible eight-hour exposure limit determined by the Occupational Safety and Health Administration. While the effects of CO and nicotine absorbed by nonsmokers remain unknown, the hazards of an involuntary smoking situation on a person suffering from chronic cardiovascular and pulmonary diseases are cause for concern.

167

SOCIETAL IMPLICATIONS

In spite of the fact that cigarette consumption in America has reached its lowest level in twenty years, girls in their teens and young women are now smoking more than ever before. Among all teenagers, smoking has declined 25% since 1974, yet a disturbing rise of smokers, from 25.9% to 26.2%, has occurred among girls between seventeen to eighteen years of age during the last five years. Not only has smoking increased among young females, but also they are smoking more heavily than in the past.

In an effort to reverse these trends, the American Cancer Society has sponsored studies to help explain the acceleration in smoking among teenage girls and young women. Findings reveal the importance of smoking education--and the earlier the better.

Among teenage girl smokers, 60% report starting smoking before thirteen years of age. Yet only 4% attended smoking education programs at the age of twelve in the sixth grade. While 48% did attend anti-smoking classes in school, these occurred in the seventh through tenth grades--in many cases too late.

The increase in the number of young female smokers can be linked to several sociological factors in the teenage environment. Changes in prevailing social and moral norms, as well as the new liberalized values that originated back in the sixties, have made their way to today's teens. Today's emphasis on the emotional rather than the rational, on the self and self-fulfillment, and on the informal life-style that more readily accepts drugs and sex, seem to make smoking more acceptable. Peer pressure remains a dominant influence with teenage girl smokers. All teenagers questioned, smokers and nonsmokers, consider smoking to be a major phenomenon among their peer groups, families, and all adults around them.

Though the majority of teenagers may be fully aware of the dangers of smoking, a limited amount of anti-smoking propaganda is available to combat the pervasive smoking environment surrounding the teen. Many parents are permissive with smoking, while many high schools actually designate smoking areas on campus. Unfortunately, most personal physicians and health clinics have failed to caution teens about the health hazards of smoking. As a result of the equal time provision, antismoking television commercials have been cut considerably since the banning of cigarette advertising on TV.

MAJOR CONCEPT

Maintaining a safe and healthful environment is a shared responsibility of the individual, family, and society.

OBJECTIVES
    By the end of this activity the students should be able to:
    -Plan and carry out independent library research in order to
understand the effects of smoking on the body.

MATERIALS
    -Paper, pens

VOCABULARY
    -Cancer, carbon monoxide, chronic bronchitis, cilia, circulatory
disease, coronary heart disease, emphysema, involuntary smoking,
macrophages, mainstream smoke, nicotine, respiratory disease, sidestream smoke, Surgeon General, tar

PROCEDURES
    From suggested problems and issues, the students select a
research project, forming a committee of other interested students.
Committee members conduct research on their topic. They compile
their findings in the form of a presentation to the class.
    A Forum on Smoking is then planned in which committees exhibit,
demonstrate and explain their findings to parents, teachers, and
the student body.
    Students should write to the following for more information
on smoking:
    U.S. Department of Health, Education and Welfare
    Public Health Service
    Center for Disease Control
    Bureau of Health Education
    National Clearinghouse for Smoking and Health
    Atlanta, Georgia 30333

    U.S. Department of Health, Education and Welfare
    Public Health Service
    National Institute of Health
    National Cancer Institute
    Bethesda, Maryland 20014

    In addition students should be encouraged to complete through
library research, surveys and opinion polls. As a part of the Forum
on Smoking, you should have students evaluate the evidence presented
by various committees.

Vocations and Avocations in Community Health
Grades 6-8

ACTIVITY OVERVIEW

For the purpose of acquainting themselves with career opportunities in the health sciences, the students interview professionals and volunteers who work in the health field. The students share their findings with their classmates.

SCIENCE BACKGROUND

Career opportunities in the health sciences are increasing. In addition, various ethnic groups, women, and handicapped persons are finding greater opportunities for employment in many other fields. Hospitals provide vocational opportunities other than those for nurses and physicians, such as clinicians, technicians, and practitioners, many of whom are medical specialists, highly trained in a particular branch of medicine (e.g. cardiologist). In addition, a volunteer staff frequently plays a significant role in the functioning of the hospital.

Public health departments encompass a variety of career opportunities in such areas as disease control, environmental sanitation, statistics and surveys, health education, nursing, counseling, laboratory work, occupational health, dentistry, and fluoridation programs.

SOCIETAL IMPLICATIONS

With sufficient knowledge, young adolescents can begin to identify and examine career opportunities. Comparing and evaluating requirements and the necessary preparation and experience for various types of careers are important for planning future educational and vocational goals. In addition to providing personal benefits, familiarity with the experiences of health-related careers may motivate students to take an active interest in promoting health in the community.

MAJOR CONCEPT

Primary responsibility for improving and maintaining the health of the community is a function of its members.

OBJECTIVES

By the end of this activity the students should be able to:
-Investigate and evaluate the wide range of opportunities that exist for contributing to the health of individuals in the community.

MATERIALS
    None

VOCABULARY
    —Physician Specialists: Cardiologist, Dermatologist, Obstetrician/
Gynecologist, Opthalmologist, Orthopedist, Pediatrician, Psychiatrist,
Surgeon

PROCEDURES
    1. Lead the class in a brainstorming session for the purpose
of identifying as many health related careers as possible in both
volunteer and paid professional positions.
    2. Each student selects a health related occupation and inter-
views a person working in that capacity.
    3. Invite the students to prepare written reports that include:
        a. the specific training required for the given position
        b. the job description, including day-by-day activity
        c. the salary range
        d. what the health worker likes most and least about her
            job and
        e. evaluation of this occupation as a potential for student
            community service

Resources for Teaching Health and Nutrition Sciences

Ash, Joan, and Stevenson, Michael. <u>Health: A Multimedia Source Guide</u>.
New York: Bowker, 1976. 185 pp. $16.50. Lists and describes
700 groups and organizations that provide information on health
issues--includes a good guide to sources of free and inexpensive
health education materials.

Bershad, D., and Bernick, D. <u>From the Inside Out</u>. Boston: Learning
for Life/MSH, 1979. <u>Students Guide</u>, 220 pp., $7.00. <u>Teacher's
Guide</u>, 218 pp., $7.00. Ten posters, $6.00. 118 word cards, $5.00.
Grdes 5-8. From 141 Tremont Street, Boston, MA 02111. Whimsical
and humor story-style reader provides an innovative curriculum to
facilitate healthy attitudes and behaviors; includes activities,
student worksheets, background information and resources for a
16-week course.

Engs, Ruth C., and others. <u>Health Games Students Play</u>. Dubuque:
Kendall-Hunt, 1975. 166 pp. $5.95, paperback. Grades 6 and up.
Teacher Resource. A collection of 84 structured experiences,
simulation games and experiential exercises organized into 13
topical chapters. Topics include dental health, nutrition, aging,
mental health, consumer and community health, family life and
sexuality, drugs, environmental games. Many interesting activities
that can be adapted for younger groups.

Horkheimer, Foley, and Alley, Louis E. <u>Educators Guide to Free
Health, Physical Education and Recreation Materials</u>. 13th Edition,
1980-81. Randolph: Educators Progress Service, 1980. $16.50.
Similar in scope and flaws to Saterstrom's <u>Educators Guide to Free
Science Materials</u>.

Humboldt County Office of Education. <u>Peanut Butter and Pickles: A
Nutrition Project for Pint Size People</u>. Eureka: Humboldt County
Office of Education, 1980. 407 pp., 3-ring binder, art activities,
27 page-cooking booklet. $49.00. (Sample pages available for
$2.00.) Grades K-6. From 901 Myrtle Avenue, Eureka, CA 95501.
An attractive, comprehensive and creative curriculum which includes
worksheets, learning activities and recipes that are both nutritious
and delicious. Loaded with ideas for integrating nutrition into
other subject areas, with materials for a parents' newsletter to
accompany the program.

Jenkins, Dorothy M. Human Sexuality: Curriculum Guide for a Course in Human Sexuality. Los Angeles: Los Angeles Regional Family Planning Council, 1976. 105 pp. $3.50. Teacher Resource. From 630 South Shatto Place, Los Angeles, CA 90005. A comprehensive series of 25 lesson plans which can be taught in any order and at many levels. The guide also includes a bibliography, references, suggested visual aids and films. The appendix includes pretests, diagrams, values clarification exercises, and more.

Kellogg Company. Fitness Focus. St. Paul: Kellogg Co. Nutrition Unit, 1980. Teacher's Guide, 6 pp., with additional teaching units. $2.50. Grades 5-9. From Box 9113, St. Paul, MN 55101. Uses six interesting activities to involve students in physical fitness through exercise, rest, and good eating habits.

Marbach, Ellen S.; Plass, Martha; and O'Connell, Lily. Nutrition in a Changing World. Provo: Brigham Young University Press, 1979. Preschool edition, 208 pp., $8.95. Primary edition, 118 pp., $6.95, paperback. Grades K-3. Teaches the Basic Four Food Groups, major nutrients, and their function in the body. Emphasizes nutrition education in primary grades before food biases are set. Poems, stories, songs, and plays can accompany children's experience of food through smell, taste, and touch. Fourteen units deal interestingly with shopping, consuming, raising, selecting, preparing, and sharing food as well as dining out, holidays, food from other lands, nutrients and healthy teeth. Each unit has activity worksheets and suggested resources.

Scott, Gwendolyn D., and Carlo, Mona W. Learning-Seeing-Doing: Designing Creative Learning Experiences for Elementary Health Education. New York: Prentice-Hall, 1979. 256 pp. $16.85. Grades K-8. Teacher Resource. Includes more than 117 sample lessons, learning packets for slow, average, and honor students, and suggestions for introducing health concepts at all levels.

Scott, Gwendolyn D., and Carlo, Mona W. On Becoming a Health Educator. Dubuque: W. C. Brown, 1979. 244 pp. $6.95. A well-referenced and creative guide for facilitating health education, with many suggestions for innovative and involving methods, and suggestions on evaluating teaching and learning.

Children's Resources: Books, Games, and Pictures

Allison, Linda. <u>Blood and Guts: A Working Guide to Your Own Insides</u>.
Boston: Little, Brown, 1976. Brown Paper School Book. $5.95,
paperback. Grades 5 and up. An entertaining and fact-crammed
guidebook to the human body, in the inimitable Linda Allison style
of pen and ink drawings supported by intriguing activities and low
cost experiments.

Asimov, Isaac. <u>How Did We Find Out About Germs</u>? New York: Walker
and Co., 1974. 64 pp. $4.95. Grades 5 and up. Simply written
yet scientifically informative, it traces the history of the
major discoveries, emphasizing the methods and rationales
utilized by such scientists as Spallanzani, Pasteur and Jenner.

Bedeschi, Guilio. <u>The Science of Medicine</u>. New York: Franklin
Watts, 1975. 128 pp. $6.90. Grades 6 and up. This well
organized and interesting book conveys the complex diversity of
the field of medicine. Many colorful illustrations. Brief glossary
of medical terms, index and list of further reading.

Burns, Marilyn. <u>Good for Me! All About Food in 32 Bites</u>. Illustrated
by Sandy Clifford. Boston: Little, Brown, 1978. Brown Paper
School Series. $5.95, paperback. Grades 5 and up. Another
appealing light-hearted activity-oriented book that will have
children recording their meals, making food charts, and thinking
about nutrition in the midst of experiments.

Burns, Sheila H. <u>Allergies and You</u>. New York: Messner, 1980.
63 pp. $6.97. Grades 3 and up. An engaging book directed to
children that explains allergens and shows children how they can
become detectives to discover their own allergies. Includes clear
definitions of terms, as well as photographs, drawings, and an
index.

Cobb, Vicki. <u>More Science Experiments You Can Eat</u>. New York: Harper
& Row, 1970. 128 pp. $3.95. Grades 4 and up. Explains the
processes of ripening, drying, freezing, and canning. Experiments
with food additives and flavorings lead into the discussion of
smell and taste. It is a delightful book for the young scientist-
cook.

Daly, Kathleen N. Body Words: A Dictionary of the Human Body, How It Works, and Some of the Things that Affect Its Health. New York: Doubleday, 1980. 152 pp. $10.95. Grades 4 and up. A straightforward, well-formatted, readable, and accurate dictionary of terms relating to the human body, illustrated with line drawings.

DeCaro, Matthew V. The Gray's Anatomy Coloring Book. Philadelphia: Running Press, 1980. Unpaged. $4.95. All grades. From Running Press, 38 South 19th Street, Philadelphia, PA 19103. Contains 102 illustrations from the 1974 American edition of Gray's Anatomy, reproduced in a form suitable for coloring. Includes drawings of parts of the skeleton, internal organs, muscles, arteries, veins, and lymphatic vessels. Some of the drawings of bones outline the areas where muscles are attached. Drawings are accompanied by descriptive captions. Should aid young students to appreciate the beauty of the human body.

Doss, Helen. Your Skin Holds You In. New York: Julian Messner, 1978. 64 pp. $6.97. Grades 4-7. Describes the cell structure of human skin and its function as a temperature control system and a sense organ. Discusses how to protect and care for the skin.

Goldsmith, Ilse. Anatomy for Children. New York: Sterling, 1964. $6.95. Grades 3 and up. An easy-to-read text that provides clear explanation of every body system through easily understood comparisons to everyday machines and materials. Simple experiments demonstrate how the heart pumps, how enzymes work, etc. Other health books by Ms. Goldsmith include Why You Get Sick and How You Get Well (Sterling, 1970, $6.95) and Human Anatomy for Children (Dover, 1969, $2.00, paperback).

Grossman, Robert, developer. Circulation. New York: Teaching Concepts, 1973. Game. $14.95. Grades 4 and up. From P. O. Box 2507, New York, NY 10017. Explains the workings of the circulatory system through a journey through the blood stream. Two to four players, 20 to 40 minutes.

Kimball, Richard L. You and Me: A Book About the Human Body, Its Action, Use, Measurement and Place in This World. 2nd ed. San Leandro: Educational Science Consultants, 1973. 63 pp. $3.95. Grades 1-6. A workbook with tear-out pages, includes 41 investigations based on the human body: many measurements (some could be metric) leading to graphing. An interesting book, well-related to children whose experiences in questioning and recording data lead to a knowledge of health and anatomy.

Madison, Arnold. Smoking and You. New York: Julian Messner, 1975.
64 pp. $5.95. Grades 4-6. This book clearly explains smoking's
effect on the respiratory system and the body's organs and reviews
the history and research on smoking. Clearly written and illustrated, it can serve as a reference with a helpful glossary and
index.

Newman, Gerald, editor and compiler. Encyclopedia of Health and the
Human Body. New York: Franklin Watts, 1977. $17.00. Grades 7
and up. Teacher Reference. Useful and economical school reference
whose alphabetical entries cover anatomy, body systems, diseases,
mental and physical disorders, and genetics, as well as biographi-
cal entries for physicians, scientists and other health workers.

Nourse, Alan E. Hormones. New York: Franklin Watts, 1979. $7.00.
Grades 6 and up. Good explanations of the roles and functions of
hormones in the human body. Alan Nourse is a well-known medical
author whose books for children include Fractures, Dislocations,
and Sprains (Watts, 1978, $4.90) and Lumps, Bumps, and Rashes
(Watts, 1976, $4.90).

Paul, Aileen. The Kids' Diet Cookbook. Garden City: Doubleday,
1980. 180 pp. $7.95. Grades 5 and up. This book just might
be useful for overweight kids. It includes good information
on nutrition and chart keeping, and excellent recipes. Ms. Paul
is a specialist on children's books on gardening and cooking.

Power, L. Good as Goaled. Ann Arbor: National Health Systems,
1980. Game. $15.00. Grades 4 and up. From Box 1501, Ann
Arbor, MI 48106. A bingo-like game reflecting the Dietary Goals.
It can teach up to 40 players to learn to make good food choices.

Pringle, Laurence. Lives at Stake: The Science and Politics of
Environmental Health. New York: Macmillan, 1980. 154 pp.
$8.95. Grades 6-8. Objectively covers the roles of scientists,
government, lobbyists, industry, and the public, and how they
affect the quality of our air, water, diet, and other health-
threatening aspects of our environment. Includes a list of
relevant agencies and organizations, a glossary, and an index.

Laurence Pringle is a competent and prolific author on environ-
mental issues. Other highly recommended works include Recycling
Resources (Macmillan, 1974, $6.95), Our Hungry Earth: The World
Food Crisis (Macmillan, 1976, $6.95), Pests and People (Macmillan,
1972, $6.95), and Twist, Wiggle and Squirm: A Book About Earthworms
(Crowell, 1973, $6.89), and This Is a River (Macmillan, 1972, $5.95).

Scheibel, Barbara M. _Noise: The Unseen Enemy_. West Haven: Pendulum Press, 1972. 64 pp. $1.45, paperback. Grades 7 and up. Examines the physiology and psychology of sound, its transaction to noise, and the physiological and psychological damage.

Showers, Paul. _No Measles, No Mumps for Me_. New York: T. Y. Crowell, 1980. 34 pp. $8.95. Grades K-3. Presents the scientific concepts of immunization, bacteria and viruses for young children, with superb illustrations. A lively information book, particularly appropriate for children who are getting "shots."

Silverstein, Alvin and Virginia. _The Sugar Disease: Diabetes_. Philadelphia: Lippincott, 1980. 111 pp. $7.95. Grades 5 and up. Well-researched and well-presented discussion of a disease that is the third cause of death in America after heart disease and cancer.

Tully, Marianne and Mary Alice. _Facts About the Human Body_. New York: Franklin Watts, 1977. $7.00. First Book Series. Grades 7 and up. Uses cartoons and a question-and-answer format to tour all body systems; reproductive, skeletal, respiratory, digestive, circulatory, nervous, elimination. Answers are factual and straightforward.

Wilson, Ron. _How the Body Works_. New York: Larousse, 1979. $7.95. Grades 5 and up. Teacher Resource. Colorful, detailed drawings and diagrams illustrate various body systems and functions; good sections on reproduction and puberty.

Models, Records, Films and Filmstrips

After the Ouch. Los Angeles: Churchill Films, 1979. 16 mm. Color film. 15 minutes. $220.00; $18.00, rental; $220.00, video. Grades 6 and up. Through vignettes the film tells children how to treat such common minor injuries as nose bleeds, cuts, bruises, splinters, and burns. Advice and direction is sound, well presented and medically accurate. Clever animation, including microphotography. An excellent introduction for health and personal cleanliness.

Anamods. (Models of human organs.) Fort Atkinson: Nasco. _Heart, Brain, Kidney, Eye, Ear, Lung_. $5.00 each. All grades. From 901 Janesville Ave., Fort Atkinson, WI 53538. Three-dimensional cross-sectional, medically accurate cardboard models, easily assembled on a plastic base. Each comes with a key, instructor's guide, discussion points, and activities in functional folders.

Being Healthy Series 400, Series 500, Series 600. Chicago: Nystrom, 1978. Color filmstrip series, each with four filmstrips, four cassettes, and 16 activity sheets. $140.00/set. $395.00 for three sets. Grades 4 and up. Includes usable teacher commentary, appropriate lesson plans, high quality graphics, and a multitide of good ideas for teaching children about staying healthy.

First Aid for Young People. Santa Monica: BFA Educational Media, 1979. 16 mm. Color film. 16 minutes. $265.00; $32.00, rental. Grades 5 and up. Uses television personality Tood Turquant, mannequins, and boys and girls to demonstrate first-aid treatment for three common emergencies: stopped breathing, choking, and shock, all following the most recent American Red Cross recommendations.

How Your Body Parts Function (Parts IV & V). Jamaica: Eye Gate Media, 1977. Four color filmstrips, two cassettes each set. Part IV: Your Respiratory System, 42 frames, 7 minutes. Your Muscular and Skeletal Systems, 42 frames, 7 minutes. Your Circulatory System, 42 frames, 9 minutes. Your Reproductive System, 42 frames, 9 minutes. Part V: Your Excretory System, 40 frames, 7 minutes. Your Alimentary System, 43 frames, 8 minutes. Your Nervous System, 43 frames, 8 minutes. Your Endocrine System, 44 frames, 9 minutes. $49.80/set. Grades 3-6.

Uses first-person narrative to describe each body system and its role in the whole body, with reviews at the end of each filmstrip. Straightforward if not engrossing, with clear diagrams and health implications. Your Blood includes an excessive amount of information and vocabulary, others are well-organized and clear. Set includes a skimpy lesson plan.

Smush the Fire Out. North Hollywood: Film Communicators, 1976. One color filmstrip, one cassette. 105 frames, 11 minutes. $79.00. Grades K-3. Uses children's drawings and photographs to illustrate fire prevention and safety rules in the classroom, home, and play. Shows such things as how to telephone the fire department, how to roll to extinguish burning clothing, the importance of knowing your address and of not playing with matches. Guide includes background, objectives, and activities. This is also available as a 16 mm film.

Staying Healthy. Santa Monica: BFA Educational Media, 1978. Four
color filmstrips, with four records or four cassettes. Health
Protection, 61 frames, 13 minutes. Defenses of Our Bodies, 52
frames, 8 minutes. How Some Diseases Occur, 58 frames, 11 minutes.
Our Problems with Spreading Diseases, 60 frames, 10 minutes.
$70.00/set. Grades 4-8. Accurate and up-to-date, with emphasis
on personal responsibility (diet, exercise, etc.) and prompt
diagnosis and treatment. Includes good historic background.
Guide provides synopses, concepts, questions, and activities.

Where Our Food Comes From. New York: ACI, 1975. Four color filmstrips, four cassettes. Field Crops, 76 frames, 12 minutes.
Fruits and Vegetables, 78 frames, 12 minutes. Livestock, 76
frames, 12 minutes. Fisheries, 67 frames, 12 minutes. $65.00/
set. Grades 4-6. A good child's perspective on food production
that shows where our food comes from and why and how a concern
for ecology and the environment is essential for food production.
Logically organized with appropriate vocabulary and concepts.
Guide includes summaries, questions, and activities.

III

Physical Science Activities

Humans have been challenged to understand matter and energy throughout history. Study of the physical sciences, primarily physics and chemistry, has included examination of a range of phenomena from visible light to atomic energy. Such endeavors are the activities of scientists. But children are also interested in the forms, behavior, and laws governing matter and energy. This information makes their world understandable and less chaotic. Childrens' study of the physical environment must have the same goals as study by physical scientists. Both should be directed by the goal of explaining the physical world in ways consistent with observable and reproducible phenomena. These explanations must predict the behaviors of matter. Scientists have more sophisticated instruments and explanations, but they and children adhere to similar goals.

The scale and sophistication of study varies for scientists and students. In the activities of this book we have taken an approach of requiring the child to first describe the physical environment. He or she can thus begin with a basic understanding and vocabulary. The activities require inquiry into the basic states of matter—solid, liquid and gas. They later develop the fundamentals of measurement. Energy is an important theme at the intermediate level. The dangers of acid rain, an important social issue related to chemistry, is introduced at the middle school level.

Refer to the following planning charts for a summary of all activities at each grade level. The planning charts provide an overview that should assist in the selection and organization of activities.

PLANNING CHART FOR PHYSICAL SCIENCE ACTIVITIES: GRADES K–2

| ACTIVITY | OBJECTIVES | | | | | TEACHING METHODS | RELATED CURRICULUM |
	Conceptual Knowledge	Learning Processes	Psychomotor Skills	Attitudes and Values	Decision-making Skills		
41. Describing the Physical Environment: Solids	Non-living materials have identities based on the properties of their physical state.	Observe, compare.	Handles non-toxic substances.	Curiosity and exploration of objects in environment.	—	Hands-on activity.	—
42. Describing the Physical Environment: Liquids	Non-living materials have identities based on their properties and their physical state.	Observe, compare, classify.	Handles non-toxic substances.	Curiosity and exploration of objects in environment.	—	Hands-on activity.	—
43. Describing the Physical Environment: Gases	Non-living materials have identities based on their properties and their physical state.	Observe, compare, classify.	Handles non-toxic substances.	Curiosity and exploration of objects in the environment.	—	Demonstration and activity.	—
44. Describing the Physical Environment: Forms	Living and non-living things have identities based on their properties.	Observe, compare.	Handles non-toxic substances.	Curiosity, exploration of environment.	—	Hands-on activity.	Language Arts.
45. Describing the Physical Environment: Sizes	Living and non-living things have identities based on their properties.	Observe, compare.	Handles non-toxic substances.	Curiosity, exploration of environment.	—	Hands-on activity.	Language Arts.
46. Describing the Physical Environment: Textures	Living and non-living things have identities based on their properties.	Observe, compare.	Handles non-toxic substances.	Curiosity, exploration of environment.	—	Hands-on activity.	Language Arts.
47. Describing the Physical Environment: Locations	Living and non-living things have properties based on their identities.	Observe, compare.	Handles non-toxic substances.	Curiosity and creativity, exploration and combination of objects.	—	Hands-on activity.	Language Arts.

181

Describing the Physical Environment: Solids
Grades K-2

ACTIVITY OVERVIEW
    The adjectives right, left, heavy, light, hard, soft, wet
dry, hot and cold are defined through the interaction with solid
objects in the environment. Each comparison is made in a distinctively
dichotomous situation; the relativeness of these words is not introduced. The culminating exercise is the utilization of right and left
as directions for sorting solid objects. The concept of solid is
introduced.

SCIENCE BACKGROUND
    Matter is anything that occupies space and has weight. Rocks,
water, air, metal and wood are all examples of matter. In this
activity the words matter and material are used synonymously. Some
materials are made of only one type of matter, e.g., minerals, water
and oxygen. Other materials are made of more than one type of matter,
e.g. rocks, air, organisms. Matter (or materials) in the physical
environment can be observed in three forms or physical states--solid,
liquid and gas. Materials which are solid have a definite shape and
size. Examples of solid materials are wood, ice, and gold. A solid
can be either hard or soft.

SOCIETAL IMPLICATIONS
    Being able to differentiate between the three physical states
of matter is a prerequisite to describing the environment and learning
more about changes that have occurred in living and nonliving matter
and the environment.

MAJOR CONCEPTS
    Objects can be sorted according to property. Objects can have
two or more different properties. A solid object has a definite size
and shape.

OBJECTIVES
    At the completion of this lesson the child should be able to:
    -Describe the weight of an object as either heavy or light.
    -Describe the temperature of an object as either hot or cold.
    -Differentiate between right and left.
    -Identify an object by the quality of hardness or softness.
    -Describe the moisture content of an object as either wet or dry.

MATERIALS

-A tray for each child. For example: small cardboard trays used in meat markets or old trays from the cafeteria.

-Common objects from the room and home that are heavy and objects that are light, all objects should be solid. If possible objects that are similar in properties and material but differ in weight-- for example: steel and aluminum.

-Six pieces of cloth--three wet and three dry, cotton balls, Ice cubes wrapped in aluminum foil and pieces of warm metal wrapped in aluminum foil. Note: Be sure the object does not burn the child, magazine pictures of scenes depicting hot/cold/; wet/dry and objects that are heavy and light; small cards with the contrasting words introduced in this lesson. For example: hot and cold.

VOCABULARY

-Right, left, heavy, light, hard, soft, solid, wet, dry, hot, cold, same, different, object, material, properties

PROCEDURES

1. Prepare a tray of the following objects for each child: (If you are short of materials, have two children share a tray.) cotton, wet and dry pieces of cloth, heavy and light objects, hard and soft materials and at least one example each of hot and cold objects. These should be prepared immediately before the lesson. Add any other objects you think appropriate.

2. Distribute the trays and encourage the children to explore the materials. Their attention should be directed to the objects; beyond that they should be encouraged to examine, explore and inter- act with the objects. Exploration should continue for about 5-10 minutes; the time spent should depend on interest.

3. Bring the children together and ask about the objects on their trays. Initially, have them talk about their objects. Questions such as: What did you observe about the objects? How were the objects different? What properties were the same? can be used to start the discussion. Tell me about the objects on your tray can also be used as an opening statement.

4. It may turn out that the children discuss the properties outlined in the lesson without direction from the teacher. If they tell about one piece of cloth being wet or the other dry, ask them to explain what they mean. The same is true for hot/cold and heavy/ light. If they do not discuss some of the desired words, hold up objects that can be compared and contrasted with a focus on the desired property.

5. As a summary go over the new words and print them on the board or use small cards to show the printed word in conjunction with the child's object. This activity should clarify the words and establish the operational definitions of objects, material and solid.

6. Invent the word <u>Solid</u> for the students. Tell them that all of the objects they have explored have a definite use and shape--this is what it means when we say an object is solid.

7. It is most important that the children discuss the materials. The teacher should key on areas the children do not readily understand. Here more examples should be provided.

8. Ask: <u>How many know the directions right and left</u>? For those that do not understand either give individual help or have another child explain the directions.

9. The final activity is sorting magazine pictures depicting the various words of the lesson. The pictures should be grouped on the right or left using the new words as the criteria. <u>Go through the pictures and place all the photographs of something hot on the left and something cold on the right</u>. Use the small cards of the printed words for this activity.

10. Take a field trip around the school with the new words as the focus of the trip. Follow the field trip with their explanations of objects in their environment that are hot/cold, wet/dry, heavy/light and hard/soft.

Describing the Physical Environment: Liquids
Grades K-2

ACTIVITY OVERVIEW
The students have the opportunity to examine and explore the properties of various liquids.

SCIENCE BACKGROUND
Earth materials or matter exist in three physical states--solid, liquid and gas. Wood, water, and air are all examples of matter in the three physical states.

The size of a liquid is definite, but it does not have a definite shape. Some examples of liquids are milk, honey, gasoline and oil. A liquid will assume the shape of the container into which it is poured.

SOCIETAL IMPLICATIONS
Liquids form a substantial part of the child's world. Before children understand changes in the environment they should know the three states of matter and thus be able to define many of the changes that occur in them.

MAJOR CONCEPTS
Matter exists as a liquid. Liquids can be described by their properties. Liquids have definite size but not definite shape. When liquids are mixed some properties can change.

OBJECTIVES
At the completion of this lesson the child should be able to:
-Describe the properties of liquid.
-State the changes that occur when liquids are mixed.
-Differentiate between liquid and solid objects in the environment.

MATERIALS
-Snap cap vials for each child. If supplies are short, groups of two or three children can work with one set up.
-Water, mineral oil, alcohol, or white vinegar, liquid starch, liquid detergent, corn oil, clear plastic tray or wax paper on a plate.

VOCABULARY
-Liquid, flow, fast, slow, thick, thin, pour

PROCEDURES

1. This activity should be completed on two consecutive days.

2. Distribute vials containing the liquids to the students. Make it very clear they are <u>not</u> to remove the caps.

3. Have the students observe the liquids and discuss the properties. <u>How are they alike</u>? <u>How are they different</u>?

4. At the end of the first day have the children group the liquids any way they would like. Have them explain the property they used for the grouping.

5. On the second day distribute the plastic trays or sheets of wax paper.

6. Pass out the vials.

7. Allow the children to mix <u>a few drops</u> from the vials in their plastic trays. They should then observe the properties of the liquids.

8. In general this is exploration for the children. The teacher's role is to focus their attention on the properties, similarities, differences, and changes.

9. A group discussion should follow the two days of activities. During this time the words suggested in the vocabulary should be recorded as they are used by the children to describe the liquids. Also, record any other words used in the discussion.

10. Bring a "mystery liquid" (it can be anything, see materials list) to class. Have the students describe the properties of the liquid. Mix the mystery liquid with other liquids and have the students describe the changes.

Describing the Physical Environment: Gases
Grades K-2

ACTIVITY OVERVIEW

Part I of this laboratory is intended to be an introduction to the concept of gases. Also, the interest of the children in this activity should be utilized by having them discuss the properties of bubbles. Many property words can be utilized by the children when describing the bubbles.

In Part II, the properties of gases are developed through a series of activities. With this the children are introduced to the third physical state in which objects can exist. For our purpose, a sample of air will be considered an object. The fact that air is colorless, odorless, tasteless, and assumes the shape and volume of the container in which it is contained makes it the most abstract of the physical states that has been presented. The main purpose of this lesson is to establish the concept of air and its properties.

SCIENCE BACKGROUND

Matter has weight and takes up space. Sometimes there is only one kind of matter in a material, in which case this material is called a pure substance. Examples of a pure substance are salt, sugar and oxygen. Other materials have more than one kind of matter: air and rocks are examples of this type of material.

A gas has neither a definite shape nor a definite size. Chlorine, oxygen, and ammonia are examples of gases. If you put a gas into a container, it will spread out to fill the container, and it will take the shape of the container.

SOCIETAL IMPLICATIONS

The physical state of gas is difficult for some children to conceptualize. Unlike solids and liquids, one often cannot see, feel, taste, smell or hear a gas. Yet, they are around us all the time and essential for life. Describing gases to students is like trying to describe water to fish.

MAJOR CONCEPTS

Bubbles are made by blowing air into soapy water. Bubbles vary in size. Bubbles vary in shape. Bubbles vary in color. Matter exists as a gas. Gases have neither a definite size nor a definite shape. Gases can be described by their properties. The three physical states of matter are: solid, liquid, and gas.

OBJECTIVES

At the the completion of this lesson the child should be able to:
-Identify the properties of bubbles.
-Describe the properties of bubbles.
-Describe the properties of a gas.
-Describe the three physical states of matter.

MATERIALS

Part I
-A plastic* straw for each child
-A small container for each child's soapy liquid**
-Newspapers or appropriate covers for the children's desks.

Part II
-One balloon for each child, a pinwheel for every four children, a plastic baggie for each child, a test tube with colored water, a stopper and an air bubble for each child, a plastic syringe and piece of tubing that fits over the end of the syringe, one large beaker, a small beaker (a size that fits inside the first), a cork, and a small tray for each child

VOCABULARY

-Air, gas, blow, odorless, colorless, shape, soap, bubbles, straw, blowing, tasteless

PROCEDURES

Part I
1. Pass out containers, straws and plain water.
2. Have the children blow into plain water. "Tell me what happened."
3. Provide soapy water and allow the children to play freely and at length with the materials.
4. Focus their attention on the specific characteristics of the soap bubbles. Possible questions include: "How would you describe the bubbles?" "What shape is your bubble?" "What do you have to have to make a soap bubble?" "What happens when a soap bubble breaks?" "What did you use to make bubbles?" "How do soap bubbles move?"
5. The activities should be concluded with a discussion about the children's observations.

_____

*Plastic straws can be made into a bubble pipe by (a) cutting one end of the straw and (b) spreading the tabs.
**The soapy liquid can be made by mixing the following ingredients: 1 cup of detergent, 1 cup of glycerine, 5 cups of clean water, a pinch of sugar (to toughen the bubbles), an egg beater.

Part II

1. The first portion of this activity the children are engaged in a free investigation of materials. The materials will focus their attention on air.

2. Each child should be provided a tray with the following materials: a balloon, a plastic baggie, a stoppered test tube with an air bubble, a plastic syringe and a piece of tubing. When the children get their tray of materials encourage them to explore "experiment" with the items provided.

3. After sufficient time, collect materials and start the following discussion and demonstration.

4. Show the children the following set up:

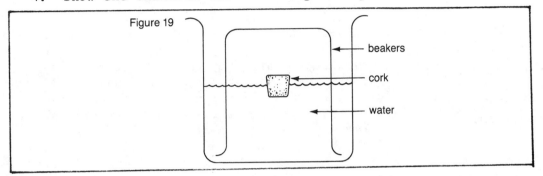

Figure 19

beakers

cork

water

As you push the inner beaker up and down have the children watch the cork. "Why does it stay where it does?" "What is in the large beaker?" "The small beaker?" At this time accept the children's responses concerning air being in the inner beaker.

5. Take a plastic baggie and make a sweeping motion with the baggie open. Close the baggie and twist the top until it is filled with air. Invent the concept of air. You may acknowledge their use of the word air or tell them air is a gas. Show them using the same materials they used during their investigation. Ask the children to describe the properties of the "stuff" in the baggie. Words such as colorless, odorless, tasteless should be "invented" for the children. Question them about the color, shape, odor and taste.

6. Have the children tell about their investigations; encourage their use of the words outlined in this activity. "Can they find other examples of air?" Encourage them to talk about their discoveries.

7. Provide each student with a picture from a magazine that shows solids, liquids and gases. Have them describe the properties of these objects in their pictures.

8. Take the students on a field trip around the school and have them describe objects that are solid, liquid and gas.

Describing the Physical Environment: Forms
Grades K-2

ACTIVITY OVERVIEW
Shapes and corresponding words are learned in this lesson. Each child has his own packet of objects used in the activities. As the child is ready the property of shape is combined with the property of color when describing his/her objects and other objects in the classroom. Charts are initially used for simple sorting tasks of one and two properties.

SCIENCE BACKGROUND
This activity continues the development of a means of describing the physical environment. A circle is a plane curve everywhere equidistant from a given fixed point, the center. A rectangle has 4 sides, 2 long and 2 short, each side having right angles. A square has right angles and 4 equal sides. A triangle is a plane figure formed by connecting 3 points not in a straight line by straight line segments; a 3-sided polygon. There are many other 2 dimensional forms that can be used to describe the environment. Likewise there are three dimensional forms such as balls, cylinder and cubes that are based on the 2 dimensional forms introduced in this lesson.

SOCIETAL IMPLICATIONS
Understanding the bases of form in nature will help students observe and communicate the complexities and subtleties of their environment. There is another important implication--aesthetics. Appreciating the beauty of nature is based on an understanding of the fundamental forms of which nature is composed.

MAJOR CONCEPTS
Objects can be described by their property of shape or form. Combining color and shape gives a better description of an object.

OBJECTIVES
At the completion of the lesson the child should be able to:
-Identify objects using the property of shape.
-Identify the following forms: irregular, circle, square, triangle and rectangle.
-Combine color words and shape words when describing objects provided in the environment.

190

MATERIALS

    -Common objects from the classroom and home and environment that have the shapes being presented.

    -A small packet of objects for each child. His or her name should appear on the packet. The actual packet could be: a manila envelope, a filing folder with sides stapled or a piece of 8½ x 11 construction paper that has been folded so two inches of paper is above the folded edge.

    The sides should be stapled. Paper art in circles, squares, triangles, rectangles and irregular shapes will be included in each packet. Each of these shapes should be provided in multiples of colors. To aid you in constructing the packet, a grid has been provided that coordinates the colors and shapes. You should make one object according to the two coordinates in the grid. At this time all objects should be about the same size; e.g., the square should be 8cm x 8cm, the rectangle 8cm x 12cm, the circle should have a diameter of 8cm, the triangle should be cut from a shape 8cm x 8cm. The irregular shape should have the same general dimensions of eight centimeters by eight centimeters. For the first portion of this activity you will only need the first three colors plus black and white for each shape. Later the other colors will be added.

Figure 20	Circle	Square	Triangle	Rectangle	Irregular
Red	X				
Yellow					
Blue					
Green					
Orange					
Purple					
White					
Black					

    As you complete the object for each child's packet mark out the area in the grid with an X. The X in the first square (see example) indicates all the red circles have been constructed for the class. When these have been prepared place them in the child's packet.

    Large (about 18cm x 21cm) examples of the shapes being presented i.e., irregular, rectangles, circle, square, triangle, should also be completed.

    -Large construction paper (18 x 24) about 4-5 sheets for each child. These will be used for sorting the shapes. There should be some (the number depends on the number of children requiring this

Figure 21

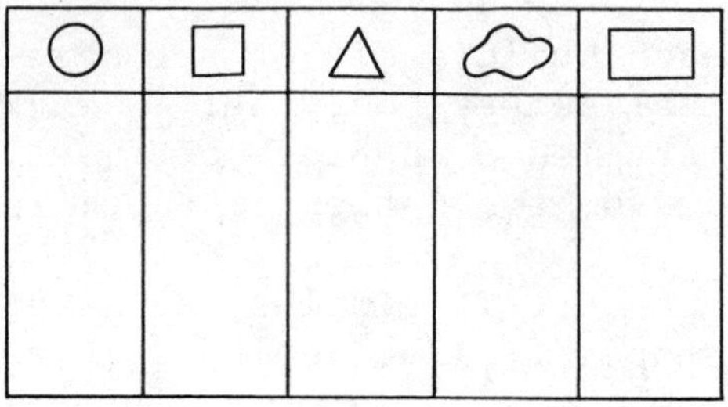

○	□	△	☁	▭

Figure 22

circle	square	triangle

Figure 23

	triangle	square
red		
yellow		
blue		
green		

level of instruction) with the iconic symbol; others with the word symbol (see Figure 22) in varying numbers of shapes. Still others should be completed in a two dimensional matrix using shapes and colors (see Figure 23).

The teacher should note that all combinations are not given; there are several hundred different combinations for the charts suggested above. You are not expected to have all combinations; but, it is certainly to your advantage to have many different sheets available at the various levels outlined.

-Index cards with the printed color words from earlier lessons and the shape words from this activity.

VOCABULARY
    -Circle, square, triangle, irregular, rectangle

PROCEDURES
    1. Bring a multiple of objects that are examples of the shapes to be learned. Many of the shapes should be common objects from the classroom and home. There are numerous objects that are examples of the shapes: windows, paper, door knobs, globes, etc.

    2. Using simple pantomime show the children examples of circles and gesture, "What is this?" After several examples show them a circle you have constructed.

    Show them the word CIRCLE on an index card. Say the word and have them repeat the word. Immediately see how many circular objects can be found in the room; use the initial objects presented. Have the children use the words in sentences when describing objects in the classroom.

    3. Repeat the procedures outlined in part 2 for squares, triangles, rectangles and irregular shapes. Vary the pace according to the needs of the children.

4. Place "I KNOW MY FORM WORDS" on the blackboard. Present the class with a shape, either one you have constructed or one from the classroom and have them tell you the shape. As the children respond record the new shape word on the board or chart. If the children know the words already, simply record the words and continue to the next activity.

5. Pass out the packets containing the colored shapes. Allow the children to look through the materials.

6. Start this activity by saying, "You know your colors; hold up a red object, a yellow object, a blue object." Help the children that seem confused.

7. "You also know your shapes; hold up a square, circle, etc. until the children have identified the objects by color and shape.

8. Use the large charts outlined in the materials section. Have the children sort the objects in their packets into appropriate piles. Start with the simple charts; as the children progress, increase the number of objects they are sorting and the properties between which they must discriminate.

Note: There must be decisions made by the teacher relative to the level, number and complexity of the sorting activity. Decisions should be based on the needs and understanding of individual students. The charts for sorting will be used extensively later. This lesson introduces the children to the charts. Their main use will be after the color, size and shape words have been introduced.

Describing the Physical Environment: Sizes
Grades K-2

ACTIVITY OVERVIEW

Big, little, large and small are operationally defined by the children. Sorting and classifying materials using one, two and three properties provides summary and reinforcement for the words and concepts of the first three lessons.

SCIENCE BACKGROUND

Big, little, large and small are concepts which are relative. Very few students will have any difficulty distinguishing between a large and a small piece of paper, or describing a rock as big or little. It is important to extend students' perceptions of size by introducing gradations, e.g., large, larger, largest.

By defining large and small amounts of time, big and little distances, perceptions of time/space can be included. Examples: it takes a larger amount of time to eat lunch and a smaller amount of time to eat a peanut; it is a big distance from school to the moon, a small distance from school to home.

SOCIETAL IMPLICATIONS

Developing a sense of perspective of objects, organisms and events in time and space is essential when describing the physical environment. The immediate environment is filled with changes--how long are they in the scale of geological time and how large are they in the scale of stellar space? Events that happen now may seem important, what impact will be recorded 50 years from now? Understanding the answers to questions such as these starts with a conceptualization of large and small, big and little and the relativeness of these terms.

MAJOR CONCEPTS

The size of an object is a property of that object. Describing an object or organism by a multiple of properties provides a better, more accurate description.

OBJECTIVES

At completion of the lesson the child should be able to:
-Name a size, form or color property of an object given him/her.
-Operationally use the word property when describing an object.
-Identify objects according to their size, i.e. large or small, big or little.

MATERIALS
    -Two pencils that are identical except for size,
    -Two pieces of paper that are identical except for size.
    -Objects and organisms in the classroom, objects and organisms
outdoors.
    -The sorting charts described and introduced in earlier activities.
As time progresses you should make more charts and increase the complexity of the charts.
    The children's packets should include other colors and shapes.
Also, for each of the boxes on the chart smaller objects should be
made. The initial sizes were: square 8cm x 8cm, the rectangle
8cm x 8cm etc. The smaller sizes needed for the new set to be included
are: square 4cm x 4cm, rectangle 4cm x 8cm. The circle diameter is
1½cm; the triangle should be cut from a 4cm x 4cm square. Again, the
irregular shape should have the same general dimensions as those
described above, about 8cm x 8cm. Use the grid provided in activity
2 as a guide.

VOCABULARY
    -Large, small, big, little, property

PROCEDURES
    1. Show the children two pieces of paper and ask them to describe
the objects. How are these objects the same? How are these objects
different?
    2. Repeat the procedures outlined in 1 using the pencils and
styrofoam spheres.
    3. As the children use the words big and large; small and
little, to describe the differences add these words to their list
under the title--I KNOW FOUR SIZE WORDS.
    4. As an immediate follow-up activity, you identify an object in
the room and ask the children to identify something smaller and something larger. For example: "Here is an eraser; name something bigger
(Chair, desk, book, etc.). Name something smaller (chalk, pencil,
paper clip).
    5. Take the children out of the classroom on a short excursion.
The objective of the excursion is to collect three objects of different
size. You need only spend a short time outside. Be sure the children
collect small objects. Have them place the objects in the plastic
bags. Return to the classroom.
    6. Have the children identify what they collected and discuss
the properties of their objects. Questions you can ask include:
Which object is largest? Smallest? Can you tell me other properties?
Color? Form? Tell about objects that are solid, liquid or gas. Let
the children do the talking. Your direction should have them focus
on the size, shape and color of the objects collected.

7. At this point the charts can be used very effectively on an individual basis. Review the use of the charts with the children. That is, they are to take the objects from their packet and place the object in the column corresponding to the property requested. To start, distribute a large sheet similar to the one below to each child:

CIRCLE	SQUARE	TRIANGLE

The order, number and type of property (circle, square, triangle, in the example given) should be varied. Children having difficulty should be given easier problems; children who learn property words quickly should be given more complex problems. Have the children sort the objects from their packet into appropriate sections on the chart. If they complete this, switch charts with another child that has finished or provide the child with a new chart. At this time it would be best to sort by one property only; the next lesson has them combine properties.

Note: There may be some difficulty in describing properties from objects collected outdoors. The difficulty often arises because distinctions are not as discrete or dichotomous as those provided in the activity. Let the <u>children</u> resolve the problem.

If some children are ready, then you may have them progress to other lessons individually. Read the lesson first then you can explain it and have them proceed.

This lesson might be split over a couple of days...the introduction and identification one day and the outdoor excursion and discussion the second day.

Describing the Physical Environment: Textures
Grades K-2

ACTIVITY OVERVIEW
The adjectives rough and smooth are introduced and operationally defined. The first activities are clearly distinguished--rough from smooth. As the lesson progresses the relativeness of these properties should become apparent to the child and other texture words can be introduced.

SCIENCE BACKGROUND
The composition or structure of a substance gives it texture. The texture of materials such as minerals is a property that often provides a key to the materials identity.

SOCIETAL IMPLICATIONS
Being able to describe the texture of a material often gives a clue to its composition and structure. This, in turn, gives a clue to any changes that have occurred to the material.

MAJOR CONCEPTS
Texture is a property that can be used to describe objects. Texture is a relative property.

OBJECTIVES
At the completion of this lesson the child should be able to:
-Use the words smooth or rough when describing the texture of an object in his/her environment.
-Change his/her description of texture when a new object is introduced that is greater or less than a texture already described.

MATERIALS
-Squares of fine grained sand paper and regular white paper. The dimensions of the squares should be about 5cm x 5cm. One set for each child.
-Five centimeter by five centimeter squares of coarse grained sand paper. The grain should be much more coarse than that used in the first comparison. One square per child.
-Small squares of sponge, corrugated cardboard, cloth (linen, burlap, corduroy) and other objects in the classroom or school that can be used to demonstrate the texture of an object.
-A golf ball and a ping pong ball, or any two objects that have the same general properties of color, form and size but differ in their textures, i.e. one object is very definitely smooth while the second is rough.
-Other common materials in the classroom and outdoors.

VOCABULARY
    -Rough, coarse, smooth, fine

PROCEDURES
    1. Hold up the two objects (golf ball and ping pong ball) and ask the children to describe the properties they observe. How are these objects alike? How are these objects different?
    2. Accept the responses of the children; they often use words such as bumpy or even to describe the objects.
    3. Using the words the children have used, either the desired words i.e. rough and smooth or words such as bumpy, introduce or reinforce the use of rough and smooth. Briefly explain that the texture of an object is described as rough or smooth.
    4. Distribute the first two pieces of paper, one sand paper, the second regular paper. Walk around to the children and have them describe the properties of the objects. The objects will most likely differ in texture and color and be similar in size and shape. Some children may use only visual clues to discriminate texture. Have them also use a tactile approach for the identification of textures.
    5. When the children understand and can use rough and smooth, add these words to their word chart.
    6. Introduce the coarse sand paper and have them describe the texture of the three objects.
    7. Remove the paper and ask the child which piece of sand paper is rough and which is smooth. If the child insists both are rough, have him describe how they differ in roughness. They are both rough; one is rougher.
    8. At this time you could:
        a. Distribute other common objects.
        b. Go on a texture hunt indoors.
        c. Go on a texture hunt outdoors.
    Note: The basic format of this lesson can be used to introduce the words: dull/shiny and heavy/light. The materials will differ; the procedures will remain approximately the same. If you introduce these words, be sure the first examples are distinctly different for the property being described. Later the relativeness of the property can be introduced.

Describing the Physical Environment: Locations
Grades K-2

ACTIVITY OVERVIEW
This lesson is specifically designed to introduce and operationally define prepositions. Since there are a large number of new words for the children, it would probably be best to extend the lesson over several days.

SCIENCE BACKGROUND
Objects and organisms exist in time and space--they have locations. Likewise events, changes in objects and organisms occur in time and space and thus can be described, at least in part, through a set of coordinates. Much work of scientists deals with the location-- accurately describing a place.

SOCIETAL IMPLICATIONS
Developing a sense of location in time and space is crucial to the accurate description of objects, organisms, and events in the student's environment.

MAJOR CONCEPTS
Objects can be described or located in space and time relative to other objects.

OBJECTIVES
At the completion of the lesson the child should be able to:
-Use prepositions to describe an object's or organism's location relative to other objects.
-Locate an object when given a description of the object's location.

MATERIALS
-At least one large cardboard box. Washing machine and refrigerator size are suggested.
-Small boxes, either provided or constructed. The size should be about 12 cm x 12 cm. These are to be used while sitting at desks and should not be so large they distract from the activity.
-A small figure or animal. These can be provided or cut out of paper.
-Provide a funny name for the figure: ALEX SNORGOLE, BENNY BEATLE, FELIX FLUGEDRUF, FRED FLAPNURD, RALPH RABBIT OR MELVIN NESFLUBER.

VOCABULARY
     -After, around, before, behind, beside, by, from, in, in front
of, into, near, on, off, out of, over, through, to under, upon

PROCEDURES

PART I

1. Place the large box in the room and have the children gather
around you and the box. If you are able to obtain several boxes, they
should be used in a similar manner.
2. Be sure the box is open at both ends.
3. Start the activities by having one child follow your commands,
then the next and so on through the class. Each command will include
a preposition or prepositional phrase. The other children should
observe and see if they can follow the directions.
4. The students should complete the following in order.
1st student - Go in the box and come out of the box.
2nd student - Place a paper on the box and take it off the box.
3rd student - Place a paper under the box.
4th student - Go to the box.
5th student - Go around the box.
6th student - Go in front of the box.
7th student - Go behind the box.
8th student - Go by the box.
9th student - Go near the box.
10th student - Throw the paper over the box.
11th student - Go beside the box and come back from the box.
12th student - Go into the box and crawl through the box.

     The activity should be repeated with the children experiencing
different aspects of the problem. For example, if in the first
exercise the individual went to the box; this time he might go near
the box. Introduce the terms before and after.
5. After this has been completed twice or perhaps three times,
depending on the children's understanding, introduce the written
preposition indicating where the child should go; for example, a
large card saying GO _____ THE BOX could be used. Small cards can
be substituted for the prepositions. Say the commands for them
initially; then place the preposition in the blank and see if the
children understand. If they do not understand, help them complete the
activity.
6. When you feel they have been operationally introduced to the
prepositions through their physical activity, the second part of the
lesson can be completed. If time permits, it would be good to introduce the second activity on the same day the large boxes are used.

7. Distribute the small boxes and figures to each child. This activity will have them complete various manipulations of the figures in coordination with the small box.

8. When all the students are ready, have them follow your directions. Start with verbal directions and gradually move toward giving directions with the cards used in the activity prior to this one.

9. Have the children complete the following activities individually at first and then in combinations. Use Fred Flapnurd for the name.
   a. Place Fred <u>in</u> the box; take him <u>out</u> of the box.
   b. Place Fred <u>on</u> the box; take him <u>off</u> the box.
   c. Place Fred <u>under</u> the box.
   d. Move Fred <u>to</u> the box.
   e. Place Fred <u>beside</u> the box.
   f. Place Fred <u>in front of</u> the box; move him <u>behind</u> the box.
   g. Place Fred <u>beside</u> the box; move him <u>over</u> the box.
   h. Place Fred <u>upon</u> the box.
   i. Place Fred <u>on</u> the box; have him go <u>under</u> and then <u>through</u> the box.

10. Depending on the children this activity can be continued using the prepositions individually or in a series of requests. As you observe the children you should note their understanding of the words. Within this lesson there is opportunity for diversity of student response. As the students progress, make a conscious effort to shift from group questions to individual questions based on the level and understanding of the student.

11. Play the game "Where is Fred Flapnurd," where you hide Fred around the classroom and the students must use questions about objects, properties, locations, etc. to determine where Fred is. Expand the game to include the school and community once the children grasp the basic ideas. A good extension of this activity is the student's identification of prepositions in a story you are reading.

PLANNING CHART FOR PHYSICAL SCIENCE ACTIVITIES: GRADES 3–5

ACTIVITY	OBJECTIVES					TEACHING METHODS	RELATED CURRICULUM
	Conceptual Knowledge	Learning Processes	Psychomotor Skills	Attitudes and Values	Decision-making Skills		
48. Measuring Objects	Things (living and non-living matter) have identities based on the way they are put together (structurally organized).	Observe, compare, measure.	Learners use and care for simple tools and equipment that require no adjustments: ruler, hammer, container, brush, etc.	Learners actively explore environment and ask questions.	Teacher and learners discuss immediate consequences of various alternatives.	Hands-on activity.	Mathematics.
49. Measuring Area	Things (living and non-living matter) have identities based on the way they are put together (structurally organized).	Observe, compare, measure.	Learners use and care for simple tools and equipment that require no adjustments: ruler, hammer, container, brush, etc.	Learners actively explore environment and ask questions.	Learners participate in identifying alternatives.	Hands-on activity.	Mathematics.
50. Interaction and Change	All groups change because members of the group interact with each other, with other groups or with the environment (living and non-living matter).	Infer.	Learners construct simple projects and models without guidance. Construct materials in experiment, construct shelter from raw material, etc.	Learners attempt to compare alternating points of view with evidence.	With help, learners rank alternatives and select one, accepting consequences.	Demonstration and hands-on activity.	Mathematics, Reading.
51. Observing Patterns: Graphing and Predicting	Groups can change and still conserve their identities. There are limits to the capacity of groups to change and still conserve their identities. When groups are changed beyond their limits, matter and energy are conserved but groups lose their identities.	Construct and interpret graphs.	Learners construct simple projects and models without guidance. Construct materials in experiment, construct shelter from raw material, etc.	Learners combine objects and materials in new ways.	Learners gather some information needed, and become aware of difference between facts and attitudes or values.	Hands-on activity.	Reading, Social Studies, Mathematics.
52. Energy Systems	Energy is the ability of matter to change into other matter.	Observe, gather, organize information.	Manipulate simple materials for observations.	Learners combine objects in new and unique ways.	Learners describe alternatives that influence self and others.	Exploration, discovery.	Social Science, Geography.
53. Sources of Energy	Energy is essential for earth processes.	Gather and organize information.	—	Learners assume responsibility for use of energy resources.	Learners gather information needed for decision.	Projects, questioning game.	Reading, Social Science.

203

Measuring Objects
Grades 3-5

ACTIVITY OVERVIEW

Measurement is a basic skill in precise descriptions of the environment. In these activities, two skills are involved--using a standard unit of measurement and comparison in measuring along a straight edge.

SCIENCE BACKGROUND

One of the identities every object has is its measurement--or description of its size when compared with other objects. The main task here is to help students acquire skill in comparing the length of objects using a standard language or measuring unit. This task involves the psychomotor skill of using a ruler--and measuring with reasonable accuracy along a straight edge.

By matching and comparing, thinking about his results, and generalizing from any experiences, a young child gradually comes to accept the idea that number, length and quantity stay the same even when the appearance of objects changes. He finally realizes that ten dominoes are ten no matter how he places them, and that a piece of string stays the same length whether he arranges it in a circle or in a straight line. He knows for sure that one cup of water remains one cup, regardless of the shape of its container. As he arranges and rearranges his dominoes and pours liquids from one container to another in different situations, he develops his ability to pay attention to several kinds of measurement at once--height and width, number and spatial arrangement.

The same experiences which enable a child to accept the fact that quantity is constant are necessary for understanding the "how" and "why" of measuring. He begins by expressing the size of another, goes on to establish standard units of his own, and gradually learns to handle conventional measuring tools with understanding. Conventional measuring devices lose much of their mystery if a child uses them alongside other tools of his own invention. Lacking this sequence of experiences, children frequently assume that conventional units of measurement are somehow essential to measurement. For some children, it seems as if length exists only when they have inches with which to measure it or that an object too large for the available scales will weigh "nothing."

SOCIETAL IMPLICATIONS

People measure to obtain information for some purpose or to satisfy curiosity, and it sometimes is necessary to measure environmental changes. Measuring in the classroom will be most effective

and interesting if it grows out of situations in which children are
actively involved. Sewing, cooking, carpentry, and caring for animals
are examples of activities that capture children's interest and provide
opportunities for measuring. Take the time to encourage natural
exploration and subsequently measurement of objects, organisms, and
events in the environment. Developing the skill is essential to
understanding the process, scale, and consequences of environmental
change.

MAJOR CONCEPT

If A is the same as B, and B is the same as C, then A must be
the same as C.

OBJECTIVES

By the end of these activities the child should be able to:

-Demonstrate how many times a measuring stick can be laid end-
to-end along a given length that is to be measured.

-Name the results of measurements in while metric units or as
between two whole number units.

MATERIALS

-Boxes, unmarked sticks, metric rulers, tooth picks

VOCABULARY

-Decimeter, centimeter, measure, ruler

PROCEDURES

1. Put a large cardboard box on one side of the room and a table
on the other. The box should be nearly (but not exactly) the same
height as the table. Ask, "Would it be possible to slide the box
under the table?" "Which do you think is taller--the table or the
box?" "Use the sticks to find the height of the box. How many sticks
high is the box?" "Use the same sticks to find how tall the table
is. How many sticks tall is the table?"

Now compare the heights of the box and the table in terms of how
many sticks high they are. Which one is the higher object? Slide
the box over to the table. Compare the heights again. Do you agree
with your measurement?

To avoid a mass movement of the students toward the box or table,
have the students get into groups and send a representative of the
group to do the measuring. Or, if you prefer, organize "shifts" so
that all students participate in the measuring.

A disagreement between measurements may be due to laying the
sticks in a crooked or diagonal line. If so, help the student
recognize the need to lay the sticks end-to-end.

Figure 25   TASK SHEET #1

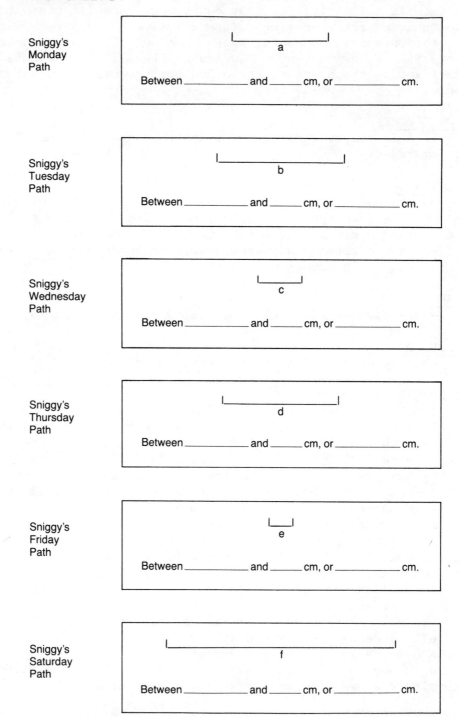

Sniggy's
Monday
Path

a

Between _____ and _____ cm, or _____ cm.

Sniggy's
Tuesday
Path

b

Between _____ and _____ cm, or _____ cm.

Sniggy's
Wednesday
Path

c

Between _____ and _____ cm, or _____ cm.

Sniggy's
Thursday
Path

d

Between _____ and _____ cm, or _____ cm.

Sniggy's
Friday
Path

e

Between _____ and _____ cm, or _____ cm.

Sniggy's
Saturday
Path

f

Between _____ and _____ cm, or _____ cm.

Figure 26   TASK SHEET #2

	A. Between ____ and ____ cm.	B. Exactly ____ cm
1. 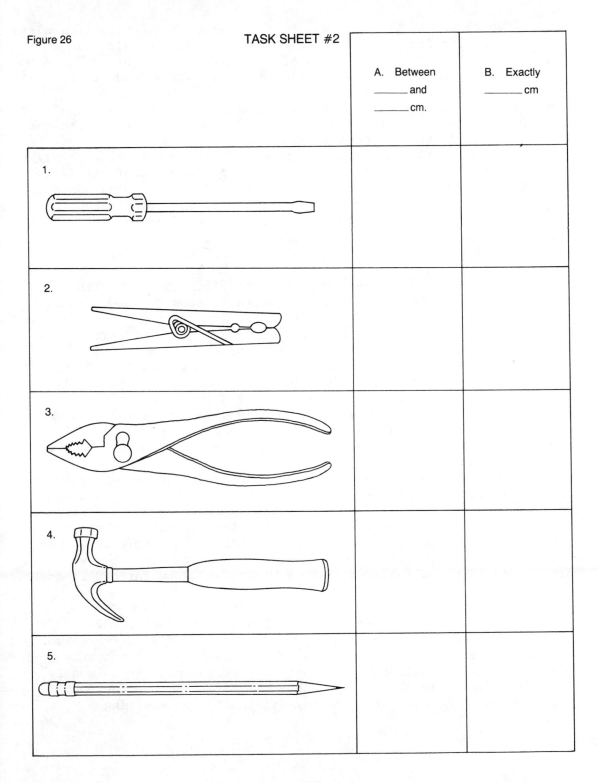		
2.		
3.		
4.		
5.		

2. "Which way is the best way to measure height--laying the rulers in a vertical straight line, end-to-end, or laying the rulers in a crooked line with some or all ends of the rulers overlapping?"

"Why do you think so?" A key idea here is that we need to be accurate in our measuring if it will be helpful to someone else. When you have disagreements, have the students show you how they found their answer. As you watch their procedure, you will likely find the reason for the different measurements of the same thing.

3. Ask the students to measure the same box, or this time it might be fun to have them measure their desk top and drawings of the feet using only one ruler. (Demonstrate this method for those who do not discover how to do this themselves. First mark one ruler's length vertically with a pencil on the box. Slide the end of the ruler to this mark. Mark another ruler's length. Continue sliding the ruler in a vertical straight line until the height of the box has been covered.) "How many ruler lengths high is the box?"

Have them continue to measure the width of the doorway with erasers and to use one of the square blocks to measure the width of their paper.

Then for a fun challenge have them draw a picture of three objects they used to measure their desk top.

All answers should be to the nearest unit length such as 2 stick lengths, 5 eraser lengths, 7 block lengths. When they have completed their measuring, it might be useful to have a large bulletin board to post their results on so that one student's data can be compared with others. In the discussion, have them tell you what might be some reasons for different answers to the measurement of the same object.

4. On a Task Sheet (see figure 25) are some lines which show how far a snail named Sniggy went each day. Use your centimeter ruler to measure his paths. Write each measurement two ways--(1) as between two whole number centimeter lengths (such as "between 2 and 3 centimeters"), and (2) as the centimeter-length to which it is closest.

When they are ready to show their results, have them tell you on which day Sniggy went the farthest, least distance, etc. How much further did he go on Thursday than on Wednesday? How far did he go on Sunday?

5. On a Task Sheet (see figure 26) use a centimeter ruler to measure the length of each item. If the measurement is between two whole centimeter units, put the results in column A. If the measurement is an exact centimeter unit, put your measurement in column B.

Posting their results on a class chart will help you and them to see who are the ones still having difficulty in measuring.

Measuring Area
Grades 3-5

ACTIVITY OVERVIEW

The concept in this activity is the identity of things based on comparisons of their areas. The learning moves from initial comparisons--"which is biggest"--to ordering based on units--"how much bigger." The new skill involved here is the use of a grid as a vehicle for "standard" comparison.

SCIENCE BACKGROUND

As a skill in describing the environment, measurement is a challenge for many young students. The measurement of an area is similar to linear description. It begins with simple comparison, is extended with comparison with arbitrary units, and culminates with comparisons of standard units. The use of footprints or body shadows enables students to quickly acquire these new skills.

You may recall that in linear measurement you first compare length of objects, order them from longest to shortest, compare them with each other and finally with a standard unit. In this initial experience, much of the sequence will be repeated--comparing footprints, ordering them from largest to smallest, and then comparing them with squares on a grid. It is probably best not to introduce square centimeters as a standard unit at this time--the psychomotor development and counting capability of your students suggests keeping the squares in the grid larger and thus the total number within comprehension.

However, describing area in terms of square units is a meaningful foundation for thinking of the area of a surface as two dimensional which can be measured and described.

SOCIETAL IMPLICATIONS

This science topic relates to the student's social development by providing him or her with a new vehicle for curiosity. Being able to think about differences in area as a vehicle of describing the physical environment enables the student to be more precise in determining changes. Also, an important emphasis in decision making here is the student participating in the identification of alternatives in how to adequately describe area--count all squares, only those that are mostly full, etc.

MAJOR CONCEPT

Comparisons of area are as simple and useful as our linear comparisons.

OBJECTIVES

By the end of these activities the student should be able to:
—Order objects based on visual perception of their area.
—Order objects based on comparison with other units of area.
—Identify or name comparisons in area for a set of objects.

MATERIALS

—Butcher or chart paper, pictures of animals and their foot prints, 1cm square grid for overhead projector

VOCABULARY

—Area

PROCEDURES

1. <u>Footprints Tell</u> — Begin this experience by asking the students who they think has the largest footprint in the room (you may need to have them tell you what a footprint is first). Then, have each pair of students trace the <u>left</u> print of their partner. These they can cut out and be sure to name whose print it is.

Now in groups of 4, have them arrange the prints from largest to smallest.

Post the largest of each group on the board and have the class rearrange them until they agree who has the largest.

Now have the students order the pictures of the footprints from largest to smallest. Then you will want them to show you how they decided and check their answer. (See figure 27 for sample footprints).

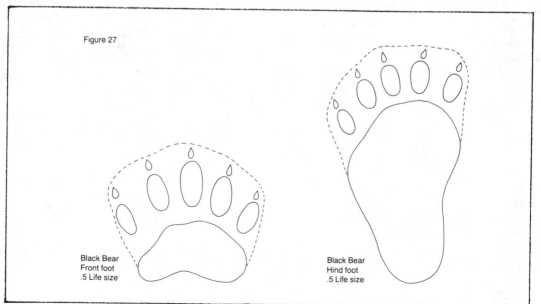

Figure 27

Black Bear
Front foot
.5 Life size

Black Bear
Hind foot
.5 Life size

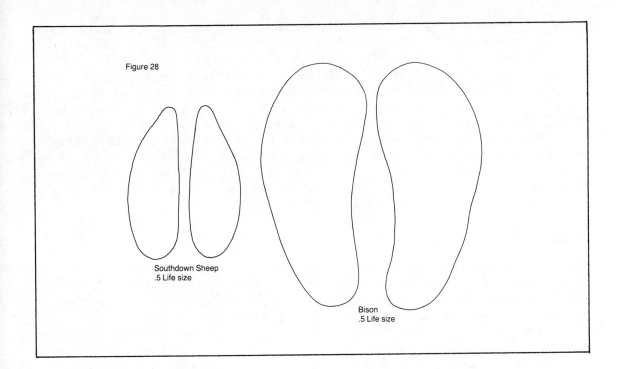

Figure 28

Southdown Sheep
.5 Life size

Bison
.5 Life size

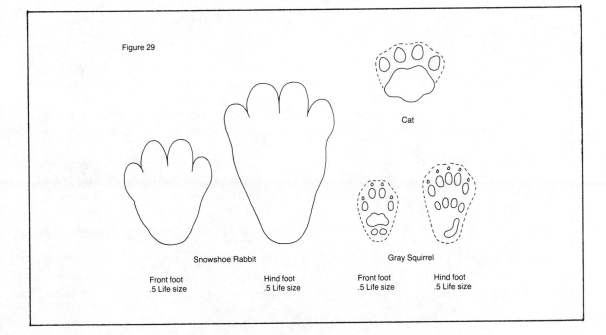

Figure 29

Cat

Snowshoe Rabbit

Gray Squirrel

Front foot
.5 Life size

Hind foot
.5 Life size

Front foot
.5 Life size

Hind foot
.5 Life size

When completed, find out what your students think they now know about what footprints tell.

2. **Who's the Biggest?** - For many of your students, bigger means length. In this activity, as with footprints, the decision about "bigger" depends on both length and width as seen when one has something "left over" when you put one object on top of another.

One way is to have the students make an estimate of the order of their area--starting back to back and comparing both height and width. Using name cards, arrange the list of children in your class from largest to smallest based on their visual estimates. Note: you likely will have many ties, e.g.:

Bill   Jane   Lilla   Tim
        George
        Joan

Now in teams of two, have one student lie down on the newsprint or paper. The partner should carefully draw the child's shadow. You might do a demonstration of this by having your children tell you how to get a piece of paper to look like Doug's shadow. These "shadows" can be decorated as you all wish. Now have your students arrange a display of the shadows of your class down the hall wall outside your room. Arrange the shadows from largest to smallest, area or space.

3. **Squares on Top** - You may want to do this as a group activity with an overhead projector. Using the largest to smallest animal footprints, have your students count (using a grid) how many squares it takes to cover the footprint. Note: both you and your students will have to decide how to count the squares that are not completely filled.

-You may wish to count only all the squares that are full.
-You may want to count all full or more than half full squares.
-You may want to count all squares that have any part of the print.

Which you do is not important, but that you agree on a way and follow it **is** **important**.

Have your students continue to count the squares for each footprint and mark their results on them. Based on their new measurement way, is there a need to change any of the order from largest to smallest?

4. **How Many?** - This is a delightful way to share your room with small groups of students in a new way.

Show them a pile of counting blocks and a box lid. Ask them to estimate how many blocks would fit in the lid (one layer only please!). Then have them try it to see.

Now look around the room and puzzle on these questions:

-How many windows could be put on the walls of the room?

-How many doors would fit on the ceiling?

-How many of our rooms would fit on the playground or in the cafeteria?

Both you and they can think of many more "How Many Fit" questions for the game.

Interaction and Change
Grades 3-5

ACTIVITY OVERVIEW

In the activities, students will use pendulums, tug-of-war, magnets and dropping balls to search for some of nature's patterns.

SCIENCE BACKGROUND

The pattern or "rule" that your students will be generating will be the simple statement of how things interact or change in a regular way. Since events we see are not caused by "magic" or accident we believe they have an explainable cause--and at this level your students are beginning their search. In this search their success is found in the way in which they can "make" it happen over and over again. The key learning process is that of inferring. The "rule" students generate is their inference as to why it happens. If the rule is intended to express a conclusion about the cause--and thus the word "because" can be used--your students have an excellent example of an inference, e.g., The pendulum swings because... On the other hand, the rule may be more of a future statement--a prediction, e.g., It will swing if you.... In either case students have gone beyond observation of the objects in events and their interaction--they are making initial interpretations. For elementary students, these interpretations should be based on first-hand experience. In later years they will have the cognitive development to enable them to deal with verbal descriptions of events. At this stage in their development, first-hand experiences are essential.

SOCIETAL IMPLICATIONS

In keeping with students psychomotor skill development, this activity permits them to construct some simple science projects, especially with the pendulum and magnet. In the more "openess" of the activities--and the opportunity to construct their own rules--you are also fostering the development of objectivity in your students. Their role is not of accepting conclusions but rather of testing or searching for evidence to support other's "rules". Their decision making development is thus serving in their awareness that a "rule" may not fit all the facts--and that one consequence of this is that they may need to change the rule. On the other hand, more than one rule may indeed fit the same facts.

MAJOR CONCEPT

Events occur in predictable patterns.

By the end of these activities, the student should be able to:
  -Construct a prediction about an event based on previous observations of that event.

MATERIALS
  -Places for swinging pendulums, string, tape, scissors, modeling clay, bunch of keys, washers.
  -Spring scales--50 pound ones work well.
  -Box of magnets and bars that are not magnets, glass plate, iron filings and string.
  -Collection of balls and scrap paper. (A balance will be useful for those who wish to measure the stuff in the balls more exactly.)

VOCABULARY
  -Prediction, interaction, change

PROCEDURES
  1. Swinging Together (See Task Card 1)
  Making a setting for students to have freedom to experiment with pendulums is essential. Out of the "play" activity they will generate rules or predictions. A simple pendulum frame will help:

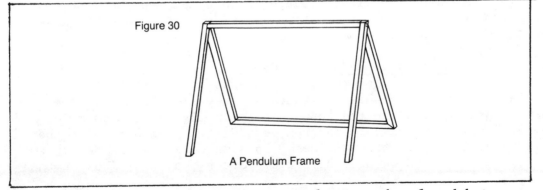

Figure 30

A Pendulum Frame

or a simple piece of 2x4 about a meter long can be placed between 2 desks and books help hold it in place; or you can use tongue depressors that you use a razor to split one end and slide the string in the split (see below).

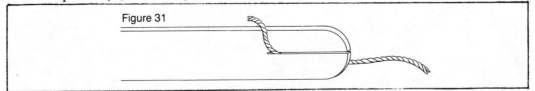

Figure 31

These depressors can be taped to the top of a desk or table.

After your students have completed Task Card #1, (see figure for sample) schedule a discussion.

In this discussion time with the students, be sure that their rules are stated so others can follow them. In fact, it might be a great idea to have them write their rules on colored construction paper. These could be posted and others could try to see if the "rule" works. If it does, they could sign their initials; if not, they could write a new one that will work.

2. <u>Move It</u>! (See Task Card 2)

In these activities, using Task Card 2 your students will have fun working together on a task that requires them to cooperate. It will work best if they work in teams of three--two to tug and one to read the scales.

When they have completed Task Card #2 and have their "rules" written, have them share their rules and maybe test some of them in your discussion group.

3. <u>Magnet Fun</u> (See Task Card 3)

You may need to help your students with the second part of this activity. Try several magnets. You will find it helpful to pour the filings off the glass plate onto a sheet of paper and then pour back into container from the paper.

In the discussion after children have completed the Task Card, attend to their rules. What was their evidence they used to make these predictions?

4. <u>Dropping Paper Wads</u> (Task Card 4)

It may be a surprise for your students to find out that objects all fall at very much the same rate, if they are about the same shape. As they fill in the results of dropping various pairs of objects, you may need to help them decide if it was almost at the <u>same</u> time or very different times. In some cases, it is better to listen to the sound when it hits the floor rather than look at the objects.

In the discussion, you should take the opportunity to have other students try out the prediction ("rule") to see how well it works.

TASK CARD #1

Swinging Together

Materials you will need: string, a bunch of keys, scissors, and modeling clay and washers.

Your teacher will show you where you can swing the pendulums.

First: Make two pendulums with washers.

Can you get them to swing together? Draw a picture or tell how you did it.

Second: What can you do to change the way the pendulum swings?

Try it and then write down your rules for changing pendulums.

Third: Find two ways to make the pendulum swing faster. Tell about them here by writing down your two rules.

Fourth: Make a pendulum with the keys, the scissors and the clay. Try your predictions to see if your new pendulum will follow your rules.

TASK CARD #2

Move It!

Materials you will need: scales.

First: If you and a friend pull the same on each other, which one of you slides first?

Can you change things, so that you can make each other slide first?

Write your "First Slide Rule" here.

Second: Have a tug-of-war with a partner, but use the scales. Each of you hold the scales.

Before you pull, what do the scales read? _____

If your friend stands still and you pull, what do you read on the scales? _____

If you stand still and your partner pulls, what do you read on the scales? _____

Now if you both pull, what do you read on the scales? _____

Third: For this you will still need partners for pulling. Try each of these tug-of-wars.

One Partner With	The Other Partner With	Scale
1. Rubber shoes	Rubber shoes	_____
2. Leather bottom on shoes	Rubber bottom shoes	_____
3. Rubber shoes	Stocking feet	_____
4. Leather shoes	Stocking feet	_____

One Partner With	The Other Partner With	Scale
5. Stocking feet	Stocking feet	_____
6. Stocking feet	Bare Feet	_____
7. Bare feet	Rubber shoes	_____
8. Bare feet	Leather shoes	_____
9. Bare feet	Bare feet	_____

What is your "rule" about what is the hardest to slide?

_____

_____

_____

What is your rule about what is the easiest to slide?

_____

_____

_____

TASK CARD #3

Magnet Fun

Materials you will need: a box of magnets and bars, iron filings, glass plate and string.

Magnets have many surprises. See if you find the surprises in these activities.

1. In the box of bars, find those that are magnets and those that are not magnets.

What is your rule—for how to find out if it is a magnet?

2. Have your teacher help you with this. Watch as she puts a plate on top of a bar magnet and sprinkles iron filings on the plate.

What happens to the filings?

Draw a picture of what you see.

3. Tie a string around a magnet and hang it up like a pendulum. Swing the magnet and watch it until it completely stops.

Try it again. Did it stop in the same position? _____

Write your rule that tells about "hanging magnet position."

TASK CARD #4

Dropping Paper Wads

Materials you will need: scrap paper and a collection of balls.

Paper wads or spit balls are things some people throw. In this experiment, you will be finding out what happens when they drop.

First arrange the balls from the heaviest to lightest. If you dropped the heaviest ball and the lightest ball at the same time, which would hit the floor the quickest?

Try it.

Check each of these pairs and fill in what you see.

	Baseball	Ping Pong	Golf	Paper Wad	Sheet of paper
Baseball					
Ping Pong					
Golf					
Paper Wad					
Sheet of Paper					

Which do you think is the most important reason for what you see?

-color of ball or paper
-shape of ball or paper
-roughness of ball or paper
-heaviness of ball or paper

Now write your rule for "dropping balls."

Observing Patterns: Graphing and Predicting
Grades 3-5

ACTIVITY OVERVIEW
In this activity students use a variety of materials--balls, pendulums and incline planes to observe patterns, graph and predict movements of objects.

SCIENCE BACKGROUND
A very helpful tool in interpreting events is the graph. Constructing the graph requires the student to organize his or her observations. Within the graph it is possible to see trends or patterns. Stating these patterns as rules or predictions then gives the student the opportunity to investigate further--or test his or her predictions.

You never get more out of a system than what you put into it. The distance you pull a pendulum back is always _more_ than the distance it swings out. Thus the limits to the capacity of objects to change their position is certainly a repeated experience. The "rules" your students develop illustrate this more general statement. The rules and their evidence illustrate ways in which you are nurturing your students' development of skills in constructing interpretations of his or her experience.

If one performs an experiment where one variable is changed and another variable measured to see how it relates to the first, the data can be used to predict the results of other experiments. In order to do this, the relationship between the two variables must be discovered. Simple number progressions are recognized readily and predictions from them can be made with confidence. However, scientific work often produces data in which relationships between two variables are not at all obvious. When this happens it is found that a relationship can often be discovered by constructing a graph of the data. This representation of the data (graph) is, therefore, a tool which will be useful in the student's study of science. You may find it necessary to use many opportunities to emphasize the graph both as a means of representing data and as an aid to prediction. As the techniques of graphing are developed they can be applied to more complex situations.

SOCIETAL IMPLICATIONS
One of the problems confronting people who study environmental, population and resource problems is that of predicting future consequences. This problem is especially true for chronic long term changes such as acid rain or CO_2 in the atmosphere. Most people can predict the results of acute short term changes (such as storms).

These activities will assist students in the skill of prediction, and especially accurate prediction. The final activity, investigating patterns in a local environment is very important to developing skills in making predictions about science related social problems.

MAJOR CONCEPT
Patterns in nature enable one to make predictions about changes in objects, organisms and environments.

OBJECTIVES
By the end of these activities each student should be able to:
-Construct a prediction given a graph of data.
-Demonstrate a test for a prediction.

MATERIALS
-A collection of balls including a rubber ball, a golf ball, a ping pong ball, a marble and chart paper. (It will help if you have a pair of children. Make several charts marking lines every decimeter; 10 lines are enough.)
-A ring stand, pendulum stand, or devices for swinging pendulums, washers, string and modeling clay.
-Two incline planes or slanted surfaces arranged in a V, marbles or cylinders such as coke cans.
-You will have to make Task Cards for the different activities. Sample Task Cards are provided in the figures which accompany the activity.

VOCABULARY
Graph, predict, pendulum, incline

PROCEDURES
1. Bounce Heights - Task Card 1
You may want your students doing this in the hall or outside the building--but it is great fun to see for yourself. Task Card #1 provides directions. (See figure 32 for a sample of the Task Card)
In your discussion, be alert to the "rules" and the evidence the student gives for his rule. The rule might be as simple as:
"Bounce height is always less than drop height."
Or it might be more complicated: "Bounce height is half the drop height."
You may need to help them think about how well the last rule fits each kind of ball.

2. <u>Swinging Stuff</u> - Task Card 2

Their rule for swings should show that a pendulum swings quite symetrically--the distance on one side matches the distance on the other side of the middle line.

The weight will not be an important factor either, although many students may think it should. The real way to make it swing faster is to shorten the string.

After they have completed Task Card #2, have them share results. In the discussion carefully listen to what rules and evidence your children present.

3. <u>Rolling Hills</u> - Task Card 3

After your children have gathered their data and plotted their graph, having them describe their rule and the evidence they used to build the rule.

4. <u>Investigating the Local Environment</u> - Task Card 4

After you have completed the first 3 parts of the activity take a "field trip" around the school and see how many patterns can be graphed in order to make predictions. Examples might include: student movement, distribution of lunches, classroom use, etc. This can be used as a summary activity. Note: The Task Card is ambiguous by intent.

TASK CARD #1

Bounce Heights

Materials you will need: a collection of different kinds of balls, chart paper and graph paper.

When you drop a ball, does it come back up to your hand, almost back up or bounce above your hand?

What can you do to make the ball bounce higher than you?

Use the charts to find out what the simple bounce (don't try to make it go higher!) of a ball is when you drop it.

Figure 32   DROP HEIGHT FROM LINE

	2	4	6	8
Rubber ball				
Golf Ball				
Ping Pong Ball				
Marble				

222

Now use the information for the rubber ball and make a graph showing bounce and drop distances for each ball.

Do this for each ball.

How high would you expect the rubber ball to bounce if you dropped it from line 3? 5? 7?

_____

_____

_____

From your graph, make up your own "Bounce Height Rule."

TASK CARD #2

Swinging Stuff

Materials you will need: washers, string and modeling clay, pendulum stand.

Hook up one of your pendulums. As you pull it back, hold your hand where you think it will swing.

Try it.

What happens?

Now measure 4 decimeters on either side of the center where the pendulum stands. Fill in this chart.

If you pull the pendulum back	Then it will swing to a line on the other side
1 decimeter	_____
2 decimeter	_____
3 decimeter	_____
4 decimeter	_____
Make a graph of your results. State a good "Pendulum Swing" rule.	_____

Which swings farther—a heavy pendulum or a light one? (Check—you can make one pendulum heavy by adding clay to the washer.)

How can you get the same pendulum to swing faster?

TASK CARD #3

Rolling Hills

Materials you will need: marbles or cylinders (such as old pop cans) and two slanted surfaces; graph paper.

Suppose you were riding down a valley and the road goes up a hill. If you coasted on your bike down the hill, would it stop at the bottom, or go on up the hill?

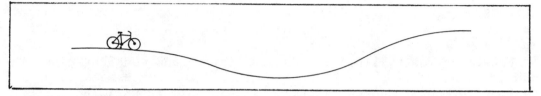

Mark where you think you would stop.

Your teacher will show you where you can test how far up a marble or cylinder will go after it rolls down an inclined plane.

On the slant surface, mark a point at each decimeter away from the middle point.

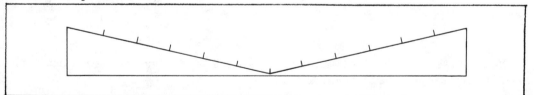

Now complete this chart:

If the point of release is	then the point it stops or reverses is
1 decimeter	_____
2 decimeters	_____
3 decimeters	_____
4 decimeters	_____

Make a graph of your results.
State a "Rule of Rolling Objects" _____

_____

_____

Will the same thing happen to a round pencil? _____

Will the "rule" work if you make the slant steeper? _____

TASK CARD #4

Investigating a Local Environment

Go outside the classroom and find patterns in your local environment. Gather information about the patterns so you can graph them.
Make a prediction about future observations. Now check and see if
your predictions were accurate.

Hints: you might consider student movements or gatherings, cars
in the neighborhood, use of materials in school, the cafeteria or
school playground.

Energy Systems
Grades 3-5

ACTIVITY OVERVIEW

This lesson uses children's intrinsic interest in materials to define energy. In addition children learn there are two types of energy--kinetic and potential. Children are also introduced to the concept of system.

SCIENCE BACKGROUND

Two things that are basic to the study of science and society are matter and energy. Matter is anything that occupies space and that has mass (which we experience as weight). Energy is the capacity to do work by pushing, pulling or chemically changing some form of matter. There are two kinds of energy--potential and kinetic. Kinetic energy is the energy of matter in motion. Potential energy is energy that matter has due to its position or condition.

Energy can be thought of in six forms--mechanical, heat, electrical, wave, chemical and nuclear. Mechanical energy is the form most commonly observed. It is the energy of machines. Heat energy is produced by the motion of molecules in a material. Electrical energy results from the motion of electrons in a substance. Sound and light are examples of wave energy. The release of energy in chemical reactions is another form of energy. Finally, nuclear energy is the result of the nucleus of an atom splitting or the fusion of the nuclei of two atoms.

SOCIETAL IMPLICATIONS

Energy is essential to our existence. Energy is used by all living organisms to move matter and change matter from one form to another. Houses are warmed and cooled, food produced and industries run on energy. The use of energy and changes in its forms is one of the central crises of our age. How can we continue to use the energy in the near future. Society presently uses energy and matter as primary resources for our products and comforts. The problem is that we use matter and energy as though it were an infinite resource and we use the environment as though it had an infinite capacity to absorb the heat and waste left as a result of our uses and transformations of matter and energy. The assumptions underlying this use of energy are presently changing and will continue to do so in the future.

MAJOR CONCEPTS

-Energy is the capacity to do work.
-Kinetic energy is the energy of matter that is moving.
-Potential energy is the energy of matter due to its position
or condition.
-A system is a collection of materials that form a whole.
-Interaction results when materials do something to one another.
-Interactions use (consume) energy.

OBJECTIVES

At the completion of this lesson the student should be able to:
-Define energy.
-Differentiate between potential and kinetic energy.
-Describe an energy system.
-Describe how energy is used in an interaction between materials.

MATERIALS

The materials are suggested for each group of two students.
You may wish to have the students work individually. Place all of
the objects for a group in a medium size baggie or on a tray.
-1 flashlight battery - size D, 1 flashlight bulb, 1 piece of
wire - 20-25 cm long, 1 rubber band, 1 pencil, 1 small rock, 1 small
balloon, 1 piece of string - 20-25 cm long

VOCABULARY

-Battery, bulb, energy, interaction, kinetic, potential, system,
wire

PROCEDURES

Note: This portion of the lesson should be conducted as an
exploration-discovery activity.
1. Distribute the materials to the children.
2. Give the simple directive: Try and see how these objects
interact.
3. After a few minutes you might suggest that some of the children
try and light the bulb using the wire and battery.
4. Allow the children to explore the materials for 10-15 minutes.
5. Take a couple of minutes and have each group explain what
they did. Examples might include: lighting the bulb, stretching the
rubber band, rolling the string up on the pencil, dropping the rock
and so on.
6. Tell the students that what they did involved energy systems,
and that you are now going to define some terms for them. Place these
definitions on the board or overhead projector.

ENERGY –	the ability of matter to change other matter
KINETIC ENERGY –	energy that matter has because it is moving
POTENTIAL ENERGY –	energy that matter has because of its position or condition
SYSTEM –	a group of objects that makes a whole
INTERACTION –	the result of objects doing something to one another

7. Have the children review what they did with the materials at the beginning of the lesson. They should use the terms energy, potential, kinetic, system and interaction in the discussion. Have them first define a system they made. Then how energy was used in the system. Ask them: What was potential and what was kinetic energy in their system? What types of interactions occurred? What What was their evidence that an interaction occurred? How does the evidence of the interaction relate to energy?

Sources of Energy
Grades 3-5

ACTIVITY OVERVIEW

Children gather information on energy sources. During a class period they use questioning techniques to determine the energy sources studied by other students. This activity is intended to introduce students to the types of energy resources.

SCIENCE BACKGROUND

Energy resources can be classified in the categories of nonrenewable, renewable and synthesized fuels. The following table summarizes many of the sources of energy in these categories. This table could be used as a summary for the activity.

Figure 33	Sources of Energy	
NONRENEWABLE	RENEWABLE	SYNTHESIZED OR DERIVED

Fossil Fuels
   Coal
   Natural Gas
   Oil Shale
   Petroleum
Nuclear
   Conventional Reactor
    Fission
   Breeder Reactor Fission
   Fusion
Geothermal
	Biomass
	Ocean Currents &
	   Tidal Energy
	Some Geothermal
	Solar
	Water (Hydro-
	   electricity)
	Wind Power
		Biofuels
		Hydrogen Gas
		Synthetic Natural Gas
		Synthetic Oil/Alcohol
		Urban Waste
		   (Bioconversion)

The following are brief definitions of some of the primary sources of energy:

Fossil Fuel – This is the use of geologically preserved plants and animals. The remains are in such a form that they can be burned to release energy. Examples include: natural gas, coal and oil. Burning fossil fuels is a major contributor to acid rain and CO_2 in the atmosphere.

Nuclear Energy - The energy released through nuclear fission or fusion. Nuclear fission is the splitting of a heavy element into two or more nuclei of lighter elements. The result is a substantial release of energy and the release of neutrons. Uranium 235 and Plutonium 239 are used for nuclear fission. Nuclear fusion is the forcing together of two nonradioactive elements to form a nucleus of a slightly heavier element. The process releases energy. For example, hydrogen isotopes can be combined to form Helium.

Geothermal - Heat energy from processes within the earth.

Biomass - The burning of wood, use of crops, food and animal waste for energy.

Solar - The use of direct radiation from the sun. Indirect forms of solar energy include wind, water, ocean currents and biomass.

Synthetic oil, gas, alcohol - energy produced derived from coal or other organic wastes.

Biofuels - alcohols and natural gas from plants and organic wastes.

SOCIETAL IMPLICATIONS

Energy resources are the driving power of the earth's spheres and of human society. The availability and types of energy resources influence each of us at the individual level and whole societies. Presently, we are heavily dependent on fossil fuels as the source of energy for our society. One half of the availability of this resource is diminishing and the cultural shocks of this realization are being felt by all of us. The symbolic announcement of the crisis was the 1973 Arab oil embargo and the increase in price of oil imports. By most reports (and conflicts) our society is now in a period of transition to the use of other sources of energy and modification of energy intensive life style.

MAJOR CONCEPTS

-Energy is essential for earth processes.
-There are many sources of energy.
-Energy is the capacity to do work.
-Energy can change forms but it is never created or destroyed.

OBJECTIVES

At the completion of this lesson the student should be able to:
-Identify several different energy sources.
-Present detailed information on one energy source.
-Describe some results of using energy sources.

MATERIALS

-Felt tip pen, 5 x 7 index cards (one per student)

VOCABULARY

-Coal, energy, garbage, geothermal, hydroelectric, petroleum, natural gas, oil shale, nuclear, tidal, solar, wind, biomass

PROCEDURES

1. One week before the lesson assign groups of two students each an energy topic. Tell them they are to gather information on the topic and be ready to answer questions from the class. You may wish to incorporate this assignment into reading and/or social studies.

2. Prepare the 5 x 7 cards by printing the name of an energy source on them.

3. On the day of the lesson-questioning game you should explain the rules of the game. Students will work in groups of four (except the two students who are answering questions).

   A. Each group can ask only two questions per round.
   B. Questions can be answered with only a yes or no.
   C. Continue questioning rounds until a group correctly identifies the energy source.
   D. A correct guess adds 5 points. An incorrect guess subtracts 5 points. The team with the highest score wins.

4. After the questioning game have the students give a summary of their energy source.

5. You may wish to pay particular attention to any energy sources that are locally important.

PLANNING CHART FOR PHYSICAL SCIENCE ACTIVITIES: GRADES 6–8

ACTIVITY	OBJECTIVES					TEACHING METHODS	RELATED CURRICULUM
	Conceptual Knowledge	Learning Processes	Psychomotor Skills	Attitudes and Values	Decision-making Skills		
54. Energy: A Primary Resource	Environments change because living and non-living matter interact.	Classify, gather, organize, and interpret information.	Use and care for tools.	Explore environment and ask questions.	Learners collect and differentiate information that affects self, others and environment.	Exploration, discovery.	Social Studies.
55. Limits to Energy Sources	There are limits to the capacity of earth materials to supply energy.	Observe, measure, gather, and organize information.	Handle substances, construct projects.	Explore environment, assume responsibility for use of natural resources.	Learners describe consequences of various alternatives.	Exploration, discovery, activity.	Social Studies.
56. Collecting and Storing Solar Energy	Earth materials have different capacities to absorb and store solar energy.	Form hypothesis, predict.	Learners construct simple projects.	Learners assume responsibility for wise use of resources.	Learners form alternatives based on information.	Hands-on laboratory explanation.	Social Studies.
57. A Source of Acid Rain: Sulfur Oxides	Earth systems change due to interactions.	Describe, observe.	—	Learners assume responsibility for changes due to resource use.	Learners form alternatives based on information.	Demonstration.	Social Studies.
58. Acid in the Atmosphere: Cloud Formation	Earth systems change due to interactions.	Observe, describe, infer.	—	Learners assume responsibility for changes due to resource use.	Learners form alternatives based on information.	Demonstration.	Social Studies.
59. Effects of Acid Rain on Materials	Earth materials change due to interactions.	Observe, describe, infer.		Learners assume responsibility for changes due to resource use.	Learners form alternatives based on information.	Demonstration.	Social Studies.

Energy: A Primary Resource
Grades 6-8

ACTIVITY OVERVIEW

Students identify activities they enjoy and then determine where the activity occurs, the evidence for energy use, the immediate source of energy, the primary source of energy and the earth spheres of the primary energy source. These observations are repeated for activities in the school and community.

SCIENCE BACKGROUND

We have five primary sources of energy that are naturally available on earth: solar, fossil fuels, nuclear, geothermal and tidal energy. Fossil fuels and nuclear energy are stored as potential energy. The other three are kinetic energy or energy due to the motion of materials.

Solar energy is the major source of energy for the earth. It is not, however, the major source that is directly used for human purposes. Solar energy is available as light and heat and is used by plants to manufacture food. Energy from the sun is renewable and clean. In the next decades we will see increased use of this energy source.

Fossil fuels such as coal, oil and natural gas, are stored chemical energy. Solar energy was the original source for these fuels. Plants and animals died and were transformed into fossil fuel through heat and pressure beneath the earth's surface. Fossil fuels are presently used extensively for energy because they have been easy to find and produce. This is now changing very rapidly. Important points about fossil fuels are that they are nonrenewable and do cause pollution.

Nuclear Energy is stored in nuclei of atoms such as plutonium and uranium. Through rearranging (through fission and fusion) of these nuclei great amounts of energy are released. Fission occurs when the nucleus of an atom such as uranium is split into two nuclei. This is a process of converting matter into energy. Fusion is the combining of lighter nuclei, for example hydrogen, into a heavier nuclei--helium in this example. Mass is again converted into energy. Nuclear energy is nonrenewable and does have other safety problems.

Geothermal energy occurs naturally within the earth. It is observed in the form of geysers, hot springs and volcanoes. Geothermal energy is restricted geologically and geographically; so while it is a continuous source of energy its use is somewhat marginal at this time.

Tidal energy is continuous and results from the gravitational attraction between the earth and the moon. There is some potential of using this source for electricity but this potential has not been fulily explored.

SOCIETAL IMPLICATIONS

It is clear that we do have an energy shortage and that a social transformation to new sources is presently underway. As a society we consume tremendous amounts of energy, some needed and some wasted. As the search for new sources of energy continues we need look no further than the five studied in this activity. The _forms_ in which these sources are used and the transfer of energy from one form to another must also be considered in our transformation to new energy sources.

MAJOR CONCEPTS

-Human interactions with the lithosphere, hydrosphere, atmosphere and biosphere can be related to energy.

-Human energy use can be traced to primary sources: solar, fossil fuels, nuclear, tidal, geothermal.

OBJECTIVES

At the completion of this activity the students should be able to:

-Identify the five primary sources of energy: solar, fossil fuel, nuclear, tidal, geothermal.

-Describe an "energy chain" from the human use of energy to a primary source.

-Identify the earth sphere in which energy is used and/or found.

MATERIALS

Observation sheets (see Procedures)

VOCABULARY

-Primary, source, solar, fossil fuel, nuclear, ecosphere, tidal geothermal, lithosphere, hydrosphere, atmosphere

PROCEDURES

1. Start a discussion by asking the students to each list five things they really like to do. They will then list several things. Then ask them to look over the list and try to identify the earth sphere most directly related to the activity. That is, the sphere with which the activity was _primarily_ associated, e.g., swimming-hydrosphere, rock collecting-lithosphere. Continue this discussion for several minutes.

    Note: Lithosphere - solid earth, ground or rocks.
           atmosphere - air surrounding the earth
           hydrosphere - water

2. Distribute the observation sheets (see figure 34).

Figure 34	OBSERVATION SHEET				
Activities	Earth Sphere Used	Evidence For Energy Use	Immediate Energy Source	Primary Energy Source	Earth Sphere of Primary Energy Source
Swimming	Hydrosphere	Motion	Food	Solar	Atmosphere

3. Continue the discussion by having the students fill in the columns for each activity. There may be some difficulty identifying the earth sphere, since students are, by definition a part of the ecosphere. But, you can have them determine the primary earth sphere. Evidence for Energy Use will be light, motion or heat. The Immediate Energy Source will vary: food, electricity, gasoline, etc. The immediate energy source should be traced to a primary source. Finally, the primary source should be located in one of the earth spheres.

4. Next ask the students to list two things they need (not want) on their list. Can they do the same for their needs. They should list things that are primary needs: air, water, food.

5. By this time the students should be fairly well introduced to the activity. The next section is to have groups of 2 students identify activities around the school and complete observation sheets.

6. The next stage is to have groups of four students identify community activities and complete an observation sheet. Direct the students' attention to different activities in the community-government, business, industry, recreation and so on.

7. Have the students complete an observation form that includes the following activities: turning a light on, playing a record player, running, riding in a car and riding a bicycle. Have the students complete the observation form for individuals living in another part of the world, e.g., a Third World Country.

Limits to Energy Sources
Grades 6-8

ACTIVITY OVERVIEW

Through simple activities and observations students realize that sources of energy are limited, and that some sources can only be used once.

SCIENCE BACKGROUND

Energy resources can be grouped as nonrenewable, renewable and synthesized or derived. The limit of a nonrenewable resource is the amount of that resource that can be found and used at reasonable cost and marginal environmental impact. In short, it is the quantity of the resource that defines the substantial limits to its use. By analogy using a nonrenewable resource is like living off your savings when you have no income. When the savings is gone, your income is gone. Renewable resources are, in theory, limitless. But in fact, there is a limit. If a renewable resource is used faster than it can be replenished, then the resource becomes depleted and ultimately is nonrenewable. Again, by analogy, using renewable resources is like living off the interest of your savings without using the capital. If use exceeds the interest rate, then capital is diminished at your rate of expenditure until your capital is depleted. In the case of renewable resources it is the rate of use that is the limiting factor.

As mentioned above, energy must be available in useful form, at reasonable costs and without harmful effects on the environment. Energy scarcity, then, does not really mean we are running out of energy sources. It means that there may be a shortage of a resource, a rise in price (such as happened in the OPEC price increases) or to a substantial amount of environmental damage.

SOCIETAL IMPLICATIONS

Examples have been mentioned of the rise in oil and gasoline prices after 1973. The oil embargo made individuals aware of another fact--the dependency of other social factors on petroleum. Energy is needed for much more than cars. Energy is needed to run machines and grow food; and, if the source of energy is oil and it becomes more expensive, so does all the products for which oil is a source of energy.

1973 was a turning point for industrialized countries. During the period from 1973 to 1980 we became cognizant of the limits to our energy resources. If we take the lesson of limits seriously and start the transition to conservative practices and alternative sources, all will be well. If, on the other hand, we do not face the reality of limited energy resources, our society will be in serious trouble.

MAJOR CONCEPTS
    -There are limits to the capacity of earth materials to supply
energy.
    -Conservation is one method of avoiding the depletion of energy.
    -Changing energy sources is one method of avoiding the depletion
of energy.

OBJECTIVES
    At the completion of this lesson the student should be able to:
    -Define conservation as the preservation of resources through
decreased use.
    -Describe the limits of several energy sources.
    -Describe methods of avoiding the depletion of resources through
(1) decreased use and (2) increased supply.
    -Define energy as the capacity to do work.

MATERIALS
    -A set of the following for each group of 2 or 3 students:
small birthday candles, matches, styrofoam cups, clock, thermometer,
test tubes, test tube holder

VOCABULARY
    -Energy, resources, heat, light, conservation

PROCEDURES
    1. Before class place a small hole in the bottom of the styrofoam
cup. Then place the candle in the bottom of the cup. (See figure 35).

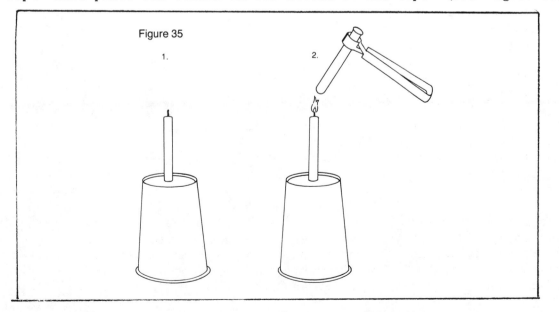

Figure 35

2. Distribute the materials to each group of students.

3. Tell the students they are going to use the candle to heat water in their test tube (see diagram 2)

4. Place 5 cm of water at room temperature in their test tube.

5. Tell the students they are to heat the water by 10°C. During the activity they should record (1) How long it takes to heat the water 10°C (2) How much (in centimeters) of their candle is used. Allow them to proceed with the activity.

6. Discuss their results when they have completed the activity. During the discussion ask them: How long do they think it would have taken to heat the water 20°C, 30°C? How long would your candle last?

PART II

1. The second part of this activity is a challenge and exploration. Challenge the students to heat their water 30°C without using all of their candle. Tell them to record what they do and the results they obtain.

2. Have the students share their results with the rest of the class.

3. During the discussion point out those ideas that represent conservation of the energy source and those that represent use of other energy sources and combinations of the conservation and use of renewable resources.

4. Extend the discussion to the limits and conservation of natural resources such as fossil fuels.

5. Have the students design their own activity to demonstrate more efficient methods to use energy.

Collecting and Storing Solar Energy
Grades 6-8

ACTIVITY OVERVIEW

In this activity the students collect solar energy using different earth materials. They then determine which materials are best for storing solar energy. The activity ends with an exploration in which the students are challenged to set up a system that will store energy efficiently.

SCIENCE BACKGROUND

Solar energy is abundant. This fact is one of the major advantages of solar energy as a resource. Solar energy falls on the upper atmosphere at a rate of about 1.3 kilowatts per square meter. (A watt is a metric unit of power. One watt equals one joule of work per second. A kilowatt is 1000 watts). On the average, about 13% of this energy arrives on the earth's surface. Here is another way of thinking of this resource. The energy equivalent of 10 barrels of oil falls on each acre of the United States each day, or over 22 billion barrels of oil per day on the contiguous 48 states. The resource is abundant. However, the amount available to use varies greatly with latitude, season and weather. Technological advances may be able to overcome some problems and convert and store solar energy for our use.

Solar energy includes more than the direct rays of the sun. It also includes the energy that results from the interaction of solar radiation with different parts of the earth's spheres. Wind power, water power, ocean currents and biomass power are also included in the use of solar energy as a resource.

There are, however, problems with the use of solar energy. The collection and concentration of the resource is difficult. Certain geographic locations are well suited for the use of solar energy while it would be substantially less feasible in other areas. Presently the cost of technology for the use of solar energy is high; but in terms of lifetime cost of energy for a home this factor is reduced somewhat.

Direct solar energy is usually collected and concentrated for use in space heating and water heating. Through the use of photovoltaic cells it can also be converted to electricity.

SOCIETAL IMPLICATIONS

Estimates range as to the use of solar energy in our society. Some think that 20 to 25 percent of U.S. energy needs could be served by the 2000 and perhaps 50 percent by 2020--if we have an all out program of research and development.

MAJOR CONCEPTS

-Earth materials have different capacities to absorb and store energy.

-Solar energy can be used as an energy source for heating.

OBJECTIVES

At the completion of this lesson the student should be able to:

-Describe some earth materials that are good for collecting and storing solar energy.

-Describe the problems of using solar energy.

-Apply ideas concerning the collection and storage of solar energy to the resolution of some social problems.

MATERIALS

-6 styrofoam cups (per group), 6 thermometers (per group), cardboard box per group (similar in size for all groups. Save the boxes for di to paper), glad wrap, sand, water, cut paper (like confetti), small pebbles, other earth materials, graph paper, clock

VOCABULARY

-Collection, control, storage, solar, variables

PROCEDURES

Part I

1. This activity is to be completed outdoors on a sunny day.

2. Fill each cup with an earth material. Have the students place sand, pebbles, water, cut paper and nothing (air) respectively in 5 containers. They are to select an earth material for the sixth container.

3. Place the cups in the box and place thermometers in the cups.

Note: Place a thermometer in the empty cup and cover the cup with glad wrap or a similar material.

4. When all cups are set up in the box be sure temperatures are stabilized at room temperature. Take the boxes outdoors.

5. Have the students record the temperature each minute for 30 minutes. After 20 minutes have them bring the cups and boxes indoors (out of the sun) and record the change in temperature for the next 20 minutes.

6. Have the students graph their results for the next day. The graph should be set up as follows:

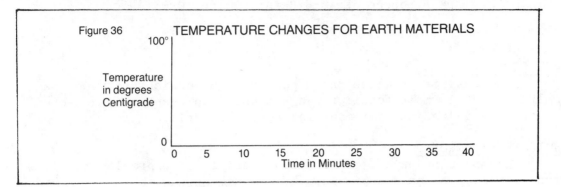

Figure 36   TEMPERATURE CHANGES FOR EARTH MATERIALS

Temperature in degrees Centigrade

7. Discuss the results on the next day:
    Which temperature increased fastest? Slowest?
    Which material held the heat energy longest? Shortest?
    What material could best be used for storing solar energy?
    How could your results be applied to heating the school?
    Classroom? Homes?

    Part II
    1. This part of the activity is a challenge--exploration.
    2. Each student group is to design a system that they think is
efficient for the collection and storage of solar energy.
    3. Inform the students that they will have one period to design
the system. They must use earth materials from the prior activity
and their system cannot be any larger than the box used in the last
activity. (You can allow for some variation on these directions).
    4. Evaluation of the student solar systems will be completed by
taking each system outdoors and placing it in the sun for 20 minutes.
Temperatures will be recorded as they were in Part I.
        Which system had the greatest increase in temperature?
        Which system maintained heat energy the longest upon returning
            to the classroom? (Use classroom temperature as a standard.)
    5. Have the students describe how they constructed their
collection/storage system.

    Part III
    1. Present the following materials and ask the students to rank
them according to the materials capacity to store solar energy.
1) Salt water, 2) a rock, 3) an empty jar, 4) a stack of paper,
5) a green plant.
    Ask the students why we do not use solar energy to warm our
classrooms, schools or homes.
    2. Have the students discuss the idea of using solar energy
instead of fossil fuels.

A Source of Acid Rain: Sulfur Oxides
Grades 6-8

ACTIVITY OVERVIEW
    A demonstration illustrates possible connections between the
sulfur found in most fossil fuels and the acid eventually detected
in the precipitation over many parts of the world.

SCIENCE BACKGROUND
    An important aspect of the acid precipitation problem is the water
incorporation of oxides produced by combustion and subsequent acid
formation. The basic chemistry of this process is given below in
Figure 37.

Figure 37

$$S_{(s)} + O_{2(g)} \longrightarrow SO_{2(g)}$$

$$SO_{2(g)} + H_2O_{(1)} \longrightarrow H_2SO_{3(ag)} \longrightarrow 2H^+_{(aq)} + SO^{2}_{3(aq)}$$

sulfurous acid

    One step which occurs in the atmosphere, that is not represented
by the demonstration, is the oxidation of the sulfur from the plus
four to a plus six oxidation state. Whether this occurs in the gaseous
state ($SO_2 + 1/2O_2 \longrightarrow SO_3$) or after dissolution ($SO_3^2 + 1/2O_2 \longrightarrow SO_4^{2-}$)
is not clear. In any case it should be mentioned that sulfuric and
not sulfurous acid actually occurs in acid precipitation.

SOCIETAL IMPLICATIONS
    In the discussion point out different sources of sulfur dioxide
that are represented here by the burning of sulfur, sources such as
volcanoes, power plants, industry, metal smelting, and transportation
should be included. Make the point that the gases (SO_2 or SO_3) can
travel long distances before and after dissolving in water, i.e., in
clouds.

MAJOR CONCEPTS
    -Acid rain forms through the chemical combination of sulfur
oxides (and nitrogen oxides) and water.
    -Burning fossil fuels is the primary source of sulfur oxides.

OBJECTIVES

After this activity students should be able to:
-Identify the sources of acid rain.
-Describe the chemical process that produces acid rain.

VOCABULARY

-Acid, acid rain, fossil fuels, sulfur oxides

MATERIALS

-Sulfur 1-2g, ordinary clear glass bottle with cork (1 liter is a convenient size), bromcresol purple indicator solution, deflagrating spoon, bunsen burner

PROCEDURES

*It is advised (and in some states required) that the instructor and students wear eye protection during this activity.

1. If a one liter bottle is being used, add about 200ml of distilled water and 5-6 drops of indicator. The solution should be gray in color indicating a pH of about 6. If this is not the case, a few drops of dilute NH_4OH to a yellow solution or dilute acetic acid to a purple solution will adjust the solution to the proper pH.

2. Fill the deflagrating spoon with sulfur (one gram) and heat over a Bunsen burner until it ignites. Insert the spoon with burning sulfur into the bottle and insert the cork (cut a notch in the cork for the deflagrating spoon). Placing white paper under and behind the bottle will make the color change more visible.

3. After the sulfur has burned it may be necessary to swirl the solution in order to dissolve sufficient gas. This occurs in much the same way that a swift moving stream will dissolve more oxygen than standing water. The indicator will change to yellow at a pH less than six.

4. Review the chemistry involved in the demonstration. Be sure to make the connection between the demonstration and the formation of acid precipitation. Discussion should include natural and human sources of sulfur oxides.

Acid in the Atmosphere: Cloud Formation
Grades 6-8

ACTIVITY OVERVIEW
The activity is a demonstration in which a cloud is created in a closed flask. Discussion is held afterwards concerning factors involved in cloud formation, the part cloud formation holds in the water cycle, and how a cloud becomes acidic.

SCIENCE BACKGROUND
The cloud formation process includes evaporation of water from standing bodies of water or evapotranspiration from plants and condensation of that water vapor on solid particles in the atmosphere. Factors influencing evaporation are heat and pressure (compressing a gas causes its temperature to rise). Condensation of water is influenced by cooling and release of pressure. An illustration of these ideas is found in the observation of evaporation in the coastal regions and condensation as water vapor moves up the side of a mountain into a zone of lower temperature, lower pressure, where precipitation is likely to occur. Solid particles on which condensation may occur are present in the atmosphere in many forms. The type of particle can influence the pH of the water involved. Dust and soil particles blown into the atmosphere are usually basic, as i.e. salt from sea spray and organic material, thus increasing the pH of the forming cloud. Lowering of pH occurs as atmospheric gases such as sulfur dioxide (SO_2) and nitrogen oxides (NO) react with water to produce sulfuric and nitric acid. The amount of solid particles and gases in the air, therefore, controls the acidity of clouds and eventual precipitation.

SOCIETAL IMPLICATIONS
Although sulfur dioxide is produced by natural sources such as volcanoes, approximately 90% of atmospheric sulfuric emissions in North America are human in origin. Electric utilities produce about 60% of the total. Nitrogen oxides are produced from both the combustion of fossil fuels and automobile exhaust. Thus it is primarily humans who have control over the amount of these gases in the atmosphere and, hence, the acidity of clouds and precipitation. We have succeeded in reducing the local acidity of precipitation by regulating the height of emission smokestacks, yet this has served only to distribute the problem of acid rain over a larger geographic area as the smoke is now released into the upper atmosphere and carried greater distances before returning to earth.

MAJOR CONCEPTS

-Heat (and pressure) is necessary to <u>evaporate</u> surface water and create <u>water vapor</u>.

-Cooling (and release of pressure) is necessary to cause <u>condensation</u> of water vapor.

-Solid particles in the atmosphere act as <u>condensation nuclei</u> for the water vapor.

A cloud is a concentration of water vapor which has condensed on solid particles.

-Particles present in the atmosphere affect the pH of the cloud.

-Gases in the atmosphere (SO_2 and NO_x) emitted by factories and automobiles react with water vapor to create acid rain.

-Through movement of the gases and clouds in the air and water on the ground, acid rain could become a problem.

OBJECTIVES

After this activity students should be able to:

-Define factors affecting the formation of a cloud.

-Describe factors influencing the pH of a cloud.

-Illustrate, by means of a simple diagram, the water cycle.

-Point out where in the water cycle acid rain begins.

-Describe how human activities affect the production and distribution of acid rain.

VOCABULARY

-Condensation, condensation nuclei, evaporation, water cycle

MATERIALS

-1 medium-sized flask, 1 stopper with hole through it, 1 inch-long glass tube (the size of the hole in stopper), 1 short piece of rubber tubing, water, matches

PROCEDURES

Part I Demonstration

1. Set up flask as shown in diagram: Insert glass tube through hole in stopper, rubber tubing over the top of the glass tube, and the stopper fit tightly into top of the flask. The flask must be completely dry for the first experiment.

2. Increase pressure in the flask by blowing hard through the rubber tubing. Pinch tubing tight between your fingers before removing your mouth.

Figure 38

3. Release pressure by releasing your fingers from the tube.

4. Record whether or not a cloud was formed (it is easier to tell if the room is darkened and a light is placed behind the flask before releasing the tube).

5. Pour 5-10 ml of water into the flask, replace the stopper, and swirl the water around a bit to wet the sides of the flask.

6. Repeat steps 2 through 4.

7. Rinse flask once more with the water already in it.

8. Light a match, remove the stopper, and let some of the smoke from the match enter the flask by holding the flask at an angle (so that the hole does not face straight up). Replace the stopper in the flask tightly.

9. Repeat steps 2 through 4.

10. Discuss the activity, using discussion questions and scientific background provided.

Part II - Discussion

1. What effect do you think blowing in the flask had?
2. What happened when the tube was released?
3. Why didn't a cloud form in the dry flask?
4. Why didn't a cloud form in the second experiment?
5. What conditions need to be present for cloud formation?
6. Where do we find the best conditions for evaporation?
7. What conditions cause a cloud to dissipate?
8. Where are these likely to be found?
9. If there was sulfur dioxide (like that produced in the previous experiment) present in the flask, what effect do you think that would have had?
10. Where are the greatest concentrations of sulfur dioxide or nitrogen oxides? Why is that so?
11. Do you know of any methods used to reduce that concentration? (tall stacks, scrubbers)
12. Do you think these methods have been effective?
13. Can you think of any other problems these actions might have caused?

246

A means for connecting sulfur-producing area to local acidity of precipitation is to have the students study wind patterns, evaporation rate, and air quality in their area.

In the classroom, students could use maps and satellite photographs to monitor the movement of clouds across the nation for a week's time.

Outside, students could construct weather vanes or pinwheels and use anemometers to measure direction and speed of lower elevation winds. The students should then determine how the wind patterns at each elevation might contribute to the acid precipitation problem in their area.

To measure evaporation rate, a wet and dry-bulb thermometer may be set up outside and measured once or twice a day for a week. Students should develop hypotheses as to why evaporation will differ from early morning to afternoon, from day to day and from season to season.

Air quality may not be readily measured by the students and it may be necessary to consult local airports or weather stations for this data.

As students discover the relationships of evaporation, air quality, wind speed and direction, and acid rain, they should obtain a clearer picture of the acid rain problem and a better idea of how acid rain may potentially affect their community and environment.

Effects of Acid Rain on Materials
Grades 6-8

ACTIVITY OVERVIEW

This demonstration shows the effect of a strong acid on selected materials.

SCIENCE BACKGROUND

For as many samples as possible describe the reaction through equations.

Figure 39
For Limestone

$$CaCO_{3(s)} + H_2SO_{4(aq)} \longrightarrow CaSO_{4(aq)} + CO_{2(g)} + H_2O$$

SOCIETAL IMPLICATIONS

The reactions of 3M H_2SO_4 are in some cases quite dramatic. Fortunately it does not rain 3M (pH 0), but rather a solution approximately 1000 times more dilute. It should be discussed that this more dilute solution will have the same effect given a sufficiently long period of acidic precipitation. You might point out to the students that millions of dollars are spent each year for the restoration of materials corroded due to acid rain.

This demonstration shows the direct effects of sulfuric acid on materials. Sulfuric acid also has the ability to dissolve certain naturally occuring compounds of heavy metals. These heavy metals can, once in solution, have their own effects on living organisms. These effects are considered by some to be more harmful to aquatic life than acid precipitation itself.

MAJOR CONCEPTS

-Acids (sulfuric and nitric) have pronounced effects on some materials.

-Acid rain corrodes many human materials such as statues and buildings.

OBJECTIVES

After this study students should be able to:

-Describe the influence of acids on materials.

-Describe the effects of acid rain on human structures.

-Relate concentration and duration to the extent that acid is harmful.

VOCABULARY
    -Concentration, duration, heavy metals, metals

MATERIALS
    -1 - 3M H_2SO_4 in dropping bottles
    -Watchglasses, petri dishes, or small beakers
    -various materials; some good choices are: concrete, marble or
limestone, metals such as zinc, aluminum, or copper, paper, fabric
(colored and white, cotton and synthetic), and leaves. Also ask
students to bring materials of their own.

PROCEDURES
    1. Place samples of the materials in different watchglasses.
Drop a few drops of the sulfuric acid solution on the samples. Let
it stand for several minutes and record any observations.
    2. Have the students describe the effects of acid on different
materials. During the discussion review the different levels of pH
involved in the acid used as compared to acid rain. Point out the
variables of time, materials and pH in the problem. The activity can
be extended by examining the effects of different acids, pH, times
and materials. You can also have the students identify any local
materials that may have been corroded due to acid rain. Head stones,
statues and building facades are good places to begin this investigation.

Resources for Teaching Environmental and Physical Science

Children's Resources: Books, Games, and Pictures

Ackins, Ralph. Energy Machines. Milwaukee: Raintree, 1980. 32 pp.
$9.95. Grades 2-4. One of a series of books on machines issued
by Raintree, this one deals with machines involved in finding and
transporting energy--including solar and nuclear energy. It
includes Communications Machines (newspapers, telephones,
satellites) and Fastest Machines.

Alexander Graham Bell Association for the Deaf. World Traveler
(Science). Washington, D.C.: Bell Association. Six 16-page
booklets. $2.75/set, quantity reduction. Grades 2 and up.
From World Traveler (Science), Box 3618, Washington, D.C. 20007.
Series of booklets illustrated with National Geographic photos
and written at the third grade level. Titles: The Sun, Energy,
Small World (microscopes), Animals That Travel, The Human Body,
and Shapes in Nature.

Branley, Franklyn M. C. Color from Rainbow to Lasers. New York:
T. Y. Crowell, 1978. $8.95. Grades 6-8. Uses simply described
experiments to amplify discussions of such things as theories
of color vision, psychology of color, measurement of hues, and
examination of the color spectrum.

Brown, Alford Eugene. Absolutely Mad Inventions. New York:
Dover, 1970. 125 pp. $1.50, paperback. Grades 5 and up.
Teacher Resource. "A collection of follies," 57 Rube Goldber-
gish inventions that were actually submitted to the patent
office, complete with actual descriptions and illustrations.
Interesting models for physics, fantasy, descriptive writing,
and technical illustration.

Brown, William, and White, Edwin. ESS Activity Cards. Virginia
Beach: Observe, 1978. Three sets of cards. $5.95 to $7.95/set.
From P.O. Box 62078, Virginia Beach, VA 62078. Grades 4 and up.
Three sets of activity cards, A-Blocks, Batteries and Bulbs,
and People Pieces (22 to 32 cards each) correlate with ESS
Readers (based on the McGraw-Hill set). The cards pose questions
that require students to discover the answers through safe
manipulative activities with easily obtainable materials.

Burns, Marilyn. This Book is About Time. Boston: Little, Brown, 1978. $5.95, Brown Paper School Book. Grades 5 and up. Teacher Resource. Explores various concepts of time such as body time, reaction time, historical calendars (such as Egyptian and Chinese) that came from observation of the skies, with suggestions of ways of making such exotic time markers as water clocks and sun dials with easy-to-locate materials.

Caney, Stephen. Inventions and Contraptions. New York: Workman Publishing, 1980. 256 pp. $12.50, $5.95 for paperback. Grades 4 and up. Teacher Resource. Young inventors can read the history of 50 landmark inventions and ponder the author's list of related contrivances still waiting to be invented.

Condit, Martha Olson. Something to Make: Something to Think About. New York: Four Winds, 1976. 39 pp. $4.95. Grades 1-3. A do-it-yourself book that suggests materials and provides directions for seven interesting projects. Very nicely illustrated by Beatrice Darwin. These projects are followed up by valuable hints on "something to think about."

Corbett, Scott. Home Computers: A Simple and Informative Guide. Boston: Atlantic-Little, Brown, 1980. 118 pp. $7.95. Grades 5 and up. An introduction to small computers suitable for home use for fun and work. Includes glossary and index.

Crews, Donald. Light. New York: Greenwillow, 1981. $7.95. Grades 1-4. A rather subtle picture book, essentially a collection of paintings of light in contrasting contexts (such as city/country) or concentrations (as day/night). Certainly a consciousness-raiser in its pictures of headlights/taillights, and glimmering lights.

Elementary Science Box. Inglewood: Educational Insights, 1974. Box of cards. $5.95 plus postage and handling. Grades 4 and up. From Dept. W-45, 211 S. Hindry Avenue, Inglewood, CA 90301. Includes 135 experiments on subjects like magnetism, electricity, sound, light, aerodynamics. It is correlated with two Science Project Books of 64 pages each, one for teachers and one for students.

Epstein, Sam and Beryl. Look in the Mirror. New York: Holiday, 1973. Unpaged. $4.50. Grades 1-4. This lively book suggests approximately 20 simple activities leading to the exploration of the characteristics and uses of mirrors, using common objects found in the home or school.

Gardner, Beau. _The Turn About, Think About, Look About Book_. New York: Lothrop, Lee & Shepard, 1980. $6.95. All grades. A remarkably beautiful and interesting book whose square pages each contain a thought-provoking, brightly colored pattern that can be examined from each of its four separately captioned edges. A most interesting study in form and perception.

Kettelkamp, Larry. _Lasers: The Miracle Light_. New York: Morrow, 1979. 126 pp. $6.95. Grades 6 and up. An up-to-date coverage of a difficult subject, with sufficient background to clarify the principles involved. Well organized, with many diagrams and photos (including some of women scientists and engineers). Includes an index.

Knight, David C. _Silent Sound: The World of Ultrasonics_. New York: Morrow, 1980. 96 pp. $6.67. Grades 4-8. Clear and comprehensive treatment of ultrasound and its production and utilization by the military, industry, and medicine, with speculation on future uses.

Moorman, Thomas. _What Is It Really Like Out There?: Objective Knowing_. New York: Atheneium, 1977. 87 pp. $5.95. Grades 6 and up. Translates basic philosophy into simple language for beginners. Carefully explains the strengths and weaknesses of such ways of knowing as survey investigations. Author has a definite knack for simplifying difficult concepts that could be helpful for teachers as well as students.

Mullin, Virginia L. _Chemistry Experiments for Children_. New York: Dover, 1968. 96 pp. $2.00 paperback. Grades 3 and up. Teacher Resource. Includes 40 simple experiments dealing with air, water, solutions, diffusions and osmosis, crystals, fire, photography, acids and bases, and everyday things. It includes chapters on laboratory techniques and on setting up an inexpensive laboratory.

Ploutz, Paul F., developer. _Elements_. Athens: Union Printing Co., 1970. Game. $13.00. Grades 6 and up. From 17 West Washington Street, Athens, OH 45701. A competitive board game designed to teach the Periodic Chart of the Elements and the names of 105 elements. Has four games and eight variations for two to six players, from 20 to 60 minutes.

Reuben, Gabriel. _Electricity Experiments for Children_. New York: Dover, 1960. 87 pp. $2.00, paperback. Grades 5 and up. A step-by-step guide to 55 safe experiments, demonstrations and projects in magnetism, electricity, and electronics. All use inexpensive materials available in homes, drug stores, and hardware stores.

Schneider, Herman and Nina. _Science Fun for You in a Minute or Two: Quick Science Experiments You Can Do_. New York: McGraw-Hill, 1975. 64 pp. $6.95. Grades 3-6. Uses the format of a child's day (staring at the ceiling while in bed, brushing teeth, breakfast, etc.) to suggest 26 quick physical science activities. Most are stimulating and will generate questions, inferences, and solutions.

Senechal, Marjorie, and Fleck, George. _Patterns of Symmetry_. Amherst: University of Massachusetts Press, 1977. 152 pp. $12.00, cloth. Grades 6 and up. Teacher Resource. This beautifully illustrated book shows the common thread, symmetry, which interlinks areas of human thought in art and science. Presents the symmetry explored by ancient and modern culture, and recommends further studies.

Simo, Connie; Wells, Kappy; and Wells, Malcom. _Sandtiquity_. New York: Taplinger, 1980. 112 pp. $10.95. $4.95, paperback. All grades. A fascinating book for a field trip at a beach, written by an architect, a sculptor, and a photographer. Shows (with photographs) and tells (with clear instructions) just how to use damp sand and a straight-edge stick (such as a shingle, ruler, or a bit of fence) to create such architectural structures as pyramids, ancient buildings, and modern dams. Incorporates a knowledge of history, physics, architecture, and engineering.

Simon, Seymour. _Mirror Magic_. New York: Lothrop, Lee & Shepard, 1980. 48 pp. $7.95. Grades 2-6. An introduction to mirrors that includes such uncomplicated but interesting mirror activities as making a periscope and mirror writing. Mr. Simon is another very prolific author of children's science books. Other titles include: _Life on Ice_ (Watts, 1976, $9.90), _The Optical Illusion Book_ (Four Winds, 1976, $8.95), and _The Paper Airplane Book_ (Viking, 1971, $7.50), and a series involving Einstein Anderson, science sleuth.

Stein, Sara. The Science Book. New York: Workman Publishing, 1980. $5.95, paperback. Grades 3-7. This supplemental text of photographs, drawings, and experiments describes natural phenomena and suggests ways of answering the "why" questions students ask. Ms. Stein is the author of many children's books dealing with care of such pets as gerbils, guppies, and puppies.

Webster, David. How to Do a Science Project. New York: Franklin Watts, 1974. 61 pp. $5.90. Helpful introduction to research projects and the scientific method, with many suggestions for preparing reports, demonstrations, and displays.

Weiss, Malcom. Seeing Through the Dark: Blind and Sighted Vision Shared. New York: Harcourt Brace Jovanovich, 1976. $5.95. Grades 6 and up. Deals with sight in a way that encourages young readers (and teachers!) to examine subjects from multiple points of view.

Wyler, Rose. What Happens If . . .? Science Experiments You Can Do By Yourself. New York: Walker, 1974. 48 pp. Grades 2-4. Simple science experiments presented with copious illustrations.

Zubrowski, Bernie. Ball-Point Pens. Boston: Little, Brown, 1979. 64 pp. $6.95, paperback. A Children's Museum Activity Book. Grades 4 and up. An exciting collection of discovery experiments using discarded ball-point pens and inexpensive miscellanies like paper clips and string. Projects include hydrometers, thermometers, eye droppers, equal arm balancers, prisms, and more. The book provides clear illustrations and precise instructions as well as scientific and historical information and questions designed to move students through guided, modified, and free discoveries of their own.

Films and Filmstrips

Attraction of Gravity. Santa Monica: BFA Educational Media, 1975. 16mm. Color film. Nine minutes. $150.000; $20.00 rental. Grades 4-8. Interestingly duplicates the classic experiments of Cavendish and Bays that illustrate the relationships between mass, distance and the forces of gravity.

Color: A First Film. Santa Monica: BFA, 1979. 16 mm. Color film. 13 minutes. $220.00; $26.00 rental. Grades 1-5. An illustration of the importance of colors in our lives is followed by experiments that analyze white light and combine colored primary colors.

Cosmic Zoom. New York: National Film Board of Canada, 1970. 16 mm.
Color film. Eight minutes. $145.00. All grades. An unusual
film (also available as a book) that starts by focusing on a boy
fishing and changes perspective up: first moving up in stages--
up to the farthest reaches of the universe--then back to the boy
and down to magnified smaller units inside the boy--to the last
atom of a living cell. Excellent for perspective on the universe
and our role in it.

Heat and Hemispheres. New York: Sterling Educational Films, 1969.
16mm. Color film. 11 minutes. $120.00. Grades 1 and up.
Uses experiments with heat, metal objects and thermometers to
explain interrelations between heat and hemispheres, sun and
seasons.

History of Measurement. Burbank: Walt Disney Educational Media,
1976. Five color filmstrips, five records, five cassettes.
Language of Measurement, 45 frames, 6 minutes. Long and Short
of It, 63 frames, 9 minutes. Weighty Problem, 67 frames, 9
minutes. Measuring the Unknown, 57 frames, 7 minutes. Measuring
the Future, 64 frames, 9 minutes. $88.00/set. Grades 4-7.

Good background and overview of the history of measurement, which
indicates how trade, science, inventions, etc., depend upon a
standardized system. Future introduces the metric system. Guide
includes an excellent history, as well as summaries and vocabularies
of each filmstrip, along with suggested activities and a bibliography.

Reflections on Time. Chicago: Encyclopedia Britannica. 16 mm.
Color film. 22 minutes. $290.00 Grades 4 and up. A film whose
provocative questions force students to consider time subjectively
as well as objectively and geologically. Very popular and
stimulating for students.

IV

Earth and Environmental Science Activities

The earth and environmental sciences include study of the lithosphere, usually thought of as the hard outer surface or crust of the earth; the atmosphere, or the air surrounding the earth; the hydrosphere, or water; the biosphere, or realm of life on earth; and the celestial sphere, or outer space. The interactions between these spheres create many of the problems and issues related to our theme of science and society. Think of the topics one hears about almost daily: population, food, arable land, fossil fuels, water shortages, forests, and pollution. All can be identified with a particular aspect of the earth and environmental sciences.

As our understanding of traditional earth science topics such as geology, meteorology, and astronomy has increased, so has our understanding of interdisciplinary topics such as population growth, environmental abuse and resource use. In the last twenty-five years discussions of ocean management, environmental impacts, environmental hazards, and energy policies have increased. Appropriate introductions to these topics should be a part of elementary and middle school science programs.

The activities presented in this volume have a different emphasis than activities associated with traditional topics such as rocks, minerals, weather, and dinosaurs. We have designed activities that introduce children to the environment and changes that occur in it. Their understanding of conservation, resources, population and pollution is developed through the activities.

The planning charts give further details about the objectives and methods for each activity. Reference to the planning charts should assist you in deciding which activities are best for your students and your existing science program.

PLANNING CHART FOR EARTH AND ENVIRONMENTAL SCIENCE ACTIVITIES: GRADES K-2

ACTIVITY	Conceptual Knowledge	Learning Processes	Psychomotor Skills	Attitudes and Values	Decision-making Skills	TEACHING METHODS	RELATED CURRICULUM
			OBJECTIVES				
60. Describing the Environment: Objects Organisms and Colors	Living and non-living things have identities based on their properties.	Observe.	Handle non-toxic substances.	Curiosity, exploration of environment.	—	Hands-on activity.	Language Arts.
61. Earth Materials: Natural and Synthetic	Natural and synthetic materials have identities based on their properties.	Observe, compare, classify.	Handle non-toxic substances.	Objectivity—listening to alternative points of view.	Identify information needed for decisions.	Question-ing and activity.	Social Studies.
62. Changes in the Environment	All things change due to interaction with other objects. Identity is conserved in some changes.	Observe, compare.	Handle non-toxic substances.	Curiosity and creativity, exploration and combination of objects.	Identify information needed for decisions.	Explora-tion, dis-covery.	—
63. Measuring Changes in the Environment	All things change due to interaction with other objects. Changes can be measured.	Measure.	Use simple tools and equipment.	Objectivity in observation and measurement.	Gather information needed for decisions.	Hands-on activity, problem solving.	Math.
64. Are Changes Good or Bad?	Changes can be good, bad or neutral depending on personal perceptions.	Observe, compare.	Handle non-toxic substances.	Responsibility for environmental changes.	Discusses immediate consequences of change.	Discus-sion.	Social Studies.
65. Changing Earth Materials: Solids, Liquids and Gases	Earth materials change due to interaction with other materials.	Observe, compare.	Handle non-toxic substances.	Creativity in combination of earth materials.	Learn and discuss consequences of change.	Explora-tion, dis-covery.	—
66. Studying an Environment	Environments have identities based on their properties, materials, and organization.	Observe, compare.	Learners care for plants and animals.	Responsibility for care of plants and animals.	Formulation of alternatives for decision.	Project.	—
67. The Environment Outside of the Classroom	Environments change through interaction with living and non-living things.	Observe, compare.	—	Responsibility for use of natural resources, self, and others.	Gather information needed for decision.	Field trip.	Social Studies.

Describing the Environment: Objects, Organisms, and Colors
Grades K-2

ACTIVITY OVERVIEW

The child is introduced to the concepts of objects and organisms. In addition color words are reviewed. Objects and organisms from the classroom are used as the focal point of the activity. The noun <u>object</u> replaces the name of "things" in the child's environment. Any non-living thing that can be seen or felt is an object. Living objects are <u>organisms</u>. Words used to describe objects and organisms are the properties of the object. Color is a property emphasized in this lesson.

SCIENCE BACKGROUND

This activity is intended to establish vocabulary and a means of describing the environment. Because of this primary emphasis the focus on science concepts should be secondary. After the introductory activities in which students learn how to describe their environment the focus shifts to science concepts, processes, skills, attitudes and decisions appropriate to the grade level.

All objects and organisms have characteristics called properties. Describing the properties of objects or organisms is the method used to differentiate them from each other. There are two main types of properties—physical and chemical. The physical properties of an object or organism are those qualities we can observe with our five senses. Also, the physical properties include: color, odor, taste, weight, hardness, texture, elasticity, boiling and melting points, solubility, conductivity and malleability. Our emphasis in these activities is on the physical properties of matter.

One of the most obvious physical properties of matter is color. When white light strikes an object, all the colored lights except one are absorbed by the object. This one colored light is reflected to the eye and we say the object is a certain color. For example, grass absorbs all the colored lights except green, which is reflected to the eye and we say grass is green. A red rock looks red because all the colors of white light have been absorbed except red which is reflected to the eye. When all the colored lights are reflected to the eye, the object appears white. When all the colored lights are absorbed by the object it appears black because not one light is reflected to the eye. Black is actually the absence of all color, not a color.

The primary colors in colored lights are red, green, and blue. The primary colors of paints are red, yellow and blue. Every other color can be made by mixing different combinations of these primary colors. When colored paints are mixed, the results are different

than when colored lights are mixed. Because the paints are not
completely pure they reflect small amounts of other colors.
    The blue of the sky is actually due to dust. The dust in the
air scatters some of the blue color of sunlight and it is reflected
to the eye.

SOCIETAL IMPLICATIONS
    Being able to describe the environment clearly is the first level
of understanding the objects, organisms, and events that occur and have
an effect on each other. Learning common terms such as objects and
organisms increases our ability to communicate about the environment.
Color is an important and easily observed property of objects and
organisms. It is also a property that often indicates a change has
occurred.

MAJOR CONCEPTS
    -All non-living things in the environment can be referred to as
objects.
    -Living things in the environment can be referred to as organisms.
    -Living and non-living things have identities based on their
properties.
    -All objects and organisms can be described by their properties.
    -The property of color (or lack of color) can be used to describe
objects.

OBJECTIVES
    At the completion of the lesson the child should be able to:
    -Use the word object when referring to things in his/her environ-
ment.
    -Identify objects using the property of color.
    -Identify the colors: red, green, blue, orange, yellow, purple,
black and white.

MATERIALS
    Objects in the classroom

VOCABULARY
    -Object, red, green, orange, yellow, blue, purple, white, black,
properties

PROCEDURES
    1. Point to an object in the classroom and ask: What is this
object? Repeat this procedure for several objects in the room. The
children will respond with answers such as: a desk, the blackboard,
a pencil, a student, a plant, etc.

2. Hold up a piece of paper and ask: <u>What is this object</u>? Emphasize the word <u>object</u>. As soon as the children respond, point out the fact that you have referred to all the things as objects.

3. Reverse the questions used earlier. <u>What is the door</u>? <u>pencil</u>? <u>desk</u>? All are objects. Point out that <u>object</u> is just another word the child will use when talking about things in his environment.

4. Repeat these procedures (2-3) for the word organism. Ask: <u>How do you know objects/organisms are different</u>? Find some objects from the classroom. Have the children tell about the object. The objects should include the following colors: red, orange, yellow, green, blue and purple. At this time accept all responses that describe properties of the object.

5. Tell the children: <u>The reason you know objects/organisms are different is because they have different properties</u>. The color of an object is one property.

6. Place I KNOW MY COLOR WORDS on the board or a chart. Review the objects described before. As the children use a color to describe an object print the color word on the board.

7. Review the color words. You find an object and ask the children for the <u>property of color</u>. Point to a color word and have the children find an object with that color.

8. This procedure can be repeated for objects that are black and white.

Note: You should respond to the level of the child. If colors are known, progress faster; in other cases more review and a slower progression may be required.

Continually use the word OBJECTS when referring to non-living things in the classroom. Use the word ORGANISM when referring to living things. Likewise, use the word PROPERTY. The children will not use the word immediately. If you use it, and encourage them to use these words, soon the words will be theirs.

These words are <u>not</u> spelling words. They are intended to be incorporated into the child's vocabulary. Be sure the child has directly experienced the word. In other words, you are operationally defining the words.

Earth Materials: Natural and Synthetic
Grades K-2

ACTIVITY OVERVIEW
Natural and synthetic materials are introduced and described
in this lesson. A differentiation between object, property,and material
is established. Glass, paper, metal, plastic, cloth and wood are
examined in the lesson and later these materials are discovered within
the classroom and school.

SCIENCE BACKGROUND
The difference between natural and manmade products is an important
characteristic of materials. The use of resources for products,
the consumption of energy to produce products and the ability of the
environment to absorb and degrade waste products are all related to
the origin of objects of common human use.

Since World War II technological advancement has produced a
number of synthetic products that contribute to pollution in industrialized countries. Some of the changes are listed below.

Natural and Synthetic Products	
Natural	Synthetic
Fibers such as cotton and wool	Fibers using petroleum products
Foods	Food additives
Soap	Detergent
Natural Rubber	Synthesized Rubber
Fertilizer	Synthetic Fertilizer

SOCIETAL IMPLICATIONS
Some environmentalists argue that the introduction of synthetic
products has been the major cause of pollution. While this may be an
overstatement, it is still the case that many synthetic products such
as DDT, PCB,and food additives are products whose effects are not
clear and may indeed be harmful.

The technological production of synthetic materials is not,
however, the major source of pollution. Still we must learn to make
decisions about those products which are beneficial and those which
are harmful. As a first step in this process students should learn
to differentiate natural from synthetic materials.

MAJOR CONCEPTS
-Objects are composed of material.
-Materials have unique properties.
-Some objects are natural and some are synthetic.

OBJECTIVES
At the completion of this lesson the child should be able to:
-Identify the following materials: wood, metal, glass, plastic, paper, and cloth.
-Describe the properties of common material.
-Distinguish between an object, property and material.
-Differentiate between natural materials and man-made materials.

MATERIALS
-A small tray for each child
-At least one each of the following materials for each child's tray: paper, glass, wood, metal, plastic, and cloth. It is preferable to have more than one example of each material.
-You should also be aware of the objects within the classroom which are made of these various materials and those which are natural and man-made.
-A plant in a plastic pot
-One slotted chart for every group of three children It should be small enough to carry along with "material" cards. The general format should be as follows:

This object is made of _____		paper
paper	metal	glass
wood	cloth	cloth
plastic	glass	plastic
		metal
		wood

Note: The words on the chart are provided only for reference. Also this same format can be modified for objects that are made of more than one material; i.e., This object is made of these materials:

And this object is _____(natural, synthetic).

The teacher should have a set of materials for discussion. The set should include many common examples of natural and man-made materials. For example, PAPER; printed pages, kleenex, paper towel, cardboard, GLASS: mirror, drinking glass, eye glasses, windows, and bottles. The same is true for the other materials--wood, metal, cloth and plastic. Be sure to include an assortment of natural and synthetic products.

VOCABULARY

-Material, wood, metal, glass, plastic, natural, resource, paper, cloth, synthetic

PROCEDURES

1. Pass out the trays of materials to the children. Allow them to look at and handle the objects for a few minutes.

2. Start a discussion centering on their observations. <u>Tell me about the objects on your trays.</u> <u>What were some of their properties</u>?

3. Hold up a piece of paper and say, <u>This material is paper</u>. Then have the children find paper on their trays. You might also want to show them various forms of paper.

4. At this point turn the "invention" over to the children. <u>Who knows another material that is on their tray</u>? <u>Please describe the properties</u>.

5. Continue the discussion allowing the children to describe their objects and name the material. You may wish to record the names on the board. Also, see if the children can find objects in the classroom that are made of the same material. You can use some of your materials to start them.

6. Once the children have the idea of the lesson, have them determine which objects are natural and which are man-made. Let them come up with a first definition of these terms.

7. Bring a plant in a plastic pot to class. Have the children identify the materials (soil, plant, water, plastic) and which materials are natural and which are synthetic. Observe to see if they use the words object, property and material correctly.

The next step is an excursion around the school with slot cards (these are described under materials). Group the children in threes and provide them with the slot cards, material cards and directions appropriate to your situation. At this time they should focus their attention on objects made of only one material. The children should be given some freedom to explore their environment.

Allow them to explore materials around the school, preferably both inside and outside.

At a later date you may wish to complete this lesson. Select objects from around the room that are made of a) only one material, i.e. a glass slide and b) are made of a multiple of materials, i.e. a pencil.

Tell the children you are going to sort the objects and they have to find the reason for placing the object in one group or the other. Slowly place the objects of one material in one pile and the objects of more than one material in a second pile. Ask questions of the students and encourage their participation in the problem.

When they have discovered the solution start them on another excursion around the school with a modified slot card. (Repeat steps 6 and 7.) This slot card should allow for a multiple of materials. (See discussion under materials for this lesson.) Repeat this procedure for natural and man-made materials.

Changes in the Environment
Grades K-2

ACTIVITY OVERVIEW

In Part I the properties of materials are changed. The beginning of the lesson has the child change a piece of wood. Later he/she describes materials that have already been changed. After the transformation the material is still the same material. Wood blocks and wood shavings are still the material wood. This is a transition to the next section on changes.

Part II is an exploration with many objects designed to change. The concept of physical and chemical change is invented by the teacher. The concept is expanded in time and space through discussion and observation of changes past, present, and future and indoors, outdoors, and at home.

SCIENCE BACKGROUND

Matter can be modified by two very different processes: Physical changes and chemical changes. Matter is being changed in these ways all the time.

During the process of physical change, the substance remains the same, only its physical properties are changed. A piece of wood which has been sanded has changed in size and shape but it is still wood. Tearing a piece of paper into bits is another example of a physical change. When a pot boils over, a physical change is taking place because a substance is heated and expands. Cooling a substance and observing its contraction illustrates another physical change.

Matter can be changed from one of the three physical states (solid, liquid, gas) to another and this is also physical change, e.g., changing liquid water to solid ice. In a chemical change, a new substance is formed. The chemical characteristics are changed so they are different from the original substance. Burning wood, tarnishing silver, making yogurt are all examples of the process of chemical change. In order for chemical characteristics to be changed in a substance, energy--in the form of heat, light, or electricity--is either needed or given off.

SOCIETAL IMPLICATIONS

This is one of the first activities where children can start to conduct the activity with specific social implications. We are changing our environment in many ways. The bases for the changes are physical and chemical. Understanding these fundamental processes is a step toward preserving the land, water, and air since these are important to human existence. And, the limits to which the environment can be changed and still support life in a beneficial way are narrower than we usually perceive them to be.

MAJOR CONCEPTS
    -Material is conserved even if it has been changed.
    -The environment is constantly changing.
    -Change is a result of interaction between objects.
    -Changes vary in rate; some are fast and some are slow.

OBJECTIVES
    At the completion of this lesson the child should be able to:
    -Identify a material in its initial state and after it is changed.
    -Explain the changes in properties of materials that have been modified.
    -Explain that change occurs when two objects interact.
    -Identify a simple change and isolate the objects that interacted and the evidence that a change occurred.

MATERIALS
    Part I
    -A tray for each child
    -A piece of balsa wood and a piece of sandpaper for each child.
    -One set of the following for each group of two children: pine, mahogany, redwood, and cedar   The shavings should be in a plastic bag.
    -A magnifier for each child
    -A piece of sandpaper for each child
    -A small (2 x 2") piece of balsa wood for each child

    Part II
    -One tray per child
    -Each tray should have the following:
        a small piece of clay
        a piece of paper and crayon
        a scissors and string
        a small glass of water
        a small magnet and paper clips
        small pieces of colored candy that will dissolve or a sugar cube
        one page of a children's picture book that changes colors when
            the page interacts with water.(Many five and dime stores have
            these books.)
        Some sponges come in a compressed form, when water is added they
            swell very rapidly--these would also add to the interactions
            on the tray.

Note: You may think of other objects for the child's tray. Generally, you should follow these guidelines: 1) they should be of interest to the child, 2) there should be an obvious change as a result of interactions the child might initiate and 3) they should not be dangerous. Any substitute you wish to make should follow these guidelines. There should be enough materials on the tray that the child is enticed to explore the objects.

VOCABULARY
-Change, interaction, past, present, future, inside, outside, rate, fast, slow, sawdust

PROCEDURES
Part I

1. Allow the children to change a piece of balsa wood with sandpaper. A tray or piece of paper should be provided to avoid a mess.

2. Walk around the class and have the children explain what they are doing. Ask questions such as What are the properties of wood? How is the sawdust like the wood? Pointing to the sawdust and balsa wood ask: Are these the same material? Are they both wood?

3. Next distribute the blocks of wood, wood shavings and magnifiers. Have the children group the objects any way they would like. Have them explain their grouping. Ask them what they observed with the magnifier. What property did you use for classification?

4. After their discussion and classification ask them to group the wood shavings with the block from which it may have come. How are these materials similar? How are they different? How did you determine they were the same material.

Note: Part I is intended to mentally establish the concept of change through experience. Therefore, an elaborate discussion of change is not necessary at this time. Part II deals with change and the interaction of objects.

Wood was chosen because it is easy to find and prepare. Any material could be used. Examples include iron and iron filings, plastic and plastic shavings.

Part II

1. Pass out the trays and encourage the children to freely explore the objects. It is very important that appropriate time is allowed for the interaction and exploration.

2. After the children have had ample time to investigate the materials draw them together for a discussion. Have the children tell about their experience. What did you do that was most exciting? Tell what you did with the objects.

During the discussion try and focus the children's attention on 1) the objects that interacted and 2) the changes that occurred. Above all allow the children to tell you about their experiences.

3. The next part of the lesson you develop, through explanation, the concepts of change and interaction. Change is the result of objects interacting. Interaction is a relationship between objects: there is usually an evidence for interaction; this evidence is change either in the objects or in the new object.

You may wish to state these concepts on the board. Develop them one at a time, perhaps over several days. There are several important concepts here; they are also very confusing to young children unless they are explained in terms of their experience; do not rush, allow the children to grow into these understandings of their environment.

4. Do some simple demonstrations and have the children explain:
What objects interacted?
What was the evidence for the interaction?
What changes occurred?

Demonstrations: (Try these before class)
Use a small cart or car that either has a magnet attached or a metal axle. Using a strong magnet pull using the magnet at a distance.

Place a clear cup of water and white vinegar on a desk. Next to this place a clear cup with bromothymal blue and water. Have the children describe these objects. Pour them together into a third clear cup. A reaction turns the liquid in the third cup yellow.

An ice cube melting is a demonstration of a slow change. This can be started early in the demonstration. The three examples can point out rate of change. Which change was fast? Which change was slow? Extension of this concept is very important. A good place to start is the classroom--inside. Have the children find changes that are occurring now in the present, changes that occurred in the past, and possible changes in the future.

Depending on the grade level and understanding of the students you may wish to invent and clarify the difference between physical and chemical changes.

Measuring Changes in the Environment
Grades K-2

ACTIVITY OVERVIEW

Common objects from the room are measured initially. When
measuring skills have been developed a field trip outdoors is planned.
Each group of two students will be assigned a "plot" of ground that
they are to measure. This project should incorporate simple, but
varied measurements.

The concept of change is continued through the use of temperature. Preliminary activities introduce the children to the thermometer.
Initially numbers are not used to indicate temperature; rather the
terms cold, cool, warm, and hot are used to describe the temperature.

SCIENCE BACKGROUND

The earth is dynamic--changing. If there is one theme that is
basic to understanding the earth and environment it is change. Earthquakes, volcanoes, erosion, thunderstorms, and ocean currents are all
examples of change in the different realms of earth science.

Earth science is an investigation of changes in the planet earth
and the celestial sphere. Measurement is one of the fundamental ways
scientists know that change has occurred. Measuring the weight,
height, length, temperature, speed, color, volume, radioactivity,
sound, speed, and so on give an indication of the present state of an
earth material or earth system. It also provides a means of comparison
for the amount, type, and rate of change. Appropriate and accurate
measurements are essential to gathering information about changes in
the earth.

SOCIETAL IMPLICATIONS

Measuring changes in earth materials and earth systems helps us
define the limits within which changes are acceptable. Air pollution
is measured daily in most major cities. Newscasts often include
reports concerning the degree of air pollution and whether it is
acceptable for human activity. This is one simple example of the
ways measurements of environmental changes are important to society.
Other examples include: temperature, water pollution, and moisture
in the air.

MAJOR CONCEPTS

-Measurement can be used to indicate the rate and the degree of
change.

-Measurement provides a more exact description of an object and
changes.

-Temperature can be measured.

-As temperature changes, the indicator on the thermometer changes.

OBJECTIVES

At the completion of this lesson the child should be able to:

-Measure a common object such as a pencil or small piece of wood.

-Measure using an arbitrary unit of measure.

-Identify standard units of measure such as inches, feet, centimeters, and meters.

-Use a thermometer to find the relative temperature.

-Report the temperature using the correct term, i.e., hot, warm, cool or cold.

MATERIALS

Part I

-Objects for the child: six small rules for each.

-A tray for each child

-Two large boxes. One box should be just about big enough to fit in the second box.

-Cuisennaire rods, or any group of objects that are similar in all dimensions except size.

Part II

-A thermometer for each child. Either an unmarked thermometer with the numbers covered (see below) or something similar. If you are using this activity with older children, you should allow them to use a numbered thermometer.

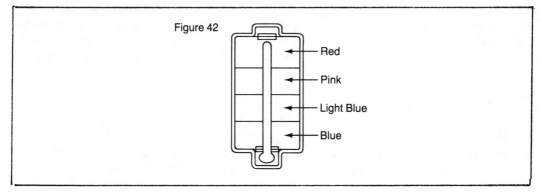

Figure 42

-Ice cubes covered with aluminum foil.

-Styrofoam cups.

-Each child should have a set of colored cards that are similar to the colors on the thermometer.

-Chart of the thermometer with the color code and appropriate words, i.e., hot, warm, cool, cold.

     —Measure, longest, widest, thermometer, temperature, hot, length,
width, warm, cool, cold, centimeters, meters, unit

PROCEDURES
     Part I
     1. Start the lesson with the two boxes and a problem: Can I get
this box in that box? The boxes should be separated and set up for
the demonstration. The children should not be able to tell whether
the box fits or not.
     2. Tell the students--These are the rules. We can move neither
box. We can use anything else (reasonable) in the room. Allow the
children to reason what might be useful. Generally, anything that
can be used to get the height and width of the box. String, long
paper, yardstick, ruler, etc. are usable.
     3. Let the children solve the problem with your direction.
     4. After the problem is solved draw the children together and
give them all three similar objects of different size, Cuisennaire
rods for example. Have each child hold up the smallest object they
have. Point out that many have different objects, and even though all
are small, some are larger than others. Repeat this with the children
finding the largest object in their collection.
     5. When this portion of the lesson is over introduce measuring
to the children. Start with a small Cuisennaire rod and simple
objects. At this time emphasize the idea of "unit". The stick they
are using is a "unit". How many "units" is the pencil, paper or
their desk. Can you put the "units" together and make a larger "unit"?
Continue this type of discussion with the children as you go from
desk to desk.
     6. Introduce the ruler. It is your decision whether you use the
metric system or the English system measurement; we strongly recommend
using the metric system.
     7. Show the children the "units" on their ruler. Allow them to
measure objects around the room or objects you have gathered and placed
on their trays.
     8. As the children work on their measuring, circulate around the
room, and discuss the concepts of length and width individually.
     9. The culminating activity of this part will be an outdoor
"measuring" trip. One thing this trip is designed to do is establish
the need for larger units of measure.
     10. Tell the children they are going outside and will stake a claim
on the school grounds. When this is done it is very important to
describe accurately the location of their claim. How are they going
to go about this? Prior to leaving the room help the children establish methods of measuring the claim. Generally it is possible to use
the city, streets and addresses, then school yard, and finally a

measurement within the yard. Some of these problems should be realized and overcome by the children.

Part II

1. Give the children two objects of different temperature. The easiest is probably two cups of water. Have the children describe the differences. If possible, play up any differences in description, i.e., warm to one child may be hot to another. Tell them you have a way to settle the discussion.

2. Distribute the thermometers and have the children examine them.

3. Next take the temperature of various objects in the classroom. For example, the ice cube, cups of water at different temperatures, the air in the room, the windows, the floor, vents, light bulbs (on and off). The first few times have the group take the temperature of the same object. You might start with the ice cube. Have them report using the colored paper that is the same as the paper on their thermometer. If the class holds up the paper, they can easily see there is a group concensus.

4. Show them the large temperature chart and tell them (also have labels) the red is <u>hot</u>, pink is <u>warm</u>, light blue is <u>cool</u> and blue is <u>cold</u>. This will give them a common vocabulary for discussion.

5. Allow the children to examine objects in their classroom. Also be sure to have them take the temperature outdoors.

6. Have the children "experiment" with the water by mixing it in different cups and seeing how the temperature changes.

7. An excellent extension of this outdoor activity is a simple counting exercise. With instruction such as "We are going to count some objects of your choice in the environment. You should know more about the objects after you counted than you did before." Objects such as: bricks, organisms, leaves, windows, materials, cars, garbage and things that the children think are pollutants can be used.

This activity introduces children to the immensity of the outside environment. Also, with the type of creativity many teachers have, addition, subtraction, division and multiplication can be applied to this activity. It might be called arithmetic with a focus on the child's environment. <u>What is being added to the environment? What is being subtracted? Is there anything being divided or multiplied?</u>

Are Changes Good or Bad?
Grades K-2

ACTIVITY OVERVIEW

The basis of many science related social problems is change in the environment. Many of these changes are bad as far as people are concerned. This activity starts with changes in the weather and a discussion of its influence as good, bad, or neutral. This discussion is then extended to observations of objects or organisms that can be seen or inferred to be increasing or decreasing in number. Later a discussion will center on these changes, measured or not, as good, bad, or neutral.

SCIENCE BACKGROUND

Change in the environment is cause for many personal decisions—value judgments—about those changes. In some cases the changes and judgments about change can be innocuous, e.g., determining that the weather is bad because it ruined your picnic. This example, and most others, should be viewed in a larger context. The same rain storm may have helped the crops, or resulted in a person's death. One important lesson learned from studying the earth is to determine which changes are indeed harmful to inhabitants and which changes are merely inconvenient. One important value makes the distinction clear—survival.

A second important lesson is to establish the time frame of changes that are deemed to be harmful. Some are very short such as the volcanic eruption of Mount St. Helens. Others are longer, such as the slow and steady pollution of the air, water, and land. Harmful changes such as the latter require us to predict what may happen in the distant future and to make changes to avoid the harmful consequences.

SOCIETAL IMPLICATIONS

Decision making is presently, and will certainly be in the future, one of the essential human attributes. Increasingly we are required to make decisions about the use of the natural world. Helping students realize that they must contribute to the decision making process is one of the new goals for science programs. The decisions must, however, be based on information, the facts of the matter, rather than opinions. Helping students to realize this goal is an important step in helping promote a better society.

MAJOR CONCEPTS

-Changes in the environment can be good, bad, or neutral.
-The environment is constantly changing.

OBJECTIVES
At the completion of this lesson the child should be able to:
-Describe changes in the environment.
-Identify changes that are good, bad, and neutral in the environment.

MATERIALS
-Charts for recording vocabulary

VOCABULARY
-Good, bad, neutral, increase, decrease, inference, observation

PROCEDURES
1. Call the students together and focus their attention on the temperature. Describe the changes in temperature that you observed. Have there been more (hot, warm, cool, cold) days recently? What do you think causes the changes in temperature? Point out some times when the temperature increased (decreased). At this time let the students determine the direction of the discussion for a period of time.

2. Shift to a discussion of weather. Is there any good weather recorded? Which weather has been bad? At this time "invent" the word neutral. Something that is neither good nor bad is a satisfactory definition at this point. What weather would you term neutral?

3. The next segment of this lesson is a field trip to the outside environment. The focus of the trip is to find objects or organisms that are increasing or decreasing. At the same time the children should make a decision about the worth of the change. Is it good, bad, or neutral? Can you measure the increases or decreases? If the children become interested, allow them to focus on some changes and actually gather data. This is a good opportunity to apply some of the experiences learned in earlier lessons. Some children will just make inferences about the changes. This is acceptable since the discussion later will distinguish between inference (guessing) and observation.

4. The heart of this lesson is the final discussion. The children should have gathered many experiences for the group discussion. The discussion should focus on the observations and judgments about the worth of the changes. Allow the children to tell about their observations. Have them differentiate between actual observations and inferences. What determines a (good, bad, neutral) change? What (objects, organisms) did you observe (increasing, decreasing)? Was the change (good, bad, neutral)?

Note: It is difficult to give directions for this discussion since it depends on student observations. The teacher's role in this discussion is facilitator, not dispenser. Be sure the children clarify, explain, and discuss their ideas.

5. The students can identify changes in the school, neighborhood, and community and determine if they are good, bad, or neutral. What other changes do they know about: pollution, population, etc. Ask them to describe what is being changed; what is the evidence for change, and if the change is good, bad, or neutral.

Changing Earth Materials: Solids, Liquids, and Gases
Grades K-2

ACTIVITY OVERVIEW
Two pieces of earth material are changed by the student. The way it is changed is entirely up to the individual. During a discussion the fundamental concept of weathering is developed. The overall scheme of change with systems is developed. The concluding activity is a field trip to find changed earth material around the school.

SCIENCE BACKGROUND
Physical changes and chemical changes are the two things that can happen to earth materials. These two changes occur all the time, e.g., bricks crumble, iron rusts. These two types of changes are very different and should not be confused.

Physical changes are easiest to observe; only the physical properties of material are changed and the material remains the same. In chemical changes the chemical properties of a material change so a new material is formed. The properties of the new material are different from those of the original material.

Examples of physical change include: the breaking up of rocks, the freezing of water, and the cooling of air. Examples of chemical change include: the melting of rocks, the addition of sulfur trioxide (SO_3) to water, and the addition of CO_2 to the air.

Energy is required or given off when a chemical change takes place. Heat, light, and electricity are the forms of energy used or omitted in chemical change.

SOCIETAL IMPLICATIONS
Changes of the environment are complex and interrelated. Some changes occur naturally while others are a result of human activity. Where are the limits? What are the trade-offs between human comfort and convenience and environmental degradation and depletion? Students will be making decisions related to issues such as these. Understanding the types, dynamics, and processes of natural and human changes of the environment are vital distinctions that should underlie human decisions concerning the use of the earth.

MAJOR CONCEPTS
- Change in nature occurs constantly.
- There are physical changes.
- There are chemical changes.
- Weathering is the breakdown of material in place.

OBJECTIVES
    At the completion of this lesson the student should be able to:
    -Explain the difference between physical and chemical change.
    -Describe examples of change in the immediate environment of
the school.

MATERIALS
    -A piece of earth material the student has collected. Generally,
rocks, concrete, and asphalt are best.
    -A plastic vial with water
    -A baggie filled with air
    -Halite or rock salt...large pieces if possible.

VOCABULARY
    -Earth, material, change, physical, chemical, evidence, inter-
action, weathering

PROCEDURES
    1. Have the students bring a piece of "earth material" to class.
    2. In a discussion bring up the following questions:
    What could cause changes in earth materials?
    How do you change something?
    How could you change a rock? A person? A liquid? A gas?
      An environment?
    How could you go about changing your earth material?
    3. Distribute a second piece of "earth material", the plastic
vial with water and the baggie.
    4. Ask the children to take their earth materials (solid, liquid
and gas) home and change them. Caution them to be careful and not do
anything dangerous.
    5. Have them record and keep track of the ways they changed
the material.
    6. The next day have a discussion about their changed materials.
Have them explain their "experiment". Could anyone get their material
back together? Describe how the materials changed.
    7. Record the different types of changes, i.e. physical change
is the breaking or reducing in size of the material. Chemical change
is the alteration of the materials. In general any breaking is
physical and application of liquids is chemical. The students will
use elaborate processes and combinations of physical and chemical
changes. Have them discuss these and try to have them isolate the
differences.
    8. The next day take the children on a trip around the school,
both indoors and outdoors. Have them find examples of the physical
and chemical alteration of earth materials.

9. Extend this activity to liquids and gases in the environment. Present these activities as challenges to the students. Can they change the earth material? What is their evidence for change? Was the change physical, chemical or both?

Studying an Environment
Grades K-2

ACTIVITY OVERVIEW

Small groups of children set up simple aquaria and observe changes. Cooperation among the children, collection of observations, and the introduction of concepts such as population, environment, and habitat are objectives.

SCIENCE BACKGROUND

Studying a small, contained environment such as an aquarium is a good way to introduce children to concepts influencing the environments in which they live. There are many interrelated and interconnected factors such as heat, light, and food, that influence the ability of an environment to sustain life. Some definitions seem an appropriate introduction.

Environment is the total of external factors that influence the life of an organism or population of organisms. Light, heat, and moisture are examples of environmental factors that influence organisms.

Population is a group of individual organisms of the same kind. All the students in the school, and guppies in the aquarium are population.

Ecology is the study of the relationships of living organisms with each other and with their environment.

These concepts incorporate the major levels of organization for the student of earth and environmental science. As study continues we shall see that environments vary, each having its own characteristics and organisms. Yet, all environmental systems are related.

SOCIETAL IMPLICATIONS

Changing environments beyond the capacity of organisms to adapt to them is a crucial problem society may be confronting. Though the problems occur at all levels in the organization of matter, the levels most perceptable to humans are: organisms - populations - communities - ecosystems - ecosphere. Other levels are also discussed and understood, for example, diseases at the cellular level due to environmental factors and pollution at the global level.

MAJOR CONCEPTS

-Birth, reproduction, and death are parts of the life cycle for organisms.

-A habitat is the place where an organism lives.

-A population is a group (two or more) of the same organism.

-An environment includes all the objects and organisms in an area.

OBJECTIVES

At the completion of this lesson the child should be able to:

-Describe aquaria habitats.

-Identify the populations in an aquarium.

-Describe birth, reproduction, and death of organisms in the aquaria.

MATERIALS

-A one gallon container for each group of two children. The cafeteria can usually save these if they are notified well in advance.

-Small plastic containers are also excellent.

-Labels

-2-3 cups of white sand per group. This is usually obtainable from lumber yards. It is also good to have some extra sand available.

-A plastic cup for each child

-A magnifier for each child

-A large 3-5 gallon container for storage of extra fish, snails, and plants

-1 bottle of liquid plant nutrient

-1 package of fish-food

-2-3 dip nets

The following can be obtained from a pet store. The quantities will depend on the number of children and groupings per aquaria. Each group should have ample quantities for their aquarium.

-guppies, 5-6 per group; duckweed, snails, elodea, eelgrass, Anacharis

VOCABULARY

-Fish, snail, plant, animal, organism, birth, reproduction, death, feeding, habitat, population

PROCEDURES

At the beginning of this section it should be noted that, due to the nature of living material, many things cannot be planned in advance. Once the aquaria are built things such as birth, death, and water evaporating will happen. Thus, it is important to be

prepared and flexible. There are numerous and varied activities
in and out of science that can be built on activity related to the
children's aquaria.

PREPARE AQUARIA

1. Several days before you obtain organisms start the lesson by
having the children clean and prepare their aquaria. Do not use soap.
Be sure both the containers and sand have been thoroughly washed.

2. Add 2-3 cups of sand to the aquaria.

3. If tap water is used allow it to stand in the container for
several days. During this time the content of chlorine and other
chemicals is reduced below a harmful level for the organisms.

OBSERVING ORGANISMS

4. When you bring the organisms, prepare a small plastic cup with
aged tap water, guppies, snails, and plants.

5. Distribute these (with magnifiers) to the children and allow
them to observe their organisms.

6. Have the children describe their organisms. Record these
descriptions on the board. Place the names of the organisms with
their description.

Questions the children should consider in their observations
include:

How do the different organisms move?
Do all plants stay at the same level?
How are the plants different? The same?
How are guppies alike? Different?

7. Have the children describe all the objects and organisms in
their environment--water, sand, and so on.

8. After description of the organisms and discussion about the
environment have the children add the organisms to their aquaria.

Note: Anacharis will float on the surface. Eel grass should
have the roots in the sand. Duckweed floats on the surface.

9. Label the aquaria. The children's names, quantity of guppies,
and plants should be included.

10. Place the aquaria in the room. They should not be placed in
direct sunlight.

11. Many events will occur in the aquaria during the next few
weeks. A few will be elaborated below. Possible suggestions and
direction are provided.

   A. Birth of guppies. How big are the young fish? Compare them
      to the adult. Which parent takes care of the young? Where
      do the babies stay most of the time? Do the babies eat the
      same things the adults do?

B. <u>Snail Eggs</u>. Where do the snails deposit their eggs? How many eggs have been laid? What do the young snails look like? How big are they?

C. <u>Death of a Fish</u>. Keep the fish in the aquarium. Use these as a learning activity. Organisms decompose upon death. What changes occur in the water? (Cloudy, due to bacteria; more algae; scum on water; odor). How does the fish's body change? What could cause a fish's death? (any selected change)? Much of the change i.e. cloudy water, odor, and different colored material is the result of bacteria growing on the wasting fish. Have the children describe the dead fish. If there are great numbers of dead fish, the odor will become very strong and offensive. Dispose of the fish after the discussion. You may wish to leave one fish in an aquarium until it completely decomposes.

D. <u>Determining male and female guppies</u>. If the children ask this question, help them design an experiment that will isolate 5-8 guppies of one kind (color) in an aquaria and 5-8 guppies of the other color in a second aquaria. Observe for a period of time and see which gives birth. The answer should then be obvious.

E. <u>Unplanned events</u>. Have the children discuss their observations, and if appropriate, plan a simple experiment that will investigate the problem. During the interim of study it is also important that you find one discussion period to establish the concepts of habitat (the place where an organism lives) and population (a group of similar organisms) and environment (all the living and non-living factors). Use the aquaria as a point of departure for these concepts.

The Environment Outside of the Classroom
Grades K-2

ACTIVITY OVERVIEW
This lesson utilizes many of the words introduced earlier as a focus words for observations of the student environment. It is a simple and straightforward attempt to apply some concepts and vocabulary to environments outside of the classroom.

SCIENCE BACKGROUND
Many of the concepts introduced earlier--physical and chemical changes, measurement, and states of matter can be applied to the study of environments. Studying a natural environment introduces many of the concepts fundamental to understanding earth systems. There are the populations of organisms (plants and animals) living and inter- acting in a certain area. This is called a community. The importance of studying the natural habitats is to see how organisms interact with one another and their physical environment.

A community of organisms interacting with one another and with their physical environments (sun, air, water, soil, wind, chemicals) is called an ecological system or ecosystem. An ecosystem is an area within which the input and output of matter and energy can be measured and related to environmental factors.

SOCIETAL IMPLICATIONS
We must understand the nature and functioning of the environment-- the interactions of the organisms and physical factors--in order to avoid the detrimental consequences of societal intervention. There is a delicate balance of natural environments. There is no better place to observe the interrelationship and functioning than in a small, natural environment.

MAJOR CONCEPTS
-Many things in the environment are relative, not absolute.

OBJECTIVES
At the completion of this lesson the student should be able to:
-Define three words from the given list.
-Present examples of the words from the immediate environment around the school.

MATERIALS
-An environment anywhere on or near the school. A list of words for reference. (It might be helpful to print the focus words on separate pieces of paper. You may wish to add words you feel appro- priate.)

VOCABULARY

-Systems, subsystems, interaction, relative, like, dislike, balance, object, color, repetition, variation, change, habitat, pollution, population, organisms, environment, community

PROCEDURES

1. The activity can be completed either individually or in groups of two.

2. Provide the children with <u>their</u> focus word (or allow them to make a choice).

3. Take them outdoors to the schoolyard or environment of your choice.

4. They are to focus their attention on examples of their word.

5. Have them report their observations to the class. Encourage them to use their words and words others have that relate to observations. They should also use the terms developed over the last 14 activities.

Note: This activity is designed to be more open than many of the others. Still, it has structure that is provided by the focus word.

-The time spent outside is an individual matter and should be decided by the teacher.

-If the children are interested, other projects and activities can emerge from this involvement.

6. Give the students different focus words and repeat the activity. Have them tell a story about their word and observations.

PLANNING CHART FOR EARTH AND ENVIRONMENTAL SCIENCE ACTIVITIES: GRADES 3–5

ACTIVITY	Conceptual Knowledge	Learning Processes	Psychomotor Skills	Attitudes and Values	Decision-making Skills	TEACHING METHODS	RELATED CURRICULUM
			OBJECTIVES				
68. Defining the Earth's Spheres	Earth's spheres have identities based on materials and organization.	Observe, classify, compare.		Learners explore environment.	—	Demonstration.	Language Arts.
69. Identifying Changes in a Terrarium	All groups and the environment change due to interaction.	Observe, classify, gather and organize information.	Learners handle and care for plants, animals, and earth materials without supervision.	Learners combine objects and materials in new ways.	Gather information and become aware of differences in environment and consequences of changes.	Team project.	Social Studies.
70. Conserving a Resource: Paper	There are limits to earth resources.	Gather and organize information.	Learners handle non-toxic substances.	Learners explore the environment.	Learners describe decisions that involve self and others.	Inquiry activity.	Social Studies, Math.
71. Recycling a Resource: Paper	Earth resources can be changed and reused.	Gather information.	Handle non-toxic substances.	Learners combine earth materials in new ways.	Learners describe alternative to disposing of waste paper.	Project.	Social Studies.
72. The Human Use of Resources	Resources are limited and sometimes not used wisely.	Observe, compare, gather information.	Use simple tools.	Learners compare alternative uses of natural resources.	Learners describe consequences of uses of natural resources.	Team project.	Social Studies.
73. The Use and Conservation of Earth Resources	Earth resources are limited and must be conserved.	Gather and organize information, infer, predict.	—	Learners attempt to compare alternative points of view with evidence.	Learners describe consequences of using earth resources.	Oral reports.	Language Arts.

285

Defining the Earth's Spheres
Grades 3-5

ACTIVITY OVERVIEW
The major encompassing units, or spheres, of the earth are defined through the use of a simple demonstration.

SCIENCE BACKGROUND
Usually earth science is divided according to discipline--geology, meteorology, astronomy and oceanography. The earth can also be studied by considering the major spheres or realms of which it is composed. The earth spheres are:

Lithosphere - Derived from the Greek word <u>lithos</u> meaning stone, and the word sphere meaning realm. The lithosphere usually refers to the crust and upper mantle of the earth. Geologists also refer to the asthenosphere, a region 75 to 175 km below the earth's surface where temperature and pressure is great enough to cause rock to flow more as liquids than solids.

Atmosphere - The air surrounding the earth. It might also be noted that atmosphere is a unit of measure for pressure. An atmosphere is equal to 1 kilogram per square centimeter.

Hydrosphere - The portions of the earth's surface that are covered by water. The hydrosphere includes oceans, lakes, rivers, ice caps, puddles, and so on.

Ecosphere - (Also biosphere) The sphere of land, water, and air in which all life is found.

Celestial sphere - This realm includes everything beyond the earth's spheres.

In the study of earth and environmental sciences, the earth spheres interact and have some effect on each other.

SOCIETAL IMPLICATIONS
One of the goals of science is to determine the similarities and differences among objects, organisms, and events that occur on earth. This too, is a goal for students' understanding of their earth. Defining the earth's spheres will help students conceptualize the identities of earth materials and organisms and the interactions and changes among the spheres.

MAJOR CONCEPTS
-Earth spheres have identities based on their materials and organization.
-Earth materials can change and still maintain their identities.
-Earth materials change due to interactions with other earth materials.

OBJECTIVES
At the completion of the lesson the child should be able to:
-Use the words - lithosphere, atmosphere, hydrosphere, biosphere and celestial sphere when referring to realms of the earth.
-Identify earth materials as belonging to one of the earth's spheres.
-Describe simple interactions between earth's spheres.

MATERIALS
-A jar with a cap
-Sand and/or pebbles
-Water

VOCABULARY
-Atmosphere, biosphere, celestial sphere, hydrosphere, lithosphere

PROCEDURES
1. Obtain a jar with a cap or lid.
2. Fill the jar half full of water.
3. Add about 4 cm of sand to the jar.
4. Shake the jar for about 10 seconds and then place it on a desk for the students to observe.
5. Ask the students to record what happened in the jar.
6. Ask the students - Why did the air bubbles go to the surface of the water? Why did the sand go to the bottom? What is above the water?
7. Place these words and definitions on the chalkboard. Go over the words and discuss the materials and properties of the different earth spheres.

Figure 43

Atmosphere - The air that surrounds the earth.
Ecosphere - The spheres of air, water,and land in which life is found
Celestial Sphere - The sky beyond the atmosphere.
Hydrosphere - The parts of the earth that are covered with water.
Lithosphere - The crust of the earth.

8. Ask the students – <u>What are two ways you can tell the difference between (among) earth spheres</u>?

9. <u>Where is the biosphere in relation to the jar</u>? <u>The earth?</u> (How far above/below the earth's surface are organisms found?) <u>In which other spheres are organisms found? How would you classify the celestial sphere</u>?

10. Bring several pieces of earth material to class--solid, liquid, and gas--have the students identify them as belonging to the different spheres. Use <u>them</u> as a part of the ecosphere, and use a planet or sun for the celestial sphere.

11. Go on a short trip outdoors and have the students use the words – lithosphere, hydrosphere, ecosphere, atmosphere, and celestial sphere to classify objects.

Identifying Changes in a Terrarium
Grades 3-5

ACTIVITY OVERVIEW

The first part of the lesson deals primarily with the construction of terraria. This is intended to be an introduction to terraria and an extension of the lesson on earth spheres. Later if you and the children so decide, specific terraria ecosystems such as desert, bog, or garden can be developed. As the children place organisms in their terraria the emphasis shifts to concepts experienced but not "invented" earlier. These are concepts such as population, habitat, environment, and the organism's response to environmental factors.

SCIENCE BACKGROUND

A community (the populations of plants and animals in a specific locality) of organisms interacting with one another and their physical environment (energy and matter) is called an ecosystem. In a sense the terrarium is a small ecosystem. The terrarium provides an ideal way for students to conceptualize the interconnectedness of the atmosphere, hydrosphere, lithosphere, and ecosphere.

The major components of the terrarium (ecosystem) are non-living and living. The non-living (abiotic) part includes the source of energy (solar) physical factors such as light, heat, and chemicals in the soil. The living (biotic) portion of the terrarium can be divided between the producers of food and consumers of food.

The students will soon find that the plants and animals in their terrarium require certain amounts of chemicals such as carbon dioxide, oxygen, nitrogen, phosphorus, and sodium. They also require certain temperatures, light, and moisture. All organisms have a range of tolerance to these chemical and physical factors. Too much or too little of any one or combination of the factors can have detrimental effects on the organism. The students will intuitively come to understand the importance of limiting factors as they try to achieve a balanced ecosystem in their terrarium.

SOCIETAL IMPLICATIONS

The terrarium is a micro example of the interdependent nature of earth systems; air keeps plants and animals alive, water and air provide needed chemicals, plants absorb carbon dioxide and give off oxygen, the soil supports plants and animals consume plants and so on. It also shows the delicate balance that exists between the various earth spheres and their ability to support life.

As a society we are coming to understand that upsetting the balance of the earth's systems can have unpredictable and undesirable effects elsewhere. One of the several important goals of studying science is to understand the interdependent nature of earth systems and how delicate the relationship is among the earth's spheres.

PROCEDURES
    Building the terraria
    1. Place the materials around the room so the children can gather materials and build their terraria.
    2. At this initial stage let them build the terraria as they see fit. The only limitations are following:
        A. Place about 3 cm of gravel on the bottom of the terraria.
        B. Soil is to be placed on top of the gravel.
        C. Do not overpopulate the terraria with bean seeds – 5-10 should be sufficient.
        D. Each group's terraria should have at least one organism of each type but not more than 10 of each type.
    3. There will be a variety of terraria developed even with these limitations. This is exactly what is intended. At this time the results of these different factors is more important than the establishment of a nice stable classroom terraria.
    4. The following information should be recorded on the terraria:
        A. Team members names
        B. Date completed
        C. Number and type of seeds planted
        D. Number and type of organisms
    5. Allow the children to place their terraria where they choose.
    6. Allow the children to observe their terraria over the next two weeks. In general, there will be a noticeable decline in the number of organisms. These should be noted and possible reasons, causes or contributing factors should be discussed by the children.
    7. When the children discuss changes in their terraria encourage them to use the terms organism, population, environment, and habitat. You may wish to define these early in the discussion.
        --a group of organisms living in a particular habitat is a population
        --a habitat defines the place where an organism lives.
        --environment includes all the factors (external) which affect an organism. What factors (light, heat, moisture) could be affecting the organism in your terraria?

    8. After a period of time the total number and kinds of organisms with which the children started should be recorded. Collect this from their original records. Have them keep track of organisms that are either missing or dead. This could be a group graphing activity. Establish a chart such as the one on the following page.

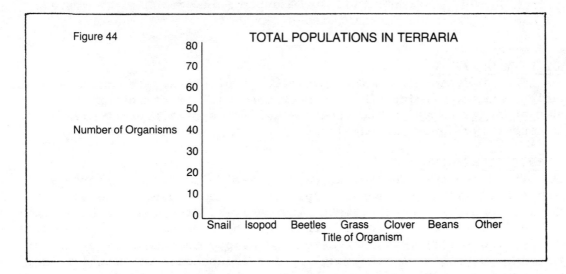

Figure 44
TOTAL POPULATIONS IN TERRARIA

Number of Organisms (vertical axis: 0, 10, 20, 30, 40, 50, 60, 70, 80)

Snail   Isopod   Beetles   Grass   Clover   Beans   Other
Title of Organism

Accumulate the total for each group. As the populations decrease reduce the size of the graph.

9. When an appropriate amount of change has been recorded have a class discussion focusing on the question - <u>Which factors do they think affected their organisms</u>? Environmental factors such as: light, air, heat, moisture, and temperature are usually listed. Which environmental factors affect them? Other people?

Note: A good follow up after the invention of environmental factors are experiments with the effect of these factors on organisms. The establishment of limits, types of responses, and natural variation in factors.

--A series of experiments can be designed to investigate the influence of various environmental factors on one animal (a second group can use plants).

--A second series of experiments can be designed to investigate the effect of <u>one</u> environmental factor and various animals (a second group can use different plants).

10. Have the children identify a population in the classroom, school, and community.

11. Have the children list three things that influenced the plants and animals in their terrarium.

12. Take the children outside and have them locate at least one habitat. The students can then design and maintain terraria representing different ecosystems: woodland, bog, desert, weed, tundra, etc.

After the preliminary activities with terraria follow up field trips around the school will have established concepts such as population, habitat, and environment. These trips should try to establish numbers and types of populations that can be found; their habitats and a description of environmental factors that may affect their existences.

Conserving a Resource: Paper
Grades 3-5

ACTIVITY OVERVIEW
The students will monitor the amount of paper used in their class during a week. During the same week they will try to determine how much paper is wasted. The students will then brainstorm to find ways of conserving paper in the class.

SCIENCE BACKGROUND
There are two fundamental ways to deal with present shortages of resources: (1) increase the supply and (2) decrease the demand. While we will continue to pursue both alternatives, it seems the best alternative is the combination of decreasing the demand, by changing life styles, and effectively increasing the supply through more efficient use and less waste of resources. These ideas are fundamental to the conservation ethic.

SOCIETAL IMPLICATIONS
Most agree that our society must start practicing greater resource conservation. Presently, we over-package and over-use resources and then try to recover some of the waste. A much simpler approach is to not use a resource such as paper in the first place. A reduction in paper packaging in the United States would not only save trees it would also save energy.

Related to the activity on paper, our society uses some 58 million tons of paper each year. This equals about 572 pounds per person. Newspapers alone account for 17% of our use of paper. About one fourth of the paper used is for containers such as paper cups.

MAJOR CONCEPTS
-There are limits to some earth resources.
-Conservation is one method of preserving resources.
-Conservation is the use of natural resources in ways that assure their future availability.
-Resources are sometimes used unnecessarily.

OBJECTIVES

At the completion of this activity the student should be able to:
-Explain that some resources are limited.
-Define waste in terms of resource use.
-Describe ways of reducing paper waste in the classroom.
-Describe the relationship between supply and demand in the classroom.

MATERIALS
    -pencils, paper (various types that are used in a typical school week), garbage bags

VOCABULARY
    -Conservation, demand, limited, reduce, resource, supply, waste, unlimited

PROCEDURES
    1. At the week's beginning count the number of sheets of paper that form the week's supply. At this time you should not worry about limiting the supply. Behave as though the supply is unlimited. Be sure to include all the different types of paper that may be used during the week. At week's end you will determine the remaining sheets of paper and thus be able to determine the amount of paper used.
    2. Place the stacks of paper in a place visible to all the students.
    3. Have each student set up a tally sheet to determine the amount and types of paper used each day.
    4. Continue the student tally for a week. Over the weekend have the students determine how much, and what types, of paper they used during the week. You should also determine the amount and types of paper used from your supply.
    5. On Monday discuss the results. During the discussion use the words supply and demand. You should also discuss any discrepancy between your tally of the supply and the student's cumulative use of paper. Bring up the topic of waste. How is paper wasted? How much paper is wasted? Can waste be prevented?
    6. Brainstorm ways that the class can reduce their use (demand) of paper and still accomplish their educational goals. Tell them they are going to try some of the measures during the week. Students may suggest: being more careful, setting up and using paper in different ways, using both sides of the paper, and reusing some waste paper.
    7. Have the class determine one or two conservation measures that they wish to use. Implement these measures over the week. Keep track of the results as you and the students did earlier.
    Note: A variation of this activity is to reduce or limit the supply. For example, each student will only have two pieces of paper a day. How will they be used?
    You could also reduce the classroom supply for the week by 1/3. Then, as the supply is depleted discuss means of conserving the remainder. Have the students determine other "resources" in the classroom and how they could be conserved.

Recycling a Resource: Paper
Grades 3-5

ACTIVITY OVERVIEW
In this activity the students will actually recycle some paper
from their classroom.

SCIENCE BACKGROUND
There is a difference between recycling and reuse. Recycling
is the collection and changing (e.g., melting) of a resource. Reuse
is the use of a product over again without changing the product. Of
course, products that are reused are cleaned and washed. This distinction
should be clear because it is not efficient to recycle some resources
that could be reused. Glass bottles serve as a good example of the
reason for this distinction. Crushing and remelting disposable glass
bottles uses 3 times more energy than it would to reuse returnable
bottles. A reasonable conclusion is to ban nonreturnable bottles and
encourage the use of returnable bottles.
Recycling has several advantages over the use of raw materials.
Recycling decreases the need for unused resources, it reduces waste
and can save energy in the production of materials. In addition it
can reduce pollution and land use.

SOCIETAL IMPLICATIONS
Recycling half the paper thrown away each year would conserve
trees and save enough energy to provide electricity for 10 million
people annually. The same amount of electricity would be saved if
our society used returnable bottles instead of the 60 billion throw-
away containers produced annually. In spite of these unsightful
statistics, our society does little recycling. Instead we produce,
use, discard, burn, and bury virtually billions of dollars of resources
annually. Recycling is a viable alternative to resource use. During
World War II the United States recycled approximately 35% of its paper;
compared to 15% recycled in 1975.

MAJOR CONCEPTS
-Some earth resources can be recycled.
-Recycling is the collection and changing (melting) of a resource
so it can be used again.
-Reuse is using a resource again without changing the material.

OBJECTIVES
    At the completion of this activity the student should be able to:
    -Define recycle.
    -Define reuse.
    -Differentiate between reuse and recycle.
    -Describe the process of recycling paper.

MATERIALS
    -Blender (or egg beater), iron, 2 small frames for each group
(you might use small 6" x 6"), water color frames, paper towels for
blotters, 2 dishpans, sponge, staple water, wastepaper from the class,
wire screen

VOCABULARY
    -Deckle, mold, reuse, recycle, slurry

PROCEDURES
    1. Make two small frames per group. The frames should be the
same size.
    2. Staple wire screen to one frame (the mold).
    3. Tear up the waste paper (newspaper and sketch paper are best)
and soak it in a dishpan of warm water. (You may wish to add detergent or bleach to the water. This will result in lighter paper.)
    4. Place the soaked paper in a blender and blend (or beat) it.
Place the blended paper (slurry) into the second dishpan.
    5. Have the students place the empty frame (the deckle) on top of
the mold frame (screen side up).
    6. The students should dip both frames into the dishpan of
slurry.
    7. They should raise the frames slowly out of the water. Allow
the water to drain back into the dishpan, then remove the top frame.
    8. Turn the screen over and place it on a paper towel blotter.
    9. Sponge dry the screen.
    10. Remove screen while leaving recycled paper (called wet leaf)
on the blotter. Place another piece of blotter paper on top of the
"wet leaf."
    11. Iron the papers dry (do not remove blotters).
    12. Remove blotters and examine the recycled paper.
    13. Use the recycled paper to write a note to your parents or a
friend.
    14. In a discussion define recycling and reuse for the students.
    15. Have the students determine ways they can 1) recycle paper
and 2) reuse paper.

    16. Present the students with pop bottles, aluminum pop cans,
milk bottles,and old cloth. Ask them which materials could be reused

and which could be recycled. Have them describe how the above materials could be recycled and/or reused.

17. Set up a recycling center for the school. You could start with aluminum cans and/or paper.

The Human Use of Resources
Grades 3-5

ACTIVITY OVERVIEW
In this lesson students explore the natural resources that are used in the production of a common product.

SCIENCE BACKGROUND
The term resources refers to the total amount of a material that exists on the earth. Many of the resources cannot be obtained at reasonable costs; so, they are in effect not available for human use. New discoveries, improved technology, and increased prices can make the mining of resources feasible. Conservation and recycling, reusing substantially and using existing resources longer can also effectively make resources more available. Note that several of these changes directly relate to the human side of the equations and infer such things as changes in life style.

SOCIETAL IMPLICATIONS
Our society is one of high consumption of resources and energy combined with low recycling and reuse of waste. There are a couple of often cited facts that relate to the background for this activity.
      -In the last 35 years we have achieved a high standard of living; to do so we have used more mineral resources and fossil fuels than all the peoples of the world have used throughout history.
      -Each year we use about 33 percent of the total world's consumption; yet we represent only 5 percent of the population.
The human use of resources is necessary. But the question must be asked--is our present life style conducive to our own well being, much less the rest of the earth's populations?

MAJOR CONCEPTS
      -Resources are limited.
      -Many resources are used in the preparation of common products.

OBJECTIVES
At the completion of this activity the student should be able to:
      -Diagram the resources used in the preparation of a common product.
      -Describe the interdependence of many resources in the preparation of products for human use.

MATERIALS
      -Large pieces of butcher paper
      -Colored pencils or pens
      -Packaging materials from a commonly known product

VOCABULARY

—Consumer, interdependence, energy, preparation, resource, product

PROCEDURES

1. This activity is best done with a "field trip" to obtain the materials to be analyzed. You might, for example, plan to lunch at McDonald's or some other place of interest to the students and convenient to the school. An alternative is to have the students save all the materials (except perishables) from a trip to a fast food restaurant.

2. Divide the class into groups of 2 or 3. Have each group analyze one set of package materials from their trip. Have them also analyze the food that was packaged. Be sure they include any condiments used.

3. Use a large piece of butcher paper to diagram the products. Start with the package materials and food in the center. Then draw lines out from the center showing the raw materials for the product. For example paper ◄——— tree - or - meat ◄——— cattle.

Depending on the level and interest of the group, continue this activity by having them include the types of energy required to transform the raw materials. Likewise they can continue the diagram back to primary energy sources and raw materials.

4. Have the groups present their charts to the class.

5. Point out the interdependence and interrelationships in the raw materials to consumable products sequence. Ask the students to determine if it was necessary/unnecessary in the sequence. How can things be changed if raw materials become scarce?

Note: It is not the objective of the lesson to be pro or con concerning the specific product or producer, e.g., McDonalds. This is an information gathering activity.

6. Ask the children how they would be willing to change in order to save some of the resources.

The Use and Conservation of Earth's Resources
Grades 3-5

ACTIVITY OVERVIEW
Students are introduced to several of the earth's resources through oral/written reports by other students. The reports include a description of the resource, its use, limits, and means of conservation.

SCIENCE BACKGROUND
Will we have enough? This is an important question concerning our use of the earth's resources. But first, what is a resource? Abundance or scarcity of a material depends, in part, on how we define resource. In a broad sense a resource is anything needed by an organism, population, or ecosystem. We must enter the human use of resources into this simple definition. The usefulness or uselessness of a resource can change because of humans. Specifically, we must consider three things as they relate to the use and conservation of earth's resources: (1) technological advances for improving, extending, using efficiently and recycling; (2) the economics of recovery and production; and (3) the environmental impact of mining; processing and production. Examples of the three points include more efficient use of coal to produce electricity through technological advances; finding and mining scarce materials increases the price of products until they are too expensive for human use; environmental damage or the use of highly toxic substances, such as lead or mercury, also influences the human use of a resource.

Resources can be grouped as seen in Figure below.

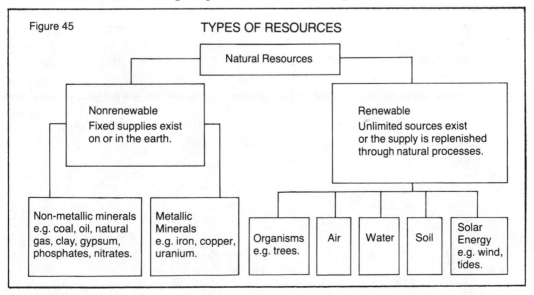

SOCIETAL IMPLICATIONS

In the future decades resource use by industrial societies will probably increase. At the same time many less developed countries are also planning on developing which will increase their use of resources. The combined use of resources such as fossil fuels, wood, food, and metals could cause critical depletion that would, in turn, influence other social factors such as economic instability and population growth.

MAJOR CONCEPTS

-A resource is anything needed by an organism, population, or ecosystem.
-Some resources are renewable.
-Some resources are nonrenewable.
-As resources become scarce conservation measures may be used.

OBJECTIVES

At the completion of this activity the student should be able to:
-Define resource.
-Differentiate between renewable and nonrenewable resources.
-Describe some conservation measures for earth resources.

MATERIALS

-Pencil, paper, library, time

VOCABULARY

-Conservation, preservation, resource, renewable, nonrenewable

PROCEDURES

1. Have the students select a topic for their written and oral report. The broad topic is "The Conservation of Earth's Resources." Each student should select a specific resource on which to report. Some topics include: Air, Water, Food, Land Use (Parks, Wilderness, etc.) Minerals, Energy (fossil fuels, nuclear, geothermal, solar, etc.) and Wildlife.

2. Tell each student that the report should include a description of the resource, where it is found, what it is used for, its abundance (or shortage) and possible conservation measures. If there are controversial topics, the student should try and present arguments for and against use and/or conservation of the resource.

3. Give the students two weeks to work on the report. Some time for their work should be provided during school.

4. Students should present their reports orally and turn in their written report. Suggested length of the oral report is 5-10 minutes. Suggested length of the written report is 3-4 pages.

PLANNING CHART FOR EARTH AND ENVIRONMENTAL SCIENCE ACTIVITIES: GRADES 6–8

ACTIVITY	OBJECTIVES						TEACHING METHODS	RELATED CURRICULUM
	Conceptual Knowledge	Learning Processes	Psychomotor Skills	Attitudes and Values	Decision-making Skills			
74. Population Growth	Environments change because living and non-living matter interact.	Graph, infer, predict, form hypothesis.	Writing, computing.	Combine ideas in new ways.	Learners.describe situations that require decisions.	Problem solving.	Math.
75. Finding Resources	There are limits to environmental change.	Infer, predict, graph.	Handle non-toxic substances.	Combine objects and materials in new ways.	Learners describe situations that require decisions.	Exploration, discovery.	Social Studies.
76. Consuming Resources	There are limits to environmental change. Environments can lose their identity.	Graph, infer, predict, describe relation of variables.	Handle non-toxic substances.	Learners seek alternative points of view.	Learners clarify consequences of alternatives.	Simulation.	Social Studies.
77. Distributing Resources	There are limits to the capacity of the environment to change.	Interpret, gather information.		Learners act on attitudes, state a position.	Learners describe immediate and long-term consequences of decision.	Simulation.	Social Studies.
78. Pollution and the Earth's Spheres	When the capacity to change is exceeded, environments lose their identities.	Observe, interpret, infer, predict.		Learners seek multiple sources of evidence.	Learners form alternatives and identifies consequences.	Inquiry.	Social Studies.
79. Noise Pollution	Environments change because living and non-living matter interact.	Observe, classify, gather information.	Learners use materials.	Learners combine objects and materials in new ways.	Learners describe immediate and long term consequences.	Exploration, discovery.	Social Studies.
80. Is Wind Power a Feasible Energy Source?	Environments change because living and non-living matter interact. Energy is required for interactions.	Observe, classify, infer.	Handle non-toxic substances.	Learners explore environment and ask questions.	Learners describe immediate and long-term alternatives.	Exploration, discovery.	Social Studies.
81. Air Pollution: A Demonstration of Thermal Inversion	When the capacity to change is exceeded, environments lose their identity.	Observe, infer.		Learners demonstrate need to use environment wisely.	Learners describe immediate and long-term consequences.	Demonstration.	Social Studies.
82. Population, Resources and Environment	Environments have identities based on properties and change because living and non-living matter interact.	Gather and organize information.	Writing.	Exploration of ideas.	Learners describe situations that require decision.	Oral and written reports.	Social Studies.

301

Population Growth
Grades 6-8

ACTIVITY OVERVIEW
     A riddle on exponential growth rates starts the activity. The
students then plot graphs for exponential growth rates and discover
the slow early growth and rapid later growth that presents problems.

SCIENCE BACKGROUND
     The activity graphically presents the concept of exponential
growth. The form of the graph is a "J"⌐ shaped curve. This is
the curve that results when any population grows by doubling, e. g.,
1, 2, 4, 8, 16, 32, 64, 128, and so on. Growth seems slow at first
and then it increases very rapidly as the bend in the "J" is reached.
(see Table and Figure in the procedures).

SOCIETAL IMPLICATIONS
     It is estimated that by the year 2000 the world's population will
be 6.35 billion. This is an increase of more than 50% over the 1975
population of 4.0 billion. The world population growth rate is in
the step part of the J curve. There are approximately 200,000 new
persons on earth each day, 1.4 million a week and about 72 million a
year. All of these new persons are to be housed, fed, clothed, and
cared for by the resources presently available, because resources are
not also increasing at a geometric rate. Those resources that can be
increased, e.g., food, do so at an arithmetic rate. Over 1/3 of the
earth's population is already in need of food, housing, clothing, and
other essentials.
     The population growth rate seems to be leveling off. In order
to sustain those living on earth this trend will have to continue.

MAJOR CONCEPTS
     -The present rate of population growth is exponential.

OBJECTIVES
     At the completion of this activity the student should be able to:
     -Identify an exponential growth rate.
     -Describe the consequences of population growth.
     -Construct a graph showing an exponential growth rate.

MATERIALS
     Film: World Population - order from Southern Illinois University,
Carbondale, Illinois
     -Graph paper, pencils

VOCABULARY
     -Population, growth, exponential, linear

PROCEDURES
     Note: This activity has one simple objective – to leave the
student with an understanding of the exponential growth of a population.
Later lessons can deal with birth rate/death rate and problems of overpopulation.
     1. Start with what is now a famous French riddle. Just before
the end of a class give the students the riddle as homework.

     There is a lily pond that has a single leaf.
     Each day the number of leaves doubles.
     On the second day there are two leaves.
     On the third day there are four leaves.
     On the fourth day there are eight leaves.
     On the thirtieth day the pond is full.
     When was the pond half full?

     Leave the students with this riddle as homework. (the answer is
the 29th day).
     2. On the next day start the class with the film "World Popula-
tion." (See Materials). This is a four minute silent film that
illustrates world population growth extraordinarily well. Do not say
anything about the film, simply start the projector. The students will
be amazed at the rate of population growth depicted in the last seconds
of the film. They will then have a first conceptualization of the
problems of exponential growth. Discussing the film and the riddle
should provide an excellent introduction to population growth rates.
     3. Depending on the level of the class have them graph an
exponential growth rate. You can use a simulation of two female
rabbits that each have two offspring a month. And these, in turn have
two offspring a month and so on. (See Figure 46). Tell the students
to plot this for a school year of nine months.

Figure 46
Simulated Growth of Rabbits for a School Year

2 x 2 = 4	1st month (Sept.)
4 x 2 = 8	2nd month (Oct.)
8 x 2 = 16	3rd month (Nov.)
16 x 2 = 32	4th month (Dec.)
32 x 2 = 64	5th month (Jan.)
64 x 2 = 128	6th month (Feb.)
128 x 2 = 256	7th month (Mar.)
256 x 2 = 512	8th month (April)
512 x 2 = 1024	9th month (May)

4. A second, more difficult problem can be presented as a challenge. Have the students determine (and graph) the thickness of paper pages that double. Show them the thickness of a piece of paper and ask them to estimate how thick it is (about 0.1 millimeter or 1/254 inch). Tell them to first estimate the thickness of paper they would have if they doubled the thickness 50 times, i.e., 1st = 0.2, 2nd = 0.4, 3rd = 0.8, 4th = 1.6, 5th = 3.2, 6 = 6.4. Have them figure this exponential rate up to 50. And then, very importantly have them graph the results. Graphing will clearly demonstrate the slow beginning of growth and then the sudden increase (See Figure 47 below) of the   shaped curve. (Note: in completing this challenge the students will have to change from millimeters to meters to kilometers in order to graph the changes)

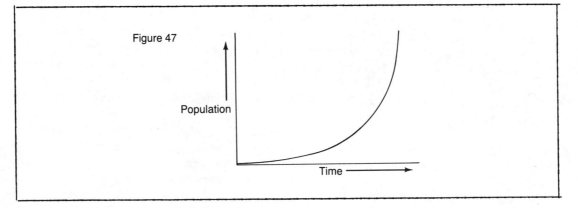

Figure 47

Population

Time

5. Discuss the results of their activity. Apply these ideas to world population growth. Be sure to use your "resident experts."
6. Give the students several growth curves and have them identify an exponential curve and an arithmatic or linear growth rate.

Finding Resources
Grades 6-8

ACTIVITY OVERVIEW

Finding pennies hidden around the room is used to simulate the difference between reserves and resources. As the activity continues the students experience the important factors in finding new resources: technology, economics, and environmental effects are developed. The concepts of this activity relate to many resources, including energy.

SCIENCE BACKGROUND

As population and affluence increase there is also an increased demand for resources--those earth materials needed by persons, populations, and ecosystems. With resource depletion there is continued exploration and extraction of resources by those who provide resources. But, as it turns out, as resources are depleted, new reserves are not as easy to find. Exploration is longer, harder, and uses more sophistiscated technologies, and likewise extraction is longer, harder, and uses more complex equipment. These two factors increase the potential for environmental damage.

The availability of many resources can be increased through recycling, reuse, conservation, and substitution. These measures, however, require a shift in present attitudes and values.

SOCIETAL IMPLICATIONS

The human use of resources and the possibility of changing attitudes and values is not unrelated to economics. As available resources are depleted it costs more to find, extract, and produce resources for use. As resources become less available the costs continue to increase. This may result in further exploration and use of resources in forms not usable at early times, for instance, using lower grade ores can become economically feasible. The increase in costs can also stimulate other approaches such as recycling, reuse, and substitution. Greater use of small, gas efficient cars, is an example of this process and the resulting changes in public attitudes and values.

MAJOR CONCEPTS

-Resources are earth materials needed by individuals, populations, or ecosystems.

-Resource refers to the total amount of an earth material.

-Reserves refers to the amount of an earth material in known locations.

-The use of resources depends on technology, economics, and the environmental effects of obtaining the resources.

OBJECTIVES

At the completion of this activity the student should be able to:

-Define resource.

-Describe the difference between reserves and resources.

-Describe the role of technology, economics, and environmental effects on the extraction and use of resources.

MATERIALS

-100 pennies, tweezers, toothpicks, small mirrors

-Other items commonly available in the classroom

VOCABULARY

-Economics, environmental impact, exploration, reserves, resource technology

PROCEDURES

1. Place the 100 pennies around the room. About 25 should be in locations that are visible and very easy to reach. The remaining 75 should be placed out of view and in places such as under chairs, under paper and boxes, on ledger, between tiles, in erasers, etc.

2. Divide the students into groups of four. Tell them that the activity simulates the exploration and extraction of earth materials (resources) that are needed by individuals, populations or ecosystems. There are pennies located around the room that represent resources.

3. First, have the students go on an <u>exploration</u>. Give each group five minutes to look around the room to determine how many pennies are in the room. The rules of the exploration are: 1) they cannot touch, turn over, dig up or otherwise change anything in the room; and 2) they cannot collect any pennies; all pennies must remain where they are. Give the groups five minutes to explore for the pennies.

4. Call the class together and have the different groups report on the number of pennies they observed. Place the numbers on the board along with the definitions:

Reserves - the amount of an earth material in known locations.

Resources - the total amount of an earth material

Figure 48

GROUPS	1	2	3	4	5	6	7
RESERVES							
ESTIMATES OF RESOURCE							

5. Ask the groups to estimate the resources (pennies) that are in the classroom. Record these on the chart.

6. In the next portion of the activity the students are to actually "mine" the resources. Tell the students that they are to keep track of the number of pennies they find and obtain each minute. Do not indicate how many are available or where they are located. But, indicate that the students must use tweezers, toothpicks, mirrors or other items to <u>look</u> under items for pennies, extract pennies, turn over things and so on. That is, they cannot simply turn a book over and look for a penny; they cannot lift up a desk and remove a penny from under a leg.

7. Allow the student-groups 20 minutes to obtain as many pennies as possible.

8. Have them complete a graph of the number of pennies found each minute over the twenty minutes. In general their graphs will look like Figure 49. With time there will be a steady decrease in the number of pennies found.

Figure 49

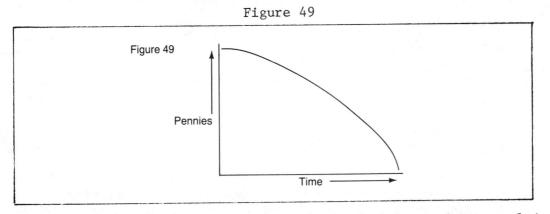

9. Discuss the activity. Start by having the students explain what happened as their extraction of resources continued. Determine if they found all of the resource (no pennies left). <u>How close were they in their estimates of the resource?</u> <u>What problems did they experience with time?</u> <u>How is this like the actual extraction of resources?</u> Be sure to point out their increased use of "technology" (tweezers, mirrors); the possible environmental effects (turned over books, papers, chairs); and the economics (it took more time, energy and technology to obtain fewer pennies as the period progressed).

10. You can bring in examples of natural resources.

Consuming Resources
Grades 6-8

ACTIVITY OVERVIEW

For several rounds the students decide on the amount of a resource they would like. By keeping track of the resource and their use of the resource they are led to a basic understanding of supply and demand The concepts of scarcity and depletion are also introduced. The activity ends with a discussion that relates these ideas to the use of natural resources.

SCIENCE BACKGROUND

Many of the problems of resources are related to the fundamental concepts of supply and demand. When scarcities of an earth material such as fossil fuels exist, some try to increase the supply while others try to decrease the demand. In the case of the former position, the proponents argue that scarcity increases prices, which in itself decreases demand, and also subsidizes further exploration for the resource and thus a greater supply. On the other hand, some argue that supplies are finite, no amount of technology or price increases can produce materials that do not exist. So, we must reduce the demand for the material and maintain the present and any future supply through reuse, recycling and conservation.

SOCIETAL IMPLICATIONS

The usual view of supply and demand as it relates to consuming resources is simple--prices fall when supply is great and prices rise when supply is limited. But this is not the case due to complex social interactions. Here are several factors that influence prices that are not directly a result of the availability of the resource. (1) The government and industry exercise some control over the supply of resources. (2) The actual price of a product has many hidden costs that have little to do with the resource. (3) The energy used to recover a resource can limit its use.

MAJOR CONCEPTS

-There is a relationship between supply and demand of resources.

OBJECTIVES

At the completion of this activity the students should be able to:
-Graph a simple problem of supply and demand.
-Explain the relationship between supply and demand.

MATERIALS
       -A large clear container
       -1500 raisins (depending on your preference, M & M's, peanuts
or other edibles can be used. They should be food that students like).
       -Graph paper, pencils, plastic baggies

VOCABULARY
       -Demand, resources, scarcity, supply

PROCEDURES
       1. Prior to the activity count out a thousand raisins and place
them in the container.
       2. At the beginning of the activity be sure the container with
raisins is visible to all students.
       3. Distribute the graph paper and help the students set up a
graph such as Figure 50. Use the overhead or chalkboard to assist
them.

Figure 50

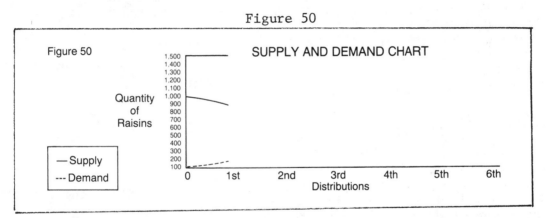

       4. To start, distribute one raisin to each student and record
the numbers on the chart. Supply should be at 1000. Demand should
start at 0. After the first round subtract the number of raisins
consumed from the supply. Keep track of the demand on the lower
portion of the graph. See Figure 1 for the first round of a class of
30. You will continue this graph procedure as the rounds of distribution continue.
       5. Ask the students if they want one or two raisins per person.
Have them raise their hands to vote for one or two. Distribute the
raisins according to their vote. Have them record the results on their
graph.
       6. Now ask if they want two or four raisins. Vote and then
distribute the raisins according to their preference. Graph the
results. (Note: they do not have to eat the raisins, they can be
saved and eaten later, use the plastic baggies for this purpose).

7. Repeat these procedures using the following options:
   4 or 8 raisins
   8 or 16 raisins
   16 or 32 raisins

Sometimes the students will realize that they cannot continue taking the largest number. You can have them use their graphs to project how many raisins will be needed to meet the demand of each round.

8. When the students realize what is happening with the supply of raisins invent the concept of scarcity. There is a scarcity when the demand for an earth material is approaching the supply of the material.

9. Stop the activity and discuss the following questions. How would you define supply? What is demand? What does it mean when we say a resource is being depleted? What could be done to reduce the scarcity of raisins? Are raisins renewable or nonrenewable? What would happen if there were no more raisins in the world? How could you use the raisins you saved? Would they be worth more, less, the same as when we had a large supply of raisins? Why? What could be done to make the supply of raisins last longer?

10. As the students answer these questions you can extend their understanding to the actual concepts of supply and demand; simple economics, recycling, renewable and nonrenewable resources, reuse, distribution and so on.

11. Give the students the following information:
   1) the number of students in the school
   2) the estimated pieces of paper used a day
   3) the estimated increase in paper use over the next nine
      months will be 2% a month.

Note: you can use different numbers in the problem depending on the level of students. Have the students plot out the increased demand for paper. Then have them explain what this will do if the supply of paper is fixed for each month. If the supply can be increased (or decreased) each month.

Distributing Resources
Grades 6-8

ACTIVITY OVERVIEW

Students are involved in a simple simulation game concerning the distribution of resources. First they make individual decisions about distribution to other groups who want and need resources. Then they work in groups to make the same decisions. The lesson ends with a discussion of the complex nature of distributing resources.

SCIENCE BACKGROUND

As population increases and the disparity between rich nations and poor nations also increases decisions will have to be made about the distribution of resources. Affluent nations must evaluate their use of resources while less developed nations must strive to become more self sufficient. All of this is occurring while we daily hear that resources are being depleted. The activity focuses on the problems of making decisions.

SOCIETAL IMPLICATIONS

If we consider food, then we are in a position to make decisions about distribution. Students should also realize that when we consider fossil fuels we are in the position of need, not distribution of surplus.

Many of the decisions concerning resources are directly related to the availability of the resource. As you can imagine, the distribution of resources is very much related to social, political, and economic factors for a country. These facts provide a good connection between this science activity and other social science lessons. Other topics that might come up during the activity are: conservation, waste, recycling, reuse, pollution, renewable and nonrenewable resources.

MAJOR CONCEPTS

-When resources are scarce decisions must be made about their distribution.

OBJECTIVES

At the completion of this activity the student should be able to:

-Give reasons for distributing resources to one group and not another.

-Show a realization that decisions concerning earth's resources are complex and interrelated.

MATERIALS

-Data sheets to record information and decisions (See Procedures).

VOCABULARY
   -Distribution, decision, resource, scarcity

PROCEDURES
   1.   Give each student a data sheet and ask him/her to complete
the questions individually. (See Figure 51 below)
   2.   After the students have made their decisions divide the class
into groups of four or five. Inform the groups that they are to reach
a decision about distributing resources.
   3.   You should talk to each group about the procedures and answer
any questions they have.
   4.   Have each group present their decisions and give their reasons
for distributing the resources as they did.

Figure 51

DATA SHEET FOR DISTRIBUTING RESOURCES
   Your problem is to decide how to distribute resources among
three groups who have requested your help. For this activity we are
using the term resources to include many different things such as
food, minerals, fuels and other items needed by people. Here is the
only information you have to make your decisions.
   You have 300 units of resources
   You presently use 200 units of resources
   You can survive on 100 units of resources
Three groups want some of your resources. Here are their situations:
   Group 1 - needs 250 units of resources to survive
            wants 250 units of resources
   Group 2 - needs 100 units of resources to survive
           - wants 200 units for survival and improvement
   Group 3 - needs 50 units for survival
           - wants 100 units for improvement.
   Group 4 - needs no units for survival
           - wants 200 units for improvement
   Your problem is to decide how you will distribute the resources.
Complete the chart below.

INDIVIDUAL DECISIONS

Distribution of Resources	Group 1	Group 2	Group 3	Group 4
Reasons for Decision				

GROUP DECISIONS

Distribution of Resources	Group 1	Group 2	Group 3	Group 4
Reasons for Decision				

5. After the group decisions start a discussion of the decisions. On what did they base their decisions? What other information would they have requested? Would they change their decisions if more units of resources were available? Would they be willing to change their life style in order to allow more units of resources to be available for distribution? Continue the discussion with students along their lines of interest.

Pollution and the Earth's Spheres
Grades 6-8

ACTIVITY OVERVIEW
>   Pollution in the different earth spheres--lithosphere, hydrosphere, atmosphere and ecosphere--is detected and classified using the human senses.

SCIENCE BACKGROUND
>   Pollution is defined as an undesirable change in the properties of the lithosphere, hydrosphere, atmosphere, or ecosphere that can have deleterious effects on humans and other organisms. A part of the task for students in this activity will be to decide what an undesirable change is; or what is undesirable to them. This lies at the heart of their study of pollution and that of any other group. One country's ban of DDT is another country's reduction in much needed food. One person's smoke pollution is another's sweet smell of success.
>   Students will observe two types of pollutants--degradable and nondegradable. A degradable pollutant is one that can be reduced, decomposed or otherwise removed through natural processes or processes that assist nature, e.g., sewage disposal plants. Degradable products are further divided into rapidly and slowly degradable pollutants. DDT and radioactive wastes are examples of the latter while crop wastes are examples of the former.
>   A nondegradable pollutant is not decomposed, or removed through natural processes. Iron, mercury, and many synthetic products are nondegradable. Nondegradable and slowly degradable pollutants must be maintained below harmful levels in the different earth spheres.

SOCIETAL IMPLICATIONS
>   We return to the discussion of "undesirable change" as the main social implication of pollution. In many cases members of society must make value judgements about the costs and benefits of pollution. Needless to say these are controversial issues. In most cases we do not have all the information needed to make a decision; and in some we do not want to wait until the information is available. If we wait, tragedy will no doubt follow in some of the cases.

MAJOR CONCEPTS
>   -Earth study can be divided into the lithosphere, atmosphere, hydrosphere and ecosphere.
>   -The earth spheres can be polluted.
>   -Pollution is an undesirable change in the properties of the lithosphere, hydrosphere, atmosphere or ecosphere that can have deleterious effects on organisms, including humans.

OBJECTIVES

At the completion of this activity the student should be able to:
- Define pollution
- Detect pollution in the different earth spheres using the senses.
- Predict the harmful effects of pollution.
- Infer what must be done to reduce pollution.

MATERIALS

Observation sheet (see Procedures)
Pencil

VOCABULARY

-Lithosphere, atmosphere, hydrosphere, ecosphere, pollution, senses

PROCEDURES

1. Tell the students they are going to classify pollution in their neighborhood and city. The classification will be based on their senses--sight, touch, hearing, taste, and smell--and the different spheres of the earth--lithosphere, hydrosphere, atmosphere, and ecosphere.

2. Provide the students with brief definitions of the terms with which they may not be familiar.

Lithosphere - the crust of the earth, e.g., rocks, soil.
Hydrosphere - the earth's water in its various forms--both on the surface and in the air, e.g., lakes, vapor.
Atmosphere - the gases that surround the earth, e.g., air.
Ecosphere - the spheres in which life is found, e.g., air, water, land.
Pollution - undesirable changes in the properties of the lithosphere, hydrosphere, atmosphere or ecosphere.

3. Give each student a copy of an observation sheet such as the one given below. The students should collect observations and examples over a week.

Figure 52
OBSERVATIONS OF POLLUTION AND EARTH SPHERES

Physical Senses	Lithosphere	Hydrosphere	Atmosphere	Ecosphere
Sight				
Touch				
Hearing				
Taste				
Smell				

Record the types of pollution observed in the different earth spheres.

4. After a week discuss the students' observations. They may not have completed all the squares. Discuss why this occurred. Ask if they had any trouble deciding how to classify some of their observations.

5. Ask the students to identify the source of the pollution and predict what might happen if the pollution continued. How could the pollution be reduced? What changes would the reduction of pollution require? Questions such as these should stimulate further discussion. Ask the students if there are types of pollution they could not detect. If so, what are they, in which spheres do they exist, and how can they be detected.

Noise Pollution
Grades 6-8

ACTIVITY OVERVIEW
In this activity the students use a simple scale to map noises around the school. They discuss the effects of noise pollution and ways to reduce the problem.

SCIENCE BACKGROUND
Noise is defined as unwanted sound. But this definition leaves something to be desired because one person's music may be another's noise. The decibel (db) is the unit of measure for either sound intensity or sound pressure exerted on the eardrum. The decibel scales for both sound power (intensity) and sound pressure are logarithmic rather than arithmatic.

The frequency or pitch of sounds can also have an annoying effect. High-pitched sounds annoy more than low-pitched sounds. By correcting for loudness, and pitch, scales have been designed to rank noises according to sound pressure. Students will use a sound pressure scale to determine various noises in their environment.

SOCIETAL IMPLICATIONS
The number of individuals with acute and significant hearing loss is raising rapidly. And many younger individuals are reporting hearing losses. In the mid 1970's about 15 million Americans had an acute hearing loss and 30 million had a significant hearing loss. Some 5 million children under the age of 18 have impaired hearing. The 1974 Census showed that almost 50% of American households report that their neighborhoods are too noisy.

The effects of noise range from annoyance to physical and psychological problems. Noise has been correlated with any number of medical ailments in the general category of stress related illnesses. Environmental noise can be disturbing enough but occupational noise is a much more serious problem.

MAJOR CONCEPTS
-Noise is an unwanted sound.
-Decibel is a unit of measuring sound.
-Noise is a form of pollution that has an effect on humans.

OBJECTIVES
At the completion of this activity the student should be able to:
-Define noise pollution.
-Use a decibel scale to determine noise levels.
-Relate noise pollution to annoyance, disruption, hearing impairment and physical and psychological effects.

MATERIALS
   -Cassette tape recorder and tape
   -Paper, pencil
   -Decibel Scale (see Procedures Figure 53)
   -Map of the school (building and grounds)

VOCABULARY
   -Noise, decibel

PROCEDURES
   1. Periodically over several days use the tape recorder to record
the noise level in the classroom. (Two-three minute intervals twice
a day for five days is suggested).
   2. Select a day and play back the tape for the students. Ask
them to list the different types of noises. Also ask them how they
felt hearing the noise they produced.
   3. On the next day form groups of two students each. Tell them
they are going to study noise in and around the school. Distribute
maps of the school (you may have to use a sketch you have prepared).
Assign locations for the different student groups. It would also be
important to record the noises at three or four different times during
the day.

   4. Have the students go to their location and remain there for
10 minutes. During this time they should record all the different
noises they hear. Repeat this procedure at different times, e.g.,
lunch, recess, during class, assemblies, if at all possible.
   5. Distribute the decibel scale (see Figure 53   ) and the
school maps. The students can then rate the noises they have recorded.
Use the "school example" column to list the noises heard around the
school. Use the school maps to make a "noise map" of the school.
   6. Discuss how the students feel in noisy places. What produced
the most noise around the school? The least? What noises could be
eliminated? Reduced? What was the most common noise? How can noise
pollution be reduced in the school? Community?

Figure 53

DECIBEL SCALE

Sound Pressure	Effect with Prolonged Exposure	Example
140	Eardrum ruptures	Jet take-off (very close)
120	Threshold of pain	Live rock music Jet take-off (60 meters) Siren Discotheque
100	Serious hearing damage	Thunder Close car horn Power mower Garbage truck Subway
80	Very loud Hearing loss	Garbage disposal Noisy office Food blender
60	Intrusive Loud	Restaurant Playground Noisy classroom Use of telephone difficult Traffic
40	Moderate	Library Avg. living room
20	Very quiet	Whisper Rustling leaves
0	Threshold of audibility	Breathing

Is Wind Power a Feasible Energy Source?
Grades 6-8

ACTIVITY OVERVIEW

Hourly observations of wind velocity are recorded over a month. During the fourth week the students prepare a "feasibility report" on wind powered electricity for their area. The reports are presented to the class and students decide if wind power is feasible at their location.

SCIENCE BACKGROUND

The sun is the primary source of energy for wind power. Windmills have long been used to pump water, grind grain, and in recent years to produce electricity. Wind is reasonably available, free, renewable, clean, safe, and has a fairly well developed technology. Estimates are that wind could provide 7 to 19 percent of all electricity in the United States by the year 2000 if we started an all out crash program to develop the resource now. To date, the research and development effort has been modest.

Wind turbines have been developed. Usually they are 5 to 10 stories high and have 20 to 30 meter blades. Large wind turbines are more efficient than small ones for two reasons: 1) electric production increases with the square of the rotor blade diameter, e.g., a 20 meter diameter rotor produces 4 times as much power as a 10 meter rotor; and 2) wind power increases as the cube of wind velocity, e.g., an 18 kilometer-per-hour wind produces 8 times as much power as a 9 kilometer per hour wind. The over all efficiency of wind turbines is about 15 to 30 percent of the energy in the wind depending on the wind turbine.

SOCIETAL IMPLICATIONS

The estimated potential for wind energy use for most of the United States is fair. It is very high in some locations such as Wyoming and parts of Kansas, Oklahoma, and Texas. The central plains generally have a moderate to high potential for the use of wind energy to generate electricity.

Wind power does have its drawbacks. Its use is limited to areas where the wind is steady at moderate speeds. A minimum of 8 m.p.h. is needed to generate electricity. A second problem is storage of energy for windless days. There are various combinations of charging batteries, using a flywheel, pumping water to levels that could be stored and released and combinations of wind and conventional generators to overcome the storage problem. There is also the fact of visual pollution when numbers of wind turbines are concentrated in regions of high winds.

MAJOR CONCEPTS
-Wind is a form of energy that can be used to produce electricity in some regions.

OBJECTIVES
At the completion of this lesson the student should be able to:
-Explain the possibilities of using wind power where she/he lives.
-Describe the advantages and disadvantages of wind power.
-Graph the daily wind speeds over a month period.

MATERIALS
-Chart for measuring wind velocity (see Figure 54)
-Daily log for recording wind velocity hourly.

VOCABULARY
-Beaufort Scale, breeze, feasibility, solar energy, power, wind, gale

PROCEDURES
1. Over a month have the students measure the wind velocity on an hourly basis. They will record their observations in a daily log.
2. Use a Beaufort Scale in measuring the velocity (See Figure 54).

Figure 54
WIND POWER

Beaufort Number	Velocity (in M.P.H.)	Wind name	Observations
0	less than 1	calm	smoke rises vertically
1	1- 3	light air	smoke drifts slowly
2	4- 7	slight breeze	leaves rustle
3	8-12	gentle breeze	small twigs move
4	13-18	moderate breeze	branches move
5	19-24	fresh breeze	small trees sway
6	25-31	strong breeze	large branches move
7	32-38	moderate gale	whole trees move
8	39-46	fresh gale	twigs break off trees
9	47-54	strong gale	branches break
10	55-63	whole gale	trees snap
11	64-75	storm	severe damage
12	above 75	hurricane	widespread destruction

3. Have the students graph their hourly observation over a month.

4. The students should keep a daily log of the wind speeds.

5. After three weeks assign a short report on using wind to generate electricity. The object of the report is to provide some background on wind as an energy source and determine the feasibility of using wind power at your location. Have the students work in groups of 3 or 4 on the "Feasibility Study."

6. Have the students present their reports and see if the groups can arrive at a concensus about the use of wind power as an energy source. This project can provide an excellent opportunity to introduce ideas such as economic and political feasibility of such a project.

Air Pollution: A Demonstration
of Thermal Inversion
Grades 6-8

ACTIVITY OVERVIEW
This activity presents the concepts fundamental to a thermal inversion through a demonstration. A post-demonstration discussion relates the concepts to the problem of air pollution.

SCIENCE BACKGROUND
The normal atmosphere condition is one of the decreasing temperatures with altitude. On occasion the reverse--a thermal inversion--occurs. In the case of a thermal inversion a layer of cool air is contained beneath a layer of warmer air. If this situation exists for an extended period of time, air pollution levels can rise to harmful levels. (See the diagram with the activity).

SOCIETAL IMPLICATIONS
Many air pollution disasters have resulted from thermal inversions. Thermal inversions are more likely in the fall or winter when solar radiation cannot reach the ground to create a warm layer and when there is increased use of fuel for warmth. The conditions for thermal inversions are especially high on the two coasts of the United States.

MAJOR CONCEPTS
-A thermal inversion occurs when a cold air mass is trapped under a warm air mass.
-Thermal inversions can result in greatly increased levels of air pollution.
-Environments of the earth change due to interactions of matter and energy.

OBJECTIVES
At the completion of this lesson the student should be able to:
-Define thermal inversion.
-Explain the relationship between a thermal inversion and air pollution.
-Identify the harmful effects of thermal inversion.

MATERIALS
-2 clear glass containers such as milk bottles (See Figure 55).
-2 large containers that will hold the glass containers and liquids (see Figure 55)
-A source of smoke (A small, postage stamp size paper soaked in 5% solution of potassium nitrate, KNO_3 and allowed to dry is suggested)
-Ice, hot tap water, matches, tweezers

VOCABULARY
   -Thermal Inversion, pollutants

PROCEDURES
   1. Conduct this as a silent demonstration.
   2. Place the glass bottles mouth to mouth in one container (see Figure 55).
   3. Add ice to the container and allow the ice to cool the bottle for five minutes.

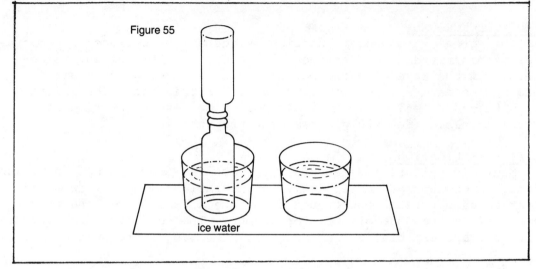

Figure 55

ice water

   4. Using the tweezers, ignite the source of smoke and drop it into the lower bottle.
   5. Let the bottles remain for several minutes.
   6. Lift the two glass bottles and place them into the second container. Add hot water to the container.
   7. Provide time for the students to observe what happens.
   8. Discuss the results. First have the students summarize what you did and what happened. <u>Ask them how the ice affected the air?</u> <u>Does cooling air make it more or less dense?</u> <u>What was the effect of hot water on the smoke?</u> <u>What happened in the bottle?</u> <u>What is the normal structure of the atmosphere?</u> <u>Does it get cooler or warmer as you increase in altitude?</u> Define a thermal inversion for the students.
             THERMAL INVERSION: A layer of dense cool air is trapped beneath
                                 a layer of light warm air.
      Ask the students to explain how this could influence air pollution in a region.
   9. Use a diagram similar to Figure 56 to describe the relationship of thermal inversions to air pollution.

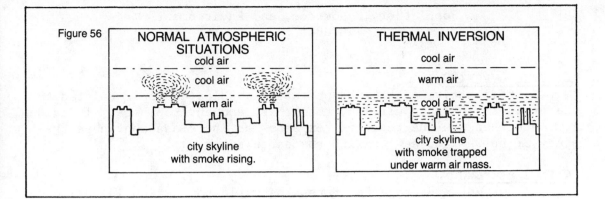

Figure 56

NORMAL ATMOSPHERIC SITUATIONS

cold air

cool air

warm air

city skyline
with smoke rising.

THERMAL INVERSION

cool air

warm air

cool air

city skyline
with smoke trapped
under warm air mass.

Population, Resources, and Environment
Grades 6-8

ACTIVITY OVERVIEW

In this activity the students study a selected topic related to
the broad topics: population, resources, and environments. Individual
students then are the resident "experts" as the class continues the
study of human interaction with the earth spheres.

SCIENCE BACKGROUND

At current and projected rates the world population is estimated
to be 6.35 billion people by the year 2000. In 1975 it was 4 billion,
in 1850 it was one billion, and in 1650 it was about ½ million. These
statistics give some idea of the accelerating rate at which the human
population is growing. The increasing population brings increasing
demands for resources and disposal of wastes.

Foor supplies need to be increased. Different energy resources
need to be developed. Air, water, and soil need to be protected from
pollution. While water is abundant on earth, it is scarce in many
locations where it is needed for irrigation and food production. The
litany could continue. But the situation should be clear. There is
an interaction among population growth, resource use, and pollution.

The interaction among population, resources, and the environment
is important to understand for it is primarily a human interaction
with earth's spheres.

SOCIETAL IMPLICATIONS

Is the prospect hopeful or hopeless? The answer is--it depends.
It depends on whether we have the capacity to change those things we
must, to develop new technologies where appropriate and, in general,
to start these changes now. Rather than crying doomsday, it is
better for students to gain some information on the problems and
develop concepts fundamental to their full understanding of the
situation. If hope is to be found, it will in part depend on the
decisions our students make.

MAJOR CONCEPTS

-The lithosphere, atmosphere, hydrosphere, and ecosphere can
change and still conserve their identities.
-There are limits to the capacities of the earth's spheres to
change.
-Human interaction with the earth's spheres has resulted in
significant changes.

OBJECTIVES

At the completion of this activity the student should be able to:
-Discuss an aspect of the human interaction with earth's spheres.
-Relate his/her topic to future activities on population,
resources,and environment.

MATERIALS

-Pencil, paper, library

VOCABULARY

-Population, resources, pollution, atmosphere, interaction,
lithosphere, hydrosphere

PROCEDURES

1. Students are to select a topic (suggested topics are provided
in Figure 57) and prepare a written and oral report on the topic. You
can also suggest that the students may compile interesting facts and
figures on his/her topic.

2. A brief (5 minutes) presentation of the topic will be given
two weeks after the assignment.

3. The activity and the student's role extends beyond the oral
presentation. The student becomes the "resident expert" in his/her
topic as future activities are completed on the related themes of
population, resources,and environment. Several of the future activities
are concerned with general concepts relating to population, e.g.,
problems in exploration, types of pollution, and not specific
information about these topics. The role of the "resident expert"
is to provide some of the extra information during discussions of
the activities.

Figure 57
Possible Topics for Student Reports

-Population
    -Zero population growth
    -Limiting population growth
    -Different views of population
        problem
    -Density of Populations

-Food
    -Green Revolution
    -Use of the Sea
    -Malnutrition
    -Famine, Disease
    -World Hunger
    -Geography of Hunger
    -"New" Foods

-Energy
    -Fossil Fuels   -Hydroelectric
    -Nuclear   -Tidal energy
    -Solar   -Ocean Currents
    -Wind   -Biomass
    -Geothermal   -Synthetic Fuels

-Water
    -Desalinization of Sea Water
    -Pollution

-Land
    -Wilderness Areas
    -Parks
    -Urban Development
    -Conservation and Preservation
    -Soil Pollution
    -Forests
    -Surface Mining
    -Wildlife

-Minerals
    -Exploration
    -Mining
    -Renewable & Nonrenewable
    -Resources vs. Reserves

-Pollution
    -Definition of Pollution
    -Types of Pollution
    -Air Pollution
    -Waste Disposal
    -Environmental Pollution
    -Technology
    -Balance in Nature
    -Environmental Impacts of
        Growth

Resources for Teaching Earth
and Environmental Sciences

Teacher Resources

Denver Public Schools and Colorado State University. Best of Energy
Book. New York: Cambridge/Basic Skills, 1980. Vol 1 (Grades
1-3), $7.95. Vol. 2 (Grades 4-6), $7.95. Both, $14.00. Grades
K-6. Teacher Resource.

An interdisciplinary curriculum developed by the Denver Public
Schools, wonderfully illustrated short activity-oriented lessons
grouped into subjects like art, language, math, science and
social studies. Activities are generally 15 minutes or less, or
independent. Includes bibliographies of films, books, and
teachers' references.

Each lesson provides background information, states concepts and
skills to be developed, lesson time, grade level, materials list,
step-by-step procedures, source, bibliography, film listing,
and an activity section.

Humanistic Environmental Education (Green Box). Eureka: 1978.
Kit with student cards, teacher booklets, program rationale.
$40.00 (Sampler available for $3.00). Teacher Resource.
From 555 H Street, P.O. Box 1408, Eureka, CA 95501.

An environmental awareness activity box with 5 think cards, 96
do cards, 250 show cards, and booklets on environmental awareness
for different sites (rural, industrial, urban, historical) as well
as 15 outdoor and 15 indoor investigations for school sites.

Lipschitz, Ceil. An Ecology Craftsbook for the Open Classroom. New
York: Center for Applied Research in Education, 1975. 208 pp.
$12.95. Grades 1-6. Teacher Resource

A book developed by a New York City classroom teacher with her
colleagues and students. Includes many ingenious ways to recycle
used materials in arts and crafts and ecology lessons, indoors
and out for grades 1-6. Suggests grade levels for projects, as
well as diagrams and instructions and an indication of the amount
of supervision needed. Has good overall suggestions for storing
materials and organizing the classroom.

McCollum, Daniel A. Your Life and Mine: Problems and Projects in
Conservation. Memphis: Wimmer Brothers Books, 1977. Teacher's
manual, $5.00; Student's manual, $3.25. From Box 18408, Memphis,
TN 18408.

High-quality curriculum materials accompanied by a superb teacher's
manual. Focus on minimizing negative effects on the environment,
and maximizing students' involvement in conservation.

National Center for Appropriate Technology. Appropriate Technology
Curriculum. Butte: N.C.A.T., 1980. $5.00. Grades 5-6 From
P.O. Box 3838, Butte, MT 59701.

Covers conservation, recycling, transportation, renewable resources,
nutrition, and energy production and uses with ten lesson plans
and quizzes, instructions for making inexpensive models, a poster,
illustrated handouts, and bibliographies for students and a list
of sources for teachers.

National School Boards Association. Energy Education and the School
Curriculum. Washington, D.C., NSBA, 1980. 40 pp. $7.50, discounts
for quantity. Teacher Resource. From Information Services Dept.,
1055 Thomas Jefferson Street NW, Washington, D.C. 20007.

A primer for school districts developing an energy curriculum,
with examples of successful programs, and suggestions for implementing programs and gaining community support.

Sale, Larry L., and Lee, Earnest W. Environmental Education in the
Elementary School. New York: Holt, Rinehart and Winston, 1972.
203 pp. $5.95.

A teacher textbook emphasizing major ecological concepts and
processes and varied approaches for student investigations.
Includes many relevant practical suggestions.

Scherer, Donald. Personal Values and Environmental Issues: A Handbook
of Strategies Related to Issues of Pollution, Energy, Food,
Population and Land Use. New York: A & W (Hart), 1978. 214 pp.
$6.95.

Presents 40 strategies to clarify personal values on major
environmental issues. Techniques that would be useful for both
students and teachers include "likes/dislikes" and "food consumption diary."

Simons, Robin. _Recyclopedia: Games, Science Equipment and Crafts from Recycled Materials_. Boston: Houghton Mifflin, 1976. 118 pp. $7.95; $3.95, paperback. Grades 3 and up. Teacher Resource.

Originally developed by the Boston Children's Museum, these are the best of a series of well-researched and ingenious directions for children and adults to use in making games, musical instruments, scientific apparatus and other classroom items from scrap and inexpensive materials. Field-tested with thousands of children.

Soil Conservation Society of America. _Conservation Science Fair Projects_. Washington, D.C.: Science Clubs of America, 1975. 32 pp. $1.00. All grades. From 1719 N Street NW, Washington D.C. 20036.

Ideas for projects in all phases of conservation—soil, water plants, pollution, wildlife, etc., with selected annotated references.

Stapp, William B. and Cox, Dorothy A. _Environmental Education Activities Manual_. Author, 1979. 776 pp. $12.00, paperback. Grades K-12. From Dorothy A. Cox, 32493 Shady Ridge Drive, Farmington Hills, MI 48018.

Completely rewritten, this new edition contains 300 activities written by teachers for teachers, as well as interdisciplinary environmental education suggestions. Grade level activities are geared to basic environmental education concepts.

Stapp, William B., and Liston, Mary Dawn. _Environmental Education: A Guide to Information Sources_. Detroit: Game Research Co., 1975. 225 pp. $18.00. Teacher Resource.

This well-organized guide to learning resources in environmental education is one of the 12 guides in the "Man and the Environment Information Guide Series."

University of Southern California, Department of Mechanical Engineering.
Solar Energy Curriculum for Elementary Schools. Los Angeles:
USC, 1980. Price not available. Grades K-6. From Seymour
Lampert, USC, Mechanical Engineering Department, Los Angeles,
CA 90007.

Many hands-on activities (reviewed by teachers) with lesson plans,
overviews, learning objectives, vocabulary lists, and teaching
strategies. Topics include the scientific method, energy and
life, the sun and light, forms of energy, energy measurement, and
energy and society.

Zero Population Growth. _Population Activities_. Washington, D.C.:
Zero Population Growth, 1980. Packet. $10.00. Grades 1-6.
From Population Education Materials, 1346 Connecticut Avenue NW,
Washington, D.C. 20036.

This packet includes 20 new teaching activities and games for
elementary students that require little preparation and only a few
inexpensive materials. ZPG is the source of _many_ good instructional resources. Send for their catalog.

Children's Resources: Books, Games, and Pictures

Adams, Florence. _Catch a Sunbeam: A Book of Solar Study and Experi-
ments_. New York: Harcourt, Brace, Jovanovich, 1978. $7.95.
Grades 4-6.

Sixteen experiments including a solar cooker, sundial, and using
a watch for a compass.

American Forest Institute. _Possum Creek Valley_. Washington, D.C.
AFI, 1978. Game. $1.50. Grades 6 and up. From AFI, 1619
Massachusetts Avenue, NW, Washington, D.C. 20036.

Intended to give students a feel for the problems involved in
forest management when impacted by population pressures on water,
recreation, and timber. Pieces should be copied through spirit
duplicator, overhead projector or other means. It takes 1 to 4
hours to play with 6 teams totalling 12 to 40 players.

Anderson, Margaret Jean. _Exploring City Trees and the Need for Urban Forests_. New York: McGraw-Hill, 1976. 102 pp. $6.95. Grades 4-6.

The final chapters include a specific discussion of how city trees lower temperature in summer, help purify both air and water, and serve as an index to pollution levels. Other chapters include some simple but instructive activities and observations.

Asimov, Isaac. _How Did We Find Out About Oil?_ New York: Walker, 1980. 61 pp. $6.95. Grades 4 and up.

A compact but comprehensive overview of oil, with a discussion of how living systems create oil, an account of the early history of petroleum, and the modern history of oil from whales to coal gas to petroleum. Includes such issues as politics, peace, and the threat to the biosphere from carbon dioxide buildup.

Asimov, Isaac. _How Did We Find Out About Solar Power?_ New York: Walker, 1981. $7.85. Grades 5 and up.

Another of Asimov's _History of Science_ series. This one covers the history of solar heating devices from Greek and Roman times to the present.

Bartlett, Margaret F. _Where Does All the Rain Go?_ New York: Coward, McCann, 1973. 47 pp. $5.99. Grades K-3.

An uncomplicated outline of where rain goes and how it supports life. Besides having the ability to erode barren land, rain can collect in forest earth, swamps, and underground rock; evaporate through plants; or travel through streams and rivers to the ocean where it begins its cycle over again.

Berger, Melvin. _Pollution Lab_. New York: John Day, 1974. 128 pp. $8.79. Grades 3-6.

A behind-the-scenes look at some important laboratories dealing with water pollution, sewage treatment, biological pollution, pollution by oil and hazardous materials, air pollution, solid wastes, radiation, and pesticides. One of a Scientists-At-Work series by Berger. Other titles are: _The National Weather Service_, _South Pole Station_, _Animal Hospital_, _Oceanography Lab_.

Caldicott, Helen. <u>Nuclear Madness: What You Can Do</u>! Brookline:
Autumn Press, 1978. 120 pp. $3.95, paperback. Grades 5 and up.

Personal experiences of an anti-nuclear activist who is showing
how an aroused citizenry can move the government to ban nuclear
power. Includes bibliography.

Christian Science Monitor. <u>Energy '80</u>. Boston: Christian Science
Monitor, 1980. 28-page reprint. $.75, quantity discount.
From Reprints Service, P.O. Box 527, Back Bay Station, Boston,
MA 02117.

A collection of current reprints that cover a wide range of
energy topics from Congressional debates to household hints.

Collis, Margaret, and others. <u>Using the Environment</u>. Sponsored by
the Schools Council, the Nuffield Foundation and the Scottish
Education Department. Macdonald Education, 1975. 6 volumes.
$7.50 each. From: Macdonald-Raintree, Inc., 205 West Highland
Ave., Milwaukee, WI 53203. Minimum order: 6 titles.

These attractive and thought-provoking volumes complete the
British Nuffield Foundation's science project series for
youngsters between the ages of 5 and 13, ranging from <u>Early
Explorations to Investigations</u> (in two volumes) of increasing
depth on plants, animals, common materials, weather, life
cycles, landscapes, observation, to <u>Tackling Problems</u> (for
children over 11), with an excellent resource book <u>Ways and Means</u>.

Cummings, Richard. <u>Make Your Own Alternative Energy</u>. McKay, 1980.
192 pp. $8.95. Grades 6 and up.

Alternate energy systems plus step-by-step instructions for
making machines and models. Other "Make Your Own" books by
Richard Cummings deal with "Model Forts and Castles" and
"Dollhouses."

Bendick, Jeanne. <u>Science Experiences: Ecology</u>. New York: Franklin
Watts, 1975. 72 pp. $4.90. Grades 3-7.

Well-developed and stimulating introduction to ecology. Emphasizes
the chain of life, and touches on many related topics, including
the water and oxygen cycles, the interdependence of all living
things and adaptation.

The Daily News (Longview, WA) and The Journal American (Bellevue, WA). Volcano: The Eruption of Mount St. Helens. Seattle: Madrona Press, 1980. 96 pp. $6.95. Grades 4 and up.

Spectacular photos of before and after the eruption chronicle the devastation of May 18. Includes human interest stories and an eruption chronology.

Ellison, Vivian. Chemical Invasion: The Body Breakers. West Haven: Pendulum Press, 1972. 58 pp. $1.45, paperback. Grades 7 and up.

Discusses internal pollution of our body environments through sprays, chemical additives, drugged livestock, fish from polluted waters, radiations, air pollution, and some voluntary addictions such as tobacco, alcohol and drugs.

Faber, Ron, and Platt, Judity, developers. Pollution. Cambridge: Abt Associates, 1973. Game. $26.00. Grades 5 and up. From 55 Wheeler Street, Cambridge, MA 02138.

Each team starts with the same amount of money to contend with the same amount of air, noise, and water pollution. Team members are factory owners or community representatives, who have to face the costs and consequences of pollution. Takes about ½ to 1½ hours to play, with 12 to 16 players.

Fields, Alice. The Sun. New York: Watts, 1980. 48 pp. $6.45. Grades 1 and up.

A simple but interesting book on the sun prepared in reference-book format. Includes experiments, information on the sun's size and structure, its relationships in the universe and in the solar system, its effect on our weather and atmosphere, and solar energy applications. Includes a few simple experiments with safeguards.

Hennings, George and Dorothy G. Keep Earth Clean Blue and Green: Environmental Activities for Young People. New York: Citation Press, 1976. 250 pp. $5.95 paperback. Grades 3 and up. Teacher Resource.

Covers a multitude of activities from library research to laboratory investigations and surveys, as well as cross-disciplinary projects involving music, art and poetry. Major emphasis is integration of social studies.

Israel, Elaine. The Great Energy Search. New York: Messner, 1974.
64 pp. $5.95. Grades 5 and up.

Opens with an historical survey of the fuels we have used--food,
wind, water, coal, steam and gasoline--and then focuses on today's
fuels--coal, oil, natural gas and electricity and the problems of
supply. Alternative sources--solar energy, nuclear power and
geothermal power--are discussed.

Kalina, Sigmund. Three Drops of Water. New York: Lothrop, Lee &
Shepard, 1974. 64 pp. $6.44. Grades 2-6.

A lucid cohesive test covering water cycles and pollutions. It
traces the path of three hypothetical water drops from their
frozen state on a mountain top, through their melting and movement into larger and larger bodies of water, to absorption by a
cloud and return to earth in the form of rain and snow. En route,
they pass through waterways in various states of health,
supporting different kinds of animal and plant life.

Koehler, Sherry, editor. It's Your Environment: Things to Think
About--Things to Do, from the Environmental Action Coalition.
New York, Scribner, 1976. 217 pp. $7.95. Grades 3-7. Teacher
Resource.

A large, informal book on activities and environments, with
humorous illustrations, compiled from ECO-NEWS, mostly for
city kids, containing "things to think about and things to do."
It has a good combination of large issues (climate, energy) and
specific city pollutions (roaches, dogs), with an emphasis on
problem-solving.

Landahl, John, and others. Population Education Task Cards. Graphics
by Tom Peterson. Seattle: Dolphin Enterprises, 1974. 23 cards
in packet. $5.25, single set; $3.95 or less for multiple copies.
Grades 5 and up. From 1207 N.E. 103rd Street, Seattle, WA 98125.

Each nine-inch-square task card contains a well-thought-out
activity related to population, ranging from simple (count the
number of blades of grass in a square inch and measure out the
area required for a million blades) to considerably more complex.
These activities, field tested for junior and senior high
students, seem appropriate also for bright 5th and 6th grade
students and can be modified for younger students. Can be used
as a unit, or incorporated into math, science, and social studies.

Lauber, Patricia. *Too Much Garbage*. Champaign: Garrad, 1974. 64 pp. $5.97. Grades 2-6.

Shows the problems of garbage through the viewpoints of a typical family. Aspects of solid waste disposal, the loss of resources, waste of energy, threats to health, and aesthetics are all vividly discussed for young children.

Mount St. Helens Curriculum Materials Project. *Mount St. Helens: Classroom Activities*. Vancouver: Mount St. Helens Curriculum Materials Project, 1980. Price not given. Grades 2-12. From Educational Service District 112, 1313 NE 134th St., Vancouver, WA 98665.

High quality activities in subject areas from which teachers can select. In three parts: a 52-page student tabloid and teacher's guides at the elementary and secondary level. The tabloid deals with volcanoes, Mt. St. Helen's history, events leading to the eruption and the effects.

McClung, Robert M. *Mice, Moose, and Men: How Their Populations Rise and Fall*. New York: Morrow, 1973. 64 pp. $6.74. Grades 4 and up.

A fascinating introduction to the complex subject of population dynamics, with suggestions for further reading.

Miles Betty. *Save the Earth: An Ecology Handbook for Kids*. New York: Knopf, 1974. 96 pp. $6.99; $2.50, paperback. Grades 3-5.

This activists' handbook, by a teacher at the Bank Street College of Education, is illustrated with attractive photographs and diagrams which manage to integrate concepts and information and yet remain appealing. It provides background information and projects on land, air, and water. Many other projects involve community surveys on such things as water use and pollution.

Navarra, John Gabriel. *Earthquake!* Garden City: Doubleday, 1980. 96 pp. $7.95. Grades 5 and up.

Concise but authoritative treatment on the causes, measurement, and prediction of earthquakes; includes a bit on the theory of plate tetonics.

Penn City. Reading: Nolde Forest Environmental Education Center.
    Game. Price not provided. Grades 4 and up. From Director,
    Simulation Games, Nolde Forest Environmental Education Center,
    Box 392, R.D. No. 1, Reading, PA 19607.

This six-weeks land-use game for intermediate elementary children
involves developing a 350 acre site in an expanding metropolis,
with preliminary research. This source has developed other
environmental games, including games for primary children.

Perl, Lila. The Global Food Shortage: Food Scarcity on Our Planet
    and What We Can Do About It. New York: Morrow, 1976. 127 pp.
    $5.95. Grades 5 and up.

This well-organized and moving book deals in separate sections
(sometimes based on Ms. Perl's personal experiences in developing
countries) with the population explosion, the relationship between
energy use and food supply, patterns of food distribution within
the global community, ways to improve the distribution and
possibilities for expanding our food supply. Serious and informed,
though not discouraging: an important book for thinking children.

Pringle, Laurence. Chains, Webs, and Pyramids: The Flow of Energy
    in Nature. New York: Crowell, 1975. 34 pp. $5.50. Grades 3-6.

A thoughtful introduction to food chains and their importance in
the maintenance and balance of nature. Explains some of the
methods used to trace the flow of food energy. Handsome and
delicate illustrations.

Pringle, Laurence. Nuclear Power: From Physics to Politics. New
    York: Macmillan, 1979. 144 pp. $7.95. Grades 6 and up.

Carefully researched and clearly written, it surveys the development of nuclear power, reviews the accident at Three Mile Island
reactor and takes a provocative look at the nuclear controversy.

Pringle, Laurence P. Recycling Resources. New York: Macmillan,
    1974. 119 pp. $5.95. Grades 6 and up.

Suggests a class trip to a landfill or incinerator. Gives
statistics in a way that catches children's interest and concern.
Final chapters deal with the future and legislative, monetary and
attitudinal problems. Includes an index and graded list of
additional readings. Appropriately printed on recycled paper.

<u>Put Your Garbage to Work</u>. Pittsburgh: Creative Recycling Center, 1980. Educational packet including 24" x 35" poster, fact sheets, and activity suggestions. $3.50. Grades 4 and up. Teacher Resource. From Creative Recycling Center, 4614 Liberty Avenue, Bloomfield, Pittsburgh, PA 15224.

Identifies a dozen different kinds of household discards and provides fact-sheets and suggested activities for using these discards.

Sorvall, Vivian. <u>Water Pollution: Our Troubled Water</u>. West Haven: Pendulum Press, 1972. 63 pp. $1.45, paperback. Grades 7 and up.

Examines physiology, water cycle, and consequences of pollution of the simple fluid we take for granted. It accounts for 71% of the human body, is necessary for drinking, growth, and cleanliness.

Sternberg, Barbara. <u>Who Keeps America Clean</u>? New York: Random House, 1976. 73 pp. $2.50, paperback. Grades 4 and up.

This illustrated guide is part of a paperback series which uses photos with lively first-person accounts of men and women working in the fields: <u>Adventures in the World of Work</u>. The adventurers in this volume include a civil engineer, environmental chemist, and wild-life manager (all women) as well as a sewage plant operator, manager of a recycling plant, noise pollution inspector, environmental writer, and a (male) sixth grade teacher who tells how he incorporates environmental interests into his classroom.

This book has descriptions of other interesting environmental positions and addresses of organizations to contact for more information.

Stevens, Leonard. <u>How a Law is Made: The Story of a Bill Against Air Pollution</u>. New York: T. Y. Crowell, 1970. 109 pp. Grades 5 and up.

Uses the story of an air pollution bill to introduce the politics of law-making, the pressure groups, the interactions between law makers and the citizen's role. Impressive content with an easy, narrative approach and a sixth grade reading level.

Simon, Seymour. *Projects with Air: A Science at Work Book.* New York: Franklin Watts, 1975. 96 pp. $4.90. Grades 4 and up.

Describes 27 activities dealing with air and gases, and lists materials needed. The concepts involved are simply explained and applications are suggested. The book is adequately illustrated with black-and-white drawings.

Watson, Jane Werner. *Alternative Energy Sources.* New York: Franklin Watts, 1979. 64 pp. $5.45. First Book Series. Grades 4-8.

A clear and restrained presentation of a difficult, controversial topic. Suggests ways to use sun and wind power, geothermal energy, and how to convert our waste materials into energy. Illustrated with black-and-white photographs, this book includes a glossary and index.

Learning About Weather. David C. Cook Publications, 1978. 16 pictures, 12" x 17" with 32-page *Guide.* $5.50. Grades 2-6.

Colorful photos that illustrate weather phenomena clearly backed by a 32-page guide with background information, a story, discussion starters, and a bibliography for each print. Prints deal with sunshine, winds, clouds, rainbows, lightning, hail, snow, ice and frost, tornadoes, hurricanes, drought, fog, smog, weather forecasters, and weather satellites (the last a drawing). The back of each print lists five questions, background information (for the student).

Wesley, John, developer. *Ecopolis.* Lakeside: Interact, 1971. Game. $14.00. Grades 5-12. From P.O. Box 262, Lakeside, CA 92040.

Involves students in 150 years of North American history, and provides them with an opportunity to solve current problems in the city of Ecopolis. A simulation game with 18 to 35 players, which requires about 12 or 15 forty- to fifty-minute periods. Interact also publishes other ecology games.

Films and Filmstrips

Backyard Alternative Energy. Lawrence: Centron Films, 1980. 16 mm.
Color. 25 minutes. $525.00; $52.50, rental. Grades K-9.

A brief presentation of some alternative energy devices used in
the United States today, including water mills, wind generators,
solar greenhouses, and pedal power.

Coal: The Rock that Burns. Lawrence: Centron Educational Films,
1976. 16 mm. Color film. 13 minutes. Economic Geography
Series. $235.00. Grades 2 and up.

Illustrates where and how coal was formed, how it is mined and
moved to the consumer. Covers areas such as strip mining and
reclamation of strip mining sites.

Discovering Fossils. Chicago: Coronet, 1977. Four color filmstrips, with four cassettes or four records.

Collecting Small Fossils, 64 frames, 11 minutes. Digging for
Dinosaurs, 55 frames, 11 minutes. Reconstructing Prehistoric
Eras, 55 frames, 11 minutes. Clues to Dating Fossils, 57 frames,
12 minutes. $65.00/set. Grades 4-9.

An interesting presentation on how fossils are formed, collected,
studied, and compared; provides a good introduction to scientific
method and should fascinate children interested in dinosaurs,
fossils, or prehistory. Good photography and audio quality.
Guide introduces scientific vocabulary and includes general
objectives, instructional design, activities and projects,
pre- and post-viewing questions.

Energy Sources of the Future. New York: McGraw-Hill, 1974.
16 mm. Color film. 15 minutes, with teacher's guide.
$240.00; $12.50, rental. Grades 5-8.

A quick overview of ten sources of alternate energy (shales,
underground coal gasification, repulsive magnetic levitation,
superconductivity, nuclear power, solar energy, wind, steam,
tides, and garbage). Stresses the ideas of choice and citizen
responsibility along with showing the processes of use and
recovery.

Garbage. Seattle: King Screen Productions, 1968. 16 mm. Color
    film. 11 minutes. $125.00. Grades 2 and up.

Visual exploration of the sea of garbage that threatens to overwhelm us; follows garbage from kitchen and cafe to the dump and
beyond. No narration.

Garbage. Santa Monica: BFA, 1970. 16 mm. Color film. 11 minutes.
    $165.00; $20.00, rental. All Grades.

Another visual essay on garbage considers the garbage can as art,
garbage disposal, and garbage as a menace threatening to engulf
the world.

Geology. Santa Monica: BFA Educational Media, 1977. Four color
    filmstrips, four cassettes.

Things that Build Up the Earth, 50 frames, 7 minutes. Things
that Tear Down the Earth, 50 frames, 7 minutes. Water Cycle,
47 frames, 8 minutes. Mountains and Rocks, 49 frames, 8 minutes.
$56.00/set. Grades 4-6.

Good explanation of geologic concepts and forces at the middle
grade level, well illustrated with photos from the U.S. Geodetic
Survey. Guide includes objectives, vocabulary, and discussion
questions that require deductive thinking

Joey's World. Santa Monica: Stephen Bosustow Productions, 1974.
    16 mm. Color film. Also 3/4" videocassette. $300.00; $15.00/
    day rental. Grades 3 and up.

A mood/think piece on the kind of world awaiting Joey, the 7-
year-old son of the narrator in the next quarter century. Joey
is shown playing--unaware of our tremendous consumption of raw
materials. The point is that we need to conserve, reuse, recycle
and weigh our uses of materials.

Oceans: A Key to the Future. United Learning, 1977. Five color
    filmstrips, five cassettes.

Past, Present and Future, 50 frames, 9 minutes. Storehouse of
Food, 52 frames, 11 minutes. Storehouse of Raw Materials, 39
frames, 9 minutes. Storehouse of Power, 38 frames, 9 minutes.
Changing the Oceans, 48 frames, 11 minutes. $75.00/set. Grades
5-8.

A stimulating presentation of human interdependence with the sea
that emphasizes the oceans' potential for meeting our demands for
food, power, and raw materials, thus providing a context for
information on the oceans' size, depth, physical features and
composition, life forms, life zones and relationship to land
masses and waterways. Visuals combine photography, drawings,
painting and diagrams. Guide includes summaries, quizzes, objectives

Persistent Seed. New York: National Film Board of Canada, 1963.
16 mm. Color film. 15 minutes. Rental only. Grades 3 and up.

Visuals and natural sounds--but no narration--shows the growth
of a seed amidst cement blocks and bulldozers.

Rivers: Roots of the Ocean. Burbank: Walt Disney Educational Media,
1979. Five color filmstrips, 85 frames each; five cassettes, 15
minutes each. $115.00/set.

A well paced series on the past, present, and future of the
Colorado, Nile, Mississippi, Amazon, and Thames Rivers--covering
for each, the river's relation with the ocean, its sources and
natural wealth, its influence on the environment, and its ecological
balance today. Most of these rivers, of course, have been
threatened or are still threatened by pollution and detrimental
changes caused by people.

Rubbish to Riches. Glendale: Aims Instructional Media, 1979. 16 mm.
Animated color film. 11 minutes $215.00; $25.00 rental. Grades
5 and up.

A general introduction to methods of converting trash to valuable
resources; includes systems for generating methane from landfill
as well as means of recovering and recycling combustible and
noncombustible items from dumps.

The Water Planet with Jacques Cousteau. Irvine: Doubleday Media, 1970.
16 mm. Color film. 20 minutes. Undersea World Series. Rental
only. Grades 5 and up.

According to Cousteau, Earth is the only water planet and--if we
don't take care of it--there won't be any more. Tells how to take
care of and avoid overexploiting our sea resources.

<u>Seasons: Man's and Nature's</u>. Los Angeles: Oxford Films, 1972.
16 mm. Color film. 11 minutes. $170.00. All Grades.

Rich in content, color, and detail, this brief film presents
images of many facets of the seasons. Evocative for science or
artistic expressions. Relates well to units on ecology, science,
weather, or seasons.

General Resources for Teaching about Science and Society

General Resources for Teaching About Science and Society

This is an extensive, but not exhaustive, personal selection, limited almost exclusively to in-print trade books, games, films, and filmstrips, including many resources that lead to other sources of information.

Materials were selected for intrinsic quality, with some preference being given for inexpensive materials, materials that emphasize activities, and/or the interconnectedness between science and the rest of the world. The resources in this section include general references, sources for information, professional textbooks, organizations, and periodicals. There are resources specifically for biology, health, physical and earth sciences at the end of each section.

Theory into Practice

The books in this section lean towards theory. Those in the following section are practical in nature.

Barman, Charles R., and others. Science and Societal Issues: A Guide for Science Teachers. Ames, Iowa: Iowa State University Press, 1982, 145 pp.

Helps students confront controversial issues and make personal decisions, and helps teachers think through problem areas. Mostly for the secondary teacher, but many issue-oriented areas, such as energy choices, the metric system, automobile safety restraints, etc., are relevant for the elementary teacher.

Bybee, Rodger and Sund, Robert. Piaget for Educators. Columbus: Charles E. Merrill and Company, 1982. 318 pp. $14.95.

Presents Piaget's theory in the context of education and school. Numerous activities and practical suggestions are provided. A valuable resource for teachers at all levels.

Charles, Cheryl, and Samples, Bob, editors. Science and Society: Knowing, Teaching, Learning. Washington, D.C.: National Council for the Social Studies, 1978. 88 pp. $4.95.

A fairly cohesive collection of essays by well credentialed scholars and visionaries, including such names as Margaret Mead, Jonas Salk, and Carl Rogers. Sections consist of essays on science-related issues with educator's responses focusing on classroom implications.

Good, Ronald G. How Children Learn Science: Conceptual Development and Implications for Teaching. New York: Macmillan, 1977. 337 pp. $10.95.

Presents selected concepts in science and mathematics, and ideas concerning mental structures related to the concepts. Part I reviews Jean Piaget's work. Part II considers research studies on cognitive development. Part III describes Piaget's stages of cognitive development. Part IV examines intellectual requirements of concepts in elementary science texts and programs in the first, third, and fifth grades. Part V describes five roles for science teachers, with appropriate conditions. Part VI provides concrete ideas for helping youngsters learn science through investigations. Appendices include a self-test and background materials.

Hofman, Helenmarie, and Ricker, Kenneth S. Sourcebook: Science Education for the Physically Handicapped. Washington, D.C.: $6.00, spiral bound.

Includes chapters on law and the handicapped, teacher training, resources, careers; and visual, auditory, and orthopedic handicaps; as well as a position statement and recommendations.

Lawson, Anton E. 1980 AETS Yearbook: The Psychology of Teaching for Thinking and Creativity. Association for the Education of Teachers in Science, 1979. 319 pp. $7.00, offset from ERIC/ SMEAL.

This seventh yearbook of the Association contains papers that involve the relationship of teaching thinking and creativity in the context of science education, with a forward by Jean Piaget and chapters by such notables as Robert Gagne.

Olson, Robert W. _The Art of Creative Thinking_. New York: Harper & Row, 1980. 265 pp. $4.95, paperback.

Based on research and experiments in ways to stimulate creativity, the book gives techniques and exercises to develop creative ability

Romey, William D. _Teaching the Gifted and Talented in the Science Classroom_. Washington, D.C.: National Education Association, 1980. 64 pp. $4.50.

An intelligent perspective on giftedness as it relates to science teaching and the role of the scientist. Includes many motivational devices for stimulating excellence and many intriguing science activities. Includes a 54-item bibliography. Part of NEA's series on _Teaching the Gifted and Talented in the Content Areas_. A similar work on mathematics costs $3.50.

Simpson, Ronald D., and Anderson, Norman D. _Science, Students & Schools: A Guide for the Middle & Secondary Teacher_. New York: Wiley, 1981. 400 pp. $16.95.

Covers traditional topics such as planning, laboratory teaching, test construction, teaching strategies, and individualizing, plus human relations models, teaching exceptional and multicultural students, and ways of handling controversial issues.

Thelen, Judith. _Improving Reading in Science_. Newark: International Reading Association, 1976. 55 pp. $3.50. Available from IRA, Newark, DE 19711.

Little booklet helpful for improving science reading skills. The five-step plan suggests ways to help students read to learn, with twenty exercises that illustrate how to carry out each step.

Todd, Vivian Edmiston, and Armstrong, Terry. _Beginning Everyday Science Early_. San Jose: Lansford Publishing Co., 1980. 36-page booklet. $4.50. With 11 color overhead transparencies, $99.50.

Booklet outlines the values and methods of teaching science early, and suggests how to choose and organize a science curriculum. Transparencies are recommended for workshops.

Trojcak, Doris A. Science with Children. New York: McGraw-Hill,
    1979. 384 pp. $23.65.

A translation of largely Piagetian theory into practice that
provides an understanding of how children learn science, what
type of science activities are meaningful to children, and how
to plan and present appropriate encounters with science for
children. Well structured and full of detailed suggestions on
projects indoors, outdoors, and in the classroom.

Wadsworth, Barry J. Piaget for the Classroom Teacher. New York:
    Longman, 1978. 304 pp. $5.95.

Piagetian thought well selected and applied to classroom teaching.

Activities, Provisions, Sources, and Practices

Abruscato, Joe, and Hassard, Jack. The Whole Cosmos, Catalog of
    Science Activities for Kids. Santa Monica: Goodyear Publishing,
    1977. $10.95. All grades; Teacher Resource. Available from
    1640-5th Street, Santa Monica, CA 90401.

A reading and learning experience for science teachers and
students, this catalog includes science activities, creative
arts activities, puzzles, games, and biographies of scientists
in life, physical, earth, and aerospace sciences.

The same authors have prepared The Earthpeople Activity Book
(same price, same source) that includes ideas, games and
projects from and for past, present, and future earthpeople,
with good activities in archaeology, anthropology, and ecology
for middle-graders.

Bartholomew, Rolland B., and Cawley, Frank E. Science Laboratory
    Techniques: A Handbook for Teachers and Students. Menlo Park:
    Addison-Wesley, 1980. 311 pp. $12.50, spiral bound. Teacher
    Resource.

Covers major demonstration and laboratory techniques for all
levels, including general biology (as sterilizing, making leaf
prints), earth sciences, chemistry, and physics, with helpful
appendices.

Bergman, Abby Barry, and Jacobson, Willard. <u>Science for Children</u>:
   <u>A Book for Teachers</u>. New York: Prentice-Hall, 1980. 567 pp.
   $17.95.

   This book offers a wealth of typically organized, tested science
   project ideas. Includes techniques for gearing a science program
   to each individual child's conceptual and perceptual ability.

Blackwelder, Sheila. <u>Science for All Seasons: Science Experiments</u>
   <u>for Young Children</u>. New York: Prentice-Hall, 1980. 272 pp.
   $11.95, cloth. Grades K-6. Teacher Resource.

   Activities that answer questions and teach problem solving
   techniques as well as answering specific children's questions.

Fyffe, Darrel, and others. <u>My Side of the Mountain: Science</u>
   <u>Webs and Activities</u>. Bowling Green: Bowling Green State
   University, 1979. Teacher Resource. Available from Bowling
   Green, OH 43403.

   A matrix listing the interrelationships between personal survival
   science, air and weather, animals, plants, ecology, senses, and
   food. Lists activities to develop the concept of science and
   the environment interrelated.

Gross, Phyllis. <u>Teaching Science in an Outdoor Environment</u>. Berkeley:
   University of Calirornia Press, 1972. 175 pp. $3.95, paperback.
   Teacher Resource.

   Includes many suggestions, starting points, and activities for
   learning science in an outdoor environment, starting with the
   school environment and moving out to vacant lots, private and
   public lands. Includes interesting, creative, and self-
   actualizing activities appropriate for independent study,
   class projects, and field trips.

Humphrey, James H. <u>Teaching Elementary Science Through Motor</u>
   <u>Learning</u>. Springfield: C. C. Thomas, 1975. $8.75.

   Based on the premise that children will learn better when
   academic learning occurs through physical activity. Provides
   specific game-like motor activities for studying areas like the
   earth and the universe, conditions of life, chemical and
   physical changes. Included for each area are applications to be
   made and the concepts to be learned.

McCormack, Alan J. Outdoor Areas as Learning Libraries: CESI Source-book. Council for Elementary Science, International, 1979. 216 pp. $6.50, offset. From ERIC/SMEAL.

Provides ideas for outdoor learning experiences, appropriate for grades one and up, in areas surrounding the school.

McGiffin, Heather, and Brownley, Nancie, editors. Animals in Educa-tion: A Resource for Biology Teachers. Washington, D.C.: Humane Education, 1979. $9.95. Teacher Resource. Available from National Association for the Advancement of Humane Education, 2100 L Street NW, Washington, D.C. 20037.

Includes 16 articles addressing the controversy on the use of live animals in elementary and high school projects; also includes HSUS guidelines for the use of live aniamls in biology classes and science fairs, with a discussion of state legislation on this topic.

Other publications of the HSUS include a magazine for teachers, Humane Education, quarterly, $7.00; another magazine for children, Kind, 6 issues/year, $4.00, quantity discount; a good book on Careers Working with Animals ($6.95); and $6.00 Superpackets of humane education games, projects, and worksheets.

Orlans, F. Barbara. Animal Care from Protozoa to Small Mammals. Reading: Addison-Wesley, 1977. 374 pp. $10.95. Teacher Resource.

A practical compendium for teachers on how to find, order, culture, feed, care for, handle, and teach about living animals. About half the book is devoted to vertebrates, half to invertebrates, (excluding birds) wild mammals, domesticated carnivores, monkeys, and ungualates. Emphasizes the proper handling of laboratory animals, with practical directions (how to pick up frogs, how to make cages, etc.).

Radford, Don. <u>Science from Toys: Stages 1 & 2, and Background: A Unit for Teachers</u>. London: Macdonald Education, 1972. A School Council Publication. 92 pp. $7.50. Available from Macdonald-Raintree, 205 W. Highland Avenue, Milwaukee, WI 53203. Teacher Resource.

An interesting volume that includes the history of toys as well as correlating educational uses of toys with Piagetian stages. Arranges toys by types (spinning toys, toys that make sounds or music, etc.) and for each type suggests such educational applications as illustrative materials, principles to be investigated, etc. Includes charts for each type of toy and an index to objectives.

A companion volume, <u>Science, Models and Toys: Stage 3</u>, explores the uses of toys for older children.

Schmidt, Victor E., and Rockcastle, Verne N. <u>Teaching Science with Everyday Things</u>. New York: McGraw-Hill, 1968. 167 pp. $8.95. Teacher Resource.

A practical, attractive little book, based on years of university experience in teaching science teachers. It includes about 100 activities in all areas of science, well designed to encourage pupil participation.

Trowbridge, L.; Bybee, R.; and Sund, R. <u>Becoming A Secondary School Science Teacher</u>. (Columbus: Charles E. Merrill and Company, 1981).

Contains many ideas and methods appropriate for teachers at all levels, but especially junior high and middle school.

Sources for More Information

Newman, Michele M., and McRae, Madelyn A., compilers and editors. <u>Films in the Sciences: Reviews and Recommendations</u>. Washington, D.C.: American Association for the Advancement of Science, 1980. 184 pp. $14.00.

Summarizes, reviews, and evaluates nearly 1,000 films in all areas of science, with reviews arranged by Dewey Decimal Number. Includes indexes by subject, title, and film distributor.

Saterstrom, Mary H., and Renner, John W., editors. <u>Educators Guide</u>
   <u>to Free Science Materials</u>. 21st Edition, 1980-1981. Randolph:
   Educators Progress Service, 1980.

The current edition of this ongoing guide includes almost 2,000
free items: 1,125 films, 35 filmstrips, 31 slide sets, 49 audio-
tapes, 161 videotapes, 1 script, 5 transcriptions, and 519 print
items--about 30% starred items new to this edition. It is divided
into subject areas--from aerospace and biology through physics
and teacher references. For each item, it includes title, source,
type of media, length, date when available, usually not the
audience or grade level. While it includes many good items (at
a desirable price), it is unselective. For example, its environmental education films (mostly by industrial sources) include some
by notorious polluters. It should be used with care and discrimination.

Woodbury, Marda. <u>Selecting Materials for Instruction: Subject</u>
   <u>Areas and Implementation</u>. Littleton: Libraries Unlimited, 1980.
   335 pp. $19.50. Teacher Resource.

Provides extensive criteria and resources for the different
subject fields, with separate chapters on science, mathematics,
environmental education, affective education, health education,
narcotics, nutrition, and sex/family life education, among others.
Each chapter leads to organizations and resource bibliographies,
as well as to standards and suggestions that simplify the process
of selection.

This is one of a series of three volumes that cover the process
of selection thoroughly. <u>Selecting Materials for Instruction:</u>
<u>Media and the Curriculum</u> ($18.50) covers requirements and sources
for different media, as toys, games, films, and has a thorough
chapter on free materials, which considers the problems of selecting
free science materials. <u>Selecting Materials for Instruction:</u>
<u>Issues and Policies</u> ($18.50) provides an overview of policies and
criteria, with chapters on teacher, parent, and student roles in
selection, and on selecting for individualization, gifted children,
and special education.

Information on Games

Many of the activity books also include activities that could be considered games or simulations.

Davis, Arnold R., and Miller, Donald C. Science Games. Belmont: Fearon-Pitman, 1974. 30 pp. $2.95, paperback. Grades 1-6.

Describes 52 inexpensive games for elementary science classes which can be made by students or teachers and require only a minimum of equipment. For each game, the book provides objectives, number of players, materials required, if any, and procedures.

Ellington, H. I., and others. Games & Simulations in Science Education. New York: Nichols Publishing, 1980. 180 pp. $23.75. Available from W. G. Nichols, Inc., P.O. Box 96, New York, NY 10024.

Reviews the role of games and simulations in science education, and contains a comprehensive collection of data sheets on the science-based exercises that are currently available.

Horn, Robert E., and Cleaves, A., editors. The Guide to Simulations/ Games for Education and Training. 4th Ed. Beverly Hills: Sage, 1980. 2 volumes. $49.95 for both: Vol. 1: Academic Simulations/ Games, and Vol. 2: Business Games.

The basic guide to simulations and games with more than 1,400 separate games in the current edition. Half of the entries in this edition are new, with games listed for all levels (with information on source, number and age level of players, etc.). Separate chapters include games on the future, ecology, and science, with introductory essays on each subject area.

Hounshell, Paul B., and Trollinger, Ira R. Games for the Science Classroom: An Annotated Bibliography. Washington, D.C.: National Science Teachers Association, 1977. 24 pp. $3.75, paperback.

Includes 1977 information on how to choose, order, or prepare more than 100 science games, along with summaries of their rules. Commentary includes purpose of each game and its usability in the classroom.

Reese, Jay, Simulation Games and Learning Activities Kit for the Elementary School. West Nyack: Parker, 1977.

A book-form kit that provides charts, forms, maps, and procedures for a wide variety of learning games and simulations.

Organizations and Information Sources

The few organizations listed here are some of the many that could be helpful to elementary and junior/middle school science teachers. Many more are incorporated and described in Woodbury's series on Selecting Materials for Instruction. Her Subject Areas and Implementation is especially valuable for areas related to science, environmental education, health education, sex education, nutrition education, and drug education.

American Association for the Advancement of Science (AAAS)
    1776 Massachusetts Avenue NW
    Washington, D.C. 20036 (202) 467-4400

    Its publications include many that review elementary (and other) science materials.

Animal Welfare Institute
    P.O. Box 3650
    Washington, D.C. 20002

    This group produces some valuable items for teachers. Their First Aid and Care of Small Animals (46 pp.) is free and useful. Their Humane Biology Projects is worth looking into.

Center for Science in the Public Interest (CSPI)
    1757 S Street NW
    Washington, D.C. 20009 (202) 332-9110

    A public service organization whose well researched and attractive publications on food and nutrition balance corporate offerings. Their monthly magazine Nutrition Action includes news, activities and reviews.

    Their Creative Food Experiences for Children by Mary Goodwind (1974) is well set up for teaching with activities, games, recipes, and facts. Their Nutrition Scoreboard and Chemical Cuisine are attractive and accurate posters.

ERIC Clearinghouse for Science, Mathematics, and Environmental Education (ERIC/SMEAC)
    Ohio State University
    1200 Chambers Road, Third Floor
    Columbus, OH 43210 (614) 422-6717

ERIC/SMEAC cont'd
Like other ERIC Clearinghouses, this processes documents and articles for inclusion in Resources in Education (RIE) and Current Index to Journals in Education (CIJE). Additionally, it has an extensive publication program whose materials are listed in a free catalog. Compiles many summaries of research and practice.

The ERIC Clearinghouse for Social Studies/Social Science Education (855 Broadway, Boulder, CO 80302) also has some materials in the areas where social studies impinge on science (for example, environmental education).

Food and Nutrition Information and Educational Materials Center
National Agricultural Library
U.S. Department of Agriculture
10301 Baltimore Blvd.
Beltsville, MD 20705 (301) 344-4719

Disseminates information on food and nutrition to those teaching nutrition to children. Information includes books, pamphlets, films, tapes, manuals, programmed materials, etc. It also compiles bibliographies of loan materials and distributes these free to nutrition educators as long as the supply lasts.

Hatheway Environmental Education Institute
Massachusetts Audubon Society
Great South Road
Lincoln, MA 01733 (617) 259-9500

Specializes in teacher training and in developing and collecting curriculum materials in environmental education; publishes The Curious Naturalist as well as bibliographies on environmental education.

National Association of Biology Teachers
11250 Roger Bacon Drive
Reston, VA 22090

An organization that recognizes the importance of biology education at all grade levels. It has a monthly publication--The American Biology Teacher and other materials for teachers.

National Nutrition Education Clearinghouse (NNECH)
2140 Shattuck Avenue
Berkeley, CA 94704   (415) 548-1363

A Clearinghouse of the Society of Nutrition Education with a
substantial library of more than 8,000 items, and an ongoing
publication program; it compiles bibliographies and evaluates
teaching materials.

Their Journal of Nutrition Education reviews books, current
research, and curriculum materials. Other publications include
guides to audiovisuals, elementary teacher materials, sources,
etc.

National Science Teachers Association (NSTA)
1742 Connecticut Avenue NW
Washington, D.C. 20009   (202) 265-4150

An organization of science teachers, founded in 1944, whose
membership includes Science and Children (entered under the
Periodicals section) as well as the NSTA News-Bulletin and a
discount on many supplementary publications.

Publications include a how-to-do-it series, a Careers series,
Elementary Science Packets (about $3.00 each) that list resources.
These include Environment and Energy. Other publications worth
acquiring are Hunger: The World Food Crisis and Population:
The Human Dilemma

Orienteering Services
308 West Fillmore
Colorado Springs, CO 80907

A useful group for outdoor science teachers who want to develop
map skills along with other programs. Offerings include a very
helpful workbook, Your Way with Map and Compass (student's
edition, $1.95, paperback; teacher's edition, $2.95, paperback).
A filmstrip program, Adventures with Map and Compass costs
$90.00. Write for their catalog.

The Science Man
4738 N. Harlem
Harwood Hts., IL 60656   (312) 867-4441

This publisher and distributor issues a stimulating catalog of
science books and supplies "hand-chosen for their creative
philosophy and their subject materials." Their off-beat table of
contents includes, among others: "the kitchen sink," energy
awareness, action learning, getting better, "time, space, and
seasons," pint-sized size, teacher stuff, and interdisciplinary
encounters.

Selective Educational Equipment (SEE), Inc.
3 Bridge Street
Newton, MA 02195

Specializes in inexpensive activity-oriented and manipulative
items, as rain gauges, student activity cards--all carefully
selected to involve students in their own education. Send for
their catalog.

Sex Information and Education Council of the U.S. (SIECUS)
137 North Franklin Street
Hempstead, NY 11550   (516) 483-3033

A basic resource and clearinghouse on materials and information
related to human sexuality and sex education; it creates and
distributes original books, study guides, and bibliographies,
as well as reviewing other materials in its bimonthly SIECUS
Report.

Periodicals

This section includes periodicals for both teachers and students,
emphasizing those that suggest activities and/or review books, games,
and media materials.
Other review sources are librarians' publications, e.g. Booklist
(which reviews audiovisual materials also), Library Journal, School
Library Journal, and others. The Educational Film Library Association's
Sightlines and Landers Film Reviews are the best review sources for
educational films.

Science education articles in other publications can be followed
through two periodical indexes: Education Index is frequently found
in large public libraries; Current Index to Journals in Education (CIJE)

is available at many schools of education and district-level libraries. Computer searches of <u>CIJE</u> are available through sources that search ERIC.

<u>American Education</u>. 10 issues/year. $12.00. From Superintendent of Documents, Government Printing Office, Washington, D.C. 20402.

> Issued by the U.S. Department of Education and reflecting the federal interest in education at all levels. Reports on U.S. government publications, federal funds, research developments and statistics.

<u>Appraisal: Children's Science Books</u>. 3 issues/year. $12.00. From Appraisal, Children's Science Book Review Committee, 13 Appian Way, Cambridge, MA 02138.

> An interesting review journal that combines excellent evaluative annotations and ratings by children's librarians and science specialists. Includes rating and grade level for each book-- covers 70 to 80 books per issue.

<u>The Computing Teacher</u>. Currently 7 issues/year. $14.50/9 issues. From Computing Center, Eastern Oregon State College, La Grande, OR 97850.

> A journal for persons interested in the instructional use of computers covering the impact of computers on curriculum, teaching computing, and using computers. Ongoing departments include film reviews, book reviews, and software reviews, and general news and information for the elementary grades.

<u>Creation/Evolution</u>. Quarterly. $8.00/year; $2.50 individual issues; discount rates for copies to be distributed to legislators, school boards, students, etc. From P.O. Box 5, Amherst Branch, Buffalo, NY 14226.

> A nonprofit journal about 48 pages per issue, dedicated to promoting evolutionary science and answering the arguments of creationists, with articles, reports, and updates on the status of creation bills and resolutions.

<u>Instructor</u>. 9 issues/year. $14.00. From Instructor Publications, Instructor Park, Dansville, NY 14437.

A journal for elementary school teachers that review about 500 books, nonprint materials, and professional books each year. Its reviews of science materials are in the October, December, January, and March issues; its reviews of films and filmstrips occur in October, December, February, and April. It occasionally issues bibliographies on science topics, usually in the October issue.

<u>Journal of Environmental Education</u>. Quarterly. $10.00/year for individuals; $15.00/year for institutions. From Heldref Publications, 4000 Albemarle Street NW, Suite 500, Washington, D.C. 20016.

An award-winning multidisciplinary resource devoted to research and practice in environmental education and communication. Includes project reports, critical essays, and research articles.

<u>Journal of Nutrition Education</u>. Quarterly. $20.00 personal subscription; $25.00 institutions. From Society of Nutrition Education, 2140 Shattuck Avenue, Suite 1110, Berkeley, CA 94704.

Includes substantial, thoughtful reviews of books, games, reports, charts, audiovisuals, classroom materials, and professional readings--about 70 items per issue.

<u>National Geographic World</u>. Monthly. $6.95/year. From National Geographic Society, Department 00481, 17th and M Streets NW, Washington, D.C. 20036.

A children's magazine with many articles that are useful for studying our natural and human-created environment, with features like "Easter Ornaments," "Rooftop Ideas," and "Fun Pack,"

<u>Odyssey</u>. Monthly. $9.95/year, quantity discount. From P.O. Box 92788, Milwaukee, WI 53202.

An astronomy and outer-space magazine highly popular with kids, guaranteed to be read. Includes ongoing articles on astronomy and space travel, with columns like Kepler's Corner, NASA News; also distributes inexpensive full-color <u>Space Cadet Posters</u>.

<u>Ranger Rick's Nature Magazine</u>. 10 issues/year. $9.50 for members of
Ranger Rick's Nature Club. From National Wildlife Federation,
1412-16th Street NW, Washington, D.C. 20036. Grades 4 and up.

Colorful nature magazine of about 48 pages, with many accurate
articles and activities. <u>Activity Guides</u> to accompany this
publication are about 8 pages each, and cost $3.00 for 10 issues.

<u>Your Big Backyard</u> (also issued by NWF) is for preschool and primary
children (10 issues/year for $7.50). Each issue contains about 20
pages, with a separate page of suggestions for parents and teachers,
and many built-in exercises. It is available from 8925 Leesburg
Pike, Vienna, VA 22180.

<u>Science Activities</u>. Quarterly. $10.00/year for individuals; $15.00 for
for institutions. From 4000 Albemarle Street NW, Washington,
D.C. 20016.

A periodical which cuts a wide swath, from observation of grasshoppers to astronomical photography. Emphasizes activities, mostly
at the high school level, though many can be translated downward
through the grades. It reviews about eight books per issue.

<u>Science and Children</u>. 8 issues/year. $20.00 includes membership.
From National Science Teachers Association, 1742 Connecticut
Avenue NW, Washington, D.C. 20009.

The national professional journal for elementary and middle school
teachers, with good articles and reviews of 20 to 25 books per
issue. The March issue includes an annual annotated list of about
100 recommended science books prepared by a joint committee of the
NSTA and the Children's Book Council. The list is also available
free of charge from the Children's Book Council, 65 Irving Place,
New York, NY 10013 with first-class postage for 2 ounces.

<u>Science Books and Films</u>. 5 issues/year. $17.50. From American
Association for the Advancement of Science, 1515 Massachusetts
Avenue NW, Washington, D.C. 20005.

An easy-to-use review journal, arranged by Dewey Decimal System,
that reviews about 250 trade and textbooks and 50 to 60 films
and filmstrips in each issue. Appraisals (from highly recommended
to not recommended) and grade levels can be seen at a glance. Items
reviewed are appropriate for elementary, junior and senior high,
college students, professionals and general audiences. The bulk
of the material may be for older audiences.

<u>Scientific American</u>. Monthly. $21.00/year, $2.00/issue. From 415
    Madison Avenue, New York, NY 10017.

The December issue of this journal includes an annual conspectus
    on books on science and technology for younger readers. The
    December 1980 issue, for example, included long narrative reviews
    of 25 very interesting and diverse books.

TELEVISION
MARKETING

TELEVISION MARKETING

Network,
Local,
and Cable

DAVID POLTRACK

MCGRAW-HILL BOOK COMPANY

New York   St. Louis   San Francisco   Auckland
Bogotá   Hamburg   Johannesburg   London
Madrid   Mexico   Montreal   New Delhi
Panama   Paris   São Paulo   Singapore   Sydney
Tokyo   Toronto

Library of Congress Cataloging in Publication Data

Poltrack, David.
  Television marketing.

  Includes index.
  1. Television advertising.   2. Cable television
advertising.   I. Title.
HF6146.T42P64   1983   659.14′3   83-851
ISBN 0-07-050406-7

1 2 3 4 5 6 7 8 9 0   DOCDOC   8 9 8 7 6 5 4 3

ISBN 0-07-050406-7

The editors for this book were William R. Newton and
Patti Scott, the designer was Elliot Epstein, and the
production supervisor was Teresa F. Leaden. It was set in
Melior by J. M. Post Graphics, Corp.

Printed and bound by R. R. Donnelley & Sons Company.

This book is dedicated
to my wife, Leslie,
whose inspiration shaped it
from conception to completion.

ABOUT THE AUTHOR

David F. Poltrack began in advertising after receiving his B.A. degree magna cum laude from Notre Dame. At Ted Bates Advertising, he rose rapidly from an assistant media buyer to media group manager.

Since 1969, when he joined CBS in the Television Stations Division, David Poltrack has served as director in a variety of important marketing positions. He moved over to the CBS network as vice president, Marketing Services, in 1979, where his responsibilities included audience and market research, market planning, sales promotion, merchandising, and audiovisual production. In 1982, he assumed the position of vice president, research, for the CBS broadcast group responsible for all CBS research in the areas of television, radio, and cable.

A resident of New Canaan, Connecticut, David Poltrack received his M.B.A. degree from New York University. As an adjunct associate professor at NYU he currently teaches a number of courses in advertising and marketing.

Contents

Preface

In the relatively short time span of four decades television has evolved from a medium offering a limited selection of programs delivered to the viewer in a low-quality black-and-white format to a medium providing a vast array of program options delivered in color enhanced by dazzling special effects. During that period television has been established as the primary form of commercial communication for the nation's leading business concerns. This year, 1983, over $12 billion will be invested in television advertising. This medium represents the major component of the marketing programs of several thousand individual brands and business enterprises. An understanding of television advertising and the television advertising marketplace is, therefore, vital to today's marketing executive.

The television advertising industry is highly specialized. Commercial production houses create commercials. Media planners design the advertising campaigns. Media buyers purchase television time from media sales representatives. The foundations of two major industries, the advertising industry and the television industry, are rooted in the buying and selling of television time for the presentation of commercial messages. Yet only a fraction of the individuals employed in these two industries are directly involved in the television advertising process, and those involved are usually only involved in a narrow functional role.

This book is designed to provide an overview of the entire television advertising process for those involved, either directly or indirectly, in that process. For the *marketing executive*—the brand manager or account executive—responsible for integrating television advertising into the marketing plan, this book provides an insight into how the television advertising process can be managed in order to maximize its contribution to that marketing plan. For the *media buyer, media planner, commercial producer, television sales representative, market research executive*, and the other executives involved in one specific facet of television advertising, this book provides an understanding of the other facets of television advertising and how the various facets are interrelated. For the *student of marketing* this book provides an in-depth study of one of its most critical and fascinating aspects.

The book begins with a discussion of television audience measurement, the all-important method for establishing the value of television time. The lexicon of the business is also presented. Next, two chapters each are devoted to the national network television, local television, and cable television markets. One chapter presents the players in each market, the three television networks, the local market television stations, and the cable television networks and systems. Each second chapter then focuses on the dynamics of each television advertising market. Subsequent chapters cover the production of the television commercial, the legal and regulatory aspects of television advertising, the planning of the television campaign, the combination of television advertising with advertising in other media, measuring the effectiveness of the television advertising campaign, establishing the television advertising budget, and direct marketing on television.

I have found my fifteen years as a participant in the world of television advertising, first as a member of the media department at Ted Bates Advertising and then as an executive with both the television stations and television network divisions of CBS, to have been stimulating and rewarding. It is my hope that this book will effectively demonstrate the excitement and dimension of television advertising to the reader.

Many individuals contributed to the preparation of this book. My colleagues at CBS: Mike Eisenberg, Dave Fuchs, Hal Gessner, Jeremy Handelman, Paul Isacsson, Nancy Mendelson, Bernie Saperstein, Dan Scher, and Penny Vare-Armonas. At Arbitron: Pierre Megroz. At A.C. Nielsen: William Behanna. At Simmons Market Research Bureau: Ed Barz and Randy Brown. At Broadcast Advertising Reports: Pro Sherman.

Special thanks to Joe Dicerto, my technical advisor, and Terri Kalyn for her tireless work in the preparation of the manuscript.

David Poltrack

TELEVISION
MARKETING

1

Changing
Television Landscape

The television age began in 1931, when the Federal Communications Commission (FCC) allowed NBC to broadcast the first television signal in New York. By 1950 it was clear that television was the medium of the future. From the beginning it was funded by advertising. It took the three TV networks only until 1951 to reach profitability. By 1960 advertising revenues had jumped to $472 million, compared with $35 million ten years earlier. The 1970 figure was $1.5 billion, and by 1982 the networks were at the $6 billion mark.

The early relationship between television and the advertising community centered on the advertisers providing programming to the networks. The early network schedules included such programs as the *Texaco Star Theater*, the *Philco TV Playhouse*, the *Colgate Comedy Hour*, the *Gillette Cavalcade of Sports*, and the *Kraft Television Theater*. Gradually the emphasis shifted from program sponsorship to a less risky strategy of scattering commercials throughout the network schedules. With this change the advertisers gradually withdrew from program production. Today very few network television programs are client-furnished. Instead, most programs are developed by independent producers and bought by the networks.

The network television marketplace has gradually evolved into eight distinctive markets, coinciding with eight "dayparts": primetime (Monday to Saturday, 8–11 p.m., Sunday, 7–11 p.m.), morning, daytime, news, late night (Monday–Friday, 11:30 p.m. to conclusion), children's programming, sports, and specials. Primetime is the most important daypart, representing the highest viewing level period of the day and accounting for more than 40 percent of all network television adver-

1

tising revenues. Sports and news are two dayparts that have been growing in significance over the years.

The major advertising agencies and their clients dominate the buying
of network time; nine advertisers account for 25 percent of all network
advertising dollars, whereas it takes the bottom 491 network advertisers
to make up another 25 percent. They buy network television time in
three stages. The *upfront market* begins in May for the following television season (September of year 1 through August of year 2). The major
advertisers will lock up key inventory during this period. The *scatter
market* precedes each quarter-year. During these times major advertisers
fill out and adjust their schedules, and seasonal advertisers purchase
their initial schedules. The *opportunistic market* continues throughout
the year. This is when all remaining inventory is sold. If the upfront
market and scatter market have been strong, little inventory will be left
for the opportunistic market. If, however, these markets have been weak,
advertisers can get very good deals during the opportunistic market.
The network television market is covered in greater detail in Chapters
3 and 4.

The growth of television networks has been paralleled by the growth
of television stations. Originally the television station marketplace was
dominated by VHF network affiliates. Today the less powerful UHF
stations are coming into their own, and the independent television
stations are providing the network affiliates with strong competition.

The local television station advertising marketplace has a local and
a national component. The local advertiser has become a more important client for the local station, and the portion of a television station's
revenue this client provides has been growing, partly because of the
recent entry of major retailers into the television medium. Fueled by
an aggressive industry market development effort, retail advertising on
television has grown dramatically in the past decade. Chapters 5 and
6 focus on the local television station and buying time in the local
television market.

Any discussion of the changing television landscape immediately
evokes the emerging world of cable television. Cable television was
born in 1948, when Community Antenna Television began offering
homeowners better television reception through a cable hookup with
a master antenna. A combination of limited service and government
restrictions kept the growth of cable television down until the 1970s.
In 1972, the FCC began lifting its restrictions on cable television. Then,
in 1975, Home Box Office began offering pay television service via
satellite to cable system subscribers throughout the country; the cable
revolution had begun in earnest. By 1981, some 4500 cable systems
were in operation, and another 6000 were in various stages of devel-

opment. In all, there were 22 million subscriber homes, 11 million of which were receiving some pay service. It is estimated that 60 percent of all U.S. television homes will be cable television subscribers and 45 percent will be purchasing some pay service by 1990.

The implications of the growth of cable television for the advertiser are twofold. First, the advertiser has to consider the impact of cable television growth on the television networks and television stations, the primary sources of advertising impressions. Future television campaign planners must adjust for this new competition. Second, the advertiser must assess the advertising opportunities provided by the new cable services. These include the national advertising availabilities offered by the advertiser-supported cable networks, the local and regional advertising opportunities offered by the local cable systems and multiple-system operators, and the as yet unavailable advertising potential represented by the pay cable services.

In addition to cable television, there are many other newcomers on the television horizon. Direct-broadcast satellite (DBS), low-power television (LPTV) stations, and subscription television (STV) all represent even further fragmentation of the television audience. High-definition television and teletext will enhance the advertising potential of the medium. The videotape recorder and video disk player will also change how television is used. And in the more distant future are interactive, two-way cable communication and videotext systems connecting the television, telephone, and home computer in a complete home communications system. Chapters 7 and 8 attempt to put this dynamic medium in perspective.

To understand the television advertising marketplace, it is necessary to understand the product of that marketplace, the television audience. The television advertising marketplace has been likened to a commodity market with prices in constant flux. Its unique elements are the nature and dynamics of the inventory of audience impressions. Unlike other commodities, audience impressions are not directly measurable. Instead, research is used to estimate the sizes of past audiences, and future audiences are predicted from these measurements. Also, viewing patterns change constantly, making the prediction of future audiences based on past audiences anything but a precise science. Thus the subjectivity of buyers and sellers as they attempt to interpret research data must be added to the volatility normally found in a commodity market. The advertiser that enters into negotiations for television time should be well versed in the art of ratings research. Chapter 2 provides an introductory course on types of research, major research suppliers, and terminology of the trade.

Once the advertiser has mastered the rudiments of audience measurement, it is necessary to advance to the more complex aspects of planning the television campaign. All television advertising campaigns are composed of audience impressions. These audience impressions represent a certain number of viewers being exposed to a specific number of commercial messages. The number of *different* viewers exposed to at least one message constitutes the *reach* of the campaign. The number of commercials to which each viewer is, on average, exposed constitutes the *frequency* of the campaign. The television campaign planner will endeavor to maximize the reach of the campaign without reducing the frequency below an effective level.

The minimum level of exposure required for effective communication of the commercial's message is one of the most widely researched and debated issues in advertising research today. The planner attempting to find the right mix for a particular campaign will have to address the issues of commercial audience versus program audience, the timing of the campaign, the complexity of the commercial message, the competitive advertising activity, and the proper mix of national network and local spot television, as well as the basic questions of how much is enough and how much is too much.

Chapter 10 explains these issues, summarizing the key research findings and attempting to mold them into an effective road map for the television campaign planner. Chapter 14 then takes the planner from the theoretical to the practical application through the presentation of a basic format for establishing a television advertising budget.

As the television campaign planner charts the course, a tendency toward too narrow a focus will have to be avoided. In most cases, the television campaign will be but one component of a multimedia advertising campaign, and that campaign but one element of a total marketing program. The planner must be familiar with the synergistic qualities of various media when used in combination with television. Chapter 11 introduces the concept of the media mix and discusses the effective integration of the television campaign with advertising in other media.

Effective television advertising is more than the purchase of time. It is communication of the commercial message to the viewer, and the most important determinant of the effectiveness of commercial communication via television is the commercial itself. The composition of the television commercial and its creative execution will, in all likelihood, overshadow the media planning considerations. What to say? How to say it? How much to spend on production? These questions are all critical to the success of the campaign.

Before the advertiser begins the creative process of developing a commercial, knowledge in these areas is essential. The advertiser must be familiar with the commercial production process. What can be done?

What cannot be done? And how much will a given commercial execution cost? Also, the advertiser must be familiar with what cannot be said. Each commercial must be designed to conform with government regulations and the self-regulatory strictures of the advertising and broadcasting industry. Chapter 9 deals with the commercial and its creation, from concept testing to finished production. Chapter 13 covers advertising regulation and the commercial clearance process.

Finally, no television advertiser is more affected by the current dynamics of the television marketplace than the direct-response marketer. Cable television and such innovations as teletext and interactive cable represent vastly expanded direct-marketing opportunities via television. Chapter 15 focuses on these new vistas for the direct-response advertiser.

Yes, the television landscape is changing dramatically. This book is designed to prepare the advertiser for that change by providing a sound foundation for executing television campaigns and for dealing successfully with the new television era that is on its way.

The Rating Game: Defining the Television Product

The commercial television industry is a unique component of the business sector. Essentially this industry functions like any other within the business community. It spends money and incurs costs to obtain money, to generate revenues. If its member firms are successful, the revenues will be greater than the costs and thus a profit will be realized. The television industry differs in the manner in which it generates revenues. Most business firms offer a product or provide a service in return for a specified financial remuneration. The television industry does manufacture a product—television programming—but it gives that product away for nothing. The television industry obtains its revenues when it sells the users of its primary product—or, more precisely, access to the users of its primary product—to advertisers.

This unique form of business enterprise leads to a two-stage marketing process for the television network and the television station. First, the television audience must be attracted to the program offerings. Second, that audience must be marketed to advertisers. Before a television executive can move from the first marketing stage to the second, there must be an interim step: the audience must be defined.

The advertiser wants to know how many people will see and hear the commercial message and who they will be. Will they be women or men, old or young, rich or poor? All these demographic considerations will affect the price the advertiser is willing to pay.

The necessity for this interim step presents the television marketing and sales executives with a problem. Actual measurement of the entire audience for a program is impossible. With 80 million plus television households in the country, there is no effective way to keep track of each household's viewing. To solve this dilemma, the television industry has turned to the science of statistics. It employs research companies to measure the television audience. These companies use carefully selected samples from the television household universe. They measure, through a variety of devices, the viewing of the people in these samples and, using the science of statistics, project total U.S. viewing levels from these measurements. These measurements and the firms providing them are the subject of this chapter. Before we get into specifics, it is necessary to spend some time on the terminology, or lexicon, of the business.

TELEVISION MEASUREMENT: BASIC TERMINOLOGY

Like most businesses, the television industry has developed a lexicon of its own. Included in the television executive's vocabulary are a series of terms that help define the television audience. Most important among these terms are the rating, HUT and PUT, share, GRPs, and the CPM.

Rating

The *rating* of a television program refers to the percentage of television homes that watched that program. One rating point equals 1 percent of the total television audience. The television audience can be defined either on a household, or *homes*, basis or on a *persons* basis. The most commonly used rating is the *homes* rating, coinciding with the percentage of television households watching the program. This is the rating that you are likely to see published in the press.

So far, it seems quite simple. However, there is one major complication. What constitutes watching a program? Should a rating be confined to those households watching the entire program, or should it be expanded to cover those households that watched any of the program? Actually, there is a rating for both. On the network side, the *average audience rating*, also known as the *AA rating*, is defined as the percentage of U.S. television households that were tuned to a specific program during the average minute of the telecast. Figure 2-1 illustrates how the AA rating is calculated. The AA rating for this hypothetical 15-minute program was a 30; that is, 30 percent of the 10-home universe viewed the average minute of the program. The *total audience rating (TA rating)* is defined as the percentage of U.S. television households that watched any part of the program in excess of 5 minutes. In the example, 4 out of 10 homes, or 40 percent, watched 5 or more minutes of the program. The TA rating was therefore a 40. Note in Figure 2-2 that home 4 was not counted in the TA rating, because it watched only 4 minutes of the program.

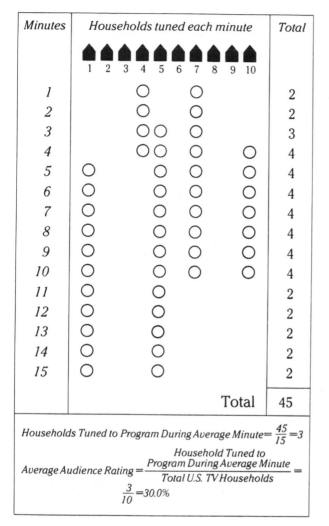

FIGURE 2-1
Average audience rating.

(From *CBS Basic Guide to Network Television*, CBS, New York, 1981.)

The AA rating is the statistic quoted most often. Actually, this rating has become identified with the term *rating*, and the TA rating is seldom used in the normal broadcaster-advertiser negotiations. After all, in most cases a commercial will run during a specified time of the telecast and not throughout the telecast. For this reason, the AA rating is a more accurate estimate of the audience for the commercial than the TA rating.

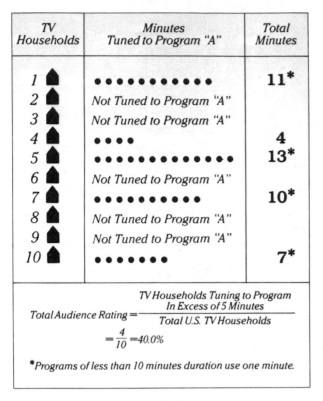

TV Households	Minutes Tuned to Program "A"	Total Minutes
1	• • • • • • • • • • •	11*
2	Not Tuned to Program "A"	
3	Not Tuned to Program "A"	
4	• • • •	4
5	• • • • • • • • • • • • •	13*
6	Not Tuned to Program "A"	
7	• • • • • • • • • •	10*
8	Not Tuned to Program "A"	
9	Not Tuned to Program "A"	
10	• • • • • • •	7*

$$\text{Total Audience Rating} = \frac{\text{TV Households Tuning to Program In Excess of 5 Minutes}}{\text{Total U.S. TV Households}}$$

$$= \frac{4}{10} = 40.0\%$$

*Programs of less than 10 minutes duration use one minute.

FIGURE 2-2

Total audience rating.

(From CBS Basic Guide to Network Television, CBS, New York, 1981.)

Unfortunately, the local-market television measurement services do not use the same precise definition as the network service. They define the rating as the percentage of television households tuned to a particular station for 5 minutes or more during an average quarter-hour. Although this distinction may seem slight, it can result in different audience estimates. A home tuned to a program for 3 minutes of its 30-minute duration would be counted in the network average-minute rating for these 3 minutes, but would be excluded from the average-quarter-hour rating in the local rating.

One final note of caution concerning the varied rating terms: Each rating provided in a national or local-market measurement report represents a percentage of the television household universe covered by that report. A 1 rating in New York, therefore, represents fewer households than a 1 rating nationally, but far more than a 1 rating in Fort Wayne, Indiana.

HUT and PUT

The rating for each station during a specified time period indicates the percentage of the potential audience that was viewing the station at that time. If the ratings of every television station available for viewing by the TV audience during a specified time were combined, this figure would equal the percentage of the potential television audience viewing television during that time. This aggregate figure is referred to as the *households-using-television (HUT) level* when the TV household au-

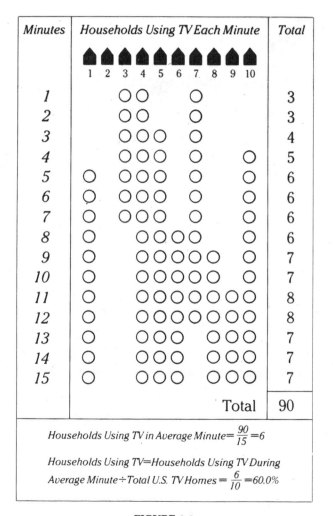

FIGURE 2-3
Households using television.
(From CBS *Basic Guide to Network Television*, CBS, New York, 1981.)

dience is measured or the *persons-using-television (PUT) level* when the total number of persons viewing television is measured. The precise definition of HUT is the percentage of TV households with their TV sets on during the average minute of each 15-minute time period.

Figure 2-3 illustrates this concept. Using the same 10-home base as Figures 2-1 and 2-2, this chart shows the total viewing, *of any station*, by the 10 homes for the 15-minute period. Averaging the homes using television during each of the 15 minutes yields six homes per minute. And 6/10 = 60 percent, the average HUT level during this 15-minute period.

HUT levels vary by time of day and season of the year. Figure 2-4 provides the HUT level during 1979 by hour for February and July. The lowest level of viewing shown is between 7:00 and 8:00 a.m. in July, when only 8 percent of TV homes were tuned in during the average minute. The highest viewing period is between 9:00 and 10:00 p.m. in January, when 66.5 percent, or almost two-thirds, of all TV households were tuned in during the average minute.

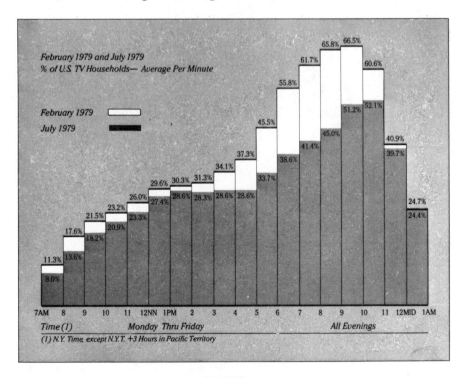

FIGURE 2-4

Hour-by-hour estimates of households using television.

(From "National TV Ratings," NTI, A.C. Nielsen, Chicago, Jan. 29–Feb. 25 and July 2–July 29, 1979.)

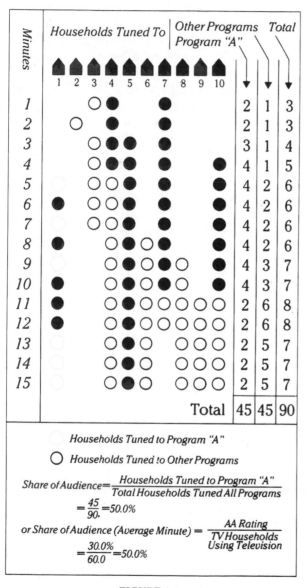

FIGURE 2-5

Share of audience.

(From CBS Basic Guide to Network Television, CBS, New York, 1981.)

Share

Once each station's rating and the HUT level are known, it is possible to calculate each station's share of audience. In our example the program achieved an AA rating of 30 (Figure 2-1) in a time period during which 60 percent of all TV households were viewing television (Figure 2-4). This translates to a 50 percent share of audience for program A (30/60 = 50 percent). Figure 2-5 illustrates this concept.

Share of audience is used to measure a program's strength vis-à-vis other programs. Over time it can be employed to determine whether a program is gaining or declining in relative audience popularity. The share measure also can be used to evaluate the program's relative appeal by season, by time period, and by market.

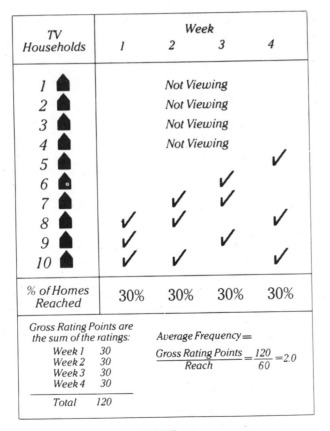

FIGURE 2-6

Gross rating points.

(From CBS *Basic Guide to Network Television,* CBS, New York, 1981.)

Gross Rating Points

An advertiser's television schedule will usually consist of commercials on several different programs. Each program has a rating. By adding these ratings it is possible to compare the relative magnitude of advertisers' schedules. The sum of the ratings for a series of programs is referred to as a *gross rating point (GRP) level*. Figure 2-6 shows the number of homes that watched a program during each of 4 weeks. Each week 3 of the 10 homes viewed the program, generating a 30-rating level. An advertiser that ran in the program each week would have garnered four 30-rated announcements. This translates to 120 GRPs.

The important element in the GRP concept is the *gross* aspect of the measurement. Note that in some cases the program attracted the same households for 2 or 3 of the 4 weeks. In other households (households 5 and 6) the program was viewed only once. So each 30 rating consists of some households that are included in the other three 30 ratings and others that are not. The 120 total includes multiple-episode-viewing households several times. Therefore, it is a gross audience measure.

The total number of households viewing the four telecasts was equal to 120 percent of the total TV homes. Of course, not 120 percent of all TV homes viewed the four programs (an impossibility). Actually, only 60 percent of the households, or 6 out of 10, viewed any of the four telecasts; but since they viewed an average of two telecasts each, the GRP level was 120. Gross audience levels expressed in television homes, as opposed to rating points, are called *gross impressions*. In the example, the gross impressions were 12, the sum of all households' viewing frequency. The GRP concept is a critical one, because advertisers' television campaigns usually are planned on a GRP basis.

Cost per Thousand

There is a wide divergence in the rating levels of various television programs. A late-night or early-morning program may generate only a 1 or 2 rating, whereas a top 10 primetime program will break the 30-rating barrier. The cost of advertising on television programs varies by rating level. However, many other factors influence the cost of advertising on a given television program, factors such as audience composition, time of year, program content, and merchandising considerations. These factors prevent television advertising costs from varying in perfect synchronization with the rating level. Media buyers, therefore, require some other measure to facilitate the relative efficiency of advertising on one program versus another. The measure they have chosen is *cost per thousand (CPM)*.

The CPM is simply the cost per 1000 homes or viewers delivered by the program. A CPM home would be derived by dividing the cost of the commercial unit for the program by the total homes (in thousands) watching the program. For example, if a 30-second unit in a primetime program cost $100,000 and the average audience for that program consisted of 20 million homes, the CPM would be found by dividing the cost ($100,000) by the thousands of homes (20,000):

$$\frac{\$100,000 \text{ (unit cost)}}{20,000 \text{ [number of homes (000) viewing]}} = \$5.00 \text{ cost per thousand}$$

The CPM homes for this program would be $5.00. Television buyer-seller negotiations center on the CPM. Buyers are looking for maximum efficiency (low CPM), whereas sellers seek to maximize total revenue (high CPM). Alternative daypart mixes and stations will be evaluated by the buyer on a CPM basis.

It is more than likely that the CPM used in negotiations will not be the CPM homes, but the CPM for some target demographic group. Buyers seeking to reach adults aged 25–54 with their advertising message will choose the programs that deliver this audience most efficiently. The calculation is the same, except that in this case the denominator is the total adults aged 25–54, rather than the total homes, viewing each program.

A frequently used substitute for the CPM is the cost per point. The *cost per point* is the unit cost divided by the rating delivered by the program. In the example, the 20 million homes would translate into approximately a 25 rating. Dividing the $100,000 unit cost by this 25 rating yields a $4000 cost per point:

$$\frac{\$100,000 \text{ (unit cost)}}{25 \text{ (AA rating)}} = \$4000 \text{ cost per point}$$

Media planners use the cost per point to relate budgets to GRP levels. If a plan calls for 500 GRPs, the cost per point can be used to calculate the budget required. If the television budget has been established at $1 million, the cost per point can be employed to estimate the GRP level that can be planned at that budget level.

Although the cost per point is used widely by media planners, its overall use in the buying and selling process is far below that of the cost per thousand, for two basic reasons:

1. The cost per point does not have the same base from market to market and, therefore, does not allow for comparisons either across markets or between network television and local-market television. Since a national-market rating point equals far more

homes than a New York market rating point, and since a New York market rating point equals far more homes than a Dallas market rating point, comparison of the national network cost per point, the New York cost per point, and the Dallas cost per point is meaningless. The CPM, however, with its total-homes or total-viewers base, does allow for network-to-local television and cross-market comparisons.

2. The cost per point is not a sensitive enough measure for use in making buying decisions. For example, take two programs, A and B. Both have a 5 rating. Program A costs $18,000. Program B costs $20,000. Comparing these programs on a cost-per-point basis would lead the buyer to select program A over program B. [See Figure 2-7(a).] However, program A's rating is actually a 4.5 rounded to a 5.0, whereas program B's rating is a 5.4, also rounded to a 5.0. If the buyer uses the CPM instead of the cost per point, the total audience in the denominator will reflect the unrounded delivery of the two programs, and program B will be chosen. [See Figure 2-7(b).] Obviously, The CPM alternative is superior, since it does not involve rounding. For this reason buyers and sellers prefer to use this more sensitive measurement.

$$\text{Cost per point (CPP)} = \frac{\text{Cost}}{\text{Rating}}$$

Program A: $\qquad \text{CPP} = \frac{\$18,000}{5} = \$3600$

Program B: $\qquad \text{CPP} = \frac{\$20,000}{5} = \$4000$

(a)

$$\text{Cost per thousand (CPM)} = \frac{\text{Cost}}{\text{Total homes}}$$

Program A: $\qquad \text{CPM} = \frac{\$18,000}{3,600,000} = \$5.00$

Program B: $\qquad \text{CPM} = \frac{\$20,000}{4,300,000} = \$4.65$

(b)

FIGURE 2-7

(a) Cost per point. (b) Cost per thousand.

These terms represent the basic analytical tools used in the planning, buying, and selling of television time. But before the analysis can begin, someone has to provide the numbers. That is the function of the television rating services.

TELEVISION MEASUREMENT SERVICES

Measuring the National Television Audience: The Nielsen Television Index

The major research supplier to the television industry is the A.C. Nielsen Company. It is the nation's largest market research company. The Nielsen food and drug index is the official scorekeeper of the marketing wars fought daily by marketers in the nation's major supermarkets and drug chains. So it was only natural that when these marketers turned to television as their major advertising medium, they turned to Nielsen for audience estimates. Television audience measurement research is conducted on two levels, national and local. On the national level Nielsen has no competition. On the local level, a second firm, Arbitron, competes with Nielsen.

The basic national television measurement service provided by Nielsen is the Nielsen television index, known in the trade as NTI. This report is issued biweekly (except for 4 nonreport weeks). Audience estimates are developed through the use of two continuing samples, a 1200-household meter sample (to be expanded to 1700 households in 1983) and a 2400-household diary sample.

The meter sample measures household viewing patterns. Cooperating households' televisions are equipped with a Storage Instantaneous Audimeter, which automatically records every minute of television set operation by channel. This information is fed daily by the Audimeter to a central Nielsen computer for processing. Daily reports of viewing are provided to the networks and other subscribers on a 1-day-delay basis. Each week ratings are summarized in the "Fast Weekly Household Audience Report," which provides HUT and rating levels by daypart and rating and share data alphabetically by program. It also reports the number of television stations carrying each program and the percentage of total U.S. coverage they represent.

The meter sample records only tuning; it provides no data on who is viewing. The separate 2400-household diary sample provides this essential "who is watching" component of the overall Nielsen television audience measurement service. The cooperating households in this sample record viewing by all household members in a closed-end diary known as an Audilog. An Audilog is provided for each television set in the household. Viewing is recorded on a quarter-hour basis. Each television set in a diary sample household also is equipped with a Recordimeter, which counts the number of hours that the set is used during the week. Nielsen compares the Recordimeter time record with the diary time to check on diary entries. Where there are notable discrepancies, the diary is eliminated from the final sample.

Viewing estimates from the 1200-household meter and the 2400-household diary samples are combined into 17 biweekly reports. The household viewing estimates from the meter sample provide rating, share, and projected household information for each program aired during the 2-week period covered by the report. The *persons-viewing* estimates obtained from the diary households are expressed as viewers per 1000 viewing households. Persons-viewing data are broken down into key demographic groups:

Total persons	Total men
2 +	Aged 18–34
Total women	Aged 18–49
Aged 18–34	Aged 25–54
Aged 18–49	Aged 35–64
Aged 25–54	Aged 55 +
Aged 35–64	Teens
Aged 55 +	Aged 12–17
Working women	Female
Lady of the house	Aged 12–17
Children	
Aged 2–11	
Aged 6–11	

The user need only multiply the viewer-per-1000 number provided for each demographic group by the number of households (in thousands) provided from the meter sample to obtain an estimate of the number of viewers from that demographic group watching each program.

Figure 2-8 is a sample page from one of these reports. Note that there are several entries from each program. If we focus on the *Dukes of Hazzard* entry, the first line of data, the A line, is the average audience for the entire program. The second line, the B line, is the average audience for that program over the entire season. The Nielsen season begins with the "2nd September" report. In the first column, to the right of the title on the first line, are a series of numbers. The first—14 in this case—is the number of telecasts included in the B-line season-to-date averages. The two lines of data under the B line are the individual half-hour audience levels for each half hour of the telecast. The time

PROGRAM AUDIENCE ESTIMATES (Alphabetic)　　2ND FEB. 1981 REPORT

AUDIENCE COMPOSITION — VIEWERS PER 1000 VIEWING HOUSEHOLDS BY SPECIFIED CATEGORIES

EVENING CONT'D

CBS WEDNESDAY NIGH-CONT'D

Program / Time	KEY	AVG AUD %	SHARE %	AVG AUD (0,000)	TOTAL PERSONS (2+)	LADY OF HOUSE	WORK-ING WOM.	WOMEN TOTAL	W 18-34	W 18-49	W 25-54	W 35-64	W 55+	MEN TOTAL	M 18-34	M 18-49	M 25-54	M 35-64	M 55+	TEENS TOTAL	TEENS FEM.	CHILD. TOTAL	CHILD. 6-11
10.00-10.30	A	16.5	25	1284	1723	752	333	825	292	542	489	407	228	600	241	367	320	293	187	199	94	99	82^
10.30-11.00	A	16.5	26	1284	1725	750	344	824	295	541	488	414	224	600	235	359	314	303	191	215	113	86^	74^
11.00-11.30	A	15.7	28	1221	1478	734	315	823	295	504	491	416	244	520	167^	308	287	277	170^	115^	60^	20^	20^

CHARLIE'S ANGELS — SAT. 8.00P 60 ABC PD — T/C THIS SEASON 5 — NO OF STATIONS 199 — PROG COVERAGE WK1 199 WK2 98 (99)

Program / Time	KEY	AVG AUD %	SHARE %	AVG AUD (0,000)	TOTAL PERSONS (2+)	LADY OF HOUSE	WORK-ING WOM.	WOMEN TOTAL	W 18-34	W 18-49	W 25-54	W 35-64	W 55+	MEN TOTAL	M 18-34	M 18-49	M 25-54	M 35-64	M 55+	TEENS TOTAL	TEENS FEM.	CHILD. TOTAL	CHILD. 6-11
8.00-8.30	A	14.8	25	1151	1938	710	268	802	324	436	328	271	300	591	170	281	254	270	252	255	171^	290	205
8.00-8.30	B	15.3	25	1190	1968	723	274	815	288	429	366	313	321	612	175	311	280	285	246	215	134	326	232
8.30-9.00	A	13.4	23	1043	1953	712	250	811	309	424	324	285	315	578	160	267	238	262	258	260	184	304	214
8.30-9.00	A	16.2	27	1260	1915	708	281	791	334	441	327	256	289	596	176	289	265	274	245	251	161	277	193

CHIPS — 2 SUN. 8.00P 60 NBC OP — T/C THIS SEASON 9 — PROG COVERAGE WK1 207 WK2 99

Program / Time	KEY	AVG AUD %	SHARE %	AVG AUD (0,000)	TOTAL PERSONS (2+)	LADY OF HOUSE	WORK-ING WOM.	WOMEN TOTAL	W 18-34	W 18-49	W 25-54	W 35-64	W 55+	MEN TOTAL	M 18-34	M 18-49	M 25-54	M 35-64	M 55+	TEENS TOTAL	TEENS FEM.	CHILD. TOTAL	CHILD. 6-11
	A	21.4	32	1665	2456	717	243	810	316	523	437	337	236	774	383	565	474	332	157	266	104^	606	397
	B	19.8	29	1540	2292	717	281	810	340	535	443	343	218	763	327	538	476	358	168	259	94	460	309

DUKES OF HAZZARD — FRI. 9.00P 60 CBS CS — T/C THIS SEASON 14 — NO OF STATIONS 205 — PROG COVERAGE WK1 204 WK2 99 (99)

Program / Time	KEY	AVG AUD %	SHARE %	AVG AUD (0,000)	TOTAL PERSONS (2+)	LADY OF HOUSE	WORK-ING WOM.	WOMEN TOTAL	W 18-34	W 18-49	W 25-54	W 35-64	W 55+	MEN TOTAL	M 18-34	M 18-49	M 25-54	M 35-64	M 55+	TEENS TOTAL	TEENS FEM.	CHILD. TOTAL	CHILD. 6-11
9.00-9.30	A	26.4	43	2054	2160	709	266	773	294	464	408	369	246	611	220	373	320	311	203	217	126	559	367
9.00-9.30	B	27.4	44	2155	2155	733	272	801	291	474	420	368	267	638	220	379	342	323	212	204	102	512	364
9.30-10.00	A	25.4	42	1976	2179	706	275	774	294	451	414	375	242	618	228	383	327	316	205	214	131	573	372
9.30-10.00	A	27.5	44	2140	2129	708	254	766	290	451	402	359	251	601	209	362	313	306	205	220	124	542	359

DYNASTY — 2 MON. 9.00P 60 ABC GD — T/C THIS SEASON 4 — PROG COVERAGE WK1 198 WK2 99

Program / Time	KEY	AVG AUD %	SHARE %	AVG AUD (0,000)	TOTAL PERSONS (2+)	LADY OF HOUSE	WORK-ING WOM.	WOMEN TOTAL	W 18-34	W 18-49	W 25-54	W 35-64	W 55+	MEN TOTAL	M 18-34	M 18-49	M 25-54	M 35-64	M 55+	TEENS TOTAL	TEENS FEM.	CHILD. TOTAL	CHILD. 6-11
9.00-9.30	A	16.0	23	1245	1671	816	339	850	297	509	475	445	245	621	194	337	297	305	217	150^	106^	50^	48v
9.00-9.30	B	19.0	27	1478	1782	802	338	856	314	512	482	401	260	648	231	351	333	305	219	155^	117^	112^	78
9.30-10.00	A	15.3	22	1190	1732	829	343	864	285	504	485	470	251	636	189^	343	310	317	226	155^	117^	77^	72^
9.30-10.00	A	16.6	24	1291	1620	806	335	841	309	518	465	423	243	608	198	334	284	296	209	146^	96^	25v	25v

EAST OF EDEN—PART II(S) — 1 MON. 9.00P 114 ABC GD — PROG COVERAGE WK1 200 WK2 99

Program / Time	KEY	AVG AUD %	SHARE %	AVG AUD (0,000)	TOTAL PERSONS (2+)	LADY OF HOUSE	WORK-ING WOM.	WOMEN TOTAL	W 18-34	W 18-49	W 25-54	W 35-64	W 55+	MEN TOTAL	M 18-34	M 18-49	M 25-54	M 35-64	M 55+	TEENS TOTAL	TEENS FEM.	CHILD. TOTAL	CHILD. 6-11
9.00-9.30	A	28.1	42	2186	1627	760	342	859	329	529	493	426	244	618	210	356	365	315	205	105^	67^	45^	40^
9.30-9.30	A	25.9	36	2015	1706	760	344	849	329	510	481	413	246	648	248	384	379	305	204	122	76^	87^	73^
9.30-10.00	A	28.5	41	2217	1635	757	344	865	329	532	495	427	245	622	210	361	364	316	206	99^	64^	49^	42^
10.00-10.30	A	29.0	44	2256	1598	756	340	860	331	539	495	436	240	607	198	347	363	320	206	101^	66^	30^	25v
10.30-11.00	A	29.1	46	2264	1574	769	343	866	326	537	502	432	249	594	184	335	354	325	202	96^	63^	18v	18^

KEY　A CURRENT REPORT　B SEASON AVERAGE　　FOR EXPLANATION OF SYMBOLS, SEE PAGE A

FIGURE 2-8

(From "Program Audience Estimates," A.C. Nielsen, Chicago, 1981.)

frame covered is shown to the left under the title. Also given in this section of the report are the clearance statistics—the number of stations carrying the program (205 and 204 in weeks 1 and 2 of this report period, respectively) and the percentage of the United States that these stations covered (99 percent for both weeks).

Another section of this report, shown in Figure 2-9, provides household viewing information by night of the week. In this section, AA ratings and share-of-audience percentages are given for each program on each network. The bottom line of each network section provides the AA rating by quarter hour. The line above the bottom line gives the share. The first share figure shown is the overall share of the program; the other shares shown, followed by asterisks, are individual half-hour shares. The line above this line provides the overall AA rating for the show (the first number) and each half-hour rating (the numbers followed by asterisks). The top line contains one figure per program—the projected households (in thousands) viewing that program during the average minute. Above the program title is the total number of households viewing 5 minutes or more of the program, expressed as a TA rating (the lower line) and in households (the upper line).

What this section tells the person using the report is that on Friday, February 20, 1981 (week 2), *Dukes of Hazzard* obtained an AA rating of 25.5, which translates to 19,840,000 viewing households per average minute of telecast. This represented a 41 percent share of all household viewing from 9 to 10 p.m. The *Dukes of Hazzard* audience increased from a 23.1 rating level during the first quarter hour to a 24.6 during the second, a 26.0 during the third, and a 28.2 during the final 9:45–10:00 p.m. (EST) quarter hour. On a half-hour basis, this averaged to a 23.9 AA rating and 39 percent share for the 9:00–9:30 p.m. (EST) half hour and a 27.1 AA rating and 43 percent share for the 9:30–10:00 p.m. (EST) half hour. During the course of the *Dukes of Hazzard* broadcast, 32.1 percent of all U.S. television households watched 5 or more minutes of the program, which translates to 24,970,000 households.

In addition to these important program audience and household viewing estimates, each biweekly NTI report provides the following summary statistics:

1. Comparisons of AA estimates by selected program types
2. NTI estimates of TV usage by daypart
3. National TV Nielsen ratings of persons-viewing data for top programs
   - Households
   - Total persons
   - Women aged 18 +

Nielsen NATIONAL TV AUDIENCE ESTIMATES

EVE. FRI. FEB. 13, 1981

TIME	7:00	7:15	7:30	7:45	8:00	8:15	8:30	8:45	9:00	9:15	9:30	9:45	10:00	10:15	10:30	10:45
ABC TV																
TOTAL AUDIENCE (Households (000) & %)					3,380 / 17.2		11,590 / 14.9		15,950 / 20.5							
Program					BENSON		I'M A BIG GIRL NOW (OP)		ABC FRIDAY NIGHT MOVIE (INMATES: A LOVE STORY)							
AVERAGE AUDIENCE (Households (000) & %)					1,980 / 15.4		10,660 / 13.7		10,040 / 12.9	12.4*		13.1*		12.8*		13.4*
SHARE OF AUDIENCE %					26		22		21	20*		21*		21*		23*
AVG. AUD. BY ¼ HR. %					15.0	15.8	13.9	13.6	12.0	12.7	12.9	13.3	13.0	12.7	13.2	13.6
CBS TV																
TOTAL AUDIENCE (Households (000) & %)					6,800 / 21.6				24,970 / 32.1							
Program					INCREDIBLE HULK (OP)				DUKES OF HAZZARD				DALLAS			
AVERAGE AUDIENCE (Households (000) & %)					2,530 / 16.1	14.6*		17.7*	21,240 / 27.3	26.9*		27.8*	23,810 / 30.6	30.7*		30.6*
SHARE OF AUDIENCE %					27	24*		29*	44	44*		45*	52	51*		52*
AVG. AUD. BY ¼ HR. %					14.2	15.0	16.7	18.6	26.3	27.4	27.6	28.1	30.4	31.0	31.2	29.9
NBC TV																
TOTAL AUDIENCE (Households (000) & %)					6,490 / 21.2		16,180 / 20.8		12,840 / 16.5				7,940 / 10.2			
Program					HARPER VALLEY		BRADY GIRLS GET MARRIED (OP)		NERO WOLFE				NBC MAGAZINE			
AVERAGE AUDIENCE (Households (000) & %)					4,780 / 19.0		14,160 / 18.2		10,430 / 13.4	13.3*		13.5*	6,220 / 8.0	8.1*		7.9*
SHARE OF AUDIENCE %					32		30		22	22*		22*	14	14*		14*
AVG. AUD. BY ¼ HR. %					18.5	19.5	18.8	17.7	13.4	13.2	13.7	13.4	8.2	8.0	7.9	8.0

EVE.FRI. FEB.20, 1981

U.S. TV Households: 77,800,000

ABC TV (W)

	BENSON (OP)		ABC FRIDAY NIGHT MOVIE — THE INTRUDER WITHIN			DEMO REPLY–PRES. ADDRESS (SUS)
TOTAL AUDIENCE (Households (000) & %)	15,330 / 19.7	18,050 / 23.2				
AVERAGE AUDIENCE (Households (000) & %)	13,850 / 17.8	10,110 / 13.0				
SHARE OF AUDIENCE %	30	21	13.8* 23* 13.9	14.0* 22* 14.1	14.3* 23* 13.7	
AVG. AUD. BY ¼ HR. %	17.1	9.9	13.9	14.1	13.7	
	18.4	9.8* 16* 9.7		14.8		

CBS TV (E E K 2)

	INCREDIBLE HULK (OP)		DUKES OF HAZZARD		DALLAS	
TOTAL AUDIENCE (Households (000) & %)	16,650 / 21.4		24,970 / 32.1		32,750 / 42.1	
AVERAGE AUDIENCE (Households (000) & %)	11,980 / 15.4	13.8*	19,840 / 25.5	23.9*	27,070 / 34.8	32.5* 37.1*
SHARE OF AUDIENCE %	25	23*	41	39*	58	53* 64*
AVG. AUD. BY ¼ HR. %	13.4	14.2	23.1	24.6	32.1	33.0 36.8
	16.8	17.1* 28* 17.3	26.0	27.1* 43* 28.2	37.3	14.3* 23* 13.7 ...

NBC TV (2)

	HARPER VALLEY	BRADY GIRLS GET MARRIED (OP)	NERO WOLFE		NBC MAGAZINE	DEMOCRATIC RESPONSE–NBC (SUS)
TOTAL AUDIENCE (Households (000) & %)	14,390 / 18.5	20,150 / 25.9	13,690 / 17.6		6,540 / 8.4	
AVERAGE AUDIENCE (Households (000) & %)	13,070 / 16.8	17,970 / 23.1	10,740 / 13.8	14.1*	5,760 / 7.4	
SHARE OF AUDIENCE %	28	38	22	23*	12	
AVG. AUD. BY ¼ HR. %	16.6	22.8	14.1	14.0	7.6	
	16.9	23.5	14.0	13.5* 22* 13.1	7.2	

TV HOUSEHOLDS USING TV

WK. 1 (See Def. 1)	55.0	56.8	57.8	58.4	59.2	61.2	59.6	61.3	60.7	62.0	61.3	61.8	60.1	59.6	57.6
WK. 2	56.6	57.3	56.9	58.4	59.1	60.6	61.0	61.4	60.8	62.2	61.4	63.0	62.6	61.2	57.3

For explanation of symbols, see page A.

FIGURE 2-9

(From "National TV Audience Estimates," A.C. Nielsen, Chicago, 1981.)

23

NTI CALENDAR — 1980-'82

SHOWING NATIONAL TV-RATINGS REPORT INTERVALS

Fast Weekly Households Ratings are published 52 weeks and Fast MNA TV Ratings are published 50 weeks a year.

SEPTEMBER '80

M	T	W	T	F	S	S
1	2	3	4	5	6	7
8	9	10	11	12	13	14
15	16	17	18	19	20	21+
22	23	24	25	26	27	28+
29	30					

OCTOBER '80

M	T	W	T	F	S	S
		1	2	3	4	5+
6	7	8	9	10	11	12+
13	14	15	16	17	18	19+
20	21	22	23	24	25	26+
27	28	29	30	31		+

NOVEMBER '80

M	T	W	T	F	S	S
					1	2+
3	4	5	6	7	8	9+
10	11	12	13	14	15	16+
17	18	19	20	21	22	23+
24	25	26	27	28	29	30+

DECEMBER '80

M	T	W	T	F	S	S
1	2	3	4	5	6	7+
8	9	10	11	12	13	14+
15	16	17	18	19	20	21+
22	23	24	25	26	27	28††
29	30	31				+

JANUARY '81

M	T	W	T	F	S	S
			1	2	3	4+
5	6	7	8	9	10	11+
12	13	14	15	16	17	18+
19	20	21	22	23	24	25+
26	27	28	29	30	31	+

FEBRUARY '81

M	T	W	T	F	S	S
						1+
2	3	4	5	6	7	8+
9	10	11	12	13	14	15+
16	17	18	19	20	21	22+
23	24	25	26	27	28	+

MARCH '81

M	T	W	T	F	S	S
						1+
2	3	4	5	6	7	8+
9	10	11	12	13	14	15+
16	17	18	19	20	21	22+
23	24	25	26	27	28	29+
30	31					

APRIL '81

M	T	W	T	F	S	S
		1	2	3	4	5+
6	7	8	9	10	11	12+
13	14	15	16	17	18	19+
20	21	22	23	24	25	26††
27	28	29	30			+

MAY '81

M	T	W	T	F	S	S
				1	2	3+
4	5	6	7	8	9	10+
11	12	13	14	15	16	17+
18	19	20	21	22	23	24+
25	26	27	28	29	30	31

JUNE '81

M	T	W	T	F	S	S
1	2	3	4	5	6	7
8	9	10	11	12	13	14
15	16	17	18	19	20	21
22	23	24	25	26	27	28†
29	30					+

JULY '81

M	T	W	T	F	S	S
		1	2	3	4	5+
6	7	8	9	10	11	12+
13	14	15	16	17	18	19+
20	21	22	23	24	25	26+
27	28	29	30	31		+

AUGUST '81

M	T	W	T	F	S	S
					1	2
3	4	5	6	7	8	9
10	11	12	13	14	15	16
17	18	19	20	21	22	23
24	25	26	27	28	29	30†
31						

SEPTEMBER '81

M	T	W	T	F	S	S
	1	2	3	4	5	6
7	8	9	10	11	12	13
14	15	16	17	18	19	20+
21	22	23	24	25	26	27+
28	29	30				

OCTOBER '81

M	T	W	T	F	S	S
			1	2	3	4+
5	6	7	8	9	10	11+
12	13	14	15	16	17	18+
19	20	21	22	23	24	25+
26	27	28	29	30	31	+

NOVEMBER '81

M	T	W	T	F	S	S
						1+
2	3	4	5	6	7	8+
9	10	11	12	13	14	15+
16	17	18	19	20	21	22+
23	24	25	26	27	28	29+
30						+

DECEMBER '81

M	T	W	T	F	S	S
	1	2	3	4	5	6+
7	8	9	10	11	12	13+
14	15	16	17	18	19	20+
21	22	23	24	25	26	27††
28	29	30	31			+

JANUARY '82

M	T	W	T	F	S	S
				1	2	3+
4	5	6	7	8	9	10+
11	12	13	14	15	16	17+
18	19	20	21	22	23	24+
25	26	27	28	29	30	31+

FEBRUARY '82

M	T	W	T	F	S	S
1	2	3	4	5	6	7+
8	9	10	11	12	13	14+
15	16	17	18	19	20	21+
22	23	24	25	26	27	28+

+ Includes Audience Composition (optional)

† Fast Weekly Household (FWH) Reports Only

†† FWH and FMNA Reports Only

FIGURE 2-10

Nielsen's "black weeks."

(From "National TV Ratings," NTI, A.C. Nielsen, Chicago, Sept. 1, 1980.)

- Men aged 18+
- Women aged 18–49
- Women aged 55+
- Men aged 18–49
- Men aged 55+

These biweekly NTI reports are commonly referred to as the *pocketpieces* because of their pocket-size format. In addition to the 17 complete pocketpieces, seven household-data-only reports are issued each year. In total, 48 weeks of viewing are reported in the pocketpieces. The remaining 4 weeks are known as the "black weeks" (see Figure 2-10). During these weeks, no complete NTI reports are issued; however, household audiences are measured and rating information is available for these weeks in the "Fast Weekly Household Rating Reports."

The demographic detail provided in the biweekly NTI reports is limited to basic age dimensions and the two *lady-of-the-house* and *working-women* groups. Further demographics are provided in the "Market Section Audience Report," issued nine times per year, and the two-volume "National Audience Demographics Report," issued eight times per year. The "Market Section Audience Report" includes estimates of U.S. television usage and household program average audiences for the entire United States and by market section. The market sections included are territory, county size, household income, selected upper demographics, education of head of house, and occupation of head of house, as well as the basic age demographics. The "National Audience Demographics Report" is the most comprehensive audience report provided by Nielsen. Volume 1 provides eight tables of summary data, cross-tabulated by basic age breaks. Volume 2 provides four tables of summary statistics with market section detail. Figure 2-11 lists the 12 table titles.

In addition to these regular reports, the Nielsen NTI service is supplemented regularly by reports measuring trends in viewing levels and focusing on summary statistics by program type. At the end of each television season, NTI publishes its annual "Nielsen Report on Television, 19__," highlighting significant viewing trends.

The national television audience is by far the most comprehensively measured media audience. The NTI research service costs the networks about $7 million collectively each year. Agencies and advertisers pay a far lower rate, which varies in accordance with the percentage of service to which they subscribe. An advertiser or agency subscription rate for the entire service varies by network billings. Major advertiser and agency bills run into six figures.

This report, in two volumes, is issued eight times a year, with each issue based on four measured weeks. One-time-only and special programs telecast during the second September report are included in the October NAD report, and programs telecast in the first or second January report are included in the February report.

Volume 1: Total U.S. Audiences

This volume estimates U.S. television usage for both households and persons. Persons data by age breaks are reported as follows for men, women, and children:

Table 1: Estimates of average hours of TV usage per week.

Table 2: Estimates of television usage by daypart.

Table 3: Summary of network program audience estimates by type.

Table 4: Estimates of individual network program audiences (total duration)—evening, Monday–Friday daytime, Saturday and Sunday daytime.

Table 5: Television usage and network programs' audience estimates by half hours (percent) in time period sequence.

Table 6: Estimates of television usage by daypart for lady of house and working women.

Table 7: Estimates of network program audience by type—lady of house and working women.

Table 8: Estimates of individual network program audiences (total duration)—lady of house and working women—evening, Monday–Friday daytime, Saturday and Sunday daytime.

Volume 2: Audiences by Market Sections

This volume estimates U.S. television usage and sponsored network program audiences for both households and persons in composite form and by market sections. Persons data are reported by age breaks for men, women, and children. Market sections: territory, county size, household size, presence of nonadults, household income, and selected upper demographics. Data reported are as follows:

Table 9: Estimates of average hours of TV usage per week.

Table 10: Estimates of television usage by dayparts.

Table 11: Summary of network program audience estimates by type.

Table 12: Estimates of individual network program audiences (total duration)—evening, Monday–Friday daytime, Saturday and Sunday daytime.

FIGURE 2-11

National audience demographics report.

(From A.C. Nielsen, Chicago, 1981.)

Despite its comprehensiveness the NTI service does not meet all television audience measurement needs. Important missing elements include data on an individual market level. After all, the retailer advertising in Dallas is interested in the Dallas market audience, not the national audience. The local broadcaster and advertiser can turn to one of two local-market television measurement services to meet their needs.

Measuring the Local Television Audience: Arbitron and NSI Services

Unlike the national situation, where there is only one game in town, the local-market television measurement contest has two competitors: the Arbitron "Television Market Reports" and the Nielsen station index (NSI). The best place to start to talk about these two services is to discuss what they have in common.

Each service offers periodic surveys of television viewing by television market; however, each defines a television market slightly differently. All TV markets are measured for 4 weeks at a time during November, February, May, and July. These survey periods are known in the trade as the "sweep" periods. Selected markets are surveyed also during October, January, and March by both services; and 52-week measurement is provided for New York, Los Angeles, Chicago, Philadelphia, and San Francisco. All surveys are based on a diary method of audience measurement, except the 52-week measurement markets, in which a mixed meter-diary methodology is employed. Each report contains several sections breaking out audiences by daypart, quarter hour, and program. Household and basic age demographic data are provided. Although neither service offers a total-audience type of rating information, they both include cumulative audience figures by daypart. For the researcher desiring more specific information about audience duplication and accumulation, the services offer online computer systems, ARB-AID and NSI+. These systems are discussed further in later chapters.

The battle for recognition as the local-market rating service is closely contested. Both services are roughly equal in terms of local-station support; however, Nielsen is still stronger in major national advertising agencies, because of the strength of its companion NTI service. One place where Arbitron does seem to lead is in the acceptance of its ADI as the official television market designation. Further discussion of these local-market television measurement services will require treating them separately.

ARBITRON

The Arbitron Company is a division of Control Data Corporation. The essential business of Arbitron is the measurement of television and radio audiences. Arbitron's dominance in the radio audience measurement field is comparable to Nielsen's position in national television audience measurement. Various competitors have come and gone during the years, but Arbitron has always been the leader, and today it has no competition that covers all radio markets.

Arbitron's television audience measurement service began in 1949, preceding its radio service. Sweep period reports are issued for 212 areas of dominant influence (ADIs). An *ADI* is defined as "an area that consists of Arbitron sampling units in which the home market commercial stations and satellite stations reported in combination with them received a preponderance of total viewing hours."[1] A complete list of the 1981–1982 ADIs is provided in Table 5-1.

The ADI is only one of three universe descriptions used by Arbitron in its television reports. The *metro* area originally consisted of "all counties included in the market's SMSA, counties in which were located the market stations' cities of license or identification plus others included due to historical industry precedent."[2] In June 1975, Arbitron revised this policy to take into account actual viewing patterns; however, some traditional metro counties remained assigned to their original metros even though the home market station(s) did not "exert dominant influence" in these counties.[3]

The third universe description Arbitron uses is the *total survey area* (*TSA*). The TSA is the broadest coverage area, defined as "a geographic area comprising those counties in which, by Arbitron estimates, approximately 98% of the Net Weekly Circulation of commercial home market stations occurs, exclusive of counties located outside the local market area reached solely by sky satellite transmission."[4]

The Arbitron "Television Market Report" contains ratings on both an ADI and a metro basis. TSA audiences are shown in thousands only. The Arbitron rating is slightly different from the NTI average audience rating. The Arbitron rating is defined as "the estimated percent of television households, or persons within those households, tuned to a particular station for five minutes or more during an average quarter-hour of the reported time period for the ADI, Metro or Home County."[5] The qualifying statement "for five minutes or more" is not included in the more sensitive NTI average-minute audience definition; therefore, some households that would be included in an NTI average audience rating would be excluded from the Arbitron rating.

With the exception of New York, Los Angeles, Chicago, Philadelphia, and San Francisco,[6] where meters are used, all Arbitron audience estimates are obtained from a diary sample. Each participating household keeps a diary of its TV viewing for 1 week. Four weeks of sampling are combined in each report. A minimum sample of 200 per market is required. Actual sample sizes run from approximately 1500 each for top 10 markets, to 1000 each for middle-size markets, to 200 to 300 for the smaller markets. The actual Arbitron survey schedule for the 1980–1981 television season is shown in Table 2-1.

Arbitron uses meters to measure television audiences in New York, Los Angeles, Chicago, Philadelphia, and San Francisco. These meter samples provide 52-week household viewing data. Meter samples average 500 households per market. During the periods shown in Table 2-1, diary samples are employed in these markets also. Persons-viewing information from these diary samples is matched to the household viewing levels obtained from the meter sample to generate the full audience estimates provided in the Arbitron "Television Market Reports" for these markets. This mixed meter-diary sampling technique is also used by Nielsen in its NSI reports for metered markets. This has caused researchers some concern. To the extent that two different methodologies are being used in meter markets and smaller, diary markets, how comparable are the audience levels recorded in these two markets? This question is explored further later in this chapter.

Each Arbitron report has three basic sections. The daypart audience estimates summary section provides average audience statistics by station for 20 different dayparts. It includes ADI and metro rating and share data; TSA audiences (in thousands) on a households and persons basis; TSA cumulative audience levels on a households, men, women, and working-women basis; ADI ratings on a key-demographics basis; a four-report share trend for each station; and a section showing the distribution of each station's audience both within the ADI (metro versus nonmetro) and outside the ADI. Figure 2-12 presents a sample

TABLE 2-1
ARBITRON REPORT PERIODS FOR
1981–1982

September 23–October 20

*October 28–November 24

January 6–February 2

*February 3–March 2

March 3–March 30

*April 28–May 25

*July 7–August 3

---

*Sweep periods.

Daypart Audience Estimates Summary

TOTAL SURVEY AREA, IN THOUSANDS (000's)

DAYPART AND STATION	ADI RTG	ADI SHR	FEB '82	NOV '81	JUL '81	MAY '81	METRO RTG	METRO SHR	TV HH	PERS TOT 2+	18+	18-49	12-24	12-34	18-34	WMN TOT 18+	18-49	12-24	18-34	25-49	25-54	WKG WMN 18+	MEN TOT 18+	18-49	18-34	25-49	25-54	TEENS 12-17
MON–FRI 7.00A–9.00A																												
KVBC	6	26	24	30	38	25	6	26	12	14	14	7	1	4	4	7	4	–	2	3	3	2	7	3	2	3	3	–
KVVU	6	26	24	28	13	27	6	26	12	16	4	3	2	4	3	4	2	1	2	2	2	1	1	1	1	2	2	1
KLAS	2	10	28	9	16	18	2	10	5	6	5	2	–	2	2	2	1	–	–	1	1	–	3	2	2	–	–	–
KTNV	8	34	35	34	33	30	8	34	16	19	18	11	3	6	5	11	7	2	3	6	7	2	6	3	–	3	4	1
* KLVX	**		**																									
HUT/TOT	24		27	29	22	24	23		45	54	41	23	6	16	14	24	14	3	7	12	13	5	17	9	5	8	9	2
(continued)																												
KTNV	12	22	20	28	8	18	12	22	23	38	32	19		14	11	14	9	3	3	3		5	17	10	6	8	9	3
KLVX	1	1	2	2	**	2	2	1	2	2	2	1			1	1	1						1	1				
HUT/TOT	54		61	61	52	53		54	103	168	142	87	32	63	50	70	45	16	25	32	38	26	71	42	25	33	38	11
7.00P–7.30P																												
KVBC	6	10	12	13	17	10	5	10	11	19	15	13	6	11	9	6	6	3	3	4	5	3	9	8	5	5	5	2
KVVU	28	50	43	41	51	49	29	51	54	92	77	53	24	41	33	38	28	12	17	19	22	18	39	25	16	18	21	8
KLAS	12	21	26	27	28	23	12	21	22	34	29	13	4	8	6	17	7	2	3	6	7	5	11	6	3	5	5	2
KTNV	10	18	17	23	5	19	10	17	20	32	29	17	3	11	10	12	8	2	5	7	7	3	17	10	5	8	10	1
KLVX			1		**	1																						
HUT/TOT	56		64	63	53	56		56	107	177	150	96	37	71	58	73	49	19	29	36	41	29	76	49	29	36	41	13

LAS VEGAS

DPS–1

MAY 1982 DAYPART SUMMARY

* ESTIMATES EXCLUDE QTR-HRS STATION WAS NOT ON AIR
** SHARE/HUT TRENDS NOT AVAILABLE
+ COMBINED PARENT/SATELLITE

Daypart Audience Estimates Summary

Daypart Summary

DAYPART AND STATION	TSA (000's) CHILDREN 2-11	6-11	CUMES (000's) TSA TV HH	WMN TOT	WMN 18-49	MEN TOT	ADI TV HH	PERSONS TOT 2+	18+	18-49	12-24	12-34	18-34	WOMEN TOT 18+	18+	12-34	18-34	25-49	25-54	WKG WMN 18+	MEN TOT 18+	18-49	18-34	25-49	25-54	TNS TOT 12-17	CHILD 2-11	6-11	PERCENT DISTRIBUTION METRO	ADI	ADJACENT ADI'S #1	#2	#3	TV HH RTGS IN ADJACENT ADI'S #1	#2	#3
MON-FRI 7.00A-9.00A																																				
KVBC	1		31	24	13	19	31	3	4	3	1	2	2	4	3	1	3	3	3	2	4	2	2	3	3	2	1	1	98	99						
KVVU	10	5	40	18	14	7	38	3	3	1	2	2	2	2	2	1	1	2	2	2	2	1	1	1	1		14	11	94	97	3					
KLAS			19	11	6	12	19	1	1	1		1	1	1	1		1	1	1	1	2	1	1	2	2		1	1	96	96						
KTNV	1	1	37	32	23	20	37	4	5	4	2	3	3	6	6	3	4	6	7	3	10	3	3	3	3	2	1	1	95	99						
* KLVX			3	1	1	1	3																						99	99	1					
TOT/PVT	12	6	308	250	139	160	99	12	12	10	6	8	9	15	12	8	11	13	14	7	10	7	7	9	9	5	16	14	95	99						
9.00A-4.30P																																				
KVBC	1		76	60	34	39	72	2	2	2	1	1	2	3	3	2	2	2	3	1	1	1	1	1	1	1	1	1	96	97			3			
* KVVU	1	1	102	73	50	59	98	3	3	3	2	2	2	4	4	2	3	3	4	2	3	2	2	2	2	1	2	2	96	97		3				
* KLAS	4	2	103	75	52	53	100	3	3	3	3	3	2	4	4	4	5	4	4	3	3	2	2	1	1	4	5	5	98	99		1				
* KTNV	1		75	56	38	40	75	3	3	3	3	3	3	5	4	5	5	4	4	3	1	1	1	1	1	2	1	1		99		1				
7.00P-7.30P																																				
KVBC	2	1	26	18	15	19	26	4	4	5	5	5	5	4	4	5	5	4	4	4	5	6	6	5	5	5	3	3	95	99	1					
KVVU	6	4	94	74	56	75	92	19	21	21	22	20	20	22	22	22	21	20	21	24	21	19	20	18	19	18	9	8	99	99						
KLAS	4	2	52	40	20	33	52	7	8	5	3	4	4	6	6	6	4	6	6	7	6	7	7	5	5	3	6	6	99	99	4					
KTNV	3	1	42	28	19	38	41	7	8	7	3	5	10	10	6	3	6	7	7	5	9	6	6	8	8	4	4	3	92	96						
KLVX			2	2	1	1	2																						97	99	1					
TOT/PVT	15	8	488	424	259	409	162	38	42	38	35	35	36	43	39	35	37	39	40	41	42	38	37	36	38	30	22	22	97	99						

MAY 1982 DAYPART SUMMARY

DPS-2

ADJACENT ADI # 1 — LOS ANGELES
ADJACENT ADI # 2 — PHOENIX (FLAGSTAFF)
ADJACENT ADI # 3 — SALT LAKE CITY

LAS VEGAS

FIGURE 2-12

(From Arbitron, "Daypart Audience Estimates Summary," New York, 1982.)

31

Weekly Program Estimates

Time Period Average Estimates

DAY AND TIME / STATION PROGRAM	WEEK-BY-WEEK ADI TV HH RATINGS WK 1 4/28	WK 2 5/5	WK 3 5/12	WK 4 5/19	ADI TV HH RTG	ADI TV HH SHR	ADI TV HH SHARE/HUT TRENDS FEB '82	NOV '81	JUL '81	MAY '81	METRO TV HH RTG	METRO TV HH SHR	TOTAL SURVEY AREA, IN THOUSANDS (000's) TV HH	PERSONS 18+	PERSONS 12-24	PERSONS 12-34	WOMEN TOT 18+	WOMEN 18-49	WOMEN 12-24	WOMEN 18-34	WOMEN 25-49	WOMEN 25-54	WKG WMN 18+	MEN TOT 18+	MEN 18-49	MEN 18-34	MEN 25-49	MEN 25-54
	1	2	3	4	5	6	58	59	60	61	8	9	11	13	15	16	18	19	20	21	22	23	24	25	26	27	28	29
▲ RELATIVE STD-ERR THRESHOLDS (1 σ) 25%	15	12	16	14	4						4		22	33	35	34	26	25	31	28	22	22	20	25	25	27	22	22
50%	4	3	4	3	1						1		5	8	9	9	6	6	9	7	6	6	5	6	6	7	6	6
TUESDAY																												
10:30P-11:00P(CNTD)																												
KTNV HART TO HART	6	16	34	10	17	32	32	32	45	22	17	33	32	41	11	24	24	17	6	10	13	15	11	18	12	8	10	11
KLVX PTV	–	2	2	–	1	2	2	1	**	**	1	2	2	2	1	2	1	1	1	1	1	1	1	1	1		1	1
HUT/TOTAL	53	47	64	43	52		47	51	40	49	52		101	134	36	77	71	52	19	32	40	47	31	63	47	31	35	38
11:00P-11:15P																												
KVBC 11P CH 3 NWS	4	2	3	7	4	13	15	20	17	22	4	14	7	9	2	4	5	3	1	2	2	2	1	5	3	2	2	3
KVVU BURNS-ALLEN	6	5	8	11	8	25	17	19	25	16	8	25	14	22	10	15	11	9	5	7	5	5	6	12	10	8	5	5
KLAS NWSCEN 8 EVE	9	7	7	11	9	29	43	28	28	35	9	30	17	23	3	7	11	7	1	4	7	8	3	12	8	4	6	7
KTNV NW 13 LT	9	9	9	10	9	31	22	30	31	25	9	32	18	24	2	5	9	5		2	5	5	4	15	6	3	5	7
KLVX PTV	–	–	2	–			3		**	**			1	1		1	1	1		1	1	1	1					
HUT/TOTAL	28	24	32	36	30		30	34	30	24	30		57	79	17	32	37	25	7	16	20	21	15	44	27	17	18	22
11:15P-11:30P																												
HUT/TOTAL	3	1	3	3	2		4	6	7	3	2		4	4	1	1	2	1			1	1	1	2	2	1	1	1
WEDNESDAY																												
4:00P- 4:30P																												
KVBC BONANZA	2	4	6	7	5	13	24	21	24	20	5	13	9	11	3	4	6	4	2	2	2	2	2	5	3	1	2	2

LAS VEGAS TPA-17 TUE/WED MAY 1982 TIME PERIOD AVERAGES

- * SAMPLE BELOW MINIMUM FOR WEEKLY REPORTING
- ** SHARE/HUT TRENDS NOT AVAILABLE
- – DID NOT ACHIEVE A REPORTABLE WEEKLY RATING
- ‡ TECHNICAL DIFFICULTY
- \+ COMBINED PARENT/SATELLITE
- ▲ SEE TABLE ON PAGE iv

Time Period Average Estimates

Station Break Average Estimates

Daily

LAS VEGAS

MAY 1982 TIME PERIOD AVERAGES   TPA-18   TUE/WED

FIGURE 2-13

(From "Weekly Program Estimates: Time Period Average Estimates," Arbitron, New York, 1982.)

daypart audience estimates summary. A separate summary is provided for network programming only, divided into the 11 basic network dayparts.

The second major section of the Arbitron report is the time period average estimates summary. This section presents audience data by station, on a detailed basis. For most time periods, audiences are reported on a half-hour by half-hour basis. From 11:00 to 11:30 p.m. each day, quarter-hour by quarter-hour data are provided. After 4 p.m. (EST) these time period averages are shown by individual day. Before 4 p.m., time period averages on weekdays are provided only on a Monday–Friday basis. Saturday and Sunday time period audiences are reported individually for the entire day.

The time period average estimates section (Figure 2-13) provides the same basic audience detail as the daypart summary section. However, there are some differences: ADI ratings are reported for each of the 4 measurement weeks, demographic breakouts are more limited than in the daypart summary, and no cumulative audience data are provided.

The program audience estimates section provides audience data on a program-by-program basis. If two programs ran during the same time period (2 weeks each), there would be a listing for each program in this section. If the same program ran at different times and/or on different days during the survey period, audience data would be reported for each telecast and for all telecasts averaged. The first two columns of Figure 2-14 show the number of weeks and the number of quarter hours of telecast for each program listed.

NIELSEN STATION INDEX

A.C. Nielsen's "Nielsen Station Index (NSI) Reports" complement this firm's national service, providing regular 4-week reports of market-by-market television viewing. The NSI survey schedule is similar to that of Arbitron, with the four basic sweep measurements and several supplemental surveys in major markets. NSI survey results are published in "Viewers in Profile (VIP) Reports." Table 2-2 gives the NSI survey schedule for the 1981–1982 season.

The NSI market designation is the *designated market area (DMA)*. For a county to be included in a DMA,

> a) the commercial stations assigned to the NSI market must achieve the largest share of the 9 AM to 12 midnight average quarter-hour household audience in the Metro/Central Area, or
>
> b) one commercial station in the Metro/Central area must achieve a larger share of the 9 AM to 12 midnight average quarter-hour household audience than any commercial station outside the market.[7]

TABLE 2-2
NSI REPORT PERIODS FOR
NIELSEN, 1981–1982

September 24–October 21

*October 29–November 25

January 7–February 3

*February 4–March 3

March 4–March 31

*April 29–May 26

*July 8–August 4

---

*Sweep periods.

Figure 2-15 shows the 205 DMAs and their television household counts for the 1981–1982 season.

The NSI service uses three other geographical designations to report audiences. The metro area coincides with Arbitron's metro. Nielsen defines the *metro* area as the SMSA(s) of the originating TV station market(s) brought to county lines by including all counties with 50 percent of their population in the metro area. The NSI area designation is comparable to the Arbitron total survey area; however, it includes the geographic area accounting for 95 percent of all home station viewing versus Arbitron's 98 percent.

The NSI report also features a *station total area* audience summary that includes *all* viewing to a station within and without the NSI area. Unlike Arbitron, NSI includes satellite-fed coverage in this figure. The NSI rating is identical to the Arbitron rating using the "5 minutes or more" criterion as opposed to the "average minute audience" criterion employed by Nielsen's own NTI service. Diaries are used to obtain viewing data in all but the six metered markets, where a mixed meter-diary system is employed. Sample sizes range from 200 to 2000 in diary markets and 300 to 600 in the six meter markets (September 1982).

NSI "Viewers in Profile Reports" are divided into three main sections, similar in format to the Arbitron reports. The daypart summary provides summary audience statistics for 21 separate daypart designations. These statistics include the DMA household rating and share plus a four-book share trend, DMA persons ratings for 16 demographic breaks, station total-audience levels for 20 demographic breaks, a distribution of audiences by home and adjacent DMAs, and the cumulative household audience percentage and count for each station. Figure 2-16 provides a sample page from this section of an NSI report.

Weekly Program Estimates

Program Audience Estimates

TIME AND STATION		TELE-CASTS		WEEK-BY-WEEK ADI TV HH RATINGS				ADI TV HH			METRO TV HH			
DAY	PROGRAM	# OF WKS	# OF QTR-HRS	WK 1 4/28	WK 2 5/5	WK 3 5/12	WK 4 5/19	RTG	SHR	HUT	RTG	SHR	HUT	
				1	2	3	4	5	6	7	8	9	10	
▲ RELATIVE STD-ERR 25%														
THRESHOLDS (1 σ) 50%														
6:00P KTNV														
AVG BENNY HILL		40		16	14	11	13	13	25	53	13	25	53	
6:30P KVBC														
MON ASATURDY NGHT		16		7	5	3	9	6	11	54	6	10	54	
TUE ASATURDY NGHT		16		9	12	4	6	8	16	53	8	16	53	
WED ASATURDY NGHT		16		8	6	3	10	7	11	60	7	11	60	
THU APOINT BLANK		2		3				3	5	56	3	5	56	
ASATURDY NGHT		16		4	7	5	7	6	11	54	6	11	54	
FRI ASATURDY NGHT		16		4	8	5	7	6	13	45	6	13	46	
SAT AACTN SENIORS		8		4	5			2	6	34	2	6	35	
SUN WILD KINGDOM		8		11	5	15	12	11	25	43	11	25	43	
AVG AACTN SENIORS		16		1	1	1	2	1	6	20	1	6	21	

	TV HH	PERSONS									WOMEN								WKG WMN 18+
		TOT 2+	18+	18-49	12-34	12-24	18-34	TOT 18+	18-49	18-34	12-24	18-34	25-49	25-54					
	11	12	13	14	15	16	17	18	19	20	21	22	23	24					
	22	52	33	30	35	34	32	26	25	31	28	22	22	20					
	5	13	8	7	9	9	8	8	9	9	7	6	6	5					
	26	41	35	22	12	18	14	15	9	3	6	7	8	6					
	11	19	15	13	6	12	9	6	6	2	4	4	4	3					
	16	29	24	21	10	18	17	10	9	4	8	6	7	4					
	13	23	18	17	6	14	12	7	6	3	5	4	5	3					
	5	5	9	5	5	5		4	4	1									
	11	16	13	10	2	6	5	5	4	3	3	4	5	2					
	11	19	14	12	10	13	9	6	4	4	3	3	3	3					
	4	5	5	2				2	1				1						
	21	37	31	18	7	11	7	13	7	2	4	6	7	5					
	2	3	3	1				1											

WED AENTRTNMT TON		4		13	10	15	20	14	22	66	14	20	66	
THU AENTRTNMT TON		8		11	10	11	10	11	20	56	11	20	56	
FRI AENTRTNMT TON		8		9	11	5	9	8	17	48	9	18	49	
AVG ENTRTNMT TON		40		10	9	14	12	11	20	56	12	21	56	
KTNV														
MON AYOU ASKD FOR		8		7	9	3	5	6	10	57	5	9	57	
TUE AYOU ASKD FOR		8		10	9	3	5	7	11	55	5	9	55	
WED AYOU ASKD FOR		8		9	9	3	8	7	11	66	7	11	66	
THU AYOU ASKD FOR		8		9	5	1	7	6	10	56	5	10	56	

	TV HH	TOT 2+	18+	18-49	12-34	12-24	18-34	TOT 18+	18-49	18-34	12-24	18-34	25-49	25-54	WKG WMN 18+
	27	39	37	18	6	9	12	22	11	4	5	8	10	6
	21	32	28	12	4	9	6	17	8	5	3	7	8	4
	16	24	21	11	5	8	6	12	7	3	3	5	8	4
	22	31	29	15	5	10	9	17	9	6	3	7	8	5
	11	23	17	11	3	6	4	7	5	2	2	4	4	2
	10	23	14	12	3	6	3	6	4	2	1	4	4	2
	15	27	20	8	2	6	4	9	4	2	3	3	4	1
	12	22	18	11	3	8	6	8	5	3	3	3	3	2

LAS VEGAS

MAY 1982 PROGRAM AUDIENCES

Program Audience Estimates

TIME AND STATION — DAY / PROGRAM	TOTAL SURVEY AREA, IN THOUSANDS (000's) — MEN TOT 18+	MEN 18-49	MEN 18-34	MEN 25-49	MEN 25-54	TEENS TOTAL 12-17	CHILDREN 2-11	CHILDREN 6-11	ADI TV HH RTG	ADI TV HH SHR	ADI TV HH HUT	ADI RATINGS — PERSONS TOT 2+	PERSONS 18+	PERSONS 18-49	PERSONS 12-24	PERSONS 12-34	PERSONS 18-34	WOMEN TOT 18+	WOMEN 18-49	WOMEN 12-24	WOMEN 18-34	WOMEN 25-49	WOMEN 25-54	WKG WMN 18+	MEN TOT 18+	MEN 18-49	MEN 18-34	MEN 25-49	MEN 25-54	TNS TOT 12-17	CHILD 2-11	CHILD 6-11
	25	26	27	28	29	30	31	32	5	6	7	35	36	37	38	39	40	41	42	43	44	45	46	47	48	49	50	51	52	53	54	55
▲ RELATIVE STD-ERR THRESHOLDS (1 σ) 25%	25	25	27	22	22	28	43	32	4			3	3	4	11	5	7	4	7	21	12	8	7	11	5	7	12	8	7	20	18	23
50%	6	6	7	6	6	8	12	10	1			–	–	1	3	1	1	1	1	6	3	2	2	3	1	1	3	2	2	6	5	7
6:00P KTNV																																
AVG BENNY HILL	20	13	9	7	9	4	2	2	13	25	53	8	9	8	11	9	9	8	7	6	7	7	8	8	11	10	11	7	8	9	3	6
6:30P KVBC																																
MON ^SATURDY NGHT	9	7	5	6	6	4	1	1	6	11	54	4	4	5	6	6	5	4	4	5	5	5	4	5	5	6	6	6	6	8	1	2
TUE ^SATURDY NGHT	14	13	9	7	7	2	3	2	8	16	53	6	7	8	9	9	10	6	7	7	9	6	6	5	8	10	11	7	7	3	5	6
WED ^SATURDY NGHT	11	10	7	8	8	2	3	2	7	11	60	5	5	6	6	7	7	4	5	6	6	4	4	4	6	8	9	8	7	4	4	4
THU ^POINT BLANK	4								3	5	56	2	2	2		2		2							2							
^SATURDY NGHT	7	6	2	6	6	1	2	2	6	11	54	3	4	4	2	3	3	3	3	2	4	4	4	3	4	5	3	6	5	3	3	5
FRI ^SATURDY NGHT	9	7	6	4	4	4	1	1	6	13	45	4	4	5	9	6	6	3	3	7	4	3	3	5	5	6	8	4	3	9	1	1
SAT ^ACTN SENIORS	2	1		1	1				2	6	34	1	1	1				1				1			1	1	1	1	1			
SUN WILD KINGDOM	18	10	3	9	10	4	2	2	11	25	43	8	9	7	6	5	4	7	6	4	4	6	7	7	10	8	4	9	9	9	3	4
AVG ACTN SENIORS	1	1		1	1				1	6	20	1	1					1							1			1	1			
AVG POINT BLANK	4								2	4	43		2	2		2		2							2							
FRI ^MASH-S 2	37	26	15	17	19	6	7	4	26	54	48	17	19	19	20	17	18	18	18	18	18	16	16	21	20	19	18	17	17	13	10	11
AVG MASH-S 2	43	30	19	20	23	8	9	5	29	51	56	20	22	22	24	21	22	21	22	23	21	20	20	24	24	23	23	21	21	18	12	11
KLAS																																
MON ^ENTRTNMT TON	11	7	3	5	5	1	2	1	11	20	57	7	8	6	4	4	5	10	8	4	6	8	9	6	6	5	4	5	5	1	2	3
TUE ^ENTRTNMT TON	10	8	4	7	7	1	2	2	12	22	55	6	8	7	5	5	7	10	8	9	8	6	6	8	6	6	5	7	6	2	3	5
WED ^ENTRTNMT TON	15	7	4	5	6	1	1	1	14	22	66	8	10	7	5	6	7	13	9	8	10	9	10	8	8	5	5	5	5	2	2	3
THU ^ENTRTNMT TON	11	4	2	4	5	3	1		11	20	56	7	8	5	4	4	4	10	6	6	6	7	8	6	6	3	2	4	5	5	2	1
FRI ^ENTRTNMT TON	9	5	3	3	3	2	1	1	8	17	48	5	6	4	4	4	4	7	5	5	4	6	6	5	5	4	4	3	3	4	1	3
AVG ENTRTNMT TON	11	6	3	5	5	1	1	1	11	20	56	7	8	6	5	5	5	10	7	6	7	7	8	7	6	5	4	5	5	3	2	3
KTNV																																
MON ^YOU ASKD FOR	10	6	2	6	6	2	5	3	6	10	57	5	5	4	3	3	3	4	4	3	3	4	4	2	5	5	3	6	5	3	7	8
TUE ^YOU ASKD FOR	9	5	1	5	6	3	6	4	5	9	55	5	4	3	2	3	2	3	3	2	3	4	4	3	4	4	1	5	5	6	9	10
WED ^YOU ASKD FOR	11	4	2	4	6	1	6	4	7	11	66	5	5	3	2	3	3	4	3	2	3	3	3	2	6	3	3	4	5	3	9	8
THU ^YOU ASKD FOR	10	6	3	6	7	1	3	2	6	10	56	4	5	4	3	4	4	4	4	3	4	4	3	3	5	5	4	6	6	3	4	4

MAY 1982 PROGRAM AUDIENCES PAV-18 LAS VEGAS

Program Audiences

FIGURE 2-14

(From "Weekly Program Estimates: Program Audience Estimates," Arbitron, New York, 1982.)

DESIGNATED MARKET AREAS RANKED BY TV HOUSEHOLD UNIVERSE ESTIMATES
ALPHABETICAL SEQUENCE

RANK	DESIGNATED MARKET AREA	TV HOUSEHOLDS JAN. 1982
155	ABILENE-SWEETWATER	101,230
174	ADA-ARDMORE	65,440
50	ALBANY-SCHENECTADY-TROY	463,300
153	ALBANY, GA	119,900
66	ALBUQUERQUE,FARMINGTON	350,710
175	ALEXANDRIA, LA	65,420
162	ALEXANDRIA, MN	87,090
204	ALPENA	15,360
120	AMARILLO	170,890
165	ANCHORAGE	77,850
16	ATLANTA	1,062,690
106	AUGUSTA	196,950
89	AUSTIN	242,380
148	BAKERSFIELD	125,360
20	BALTIMORE	835,150
151	BANGOR	120,620
91	BATON ROUGE	235,920
126	BEAUMONT-PORT ARTHUR	159,240
146	BECKLEY-BLUEFIELD-OAK HILL	131,170
201	BEND	24,800
168	BILLINGS	71,340
185	BILOXI-GULFPORT	56,740
127	BINGHAMTON	158,910
40	BIRMINGHAM,ANNISTON	563,670
142	BOISE	141,370
6	BOSTON,MANCHESTER,WORCESTR	1,920,160
32	BUFFALO	613,110
96	BURLINGTON-PLATTSBURGH	225,270
179	BUTTE	61,430
184	CASPER-RIVERTON	56,890
76	CEDAR RAPIDS-WATRLOO,DUBUQ	313,950
75	CHAMPAIGN&SPRNGFLD-DECATUR	316,150
46	CHARLESTON-HUNTINGTON	490,840
115	CHARLESTON, SC	178,990
31	CHARLOTTE	613,740
93	FT. WAYNE	232,140
170	GAINESVILLE	69,170
205	GLENDIVE	5,000
190	GRAND JUNCTION-MONTROSE	50,470
39	GRAND RAPIDS-KALMZOO-B.CRK	566,750
177	GREAT FALLS	64,640
67	GREEN BAY	347,130
52	GREENSBORO-H.POINT-W.SALEM	449,510
98	GREENVILLE-N.BERN-WASHNGTN	218,560
38	GREENVILLE-SPART-ASHEVILLE	574,160
173	GREENWOOD-GREENVILLE	65,580
134	HARLINGEN-WESLACO-BROWNSVL	151,020
48	HARRISBURG-LNCSTR-LEB-YORK	473,620
196	HARRISONBURG	31,670
25	HARTFORD & NEW HAVEN	707,810
163	HATTIESBURG-LAUREL	82,220
78	HONOLULU	300,560
11	HOUSTON	1,255,010
90	HUNTSVILLE-DECATUR,FLORNCE	239,160
159	IDAHO FALLS-POCATELLO	91,450
22	INDIANAPOLIS	804,420
85	JACKSON, MS	260,260
192	JACKSON, TN	43,450
63	JACKSONVILLE	371,510
77	JOHNSTOWN-ALTOONA	312,520
176	JONESBORO	65,330
121	JOPLIN-PITTSBURG	168,950
28	KANSAS CITY	688,930
61	KNOXVILLE	392,380
137	LA CROSSE-EAU CLAIRE.	149,600
193	LAFAYETTE, IN	41,320
107	LAFAYETTE, LA	194,130
167	LAKE CHARLES	71,640
99	LANSING	213,810
200	LAREDO	28,610
191	OTTUMWA-KIRKSVILLE	44,050
79	PADUCAH-C.GIRARDEAU-HARRBG	298,560
171	PANAMA CITY	66,880
183	PARKERSBURG	57,490
97	PEORIA	221,050
4	PHILADELPHIA	2,400,780
24	PHOENIX,FLAGSTAFF	727,150
12	PITTSBURGH	1,202,490
73	PORTLAND-POLAND SPRING	322,720
23	PORTLAND, OR	789,360
199	PRESQUE ISLE	29,600
33	PROVIDENCE-NEW BEDFORD	601,880
150	QUINCY-HANNIBAL-KEOKUK	122,560
41	RALEIGH-DURHAM	530,890
160	RAPID CITY	90,580
136	RENO	150,700
55	RICHMOND-PETRSBG,CHARLTSVL	429,540
65	ROANOKE-LYNCHBURG	360,390
71	ROCHESTER	333,520
109	ROCKFORD	185,820
189	ROSWELL	52,770
21	SACRAMENTO-STOCKTON	833,700
164	SALISBURY	79,000
44	SALT LAKE CITY	522,960
195	SAN ANGELO	34,720
45	SAN ANTONIO	502,930
27	SAN DIEGO	699,110
5	SAN FRANCISCO-OAKLAND	1,950,270
119	SANTABARBRA-SANMAR-SANLUOB	172,030
111	SAVANNAH	182,700
14	SEATTLE-TACOMA	1,093,860
57	SHREVEPORT	
130	SIOUX CITY	153,740
100	SIOUX FALLS(MITCHELL)	210,150
81	SOUTH BEND-ELKHART	277,660

Rank	Market	Households	Rank	Market	Households	Rank	Market	Households
80	CHATTANOOGA	286,150	108	LAS VEGAS	190,550	72	SPOKANE	331,800
182	CHEYENNE-SCOTTSBLF-STERLNG	57,940	83	LEXINGTON	266,960	95	SPRINGFIELD-HOLYOKE	228,530
3	CHICAGO	2,944,860	194	LIMA	39,640	84	SPRINGFIELD, MO	264,190
145	CHICO-REDDING	135,630	86	LINCOLN & HSTNGS-KRNY PLUS	251,130	180	ST. JOSEPH	60,650
26	CINCINNATI	707,560	56	LITTLE ROCK-PINE BLUFF	429,150	17	ST. LOUIS	1,029,430
166	CLARKSBURG-WESTON	75,140	2	LOS ANGELES,PALM SPRINGS	4,214,600	53	SYRACUSE,ELMIRA	446,770
9	CLEVELAND,AKRON	1,402,020	43	LOUISVILLE	528,190	132	TALLAHASSE-THOMASVILLE	152,290
103	COLORADO SPRINGS-PUEBLO	201,410	135	LUBBOCK	150,750	18	TAMPA-ST.PETERSBG,SARASOTA	1,028,780
129	COLUMBIA-JEFFERSON CITY	154,190	138	MACON	148,590	118	TERRE HAUTE	172,980
94	COLUMBIA, SC	231,240	105	MADISON	199,140	60	TOLEDO	401,590
143	COLUMBUS-TUPELO	137,030	186	MANKATO	56,440	152	TOPEKA	120,040
116	COLUMBUS, GA	174,100	188	MARQUETTE	54,000	139	TRAVERSE CITY-CADILLAC	147,700
37	COLUMBUS, OH	576,840	141	MASON CITY-AUSTIN-ROCHESTR	144,150	82	TRI-CITIES: TN-VA	274,550
131	CORPUS CHRISTI	152,760	154	MEDFORD-KLAMATH FALLS	113,960	87	TUCSON(NOGALES)	250,380
10	DALLAS-FT. WORTH	1,355,900	36	MEMPHIS	581,190	58	TULSA	420,190
74	DAVENPORT-R.ISLAND-MOLINE	320,030	169	MERIDIAN	69,430	198	TWIN FALLS	30,030
51	DAYTON	460,350	13	MIAMI-FT. LAUDERDALE	1,099,690	158	TYLER	94,560
19	DENVER	858,930	29	MILWAUKEE	679,100	157	UTICA	97,390
69	DES MOINES-AMES	340,560	15	MINNEAPOLIS-ST. PAUL	1,071,370	101	WACO-TEMPLE	207,830
7	DETROIT	1,658,910	144	MINOT-BISMARCK-DICKINSON	136,430	8	WASHINGTON, DC,HAGERSTOWN	1,467,620
161	DOTHAN	87,580	172	MISSOULA	65,630	178	WATERTOWN	62,010
117	DULUTH-SUPERIOR	173,440	62	MOBILE-PENSACOLA	383,590	133	WAUSAU-RHINELANDER	151,810
104	EL PASO	200,330	112	MONROE-EL DORADO	181,550	68	WEST PALM BEACH-FT. PIERCE	345,320
140	ERIE	147,410	114	MONTEREY-SALINAS	179,660	110	WHEELING-STEUBENVILLE	185,420
123	EUGENE	166,010	113	MONTGOMERY	181,490	125	WICHITA FALLS&LAWTON	161,260
187	EUREKA	55,170	30	NASHVILLE,BOWLING GREEN	675,810	59	WICHITA-HUTCHINSON PLUS	404,170
88	EVANSVILLE	245,390	35	NEW ORLEANS	590,880	49	WILKES BARRE-SCRANTON	469,230
202	FAIRBANKS	20,360	1	NEW YORK	6,409,720	128	WILMINGTON	156,280
102	FARGO-VALLEY CITY	207,010	47	NORFOLK-PORTSMTH-NEWPT NWS	480,380	122	YAKIMA	167,620
54	FLINT-SAGINAW-BAY CITY	443,610	203	NORTH PLATTE	15,740	92	YOUNGSTOWN	233,880
156	FLORENCE, SC	98,670	149	ODESSA-MIDLAND	123,930	181	YUMA-EL CENTRO	58,810
64	FRESNO(VISALIA)	365,030	42	OKLAHOMA CITY	528,260	197	ZANESVILLE	30,130
124	FT. MYERS-NAPLES	164,610	70	OMAHA	337,630			
147	FT. SMITH	127,280	34	ORLANDO-DAYTONA BEACH	595,990			

FIGURE 2-15

Nielsen TV household estimates.

(From "Designated Market Areas," A.C. Nielsen, Chicago, 1982.)

SAN FRANCISCO—OAKLAND, CA

MARCH 1981

DAYPART TIME (PTZ) STATION	METRO HH RTG	METRO HH SHR	DMA HH RTG	DMA HH SHR	SHARE TREND FEB '81	NOV '80	JUL '80	MAR '80	WOMEN 18+	18-34	18-49	25-49	25-54	WKG	FEM PER 12-24	12-24	MEN 18+	18-34	18-49	25-49	25-54	TNS 12-17	CHILD 2-11	6-11
MON.–FRI.																								
7.00AM-9.00AM																								
KBHK 44 I	2	9	2	10	13	15	15	12	4															4
KGO 7 A	5	28	5	30	30	30	36	33	4	1	1	1	1	2	1	1	3	2	1	1	2	2	4	
KGSC 36 I	<<		<<	10	9	9	3	7		1	1	1	1	1				1					1	2
KPIX 5 C	2	13	2		9	9	7	7	1	1	1	1	1	1		1	2	1	1	2	2	2		
KQED 9 P	<<		<<	16	15	16	17	16							1									
KRON 4 N	3	18	3		NR	NR	14	NR	2	1	1	1	1	1	1	1	2	1	1	1	1	1	11	7
KTSF 26 I	<<		<<	17	15	13	4	16								1						1	1	1
KTVU 2 I	3	16	3		6	4	NR	NR								6							19	13
KTZO 20 I	1	5	1	5	17	17	15	18	9	7	7	8	8	5			6	5	5	5	5	5		
HUT/PUT/TOTALS *	19		18																					
9.00AM-NOON																								
KBHK 44 I	4	24	1	5	5	4	7	3	4	4	3	3	3	2	4	2	1	1	1	1	1	1	1	1
KGO 7 A	4	24	4	22	26	26	33	22	4	5	3	3	3	3	4	3	1	1	1	1	1	1	1	1
KGSC 36 I	<<		<<																				2	2
KPIX 5 C	4		5	25	25	24	24	18	4	5	4	3	3	2			1	1	1	1	1	1	1	1
KQED 9 P	1	7	1	6	6	6	5	5	1														2	3
KBON 4 N	3	18		16	12	16		22																

For explanation of symbols, see page 3.

NSI AVERAGE WEEK ESTIMATES

SAN FRANCISCO—OAKLAND, CA

DAYPART SUMMARY

STATION TOTALS (000)

DAYPART TIME STATION: MON.–FRI. 7:00AM–9:00AM

	CUME DMA HH % AVG WK	CUME 4 WK	FEB '81 AVG WK STAT TOT HH (000)		HH	PERSONS 2+	PERSONS 18+	WOMEN 18+	W 18-34	W 18-49	W 25-49	W 25-54	W 50+	WKG	FEM PER 12-24	PER 12-24	MEN 18+	M 18-34	M 18-49	M 25-49	M 25-54	TEENS 12-17	TEENS GIRLS	CHILD 2-11	CHILD 6-11
	49	49	50		51	52	53	54	55	56	57	58	60	61	62	63	64	65	66	67	68	70	71	72	73
KBHK	13	21	242		41	51	16	9	5	7	5	6	2	3	4	13	7	4	7	5	5	10	2	26	17
KGO	19	34	367		110	143	136	84	23	46	36	41	38	19	12	15	52	15	23	20	23	2	2	5	1
KGSC			61		7	3	2	1				1	1				1								
KPIX	11	24	195		35	39	25	19	6	9	8	10	10	6	1	1	6	1	3	3	3	2		14	1
KQED			44		3	3	1	1	1	1	1	1												2	
KRON	11	24	222		58	75	74	44	5	9	9	14	35	8	2	3	30	8	17	16	18	2	2		
KTSF					3																				
KTVU	15	24	312		91	148	18	13	10	11	7	9	2	2	9	16	5	2	3	2	2	11	5	119	57
KTZO	5	11	106		18	15	6	4		3		2	2	2		5									

HUT/PUT/TOTALS *

	CUME DMA HH % AVG WK	CUME 4 WK	FEB '81 AVG WK STAT TOT HH (000)		HH	PERSONS 2+	PERSONS 18+	WOMEN 18+	W 18-34	W 18-49	W 25-49	W 25-54	W 50+	WKG	FEM PER 12-24	PER 12-24	MEN 18+	M 18-34	M 18-49	M 25-49	M 25-54	TEENS 12-17	TEENS GIRLS	CHILD 2-11	CHILD 6-11
	49	49	50		51	52	53	54	55	56	57	58	60	61	62	63	64	65	66	67	68	70	71	72	73
KGSC	7	10	107		25	40	37	24	5	12	6	9	12	7	4	8	13	8	8	8	8	9	7	12	7
KPIX	31	53	631		254	403	379	208	42	88	78	90	120	69	17	34	171	41	92	81	92	12	7	2	1
KQED	4	13	71		25	32	29	17	2	5	5	5	11	4			12	8	8	9	9	1	2	10	8
KRON	14	37	278		89	134	120	61	11	27	23	31	35	26	5	10	58	16	27	24	27	4		1	1
KTSF			7		7	7	7	2	2	2	2	2		1			5	2	4	4	4			1	
KTVU	37	52	921		434	836	632	339	168	232	153	186	107	127	133	249	294	136	200	135	156	106	55	98	67
KTZO	4	8	97		34	71	42	23	4	10	9	15	13	4	4	18	19	11	11	8	8	15	3	14	10
HUT/PUT/TOTALS *					1258	2210	1790	990	334	546	400	483	444	355	238	432	800	270	472	367	418	181	92	239	155

FIGURE 2-16

Daypart summary.

(From "Viewers in Profile," A.C. Nielsen, Chicago, 1981.)

MARCH 1981

41

SAN FRANCISCO—OAKLAND, CA

STATION

DMA HH | **DMA RATINGS**

STATION / DAY	PROGRAM	RATINGS WEEKS 1 2 3 4 5 6	MULTI-WEEK AVG RTG SHR	SHARE TREND '81 '80 NOV FEB	BAR '80	HUT

R.S.E. THRESHOLDS 25·% (1 S.E.) 4 WK AVG 50·%

KRON

Day	Program
SUN	OAKLAND A'S
AV7	EYE NWS
NOR	EYE NWS
MON	NWSCENTER 4
TUE	NWSCENTER 4
WED	NWSCENTER 4
THU	NWSCENTER 4
FRI	NWSCENTER 4
AV5	NWSCENTER 4
SAT	LAWRENCE WELK
SUN	MUPPETS

KTSF

Day	Program
MON	FLYING NUN
TUE	FLYING NUN
WED	FLYING NUN
THU	FLYING NUN
FRI	FLYING NUN
AVS	FLYING NUN
SAT	TOKYO TV
SUN	TOKYO TV

KTVU

Day	Program
MON	STS-SAN FRAN
TUE	STS-SAN FRAN
WED	STS-SAN FRAN
THU	STS-SAN FRAN
FRI	STS-SAN FRAN
AVS	STS-SAN FRAN

See Program Index for complete details of program start time, duration and weeks of telecast.

MARCH 1981

PERSONS — WOMEN — FEM — PER — MEN — TNS — CHILD

42

NSI AVERAGE WEEK ESTIMATES

SAN FRANCISCO–OAKLAND, CA

STATION TOTALS ('000)

TIME / STATION / DAY PROGRAM	HH	PERSONS 2+	PERSONS 18+	PERSONS 18+	WOMEN 18-34	WOMEN 18-49	WOMEN 25-49	WOMEN 25-54	WOMEN 25-64	WOMEN 50+	WKG	FEM PER 12-24	FEM PER 12-24	MEN 18+	MEN 18-34	MEN 18-49	MEN 25-49	MEN 25-54	MEN 25-64	TEENS 12-17	TEENS GIRLS	CHILD 2-11	CHILD 6-11
R.S.E. THRESHOLDS 25÷% / (T.S.E.) 4 WK AVG 50÷%	*38/10*	*76/19*	*59/15*	*41/10*	*22/11*	*40/10*	*33/8*	*34/9*	*33/8*	*36/9*	*36/9*	*44/12*	*57/15*	*41/10*	*45/12*	*43/11*	*34/9*	*35/9*	*36/9*	*52/14*	*43/12*	*62/16*	*55/15*
6.00PM																							
KPIX MON EYE NWS	287	445	420	241	40	96	87	103	150	145	79	14	27	178	33	80	77	100	123	13	5	12	9
NOR EYE NWS	*289*	*441*	*419*	*242*	*39*	*93*	*85*	*100*	*148*	*148*	*77*	*11*	*24*	*177*	*34*	*77*	*73*	*97*	*121*	*11*	*3*	*11*	*8*
TUE EYE NWS	227	345	329	181	33	77	68	81	118	104	55	14	33	148	37	78	65	76	96	11	5	5	5
WED EYE NWS	224	345	347	187	29	74	67	75	112	113	54	9	24	160	31	85	75	86	108	8	5	5	7
THU EYE NWS	223	359	320	192	23	58	54	67	103	134	46	6	18	128	20	53	47	58	78	7	1	7	4
FRI EYE NWS	235	334	320	190	32	69	60	70	109	121	48	12	26	157	31	73	64	73	104	8	3	8	9
AV5 EYE NWS	*240*	*368*	*347*	*199*	*32*	*75*	*67*	*80*	*119*	*124*	*57*	*11*	*26*	*155*	*30*	*73*	*66*	*79*	*102*	*9*	*3*	*14*	*9*
NOR EYE NWS	*240*	*372*	*354*	*198*	*31*	*74*	*67*	*79*	*118*	*124*	*56*	*11*	*25*	*154*	*30*	*73*	*65*	*78*	*102*	*8*	*3*	*9*	*7*
SAT CBS SAT NWS	149	223	204	99	30	59	47	55	69	40	37	15	26	105	27	67	60	72	82	7	3	12	11
SAT EYE NWS	139	197	176	91	24	47	40	50	66	44	36	16	16	85	11	45	33	54	70	8	3	12	10
SUN CBS NWS-SUN		*215*	*300*	*164*	*12*	*50*	*49*	*73*	*104*	*114*	*57*	*4*	*13*	*135*		*36*		*43*	*78*	*8*	*3*	*7*	*7*
KTZO MON BONANZA	30	54	39	18		8	8	12	12	10	4	2	16	21	3	13	13	13	21	6	2	15	9
TUE BONANZA	33	43	31	11		4	4	7	8	6	4	6	20	20	17	17	7	7	9	20	6	7	5
WED BONANZA	42	93	65	40		4	4	26	26	35	4	5	25	25		14	14	14	25	22	2	8	8
THU BONANZA	27	60	34	18	7	17	15	15	15	1		3	5	16	4	6	5	5	16	3	3	3	3
FRI BONANZA	26	71	37	24	9	12	12	18	18	12		3		13	3	10	8	8	12	11	3	26	18
AV5 BONANZA	*32*	*64*	*41*	*22*	*3*	*9*	*9*	*16*	*16*	*13*	*3*	*3*	*14*	*19*	*5*				*17*		*3*	*12*	*9*
6.45PM																							
KTZO SUN TIME MACHINE	27	48	36	22	13	22	19	19	19	19	6	11	11	14		14	14	14	14	9		3	3
	51	52	53	54	55	56	57	58	59	60	61	62	63	64	65	66	67	68	69	70	71	72	73

MARCH 1981

For explanation of symbols, see page 3.
For RSE explanations, see page 2.
See Time Period for complete competitive and post 1:15AM programming.

FIGURE 2-17

Program averages.

(From "Viewers in Profile," A.C. Nielsen, Chicago, 1981.)

SAN FRANCISCO—OAKLAND, CA

TUESDAY 6.30PM— 8.00PM

DMA HH

STATION	PROGRAM	WEEKS 1	2	3	4	MULTI-WEEK AVG RTG	SHR	FEB '81	NOV '80	MAR '80
6.30PM	R.S.E. THRESHOLDS 25%	4	4	4	4	4	2			
	(1 S.E.) 4 WK AVG 50%	1	1	1	1	1	LT			
KBHK	GOOD TIMES	7		9	7	8	14	18X	13	11
KGO	#NWS SCENE 2					15	27	26	26	27
	NWS SCENE 2	14	15	13		14	26			
	OSCAR SPCL				17	17	28			
KGSC	GUNSMOKE	1	1		1	1	1	3X		
KPIX	EYE NWS	12	9	11	13	11	20	19X	20	21
KQED	MACNEIL&LEHRER	1	1	1	1	1	3	2X	1	2
KRON	NWSCENTER 4	5	7	5	7	6	10	9X	12	10
								NR	NR	NR
KTZO	WARRIORS BKBL	4				5	8	5X	3	NR
	BARNEY MILLER	1		10	2	10	15			
	STARSKY&HUTCH	2	2	2		3	3			
	HUT/PUT/TOTALS *	64	58	61	66	62		61	63	61

DMA RATINGS

	PERSONS			WOMEN						FEM PER		MEN					TNS		CHILD	
	2+	18+	12-34	18+	18-34	25-49	25-54	WKG		12-24	12-24	18+	18-34	18-49	25-49	25-54	12-17	12-17	2-11	6-11
col	14	15	16	17	18	19	20	21	22	23	24	25	26	27	28	29	30	31	31	32
	2	2	3	2	2	3	3	4	4	8	5	2	6	7	4	7	11	3	10	13
	LT	LT		5	5	3				2	2		1	1	1	3	3		3	3
	6	5	9	5	9	6	4	3	4	13	11	5	9	6	5	4	9	9	9	8
	11	12	7	12	8	10	11	12	10	7	7	12	7	10	11	10	7	5	5	4
	10	11	6	16	6	7	9	10	7	4	5	11	6	9	11	10	5	5	5	4
	13	13	12		15	17	18	18	16	15	13	8	8	11	11	10	13	8		
	1	1	1	9	4	7	8	8	7	2	3	8	5	7	8	8	2		1	1
	7	1	1	1	1	1	1					1	1	1	1	1			1	2
	3	4	2	5	3	2	4	6		4	3	4	2	2	2	1				
	3	3	3	2	2	2	2			1	1	5	6	6	6	7	1	1	1	1
	9	8	7	8	6	8	8	8		4	5	7	6	6	8	8	10	12	12	12
	1	1	2	1	1	1	1	1		2	2	1	1	2	1	1	2	2	1	1
	3	4																	29	32
	44	48	37	50	40	43	44	46	46	39	35	45	37	40	43	42	34	42	29	32

TUESDAY 6.30PM— 8.00PM

MARCH 1981

44

NSI AVERAGE WEEK ESTIMATES — SAN FRANCISCO–OAKLAND, CA

STATION TOTALS (000)

	HH	PERSONS		WOMEN						MEN					TEENS		CHILD	
	HH	2+	18+	18+	18-34	18-49	25-49	25-54	WKG	18+	18-34	18-49	25-49	25-54	12-17	GIRLS	2-11	6-11
	51	52	53	54	55	56	57	58	61	64	65	66	67	68	70	71	72	73
	38/10	76/19	59/15	41/10	42/11	40/10	33/8	34/9	36/9	41/10	45/12	43/11	34/9	35/9	52/14	43/12	62/16	55/15
KBHK	162	301	177	89	70	81	34	34	31	88	68	77	43	43	57	35	67	39
KGO	319	545	477	247	70	133	107	134	88	229	52	122	98	112	33	17	36	16
	312	521	468	228	53	104	87	116	73	240	49	115	97	113	23	11	30	18
	340	618	504	305	121	219	168	188	133	198	61	142	103	108	62		53	12
	16	36	33	21						13								
	236	359	345	193	33	83	74	91	58	152	36	80	68	82	9	4	3	5
	34	54	43	26	5	5	3	3	4	17	3	9	9	9			5	
	115	169	168	96	28	40	18	40	50	72	15	21	13	15	1	1	11	3
	5																	
	6																	
	<<																	

DAY	TIME BREAK	STATION
	6.30PM	KBHK
		KGO
		KGSC
		KPIX
		KQED
		KRON
		KTSF

STATION TOTALS (000)

	HH	HH	WOMEN		MEN		CHILD
	DMA RTG	HH	18+	18-49	18+	18-49	2-11
	7	51	54	56	64	66	72
	2/17	38/10	41/10	40/10	41/10	43/11	62/16
KBHK	8	180	83	77	92	84	85
KGO	15	318	247	126	230	115	27
KGSC	1	15	20	3	12		3
KPIX	11	229	184	79	151	81	5
KQED	2	36	14	3	9	9	31
KRON	6	120	101	47	72	24	
KTSF	**	4					

MARCH 1981

For explanation of symbols, see page 3.
For RSE explanations, see page 2.

FIGURE 2-18
Four-week averages.
(From "Viewers in Profile," A.C. Nielsen, Chicago, 1981.)

45

The program average section offers audience figures for each program telecast during the survey period. For programs appearing more than once a week, such as newscasts, weekly averages are given also. In this section DMA household ratings are provided for each week that the show was aired. Figure 2-17 is a sample of this section.

The time period section of the NSI report breaks out audiences by time period. Monday–Friday listings begin with 6:00 a.m. and run by half hour to 5:00 p.m., with the inclusion of a 12:15 p.m. break. From 5:00 p.m. to 8:00 p.m. audiences are reported by quarter hour. Monday–Friday listings pick up again at 10:30 p.m. with a 10:30 and an 11:00 p.m. break, then continue on a quarter-hour basis through 2:00 a.m. Individual weekday listings begin at 4:30 p.m. and go through 2:00 a.m. From 7:30 to 11:00 p.m. audiences are reported only by half hour. Saturday and Sunday audiences are reported by half hour through 3:30 p.m., by quarter hour from 3:30 to 7:30 p.m., by half hour from 7:30 to 11:00 p.m., and by quarter hour from 11:00 p.m. to 2:00 a.m. A separate line of audience data is provided by station for each program airing in that time period during the 4 weeks. Also 4-week averages are given for each time break. Figure 2-18 is a sample of this section. A fourth NSI section reports a four-book share trend against key demographic audiences for selected time periods.

METHODS OF TELEVISION MEASUREMENT: METER VS. DIARY

Meter measurement consists of the electronic recording of whether or not a television set is on—and, if so, to which channel it is tuned—through an attachment to the set. *Diary measurement* consists of the placement of television viewing diaries in the cooperating homes. Diarykeepers in those homes record the viewing of each household member in these diaries. Each method has a major advantage and a major disadvantage.

The major advantage of meter measurement is that, because the meter works automatically, it accurately records all television set operation.

The major disadvantage is that the meter only reports whether or not the set is on and, if so, to which channel it is tuned. It does not report who is viewing or whether, indeed, anyone is viewing. If the set is left on, unattended, the meter keeps recording just as if the whole family were in front of the set.

The major advantage of diary measurement is that it allows for the reporting of each family member's viewing separately. This method of audience measurement produces data on persons, or demographic viewing data, as well as the less discriminating data on number of homes viewing.

The major disadvantage of diary measurement is that its accuracy is dependent upon the diligence of the diarykeeper in recording the family's viewing. Diarykeepers may forget to record some viewing or may incorrectly record some viewing. This is particularly true of viewing at times when the diarykeeper is not present.

It is generally assumed that meter measurement overestimates television audiences and diary measurement underestimates television audiences. It is also assumed that the degree of overestimation and underestimation varies by program and time period. Meter measurement may overstate late-night viewing and dinner hour viewing, since it is during those times that a television set is most likely to be left on, unattended, for some duration.

The broadcasting industry has invested substantially in research on the meter vs. diary issue. Most of this research has been conducted by Statistical Research Inc. on behalf of CONTAM (Committee on Nationwide Television Audience Measurement) and COLTRAM (Committee on Local Television and Radio Audience Measurement). These committees were established by national broadcasters to monitor the quality of the research provided by the major television research suppliers. Similar research has been conducted for the New York Ratings Committee, a local group similar in purpose to the national COLTRAM.

While the results of these studies have not been conclusive, they generally attest to the accuracy of meter measurement in recording household viewing. Studies on the quality of the data on audience composition and demographic viewing patterns provided by the diary method, however, have indicated some general weaknesses in the diary measurement approach. Viewing by children, teenagers, and young adults tends to be understated in diaries, since these segments of the television viewing audience are less likely to be primary diarykeepers and, even when they do keep diaries, are less diligent in reporting than older adults. Programs likely to be viewed by children and teenagers in the absence of the adult diarykeeper will sometimes not be recorded. Diary measurement also reports lower late-night viewing levels than meters do. This may be both because of the failure of diarykeepers to report late-night viewing and because of meter overstatement resulting from unattended television sets.

The Marriage of Meters and Diaries

The national Nielsen television index (NTI) and the other major services augment their meter data by using separate diary samples to obtain the vital "who is viewing" information. The rating services then apply the audience composition estimates obtained from the diaries to the total viewing-level measurement obtained from the meter sample. This methodology can, however, result in some data distortion, as shown in the following example.

> Program A has an audience that is predominantly made up of children and teenagers. According to the meter sample, 10 percent of the homes viewed this program. The diary sample reveals that a child was viewing in 8 out of every 10 homes watching program A, a teenager in 5 out of every 10, and an adult woman in 4 out of every 10. However, only 8 percent of the total homes measured in the diary sample reported viewing program A. Thus, assuming that the meter is correct, 2 out of every 10 diary homes failed to report their viewing of program A. And, although we cannot actually know the audience composition of those nonreporting homes, by transferring the audience composition of the diary sample to the meter results, we are assigning the same audience composition to the nonreporting homes as we do to the reporting homes. However, the diarykeeper in most cases is an adult woman, and it seems unlikely that the viewing participation for adult women in nonreporting diary homes was at the same 4 out of 10 level as the viewing participation for adult women in reporting diary homes.

Despite the possibility of such distortions, the meter-diary combined approach remains the most accurate means of measurement feasible today. However, the challenges of an increasingly complex viewing environment will require improved methods of audience measurement if the rating services are to maintain their credibility in the advertising community.

The People Meter: The Ultimate Answer

The fragmentation of viewing resulting from new cable programming options has compounded the shortcomings of the diary method. It is generally recognized that a method of viewing measurement that depends on the accuracy and diligence of an unprofessional diarykeeper breaks down when the viewing options increase from 3 or 4 to 20 or more. These new options do not have the identification of the network affiliates or the major independent stations. Even if the diarykeepers know what movie was watched and by whom, they are often unable to report on what channel they viewed it.

The answer to this problem seems to be some form of electronic measurement of *individual* as opposed to *household* viewing. "People meters," which measure the viewing of each family member, are already being used in Europe. While the results of the European experiments have been promising, application of the people meter techniques in the United States has not yet taken place. One reason for this is the huge cost involved. Today, the networks underwrite the major portion of television audience measurement. Current methodology is adequate for measuring the large network audiences, and there is thus little incentive for the networks to increase their already substantial investments in research to improve that methodology. And the small cable services are not yet in a position to take on the cost of such research. Nevertheless, the introduction of the people meter does not seem far away. Competition among research companies is likely to lead them to this approach. The advertising agencies and advertisers themselves will put increased pressure on the networks to improve the audience measurement techniques for their industry. The maturing cable industry will also contribute more to advancing the state of audience research since it stands to gain from a more accurate measurement of its audience.

DAYPARTS AND THEIR AUDIENCES

Television viewing varies significantly by time of day. This variation is demonstrated in Figure 2-4, which provides hour-by-hour HUT levels. However, HUT levels are not the only audience variable that changes by time of day; audience composition is dynamic also. To take into account the differences in the "audience" they are selling during different time periods, broadcasters have found it convenient to divide their day into various dayparts and to sell time on that basis. Network dayparts are those dominated by network-originated programming, whereas local dayparts are those predominantly programmed by the local stations.

Network Dayparts

There are eight network dayparts. These dayparts are not strictly defined by a time specification; they represent program groupings reflecting similar audience composition. The eight dayparts are morning, daytime, news, primetime, late night, children's programming, sports, and specials. These dayparts are discussed in depth in Chapters 3 and 4; however, at this point it is useful to define each in terms of the type of audience it attracts. (*Note:* All times given are Eastern standard time. Central and Mountain times are 1 hour earlier. Pacific time follows Eastern standard time format.)

MORNING [MONDAY–FRIDAY, 7 A.M.–9 A.M. (EST)]

As Figure 2-4 shows, HUT levels are lowest during these morning hours. The three network news and information programs attract an adult audience, more female than male. A significant number of children watch television during these morning hours. *Captain Kangaroo* on

TABLE 2-3

EARLY-MORNING NETWORK NEWS
(MONDAY–FRIDAY) AUDIENCE
COMPOSITION BY AGE AND SEX

	Audience (000)	Distribution (%)
Total people 2+	9480	100.0
Women		
18+	5520	58.2
18–34	1280	13.5
35–49	1230	12.9
50+	3010	31.8
25–54	2630	27.7
18–49	2510	26.4
Men		
18+	2730	28.8
18–34	550	5.8
35–49	550	5.8
50+	1630	17.2
25–54	1190	12.5
18–49	1100	11.6
Teens	410	4.3
Children	820	8.7

Source: NTI/NAD July, November 1978; February, May 1979.

CBS-TV, now shown on weekend mornings, used to go on at 8:00 a.m. and was the only network program offered for the young viewer; however, cartoons and off-network situation comedies on the independent stations fill this void.

The three network news and information programs deliver a composite average annual rating of 12.5. Table 2-3 provides a profile of the audience attracted by these programs.

DAYTIME [MONDAY–FRIDAY, 10:00 A.M.–4:30 P.M. (EST)]

From 10 a.m. on, the daytime audience is dominated by adult women viewers. Game shows, serial dramas (soap operas), and off-network situation comedies are the basic program types offered. Table 2-4 provides household and key demographic viewing levels for the Monday–Friday, 10:00 a.m.–4:30 p.m. time period. Table 2-5 shows overall

TABLE 2-4
MONDAY–FRIDAY DAYTIME
(10:00 A.M.–4:30 P.M.) RATINGS BY
SELECTED DEMOGRAPHICS

	Households			Women 25–54			Women 18–49			Women 50+		
	Audience (000)	Rating	Index	Audience (000)	Rating	Index	Audience (000)	Rating	Index	Audience (000)	Rating	Index
Total, United States	19,030	25.7	100	7,300	18.0	100	8,310	17.2	100	6,730	22.7	100
Household size												
1–2	7,310	19.0	74	1,440	13.6	76	1,550	13.1	76	4,760	22.4	99
3–4	7,320	29.6	115	3,570	18.7	104	4,150	18.2	106	1,460	22.4	99
5+	4,440	39.9	155	2,290	21.2	118	2,610	19.1	111	510	29.3	129
Household income												
Under $10,000	7,390	27.3	106	2,020	23.4	130	2,490	21.8	127	3,620	25.8	114
$10,000–14,999	3,400	24.9	97	1,500	20.2	112	1,690	18.5	108	990	21.5	95
$15,000–$19,999	3,290	27.6	107	1,450	18.4	102	1,680	18.4	107	750	21.2	93
$20,000+	4,950	23.0	89	2,330	14.1	78	2,450	13.2	77	1,370	18.6	82

Source: NTI/NAD July, November 1978; February, May 1979.

TABLE 2-5

**MONDAY–FRIDAY DAYTIME
(10:00 A.M.–4:30 P.M.) AUDIENCE
COMPOSITION BY AGE AND SEX**

	Audience (000)	Distribution (%)
Total people		
2+	26,530	100.0
Women		
18+	14,940	56.3
18–34	5,250	19.8
35–49	3,060	11.5
50+	6,640	25.0
25–54	7,300	27.5
18–49	8,310	31.3
Working women	2,770	10.4
Men		
18+	4,900	18.5
18–34	1,500	5.7
35–49	820	3.1
50+	2,580	9.7
25–54	1,920	7.2
18–49	2,320	8.7
Teens	2,550	9.6
Children		
2–11	4,140	15.6

Source: NTI/NAD July, November 1978; February, May 1979.

audience composition for the time period, and Table 2-6 breaks down this composition by program type.

NEWS (VARIOUS TIMES)

The network *news* daypart is actually a misnomer, for it is not confined to any part of the day; it includes all network news programming, no matter when it runs. However, the central element of each network's news is its daily news program, airing during the early evening hours. The three network weeknight news broadcasts attract a collective average annual household rating of 37.5. Table 2-7 shows the composition of this audience.

MONDAY–FRIDAY DAYTIME
(10:00 A.M.–4:30 P.M.) AUDIENCE
COMPOSITION BY PROGRAM TYPE

	Game shows		Situation comedies		Serial dramas	
	Audience (000)	Distribution (%)	Audience (000)	Distribution (%)	Audience (000)	Distribution (%)
Total people						
2+	5700	100.0	6880	100.0	7260	100.0
Women						
18+	3160	55.4	3060	44.5	5050	69.6
18–34	930	16.3	1180	17.2	1870	25.8
35–49	580	10.2	680	9.9	1050	14.5
50+	1650	28.9	1200	17.4	2130	29.3
25–54	1350	23.7	1520	22.1	2520	34.7
18–49	1510	26.5	1860	27.1	2920	40.3
Men						
18+	1260	22.1	1370	19.9	1070	14.7
18–34	330	5.8	560	8.1	320	4.4
35–49	200	3.5	220	3.2	170	2.3
50+	730	12.8	590	8.6	580	8.0
25–54	420	7.4	560	8.1	420	5.8
18–49	530	9.3	780	11.3	490	6.7
Teens	490	8.6	1080	15.7	600	8.3
Children						
2–11	790	13.9	1370	19.9	540	7.4

Source: NTI/NAD July, November 1978; February, May 1979.

TABLE 2-7
EARLY EVENING NETWORK NEWS
(MONDAY–FRIDAY)
AUDIENCE COMPOSITION BY
AGE AND SEX

	Audience (000)	Distribution (%)
Total people		
2+	42,160	100.0
Women		
18+	20,620	48.9
18–34	4,980	11.8
35–49	3,800	9.0
50+	11,840	28.1
25–54	8,820	20.9
18–49	8,780	20.8
Men		
18+	16,360	38.8
18–34	4,270	10.1
35–49	3,120	7.4
50+	8,970	21.3
25–54	7,320	17.4
18–49	7,390	17.5
Teens	2,130	5.1
Children	3,050	7.2

Source: NTI/NAD July, November 1978; February, May 1979.

PRIMETIME [MONDAY–SATURDAY, 8 P.M.–11 P.M. (EST);
SUNDAY, 7 P.M.–11 P.M. (EST)]

The viewing levels of Figure 2-4 peaked from 8 to 11 p.m. For this reason these 3 hours, and an additional hour from 7 to 8 p.m. on Sunday, are known as network *primetime*. In the course of the average week, over 90 percent of all people in the United States view some primetime television. Tables 2-8 and 2-9 provide both primetime HUT levels and viewing levels for the key demographic breaks for women and men. Table 2-10 shows the composition of the primetime audience.

LATE NIGHT [MONDAY–SUNDAY, 11:30 P.M.–2:00 A.M.
(EST)]

The Tonight Show has become synonymous with late-night television over the years; however, today the viewer has many alternatives from which to choose. Off-network reruns and feature films offer *The Tonight*

PRIMETIME USAGE LEVELS BY
SELECTED DEMOGRAPHICS
ON WOMEN

	Households			Women 25–54			Women 18–49			Women 50+		
	Audience (000)	Rating	Index	Audience (000)	Rating	Index	Audience (000)	Rating	Index	Audience (000)	Rating	Index
Total, United States	42,700	57.6	100	18,900	46.7	100	21,000	43.5	100	14,700	49.8	100
Household size:												
1–2	19,060	49.7	86	4,930	46.6	100	5,290	44.8	103	10,500	49.3	99
3–4	15,860	64.3	112	9,110	47.7	102	10,180	44.6	103	3,450	52.7	106
5+	7,780	70.6	123	4,860	45.2	97	5,530	40.6	93	750	43.4	87
Household income:												
Under $10,000	14,780	54.7	95	4,320	50.2	107	5,260	46.1	106	7,160	51.0	102
$10,000–$14,999	7,630	56.0	97	3,470	46.7	100	4,140	45.4	104	2,310	50.1	101
$15,000–$19,999	7,190	60.5	105	3,590	45.8	98	4,100	45.0	103	1,750	49.6	100
$20,000+	13,100	60.8	106	7,520	45.5	97	7,500	40.4	93	3,480	47.1	95
Presence of nonadults:												
Any 6–11	10,080	66.4	115	6,790	46.0	99	7,220	44.8	103	580	52.7	106
Any 12–17	10,930	68.9	120	6,700	45.6	98	6,900	41.4	95	1,380	48.1	97
Selected upper demos:												
$15,000+, with nonadults	11,690	66.7	116	7,240	44.2	95	7,830	41.3	95	1,160	53.0	106
$15,000+, HOH POM*	6,850	56.4	98	3,890	41.3	88	3,910	37.5	86	1,460	47.1	95
$15,000+, HOH												
1+ yrs. coll.	8,630	57.4	100	4,770	43.1	92	4,910	39.0	90	1,820	47.8	96
4+ yrs. coll.	6,530	51.2	89	3,340	39.2	84	3,550	36.2	83	1,480	46.3	93

*HOH = head of household; POM = professional, owner, or manager.

Source: NTI/NAD July, November 1978; February, May 1979.

TABLE 2-9
PRIMETIME USAGE LEVELS BY SELECTED DEMOGRAPHICS ON MEN

	Households			Men 25–54			Men 18–49			Men 50+		
	Audience (000)	Rating	Index	Audience (000)	Rating	Index	Audience (000)	Rating	Index	Audience (000)	Rating	Index
Total, United States:	42,700	57.6	100	15,820	41.2	100	17,320	37.7	100	11,370	47.3	100
Household size:												
1–2	19,060	49.7	86	4,340	42.3	103	4,780	41.1	109	7,050	46.8	99
3–4	15,860	64.3	112	7,550	42.0	102	8,310	39.0	103	3,390	49.8	105
5+	7,780	70.6	123	3,930	38.9	94	4,230	32.5	86	930	43.7	92
Household income:												
Under $10,000	14,780	54.7	95	3,080	50.0	121	3,890	45.7	121	4,080	48.9	103
$10,000–$14,999	7,630	56.0	97	2,870	39.8	97	3,310	38.0	101	1,960	49.5	105
$15,000–$19,999	7,190	60.5	105	3,420	41.6	101	3,680	39.6	105	1,740	48.9	103
$20,000+	13,100	60.8	106	6,450	38.8	94	6,440	33.4	89	3,590	44.3	94
Presence of nonadults:												
Any 6–11	10,080	66.4	115	4,860	38.8	94	4,980	36.8	98	570	41.9	89
Any 12–17	10,930	68.9	120	4,650	38.9	94	4,900	34.0	90	1,560	45.2	96
Selected upper demos:												
$15,000+ with nonadults	11,690	66.7	116	6,180	38.8	94	6,470	35.4	94	1,390	47.6	101
$15,000+, HOH	6,850	56.4	98	3,580	37.3	91	3,540	33.5	89	1,450	41.1	87
POM*												
$15,000+, HOH 1+ yrs. coll.	8,630	57.4	100	4,440	38.5	93	4,500	34.8	92	1,710	42.4	90
4+ yrs. coll.	6,530	51.2	89	3,200	36.5	89	3,350	34.3	91	1,260	42.0	89

*HOH = head of household; POM = professional, owner, or manager.

Source: NTI/NAD July, November 1979; February, May 1979.

TABLE 2-10

PRIMETIME (MONDAY–SUNDAY,
8:00–11:00 P.M.) TV USAGE,
AUDIENCE COMPOSITION BY AGE
AND SEX

	Audience (000)	Distribution (%)
Total people		
2+	82,670	100
Women		
18+	35,710	43
18–34	12,730	15
35–49	8,270	10
50+	14,710	18
25–54	18,940	23
18–49	21,000	25
Working women	12,470	15
Men		
18+	28,580	35
18–34	10,700	13
35–49	6,600	8
50+	11,280	14
25–54	15,800	19
18–49	17,300	21
Teens	8,200	10
Children		
2–11	10,180	12

Source: NTI/NAD July, November 1978; February, May 1979.

Show tough competition. On weekends only NBC-TV offers network programming, with its Saturday Night Live reruns on Saturday and movies on Sunday.

The Monday–Friday late-night audience is essentially adult, more particularly young adult. Table 2-11 profiles the weekday late-night audience. Figure 2-19 shows the overall HUT levels by various household characteristics for late-night television.

CHILDREN'S PROGRAMMING (VARIOUS TIMES)

The three networks present children's programming at various times during the week; however, the major block is found on Saturday be-

TABLE 2-11

LATE-NIGHT (MONDAY–FRIDAY, 11:30 P.M.–1:00 A.M.) AUDIENCE COMPOSITION BY AGE AND SEX

	Audience (000)	Distribution (%)
Total people		
2+	29,090	100.0
Women		
18+	14,260	49.0
18–34	5,350	18.4
35–49	3,720	12.8
50+	5,190	17.8
25–54	8,300	28.5
18–49	9,070	31.2
Working women	5,070	17.4
Men		
18+	11,310	38.9
18–34	5,040	17.3
35–49	2,870	9.9
50+	3,400	11.7
25–54	6,640	22.8
18–49	7,910	27.2
Teens	2,540	8.7
Children	980	3.4

Source: NTI/NAD July, November 1978; February, May 1979.

FIGURE 2-19

Monday–Friday late-night quality profile. Ratings are by household (11:30 p.m.–1:00 a.m.)

(From "National Audience Demographics," A.C. Nielsen, Chicago, July, November 1978; February, May 1979.)

tween 8 a.m. and 2 p.m. More than 60 percent of the audience during this time period is composed of children and teenagers. (See Table 2-12.)

SPORTS (VARIOUS TIMES)

Like children's programming, sports programming can be found almost anywhere on the three networks' schedules. However, it also is concentrated on weekends, in this case Saturday and Sunday afternoons. Figure 2-20 provides the audience composition of various sports on television. Although men are, as expected, the dominant audience segment, women are significantly represented in all TV sport audiences, particularly those of tennis and golf.

TABLE 2-12

SATURDAY CHILDREN'S PROGRAMS (8:00 A.M.–2:00 P.M.), AUDIENCE COMPOSITION BY AGE AND SEX

	Audience (000)	Distribution (%)
Total people		
2+	7060	100
Children		
2–11	3620	51
6–11	2220	31
Teens		
12–17	1010	14
Adults		
18+	2430	35
18–34	1370	20
35–49	460	7
50+	600	8
25–54	1260	18
18–49	1830	27
Women		
18+	1370	20
18–34	780	11
35–49	260	4
50+	330	5
25–54	770	11
18–49	1040	15

Source: NTI/NAD July, November 1978; February, May 1979.

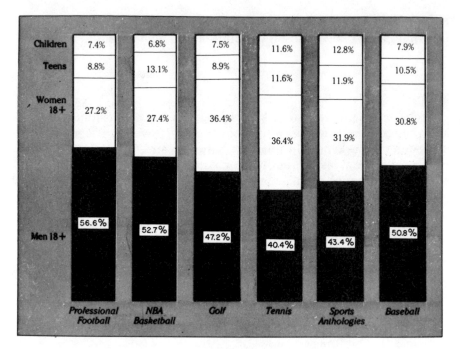

FIGURE 2-20

Audience composition of selected sports on network television for 1978.
(From "Sports 1978," NTI, A.C. Nielsen, Chicago, 1978.)

SPECIALS (VARIOUS TIMES DURING PRIMETIME)

A portion of each of the three networks' primetime schedules is treated separately by the networks. This portion consists of programs that are not regularly scheduled series or movies, but are, instead, one-time-only of periodic *special* presentations. Specials collectively have essentially the same audience composition as regularly scheduled prime-time programming; however, many specials are designed to reach selective portions of that audience. Major dramatic specials are meant to attract the more educated and affluent television viewer, animated specials are targeted to the children in the primetime audience, and *block-buster* feature film specials such as *Gone with the Wind* and *Rocky* are presented in the hope of attracting larger-than-average shares of all audience segments.

Local Dayparts

In addition to the eight network dayparts, there are four portions of the day during which the majority of programming is originated locally.

EARLY FRINGE [MONDAY–FRIDAY, 4:30 P.M.–6:00 P.M.
(EST) APPROXIMATELY] AND EARLY NEWS
[MONDAY–FRIDAY, 6:00 P.M.–7:30 P.M. (EST)
APPROXIMATELY]

These two local dayparts are listed together because they are combined in different stations. Traditionally, a network-affiliated station will follow the network's daytime schedule with entertainment programming of its own, usually off-network series, movies, or syndicated talk shows such as *The Merv Griffin Show* and *The Mike Douglas Show*. These programs will be followed, in turn, by a local news program. Independent stations will continue with off-network reruns, in effect counterprogramming the affiliates' news programming. Some affiliates begin their news programming as early as 4:30 p.m., running straight news through 7:30 p.m. (including the half-hour network news); however, the normal mix is 1 hour of entertainment programming and 1 to 1½ hours of news.

The entertainment portion of a station's Monday–Friday, 4:30–7:30 p.m. (EST) lineup is commonly referred to as *early fringe*. This programming is designed to attract either an older female audience (the talk shows) or a young adult, children, and teenager audience (movies and off-network situation comedies). The news portion of each station's lineup attracts a predominantly adult audience similar to that of the network newscasts. Since the news is likely to be the last element, airing from 6 to 7 p.m. (EST), it attracts a substantial male and working-women audience. Overall, this time period is one of rapidly rising viewing levels. Figure 2-4 demonstrates that HUT levels build from about 30 percent at 4 p.m. to 50 percent by 8 p.m.

PRIMETIME ACCESS [MONDAY–SATURDAY, 7:30 P.M.–8:00
P.M. (EST)]

The primetime access rule, adopted by the FCC in 1970, requires each station affiliated with a network to broadcast at least half an hour of local programming during the primetime hours of 7–11 p.m. each day except Sunday. Common practice established Monday–Saturday, 7:30–8:00 p.m. (EST) as the "access" half hour. Programs broadcast at this time range from game shows to animal shows, off-network situation comedies (only allowed in markets below the top 50), and local news and information programs. The HUT level during the access period is approximately 50 percent. Audience composition varies by program type, with game shows and news and information series attracting an older adult audience and off-network situation comedies attracting younger adult and nonadult audiences. We discuss primetime access and the primetime access rule further in subsequent chapters.

LATE NEWS [MONDAY–SUNDAY, 11:00 P.M.–11:30 P.M. (EST)]

Almost every television station in the country that is affiliated with one of the three networks follows its network's primetime lineup with a half hour of news. This late-news programming often achieves rating levels comparable to those of primetime programs. Late-news audiences are predominantly adult, with a much younger profile than early-news audiences. They also tend to be better educated and more affluent than early-news audiences. HUT levels during the late-news half hour are in the 40 to 45 percent range, with very little seasonality.

BEYOND RATINGS: THE QUALITATIVE DIMENSION

Although the combination of the national NTI service and the local-market NSI and Arbitron services provides a comprehensive base of audience measurement, this measurement is confined to a narrow demographic perspective. NTI offers some income, occupation, and education data in its NAD (national audience demographics) reports, but its ongoing measurement is limited to the basic age group segments. The local services provide age breakouts only. Advertisers would like more demographic detail and some measure of product usage. To provide this type of information, the television research suppliers would have to increase their sample size substantially, an expansion that would make their services prohibitively expensive.

Other research suppliers have attempted to fill this void. Comprehensive demographic and product usage audience analysis is offered to the magazine industry by the Simmons Market Research Bureau and Mediamark Research Inc. (MRI). Both services use large sample surveys to measure magazine audiences and define these audiences according to demographic and product usage specifications. Each service also includes a television audience measurement section. A brief profile of the Simmons and MRI services follows. Further discussion of these services is included in Chapter 11.

Simmons Market Research Bureau's "Study of Media and Markets"

Adults in 15,000 sample households are interviewed to measure newspaper and magazine reading, defined along 24 demographic dimensions, including sex, age, employment, education, occupation, race, marital status, family size, home ownership, and geography. Approximately 12,000 of these 15,000 respondents complete a marketing questionnaire covering over 500 product usage categories. Approximately 4000 respondents keep a 2-week television viewing diary. These television viewing data are supplemented by a section covering major television events such as the Superbowl and the Academy Awards in a roster format. Television diaries are distributed in the second quarter each year. The survey is published in the fall.

Simmons reports television data by daypart and by program. The subscriber to this study can determine which programs the heavy user of its product is likely to view. This subscriber also can obtain an extensive 24-item demographic profile of each program's audience. Simmons also offers a psychographic profile of the viewer along 20 "self-concept" and 10 "buying style" parameters.

Mediamark Research Inc.

MRI employs a sample of approximately 20,000 adults to provide a media and product usage data bank similar to that of Simmons. Demographic and product usage details parallel those of Simmons. However, viewing is handled differently. Instead of using a diary, MRI includes daypart viewing questions in its basic questionnaire and individual program viewing questions in its marketing survey. These questions allow MRI to obtain TV viewing data for its full sample.

Limitations

Both surveys provide the advertising planner with valuable information concerning the qualitative variations in television audiences. However, they have significant limitations and are, therefore, usually used as supplements to, as opposed to substitutes for, the basic Nielsen and Arbitron services. Among these limitations are the following:

- The weaknesses inherent in diary and/or roster techniques of television audience measurement are present here.

- In the case of Simmons, the limited time frame of the 2-week diary is a liability.

- Viewing data for special events are often collected from respondents at different times of year.

- Unless the viewing level for a measured program and usage of a product are both high, cross-tabulations will involve small sample segments and will be subject to substantial statistical error.

- The delay in publication of reports results in the inclusion of many canceled or rescheduled programs and the exclusion of a significant number of new programs.

TELEVISION ADVERTISERS' REFERENCE SOURCES

The two television rating services and the supplementary Simmons and MRI reports provide the audience data banks essential to the planning and buying of television advertising. However, they alone do not equip the television planner completely. Following are some reference sources that together provide the planner with all the tools necessary to perform efficiently and effectively. We refer to these sources throughout the text.

Broadcast Advertisers Reports

Broadcast Advertisers Reports (BAR) provides television advertising expenditure estimates on both a network television and local television market basis. The network BAR service includes weekly reports as well as monthly and quarterly summaries. Spending is recorded by advertiser and by product category. For each spending unit reported, actual schedules, dollars per program, and network totals are offered. Network advertising is monitored by specially trained BAR monitors. Dollar assignments are based on data obtained from the networks and major advertising agencies.

BAR's local service is available in 75 television markets. Full-time (52-week) monitoring is provided only in New York, Chicago, and Los Angeles. For all other markets, 1 week per month is monitored. The BAR Cume (cumulative expenditures) report combines advertiser spending for all markets with weekly levels projected to the full month.

Leading National Advertiser Reports

Leading national advertiser (LNA) reports estimate media expenditures for all national advertisers for six media: network TV, spot TV, magazines, newspaper supplements, network radio, and outdoor. Television figures are from BAR. LNA reports are issued quarterly. Each report consists of two volumes, one by advertiser and the other by product category.

Media Market Guide

This quarterly report estimates local television market prices for the upcoming quarter. Unit prices, AA levels, and cost-per-rating-point statistics are provided by daypart for daytime, early fringe, early news, primetime access, primetime, late news, and late fringe. Comparable pricing information is given for the other local media as well. Some basic market statistics are included, too.

Standard Rate and Data Service

Standard Rate and Data Service (SRDS) provides media buyers and planners with monthly reports of the advertising rates charged by various media. For such media as newspapers and magazines, this service is invaluable because it provides up-to-date compilations of the often complex rate cards. For radio and television, it is less useful because negotiated rates often are not reflected in station rate cards. The SRDS user often will find the TV station rate cards either out of date or employing wide price ranges that make them practically useless. Nevertheless, SRDS does provide the buyer with valuable information, including a list of key station personnel, the representative firm(s) handling that station, and the network affiliation of that station. Also SRDS offers the planner basic demographic and economic data for each television market.

Television Bureau

Television Bureau (TVB) is the trade organization of the television industry. Whereas the NAB is essentially a lobbying organization, TVB is a selling organization. Its mission is to promote television as an advertising medium. In doing so TVB compiles a great deal of data about the medium. Audience, viewing levels, expenditure summaries, and cost information are published regularly by TVB. In addition, custom research and case history materials are available. A large videotape library is available to the advertiser seeking to examine creative alternatives. Special analyses will be done for advertisers. We recommend an orientation trip to TVB before beginning the television planning and buying process.

Television Factbook

The *Television Factbook* is an annual compilation of the basic facts and figures for the television industry. It contains in-depth ownership profiles for television stations and cable systems, provides summary FCC financial figures for each TV market, and offers NSI and Arbitron market statistics. Individual station listings also include technical data and coverage statistics.

SUMMARY

This chapter introduced some of the lexicon of the broadcast industry. The all-important techniques of audience measurement were discussed, and the products of the various rating services were delineated. The broadcast dayparts were defined in terms of audiences they attract. A brief look was taken beyond the ratings to the more qualitative Simmons and MRI audience measurement services. Finally, the basic reference services available to the television advertising planner and buyer were introduced.

The next four chapters discuss the two television advertising marketplaces—the networks and the local stations—and introduce the buying and selling of time within those markets.

NOTES

1. Description of Methodology, Arbitron "Television Market Reports," October 1980, page 3.

2. Ibid., page 2.

3. Ibid., page 2.

4. Ibid., page 5.

5. Ibid., page 66.

6. Dallas, Washington, Detroit, and Miami are to be added in 1983.

7. "Reference Supplement 1979–1980, NSI Methodology Techniques and Data Interpretations," page 11.

3

Network Television

All three national television networks, ABC-TV, CBS-TV, and NBC-TV, were preceded by radio networks owned by their respective parent companies. The National Broadcasting Company introduced the first truly national radio network on November 15, 1926. Its broadcast was carried by 25 stations representing 21 different cities.[1]

CBS had several false starts before William Paley set it on the right track. It had its origins with the United Independent Broadcasters, founded in 1927 by Arthur Judson. Columbia Phonograph purchased this failing enterprise and renamed it the Columbia Phonograph Broadcasting System in September 1927. Jerome H. Loucheim of Philadelphia bailed out Columbia Phonograph a short while later. The name was changed again, this time to the Columbia Broadcasting System. Paley bought controlling interest in 1929, beginning one of the great success stories of the United States.

By 1943 RCA had split its NBC operation into two networks, the red and the blue. When the FCC decided that multiple-network owners would not receive station licenses, NBC sold its blue network to Edward J. Noble. Noble renamed it the American Broadcasting Company, and ABC was born.

The birth of the three television networks was more a process of natural evolution than of entrepreneurship. Again NBC was first. In 1931 the FCC allowed NBC to broadcast the first television signal in New York. By 1940 it was broadcasting regularly, and in June 1941 it received the first television station license. By 1949 there were 108 licensed TV stations, and all three companies had begun building television networks.

Affiliates

Limited in the number of stations they could own—five VHF and two UHF each[2]—the networks had to convince other station owners to carry their programming if they expected to represent themselves as national networks. NBC and CBS were able to attract affiliates quickly. With the high cost and experimental nature of television production, stations welcomed affiliation with one of these sources of programming. As an added incentive, each station was compensated for carrying the network's programming and the advertising it contained. The station could also sell a limited amount of local advertising time around each network program.

ABC had a tougher time. It lacked the financial and talent resources of NBC and CBS. This third network did not really become a factor in the network marketplace until the middle 1950s, following a merger with United Paramount Theaters. The slow start hurt ABC in the affiliate sign-up race, and often ABC had to settle for the weakest station in a market. Actually, in many one- and two-station markets ABC had no primary affiliate at all.

Today each television network has more than 200 affiliates reaching virtually all U.S. television households. ABC was able to entice several affiliates to switch networks when it rose to supremacy in 1976. Each network has its strong and weak affiliates, but for all practical purposes their affiliate lineups are at parity today. This network-affiliate relationship is discussed further in Chapter 5.

PROGRAMMING

A television network is essentially a programming service. Its economic livelihood depends on presenting programming that will attract the largest possible audience and then selling access to that audience to advertisers in the form of commercial announcements. The drawing power of a network's programming will determine the quality of its affiliates, the amount of its programming each affiliate will carry (an affiliate is not contractually obligated to carry the full network lineup), the size of each affiliate's audience, and thus the audience that the network will be able to offer its advertisers.

Each network broadcasts more than 90 hours of programming each week. Table 3-1 shows the basic schedule structure for the three networks during 1982.

Dayparts

PRIMETIME

Each network's inventory of primetime programming is quite similar. Situation comedies, dramatic series, theatrical and made-for-television movies, and variety programs are featured during the primetime hours when audiences—and, therefore, potential advertising revenues—are largest. Originally the networks produced almost all their primetime programming. However, a combination of economics and government action has forced the networks to rely almost entirely on independent producers for their programming these days. In 1972 the Justice Department sued the three networks on antitrust grounds, seeking to prohibit them from supplying their own programming. This case was concluded in 1980, a full 8 years later, with ABC-TV and CBS-TV finally following NBC-TV and signing consent decrees. For the 1981–1982 primetime season, only five weekly series programs and an occasional special were produced by the networks themselves. Table 3-2 lists the major producers represented on the three 1981–1982 schedules.

The composition of the primetime program schedules has changed with the change in demographics of the television audience throughout the years. Prior to 1960, variety programs represented the major component of each network lineup. *Arthur Godfrey's Talent Scouts, The Jackie Gleason Show, The Ed Sullivan Show, The Red Skelton Show,* and *The Jack Benny Show* were among the most watched each year. During the late 1950s and early 1960s, westerns became the most popular program form. For the 1959–1960 season, nine of the top 20 series were westerns, led by *Gunsmoke, Wagon Train,* and *Have Gun, Will Travel,* the top three programs.

The 1960s was an eclectic decade. Situation comedies dominated; yet the types of situation comedies on top of the ratings early in the decade were substantially different from those emerging at the end of the decade. *The Beverly Hillbillies, Gomer Pyle, U.S.M.C.,* and *The Andy Griffith Show* led all programs in the early period. These shows were simplistic and rural in appeal. By the time the 1960s came to a close, they had been replaced by a more sophisticated brand of comedy. *All in the Family* broke the mold, and Norman Lear was soon followed by Grant Tinker and MTM Productions in presenting controversial subject matter in a literate, humorous context.

In addition to *All in the Family, The Mary Tyler Moore Show* and *M*A*S*H* continued playing in the 1980s, to take their place among television's all-time most watched programs. While these programs were targeted to the more educated and affluent young adult audience, ABC-TV was directing its programming to the growing young urban market.

70

TABLE 3-1
THREE-NETWORK SCHEDULE STRUCTURE FOR 1982

Daypart	ABC	CBS	NBC
MONDAY–FRIDAY			
Morning 6 a.m.–9 a.m. (EST)	*ABC News This Morning, Good Morning America*	*CBS Early Morning News, CBS Morning News*	*Early Today Today Show*
Daytime 10:00 a.m.–4:30 p.m. (EST)	5.5 hours: Serials, game shows, reruns of primetime series	6 hours: Serials, game shows, news, reruns of primetime series	6 hours: Serials, game shows
News 7:00 p.m.–7:30 p.m. (EST)	*ABC World News Tonight*—half hour	*CBS Evening News with Dan Rather*—half hour	*NBC Nightly News*—half hour
Primetime 8 p.m.–11 p.m. (EST)	Miscellaneous entertainment programming	Miscellaneous entertainment programming	Miscellaneous entertainment programming
Late night 11:30 p.m.–2:00 a.m. (EST)	*ABC Nightline* (news), *The Last Word*, 12 m–1 a.m.	Reruns of primetime series, movies	*Tonight Show, David Letterman, SCTV Network*
Late late night 2 a.m.–6 a.m. (EST)		*Nightwatch*, 2–6 a.m.	*NBC News Overnight*, Monday–Thursday, 1:30–2:30 a.m., Friday, 2–3 a.m.
SATURDAY			
Children's programming 8 a.m.–2 p.m. (EST)	Entertainment and informational programming for children	Entertainment and informational programming for children	Entertainment and informational programming for children

SATURDAY (continued)

	ABC	CBS	NBC
Sports, various 2:00 p.m.–6:30 p.m. (EST)	Sports programming of varying duration	Sports programming of varying duration	Sports programming of varying duration
News 6:30 p.m.–7:00 p.m. (EST)	—	CBS Saturday News—Bob Schieffer	NBC Nightly News—Saturday
Primetime 8 p.m.–11 p.m.	Miscellaneous entertainment programming	Miscellaneous entertainment programming	Miscellaneous entertainment programming
Late night 11:30 p.m.–1:30 a.m.	ABC Weekend Report—Saturday (15 minutes)	—	Saturday Night Live (11:30 p.m.–1:00 a.m.)

SUNDAY

	ABC	CBS	NBC
Children's programming	Entertainment programming (10:30 a.m.–12 noon)	Entertainment programming (8 a.m.–9 a.m.)	Entertainment programming (8 a.m.–9 a.m.)
News/informational/religious	Issues and Answers, Directions (religious)	Sunday Morning (9:00–10:30 a.m.), For Our Times (religious, 10:30–11:00 a.m.), Face the Nation (11:00–11:30 a.m.)	Meet the Press (12:30–1:00 p.m.)
Sports, various 12 noon–6:30 p.m.	Sports programming of varying duration	Sports programming of varying duration	Sports programming of varying duration
News 6:30–7:00 p.m.	ABC World News Tonight—Sunday	CBS Evening News—Morton Dean	NBC Nightly News—Sunday
Primetime 7–11 p.m.	Miscellaneous entertainment programming	Miscellaneous entertainment programming	Miscellaneous entertainment programming
Late night 11 p.m.–2 a.m.	ABC Weekend Report—Sunday	CBS Sunday News with Ed Bradley	NBC Late Night Movie (11:30 p.m.–12:30 a.m.)

TABLE 3-2
MAJOR INDEPENDENT PRODUCERS
OF THE 1981–1982 PRIMETIME
SEASON

Producer	No. of programs	No. of hours
1. Universal	7	7.0
2. Paramount	9	5.5
3. MGM	4	5.0
4. Aaron Spelling/Spelling Goldberg	4	4.0
5. Columbia	4	3.5

Laverne & Shirley, Happy Days, and *Charlie's Angels* helped catapult ABC-TV into the number one position in 1976. The detective show and medical show also proliferated during the 1970s. *Hawaii Five-0, Mannix, Adam 12, Police Woman,* and *The Rockford Files* were among the most popular detective and action adventure series. *Marcus Welby, M.D.* and *Medical Center* were the standouts of the medical show genre.

As the 1980s began, the three network schedules were essentially a mixture of situation comedy, action adventure, and dramatic series. *The Barbara Mandrell Show* (NBC) was the only variety series. Westerns were attempting a comeback with *Bret Maverick* and *Best of the West. Dallas,* representing a new nighttime serial form, rose gradually to gain its place as one of TV's all-time winners. *Dynasty* soon followed and built a strong following of its own. But perhaps the most talked-about change in primetime programming was a change in content, not in form. Throughout the 1970s the networks were becoming more and more liberal in terms of both the subject matter covered by primetime programming and the manner in which it was covered. This led to a backlash as the decade ended. Decrying the growing roles of sex and violence in television programming, social and religious groups such as the PTA and Moral Majority led organized drives to "clean up" network television. These pressure group tactics have had their effect, and the networks are leaning toward softer, toned-down situation comedies and action adventure series.

Two other additions to the networks' primetime lineups were the news magazine series and motion pictures made for television. The CBS news magazine series *60 Minutes* moved into the top 20 in 1976 and reached the number one spot for the 1979–1980 season. ABC-TV and NBC-TV followed with their own news magazine programs, *20/20* and *NBC Magazine*, respectively. These two networks also introduced a lighter version of the magazine show concept with *Real People* (NBC) and *That's Incredible!* (ABC).

Motion pictures made for television began to play an increasingly important role as the networks looked for an alternative to the expensive theatrical features of the past. These TV movies range from standard 2-hour features to the multipart miniseries, such as "Roots" and "Shogun," two of television's all-time ratings champions.

Table 3-3 lists the top-performing programs through the years, led by the 1980 "Who Shot J.R.?" episode of *Dallas*.

TABLE 3-3

**NTI TOP 20 PROGRAMS,
AVERAGE AUDIENCE ESTIMATES
(PROJECTED HOUSEHOLDS)***

Rank	Program name	Telecast date	Network	Duration (minutes)	Average audience (000)
1	*Dallas*	Nov. 21, 1980	CBS	60	41,470
2	"Roots"	Jan. 30, 1977	ABC	115	36,380
3	Super Bowl XIV	Jan. 20, 1980	CBS	178	35,330
4	Super Bowl XIII	Jan. 21, 1979	NBC	230	35,090
5	Super Bowl XV	Jan. 25, 1981	NBC	220	34,540
6	Super Bowl XII	Jan. 15, 1978	CBS	218	34,410
7	*Gone with the Wind*—Pt. 1 (Big Event Pt. 1)	Nov. 7, 1976	NBC	179	33,960
8	*Gone with the Wind*—Pt. 2 (Mon. Night Mov.)	Nov. 8, 1976	NBC	119	33,750
9	"Roots"	Jan. 28, 1977	ABC	120	32,680
10	"Roots"	Jan. 27, 1977	ABC	60	32,540

TABLE 3-3 (*Continued*)

Rank	Program name	Telecast date	Network	Duration (minutes)	Average audience (000)
11	"Roots"	Jan. 25, 1977	ABC	60	31,900
12	Super Bowl XI	Jan. 9, 1977	NBC	204	31,610
13	"Roots"	Jan. 24, 1977	ABC	120	31,400
14	"Roots"	Jan. 26, 1977	ABC	60	31,190
15	World Series Game #6	Oct. 21, 1980	NBC	205	31,120
15	*Dallas*	Nov. 9, 1980	CBS	60	31,120
17	"Roots"	Jan. 29, 1977	ABC	60	30,120
18	*Jaws* (Sun. Night Mov.)	Nov. 4, 1979	ABC	165	29,830
19	*Dallas*	Nov. 7, 1980	CBS	60	29,720
20	Super Bowl X	Jan. 18, 1976	CBS	200	29,440

*Projected household estimates based on reports through April 19, 1981.
Source: A.C. Nielson, NTI reports.

DAYTIME

Daytime programming is designed to appeal to the adult women who represent the majority of television viewers during the weekday hours. Daytime programming is a mix of soap operas, game shows, and reruns of primetime series. By far the most popular of these program forms is the soap opera. Popular soap operas—or serial dramas, as they are sometimes called—such as *Search for Tomorrow, Guiding Light, The Doctors, As the World Turns,* and *General Hospital* have all been on the air for more than 10 years, far longer than most primetime series. For the 1980–1981 season, the top five daytime programs were all soap operas: *General Hospital, All My Children, One Life to Live, Guiding*

Light, and *As the World Turns.* Procter & Gamble still produces its own soap operas.

The networks have yet to introduce a successful talk show to their daytime lineups, despite the popularity of such syndicated programs as *The Phil Donahue Show* and *The Merv Griffin Show,* programs that are carried by stations throughout the country. NBC-TV recently tried *The David Letterman Show,* but this entry did not even last one season during the day. It is now a late-night show. The only other innovation in daytime programming was CBS-TV's *Up to the Minute,* a news program featuring the *60 Minutes* news personalities. This program met a quick end.

SPORTS

Sports has become an increasingly important component of the networks' programming mix over the years. Table 3-4 shows the recent increase in hours of sports programming telecast by the three networks, exclusive of the Olympics, a major addition to sports programming every fourth year. Network sports programming includes the regular presentation of the major U.S. spectator sports, football, basketball, and baseball; extensive golf, tennis, and auto racing coverage; as well as telecasts of the major events in just about every other sport. A substantial amount of these "other" sports events are presented in the context of the networks' anthology series, ABC's *Wide World of Sports,* *CBS Sports Saturday* and *CBS Sports Sunday,* and NBC's *Sportsworld.*

Most network sports programming is broadcast on Saturday and Sun-

TABLE 3-4
HOURS OF SPORTS
PROGRAMMING BROADCAST BY
THE THREE NETWORKS

Year	Hours of network sports
1967	688
1975	1127
1978	1319
1979	1358
1980	1364 (+ 53.5 minutes of Olympics)

day afternoons; however, major attractions such as the Superbowl, the World Series, and championship fights are presented during primetime.

NEWS

The news designation refers to any programming produced by the networks' respective news departments. While categorized as a daypart, this programming appears throughout the entire network schedules. News begins with the three regularly scheduled early evening newscasts and includes all news specials and documentaries, all weekend news programming, the three Sunday interview programs, and, in the case of ABC-TV, its Nightline broadcast. The morning news and information programs—Good Morning America (ABC), CBS Morning News, and The Today Show (NBC)—are considered part of the daytime daypart. The three primetime news magazine programs are also considered part of that daypart.

News, like sports, has been expanding its share of the total network lineup. CBS-TV now broadcasts its all-night Nightwatch, Monday through Friday, 2–6 a.m., followed by CBS Early Morning News, 6–7 a.m., and CBS Morning News. This network had already pioneered with the 90-minute Sunday news program CBS News Sunday Morning. It has also been experimenting with Universe, a science magazine hosted by Walter Cronkite. ABC's Nightline, the first regularly scheduled late-night news program, has been expanded to include a 12 midnight to 1 a.m. news. ABC News This Morning was added, Monday through Friday, 6:30–7:00 a.m. ABC has also added This Week with David Brinkley on Sunday. NBC-TV added NBC News Overnight, Monday through Thursday, 1:30–2:30 a.m., and Friday, 2–3 a.m., and Early Today, Monday through Friday, 6:30–7:00 a.m.

It is widely held that, with the challenge of cable, the networks will turn more and more to their news departments for programming that cannot be duplicated by organizations lacking their vast news-gathering resources.

CHILDREN'S PROGRAMMING

The children's programming description has been confined in the past to the Saturday and Sunday morning programs aimed at children and teenagers. Recently this daypart has added occasional after-school specials, dramatic presentations irregularly scheduled on weekday afternoons. Government and consumer group pressures concerning violence on television and the overall quality of children's programming have led to substantial changes in the form of the networks' offerings in this daypart. Pure escapist cartoons, often considered too violent in content, have been replaced by animation and live programming designed to carry pro-social messages for children in the context of humor and entertainment. News and information series such as ABC's *Schoolhouse Rock* and CBS-TV's *In the News* have been added to the network schedules. The afternoon specials usually deal with social issues relevant to young people. Ironically, many of those "children's" programs attract substantial numbers of adult viewers. These older viewers occasionally comprise over 50 percent of the total audience of these programs. *Captain Kangaroo*, the sole regularly scheduled weekday children's program, was moved in 1982 to weekend mornings to make way for CBS-TV's expanded morning news programming.

LATE NIGHT

All regularly scheduled network programming after 11:30 p.m. (EST) is included in the *late-night* daypart. *The Tonight Show* (NBC) has become synonymous with late-night television. CBS-TV and ABC-TV are now challenging this perennial favorite with off-network reruns and some original product. All three networks have added second late-night entries. NBC-TV follows *The Tonight Show* with *Late Night with David Letterman*, while CBS-TV has a second *CBS Late Movie II* feature, consisting of a mix of off-network series and repeats of made-for-television movies and some theatrical features. Late-night network programming had moved to the weekend with NBC-TV's successful *Saturday Night Live* show (now in reruns). NBC-TV also introduced *Sunday Night Movie*. At this time, neither ABC-TV nor CBS-TV has followed NBC-TV's lead.

SPECIALS

The *specials* daypart consists of all primetime programs that are not regularly scheduled, with the exception of news and sports. The basic forms of special programming are variety, drama, movie specials, animation, and award shows. Many of television's most successful programs through the years have been specials. "Roots," "Shogun," and *Gone with the Wind* are three such programs. Specials are an important part of each network's program arsenal because they can be used for counterprogramming and for filling the time periods of failing series while replacement programs are being produced. Well-done specials are also important to each network's image, since these programs tend to dominate the annual television awards presentations.

Competitive Position

Although a strong sales and marketing team, a positive image, and the quality of a network's programming all impact on the share of advertising dollars it will attract, the major variable in the determination of network revenues is the size of its audience. CBS-TV was dominant for 20 years, before ABC-TV took over the number one position in 1976. CBS-TV dramatically recaptured first place in primetime in 1980. For the 1981–1982 season CBS-TV was number one in that daypart as well as in evening news and late night. ABC-TV led in daytime and sports. NBC-TV was not a clear winner in any daypart; however, its introduction of the popular *Smurfs* series on Saturday morning moved this network to first place in this daypart among children (CBS-TV still leads in homes). *The Tonight Show* is holding on to first place in total households but has lost its lead in the important young-adult audience. *The Today Show* is in a tight battle with *Good Morning America* for the early-morning audience lead.

The rather small differences in percentage of audience among the three networks translate to a large number of viewers. This viewer differential in turn translates to more than $100 million in advertising revenues, most of which falls directly to the bottom line as profits. It is unquestionably a high-stakes game.

NETWORK TELEVISION AS AN ADVERTISING MEDIUM

From Sponsorship to the 30-Second Spot

Television inherited radio's tradition as an advertiser-supported medium from its outset. More than satisfied with their radio advertising results, advertisers were quick to move to television, which, with its sight, sound, and motion, offered substantially greater selling potential. In the early years the television networks produced programs that were *sponsored* by advertisers. Advertising agency network programming departments would represent advertisers, presenting program concepts to the networks. A list of the top 15 programs for the 1950–1951 season illustrates the high advertiser identification with television programming. Included were *The Texaco Star Theater, The Philco TV Playhouse, The Colgate Comedy Hour, The Gillette Cavalcade of Sports,* and *The Kraft Television Theater.*

By 1951 the television networks were profitable, with network time sales jumping from $11 million in 1949 to $35 million in 1950, then $98 million in 1951. By 1960 this dynamic new advertising medium had advertising revenues of $472 million, and the networks' collective pretax profits were $33.6 million (plus another $61.6 million from their owned and operated stations).

As the demand for network television time grew and the cost of production increased, full-program sponsorship became prohibitively expensive. Major advertisers first opted for alternative-week sponsorship, sharing a full-sponsor position with another advertiser. Soon this, too, became too costly. With the networks beginning to shift programs as the ratings war grew more and more intense, sponsors could be less and less certain of a program's performance. Coupled with the high absolute cost of sponsorship, this uncertainity led advertisers to search for alternatives. The result was the *scatter-plan* approach to network advertising. The advertisers would scatter their advertising among a series of programs.

By 1960 scatter-plan advertising was the predominant form of primetime network advertising, with the 60-second unit emerging as the basic commercial announcement. However, prices continued to rise and advertisers had to search for ways to stretch their television advertising budgets. This led first to the introduction of the *piggyback* concept, in which an advertiser would purchase a 60-second unit and run two 30-second commercials for different products. By the middle 1960s most major multibrand advertisers had shifted to this strategy. The result was a logistic nightmare, with commercial allocation schedules difficult to design and execute. In addition, the single-brand advertisers were being discriminated against, since they could not divide 60-second units among brands.

In 1971, the networks officially converted to the 30-second unit base. By 1980, 87 percent of all network television commercials were 30 seconds long with 10 percent piggybacked 60-second spots. Only 2 percent of all network commercials were 60 seconds or longer.

Changing Role of the Advertising Agency

The original advertising agency was indeed an agent, much like a real estate agent, that sold newspaper space to advertisers in return for a commission from the newspaper. By the time television entered the picture, the emphasis had changed substantially. The advertising agency was contracted by the advertiser to design and place advertising. Yet the 15 percent commission from the medium remained the primary method of agency compensation. The medium would bill the agency at a commissionable rate. The agency would pass the bill along to the client, receive payment from the client, forward 85 percent of the total to the medium, and keep 15 percent as its commission.

As the cost of media escalated and the diversity of media options increased, the 15 percent commission system became a less and less effective method of agency compensation. For example, agency A might place $1 million on a television network, while agency B placed the same $1 million on 50 local-market radio stations. Both would receive the same $150,000 commission despite the fact that the time and personnel required of agency A to complete its transaction was only a fraction of that required of agency B to complete its 50 transactions.

Fearing that media recommendations might be biased toward high-priced, low-administrative-effort alternatives, many advertisers began to deviate from the straight commission system. Today the majority of advertisers employ either some adjusted form of this system or a fee basis for compensation. In a fee-basis arrangement, the advertiser pays the net media charges and then compensates the agency based on some fee formula. The fee can be set either at a specific hourly fee for the time of each person working on the account or at an established fixed amount.

The relationship between the advertising agency and the networks has changed in another significant way. When the networks were providing their own programming and advertisers were sponsoring these programs in full, often the agencies would be intimately involved in the programming process. The network programming departments at major agencies were the representatives of their client sponsors in matters regarding program selection and production. Frequently these executives played a major role in the overall production of the program. As advertisers moved to the scatter-plan approach and the networks turned to a number of independent production companies for their product, the involvement by agency representatives in program production virtually disappeared. Today agency executives are likely to be involved only in the limited number of client-furnished programs that appear on the networks (some daytime soap operas and an occasional special).

While the changes in the network television advertising marketplace and production community were altering the role of the agency executive vis-à-vis the media, changes within the agency itself were having the same effect. Automation and specialization within the media department led to a separation of the media planning and buying functions. Today it is more likely that two different operations will be involved in developing the network advertising plan and buying the network time called for in that plan.

The process is also getting more and more analytical. A proliferation of audience information and the application of computers to audience analysis have led to a more numbers-oriented approach to network television buying. As a result, the network programming department today is staffed by executives who have shown themselves to be skilled negotiators first and trained analysts second. The demonstration of an intuitive programming sense is no longer that critical, and executives found to possess it usually move on to the producer/network side of the business.

One final outgrowth of this trend to the professional negotiator-analysts within the media department has been the arrival on the scene of the media buying service, an operation devoted entirely to the purchase of space and time. The buying service can act either as an alternative to the agency media department or as a supplement to that department. Buying services are discussed further in the chapters on local-market television, for most of their activity is centered on that area.

NETWORK TELEVISION MARKETPLACE

The television advertising unit, measured in time, represents a perishable commodity. The time reserved for each commercial within a broadcast cannot be recaptured for use at some future time. Once 6:30 p.m., July 7, 1982, has passed, the 30 seconds of commercial time scheduled to begin at 6:30 p.m. has passed with it. If broadcasters did not fill that 30 seconds with a paid commercial, they lost forever the opportunity to do so. This phenomenon constitutes the very essence of a commodity market, with each seller attempting to charge what the market will bear but always remaining sensitive to the perishability of the product.

In times of full demand, the seller simply seeks the highest bidder for each commercial unit. In times of less than full demand, the process is more complex. The seller must decide whether to charge a price that will result in the sale of all units or to maintain a price floor, accepting the fact that not all units will be sold. This decision will be based on which strategy is likely to yield the maximum revenues in light of competitive actions.

In the case of full demand, the buyers seeking access to commercial time will bid up the price, with the ultimate buyers being those marketers whose assessments of the value of the commercial time are highest. Certain buyers will be priced out of the market in this situation. In the case of less than full demand, the price pressure is all downward. Psychologically, no seller is comfortable allowing a commercial unit to go unsold, for even $1 is better than nothing. However, if all competitors seek to sell every unit, the price of every unit will be forced downward, resulting in far less total revenue for all competitors combined. Therefore, if they are to protect their market, sellers must allow units to go unsold.

The dynamics of the marketplace, in the end, are determined by the independent actions of a few sellers and of a large number of buyers trying to outfinesse one another. The sellers are trying to measure the market, to find out whether a full demand or less than full demand situation prevails. This task is made extremely difficult by the number of buyers and the various buying parameters used by those buyers. On the buyer side, the goal is to get on the air for the lowest possible price, but to get on the air at any cost. The buyer's negotiating ability is limited by the fact that the effective execution of the product's marketing plan requires an effective television advertising campaign.

If these conditions were not enough to result in an extremely volatile market, the situation is compounded by seasonality, ever-increasing programming changes, and daypart-by-daypart variation. The result is a very complex marketplace in which negotiating expertise can vastly affect the price of commercial time.

This chapter and Chapter 4 cover the network television market in depth. Chapters 5 and 6 treat the national spot-local television market.

Dimensions of the Marketplace

The network television marketplace is extremely concentrated. The three networks split approximately $5.6 billion in advertising revenues in 1981. Although the buyer side is substantially less concentrated than the seller side, it is still relatively limited in numbers. Only 563 companies were active in network television in 1981. More importantly, the dollars were concentrated among a small number of major advertisers. Broadcast Advertisers Reports (BAR) regularly reports network spending by advertiser. One of the standard reports ranks these advertisers by expenditure levels and then divides them into quartiles. Table 3-5 shows the spending by quartile for calendar year 1981.

TABLE 3-5
1981 NETWORK TELEVISION
ADVERTISERS BY QUARTILE

Quartile	No. of advertisers	Average amount spent per advertiser
1	9	$158,157,330
2	22	62,487,195
3	50	27,942,880
4	482	2,893,243

Source: BAR, 1981.

As Table 3-5 demonstrates, spending is concentrated among the top advertisers. The nine target advertisers represent 25 percent of all network spending. Procter & Gamble, the largest network television advertiser, with an estimated 1981 expenditure of $393 million, equaled the bottom 357 advertisers combined in spending. This concentration extends to actual buyers of network television—the advertising agencies—as well. The top 10 agencies account for over 90 percent of all network buying.

Buyers and Sellers

With such concentration, it is not surprising that the number of people involved in the sale and purchase of network time is small. Looking first at the seller side, we find that although the organizations of the three networks are somewhat different, they all follow the same basic structure. The core of the selling force is the account executive. Each network has between 25 and 35 account executives. Of this number, approximately 15 are headquartered in New York, where about 70 percent of all network buying is done. Chicago is the number two market, with 5 to 10 account executives accounting for another 20 to 25 percent of total network revenues. The remaining offices are in Detroit and Los Angeles. Each office is staffed by two account executives.

This core sales team is supported by a phalanx of vice-presidents and support services. Each office is headed by a vice-president. These executives, in turn, report to a vice-president/general sales manager in New York. Pricing and inventory are controlled by a sales planning operation. The three networks handle this function somewhat differently. One actually delegates much of the pricing and inventory control function to the finance department as opposed to the sales department. However, the sales planning structure is essentially the same for all three networks—a vice-president in charge, supported by daypart specialists.

The basic support services are marketing services, research, and sales administration. Marketing services includes sales promotion, merchandising, and trade advertising. Research provides the audience numbers essential to the selling process. The research departments at the three networks are all independent of the sales departments, usually headed by their own team of vice-presidents who report to top management. However, the sales departments usually have their own research specialists, who turn raw audience data into efficient sales presentations. The sales administration department is responsible for processing all paperwork, scheduling commercials, and providing essential tracking reports to management. More and more, this operation is being augmented by a centralized MIS (management information systems) unit charged with the conversion of most routine sales procedures to an online computerized mode.

Each of the three networks has one vice-president of sales responsible for the entire sales organization. This person, in turn, reports to the president of the network. In total, the number of people primarily involved in the selling process at the average network is about 150, a relatively small number for a $1.9 billion enterprise.

Things are even leaner on the buyer side. The number of people involved in the network advertising decision may be substantial, starting with the vice-president of marketing or perhaps even the president of the advertising company and covering the product management there, as well as the account management group, vice-president of media, media planners, and, most importantly, the media buyers at the agency. However, the actual negotiation process involves only a few specialists. The advertising agencies' executives charged with the responsibility for the purchase of network television time come from their network programming departments.

An agency's network programming department usually has a structure parallel to that of the networks. The actual buying of time is specialized by daypart, supervised by a vice-president, and supported by research teams. The top people in the network programming department are senior officers of the agency.

Markets

The total network television market consists of eight distinctive markets coinciding with the eight television dayparts. These dayparts are morning, primetime, daytime, sports, news, specials, late night, and children's programming. Morning is included in both news and daytime for buying purposes. Table 3-6 gives the 1981 revenues by daypart.

PRIMETIME

Primetime, defined as all regularly scheduled programming, Monday–Saturday, 8–11 p.m., and Sunday, 7–11 p.m. (EST), is by far the most important daypart. Primetime brings in 43 percent of network revenues, and it is widely accepted that the stock prices and executive careers at tbe network parent companies often hinge on primetime performance. Viewing levels are highest during primetime, and so are advertising rates. The average price of a 30-second primetime com-

TABLE 3-6
1981 ADVERTISING REVENUES BY
DAYPART

Daypart	1981 Advertising revenues (000)	Percentage of total network television advertising revenues
Primetime	$2,405,982.3	43.0
Daytime	1,185,005.2	21.2
News	463,808.3	8.3
Sports	882,268.3	15.8
Specials	227,167.8	4.1
Late night	279,189.9	5.0
Children's programming	145,099.5	2.6

Source: BAR, 1981.

mercial for the 1980–1981 season was about $70,000 with shows such as *60 Minutes, M*A*S*H,* and *Three's Company* priced well above $100,000 per 30-second unit. Despite these high prices, the primetime market is the most active television advertising market, with demand for the top shows traditionally far outpacing supply.

DAYTIME

The total daytime daypart is defined as all regularly scheduled programming Monday–Friday, 7:00 a.m.–4:30 p.m. (EST). However, the networks usually split up this daypart when selling. *The Today Show* on NBC-TV, *Good Morning America* on ABC-TV, and *CBS Morning News* usually are sold separately. Their early time periods and news orientation yield adult audiences composed of both men and women, making them distinctive from the regular soap operas, situation comedies, and game shows which follow, with predominantly female audiences. The remaining Monday–Friday, 10:00 a.m.–4:30 p.m., network programming constitutes the basic daytime daypart.

Although the total advertising revenues generated by daytime programming are substantially lower than those generated by primetime, the profits from this daypart are extraordinary. Daytime programming is much less costly for the networks to produce, and is, therefore, very profitable for them.

The average 1980 price of a 30-second unit in daytime was about $15,000. The range of prices was much narrower than with primetime, with a high of $25,000 and a low of $5000. Prices for early-morning programs ranged from $2500 for the lower-rated *CBS Morning News*, to approximately $7500 each for *The Today Show* and *Good Morning America*.

Because of the concentration of women in the daytime audience, this daypart's appeal is limited to advertisers wishing to focus on the female consumer. However, as you would expect, that represents a large universe of potential users, and daytime advertising demand is comparable to that of primetime. Major packaged goods companies, such as Procter & Gamble, General Foods, and Lever Brothers, dominate daytime. Procter & Gamble and General Foods own their own shows, which the networks broadcast as part of their schedules, charging the sponsoring company for the commercial time.

SPORTS

The *sports* daypart designation applies to all sports programming, no matter where it runs. The bulk of sports dollars are invested in the major sports franchises and the regular anthology series. NFL football is the premiere sports attraction by far, accounting for almost half of all sports spending. Table 3-7 shows 1981 spending for each major

TABLE 3-7
NETWORK TELEVISION
INVESTMENT IN SELECTED MAJOR
SPORTS, 1981

Sports	1981 Revenue (000)
Baseball	$114,000
Basketball	70,000
College football	79,000
Pro football	364,000
Golf	41,000
Sports anthologies	95,000
Tennis	22,000

Source: BAR, 1981.

TABLE 3-8
TOP 10 CATEGORIES FOR 1981
SPORTS SPENDING

	Category	Spending (000)
1.	Beer	$142,465.9
2.	Passenger cars, domestic	71,534.3
3.	Passenger cars, imported	43,781.1
4.	Commercial trucks and other vehicles	28,649.9
5.	Fire, casualty, and other insurance	28,164.4
6.	Automobile parts and accessories	26,973.9
7.	Radios, TV sets, phonographs, records	25,052.2
8.	Car and truck tires and tubes	19,474.6
9.	Cameras and photographic supplies	19,450.7
10.	Office machines and equipment	19,388.3

Source: BAR, 1981.

sport and for the anthology series. The penultimate sports program is the Superbowl. A 30-second spot in this annual event went for approximately $350,000 in 1982. Regular series football prices averaged $75,000 to $100,000 per 30 seconds, with ABC-TV's primetime games on the high end. With the new billion-dollar 5-year contract beginning in 1982, these prices are sure to rise substantially. The remaining sports prices vary widely. These programs attract approximately $3000 to $4000 per rating point, with the two upscale sports attractions, golf and tennis, getting somewhat more. The Olympics is a special sports attraction appearing every fourth year. Olympics announcements, both summer and winter, are premium-priced.

Because of the predominantly male audience, sports programming traditionally attracts male-oriented advertisers. The sports advertiser base is relatively small, with only 159 advertisers spending in excess of $1 milion per year in sports program advertising. Two product categories, beer and automobiles, dominate sports advertising, representing 30 percent of the 1981 total. This daypart is also characterized by a small base of big spenders. The top five spenders in 1981 accounted for 27 percent of all sports dollars. Tables 3-8 and 3-9 show the top 10 categories and parent companies in sports spending.

TABLE 3-9
TOP 10 ADVERTISERS FOR 1981
     SPORTS SPENDING

	Advertiser	Spending (000)
1.	Phillip Morris	$71,490.7
2.	General Motors	61,646.7
3.	Anheuser Busch	50,123.3
4.	Ford Motor Co.	28,940.9
5.	Sears Roebuck & Co.	21,877.8
6.	AT&T	19,370.7
7.	Chrysler Corp.	18,515.8
8.	RCA	16,864.8
9.	Gillette	16,076.9
10.	U.S. Armed Services	13,171.3

Source: BAR, 1981.

NEWS

By definition, the *news* daypart should include all programming produced by the three networks' news divisions; however, this is not the case. The *CBS Morning News* is a news show, but it is often sold as part of daytime. The two primetime news magazines, *60 Minutes* (CBS) and *20/20* (ABC), are both produced by the news divisions, but categorized as primetime. What are included in the news daypart are the three regularly scheduled early-evening weekday programs; all news specials or documentaries; all weekend news programming, including the Sunday interview shows; and all late-night news programs.

The three regularly scheduled weekday newscasts *The CBS Evening News with Dan Rather*, *NBC Nightly News*, and *ABC World News Tonight* are the core of the network news operations and generate the majority of the news daypart revenues. In 1980, for these three programs 30-second unit costs ranged from $45,000 for *The CBS Evening News*, the audience leader, to $35,000 to $40,000 for the NBC-TV and ABC-TV entries. All three programs are usually sold out throughout the year.

The weekend newscasts tend to be lower-priced, owing in part to inconsistent scheduling and sports preemptions. The interview programs usually are sponsored by corporations interested in reaching the Washington and professional and managerial markets.

SPECIALS

A *special* program is more likely to have a single or a few partial sponsors than to have several participating advertisers with one or two announcements each. The full-sponsored special is fairly common. For the 1980–1981 season approximately 25 percent of all primetime specials were fully sponsored. Specials are divided into those developed by the network and those provided by the advertiser. Although most specials are of the former type, major advertisers do develop their own programs as well. Procter & Gamble provides the "People's Choice Awards," which is presented annually on CBS-TV. General Foods also offers its own programs. In early 1980 this advertiser presented Nurse on CBS-TV. This program was so successful that CBS-TV bought the rights to develop it as a series for the 1981–1982 season.

The full sponsorship of a special demands a major financial commitment, with top-quality dramatic productions often costing more than $2 million. If the advertiser provides the program to the network, it pays only the time charge, approximately $200,000 per half hour.

More common than full sponsorship is half or quarter sponsorship. Traditionally any advertiser with at least a quarter-sponsorship position would receive a billboard identifying that advertiser as a program sponsor. This allows the partial sponsor both to merchandise its sponsorship to the trade and to break through the clutter of advertising. Ideally, when considering partial sponsorship, the advertiser would look for programs with other partial sponsors, as opposed to several participating advertisers, since this would further reduce the clutter.

Partial-sponsorship prices are a multiple of the 30-second price. For a 2-hour special, 3 minutes, or six 30-second spots, would constitute a quarter-sponsorship position. The billboard or billboards are given as a bonus. Special programs' 30-second unit prices follow the same pattern as those of primetime. Blockbuster movies such as *Rocky* and *Jaws* will be premium-priced, often well above the 30-second price of the top regularly scheduled series, on both an absolute and a cost-per-rating-point basis.

In 1981, advertisers spent $227 million in special-program advertising. The top spender list was composed of the big primetime spenders, such as Procter & Gamble, General Foods, and McDonald's, as well as the big corporate image advertisers, including IBM, AT&T, ITT, General Electric, DuPont de Nemours, and Xerox. Kellogg's and General Mills

TABLE 3-10
TOP 10 SPECIALS ADVERTISERS
FOR 1981

	Advertiser	Spending (000)
1.	Proctor & Gamble	$31,571.3
2.	General Foods	13,955.8
3.	General Electric	9,906.2
4.	Kellogg's	7,322.8
5.	McDonald's	6,708.0
6.	Ford Motor Co.	6,035.8
7.	Polaroid	5,344.0
8.	General Motors	5,244.0
9.	Dart and Kraft	5,077.2
10.	ITT	4,276.7

Source: BAR, 1981.

were also among the top spenders, with their investments concentrated in the animated specials. Table 3-10 gives the top 10 specials advertisers for 1981.

LATE NIGHT

In 1981 *The Tonight Show* remained the premium-priced weekday late-night program, commanding an average of $30,000 to $35,000 per 30-second announcement. CBS-TV and ABC-TV got about $20,000 to $25,000 for their first features. Note that with the introduction of its *ABC Nightline* late-night news program, ABC-TV's first program did not begin until midnight. As a result, current ABC-TV prices were somewhat lower than those of CBS-TV. In 1982 ABC-TV replaced its entertainment programming with *The Last Word,* a news program from midnight to 1 a.m.

The picture is different for the later entries. In 1981, CBS-TV dominated in this area, and its *CBS Late Movie II* went for about $10,000 per 30 seconds. The NBC-TV and ABC-TV second features averaged only about $2500 to $5000 per 30-second spot. These prices are somewhat misleading, since all three networks try to sell the earlier and later programs in combination, and actual prices are subject to negotiations.

Late-night advertising is concentrated among advertisers seeking a total adult audience. Many low-budget advertisers use this daypart because of its low unit cost compared with that for primetime. *The Tonight Show* has the added value of merchandisability to the trade, even live commercials. This is a big attraction to the smaller advertiser seeking a relatively greater impact for the dollar.

CHILDREN'S PROGRAMMING

The *Children's Program* description traditionally has referred to the Saturday and Sunday morning programming aimed at the young audience. Recently, this daypart has been expanded to include the occasional after-school programs scheduled late on weekday afternoons.

Government and consumer group challenges to the concept of advertising to children and the quality of children's programming have brought about dramatic changes in the advertising content for this daypart. Strict industry codes concerning advertising have been instituted to preempt government action. The children's guidelines limit both what can be advertised during this period and what can be said in the advertising. As a result, the number of Saturday morning advertisers has not grown appreciably. In 1974, some 79 advertisers spent $72 million in this daypart. In 1981, the number of advertisers was 91, with

TABLE 3-11
TOP CHILDREN'S PROGRAM
ADVERTISERS FOR 1981

	Advertiser	Spending (000)
1.	General Mills	$23,372.1
2.	General Foods	15,661.9
3.	McDonald's	12,349.4
4.	Mattel	11,143.7
5.	Kellogg's	10,391.9
6.	Ralston Purina	7,183.6
7.	Pillsbury	6,819.3
8.	Hershey Foods	6,188.7
9.	Tomy	4,234.3
10.	Quaker Oats	3,531.9

Source: BAR, 1981.

half of all advertising dollars accounted for by only five advertisers. However, despite the shrinking base, overall daypart revenues were up to $145 million in 1981. Table 3-11 lists the top children's program advertisers in 1981.

The average price of a 30-second commercial on Saturday morning in 1981 was $25,000. The top five programs required an extra $5000. Demand for this daypart is very seasonal, peaking during the fourth quarter, the toy companies' pre-Christmas selling season. Unit prices for this quarter were as high as $25,000 to $30,000 per 30-second spot. These rates declined to about $16,000 per 30 seconds during the first quarter.

Regional Alternative

In addition to daypart selection the network television advertiser has another option when planning a network campaign. That is the increasingly popular option of buying network television on a regional, as opposed to a national, basis.

In the early 1970s the networks found themselves pressured by smaller regional marketers to offer some alternative to full network delivery. These marketers felt that access to network television represented an unfair competitive advantage for their national competitors. As their complaints drew government interest, the networks reluctantly began to offer regional packages. Advertisers could request a specific plan covering one or more predetermined regions of the country. The regional specialist at the network would attempt to match that request with similar requests covering other regions. If a match covering the entire country could be made, each advertiser's schedule would run in the region requested. This network regional operation began more as a sales service department than a selling arm; however, today the networks have found the regional buy to represent an excellent vehicle for the development of new clients.

There are many drawbacks for the regional advertiser. First, the execution of the regional schedule depends on the availability of a compatible partner. Often this requires compromises in both program selection and campaign timing. Frequently matches cannot be made at all. Second, even when partners are found, usually the match is not perfect. Holes may remain in the national map, or market interests may overlap. In the first situation the advertisers must pay for some unwanted area in order to complete the national match. In the second situation, some compromise regarding overlapping territories must be worked out among the partners.

A third drawback concerns the configurations of network feed patterns. Figure 3-1 shows the regional feed pattern for the CBS television

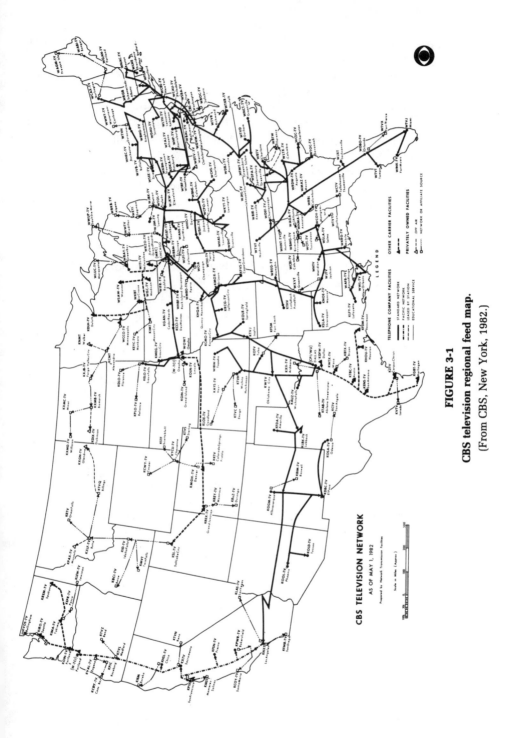

FIGURE 3-1

CBS television regional feed map.

(From CBS, New York, 1982.)

93

network. If advertisers' regional demands conform to these feed patterns, they will have to pay only a nominal charge for splitting the feeds, in addition to the regular time charges. If, however, the advertisers wish to deviate from these patterns in their division of the network, they will incur costly cut-in charges. A *cut-in* refers to a local station's cutting in on the network feed. For each market involved, a separate charge, payable to the station actually making the cut-in, is required.

Network affiliates do not like regional network buys. They feel that a regional network buy is an alternative to spot television and, as such, takes potential revenues away from them. With the rising incidence of regional network advertising and the greater and greater use of cut-ins, many affiliates have raised cut-in charges prohibitively. Thus a customized regional lineup with heavy cut-in utilization will be substantially less efficient than national network television or a straight regional feed alternative.

Despite these shortcomings, advertisers are using regionals more and more. In addition to providing the regional marketer with access to network television, regional feeds allow national advertisers to accommodate brands having varying seasonal and geographic selling patterns with a single network buy. The major use of regional feeds is found in the sports dayparts. Beer companies, oil companies, and airlines, all heavy sports advertisers, have the regionalized sales patterns that make this approach a sound alternative.

NOTES

1. Actually, AT&T owned the first radio "network," based around WEAF in New York. AT&T sold WEAF to the National Broadcasting Company—then a joint venture of RCA, General Electric, and Westinghouse—bowing to government pressure. RCA bought out General Electric and Westinghouse in 1930.

2. The differences between VHF and UHF are covered in Chapter 5.

Buying Network Television Time

THREE-STAGE NETWORK MARKET

The sale of network television time takes place in three distinct stages. The *upfront market* consists of those advertisers that make advance, full-season commitments shortly after the announcement of the new schedules. The *scatter market*, consisting of advertisers making shorter-term purchases on a quarter-by-quarter basis, follows the upfront market. The *opportunistic market* is essentially the remnant segment of the network television market, composed of week-to-week purchases of unsold time. To better understand the workings of these three distinctive markets, it will be useful to follow the buyer-seller interaction as each market evolves.

Upfront Market

Upfront negotiations are done daypart by daypart. Although the prime-time upfront market is the most important by far, the children's upfront market is traditionally the first to break. In part this is due to the fact that the schedule in this daypart is limited and the buyers are few. Also, the few advertisers want to firm up their schedules for merchandising during the crucial summer sell-in. This is especially true of the toy advertisers, the major advertisers in this daypart during the sold-out fourth quarter.

The all-important primetime upfront market begins with the return of sales management from the May affiliate conventions, regardless of whether the children's market negotiations have been concluded yet. Occasionally a special, recurring annual order may be placed earlier, but the serious negotiations begin at this time and, during the typical year, last 8 weeks. During that period in 1979, commitments totaling approximately $1.5 billion were made on behalf of 100 to 150 advertisers, commitments ranging from about $50 million each for Procter & Gamble and General Foods to as little as $1 million for smaller advertisers.

The scenario usually unfolds as follows:

1. The agency network negotiators submit a plan request to each of the three networks. Each network is provided with the budget by quarter, the demographics on which the buy is based, and any special requirements of the advertiser. The first element of gamesmanship can be seen at this point. Buyers often understate actual budgets to convince the networks that the plans requested are for 50 percent of the total budget and thus that one network will not be bought. Buyers sometimes change the emphasis on the demographics requested in order to put each network on the defensive. For example, if the advertiser were looking for total adults with a concentration on young adults, the buyer would stress the importance of total adult delivery to the network serving a superior young-adult audience, while emphasizing young adults when talking to the network with an older audience skew. Although this tactic seems sound, it is dangerous and can backfire. A potential pitfall is that the younger-skewing network may present a plan encompassing its older-audience programs and the older-skewing network may present a plan encompassing its younger-audience programs, resulting in a combined submission of inferior programs.

2. Next each network prepares a plan in accordance with the advertiser's specifications. These plans provide detailed program schedules, quarterly audience projections, pricing information, and estimated CPMs against the target demographics as well as total homes. The network is expected to make an immediate response to the advertiser's request, but in fact it does not. Since commitments of millions of dollars worth of network time are not made lightly, each major submission of an upfront plan requires the participation of sales management. Given that most plan requests occur during the same 2- to 4-week period, these requests get backed up.

   This backload introduces a second element of gamesmanship. In most years it is advantageous to take part in the earliest negotiations. First, each network is anxious to close some big deals early as a sign of both the market's vitality and its own competitive strength. These deals usually result in attractive discounts for the advertisers involved. Second, during the course of the upfront market, the networks are likely to revise rate cards upward, particularly for programs generating extraordinary advertiser interest. An advertiser may get the same discount, but it would be off a higher list price, resulting in greater absolute cost to the advertiser.

Buyers attempting to get early action on their requests often use such tactics as in-person visits to the network's sales offices and the simultaneous discussion of several clients' plans at one time. The buyer has an important ally in this effort. The network salesperson handling the account also wants the priority treatment. Whereas the networks can substitute another advertiser to cover a lost order, their salespeople depend on their key upfront clients for a large portion of their annual commissions. This all can lead to some bizarre and creative strategies. It is not uncommon for the head of sales to arrive for a lunch date and find the restaurant filled with buyers being entertained by their respective sales representatives.

3. Now the true negotiations begin. The plan has been submitted, and the buyer must respond. The buyer almost always rejects the first network offer. Changes are suggested. A revised plan is drawn up and submitted. This process can go back and forth several times. These points will be negotiated:

   a. *Programs to be included:* Each network's schedule consists of a combination of proven performers and new programs. From the advertiser's point of view, these shows can be divided into low-, medium-, and high-risk categories. As would be expected, low-risk shows carry a premium, while high-risk shows are lower-priced. The buyers usually evaluate shows separately, placing each show into one of three risk classes. This classification is subjective; however, proven winners such as *M*A*S*H* and *60 Minutes* would characterize the low-risk entries, consistent performers or strong shows moving to new time periods would constitute medium-risk programs, and newcomers appearing opposite proven competition would comprise the high-risk group. Although movies can be among the highest-rating performers, they are characterized as medium risk because of the lack of specific date and title information at the time of purchase. The exception would be the *ABC Sunday Night Movie*, which, because of its consistently high ratings, would be considered a low-risk program over the course of the season.

b. *Weight by quarter:* Demand for network television time is greatest during the fourth and second quarters and substantially lower during the first quarter. Third-quarter demand varies. During election and Olympic years, this quarter is extremely tight because of all the time taken up by convention and Olympic coverage. During other years, this quarter is relatively soft, although not as soft as the first quarter. Advertisers would prefer more weight (more spots) in the second and fourth quarters. The networks are particularly interested in building demand for the first quarter. The actual distribution of the announcements over the four quarters, therefore, becomes a negotiating tool.

c. *The option:* Orders, when they are accepted by the networks, are classified as either firm or nonfirm. A firm order is one to which the advertiser commits in full; a nonfirm order is one to which the advertiser commits only in part. In the latter case, that advertiser can, up to a predetermined date (usually 90 days before the beginning of the quarter), cancel a specified amount of the commitment. Of the $1.5 billion placed during the 1979–1980 upfront season, approximately 25 to 35 percent was nonfirm; however, less than 10 to 15 percent of these nonfirm commitments were dropped during the year. Obviously, nonfirm orders carry a higher premium than firm orders. The percentage of firm designation represents another negotiating element.

d. *Price:* Of course, the ultimate negotiating point is the price to be paid. This price can be approached from several perspectives. Essentially the network prices a plan on the basis of a rate and cost for each component program and then offers the total package to the advertiser at a *discount*. The discount reflects the network's asking price and is a function of the historical relationship with that advertiser, the composition of the plan, and prevailing marketplace conditions. This final asking price is translated by the buyer to a cost per thousand (CPM).

Because of this dual discount-CPM evaluation, negotiations can proceed on various levels. The seller attempts to get the buyer to revise the audience estimates for the programs involved upward, thereby reducing the bottom-line plan price. Although, as will be seen shortly, the network will have to honor this CPM projection eventually, the all-important concern of the network sales team is to get as many dollars committed as possible. Adjusting the discount will result in lower absolute dollars for the same inventory, and lowering the base unit price will result in lower overall revenues from the program. From the network's point of view, both situations are to be avoided.

If the network cannot get the buyer to agree to its higher audience projections, a second approach is to "sweeten" the plan. This can be done either by offering additional announcements or by upgrading the announcements from lower- to higher-rating programs. While not as satisfactory as the former alternative, this still preserves the absolute dollar value of the package.

The buyer's first line of attack is the CPM and, through it, the total price of the plan. The buyer tries to get the network to lower the total price of the plan in order to reach a target CPM level without audience projection adjustments. Failing this, the buyer attempts to get bonus units or program upgrades to sweeten the plan. The net result of these buyer-seller strategies is that most negotiations focus on the program mix and number of announcements included in the package, as opposed to the final price of the plan, which stays fixed.

e. *The hold:* Once the buyer and seller have come to terms, the plan is put on hold. A *hold* represents the network's commitment to deliver the plan at the agreed-upon price. It allows the buyer a specified time to get management approval before making the order final. Since this approval process often involves several layers of both client and agency management, it can be quite protracted. The networks usually do not like to hold inventory off the market, and they are not likely to allow a hold position to go beyond 20 days. The length of this hold position is a final negotiating element. If the advertiser has a reputation for a long approval process and/or dropping holds, the advertiser usually has to pay a slightly higher price per unit to cover the network's risk in keeping in-demand inventory off the market.

The primetime upfront market is followed by the daytime, news, and late-night upfront negotiations. Often these markets break simultaneously, or at least with significant overlap. Network sales management accords them attention in relation to their dollar value, giving daytime top priority. The number of advertisers participating is much smaller than the number participating in primetime. Whereas the primetime upfront negotiations involve over 100 advertisers, daytime involves only about 75; news, 50; and late night, 50. The percentage of inventory moved also is much less. Only about half the total inventory for these dayparts is sold upfront, compared with more than 70 percent for primetime.

With the lower dollar commitments and the simultaneous timing of these markets, sales management is less involved in these negotiations which allows several plans to be negotiated at once. Also, the program elements comprising the plans are much more limited than those for primetime. For these reasons the upfront markets for these dayparts cover a considerably shorter period of time, usually 2 to 4 weeks. As this second stage of the upfront market progresses, the primetime scatter market begins.

Scatter Market

Once the major upfront negotiations have been concluded, the scatter market begins. The scatter market consists of those advertisers wishing to purchase a flight or flights of advertising time during one or more quarters. The initial scatter market consists of advertisers wishing to make advance commitments for time in the fourth quarter. It begins about 60 days prior to the beginning of the quarter. Scatter-market negotiations proceed much as upfront negotiations, with some significant variations:

1. Scatter advertisers usually cannot tolerate the same degree of flexibility in their schedule as upfront advertisers. Given the limited timing of their campaigns (often as short as 4 to 6 weeks) and their restricted budgets relative to the upfront buyers, they must have strong assurances that the schedule will run as planned. This weakens their negotiating position.

2. The networks' ability to sell each program's inventory during the upfront season will not have been consistent across programs. Some high-demand inventory may be sold out already, while other programs are still wide open. The networks adjust their plan development process to account for this. Thus scatter negotiations involve a more limited number of program options.

These scatter-market characteristics usually benefit the seller. By the time the scatter market starts, the rate card increases will have been instituted already, and it is not uncommon to see further increases as each scatter market is in progress.

There is a fourth-quarter scenario in which the buyers can gain the upper hand. The television networks operate on a calendar-year basis. The fourth quarter represents a critical period in terms of delivering the projected or targeted annual bottom line. As the scatter market progresses, the networks' financial managers are projecting total year results. If these projections fall short of corporate goals, the networks will be called on to pursue all possible fourth-quarter business aggressively. This could lead to a buyer's market, with big discounts offered to maximize sales volume.

The 1979 fourth-quarter scatter market generated about $.5 billion in additional revenues, bringing total upfront and scatter revenues to about $2 billion for primetime alone. Children's programming, daytime, news, and late night added close to another $1 billion, bringing the total to $3 billion, or approximately 75 percent of the annual advertising revenues of the three networks. Upfront special-program and sports program sales increased this total even more. These special markets are covered separately later in the chapter.

As each subsequent quarter begins, more than 75 percent of the projected advertising revenues are already on the books. It would seem that the buyers and sellers could now turn their attention elsewhere. This is not the case. Astute buyers continue negotiations, looking for every opportunity to improve their schedules while holding funds for opportunistic purchases.

On the seller side, the economics are even more demanding. Once the networks cover their costs, every incremental dollar generated goes directly to the bottom line. The difference between $1.4 billion and $1.5 billion may represent only 7 percent in revenues; but when that $100 million (minus commissions) hits the bottom line, it can represent a variation of more than 50 percent in pretax income. The television season, with its program changes, preemptions, and alterations in audience performance, presents a volatile environment that these buyers and sellers try to negotiate in their favor on a daily basis. Add to this a number of new opportunistic buyers who build their entire network advertising programs on a week-by-week basis as the season progresses and are ready to take advantage of any and all bargains.

In-Season Opportunistic Market

With so much of their inventory sold before the season progresses, one might expect the networks to hold fast to their rate cards and the Johnny-come-lately advertiser to either pay the higher rates or be denied access to the air. However, the nature of the network television season makes things far less stable for the sellers. Consider the following factors:

1. *Program changes:* Upfront and scatter market buyers have bought specific programs in specific time periods. Many of these programs are new. What is the probability that they will survive for the fall season? In fact few will survive, and those that do are very likely to change time periods. For the 1979–1980 season, only 2 of the 17 new programs on the schedules of the three networks were around when 1980 began, and 28 of the 48 programs on the schedules had either been dropped or changed time periods.

   Every change of this nature allows the buyers of time in those programs to renegotiate their schedules. They can stay where they are, accepting time in the replacement program, or they can move with the program, providing it remains in another time period offered by the network. They also can take advantage of the change to cancel their order and take credit. Their decision is critical to the network. Inability to hold advertisers in weak time periods during schedule adjustments can result in a major loss of previously placed business for the networks.

2. *Preemption:* In addition to canceling programs, the networks often preempt programs for specials. A network runs approximately 100 hours of special programming during the television season. Most of this programming has been sold to sponsors and participating advertisers. To the extent that a special is presold, all the advertisers scheduled to run in the regular programs being preempted by the special must be accommodated elsewhere. To retain the revenues committed by these

advertisers, the network will offer them *make-goods*, or comparable substitutes. Barring the ability of the network and the advertiser to agree on a suitable make-good or make-goods, the advertiser will take credit. The negotiation of make-goods is an ongoing process throughout the year.

Not all specials are presold in their entirety. If time is still available in the preempting special when it is scheduled, the network tries to move the advertisers scheduled in the programming being preempted into the special (this is called a *move-in*). In this way, the special itself becomes the make-good. Because of the widespread stunting of specials by the networks as a consequence of their battle for primetime dominance, make-goods and move-ins are vital to the maintenance of previously committed dollars. (*Stunting* refers to the scheduling of specials in replacement for poorly performing regular programming.)

3. *Program content:* Major advertisers such as Procter & Gamble and General Foods are increasingly sensitive to program content as public interest and religious groups, decrying the proliferation of sex and violence on television, threaten boycotts of the products advertised on programs with sex and violence themes. All advertisers are given the option of pulling out of programs if they feel the content is not acceptable. However, often this is not stated in the contract; rather, it is an accommodation by the networks. Also, the networks request some written statement of the advertiser's policy before the fact.

This option is exercised most in the case of movies. Advertisers often buy a generic movie night such as the *ABC Sunday Night Movie* or the *CBS Tuesday Night Movie* before they know the titles to run on those nights. When the title is announced, the network schedules a *content view*. The advertiser's representative, usually a screening service employed specifically for this reason, views the program and either recommends that the advertiser pull out of the program or reports that the program is acceptable. The networks try to schedule these screening sessions as far in advance as possible, but with the constant program stunting and the tight production schedules involved, much advance notice may not be possible. As a result, the networks often find themselves with several last-minute pull-outs and time to sell.

This time becomes the target of the opportunistic advertiser. The network must act fast to fill the unsold time, and that opens up a buyer's market. Often programs with sex or violence themes are among the top audience performers. Everyone in the industry has a story about how an astute opportunistic buyer purchased time in a 25-rated program at the last minute for $25,000.

This type of debate about program content involves negotiations on many fronts. First, the networks fight to keep the advertisers in the program. Often they refuse to let the advertiser out of its commitment on a screening service recommendation only, insisting that the management of the advertiser view the program also. Although the dialogue is sometimes heated and often involves discussions of religious beliefs, public mores, esoteric research studies, and violence in the United States, in the end the networks grant the request of the advertiser.

The second level of negotiation involves the recommitment of this advertiser's dollars. The networks usually offer the advertiser only a limited number of options. The third level concerns the replacement of this advertiser. One need only review the program description in any week's *TV Guide* to realize that the incidence of programs with controversial subject matter in primetime is growing. It would be safe to say that each network's sales force is actively engaged in reselling at least one "content problem" program each week.

4. *Relief requests:* The world of the upfront advertiser is not always stable. Economic conditions sour, product introductions are delayed, strikes occur, crops are not harvested, and sometimes things go so well that production cannot meet demand. In these instances, advertisers often find it advantageous to recapture already committed advertising funds. Since their upfront commitments, subject to specified options, are binding, the networks are not obligated to allow advertisers to withdraw from their commitments. However, in the interest of long-term customer satisfaction, it pays to accommodate these requests when they are believed to be legitimate.

The means of accommodation is the *relief request*. The advertiser asks to be relieved of the commitment. The network then tries to resell the time. If the network is confident of selling the time at or above the original price, it unconditionally grants the relief request. If the network does not feel sure of reselling the time, it grants the request subject to resale at the previous price. Since relief requests usually are limited to a portion of a schedule or a specific time period, often the advertiser offers concessions on the balance of the schedule or other time periods to encourage the network to meet the request. These relief requests open up inventory for resale throughout the year.

5. *Audience deficiency:* Although the sales management of the three networks will adamantly deny the existence of a guaranteed CPM as a condition of any order, in fact major advertisers are protected by the networks. On a quarterly basis, all major schedules are reviewed. Those that are delivering audiences significantly lower than projected during the negotiating sessions are flagged. As the season progresses, advertisers whose schedules are not delivering as anticipated are offered *audience-deficiency announcements* (ADs) at no extra cost. These free units bring the CPM close to the projected level.

   Although the willingness of the networks to provide ADs is widely recognized, their ability to do so is not automatic. A particularly poor season could result in deficiencies of such volume and magnitude that the unsold time required to cover them all would not be available. The networks take care of their best customers first. So the quantity and quality of ADs offered are usually a function of the buyer's relationship with the network. Good buyers usually come out winners in the area.

   One network's deficiencies are usually the result of the relative success of either one or both of the other networks. If the buyer has bought all networks, she or he gets the benefits of overdelivery from the schedules on the successful networks while having the shortfall of the schedule on the less successful network covered by ADs. Knowing this, the networks are more likely to give ADs to advertisers that have committed large shares of their dollars.

6. *Option nonrenewal:* Earlier we discussed options. Only 10 to 15 percent of options are not picked up each quarter, but this still represents 2.5 percent of total primetime inventory that becomes available for sale 60 to 90 days prior to the beginning of each new quarter.

7. *Unsold time:* Although the networks sell most of the available inventory during the upfront and scatter markets, they do not sell 100 percent of that inventory. In fact, the networks deliberately fail to sell 100 percent of their inventory. They need inventory for make-goods, for audience-deficiency coverage, and for new business accounts that emerge throughout the year. Even in the most bullish of years the networks place 10 to 20 percent of their inventory on *management hold* for later sale. They know that at any time a given number of advertisers must get on the air and will pay a premium to do so. The networks want to be able to service these advertisers as well as cover the exigencies just mentioned.

All these market factors create a constantly active marketplace throughout the year. Skilled buyers will use opportunistic funds and will manipulate their schedules to take advantage of changing conditions in the marketplace. It is during these opportunistic negotiations that the talents of the best negotiators, on both the buyer and the seller side, pay dividends to the advertisers and the networks.

The scenario just described applies to the morning, primetime, daytime, late-night, and news marketplace accurately. However, two markets—sports and specials—are unique and deserve separate treatment.

SPORTS MARKET

The upfront sports market takes place on an individual sport basis. For the premiere sports attraction, NFL football, this market can open up the day after the Superbowl concludes the previous season's schedule. However, most serious negotiations follow the announcement of the new season schedules. Advertisers must move quickly here, since many categories, such as beer and automobiles, have elicited the interest of several brands in a football franchise. Aggressive marketers with big budgets in these categories try to gain an exclusive position on a given network. Exclusivity is granted on both a total-game and a partial-game basis to multiple-unit sponsors. These advertisers usually get opening and closing billboards as well as exclusivity.

Exclusivity is very important to big sports advertisers, since product category concentration often leads to a noisy environment for the beer, automobile, or insurance advertiser. When Ford decided not to renew its exclusivity option on CBS-TV in 1980, the NFL football telecasts wound up with six different automobile advertisers per game. NFL football and NCAA football are virtually sold out in this upfront market, which is over by the time the first preseason game is played. The situation is different for the other sports programs.

Baseball, basketball, and golf are the other full-season sports programs available to the advertiser. Each has its upfront market. These markets, like the football market, usually begin when schedules are announced after the conclusion of the preceding season. The upfront markets for these sports do not result in sellout situations, however. The baseball market is really made up of two separate markets. The first market, for the playoffs and the World Series, is a sellers' market, much like that for football. Prices are higher, and advertisers vie for exclusive deals in key categories. Negotiations begin after the last out of the previous season's World Series.

Regular-season baseball is not as attractive to advertisers. The profile of the baseball viewer is that of an older, downscale male, not exactly the most sought-after customer. Ratings are not high, and local team coverage by independent stations in major markets offers advertisers an alternative. The baseball networks, ABC-TV and NBC-TV, attempt to obviate these problems by tying in playoff and World Series participation with regular-season participation. This tactic has been reasonably effective; nevertheless, a large portion of baseball advertising inventory ends up in the opportunistic market.

The basketball market consists of NCAA and NBA basketball. In recent years NCAA basketball has outrated NBA basketball, as professional basketball has suffered a series of internal battles. Again the championship series for both college and professional basketball are the draws, with regular-season ratings being marginal. Unfortunately for the networks carrying basketball, these championships generate far less viewer interest than either the baseball or football championship. A great deal of basketball inventory finds its way into the opportunistic market—even championship basketball in soft years.

The golf coverage on television consists predominantly of PGA tour events, although more LPGA play is being covered today. Major attractions are the Masters, the U.S. Open, and the PGA championship. Golf coverage is expensive. Golf offers the most upscale audience profile of any sport. Therefore, the networks must get, and feel they should get, premium prices from advertisers for golf telecasts. The problem is that golf audiences, though upscale, are small. An average golf audience is approximately one-fourth to one-third as large as an average NFL football audience. For this reason there is some resistance to golf prices by advertisers, and a significant amount of golf inventory ends up in the opportunistic market.

All these sports franchises seem to exist in a feast-or-famine type of marketplace. The variation between upfront and opportunistic prices is often extraordinary. Why, then, do any advertisers buy upfront at all? There are two essential reasons. First, the attraction of exclusivity is a significant stimulant to upfront sales. Major male-oriented advertisers are well aware of the cumulative impact of an exclusive sports advertising franchise, and they are willing to pay a premium for such a franchise, even in minor sports. Second, effective sports marketing involves extensive merchandising tie-ins. These tie-ins require advance planning, and the advertisers involved cannot afford to wait for the opportunistic market.

The balance of sports programming consists of the three network anthology series and selected events in such sports as tennis, boxing, automobile racing, and horse racing. Hockey and soccer have had their runs on network television, but neither sport is covered regularly at present. The major tennis events are Wimbledon and the U.S. Open. Both attract an upscale audience and therefore are premium-priced. Demand is usually strong for these events, but, owing to the extensiveness of the coverage and the less than substantial total audience levels, some inventory reaches the opportunistic market. The major automobile racing events are delayed broadcasts of the Indianapolis 500 and the Daytona 500. Neither program is particularly attractive in terms of audience composition or size, but they are naturals for the automobile and automotive supply advertisers and usually sell quickly. In horse racing the Triple Crown alone draws the audiences and the advertisers, with an occasional match race generating extraordinary interest.

One sport that has not been mentioned is boxing. Boxing is a mixed bag. Less than championship fare is usually covered in the anthology programs. Major championships and fights between heavyweight contenders are reserved for primetime and often attract audiences and prices comparable to those for the World Series and NFL football. However, advertisers cannot count on a steady supply of these events in the future. Pay cable has been effective in outbidding the networks for major fights, and this trend should continue.

Last, but certainly not least, are the anthology series. Each network has such a program. ABC-TV's *Wide World of Sports* was the first and is the audience leader. CBS-TV's *CBS Sports Saturday* and *CBS Sports Sunday* and NBC-TV's *Sportsworld* are battling for second place. These programs feature a mixture of live and taped sporting events from around the world. Recently they have expanded in length. Saturday and Sunday editions are now the rule.

This expansion led to a shortage of legitimate sports activities. To fill the gap, the networks introduced their own created sports events, dubbed by the press "junk" sports. Today you can watch people demonstrate their strength by racing with refrigerators on their backs, stunt people risk their lives in assorted ways, cheerleaders compete against one another in various sports events, and celebrities do just about everything. While decried by the sports purists, the junk sports attract audiences. The celebrity games have even been moved to primetime.

The anthology series attract an audience somewhere between the NFL football audience and the minor sports audience in size. Often the profile of this audience is more similar to that of the primetime audience, with strong female representation. The anthology series also offer the sports advertiser a 52-week sports vehicle. The upfront season for sports anthologies is hard to pinpoint. Advertisers are consistently entering and leaving the market. Because of the 52-week duration of the anthologies, advertisers are more likely to buy these programs on a calendar-year basis. Negotiations of these calendar-year commitments are concentrated in the fourth quarter. The automobile marketers, however, buy on a television-season basis. Their negotiations coincide with the regular upfront market.

Despite this demand, sports anthology inventory can be found in the opportunistic market, although not usually in the same volume as most sports inventory. The opportunistic sports market is unquestionably the most active of any daypart. The three networks most likely will enter each working week with some sports inventory to sell for that weekend. The amount varies by the time of year and the programming involved, but something is always available. For this reason the opportunistic sports market is a 52-week market. Large sports advertisers, with seemingly unlimited budgets, are always ready to seize upon some opportunistic deal. Often all these negotiations continue through Friday, and sometimes they can spill over into the weekend, reaching completion just before airtime. It is an accepted fact that the sports sales team and buyers are the last to leave for the weekend.

The sports advertising marketplace attracts a unique individual to its buyer and seller ranks. The people involved are often sports enthusiasts themselves. With sports advertising usually being one component in a total sports marketing program for the major advertisers, sponsorship of an event on television is paralleled by on-site participation, extensive merchandising, and contracts with professional athletes. These sports marketing programs are coordinated by professionals who travel to each event.

The sellers, anxious to cultivate these key buyers, usually arrange for hospitalities and special functions at major events. These functions also create opportunities to entertain all the networks' clients in the geographic area surrounding the event location. Like their counterparts on the advertiser side, the sports sales managers of the three networks travel extensively, often attending major events covered by another network. This travel commitment, coupled with the small size of the sports marketing universe, has resulted in a close-knit group of people controlling the majority of sports advertising. This community of sports marketing experts is in constant flux as people move up and over to maximize their own earnings. It does indeed represent a unique part of the overall television-time sales environment.

SPECIALS MARKET

Specials are very important to a television network. They "create" inventory during high-demand periods by, in effect, allowing the network to sell the same time twice. They serve as relief help when new series programming falters. They are the most effective weapons in the program stunting wars conducted by the three networks. Most important, however, is the fact that often they attract premium dollars from advertisers seeking a definitive presence in the medium.

The upfront season for specials coincides with the primetime upfront season. The specials sales strategy has two stages. First, the network tries to sell the special on a sponsorship basis—a full-sponsorship basis ideally. Second, if this fails, the special is released to the sales force as part of the overall primetime mix to be sold on a participating basis.

The network sales manager responsible for selling specials on a sponsorship basis is faced with three handicaps:

1. Specials are expensive, especially on a full- or half-sponsorship basis.

2. Usually the product is not available at the time of sale.

3. The date on which the special will air usually is not known at the time of sale.

Because of the high price tag ($100,000 plus per 30 seconds), only a few corporations can afford the luxury of full or half sponsorship. These include large, multiple-product corporations that can allocate the time among many brands, which brings the cost per brand close to that of a regular primetime commitment, and giant corporations willing to invest heavily in corporate image promotion. For example, during the 1979–1980 season, General Motors fully sponsored "Shining Season," a dramatic special concerning one man's battle against cancer, and turned all the commercial time over to the cancer researchers. Certainly few companies are able or willing to make such a gesture in the name of corporate goodwill alone.

If a company invests an extraordinary amount of money in the sponsorship of a special program, that company wants the program to be special. The buyer is expected to find the "right" vehicle for the client company. The problem is that the buyer often has only a script by which to judge a property. To aid the buyers in their search, the networks schedule west coast screenings and briefing sessions. The major junket takes place at the beginning of the upfront season. Each buyer gets a preview of the major special projects in the works. Network creative managers, producers, directors, and writers discuss their projects. Then the buyers return to New York or Chicago to make their decisions and begin financial negotiations with the networks' sales managers.

It is obvious that the successful specials buyer must possess unusual talents. In effect, this buyer must be imbued with the spirit of show business, must understand the creative process, and must be able to evaluate such intangibles as casting, editing, and production quality. Such a buyer is usually a high-ranking advertising agency officer. Often advertisers and agencies look to the creative community when recruiting executives for these positions. In addition, outside creative consultants are commissioned to help select properties for sponsorship. As was the case with sports, the specials buyers and sellers are a small, close-knit group; however, they are more likely to be seen lunching at the Polo Lounge with a big-name television producer than in a front-row box seat at Madison Square Garden.

Occasionally, an advertiser brings a program to the networks for consideration. If the network agrees to present the program, the advertiser pays a time charge only, substantially lower than what would be charged for a fully sponsored network-produced special. Of course, the advertiser has to underwrite the production costs of the program. Few clients are in a position to undertake such a high-risk venture, and the networks are not actively seeking client-produced programming. Even after these deals are made, negotiation of scheduling and promotional considerations continues. The networks steadfastly retain total control in these areas, adding to the riskiness of the venture.

Animation is a unique special-program form. Animated shows are developed primarily to appeal to children; however, perennial favorites such as the Charlie Brown series appeal to all age groups. Most animation is scheduled around holidays, with the Christmas season being the most active. The traditional supporters of children's programming—cereal manufacturers, fast-food restaurants, candy and gum marketers, and toy and game manufacturers—are the major sponsors of animated specials. Unit costs in animated specials are lower than those in dramatic and variety specials ($65,000 versus $100,000); however, rating levels are comparable (15 to 20 GRP average). The "family" viewing environment is also ideal for marketers wishing to sell products aimed at children for whom the adult is the major decision maker.

DEVELOPING A NETWORK BUYING STRATEGY

The description of the network television buyer-seller process just given underscores its unique nature. There is no question that a buyer seeking to purchase network television time is going to make a substantial financial commitment and that the size of the return will be affected substantially by the adroitness of that buyer. For this reason each buyer should enter the market with a carefully laid-out plan, which should include the following:

1. *Careful review of the alternatives of entering the upfront, scatter, or opportunistic market, or all three.* The buyer must weigh the advantages and disadvantages of all three markets.

    Upfront:

    Advantages: Large selection of inventory, initial price lists usually lower, favored treatment by networks, long lead time for merchandising to trade.

    Disadvantages: Major commitment well in advance, many programs as yet untried, networks less willing to negotiate if market is strong.

    Scatter:

    Advantages: Shorter-term commitment, schedules more adaptable to market conditions, inventory selection still satisfactory.

    Disadvantages: In strong markets, prices substantially higher than upfront, heavy competition for remaining premium inventory in high-demand quarters, networks less flexible regarding schedule adjustments.

    Opportunistic:

    Advantages: Ability to make effective low-CPM deals, no fixed commitments.

    Disadvantages: Lack of premium-quality inventory, inability to plan campaign timing, can backfire in high-demand periods.

2. *Careful consideration of each daypart's role in the overall schedule.* Flexibility in moving weight among dayparts will attract greater network attention.

3. *Monitoring schedule.* Reviews of schedule performance with network salesperson should be planned to ensure prompt attention to audience-deficiency problems.

4. *In-depth review of effectiveness of buying strategy for future consideration.* The professional buyer not only will evaluate the performance of the schedule on a strict audience delivery–CPM basis, but also will consider such factors as:

   - Accuracy of initial audience estimates

   - Ability to upgrade original schedule

   - Working relationship with each network sales representative

   - Final schedule's realization of client's desires regarding timing, program quality, etc.

In summary, the network television buyer must realize that the job does not end when the order is placed. Regular communication with the network sales representatives before, during, and after the schedule runs offers the buyer many opportunities to improve on the original schedule ordered. The careful use of supplemental opportunistic funds can further enhance the buyer's ability to "play the market" for the client. *Flexibility* is critical in the volatile world of network television advertising, but that flexibility should be tied to a carefully thought-out plan of action, for the stakes are high.

5

Local Television Stations

In contrast to the simple three-member universe of network television, the advertiser considering local television market advertising must contend with a selection of over 200 individual markets and a choice of some 757 stations within those markets.

TELEVISION STATION UNIVERSE

In Chapter 2 the Arbitron area of dominant influence (ADI) and A.C. Nielsen designated market area (DMA) are defined. These designations are commonly recognized as representing the television market. For 1981, Arbitron listed 211 ADIs and Nielsen 205 DMAs. In most cases the ADI and DMA market designations were very similar. The ADI has found greater use in statistical circles. It is utilized by the *Television Factbook*, the Standard Rate and Data Service (SRDS), and the *Media Market Guide*, the three major sources of local television market advertising information. The ADI is also the television market measure employed by *Sales and Marketing Management* magazine in its annual *Survey of Buying Power*, a widely used source of marketing information and statistics. For these reasons in this book we also use the ADI as the television market descriptor.

Population is concentrated in the top markets. The top 10 ADIs alone represent almost one-third of U.S. television households; the top 30, over one-half; and the top 100, 86.3 percent. Table 5-1 lists the ADIs and their TV household populations for 1981.

The ADI, in essence, defines each market by the coverage of the television stations within that market. That coverage is limited by the FCC and is also, to some extent, a function of the popularity of the station's programming. In other words, the unique characteristics, tech-

TABLE 5-1

**ADI MARKET RANKINGS
FOR 1981**

Rank	Market	ADI TV households
1	New York	6,410,900
2	Los Angeles	4,140,000
3	Chicago	2,968,100
4	Philadelphia (Allentown & Wildwood)	2,385,800
5	San Francisco	1,959,000
6	Boston (Manchester & Worcester)	1,878,600
7	Detroit	1,661,400
8	Washington, D.C. (Hagerstown)	1,465,800
9	Cleveland (Akron & Canton)	1,394,800
10	Dallas–Ft. Worth	1,360,800
11	Houston	1,276,400
12	Pittsburgh	1,224,900
13	Miami (Ft. Lauderdale)	1,106,200
14	Minneapolis–St. Paul	1,094,200
15	Seattle–Tacoma (Bellingham)	1,087,000
16	Atlanta	1,085,800
17	St. Louis	1,024,300
18	Tampa–St. Petersburg	937,800
19	Denver	874,900
20	Baltimore	862,900
21	Sacramento–Stockton (Modesto)	811,400
22	Indianapolis	796,700
23	Portland, OR	788,300
24	Hartford–New Haven	785,000
25	Phoenix (Flagstaff)	731,000
26	Cincinnati	702,800
27	Kansas City	696,700
27	San Diego	696,700
29	Milwaukee	678,700
30	Nashville	655,700
31	Buffalo	608,000
32	Charlotte (Hickory)	606,400
33	Orlando–Daytona Beach	597,500
34	New Orleans	588,400
35	Columbus, OH	580,600
36	Memphis	570,200
37	Grand Rapids–Kalamazoo–Battle Creek	565,900
38	Greenville–Spartanburg–Asheville	551,000
39	Providence–New Bedford	548,900
40	Raleigh–Durham	548,400
41	Oklahoma City	533,100
42	Louisville	524,000
43	Charleston–Huntington	521,600
44	Salt Lake City	513,100

TABLE 5-1

ADI MARKET RANKINGS
FOR 1981 *(Continued)*

Rank	Market	ADI TV households
45	San Antonio	491,900
46	Norfolk–Portsmouth–Newport News–Hampton	485,900
47	Birmingham	480,700
48	Dayton	472,500
49	Wilkes-Barre–Scranton	461,900
50	Albany–Schenectady–Troy	457,400
51	Greensboro–Winston Salem–High Point	451,700
52	Harrisburg–York–Lancaster–Lebanon	445,500
53	Flint–Saginaw–Bay City	442,400
54	Little Rock	440,400
55	Shreveport–Texarkana	429,700
56	Richmond (Charlottesville)	428,300
57	Tulsa	422,900
58	Wichita–Hutchinson	408,400
59	Toledo	401,200
60	Knoxville	395,700
61	Mobile–Pensacola	387,500
62	Jacksonville	369,100
63	Des Moines	359,600
64	Fresno (Hanford & Visalla)	358,900
65	Roanoke–Lynchburg	352,200
66	Syracuse	350,500
67	West Palm Beach (Ft. Pierce–Vero Beach)	349,000
68	Green Bay	347,800
69	Omaha	336,800
70	Albuquerque	333,500
71	Rochester, NY	329,900
72	Portland–Poland Spring	322,300
73	Davenport–Rock Island–Moline/Quad City	322,000
74	Paducah–Cape Girardeau–Harrisburg	320,900
75	Spokane	320,300
76	Springfield–Decatur–Champaign	314,000
77	Cedar Rapids–Waterloo (Dubuque)	313,500
78	Bristol–Kingsport–Johnson City	286,000
79	Lexington (Hazard)	285,700
80	Chattanooga	280,300
81	South Bend–Elkhart	277,200
82	Springfield, MO	274,900
83	Johnstown–Altoona	274,400
84	Jackson, MS	271,300
85	Tucson	255,600
86	Lincoln–Hastings–Kearney	247,700
87	Columbia, SC	242,100

TABLE 5-1

ADI MARKET RANKINGS
FOR 1981 *(Continued)*

Rank	Market	ADI TV households
88	Evansville	240,900
89	Baton Rouge	240,300
90	Huntsville–Decatur–Florence	239,500
91	Youngstown	233,300
92	Austin, TX	229,300
93	Springfield, MA	227,000
94	Ft. Wayne	219,400
95	Peoria	218,600
96	Lansing	213,900
97	Sioux Falls–Mitchell	209,400
98	Fargo	209,300
98	Waco–Temple	209,300
100	Burlington–Plattsburgh (Hartford, VT–Hanover, NH)	207,700
101	Greenville–New Bern–Washington	203,300
102	Colorado Springs–Pueblo	197,900
103	Savannah	192,500
104	Madison	190,800
105	Las Vegas	190,200
106	El Paso	187,200
107	Augusta	187,100
108	Rockford	185,600
109	Columbus, GA	183,300
110	Monroe–El Dorado	179,300
111	Charleston, SC	178,900
112	Salinas–Monterey	178,500
113	Lafayette, LA	178,000
114	Amarillo	174,600
115	Duluth–Superior	173,400
116	Santa Barbara–Santa Maria–San Luis Obispo	170,100
117	Joplin–Pittsburg	168,900
118	Wheeling–Steubenville	166,500
119	Montgomery	165,700
120	Eugene	163,500
121	Yakima	163,300
122	Ft. Myers–Naples	161,700
123	Terre Haute	161,200
124	Beaumont–Port Arthur	160,300
125	Wichita Falls–Lawton	157,900
126	Wilmington	157,000
127	La Crosse–Eau Claire	156,500
128	Tallahassee	156,000
129	McAllen–Brownsville/LRGV	154,700
130	Corpus Christi	154,200

TABLE 5-1
ADI MARKET RANKINGS
FOR 1981 *(Continued)*

Rank	Market	ADI TV households
131	Sioux City	152,800
132	Wausau–Rhinelander	151,200
133	Binghamton	147,500
134	Traverse City–Cadillac	146,600
135	Reno	146,000
136	Bluefield–Beckley–Oak Hill	145,800
137	Erie	145,400
138	Lubbock	145,100
139	Macon	144,300
140	Boise	141,500
141	Topeka	139,600
142	Rochester–Mason City–Austin	138,500
143	Columbus–Tupelo	138,400
144	Chico–Redding	131,400
145	Minot–Bismarck–Dickinson	131,300
146	Quincy–Hannibal	128,500
147	Columbia–Jefferson City	124,700
148	Odessa–Midland	124,300
149	Ft. Smith	120,700
150	Bakersfield	120,300
151	Bangor	119,300
152	Medford	115,800
153	Missoula–Butte	112,200
154	Abilene–Sweetwater	111,500
155	Albany, GA	109,100
156	Utica	100,700
157	Florence, SC	98,800
158	Sarasota	95,000
159	Idaho Falls–Pocatello	93,300
160	Tyler	92,000
161	Rapid City	87,600
162	Laurel–Hattiesburg	83,000
163	Elmira	82,000
164	Alexandria, LA	81,800
165	Panama City	80,400
166	Alexandria, MN	79,300
167	Salisbury	79,200
168	Billings–Hardin	75,800
169	Clarksburg–Weston	75,500
170	Dothan	74,600
171	Watertown–Carthage	74,500
172	Lake Charles	71,600
173	Gainesville	70,300
174	Ardmore–Ada	69,100

TABLE 5-1
ADI MARKET RANKINGS
FOR 1981 *(Continued)*

Rank	Market	ADI TV households
175	Greenwood–Greenville	66,600
176	Jonesboro	66,000
177	Great Falls	63,900
178	El Centro–Yuma	58,000
179	Biloxi–Gulfport–Pascagoula	57,400
180	Eureka	54,900
181	Palm Springs	54,600
182	Meridian	54,300
183	Casper–Riverton	53,000
184	Marquette	52,400
185	Roswell	52,300
186	Grand Junction	49,900
187	Cheyenne	49,500
188	Tuscaloosa	48,700
189	St. Joseph	47,600
190	Harrisonburg	46,200
191	Jackson, TN	44,000
192	Lafayette, IN	41,200
193	Bowling Green	40,800
194	Anniston	40,700
195	Lima	39,400
196	Mankato	37,400
197	San Angelo	34,900
198	Parkersburg	34,500
199	Ottumwa–Kirksville	30,400
200	Twin Falls	30,300
201	Zanesville	30,000
202	Presque Isle	29,100
203	Laredo	28,900
204	Farmington	26,000
205	Selma	25,500
206	Bend	24,000
206	Victoria	24,000
208	Helena	16,700
209	North Platte	15,800
210	Alpena	15,100
211	Miles City–Glendive	10,800

ADI television market rankings are based on Arbitron estimates of U.S. television households as of January 1, 1982. Markets in parentheses have no ADI. However, the TV households estimates of their home counties are included in the listed ADI market.

Source: Arbitron, "ADI Market Rankings," New York, 1982.

nical and program-related, of a market's stations determine the boundaries of that market.

Television Stations

On April 30, 1939, NBC broadcast Franklin D. Roosevelt opening the 1939 World's Fair, and the first television station was on the air. By 1949 there were already 108 licensed television stations. At that time the FCC suspended station licensing. The commission spent the next few years developing an effective national TV station allocation system. The Table of Assignments established in 1952 set that system in motion, and the rush for TV station licenses was on. Today, there are more than 1000 licensed TV stations in the United States, including 757 commercial stations. The remaining stations are predominantly public educational stations, the majority of which (165) are members of the Public Broadcasting System. The nation's 757 commercial TV stations can be subdivided into very high frequency (VHF) versus ultra high frequency (UHF), affiliates versus independents, and group-owned versus independently owned.

VHF VERSUS UHF

The first television station subdivision is VHF versus UHF. These initials refer to the different wavelengths at which stations are licensed to operate. The television spectrum is divided into channels. Each channel coincides with a specific frequency. Very high frequency (VHF) stations broadcast over channels 2 to 13 (also specified as 54 to 72, 76 to 88, and 174 to 216 megahertz). Ultra high frequency (UHF) stations broadcast over channels 14 to 83 (also specified as 470+ megahertz).

The higher the channel number, the shorter the broadcast wavelength and the more sensitive the reception. This reception advantage differentiates VHF from UHF stations. VHF stations are divided into two classes, low band (channels 2 to 6) and high band (channels 7 to 13). Early station owners fought to obtain the prime low-band VHF allocations. Now that all these allocations have been made, attention is concentrated on the UHF spectrum.

To stimulate UHF growth, the FCC initiated several programs to bring those stations closer to parity with their VHF counterparts. First, the FCC regularly allows UHF stations to operate at radiated power levels that are 2 to 3 times higher than the VHF station levels. In 1962 the FCC convinced Congress to pass the all-channel law, stating that as of April 30, 1964, all television sets sold in the United States must have UHF tuners. In 1976 set manufacturers were further required to make these UHF tuners with discrete, as opposed to continuous, dialing. Prior to that, UHF tuning was like that on a radio, requiring the viewer to find the station on the dial. Now UHF tuning uses the same specific channel dials as VHF.

Perhaps the most important advance for the UHF station is the growth of cable television. Cable eliminated reception variation. Channel 68 can be received as clearly as channel 2. Also the cable operator probably will place channel 68 on an undesignated primary channel.

By 1975 more than 90 percent of all U.S. television households had sets capable of receiving UHF stations, and the 177 operating commercial UHF stations reported a collective profit for the first time. Over half these stations were profitable that year. In 1976 this profitable group represented two-thirds of all reporting UHF stations. Since 1976 the trend has been unclear. In 1980 profits were down 43 percent from 1979 for UHF stations as a group, and only 35 percent of these stations were in the black. UHF penetration is now up to 95 percent of all TV households.

The early VHF assignments were concentrated in major markets. When a station is assigned a channel number, it has exclusive use of that number over an area approximating 200 airline miles. These powerful station assignments created substantial coverage patterns, resulting in broad primary ADIs. In addition to being given prime VHF allocations, the major market stations were allowed to operate at high power levels and to employ high antennas to expand their coverage.

The critical goal of the FCC in the early years was to provide as many people with television service as possible. In less populated regions, stations were permitted to use translators and satellite stations to boost their coverage. Translators are authorized booster stations located within a station's basic coverage area which enhance coverage in areas the station's signal is not reaching effectively. Satellite stations extend the parent station's signal beyond its normal range. Satellite licenses were granted where low population density made full station service economically unfeasible.

As the population grows and shifts, these allocations present some clear problems. This is best illustrated by the case of New Jersey. New Jersey, one of the largest states in population, has no real VHF television stations of its own. (WNET, channel 13, the New York PBS station, is officially a New Jersey station, but it is essentially oriented toward New York.) New Jersey politicians have been fighting this matter for years, but the early New York and Philadelphia allocations shut out New Jersey.

These technical elements are all critical in determining the range of a TV station's coverage and thus contribute to the final ADI designations. However, the ability of stations in a particular market to attract the required "preponderance of total viewing hours" in a given county, and so have that county included in their ADI, is also a function of those stations' programming. The commercial television station universe also can be divided according to programming. Stations are either network affiliates or independent.

Network Affiliates   A network affiliate is a station that has signed an affiliation contract with one of the three networks, agreeing to carry that network's programming in exchange for some compensation. Each network has more than 200 affiliates, representing virtually total national coverage. Although each affiliate is expected to carry the majority of the network's programming, it is not contractually obliged to do so. For this reason, networks and stations enter into secondary affiliate relationships. A *secondary affiliate* is a station that is given the opportunity to carry any programming declined by the primary affiliate. Networks often enter into secondary affiliation contracts in markets with only one or two stations.

Each network affiliate is compensated according to the size of its market and the amount of network programming it carries. This compensation formula is based on the *network base hourly rate* for each market. These rates range from a high of $10,000 for New York to below $100 for smaller markets. (Actually, some smaller markets receive no network compensation and are shown as bonuses for advertisers.) Each station's network base hourly rate is published in the *Television Factbook*. In total, network compensation to affiliates in 1980 equaled $350 million.

Each network offers its affiliates more than 90 hours of programming per week. This leaves little time for local programming. Although there are variations by network and by station, a normal network-affiliate program schedule resembles that shown in Table 5-2.

Primetime is most often the major revenue generator for most affiliates, despite the fact that these stations have limited time for sale in this and other network-programmed dayparts, which contain network commercials.

Network affiliates consider their news programming to be the most important component of their local schedules. The combination of the early news preceding primetime and the late news following primetime often equals or surpasses primetime as a revenue generator, accounting for 30 to 40 percent of all station revenues on average.

Primetime access is a special programming area. The *primetime ac-*

TABLE 5-2
STATION X PROGRAM SCHEDULE*

Monday–Friday		Saturday		Sunday	
		Local		Local	
6:30 a.m. – 7:00 a.m.	Sign-on—local news update				
7:00 a.m. – 9:00 a.m.	Network news				
9:00 a.m. –10:00 a.m.	Local programming				
10:00 a.m. – 1:00 p.m.	Network daytime	8:00 a.m. – 2:00 p.m.	Network—children's	8:00 a.m. –noon	Network—miscellaneous
1:00 p.m. – 1:30 p.m.	Local programming	2:00 p.m. – 6:00 p.m.	Network sports and local public service and movies	Noon – 6:00 p.m.	Network sports and local public service and movies
1:30 p.m. – 4:30 p.m.	Network daytime	6:00 p.m. – 6:30 p.m.	Network news	6:00 p.m. – 6:30 p.m.	Local news
4:30 p.m. – 7:00 p.m.	Local programming	6:30 p.m. – 7:00 p.m.	Various	6:30 p.m. – 7:00 p.m.	Network news
7:00 p.m. – 7:30 p.m.	Network news	7:00 p.m. – 7:30 p.m.	Local news	7:00 p.m. –11:00 p.m.	Network primetime
7:30 p.m. – 8:00 p.m.	Local primetime access	7:30 p.m. – 8:00 p.m.	Local primetime access		
8:00 p.m. –11:00 p.m.	Network primetime	8:00 p.m. –11:00 p.m.	Network primetime	11:00 p.m. –11:15 p.m.	Network news
11:00 p.m. –11:30 p.m.	Local news	11:00 p.m. –11:30 p.m.	Local news	11:15 p.m. –11:45 p.m.	Local news
11:30 p.m. – 1:30 a.m.	Network late fringe	11:30 p.m. – 1:30 a.m.	Local movie	11:45 p.m. –sign-off	Local movies
1:30 a.m. –sign-off	Local movies and talk	1:30 a.m. –sign-off	Local movie		

*Based on Eastern standard time pattern.

cess rule was adopted by the FCC in 1970. The access rule limited the networks to supplying 3 hours of programming to affiliates between 7 p.m. and 11 p.m. (EST) each evening. On Sunday, the networks use the full 7 p.m.–11 p.m. period, but they must provide either news and information or children's programming from 7 p.m. to 8 p.m. The purpose of this rule is to encourage locally originated programming.

Stations have adopted the half hour from 7:30 p.m. to 8:00 p.m. as the primetime access period. Much to the chagrin of the FCC, they have not chosen to fill this time with local programming. Most primetime access programming today is supplied by national program syndicators. The most common program form is the low-budget game show. In markets below market 50 in rank, stations are allowed to run off-network strip programming. Many choose this type of programming for the access time period. The only creative original programming to emanate from the access rule is *PM Magazine* and similar local news magazine series.

Independent Stations   Independent stations are those with no network affiliation. They first appeared in major markets in which it was felt that local advertising potential could support more than the three network affiliates. Today there are more than 100 commercial independent stations, 30 of which are VHF and 90, UHF. More than three-quarters of these stations are profitable. Most major markets are served by more than one independent station.

Independent stations fall into two classes: special-interest independents and general-programming independents. Special-interest independents serve special groups within a market. There are special-interest stations serving the Spanish-speaking population in major markets such as New York and Los Angeles, as well as in smaller markets with high concentrations of Spanish-speaking people, such as San Antonio. There are also independent stations owned and operated by religious groups. Other types of special-interest independent stations include WGPR-TV in Detroit, specializing in programming for the black market; and KWHY-TV in Los Angeles and KMUV-TV in Sacramento, serving a variety of ethnic groups, in particular the Chinese- and Japanese-Americans.

Of greater interest to the advertiser are the general-programming independents that compete with the network affiliates for the broad television audience. These stations began with a program inventory made up predominantly of old films and children's programming. Today they offer a wide range of programming and represent viable alternatives to the network affiliates. Table 5-3 shows the top independent stations by total day share for the February 1981 rating period.

TABLE 5-3
TOP FIVE INDEPENDENTS' TOTAL
DAY SHARE

Market rank	Station	Market	Percentage of Monday–Sunday sign-on–sign-off share
1	KVVU-TV	Las Vegas	23
2	KPHO-TV	Phoenix	20
3T*	KMSP-TV	Minneapolis–St. Paul	18
3T	KPTV	Portland, Oregon	18
5T	WGN-TV	Chicago	16
5T	KMPH-TV	Fresno	16
5T	WNEW-TV	New York	16
5T	WTTG	Washington, D.C.	16

*T = tie.

Source: Arbitron, "Television Market Reports" New York, February 1981.

Successful independent stations rely on a basic counterprogramming philosophy to compete with the network affiliates. They concentrate their best programming during the 4 p.m.–8 p.m. (EST) time period, commonly referred to as *independent primetime*. The affiliates present a preponderance of news programming at this time of day. The independents counterprogram this older-skewing news programming with off-network reruns that appeal to children and younger adults. They move from pure children's programming to more adult-oriented programming as the hours grow later. This strategy can be illustrated by the July 1981 WNEW-TV (New York) schedule shown in Table 5-4.

WNEW began its key programming block at 4 p.m. with *The Brady Bunch*, a show chosen to appeal to children and teenagers. This type of program continued through 6 p.m., when *Chico and the Man*, a more adult-oriented offering, was presented. From 6:30 p.m. to 8:00 p.m. the appeal was to adults, with the top programs, *M*A*S*H* and *All in the Family*, placed head to head against the affiliates' network news broadcasts and access programming. Since the major market affiliates are precluded from using broadcasting off-network reruns in the access time period, the independents are able to win regularly at this time with their off-network product.

The independents continue this counterprogramming philosophy during network primetime and late fringe. They counterprogram the late news on the affiliates with another off-network rerun, one with a high young-adult appeal such as M*A*S*H or The Odd Couple. In conjunction with this tactic, they present their own primetime [10 p.m.–11 p.m. (EST)] news, preempting the affiliates' late news in the hope of attracting the early-to-bed set. In 1980, WPIX-TV in New York formed Independent Network News (INN) and began distributing its 10 p.m. news via satellite to independent stations around the country. One year later INN boasted a 57-station lineup with a monthly cumulative audience of 22 percent of all U.S. television households.

The two remaining major components of the independent station's lineup are syndicated talk shows, including The Phil Donahue Show, The Mike Douglas Show, and The Merv Griffin Show, and local sports programming. Local sports represent another logical counterprogramming weapon for independents. Network affiliates cannot provide enough time to cover the local sports franchise schedules effectively. Independents can provide this type of coverage, and usually they secure contracts with the local professional baseball, basketball, and hockey teams, as well as major colleges in their markets. Sports represent a competitive attraction for the male audience, even against the affiliate primetime programming.

A new and growing phenomenon is the joining of independent stations into ad hoc networks on a one-time-only basis for the presentation of a particular program. The most successful venture of this type to

TABLE 5-4
WNEW-TV WEEKDAY SCHEDULE,
JULY 1981

Time	Program
4:00–4:30 p.m.	The Brady Bunch
4:30–5:00 p.m.	Little Rascals
5:00–5:30 p.m.	The Brady Bunch
5:30–6:00 p.m.	Gilligan's Island
6:00–6:30 p.m.	Chico and the Man
6:30–7:00 p.m.	Carol Burnett and Friends
7:00–7:30 p.m.	M*A*S*H
7:30–8:00 p.m.	All in the Family

date has been Operation Prime Time (OPT). Operation Prime Time was formed in 1978. The concept involves convincing a number of independent stations to carry the program at approximately the same time, during the same week, to allow for effective national advertising.

The first OPT broadcast was in the fall of 1979. Subsequent productions included dramatizations of successful Gothic novels such as *Testimony of Two Men* and *The Damned* as well as special variety features. The OPT "Solid Gold" periodic review of popular music has been particularly successful. Many OPT and other ad hoc network programs have been able to generate network primetime-level ratings in the markets in which they are carried; the most successful of these programs have been able to obtain clearances in approximately 60 percent of the United States. This high clearance is obtained by adding to the base of independent stations with network affiliates which preempt their network to provide time for the OPT program.

Through the gradual upgrading of their programming, independent stations have been able to increase their share of viewing relative to the network affiliate competition; however, they in turn are being challenged by the new medium of cable. Local cable competition is particularly strong in the sports area; it has obtained many sports franchises.

Actually, the most serious current challenge to the independents from cable is a by-product of the independent station. The *superstation* is essentially an independent television station originating in one major market, but being fed by satellite to other markets throughout the country. WTBS-TV, Atlanta, owned by Turner Broadcasting, was the first superstation. Others include WGN-TV in Chicago and WOR-TV in New York. Currently, WTBS-TV is the only station that Nielsen measures regularly. Superstations compete with indigenous independent stations for audience in the markets into which they are fed by satellite. These stations, with programming similar to that of local affiliates, also offer the national advertiser an efficient way to reach audiences over a broad coverage area, although their coverage patterns are far from national.

STATION OWNERSHIP

A final criterion for the classification of television stations is the nature of their ownership. The FCC currently limits the ownership of television stations to five VHF and two UHF stations per owner. Each network owns five VHF stations. These stations are commonly referred to as network-owned and -operated stations, or network O&Os. All three networks include New York, Los Angeles, and Chicago stations in their portfolios. ABC-TV's two remaining stations are in Detroit and San Francisco, CBS-TV's are in Philadelphia and St. Louis, and NBC-TV's

TABLE 5-5
COVERAGE OF NETWORK-OWNED
STATIONS

Network	Station	Market	Net weekly circulation (000)	Percentage of U.S. television homes
CBS-TV	WCBS-TV	New York	6,342	
	KNXT-TV	Los Angeles	3,690	
	WBBM-TV	Chicago	2,653	
	WCAU-TV	Philadelphia	2,395	
	KMOX-TV	St. Louis	952	
		Five-station total	16,032	21.0
ABC-TV	WABC-TV	New York	5,984	
	KABC-TV	Los Angeles	3,725	
	WLS-TV	Chicago	2,666	
	WXYZ-TV	Detroit	1,703	
	KGO-TV	San Francisco	1,697	
		Five-station total	15,775	20.7
NBC-TV	WNBC-TV	New York	6,197	
	KNBC-TV	Los Angeles	3,742	
	WMAQ-TV	Chicago	2,620	
	WKYC-TV	Cleveland	1,338	
	WRC-TV	Washington, D.C.	1,333	
		Five-station total	15,230	20.0

Source: *Television Factbook*, Television Digest, Washington, 1981.

are in Cleveland and Washington, D.C. (See Table 5-5.) Both CBS-TV and NBC-TV tried their hands with UHF stations briefly, but they gave up these stations in 1959. Today no network owns a UHF station. Each network's five-station group covers more than 20 percent of all U.S. households, with the CBS O&Os leading in net weekly circulation.

In addition to the three networks there are more than 100 group *station owners*. These groups, combined with the networks, account for more than 400 commercial television stations, or more than half of all such stations in the United States. Table 5-6 presents the net weekly

TABLE 5-6
COVERAGE OF TOP FIVE
NONNETWORK STATION GROUPS

Group	No. of stations	Stations	Net weekly circulation (000)	Percentage of U.S. television homes
1. Metromedia	7	WNEW-TV (New York), KTTV (Los Angeles), WTTG (Washington, D.C.), KMBC (Kansas City), WTCN-TV (Minneapolis–St. Paul), WXIX (Cincinnati), KRIV-TV (Houston)	13,942	18.3
2. RKO	4	WOR-TV (New York), WNAC-TV (Boston), KHJ-TV (Los Angeles), WHBQ-TV (Memphis)	9,483	12.4
3. WGN-Continental	3	WGN-TV (Chicago), KWGN-TV (Denver), WPIX-TV (New York)	8,561	11.2
4. Westinghouse	5	WBZ-TV (Boston), KYW-TV (Philadelphia), KPIX-TV (San Francisco), KDKA (Pittsburgh), WJZ-TV (Baltimore)	8,495	11.1
5. Storer	7	WJBK-TV (Detroit), WJKW-TV (Cleveland), WAGA-TV (Atlanta), WITI (Milwaukee), WTVG (Toledo), WSBK-TV (Boston), KCST-TV (San Diego)	7,018	9.2

Source: *Television Factbook*, Television Digest, Washington, 1981.

circulation of the top five nonnetwork groups and a list of the stations comprising those groups. Note that Metromedia's net weekly circulation is comparable to that of the O&Os. The reason is that the Metromedia independent stations, such as WNEW-TV and KTTV, are carried outside their home markets via cable systems, which increases their potential audience substantially.

The rest of the U.S. commercial television stations are independently owned. Often these stations are part of local media operations that include radio stations, cable systems, and newspapers. The FCC no longer permits corporations to acquire television stations when the result would be this type of media cross-ownership; however, existing cross-ownership situations have been allowed to continue.

TELEVISION FACTBOOK LISTINGS

The annual *Television Factbook* provides for each television station a comprehensive list of coverage data, technical specifications, ownership information, network affiliation, network base hourly rates for affiliates, and net weekly circulation. A sample list for station KMOX-TV is shown in Figure 5-1.

TV STATION COMMERCIAL TIME FOR SALE

The two basic types of television stations, the network affiliate and the independent, offer substantially different menus of commercial availabilities to the advertiser. The actual number of commercials each type of station may offer for sale was established by the NAB code. The NAB code was discontinued in 1982; however, since the industry's commerical problem continues to follow the code specifications, those specifications are discussed here.

The NAB code was the official code of ethics for the television industry, established by the National Association of Broadcasters. Although a television station did not have to subscribe to the NAB code to remain on the air—it was a voluntary industry-created, not government-created, set of rules—most responsible broadcasters were subscribers. A list of these subscribers can be found in the *Television Factbook* (Services volume). The SRDS listings also give NAB code designations for subscribing stations.

The code set standards concerning the overall conduct of the broadcaster and, more specifically, what products could be advertised on television, what could be said about them, and how much advertising could be presented. The commercial load sections covered the amount of nonprogram material that could be broadcast, the amount of com-

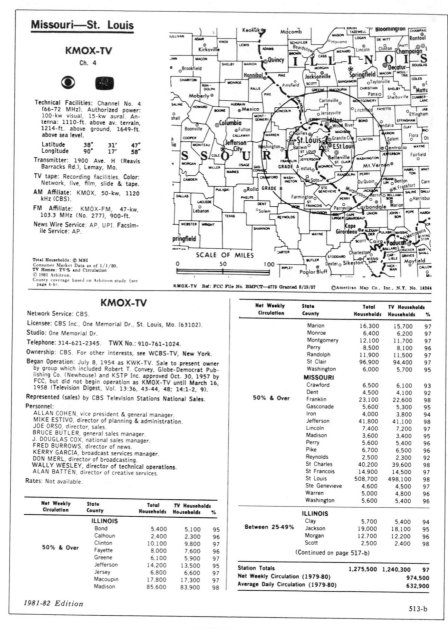

FIGURE 5-1

Sample *Television Factbook* listing.

(Reproduced with the permission of the American Map Corporation. Further reproduction prohibited.)

mercial material that could be broadcast, and the number of commercial announcements that could be broadcast consecutively. These standards varied by type of station and time of day. Nonprogram material was most limited during primetime and "children's time." Table 5-7 provides a detailed commercial pattern for both a network affiliate and an independent.

Stations could employ the *averaging* concept over the length of an individual program, exceeding the number of allowable interruptions or allowable commercial time during one part of the program as long as the average commercial time did not exceed the standards over the course of the entire program. News, weather, sports, and special events were exempt from the interruptions limitation, but not from the nonprogram material specifications. Public service announcements were not included in the consecutive announcement counts. In addition to these nonprogram material limits, credits had to be limited to 40 seconds for programs running less than 90 minutes and 60 seconds for those running 90 minutes or more.

The network affiliates' total inventory available for sale is also reduced by the network commercials they carry. The commercial loads for network programs vary by time period, program, and network. A typical network commercial time pattern would conform to that shown in Table 5-8. In primetime this time pattern would leave the affiliate with 3.5 minutes to work with each hour. However, the network also uses some time for promotional announcements. On average, the station winds up with 2.0 minutes to sell per hour. This time is most likely to be confined to the half-hour station break positions, since the networks use all the allowable in-program interruptions. Table 5-9 shows typical local-network commercial formats for each period programmed by the network.

Of course, all the inventory of the independent station is available for local sale (except when it is carrying a syndicated program with commercials inserted), and the local affiliate has total control over its local daypart inventory. The independent station counts heavily on the key area of "independent prime"—Monday through Friday, 4.p.m.–8 p.m. Local sports franchises are the other important source of independent revenue.

In summary, the local television marketer is composed of 757 commercial stations serving 211 separate markets, or ADIs. Station selection includes VHF and UHF, affiliates and independents, and group-owned as well as independently owned stations. Each has a unique profile, given its technical, managerial, and programming elements. And each station has its own commercial time limitations. The buyer of television time should take all these factors into account when dealing with that station.

TABLE 5-7

ALLOWABLE COMMERCIAL TIME ACCORDING TO THE NAB CODE

Stations	Promotional material and commercials	Program interruptions	Consecutive nonprogram announcements
Affiliates			
Primetime* Children's Saturday and Sunday†	9.5 minutes/hour and 0.5 minute promotion only	2 per half hour each program	5 nonprogram 4 commercial 3 station breaks
Children's Monday–Friday	12.0 minutes/hour	Same	Same
Other times	16.0 minutes/hour	4 per half hour each program	Same
Independents			
Primetime*	7.0 minutes per half hour	3 per half hour each program and 1 station break commercial	4 nonprogram
Children's†	Same as affiliates	Same as affiliates	Same as affiliates
Other times	8.0 minutes per half hour	Same	

*Primetime is defined as any 3 contiguous hours between 6 p.m. and midnight designated by the station.

†Children's time is any time during which programs initially designed primarily for children under age 12 are scheduled.

Source: The Television Code, 22d ed., National Association of Broadcasters, Washington, July 1981.

TABLE 5-8
TYPICAL NETWORK COMMERCIAL
TIME PATTERN

Daypart	Minutes of network commercials
Morning	5 per half hour
Monday–Friday daytime	6 per half hour
Early-evening news	5 per half hour
Primetime	3 per half hour
Late night	15 from 11:30 p.m. to 2 a.m.
Children's Saturday and Sunday	3.5 to 4 per half hour
Sports	4 per half hour

TABLE 5-9
TYPICAL LOCAL-NETWORK
ALLOCATION OF COMMERCIAL
TIME

Daypart	No. of minutes per hour	
	Network	Local
Morning	10.0	6.0
Daytime	12.0	2.0
Early-evening news	10.0	2.0
Sports	8.0	2.0
Primetime	6.0	2.0
Late night	10.0	6.0
Children's Saturday and Sunday	7.5	2.0

LOCAL-STATION MARKETPLACE

The local television marketplace is composed of two elements: the national spot television market and the local television market. The national spot television market includes all national advertisers using television advertising in one or more specific markets. These advertisers employ television in a given market or markets for various reasons:

- To supplement a network television campaign in key sales areas
- To compensate for low delivery of a network television campaign in certain markets
- To test-market new products
- To roll out a promising new product
- To test alternative media and/or creative strategies
- To obtain a more efficient alternative to network television when sales are concentrated in a limited number of markets

The local television market includes such local advertisers as banks, retailers, and local franchises.

For 1980 television station advertising revenues equaled $6.2 billion. The national spot television market accounted for 52 percent of this total, and the various local television markets, 48 percent. Since 1970 the mix of national spot and local advertising has been shifting toward local. Table 5-10 shows the revenue picture for 1970, 1975, and 1980. Local advertising moved from 30 percent of the total in 1970 to 48 percent in 1980. This local growth is concentrated in the retail sector. Retailers spend approximately $10 in newspapers for every $1 they spend in television. For this reason, stations have been focusing their developmental efforts against this segment.

TABLE 5-10
LOCAL TELEVISION STATION
ADVERTISING REVENUES

	Amount (000,000)			Percentage of total		
	1970	1975	1980	1970	1975	1980
National spot	$1234	$1623	$3244	70	55	52
Local	704	1334	2976	30	45	48

Source: "Publication title 2." Federal Communications Commission, Washington, 1982.

TABLE 5-11

TOP 10 NATIONAL SPOT
TELEVISION ADVERTISERS, 1980

Advertiser	Amount spent
1. Procter & Gamble	$125,243,500
2. General Foods	76,918,000
3. McDonald's	66,624,800
4. General Mills	61,104,300
5. Pepsico	55,640,500
6. AT&T	48,314,200
7. Coca-Cola	44,055,300
8. Lever Brothers	34,768,200
9. American Home Products	33,369,600
10. Mobil	30,814,800

Source: Quarterly press release, Television Bureau of Advertising, New York, 1981.

National Spot Television Marketplace

ADVERTISERS

Much like the network television marketplace, the national spot television marketplace is dominated by a small number of major advertisers represented by the large national advertising agencies. In 1980 the top 10 national spot advertisers (see Table 5-11) represented 15 percent of that market. Four of these advertisers were also on the network top 10 list that year, and eight made the national top 20 list. However, although the national spot market advertiser roster is topped by the same names as the network roster, the roster itself is much more extensive. In 1980, in the national spot television market 2598 advertisers were active, compared with the low 558 advertiser total in the network market.

SELLERS

The national spot market is certainly not concentrated on the seller side, with 757 commercial stations vying for national spot and local-market advertising dollars. Obviously, if a buyer for a major spot television advertiser such as Procter & Gamble had to deal with each station separately, the logistics of national spot buying would be prohibitive. National representative firms have been created to act as intermediaries between television stations and buyers and thus reduce the complex logistics of spot television buying. These firms represent many stations. Each has established markets in the major advertising centers. The buyer can negotiate the purchase of time on many stations in different markets through one of these representatives.

The *Television Factbook* lists 45 firms representing U.S. television stations. Three of the largest are John Blair, the Katz Agency, and Telerep. Blair represents 94 stations and has offices in 15 markets. Katz represents 125 stations and has offices in 18 markets. Telerep, owned by Cox Broadcasting, a major group station owner, represents 25 stations and has offices in 14 markets. Each of these representative firms performs the full selling function for its client stations. The major representative firms also provide extensive research, promotion, and MIS support to these stations. Some even have programming executives who offer program consultant services to stations. The representative firms are compensated on a negotiated commission basis. The commission can range from 5 to 20 percent, depending on the size of the station being represented.

Many major group station owners, such as the three network-owned station divisions, Metromedia, and Storer Broadcasting, have in-house national sales representatives. The network groups' national sales teams are allowed to represent only the network-owned stations; however, the other group-owned representatives can, and often do, represent outside stations as well.

BUYERS

Advertising Agencies   The top 10 agencies dominate national spot television buying to approximately the same degree that they dominate network television billings. These agencies represent 34 percent of national spot dollars, compared with 42 percent of network dollars. There is substantially less concentration, however, within the agencies.

Whereas network television buying decisions are made by a small number of senior media department specialists, often national spot television buying involves a vast cadre of buyers and assistant buyers. Spot-buying units usually are organized in one of two ways. In the *market specialist* organization, each buyer is assigned a market or group of markets. That buyer does all the buying for the agency's clients in that market. In the *account* assignment system, all buying responsibility for a particular account is put in the hands of a buyer.

The latter system is a holdover from the days when media planning and buying were integrated and often the responsibility of a single individual. Today buying and planning usually are separate units within the media department, and the buyers are not that involved in the development of a client's media strategy. As a result, the trend is toward the market specialist structure. This structure maximizes each buyer's negotiating clout with the stations, since it places a substantial number of market dollars under the specialist's control.

Media-Buying Services   Media-buying services are a significant factor in the national spot television market. They are specialty operations contracted to buy advertising space and time exclusively. These specialists first appeared in the late 1960s and early 1970s. At that time small creative specialty agencies known as "boutique" agencies were in vogue. These agencies had no service departments. The advertiser choosing to use a creative boutique for advertising production had to find some other agent to handle the media planning and buying function.

Media-buying services served that function. They worked both sides of the street, promoting themselves as media departments to the creative boutique agencies and as alternatives to full-service agency media departments to advertisers. In the latter case they emphasized how much more experience their older buyer staff had than the youth of the agency buyer corps. Many media-buying service principals were as talented in selling as in buying. Offering advertisers imaginative compensation arrangements, they found many willing clients.

Unfortunately, some of these organizations were founded by people wanting to make a lot of money fast, and they ran into the traditional financial problems associated with this type of enterpreneur. When a few major services declared bankruptcy, the media-buying service concept lost some of its luster. However, the well-run, well-financed services not only survived; they continue to thrive today. Such firms as Vitt Media, SFM, Ed Libov, and Cliff Botway provide their agency and advertiser clients with professional buying and planning in all media.

With the exception of Cliff Botway, which specializes in network television, these firms rely on national spot television buying as their major revenue producer. More and more small to medium-size agencies are finding that the well-managed media-buying service provides a breadth and quality of media service comparable to that of the top full-service agencies. As such, they are excellent complements to these smaller agencies, making them more competitive with the major agencies in the battle for accounts.

Market Characteristics

Geographically, national spot television buying is less concentrated than network buying and is more evenly spread among the regional

TABLE 5-12
TOP 50 MARKETS' SHARE OF TV HOUSEHOLDS VERSUS NATIONAL SPOT TV REVENUES, 1980

Market	Percentage of television homes	Percentage of national spot dollars	Market	Percentage of television homes	Percentage of national spot dollars	Market	Percentage of television homes	Percentage of national spot dollars
New York	8.4	7.3	Baltimore	1.1	1.2	Grand Rapids–Battle Creek–Kalamazoo	0.7	0.5
Los Angeles	5.3	6.7	Hartford–New Haven	1.0	0.8	Providence	0.7	0.5
Chicago	3.8	4.2	Denver	1.0	1.5	Oklahoma City	0.7	0.8
Philadelphia	3.2	2.9	Indianapolis	1.0	1.1	Orlando–Daytona Beach	0.6	0.7
San Francisco	2.5	3.4	Sacramento–Stockton	0.9	1.0	Raleigh–Durham	0.6	0.5
Boston	2.4	2.7	Portland, OR	0.9	1.0	Charleston–Huntington	0.6	0.4
Detroit	2.1	2.2	San Diego	0.9	1.0	Louisville	0.6	0.4
Washington, D.C.	1.8	2.0	Milwaukee	0.9	0.9	Dayton, OH	0.6	0.6
Cleveland	1.8	1.	Kansas City, MO	0.9	0.9	Harrisburg–York–Lancaster–Lebanon	0.6	0.5
Dallas–Ft. Worth	1.6	2.4	Cincinnati	0.9	1.0	Norfolk–Portsmouth–Newport News	0.6	0.5
Pittsburgh	1.5	1.5	Buffalo, NY	0.8	0.8	Salt Lake City	0.6	0.7
Houston	1.5	2.2	Nashville	0.8	0.6	Albany–Schenectady–Troy	0.6	0.5
Minneapolis–St. Paul	1.3	1.5	Phoenix	0.8	1.2	Birmingham, AL	0.6	0.5
St. Louis	1.3	1.5	Charlotte, NC	0.7	0.7	Wilkes-Barre–Scranton	0.6	0.3
Miami	1.2	1.8	New Orleans	0.7	0.9			
Atlanta	1.2	1.9	Columbus, OH	0.7	0.8			
Tampa–St. Petersburg	1.2	1.3	Greenville–Spartanburg–Ashville	0.7	0.5			
Seattle–Tacoma	1.2	1.5						

Source: Percentage of TV homes data: Arbitron, "ADI Market Rankings," New York, 1980–1981; data for percentage of national spot dollars: "Publication title?" FCC,

advertising centers, although New York and Chicago still are the major centers of buying activity. Detroit, Los Angeles, San Francisco, Atlanta, and Dallas are all significant spot television buying locations, and the major sales organizations have offices in all these markets.

Seasonality is more pronounced in the national spot television market than in the network market. The same basic pattern of strong second- and fourth-quarter demand and weaker first- and third-quarter demand holds; however, the differentials in demand are generally greater and vary by market. Growing sun belt markets such as Phoenix and San Diego, with their consistency of climatic conditions, are less susceptible to seasonal swings in demand than the established midwestern and northeastern markets.

This variation in seasonality by market is just one element of the major difference between network and national spot television, the substantial change in marketplace conditions as you move from one market to another. The national spot television market is not a single market; it is more than 200 markets, each unique. Individual market characteristics affect the relative amount of national spot television advertising dollars they attract. Table 5-12 lists the top 50 television markets and compares the percentage of television homes they represent with the percentage of national spot television revenues represented.

As a group, the top 50 markets represent a substantially greater percentage of national spot television dollars than of television homes. This is to be expected. However, the ratio varies substantially by market. Isolating three markets of comparable size—Phoenix; Columbus, Ohio; and Grand Rapids–Kalamazoo—shows Phoenix with a substantially greater percentage of national spot revenues than of U.S. television homes, Columbus with equal percentages of both, and Grand Rapids–Kalamazoo with a significantly lower percentage of national spot revenues than of U.S. television homes. The market dynamics behind these differing ratios are discussed in depth later in this chapter.

Local Advertising Marketplace

BUYERS

The local advertising marketplace is substantially more varied than the national spot television marketplace. Each individual market's local advertiser universe consists of a range of local businesses, from major retailers to "Ma and Pa" establishments. Major U.S. corporations are active in local television markets; but so are small family-owned concerns. Local television commercials range from the professionally produced six-figure variety to low-budget voice-over-slide treatments. Although the major local advertisers may be represented by a top national advertising agency, most rely on small local agencies or in-house operations for the creation and execution of their advertising programs.

The mix of large and small advertisers results in substantial variation in the composition of the local advertising marketplace. The "local" advertisers in major markets such as New York and Los Angeles are likely to be major national corporations or divisions of these corporations. These advertisers will have budgets similar to those of the large national spot television advertisers and most likely will be represented by major agencies. Production of their commercials often costs more than $100,000.

Just below these top 10 markets are a large number of smaller markets that still would earn the major market designation. Markets such as Atlanta, Houston, St. Louis, and Minneapolis–St. Paul can count many major U.S. corporations as part of their local television markets. These advertisers are more likely to be represented by local agencies that have grown substantially over the past decade as the markets matured into regional advertising centers.

Agencies such as Gardner Advertising in St. Louis, Tracy-Locke Advertising in Dallas, and McDonald & Little in Atlanta are today respected full-service agencies that have often competed successfully against the major agencies based in New York and Chicago for important national accounts. In fact, all three agencies were recently acquired by major New York agencies seeking outposts in these growing regional advertising centers (Gardner by Wells Rich Greene, Tracy-Locke by Ted Bates, and McDonald & Little by BBDO). These strong local agencies offer indigenous local advertisers the option of professional top-quality advertising support. Many of the larger advertisers have taken advantage of this opportunity; however, these markets still count on a good number of low-budget local retailers, with their minimum-cost commercials, for support.

Beyond market rank 100, the dependence of the indigenous local advertiser increases dramatically. Markets such as Sioux City, Reno, Nevada, and Corpus Christi have a local-to-national advertising revenue ratio of more than 2 to 1, compared with the overall average of approximately 1 to 1. And these accounts are truly local. In most cases their total advertising budget would not cover the production budgets of their major market counterparts. Voice-overs, slides, and local talent provide the basic commercial format many of these advertisers use.

One irony of the market-by-market variations in the television advertiser mix is that local major market businesses are less likely to enjoy the benefits of substantial television exposure than smaller market businesses. For example, a successful major market retail operation is likely to find television advertising in that market an unacceptable alternative because of the high cost of commercial production required to meet the creative standards of the market, the high unit cost of advertising time, and the waste involved in full-market television coverage when its trading area represents only a fraction of the entire market. In the smaller market, even the smallest retail operation usually can afford some television exposure, and the quality of that exposure is increasing. Local television stations are more and more able to provide the small-market advertiser with good-quality videotape production at low cost.

RETAIL SECTOR

A growing component of the local television marketplace is retail advertising. Table 5-13 lists the top 10 local advertising categories for the 75 markets measured by BAR in 1980. Just which categories represent the retail universe is the subject of some debate. Some would agree that all establishments selling directly to the consumer are retail establishments, and so all the categories shown, with the possible exception of radio stations and cable TV, should be included under the retail banner. Another point of view would limit the retail designation among these 10 categories to food stores, supermarkets, department stores, furniture

TABLE 5-13
TOP 10 LOCAL TELEVISION
ADVERTISER CATEGORIES, 1980

Category	Amount spent
1. Restaurants and drive-ins	$287,873,100
2. Food stores and supermarkets	148,708,600
3. Banks, savings and loans	140,948,200
4. Department stores	131,241,100
5. Furniture stores	111,420,100
6. Movies	102,401,400
7. Auto dealers	99,106,100
8. Discount department stores	73,505,400
9. Radio stations and cable TV	69,264,200
10. Amusements and entertainment	68,024,500

Source: Quarterly press release, Television Bureau of Advertising, New York, 1981.

stores, automotive dealers, and discount department stores. Added to this group would be the various specialty stores: drug, jewelry, dairy, carpet and floor covering, hardware, shoe, etc.

Whether the larger or smaller retail universe designation is selected, there is a pattern of growing television advertising activity in terms of the number of TV advertisers and the levels of investment in the medium. Former newspaper-only retail advertisers are moving to television as they observe the success of other retailers. A major industry effort, coordinated by the Television Bureau of Advertising (TVB), has made these advertisers more comfortable with the production and planning aspects of television advertising.

But perhaps the greatest impetus for local retail advertising on television has come from the growing availability of cooperative advertising funds from major national manufacturers or "vendors." These manufacturers offer attractive cooperative advertising allowances to local retailers as sales incentives. The allowances provide the manufacturer with valuable local television exposure for its product. They range from 100 percent funded national commercials that will be tagged with the retailer's message to matching-dollar arrangements for any retailer advertising that includes the manufacturer's product. An increasingly popular form of cooperative advertising is the doughnut commercial, which allows the retailer to open and close with a message. The vendor's product pitch falls in the middle of the commercial. Many vendors will actually have their agencies integrate the elements for the retailer.

Local retailers use these cooperative funds to build major campaigns. A local department store might employ cooperative funds from several vendors to develop an event promotion, such as a Mother's Day campaign featuring gift items for women.

SELLERS

Local advertising time is sold by the local sales force of each television station. As the advertisers and agencies vary in sophistication by market, so, too, do the seller organizations. A local advertiser purchasing time in a top 10 market deals with a sales organization consisting of several managerial levels, a large number of sales account executives, and a support operation that includes research and promotion specialists. If the advertiser is a retailer, there is a retail specialist, or perhaps an entire retail sales department, to address that advertiser's particular needs.

As the markets get smaller, so do the breadth and depth of the station sales organizations. Beyond market 50, stations are more likely to rely on their national representatives for research and promotion support, and several managerial levels will not be in evidence. Beyond market

100, the sales force may consist of just one manager and a small number of account executives. Often these executives have station responsibilities other than sales.

Although the small-market sales representative may lack the sophisticated support of the large-market account executive, more than likely she or he will be familiar with production techniques. These executives know that often a sale is contingent on helping prospective advertisers to create a commercial. The prospective advertisers' need, coupled with access to station production personnel and equipment, has made them virtual in-house creative departments for their clients.

MARKET CONFIGURATION

Whether it is a national spot television advertiser considering spot television advertising in a specific market as part of a national campaign or a local advertiser just interested in advertising in that market alone, it is vital that the advertiser understand the unique dynamics of the particular market. The one thing clear to anyone involved in television advertising over a range of markets is that there are substantial variations in the configurations, television economies, and television advertising universes. Also the advertiser must be sensitive to the intramarket changes from season to season. An in-depth comparison of the New York and St. Louis markets will illustrate these phenomena.

New York is served by six commercial television stations, three network affiliates and three independent stations. This market also has a public broadcasting station and several UHF stations serving either a portion of the total market or, in the case of WXTV, the Spanish-speaking UHF station, a particular segment of the market. In this analysis we focus on the six general market commercial VHF stations.

St. Louis also is served by three network affiliates. These affiliates are supplemented by two independent stations, one VHF (KPLR) and one UHF (KDNL). Cable television penetration is 15 percent in New York and 3 percent in St. Louis. These figures compare with a national level of more than 20 percent.

Another aspect of market configuration is time zone. New York is an Eastern standard time zone market following the television scheduling pattern of the east and west coasts. St. Louis is a Central time zone market following the pattern of the midwest. (See Table 5-14.)

TV ECONOMY

In 1980 the New York market represented 8.4 percent of all U.S. television homes; yet this market accounted for only 7.3 percent of all television station advertising revenues. St. Louis represented 1.25 per-

TABLE 5-14
NEW YORK AND ST. LOUIS
TELEVISION SCHEDULING
PATTERNS

Time period	New York	St. Louis
Daytime	9:00 a.m.–4:30 p.m.	9:00 a.m.–3:30 p.m.
Early fringe	4:30 p.m.–7:30 p.m.	3:30 p.m.–6:30 p.m.
Prime access	7:30 p.m.–8:00 p.m.	6:30 p.m.–7:00 p.m.
Primetime	8:00 p.m.–11:00 p.m.*	7:00 p.m.–10:00 p.m.*
Late news	11:00 p.m.–11:30 p.m.	10:00 p.m.–10:30 p.m.
Late fringe	11:30 p.m.–2:00 a.m.	10:30 p.m.–1:00 a.m.
Independent primetime	5:00 p.m.–8:00 p.m.	4:00 p.m.–7:00 p.m.

*Begins 1 hour earlier on Sunday.

cent of all U.S. television and 1.36 percent of all television station advertising revenues. These numbers translate to $66.18 in revenues per TV home for St. Louis and $57.24 for New York. St. Louis ranks thirty-first among the 132 ADIs for which FCC data are available. New York ranks sixty-fourth.

The New York figures would suggest a relatively depressed TV economy; however, New York represents a larger number of TV households. The St. Louis ratio of revenue to TV homes is about average for a top 50 market. Further analysis will demonstrate that these market conditions are largely explained by CPM variations that are as much the result of market dynamics as of economic conditions.

ADVERTISER UNIVERSE

The New York market derives 51.9 percent of its revenues from the national spot television marketplace and 48.1 percent from the local marketplace, while the St. Louis market shows a split of 56.3 percent national spot and 43.7 percent local. On the surface, these distributions are fairly consistent; however, a closer look unveils some substantial variations. Isolating the high-demand months of May and November reveals two very different market profiles. First, let us look at May.

Table 5-15 presents the top 20 product categories for each market in May 1980. Each market has six categories on its top 20 list that do not

	St. Louis	Amount spent (000)	New York	Amount spent (000)
1.	Restaurants and drive-ins	$143.4	Airlines	$ 1,825.2
2.	Appliance–carpet–furniture stores	142.1	Carbonated soft drinks	1,388.9
3.	Department and discount stores	131.8	Amusements and entertainment	1,287.5
4.	Beer	96.8	Restaurants and drive-ins	1,076.1
5.	Movies	91.2	Department and discount stores	959.6
6.	Banks	58.9	Passenger cars, imported	906.3
7.	Garden supplies and machinery	50.7	Games and toys	790.9
8.	Carbonated soft drinks	45.9	Watches	785.1
9.	Home improvement and building supplies	43.1	Banks	737.1
10.	Watches	38.2	Coffee, tea	689.7
11.	Food stores	35.6	Appliance–carpet–furniture stores	668.4
12.	Meats, fish, poultry	35.4	Passenger cars, domestic	608.1
13.	Candy and gum	34.4	Radio and TV stations	603.5
14.	Games and toys	32.6	Cameras, film	581.4
15.	Airlines	30.6	Wines	560.0
16.	Auto and truck dealers	30.5	Meat, fish, poultry	492.8
17.	Hotels and resorts	30.4	Candy and gum	489.9
18.	Amusements and entertainment	28.8	Movies	474.9
19.	Passenger cars, domestic	28.6	Clothing stores	427.5
20.	Cereals	28.3	Food stores	423.7
	Total	$1,157.3	Total	$15,776.6
	Percentage of market dollars	53.8	Percentage of market dollars	48.0

Source: Broadcast Advertisers Reports, "Local Market Reports," New York, 1980.

TABLE 5-16

NEW YORK AND ST. LOUIS TOP 20
ADVERTISERS FOR MAY 1980

St. Louis	Amount spent (000)	New York	Amount spent (000)
1. Target Stores	$ 37.5*	TWA	$ 556.9
2. *Silent Screen* (movie)	34.2	McDonald's	458.8
3. Busch Beer	29.2	American Express card	357.2
4. McDonald's	27.9	American Airlines	354.5
5. Wal-Mart Discount Store	24.9*	Oldsmobile dealers	285.7*
6. Burger Chef	23.8	Pathmark Supermarkets	237.7*
7. Schnuck Supermarkets	23.8*	Mello Yello soda	237.2
8. *Carney* (movie)	22.5	Channel Home Centers	228.3*
9. Kroger Supermarkets	22.4*	Jordache jeans	223.0
10. Coors beer	21.3	Pepsico	223.0
11. Ozark Vacations	20.2*	Eastern Airlines	221.7
12. Pepsico	19.8	United Airlines	221.1
13. Amoco	18.0	Buick	210.8
14. Six Flags Amusement Park	17.6*	Burger King	202.9
15. Tile Town Carpets	17.6*	Chevrolet	.190.3
16. J. C. Penney	16.6*	Kaufman Carpet	189.0*
17. Pat Riley Appliances	15.6*	Chase Bank	179.1*
18. TWA	14.7	Volkswagen	179.1
19. Mercury automobiles	14.7	Macy's	173.7*
20. K Mart	14.5*	Scott lawn products	168.9
Total	$436.1	Total	$5098.9
Percentage of market dollars	20.3	Percentage of market dollars	15.5

*Retail.

Source: Broadcast Advertisers Reports, "Local Market Reports," New York, 1980.

appear on the other market's list. For the remaining 14 categories the average variation in rank is seven places. A comparison of the two markets' exclusive top 20 entries provides valuable insight into the overall advertising profile for that market. New York includes imported passenger cars among its top 20 categories; St. Louis has auto and truck dealers. Both have domestic passenger cars. New York has cameras and film; St. Louis has garden supplies and machinery as well as home improvement and building supplies. New York has wine and coffee and tea; St. Louis has beer.

Narrowing the focus more, to individual advertisers, shows even greater diversity. (See Table 5-16.) Only two advertisers make both top 20 lists. Pepsico and McDonald's. St. Louis counts 10 local advertisers among its top 20, whereas New York only shows 6. The top 20 advertisers in St. Louis represent 20.3 percent of total market revenues, substantially more than the 15.5 percent of New York's top 20. Finally, the retail sector is much more important in St. Louis. The leading St. Louis advertiser in May was a retailer, Target Stores. Eight of the 10 local advertisers in the top 20 were retailers. In all, 19.9 percent of all St. Louis advertising revenues for May 1980 came from the retail sector. In contrast, only four retailers made the New York top 20. In total, retail represented only 10.5 percent of New York market revenue for May 1980. (See Table 5-17.)

Tables 5-18 and 5-19 present the same top 20 profiles for November 1980. The differentials are even greater. Eight of the top 20 categories on each market's list did not make the other market's list. Perhaps the most notable was sportswear, the number two category in New York. This was composed primarily of designer jeans advertising. None of the top jeans manufacturers active in New York was advertising in St. Louis at this time.

Among the top 20 advertisers in New York or St. Louis, only Ford made both lists. St. Louis numbered 11 local advertisers among its top 20, compared with only 8 for New York. The top 20 advertisers represented 21.7 percent of all St. Louis revenues, slightly higher than

TABLE 5-17

NEW YORK AND ST. LOUIS RETAIL
ADVERTISING REVENUES FOR
MAY AND NOVEMBER 1980

	New York		St. Louis	
	May	November	May	November
Total market dollars (000)	$32,986.0	$39,814.4	$2,149.4	$2,210.8
Total retail dollars (000)	3,461.9	6,020.7	427.9	465.8
Retail as a percentage of total	10.5	15.1	19.9	21.1

Source: Broadcast Advertisers Reports, "Local Market Reports," New York, 1980.

TABLE 5-18
NEW YORK AND ST. LOUIS TOP 20
CATEGORIES FOR NOVEMBER 1980

St. Louis	Amount spent (000)	New York	Amc spe (00
1. Restaurants and drive-ins	$ 182.2	Games and toys	$ 3,
2. Department and discount stores	165.0	Sportswear	2,
3. Games and toys	130.8	Department and discount stores	1,
4. Appliance–carpet–furniture stores	122.8	Restaurants and drive-ins	1,
5. Banks	79.9	Wines	1,
6. Beer	61.1	Airlines	1,
7. Radio and TV stations	59.6	Banks	1,
8. Auto and truck dealers	52.1	Amusements and entertainment	
9. Movies	48.7	Passenger cars, domestic	
10. Cereals	40.9	Sports–hobby–toy stores	
11. Food stores	40.3	Radio and TV stations	
12. Magazines and other media	38.9	Movies	
13. Watches	33.8	Watches	
14. Passenger cars, domestic	33.8	Coffee, tea	
15. Carbonated soft drinks	29.9	Appliance–carpet–furniture stores	
16. Amusements and entertainment	29.6	Cameras	
17. Meat, fish, poultry	29.0	Passenger cars, imported	
18. Small appliances— miscellaneous	25.5	Clothing stores	
19. Fire and casualty insurance	23.9	Food stores	
20. Shampoos, rinses	22.7	Magazines and other media	
Total	$1,250.5	Total	$21
Percentage of market dollars	56.6	Percentage of market dollars	

Source: Broadcast Advertisers Reports,"Local Market Reports," New York, 1980.

TABLE 5-19
W YORK AND ST. LOUIS TOP 20
DVERTISERS FOR NOVEMBER 1980

St. Louis	Amount spent (000)	New York	Amount spent (000)
Wal-Mart	$ 67.3*	McDonald's	$ 528.8
Southwestern Bell	40.7*	Toys "Я" Us	455.2*
Famous Barr	35.7*	New York Telephone	387.2*
Yellow Pages	27.8	Calvin Klein jeans	314.0
Schnuck Supermarkets	27.4*	Pathmark Supermarkets	294.8*
Mercantile Trust	26.4*	Kaufman Carpet	288.0*
Target stores	25.4*	American Airlines	287.5
Burger Chef	21.4	American Express card	258.6
Coal Miner's Daughter (movie)	20.5	Burger King	241.5
Kentucky Fried Chicken	19.1	Ford	238.0
Mark Twain Bank	18.5*	Gimbels	232.0*
WRTH radio	17.9*	Concord Watches	230.0
Ford	17.6	New York Daily News	230.0*
Pat Riley Appliances	17.5*	Two Guys	230.0*
Kroger Supermarkets	16.9*	Sasson sportswear	222.6
Cinnabar fragrance	16.8	Abraham & Straus	217.0*
Lou Fusz Motors	16.0*	Pepsico	212.0
Red Lobster Inns	15.6	Gloria Vanderbilt sportswear	209.4
Hangar 18 (movie)	15.2	TV Guide	204.2
Ground Round	15.0	United Airlines	195.3
Total	$478.7	Total	$5476.1
Percentage of market dollars	21.7	Percentage of market dollars	13.8

Broadcast Advertisers Reports, "Local Market Reports," New York, 1980.

their 20.3 percent May total. The New York top 20 represented only 13.8 percent of that market's November revenues, slightly lower than the 15.5 percent May figure. As would be expected in this pre-Christmas month, retailers were more important in both markets; however, they remained a more significant factor in St. Louis than in New York.

New York is a distinctive market; therefore, it is not surprising to find its advertiser mix quite different from that of St. Louis. However, this distinctiveness is not confined to New York. Each market is likely to have unique characteristics that will affect its advertiser mix. Los Angeles is certainly different from New York, not to mention from San Francisco, its neighbor to the north. Sun belt market profiles are quite at variance with those of the more established northeastern and midwestern markets. Even a market such as Fort Wayne, Indiana, a market expected to be "typical," has its uniqueness. In this case, Fort Wayne is so typical that national advertisers use it widely as a test market, making its advertiser mix anything but typical.

The wise marketer examines the advertiser mix of each market before investing advertising dollars. This examination should provide valuable insight into the composition of the market's consumer marketing universe, the image and market strength of the key retail operations, and the competitive environment in which they must compete.

INTRAMARKET CHANGE

Close examination of Tables 5-15 to 5-19 will uncover dramatic change in the advertiser mix for both markets from May to November. This seasonal change is often more pronounced than the market-to-market variations for any given time.

In St. Louis only six advertisers appeared on the top 20 list in both May and November. For New York the number was seven. In terms of product categories, the changes were less dramatic, but nevertheless substantial. In St. Louis five categories made the top 20 in only one of the two months, and the average rank variation from May to November was four places. In New York only 3 of the top 20 in each month did not make the list in the other month; the remaining 17 shifted an average of four rank places. Intramarket change in the advertiser mix is important to the prospective advertiser for not only the reasons just mentioned. This change affects the overall demand for television time, which in turn affects the pricing of the stations.

This introduces the most important television marketplace variable, the significant differentials in CPM among markets and within the market by time of year.

PRICING ELEMENT

In Chapter 2 the cost-per-thousand (CPM) measure was introduced. The CPM is the basic evaluative measure in buying and selling television time, and so it is used to compare the relative efficiency of television advertising in different markets and at various times of the year in each market.

CPM VARIATIONS BY MARKET

The St. Louis–New York comparison also illustrates the nature of CPM variation by market. Comparing New York and St. Louis CPMs for the first and fourth quarters of 1980 demonstrates the intermarket volatility in the cost of television advertising. (See Table 5-20.)

St. Louis CPMs are just about average for a top 50 market. New York CPMs are the lowest of the top 50 markets. Examination of Table 5-20 shows the average St. Louis CPM to have been 22 percent higher than the average New York CPM during the first quarter of 1980. This variation was highest for the daytime and early fringe dayparts— + 58 percent—and lowest for primetime—2 percent. During the fourth quarter, the St. Louis CPM premium increased to 33 percent on average. Daytime remained the daypart of greatest variation and primetime the daypart of lowest variation.

Table 5-21 compares the first- and fourth-quarter CPMs for each market by daypart. With fourth-quarter CPMs set at a base index of 100, the first-quarter indices are 86 for New York and 78 for St. Louis. The largest New York intramarket variation is in early fringe, and the largest St. Louis variation is in early news. Both these dayparts are characterized by high inventory levels, increased first-quarter audience levels, and older audience profiles. The result is a large supply of a low-demand audience segment. So it is not surprising that these dayparts are the most price-elastic in a relatively low demand period.

If we turn to the between-market variation, the news dayparts show substantially less swing from fourth-quarter to first-quarter in New York than in St. Louis. The explanation is related to the explanation of the low overall New York CPM. With three strong independents challenging the three affiliates, New York is one of the most competitive local television advertising markets. The fragmentation of the television audience in this market results in relatively low average-audience levels. When demand is high and audience levels are average or below average, the demand in this market allows the stations to sell all or at least most of their inventory at good prices. When demand is low and audience levels are high, as is the case in the first quarter, advertisers seek fewer gross rating points (GRPs) and find they can get more GRPs per unit

TABLE 5-20
NEW YORK AND ST. LOUIS CPM
COMPARISON, 1980

	First quarter			Fourth quarter		
	New York	St. Louis	St. Louis/N.Y. index	New York	St. Louis	St. Louis/N.Y. index
Daytime	$1.45	$2.29	158	$1.66	$2.79	168
Early fringe	1.58	2.49	158	2.06	3.18	154
Early news	2.32	2.59	112	2.45	3.68	150
Primetime	4.88	4.98	102	5.64	6.17	109
Late news	3.46	3.78	109	4.05	4.98	123
Late fringe	2.29	3.28	143	2.77	3.98	144
Average	2.66	3.24	122	3.11	4.13	133

Note: In this table and Tables 5-21 to 5-23, the cost per point is divided by the ADI homes per point, to yield the CPM.
Source: *Media Market Guide*, 1980.

TABLE 5-21
NEW YORK AND ST. LOUIS CPM
INDEX: FIRST QUARTER VERSUS
FOURTH QUARTER (100)

	New York	St. Louis
Daytime	87	82
Early fringe	77	78
Early news	95	70
Primetime	87	81
Late news	85	76
Late fringe	83	82
Average	86	78

Source: *Media Market Guide*, 1980.

purchased. As a result, the demand level does not allow all the stations to sell all their inventory, and there is heavy discounting.

However, the independent stations are less competitive in the news area than in the entertainment area, and so the news dayparts are less affected by the seasonal shifts in New York demand. The impact on late news is greater than that on early news because the limited inventory in that daypart pushes prices somewhat higher in the high-demand fourth quarter.

Why, then, is the opposite true in St. Louis? In this market, the news dayparts show the biggest swings in CPM from the fourth to the first quarter. Given that in every market a base of news advertisers exists, a certain level of demand for units in this daypart is always present. However, to the extent that this demand is measured in GRPs, the higher the average program rating, the less unit demand it will represent.

In St. Louis news ratings are quite high, with the top-ranking late news actually outperforming the average primetime program. These news ratings are highest during the first quarter, when demand is the lowest. They are substantially higher than the average New York news ratings. If we assume that the base of news advertisers in St. Louis is no greater than it is in New York, it will take substantially fewer news units in that market to satisfy demand than in New York. This differential will be most significant during low-demand periods, causing greater than proportionate pressure on prices.

Also, the higher St. Louis rating level for news makes this daypart a suitable alternative to primetime. Affiliates in this market can incorporate news into primetime packages with programs carrying substantially higher CPMs. The relatively low news ratings in New York do not allow for this type of packaging. In the fourth quarter, when primetime inventory is scarce, St. Louis affiliates can obtain a premium for news that their New York counterparts cannot command.

This St. Louis–New York comparison elucidates the variations in local-market television costs by market and between markets by season. Also spot television market pricing has revealed substantial daypart CPM differentials. In both markets the primetime CPM is far higher than that of the other five dayparts (+119 percent in New York and +69 percent in St. Louis). Daytime represents the other extreme. These large variations in CPM are explained by audience composition. Primetime offers the advertiser a dual adult audience, a better socioeconomic audience profile, a younger adult audience, and greater market penetration than the other dayparts.

The New York–St. Louis comparison was meant to illustrate relative marketplace conditions; however, a truly meaningful analysis of the local television market requires a broader perspective. Table 5-22 provides the 1980 annual average CPMs for the top 50 markets. Reviewing this table shows St. Louis to be an average CPM market, ranking twenty-fourth among the 50, with a $4.05 CPM versus the $4.10 average. New York, as mentioned, was in last place, with a low $2.85 CPM, whereas markets such as Baltimore and San Diego were more than double the New York level, at $6.75 and $6.15, respectively. Table 5-23 provides individual daypart indexes based on the $4.10 top 100 market annual average CPM.

By comparing high-CPM markets such as Dallas and San Diego with low-CPM markets such as Cleveland and Memphis, it is obvious that the overall vitality and growth of a market affect the demand for television time and, therefore, the relative CPM level for that market. However, this alone does not completely explain CPM variation. Baltimore is certainly not the most vital U.S. market today, and Kansas City is certainly a much stronger market economically than its low CPM level would indicate. Many other variables come into play, all having a role in the dynamics of each television marketplace.

Market Dynamics

In 1975 I conducted an extensive analysis of marketplace conditions in 22 major television markets, with the objective of isolating the variables that influenced the level of television station revenues. Using

TABLE 5-22
'ERAGE 1980 CPM FOR TOP 50
MARKETS

Market	CPM		Market	CPM
Baltimore	$6.75	26.	Indianapolis	4.05
San Diego	6.15	27.	Detroit	4.00
Dallas–Ft. Worth	6.10	28.	Oklahoma City	4.00
Houston	5.90	29.	Providence	3.90
Boston	5.50	30.	New Orleans	3.90
Denver	5.20	31.	Cincinnati	3.85
San Francisco	5.20	32.	Nashville	3.85
Phoenix	5.15	33.	Buffalo	3.80
		34.	Chicago	3.80
Washington, D.C.	5.00	35.	Grand Rapids–Kalamazoo–	3.80
Hartford–New Haven	5.00		Battle Creek	
Miami	4.90	36.	Albany–Schenectady–Troy	3.75
Portland, OR	4.65	37.	Birmingham	3.75
		38.	Louisville	3.70
Atlanta	4.65	39.	Greenville–Spartanburg–	3.50
Seattle–Tacoma	4.65		Asheville, NC	
Pittsburgh	4.55	40.	Raleigh–Durham	3.40
		41.	Los Angeles	3.40
Minneapolis–St. Paul	4.50	42.	Harrisburg–York–Lancaster–	3.40
			Lebanon, PA	
Sacramento–Stockton	4.50	43.	Norfolk–Portsmouth–Newport	3.35
Columbus, OH	4.35		News–High Point, VA	
Salt Lake City	4.35	44.	Milwaukee	3.30
Philadelphia	4.25	45.	Kansas City	3.30
Charlotte	4.25	46.	Wilkes-Barre–Scranton, PA	3.20
Tampa–St. Petersburg	4.20	47.	Memphis	3.10
Orlando–Daytona Beach	4.05	48.	Cleveland	3.10
St. Louis	4.05	49.	Charleston–Huntington	2.90
Dayton	4.05	50.	New York	2.85

Media Market Guide, 1980. Adjusted to obtain annual average. Top 50 average = $4.10. Top 100 average

TABLE 5-23
TOP 100 MARKET AVERAGE
DAYPART INDEXES

Daypart	Index
Daytime	60.0
Early evening	72.5
Early news	85.0
Primetime	170.0
Late news	120.0
Late evening	97.5

Source: *Media Market Guide*, 1980.
Base CPM of $4.10 = 100 index.

stepwise regression analysis techniques made it possible to measure the relationship between a number of dependent variables and the relative level of television advertising dollars in a market. Separate regression equations were developed for the national spot television advertising and the local advertising components of market revenues. A brief synopsis of the findings follows.

NATIONAL SPOT TELEVISION ADVERTISING

The two variables found to best predict relative national spot television revenues (expressed as the percentage of national spot television revenues over the percentage of television homes) were the market's buying power index and the market's CPM index.

The *buying power index* (BPI) is the annual measure of relative economic vitality developed by *Sales and Marketing Management* magazine and published in its annual *Survey of Buying Power*. It is a composite of each market's percentage of U.S. disposable income (50 percent weight), percentage of U.S. retail expenditures (30 percent weight), and percentage of population (20 percent weight). A high BPI represents extraordinary economic vitality in that market. It is not surprising that this variable is a powerful predictor of the relative national spot television expenditures in a market, since advertising investments are usually related to sales and a high BPI indicates a high level of consumer sales activity.

The CPM *index* is simply the CPM of market over the average CPM for all 22 markets. A high CPM index correlates with a high level of national spot television investment. The underlying relationship between these variables is less clear-cut than the BPI-revenue relationship. First, the cause-and-effect relationship is subject to challenge. One could argue that a high level of investment yields a high CPM, and not vice versa. Second, logic would say that a relatively low CPM in an economically strong market (high BPI) would attract national advertising dollars. Nevertheless, the regression analysis showed the CPM index to be a positively correlated independent variable in the national spot revenue equation when the BPI impact was taken into account.

LOCAL ADVERTISING REVENUE

The local advertising revenue component of the market dynamics equation is more complex. The local television revenue index (percentage of local television dollars over percentage of U.S. television homes) is highly influenced by the newspaper advertising variables for each market. Independent variables shown to be predictors of the local television revenue index include:

- The relative index of per-home newspaper advertising revenues
- The number of major newspapers in the market
- The percentage of gross circulation accounted for by the leading newspaper in the market
- Relative market growth
- The CPM index

These findings illustrate the fact that each market's local advertising economy is essentially newspaper-based. Newspapers preceded television and still constitute the dominant local advertising medium in all markets.

The newspaper-related variables studied reflect the relative efficiency of newspaper versus television advertising in a market. The number of newspapers required to cover a market has two effects on local television advertising investments. First, the more papers that are required, the higher the newspaper advertising base. Local advertisers pay what they must to reach their market effectively. If the competitive newspaper configuration requires them to buy advertising space in four papers to obtain full market exposure, they buy space in all four papers.

If one paper alone covers the entire market, they can afford to buy only that one paper. Thus a market such as Atlanta, with its one-paper dominance *(Atlanta Constitution/Journal)*, requires lower advertising budgets than a market such as Dallas–Ft. Worth, where four papers are required to cover the market fully.

Second, since television stations initially had to draw advertising dollars from this newspaper base, the higher the base, the greater the potential dollars for conversion to television. And, of course, more papers meant a less efficient newspaper advertising alternative, which increases the attractiveness of television, with its total market penetration. The relationship between the relative circulation of the leading newspaper and local television advertising is tied to this same competitive situation. The more dominant a single paper in a market, the more expendable the other papers will be to the advertiser, which makes it easier for the local television stations to convince that advertiser to drop those papers in favor of television.

The CPM index was the only nonnewspaper-related variable in the local television advertising revenue equation. The relationship between a high CPM and high local television advertising revenues is more easily understood than the relationship between this variable and national spot television revenues. Local advertisers are not allocating advertising dollars among markets. By necessity, they must invest advertising dollars in the local market in which they do business. There is no competition with other markets on either sales potential or cost-efficiency grounds. Instead, the television stations in a given market need only prove their relative efficiency versus newspapers. Since this efficiency advantage is usually considerable, it does not result in significant downward pressure on the CPM. In most cases, the local advertisers exhibit inelastic demand for local television time. So a market with a high CPM base will attract relatively more dollars from the total advertising universe.

CPM FACTOR

The CPM index emerged as a powerful predictor of both relative national spot television revenues and local television revenues; yet some question remains as to the causal relationship between CPM and relative revenues. An argument can be made that a high CPM index is a function of, not a cause of, high television advertising revenues. To test this argument, a third series of regression equations was generated, with the CPM index as the dependent variable. The key explanatory variables uncovered were not the relative national spot television or local television advertising variables; they were:

- The ratio of national spot TV dollars per home to local TV dollars per home

- The relative overall TV viewing level in the market

- The share of the leading independent television station in the market

The resulting equation defined the high-CPM-index market as one that has a relatively low TV viewing level and lacks a strong independent station. The ratio of national spot dollars per home to local dollars per home had an inverse relationship with the CPM index. First, the ratio of national spot to local is consistent with that uncovered in the individual revenue equations. The greater the local advertising base, the more inelastic component of the overall television advertising revenue, the stronger the underlying support for the prevailing CPM. High dependence on the national spot revenue component will require maintenance of a CPM level competitive with that of other television market alternatives, resulting in downward pressure on the CPM.

The remaining two variables, a low viewing level and the lack of a strong independent station, reduce the supply of inventory and the alternative suppliers of that inventory, respectively. Maintenance of a high CPM requires maintenance of full-demand or near full-demand conditions. This is easier in markets of relatively low inventory (audience) concentrated in the control of the three affiliates.

Table 5-24 provides the 1975 dynamics rankings resulting from the analysis. This table also shows the 1980 relative rankings of these 21 markets based on CPM (see Table 5-22). A comparison of the two ranks proves that the 1975 dynamics equations are still effective in differentiating between high- and low-CPM markets. However, there are some notable exceptions. Baltimore and Boston seem to be realizing CPM premiums far above those predicted by the equations, while the Los Angeles CPM is far lower than expected. Unusual market conditions help explain these deviations.

Both Baltimore and Boston generate high relative national spot television dollars. Approximately 60 percent of all Baltimore revenue is from the national spot market. The figure is even higher—65 percent—for Boston. The reason for these high levels lies in the bonus coverage national advertisers receive when they advertise in these markets. Baltimore stations reach outside their own ADI into the suburban bedroom communities of Washington, D.C. Washington, D.C., itself has a high national spot television base (63 percent of all revenues). Both markets benefit from corporations' desire to communicate with the nation's leaders.

TABLE 5-24

1975 DYNAMICS VERSUS 1980 CPM
RANKINGS

1975 Dynamics equation ranking*	Market	1980 CPM ranking†
1	San Francisco	6
2	Miami	8
3	Denver	5
4	Houston	3
5	Los Angeles	19
6	Atlanta	9
7	Baltimore	1
8	Indianapolis	15
9	Washington, D.C.	7
10	Dallas–Ft. Worth	2
11	Seattle	10
12	Minneapolis–St. Paul	12
13	Boston	4
14	Chicago	18
15	Buffalo	17
16	Detroit	16
17	St. Louis	14
18	Philadelphia	13
19	Pittsburgh	11
20	Cleveland	20
21	New York	21

*Dynamics ranking is a weighted average of national spot TV revenue index (0.50 weight), local TV revenue index (0.25 weight), and CPM index (0.25 weight) as predicted by the dynamics equations.

†1980 CPM is the ranking from highest to lowest CPM among these 21 markets, based on Table 5-22 CPMs.

Boston's bonus coverage emanates from its position as the business and cultural center of New England. Boston is the focus of interest for all New Englanders. The geographic concentration of this region and strong cable television penetration allow Boston stations to reach audiences far beyond the boundaries of its ADI. For this reason many national advertisers look at Boston as a one-market regional buy. They purchase Boston television to cover New England.

The depressed Los Angeles CPM can be traced to this market's unique independent station competition. Los Angeles is the only market with four competitive VHF independent stations. These stations collectively represent the highest independent station share for any market; yet, since it is split four ways, no one station gets the high share that would affect the CPM index equation. The advertiser in Los Angeles has seven viable sources of television time. This high degree of competition maintains constant downward pressure on the Los Angeles CPM.

New York CPM levels also are affected by intense independent station competition. In New York this competitive condition is compounded by high unit costs. New York unit prices are 33 percent higher than those of Los Angeles, the number two market. These high prices deter local spending. Few New York retail operations have the broad market coverage that would be required for all New York ADI viewers to represent potential customers. The combination of high unit costs and substantial waste coverage has slowed the investment of retail dollars in New York television. There are not likely to be many small retailers such as car dealers or specialty stores advertising on New York television, whereas this type of advertiser is common in smaller markets.

Annual Average:	100.0
January (12/26–1/31)	80.0
February	92.5
March	100.0
April	102.5
May	107.5
June	105.0
July	95.0
August	95.0
September	100.0
October	105.0
November	107.5
December (12/1–12/25)	110.0

FIGURE 5-2

Monthly CPM index for 1980. The annual average is 100.

TABLE 5-25

MATRIX OF IMPACT ON CPM OF THREE FACTORS: SEASON, DAYPART, AND MARKET

Market groups*	Dynamic: Warm-climate markets (1)				Dynamic: Four-season markets (2)			
Daypart	Daytime	E. fringe E. news	Prime time	L. news L. fringe	Daytime	E. fringe E. news	Prime time	L. ne~ L. frir
Demand period 1†	60 110 <u>125</u> 83	90 110 <u>125</u> 124	170 110 <u>125</u> 234	110 110 <u>125</u> 151	60 110 <u>110</u> 73	90 110 <u>110</u> 109	170 110 <u>110</u> 206	11(11(<u>11(</u> 13:
Demand period 2	70 105 <u>125</u> 92	90 105 <u>125</u> 118	170 105 <u>125</u> 223	110 105 <u>125</u> 144	70 105 <u>110</u> 81	90 105 <u>110</u> 104	170 105 <u>110</u> 196	11(10! <u>11(</u> 12'
Demand period 3	60 100 <u>125</u> 75	90 100 <u>125</u> 113	170 100 <u>125</u> 213	110 100 <u>125</u> 138	60 100 <u>110</u> 66	90 100 <u>110</u> 99	170 100 <u>110</u> 187	11■ 10■ <u>11■</u> 12
Demand period 4	50 95 <u>125</u> 59	80 95 <u>125</u> 95	170 95 <u>125</u> 202	120 95 <u>125</u> 143	50 95 <u>110</u> 52	80 95 <u>110</u> 84	170 95 <u>110</u> 178	12 9 <u>11</u> 12
Demand period 5	60 85 <u>125</u> 64	80 85 <u>125</u> 85	170 85 <u>125</u> 181	110 85 <u>125</u> 117	60 85 <u>110</u> 56	80 85 <u>110</u> 75	170 85 <u>110</u> 160	11 8 <u>11</u> 10

*Dynamic designation refers to combination of economic and competitive variables discussed in Marke~ namics section of this chapter. Indexes are: (1) 125, (2) 110, (3) 90, (4) 85.

†Demand Periods: 1 = highest demand, 11/16–12/25, index = 110; 2 = higher demand, 4/1–6/30, 10/1–? index = 105; 3 = average demand, 2/16–3/31, 9/1–9/30, index = 100; 4 = low demand–low supply, 7/1– index = 95; 5 = low demand–high supply, 12/26–2/15, index = 85.

	Nondynamic: Warm-climate markets (3)				Nondynamic: Four-season markets (4)		
aytime	E. fringe E. news	Primetime	L. news L. fringe	Daytime	E. fringe E. news	Primetime	L. news L. fringe
60	90	170	110	60	90	170	110
110	110	110	110	110	110	110	110
90	90	90	90	85	85	85	85
59	89	168	109	56	84	159	103
70	90	170	110	70	90	170	110
105	105	105	105	105	105	105	105
90	90	90	90	85	85	85	85
66	85	161	104	62	80	152	98
60	90	170	110	60	90	170	110
.00	100	100	100	100	100	100	100
90	90	90	90	85	85	85	85
54	81	153	99	51	77	145	94
50	80	170	120	50	80	170	120
95	95	95	95	95	95	95	95
90	90	90	90	85	85	85	85
43	68	145	103	40	65	137	97
60	80	170	110	60	80	170	110
85	85	85	85	85	85	85	85
90	90	90	90	85	85	85	85
46	61	130	84	43	58	123	79

How to Read

part index	60
nand period index	110
ket index	125
nposite index (0.60 × 1.10 × 1.25 × 100)	83

To summarize, economic factors (BPI), competitive media conditions (newspaper universe), relative viewing levels, and the strength of the independent stations in a market all affect the relative efficiency of television advertising in a market and the level of television advertising revenues accruing to it.

SEASONAL VARIATION

Tables 5-21 and 5-22 picture the variation in CPM levels by market and by daypart. There is a third dimension of CPM variation, the seasonal dimension. This variation is illustrated by the New York–St. Louis comparisons in Table 5-20. The seasonal factor requires a closer look.

Demand for television time is highest during May and November. May advertising activity includes heavy retail promotions centered on the change of seasons, Mother's Day, and graduations. Automotive advertising is also heavy during this month. November is the beneficiary of the Christmas season promotions.

Demand for television time is lowest during January and the mid-summer weeks. Figure 5-2 illustrates the month-to-month variation in CPM based on an index of 100 for the annual average level. January is the bargain month. Following the classic economic pattern, a high supply of audience (highest annual viewing levels) and a low demand for that audience cause downward pressure on prices. These low CPM levels benefit those advertisers for whom January represents better than average sales potential, advertising in such categories as cold remedies, coffee, and soup.

Midsummer demand is also relatively low, although not as low as during January. Also, viewing levels are lowest during this time of year, providing a better balance between supply and demand than exists in January. Therefore, CPM levels for the midsummer period are slightly higher than the January levels, although still well below second- and fourth-quarter levels. Seasonal advertisers enjoying these favorable rates include soft drink promoters and retailers with their annual summer clearance and back-to-school promotions.

INTERACTION OF VARIABLES

The cost of television time, expressed in terms of CPM, varies by market, daypart, and season. These factors do not act in isolation. The New York–St. Louis comparison demonstrates that both seasonal and daypart CPM variation can differ significantly by market. Table 5-25 attempts to provide a framework for analyzing the total impact of the variables acting in combination. Each cell contains an index number representing the multiplicative effect of the daypart, seasonal, and market dynamics variables on CPM. The composite indexes range from a high of 234 to a low of 40 (boxed cells). This means that the primetime CPM in a dynamic, warm-weather market during the highest demand period (November 16 to December 25) would be expected to be 2.34 times greater than the top 100 market all-daypart CPM average of $4.10. And the daytime CPM in a nondynamic, four-season market during the lowest demand period (December 26 to February 15) would be expected to be 0.4 times, or 40 percent, of this all-market average.

This matrix is supplied for illustrative purposes only. Although indicative of the normal relationship among the three variables and CPM, it certainly does not help explain the high CPM levels of Baltimore and Boston or the low levels of New York. The television advertising planner should refer to the available market cost data provided for each market by the *Media Market Guide*. The individual market cost statistics in this publication are updated seasonally and are the best source of prevailing market pricing.

Buying Time
in a Local
Television Market

In this chapter we present an eight-step process, illustrated by example, for buying television time in a local market. We also discuss the barter option available to the local market TV advertiser.

EIGHT-STEP PROCESS

Step 1: Avail Request

The media planning process has been completed, and a budget and plan have been developed for each market in which the product will be advertised. Now the stations must be contacted and made aware of the advertiser's desire to advertise in their market, so they can submit their proposals. The formal request for rates and commercial positions available for sale is called the *avail request*. Most stations and their representatives use fairly standardized forms containing the following information:

1. *Flight dates:* The dates during which the advertising is to run.

2. *Dayparts requested:* The parts of the day during which the advertising is to run.

3. *Demographics required:* The demographics that are of interest to the buyer, starting with the primary demographics to be used as a basis for the buy.

4. *Rating source:* The rating service and specific rating book or books that will be used to evaluate the proposals.

5. *GRP goals:* The number of rating points, by daypart, desired.

STATION X
(Salesperson: Joan Licari)

Date requested: September 1, 1981
Client: Standard Foods
Agency: XYZ
Buyer: Thomas Gallagher
Flight dates: 11/1/81 to 11/28/81

Rating source used:
November 1980 Arbitron data
Primary demographic: Women 25–54
Other demographics requested: Total women, Households

	Daypart 1, early fringe	Daypart 2, early news	Daypart 3, primetime	Daypart 4, late news
Weekly GRPs, women 25–54:	30	50	40	45

Budget: $10,000 per week

Buyer Notes:
1. Include M*A*S*H in all primetime packages.
2. Prefer Thursday and Friday for rotations.
3. Provide rationales for all estimates.
4. Submit for one-third, one half, and total budget.
5. All announcements fixed.

FIGURE 6-1

Avail request.

6. *Budget:* The budgeted dollars for the schedule.

7. *Other specifications:* Often buyers will have specific client requests and/or restrictions, such as the inclusion of a particular program in all proposals, the exclusion of programming before or after a certain time, the exclusion of programs with low adult audience composition, or the inclusion of all special programs airing during the flight dates.

At this time the client should submit all commercials for clearance if he or she has not already done so. Usually commercials are submitted for clearance to the networks prior to production. Local commercials must be submitted directly to each station's executive in charge of program practices, although most stations will accept network clearance as an acceptable condition for local clearance. The buyer should never take a salesperson's word as proof of station acceptance.

Step 2: Station Submission

Once an avail request has been submitted, the next step is the station's. The salesperson draws up a proposal based on the avail request. More than likely, several plans will be presented, representing different shares of the total budget. Often the buyer specifies in the avail request at what share levels the salesperson should prepare plans. Most buyers also request *general avails* as well as specific plans. General avails are lists of all programs in the dayparts requested, with the base price for each. Plans usually show a discounted package price below the sum of the base prices of its component programs.

Figure 6-1 shows a typical avail request, and Figures 6-2(a) to (d) the general avails and plans presented by the salesperson for station X, whom we shall call Joan Licari. Note that *The Mike Douglas Show,* early news, and late news submissions are on a multiple-day basis. These are called *rotations.* The advertiser, represented by buyer Thomas Gallagher, is not promised any specific day or time, just that the commercial will run during that week and that over the 4 weeks she or he will receive an *equitable* rotation—one for which the total rating points delivered are roughly equal to the 5-day average for the program during that period. If the advertiser wants the commercial run in a fixed position as opposed to a rotating position, she or he probably will have to pay a premium.

The primetime portions of the station X plans specify programming; however, the programs included change each week. Stations prefer to sell primetime in this manner because it allows them to get more leverage from their top shows. Often stations include primetime access

Day	Time	Program	Total homes		Total women		Women 25–54		Price ($)
			GRPs	(000)	GRPs	(000)	GRPs	(000)	
M–F	4:30–6:00 p.m.	The Mike Douglas Show	10	100.5	9	97.0	6	33.5	275
M–F	6:00–7:00 p.m.	Early news	13	131.0	10	108.0	9	50.0	475
F	7:30–8:00 p.m.	PM Magazine	16	159.0	13	120.0	12	66.5	800
M–Su	11:00–11:30 p.m.	Late news	12	121.0	10	108.0	10	55.0	650
M–F	11:30 p.m.–1:30 a.m.	CBS Late Movie	7	70.0	6	65.0	6	33.5	250
PRIMETIME									
M	9:00–9:30 p.m.	M*A*S*H	30	301.5	24	259.0	25	139.0	2000
M	8:30–9:00 p.m.	Ladies' Man	(est.) 20	201.0	16	173.0	15	83.5	1250
M	10:00–11:00 p.m.	Lou Grant	24	241.0	20	216.0	20	111.0	1700
Tu	9:00–11:00 p.m.	CBS Tuesday Night Movie	20	201.0	14	151.0	16	89.0	1350
W	8:00–9:00 p.m.	Enos	(est.) 20	201.0	13	140.5	15	83.5	1250
Th	9:00–10:00 p.m.	Magnum, P.I.	(est.) 25	251.5	23	248.5	24	133.0	1550
F	9:00–10:00 p.m.	Dukes of Hazzard	35	352.0	23	248.5	25	139.0	2000
Su	8:30–9:00 p.m.	One Day at a Time	25	251.5	19	205.0	20	111.0	1700

All audience numbers shown, except those designated as estimates, are from the November 1980 Arbitron report.

Estimate Rationale:

Ladies' Man: WKRP in Cincinnati performance Monday, 8–8:30 p.m., November 1980 Arbitron report.

Enos: Assumes 30% share based on a tired Eight Is Enough as competition for young audience. Composition based on Dukes of Hazzard special 8–9 p.m. showing, January 1980.

Magnum, P.I.: Rating based on Hawaii Five-O in its prime; composition based on Rockford Files because of James Garner–Tom Selleck similarity.

FIGURE 6-2(a)
General avails.

PLAN 1:
Women 25–54, 165 GRPs per Week

Day	Time	Program	Weekly 30s	Total homes		Total women		Women 25–54	
				GRPs	(000)	GRPs	(000)	GRPs	(000)
M–F	4:30–6:00 p.m.	The Mike Douglas Show	5	50	502.5	45	485.0	30	166.5
M–F	6:00–7:00 p.m.	Early News	5	65	652.5	50	540.0	45	250.0
M–Su	11:00–11:30 p.m.	Late News	5	60	602.5	50	540.0	50	277.5
PRIMETIME ROTATOR			2	48	483.0	38	410.0	40	222.0
Week 1									
M	10:00–11:00 p.m.	Lou Grant		24	241.0	20	216.0	20	111.0
Tu	9:00–11:00 p.m.	CBS Tuesday Night Movie		20	201.0	14	151.0	16	89.0
Week 2									
M	9:00–9:30 p.m.	M*A*S*H		30	301.5	24	259.0	25	139.0
Su	8:30–9:00 p.m.	One Day at a Time		25	251.5	19	205.0	20	111.0
Week 3									
Th	9:00–10:00 p.m.	Magnum, P.I*		25	251.5	23	248.5	24	133.0
W	8:00–9:00 p.m.	Enos*		20	201.0	13	140.5	15	83.5
Week 4									
F	9:00–10:00 p.m.	Dukes of Hazzard		35	352.0	23	248.5	25	139.0
M	8:30–9:00 p.m.	Ladies' Man*		20	201.0	16	173.0	15	83.5

*See Figure 6-2(a) for rationale.

FIGURE 6-2(b)

Station X proposal for Standard Foods.

PLAN 2:
Women 25–54, 85 GRPs per Week

Day	Time	Program	Weekly 30s	Total homes GRPs	Total homes (000)	Total women GRPs	Total women (000)	Women 25–54 GRPs	Women 25–54 (000)
M–F	4:30–6:00 p.m.	The Mike Douglas Show	3	30	301.5	27	291.5	18	100.0
M–F	6:00–7:00 p.m.	Early news	3	39	392.0	30	324.0	27	150.0
M–Su	11:00–11:30 p.m.	Late news	2	24	241.0	20	216.0	20	112.5
PRIMETIME ROTATOR									
Tu	9:00–11:00 p.m.	CBS Tuesday Night Movie (wk. 1)	1	26	264.0	19	200.0	20	112.5
M	9:00–9:30 p.m.	M*A*S*H (wk. 2)		20	201.0	14	151.0	16	89.0
W	8:00–9:00 p.m.	Enos* (wk. 3)		20	201.0	13	140.5	15	83.5
F	9:00–10:00 p.m.	Dukes of Hazzard (wk. 4)		35	352.0	23	248.5	25	139.0

PLAN 3:
Women 25–54, 54 GRPs per Week

Day	Time	Program	Weekly 30s	Total homes GRPs	Total homes (000)	Total women GRPs	Total women (000)	Women 25–54 GRPs	Women 25–54 (000)
M–F	4:30–6:00 p.m.	The Mike Douglas Show	1	10	100.5	9	97.0	6	33.5
M–F	6:00–7:00 p.m.	Early news	2	26	261.5	20	216.0	18	100.0
M–S	11:00–11:30 p.m.	Late news	2	24	241.0	20	216.0	20	112.5
PRIMETIME ROTATOR (one every other week)				25	251.5	19	200.0	20	111.5
M	9:00–9:30 p.m.	M*A*S*H, $2000 (wk. 1)		30	301.5	24	259.0	25	139.0
W	8:00–9:00 p.m.	Enos,* $1250 (wk. 3)		20	201.0	13	140.5	15	83.5

AUDIENCE							
		Total homes		Total women		Women 25–54	
	Total 30s	GRPs	(000)	GRPs	(000)	GRPs	(000)
Plan 1	68	892	8962.0	732	7900.0	660	3664.0
Plan 2	36	476	4794.0	384	4126.0	340	1900.0
Plan 3	22	290	2914.5	233	2516.0	216	1207.0

PRICING			
		CPM, $	
	Total cost, $	Homes	Total women	Women 25–54
Plan 1	35,000	3.91	4.43	9.55
Plan 2	18,750	3.91	4.54	9.87
Plan 3	13,250	4.55	5.27	10.98

FIGURE 6-2(d)

Four-week plan summaries.

in primetime packages when the ratings are comparable. Not all buyers go along with the tactic, but advertisers wishing to run in specific high-rated programs will pay a premium for them.

Step 3: Negotiation

Once each station has submitted its plans, the buyer analyzes each offer. Audience figures are checked against figures developed by the buyer. In the case of numbers reports from the specified rating source—in this example the November 1980 ARB report—this might seem redundant. However, there are subjective considerations. Rotations may be weighted differently, special editions of a program may be excluded or included in averages, and special weighting techniques may be used to account for disproportionate commercial distribution.

Where estimates are provided, there is likely to be greater disagreement. Licari provided estimates for three new programs, *Enos, Ladies'*

Man, and *Magnum, P.I.* The 20 rating level shown for the first two is equivalent to the average primetime rating for November. Given the high new-show failure rate in primetime, these estimates are fairly optimistic. The 25 rating for *Magnum, P.I.* is even more optimistic. Licari considers this a sure hit with high appeal for women because of the attraction of its star, Tom Selleck.

It is important for the buyer and seller to agree on all audience projections before price negotiation begins. The buyer is most likely to come in with more conservative estimates for these new shows and may want to lower the expected rating of a returning show based on stiffer competition this season than last. Any reduction of audience projection will affect the bottom line for the package. First Licari will try to support the estimates shown. Failing to do this, she may elicit the buyer's opinion for other shows on station X. If the buyer is particularly impressed with a new station X program not on the proposed schedule, the seller may substitute the program for one of the programs included.

Once the buyer and seller are in agreement on the audience numbers, the dollar negotiations begin. First consider the 100 percent plan, plan 1. Clearly the seller used an interesting ploy. She priced out her 100 percent submission at $35,000, less than the $40,000 budget figure supplied by the buyer. What the seller was doing was telling the buyer that he did not have to pay $40,000 for 165 GRPs, women 25 to 54, on station X. The seller would get it for him for $5000 less. If the other stations submitted plans on a 165 GRPs-for-$40,000 basis, this might be a successful tactic. Also, Licari now has $5000 to sweeten the package. Although this tactic seems effective, the other stations probably will respond by dropping their prices, and the seller runs the risk of affecting the quality of the first submission adversely to bring in the plan at this figure.

A great deal of gamesmanship goes into the budget element of negotiation. Some buyers refuse to give budgets at all, providing GRP and/ or CPM goals only. Others give budgets that are lower than the actual budgets. Just as the good buyer is eventually able to determine each seller's flexibility on pricing, so, too, the good seller is able to ascertain the real budget level from the buyer or apply an accurate adjustment factor to the budget given, based on past experience.

The station X salesperson, Licari, priced plan 1 at $35,000, a 14 percent discount from the $40,000 list value of the plan shown on the general avails. As expected, the discounts for the 50 and 33^1/$_3$ percent shares submitted are less than 14 percent, so the buyer, Gallagher, has an incentive to make a one-station buy on station X.

On the other hand, Gallagher probably asked for the three-tier submission only to obtain an initial pricing floor from Licari. Gallagher will assume that the discount of 14 percent of list price is also available for plan 2, and probably for plan 3.

The expectations of the salesperson and his or her managers are based on their relative market position. The management of a station with a 40 percent audience share expects to get at least a 40 percent revenue share. The performance of a salesperson is considered extraordinary only if she or he obtains at least this share of the dollars while providing the buyer with an equal or fair share of the audience produced by all stations combined. It is unlikely, therefore, that the buyer will be able to extract a high discount on a $33^1/_3$ percent plan, since the salesperson is aware that he or she will be providing one-third of the audience and will not want to do so for less than one-third of the dollars. One reason buyers withhold budget figures from sellers is to allow the buyers to keep the sellers in the dark concerning the share of business they are actually getting. It is not uncommon for a buyer to tell each station that it received 40 percent of the dollars. This satisfies the salesperson's desire to do better than at least one of his or her rivals.

After analyzing all submissions, Gallagher informs Licari that she is not competitive at the 100 percent level; however, because of the strength of station X in the market and the client's desire for M*A*S*H, he wants to include station X in the buy. If Licari can deliver the 50 percent plan, plan 2, at the 14 percent discount of plan 1, the order is hers. The list price of plan 2 is $20,000, and the original submission is for $18,750, a 9 percent discount. Increasing this discount to 14 percent would result in a price of $17,200, a significant reduction.

Realizing that the 100 percent order is lost, and probably also acknowledging that in a high-demand month like November it is not worth pursuing, Licari shifts her attention to holding onto at least 50 percent of the dollars. Rather than increasing the discount, she counters with some program substitutions that will increase the audience delivered, so that this new $18,750 package will deliver the same CPM as the original plan 2 would have at $17,200.

First, she recommends that her successful primetime access show, PM Magazine, be substituted for Enos in the plan's primetime package. The buyer has given Enos only a 12 rating against women aged 25 to 54, and PM Magazine delivers that rating for half the price. With a list price of $800 versus $1,350 for Enos, it really helps the package's efficiency.

Second, Licari recommends that two CBS Late Movies be substituted for one early news. These two would deliver 12 GRPs for women aged 25 to 54 versus the 9 GRPs of the early news.

Third, Licari applies the $550 saved in the Enos to PM Magazine conversion to replacing the *CBS Tuesday Night Movies* with *Magnum, P.I.*, for which the buyer shares her optimistic forecast of a 24 GRP rating for women aged 25 to 54. She also includes an additional *Mike Douglas Show.*

Gallagher responds that it looks good, but that the client will not run after 1 a.m. Licari agrees to run all *CBS Late Movie* spots prior to 1 a.m., but only guarantees the original rating average.

The actual rotation of spots is a common negotiating point, and it is one on which the smart buyer will sound out the seller even if he or she does not care. To the extent that a seller guarantees preferable rotations to some buyers, it will be impossible for him or her to provide equitable rotations to others. Table 6-1 shows the rating by half hour for a 2-hour program. The declining rating pattern is typical of late fringe programs. The network positions are loaded toward the front of the show, so, even without preferential scheduling, the local advertiser's expectations must be for less than a balanced rotation.

In Table 6-1 the straight 2-hour average rating is 6.5, but the average delivery of a local spot (the average of each position times that position's half-hour rating) is a 6.1. When four early positions are removed for preferred-treatment advertising, the average expected rating for the remaining local positions is 5.7, a full 12 percent below the 6.5 program rating. If the local station is selling everyone a 6.5 rating, obviously it cannot deliver. The unaware buyer probably will be the one with the heavy 12:30 p.m.–1:30 a.m. rotation. The station X salesperson is avoiding inequity to some degree by guaranteeing a pre-1 a.m. rotation but only the program average rotation. Standard Foods will not advertise after 1 a.m., but it is also unlikely to advertise between 11:30 p.m. and midnight.

TABLE 6-1
LATE-NIGHT ROTATION PATTERN

	11:30 p.m.–midnight	Midnight–12:30 a.m.	12:30 a.m.–1 a.m.	1 a.m.–1:30 a.m.
GRPs	9	7	6	4
Commercial positions, local	4	6	6	8
Positions assigned to preferred-position advertisers	2	2	—	—
Remaining positions	2	4	6	8

The buyer asks the seller to resubmit a formal plan, plan 4, incorporating these changes. Figure 6-3 shows this plan. Figure 6-4 compares it with plan 2. Licari has held her share of revenue with the $18,750 cost. The list price value of the plan is $21,750; therefore, the buyer is getting the 14 percent discount originally assigned to the 100 percent plan, plan 1. Gallagher looks at the new plan and says it looks good and that he will confirm the order to Licari the next day.

By now station Z begins to sense it is going to be the loser in what looks like a two-station buy. It makes a last desperation offer. Its salesperson, Tom Mason, is aggressive and is selling hard. The buyer goes back to station X, stating that station Z has resubmitted for 50 percent at a low $8.00 CPM for women aged 25 to 54. The buyer admits being reluctant to go with station Z since as the number three station it cannot provide the quality of the station X schedule. But the CPM differential is too great. If the station X salesperson can get the CPM down to $8.50, they can close the deal.

Licari can add one more *PM Magazine* or two *CBS Late Movies* at no cost, but inventory is tight and this move would definitely mean lost revenue for the station. Another alternative focuses on the fixed-rate stipulation. The avail request called for a fixed schedule, and the prices used were fixed prices. Although November is a high-demand month, it does not look as if either *The Mike Douglas Show* or the early news will sell out at fixed rates. Licari could offer preemptable rates for these programs and be quite confident that Standard Foods would not be preempted by a higher-rate advertiser. This would reduce the list price to $225 for *The Mike Douglas Show* and $425 for the early news. With four and two announcements per week, *respectively*, in these programs the total list price reduction is $1200. This more than covers the required $500 drop in the plan price.

Step 4: The Order

The seller offers the plan to the buyer, with two spots on *The Mike Douglas Show* and one early news spot preemptable by a higher-rate advertiser, for $18,250, yielding a CPM for women between 25 and 54 of $8.56. The buyer agrees, station X management accepts the order, and the buy is completed.

Who won?

The natural question to ask after completing a simulation such as this is, Who got the better deal, the buyer or the seller? Let's examine the results. Consider the buyer's perspective.

The buyer's goal was to spend $40,000 for 165 GRPs per week for women aged 25–54. The station X schedule delivered 58 percent of

PLAN 4
Women 25–54, 96 GRPs per Week

Day	Time	Program	Weekly 30s	Total homes		Total women		Women 25–54	
				GRPs	(000)	GRPs	(000)	GRPs	(000)
M–F	4:30–6:00 p.m.	The Mike Douglas Show	4	40	402.0	36	388.0	24	134.0
M–F	6:00–7:00 p.m.	Early news	2	26	261.5	20	216.0	18	100.0
M–Su	11:00–11:30 p.m.	Late news	2	24	241.0	20	216.0	20	112.5
M–F	11:30 p.m.–1:30 a.m.	CBS Late Movie	2	14	140.0	12	130.0	12	67.0
PRIMETIME ROTATOR									
Th	9:00–10:00 p.m.	Magnum, P.I.	1	27	266.0	21	219.0	22	119.5
M	9:00–9:30 p.m.	M*A*S*H		(est.) 25	251.5	23	248.5	24	133.0
				30	301.5	24	259.0	25	139.0
F	7:30–8:00 p.m.	PM Magazine		16	159.0	13	120.0	12	66.5
F	9:00–10:00 p.m.	Dukes of Hazzard	—	35	352.0	23	248.5	25	139.0
Four-week totals			44	522	5242.0	435	4676.0	382	2131.5

PRICING

Total cost	CPM		
	Homes	Total women	Women 25–54
$18,750	$3.58	$4.01	$8.80

AUDIENCE							
	Total 30s	Total homes		Total women		Women 25–54	
		GRPs	(000)	GRPs	(000)	GRPs	(000)
Plan 2	36	476	4794.0	384	4126.0	340	1900.0
Plan 4	44	522	5242.0	435	4676.0	382	2131.5
Plan 4 advantage	8	46	448.0	51	550.0	42	231.5

PRICING				
			CPM	
	Total cost ($)	Homes	Total women	Women 25–54
Plan 2	18,750	$3.91	$4.54	$9.87
Plan 4	18,750	$3.58	$4.01	$8.80
Plan 4 advantage	—	−8%	−12%	−11%

FIGURE 6-4

Plan 2 versus plan 4.

those GRPs for 46 percent of the budget. Assuming that negotiating with station Y, the other station on the schedule, turned out as well, the buyer received a 16 percent premium in an audience of women aged 25–54 for 92 percent of the original budget.

Compromises included accepting a primetime access program as part of a primetime rotation, including late fringe, in the plan, and taking three preemptable positions. The primetime access program is the critically acclaimed *PM Magazine* program, which delivers a primetime-level audience, so that is an acceptable compromise. The late fringe spots would run within the client's mandated pre-1 a.m. time frame, so that also seems acceptable. And the preemptable spots are unlikely to be preempted. All in all, it looks as if the buyer made out very well.

How did the seller do?

This is a little harder to measure. If the buyer did as well with station Y as with station X, the station X salesperson got 50 percent of the dollars for 50 percent of the audience, as would be expected. She has only the buyer's word on how much of the budget she received. As to the other half of the operation—how much of the overall audience she provided for those dollars—it is too early to tell. All buys are negotiated on the basis of audience projections; the true value of each schedule must be determined on actual audience delivery. Even though her audience figures yield the same CPM as those of station Y, this could be as much a result of her effective selling of her projections as of actual potential delivery.

On some other measures she did fairly well. By including prime access in a primetime package she effectively mixed harder-to-sell inventory with a premium-value program—in this case, M*A*S*H. Although she did not achieve her goal of keeping the full $18,750 from the originally proposed 50 percent plan 2, her reductions came from downgrading spots from fixed to preemptable rates. If the station can sell them for more, it will preempt Standard Foods. If it cannot sell them for more, it will be pleased to have Standard Foods there, even at the lower rates. One place Licari seemed to have done well was against station Z. She got the order at a CPM of $8.56 while it was shut out at $8.00. On the surface, it would seem that she also made out well.

Whether either Gallagher or Licari did well and which one did better will be determined by the execution and delivery of the schedule. We now move to the execution stage.

Step 5: Getting on the Air

Once the order is placed, the logistics of the schedule must be arranged. First, the commercials have to be sent to the station operations department. If more than one product or commercial for a given product is to be included in the schedule, an allocation form must be sent to the station traffic department stating which commercial (designated by commercial number and description) is to run in each position. It is assumed that by now all commercials have been cleared in program practices.

The station sends an official contract to the agency, stating the schedule ordered and the price agreed on. As mentioned earlier, broadcast contracts are seldom signed; however, they should be reviewed carefully by the buyer before the beginning of the schedule.

Step 6: Monitoring the Schedule

Once the schedule begins, the smart buyer will monitor its execution regularly. In the station X example, the buyer will want to make sure that the rotations are equitable and conform to Standard Foods' desire for Thursday and Friday concentration. The *CBS Late Movie* rotation must be watched to ensure that the 1 a.m. cutoff is honored.

The buyer also should watch out for separation from competing brands. Most stations guarantee at least 15 minutes' separation and occasionally extend this to full-program exclusivity when a client commits to multiple announcements in one program. Network affiliates, however, often find it difficult to protect locally placed advertising from competitors on the network. A good traffic department will try to protect advertisers from both local and network-placed competitors, but the vigilance of the buyer will increase the probability of full protection.

Despite the efforts of a vigilant buyer, a careful salesperson, and a good traffic department, and the presence of a basically fixed schedule, it is unlikely that any schedule of substance will run exactly as planned. When problems arise, the buyer and seller must work them out. Let's go back to our Standard Foods case and see how the schedule actually ran.

Figure 6-5 shows the allocation of the Standard Foods schedule established by the traffic department prior to the running of the schedule. Determination of time position within each show is not set until a few days before airing. The allocation of the Standard Foods schedule is well balanced. Note that the majority of spots are running on the preferred Thursday and Friday nights; 23 of 44 spots, or 52 percent, are on these evenings. Also when programs ran back to back, such as *The Mike Douglas Show* and the early news, an attempt was made to place multiple announcements on separate days, giving Standard Foods some exposure to that daypart's audience each day.

Let us examine what actually happened, on a weekly basis.

WEEK 1

Two problems arose for week 1. First, the network decided to preempt *Magnum, P.I.* for a special program. A *make-good* had to be negotiated. A make-good is offered whenever a spot is going to be missed or has been missed inadvertently. Barring agreement on a suitable make-good announcement, the advertiser has to take credit. Since giving credit means loss of revenue to the station, it makes every attempt to find a satisfactory replacement. Taking credit also means a loss of commission for the agency, so it, too, tries to negotiate a suitable replacement. Except when the client has specifically told the agency to recapture whatever dollars it can because of budgetary problems, a buyer usually chooses a make-good rather than takes credit.

Licari recommends that the buyer stay in the time period, since the

Program	Weekly 30s	November 1–7 M T W T F S S	November 8–14 M T W T F S S
The Mike Douglas Show	(4)	o x x x x o o	x o x x x o o
Early news	(2)	x o o o x o o	o x o x o o o
Late news	(2)	x o o x o o o	o o o o x x o
CBS Late Movie	(2)	o x o o x o o	x o o x o o o
Primetime rotator		o o o x o o o	x o o o o o o
Total 30s		2 2 1 <u>3</u> <u>3</u> 0 0	3 1 1 <u>3</u> <u>2</u> 1 0

FIGURE 6-5

Allocation of Standard Foods schedule.

preempting program, a Lily Tomlin special, should do very well with women aged 25–54. She estimates that the delivery for Lily Tomlin will be higher than the anticipated 24 rating projected for *Magnum, P.I.* The buyer is not so sure. Gallagher has merchandised the schedule to the client, and the *Magnum, P.I.* element was well received. He suggests that *Magnum, P.I.* and the *Dukes of Hazzard* be switched in rotation. He will take the *Dukes of Hazzard* in week 1 and *Magnum, P.I.* in week 4.

This change is more difficult for the seller to make. The November 5 *Dukes of Hazzard* is sold out, as is the November 25 *Magnum, P.I.* She will have to get two advertisers to switch in order to do this. Fortunately, she is able to move a November 5 *Dukes of Hazzard* advertiser into the Lily Tomlin special. The switch of an advertiser from *Magnum, P.I.* to *Dukes of Hazzard* in week 4 is easier, since the switch nets the advertiser 10 GRPs from an estimated 25 rating show to a proven 35 rating show. The first problem is solved.

The second problem concerns the early news. The Friday spot was missed because of a technical error. The buyer agrees to accept a third spot in week 2 on Friday night of that week.

WEEK 2

In week 2 the only problem concerns the late news on Saturday night. Owing to a late-running movie, the news ran from 11:30 p.m. to mid-

November 15–21	November 22–28
M T W T F S S	M T W T F S S
x x o x x o o	o x x x x o o
o o x o x o o	x o o o x o o
o o x x o o o	o o o o x o x
o x o x o o o	o o x x o o o
o o o o x o o	o o o o x o o
1 2 2 <u>3</u> <u>3</u> 0 0	1 1 2 <u>2</u> <u>4</u> 0 1

night. The buyer felt that this was not what was contracted for and that, since the ratings would be substantially depressed, he should get a make-good for this spot. The seller initially argued that because of the high anticipated rating of the movie that ran over, the news rating would be higher, not lower, than average. Therefore, no make-good was justified. The buyer persisted. Finally, a compromise was reached. The buyer would receive an extra *CBS Late Movie* in week 3 to compensate for any rating loss caused by the delayed late news.

WEEK 3

Demand for time in week 3 was extraordinary, and the station was able to sell the two preemptable spots of *The Mike Douglas Show* and one preemptable spot on the early news for higher rates. Giving the buyer the required 2-week notice, it announced that it would have to preempt for a higher-rate advertiser.

However, the buyer had not spent the entire $40,000 budget. He had $5000 left. He had convinced the client to let him hold this money for any last-minute opportunities. Such an opportunity had presented itself. The network had decided to run a 2-hour *Dallas* episode on Friday, November 19. *Dallas* was the number one show in the market, and it delivered an extraordinary 35 rating for women aged 25–54. Initially, station X wanted $3500 per 30 seconds for the program, too much of a premium. However, because of the last-minute nature of the change,

TABLE 6-2
STANDARD FOODS' STATION X SCHEDULE POSTANALYSIS, NOV. 1981 ARBITRON DATA

Day	Time	Program		Total homes		Total women		Women 25–54	
				GRPs	(000)	GRPs	(000)	GRPs	(000)
M–F	4:30–6:00 p.m.	The Mike Douglas Show		9.0	90.5	8.0	87.5	5.5	31.0
			×17	153.0	1538.5	136.0	1487.5	93.5	527.0
M–F	6:00–7:00 p.m.	Early news		12.0	121.0	9.0	97.0	8.5	47.0
			×8	96.0	968.0	72.0	776.0	68.0	376.0
M–Su	11:00–11:30 p.m.	Late news		13.0	131.0	11.0	119.0	11.0	60.5
			×8	104.0	1048.0	88.0	952.0	88.0	484.0
M–F	11:30 p.m.–1:30 a.m.	CBS Late Movie		8.0	80.0	7.0	76.0	7.5	42.0
			×9	72.0	720.0	63.0	684.0	67.5	378.0
Subtotal, fringe				425.0	4274.5	359.0	3899.5	317.0	1765.0
PRIMETIME									
F	9:00–10:00 p.m.	Dukes of Hazzard		35.0	352.0	22.5	243.0	24.0	133.5
M	9:00–9:30 p.m.	M*A*S*H		33.0	331.0	26.0	280.5	26.0	144.5
F	7:30–8:00 p.m.	PM Magazine		17.0	169.0	13.5	124.5	12.5	69.5
Th	9:00–10:00 p.m.	Magnum, P.I.		23.0	236.5	22.0	237.5	23.0	127.5
F	8:00–9:00 p.m.	Dallas		40.0	402.0	30.0	324.0	30.0	166.5
			×2	80.0	804.0	60.0	648.0	60.0	333.0
Subtotal, prime				188.0	1892.5	144.0	1533.5	145.5	808.0
					6167.0	503.0	5433.0	462.5	2573.0

it was willing to accept $2500 per 30 seconds for the additional hour. The buyer agreed to purchase two 30-second spots at this rate if *The Mike Douglas Show* and the early news were not preempted. Licari presented this offer to management as a package: two *Dallas* spots plus an upgrade of *The Mike Douglas Show* and the early news to fixed announcements for $5000. Management accepted.

WEEK 4

During week 4 the first of *The Mike Douglas Show* announcements ran in the same commercial break as that of a competitor. Again the buyer asked for a make-good. Licari knew she had to deliver, so she offered a second announcement that Friday. Gallagher did not like the idea of running two spots in a show on the same day, and he suggested a Thursday early news. Licari argued that it was unfair of Gallagher to ask for a $475 spot as a make-good for a $275 spot that did run, after all. The buyer relented and agreed to take the extra spot on *The Mike Douglas Show* on Friday.

With the schedule completed, it remains to determine how well each negotiator did.

Step 7: Postbuy Analysis

Determining how well the buyer did requires waiting for the publication of the November 1981 ARB report. The client has agreed with the agency that the schedule will be *posted* on this book. The posting of a schedule is all-important to the buyer. A sophisticated client will compare the audience delivered with the audience projected by the buyer at the time of the buy. The client hopes the buyer has done better than projected, but *not too much better*. The client has determined how much weight is needed in each market and budgeted the dollars required to meet each market's weight goal, based on agency cost estimates that most likely were supplied by the buyer. If the buyer overachieves the goal of the advertiser by a substantial amount, the client has misallocated dollars to that market. These dollars probably could have been used more effectively elsewhere. Thus overachieving goals is not always a plus—just the lesser of two evils. Ideally, the schedule would deliver audiences identical to the buyer's projections.

Table 6-2 presents the postbuy analysis for the Standard Foods schedule. Table 6-3 compares the actual performance with buyer projections for the original plan. The all-important projection for women aged 25–54 was exceeded, while the actual values for homes and total women were slightly below those projected. Based on the goal of equaling the pro-

TABLE 6-3

**ACTUAL BASE SCHEDULE
DELIVERY VERSUS ORIGINAL
PLAN 4 ESTIMATES**

	Audience					
	Total homes		Total women		Women 25–54	
	GRPs	(000)	GRPs	(000)	GRPs	(000)
Original plan 4 projection	522.0	5242.0	435.0	4676.0	382.0	2131.5
Original plan 4 actuals*	516.0	5192.5	428.0	4621.5	389.5	2167.0
Actual versus projection	(−6.0)	(−49.5)	(−7.0)	(−54.5)	+7.5	+35.5

*Does not include bonus spots or extra *Dallas* buy.

jection, but not by a substantial amount, the buyer did very well.

However, a good buyer does not stop at the initial order, but constantly tries to improve the client's position through schedule manipulation as the schedule progresses. Through make-goods this buyer added two spots to the original schedule. Table 6-4 shows his performance with these two spots included. Now he has exceeded his projections in every demographic. So the buyer has two stars, one for

TABLE 6-4

FINAL PLAN 4

	Total 30s	Audience					
		Total homes		Total women		Women 25–54	
		GRPs	(000)	GRPs	(000)	GRPs	(000)
Original plan actuals	44	516.0	5192.5	428.0	4621.5	389.5	2167
Additional no-charge units	2	17.0	170.5	15.0	163.5	13.0	73
Total	46	533.0	5363.0	443.0	4785.0	402.5	2240
Original plan projections		522.0	5242.0	435.0	4676.0	382.0	2131
Actual versus projections		+11.0	+121.0	+8.0	+109.0	+20.5	+108

AUDIENCE							
		Total homes		Total women		Women 25–54	
	Total 30s	GRPs	(000)	GRPs	(000)	GRPs	(000)
Final plan 4	46	533.0	5363.0	443.0	4785.0	402.5	2240.0
Dallas	2	80.0	804.0	60.0	648.0	60.0	333.0
Total	48	613.0	6167.0	503.0	5433.0	462.5	2573.0
Projected		612.0	6146.0	505.0	5432.0	452.0	2520.5

PRICING				
			CPM ($)	
	Total cost, $	Homes	Total women	Women 25–54
Projected	23,750	3.86	4.37	9.42
Delivered	23,750	3.85	4.37	9.23

	Total homes		Total women		Women 25–54	
	GRPs	(000)	GRPs	(000)	GRPs	(000)
Dallas projection	45.0	452.0	35.0	378.0	35.0	194.5
Dallas actual	40.0	402.0	30.0	324.0	30.0	166.5

FIGURE 6-6

Final plan 4 plus *Dallas.*

making initially accurate projections and one for upgrading the schedule in progress.

But we are not ready to make our final judgment. Remember that the buyer added $5000 to purchase two *Dallas* units during the campaign. Was this a good move? On the negative side, Figure 6-6 shows that

Dallas did not meet his projections. On the positive side, the two *Dallas* spots delivered 333,000 women aged 25–54 for $5000, translating to a $15.00 CPM. The original *Dallas* price of $3500 per 30-second spot, even with the delivery of 389,000 projected women aged 25–54, would have translated to an $18.00 CPM. Although the $15.00 CPM is significantly higher than that of the other primetime programs purchased, *Dallas* is the number one program, and a premium must be expected. When you add the *Dallas* spots to the remainder of the schedule, the bottom-line numbers are almost identical, as shown in Figure 6-6, and the buyer did best against the CPM target for women aged 25–54.

In summary, our buyer acted with professionalism and delivered a quality, well-executed schedule to the client. All advertisers should be lucky enough to have such a competent buyer working for them.

The seller did not do badly either. She ended up with $23,750 out of $40,000, a 59 percent share of the budget. She was able to accommodate all make-goods, not losing any money to credits. She sold two *Dallas* units for management. The ability to sell premium-priced inventory at short notice is certainly an attribute in a salesperson. Most of all, she maintained an excellent working relationship with a top professional buyer throughout the process. She can expect more business in the future from Standard Foods.

But one step remains.

Step 8: Billing and Payment

Each month the station sends an invoice to the agency. That invoice shows precisely when each commercial ran and states the amount due for the portion of the schedule that aired during that month. There are two areas of possible conflict. First, the buyer may discover that one or more commercials did not run as ordered. Second, the buyer may not agree with the dollars due.

For many years, slow payment was a problem in television advertising billing. Agencies usually received payment from their client for the advertising placed during the month prior to receipt or upon receipt of the bill from the station. If they found some reason for withholding payment to the station, they would have use of the client's money for the interim period. They could invest this money in interest-bearing accounts and so generate additional income. This is a classic example of what is called *playing the float*.

Station sales personnel were too busy or just not particularly interested in settling billing discrepancies, and bills often went unpaid for many months. Two things changed that indifference. First, sophisticated financial managers emerged within the broadcast management hierarchy and focused their attention on this problem. Second, a few agencies and buying services went bankrupt. These bankrupt institutions had been paid by their clients for the time bought on stations. In the Lennen and Newall case, it was ruled that the clients were not liable for the debts of Lennen and Newell made in their behalf, since they had paid the agency in good faith and the media had not made them aware of the financial situation as the bills went unpaid.

The new, uniform industry contract established on January 1, 1981, addresses the problem of discrepancies and liability. New contracts state that "payment by agency of items which are not in dispute on each invoice is due within 15 days after receipt of invoice by agency." No longer can an agency withhold payment of a $100,000 bill because of a discrepancy concerning one $1000 spot. As to liability, the contract states that the agency is solely liable for all contracts initially, but that if payment is not received on nondiscrepant items "within five weeks after the end of the month for which the invoice was received, the station may elect to notify agency and advertiser in writing of such nonpayment. From and after receipt of such notice the advertiser is solely liable for all time purchased in its name by the agency for which that advertiser has not yet remitted payment to the agency."

The second area of potential dispute involves the amount charged. Although the total package price usually is not a problem, allocations of charges by announcement can be a problem, as can allocation by month. It is important for the salesperson and buyer to agree in advance on how these allocations will be made in order to accommodate each other's fiscal calendars and postbuy evaluation procedures.

Gallagher ordered a discrepancy report from BAR. As part of its monitoring service in 75 markets, BAR provides advertisers with reports showing where competitive commercials ran too close to their commercials or where their commercials ran outside designated time periods. The Standard Foods buyer ordered a BAR analysis for his schedule and found that, in addition to the one product conflict that he had picked up, the November 11 *CBS Late Movie* announcement ran adjacent to that of a competitor. He notified Licari, and it was agreed that he would exclude the cost of this spot when paying the Standard Foods bill.

However, when the bill arrived, Gallagher noted that the allocated price for the *CBS Late Movie* spot was $215, not the $250 list price shown on the general avails. He felt he should withhold the entire $250 and notified Licari of his intention. She argued that because the plan was bought at a discount of 14 percent from list, all spots were shown at this discount level. Since the buyer actually paid 86 percent of the list price for the package, he could not fairly expect to get 100 percent back on missed announcements. The buyer agreed that this was reasonable and deducted only $215. The adjusted bill was sent to accounting for payment.

So ends our simulation. With both the buyer and the seller showing professionalism and reasonably addressing all issues, both came out winners in the end. Unfortunately this does not happen all the time, or even often enough.

Summary Chart

Table 6-5 is a chart summarizing the responsibilities of the buyer and seller during each stage of the buying process. By adhering to their responsibilities during each step, the buyer and seller should be able to minimize tension and conflict in the buying process. We conclude this chapter with a discussion of a unique form of television time buying, the barter or trade deal.

BARTER AND TRADE ADVERTISING

There is an alternative to paying cash for advertising time available to the advertiser—barter or trade. Radio and television time is a perishable commodity; unsold time cannot be stored away for future use. For this reason there is constant pressure on the station to sell all inventory, for some price. However, in less than full-demand situations, selling all inventory would require dramatic price reductions, reductions that would undermine the market's pricing structure and actually result in

TABLE 6-5
GUIDE TO EFFECTIVE PURCHASE
AND SALE OF LOCAL MARKET
TELEVISION TIME

The buyer should:	The seller should:
STEP 1: REQUEST FOR AVAILS	
Provide the salesperson with as much information as possible	Respond quickly to all avail requests
Allow the salesperson enough time to prepare a well thought out submission	Get as much guidance from the buyer as possible
Monitor the market and time the request to optimize the negotiating position	Know what the buyer expects

TABLE 6-5

**GUIDE TO EFFECTIVE PURCHASE
AND SALE OF LOCAL MARKET
TELEVISION TIME** *(Continued)*

The buyer should:	The seller should:

STEP 2: STATION SUBMISSION

The buyer should:	The seller should:
Set up personal presentation meetings for each salesperson	Present a variety of plans—give the buyer options
Allow every station to make a submission	Provide "reasonable" audience estimates with sound rationales for each
Ask for resubmissions if original submission not on target	Always make submission in person
Develop audience estimates	Be creative; do not limit submission to strict avail request if alternative approaches make sense

STEP 3: NEGOTIATIONS

The buyer should:	The seller should:
Negotiate on all levels: audience estimates, pricing, program mix, fixed versus preemptive rotations	Negotiate on all levels: audience estimates, pricing, program mix, and fixed versus preemptive rotations
Never accept a station's original proposal as final—give it the chance to resubmit	Be in contact with buyer and available during negotiating period; let buyer know that seller is flexible
Make commitments final, and do not back down on agreements	Respond quickly to buyer offers
	Accept all orders—even disappointing ones—with appreciation
	Be a good loser as well as a winner

STEP 4: THE ORDER

The buyer should:	The seller should:
Be specific when placing an order—request quick confirmation	Confirm order as soon as possible
Get written confirmation of order	Send written confirmation of order

STEP 5: GETTING ON THE AIR

The buyer should:	The seller should:
Deliver all commercials to station operations department	Make sure buyer sent commercials to operations department
Make sure commercial scheduling information has been received by station traffic department	Make sure commercial scheduling information has been received by station traffic department; obtain a copy for reference

The buyer should:	The seller should:

STEP 6: MONITORING THE SCHEDULE

The buyer should:	The seller should:
Obtain planned rotation schedules from station in advance	Work with the traffic department to ensure best rotation for buyer
Work continually to upgrade schedule through effective negotiation of make-goods	Handle make-goods quickly—in advance, when possible
Keep in contact with salesperson	Look for opportunities to upgrade buyer's schedule
	Present reasonable proposals for additional spots to buyer
	Keep in contact with buyer
	Track competitive schedules

STEP 7: POSTBUY ANALYSIS

The buyer should:	The seller should:
In cases of underachievement, let seller know as soon as possible; use in future negotiations	Do a postanalysis, and do not wait for the buyer's report
In case of overachievement, let seller know as well	In cases of underachievement, if compensation is to be made, offer additional spots quickly; if not, discuss ways to avoid future shortfall
Let client know results as soon as possible, without waiting to be asked	In cases of overachievement, congratulate and credit buyer
Evaluate performance carefully	Do postanalysis of competitive schedules for future negotiations

STEP 8: BILLING AND PAYMENT

The buyer should:	The seller should:
Communicate all special billing requirements to seller before first billing period ends	Request any special billing requirements from buyer before first billing period ends
Pay all nondiscrepant items promptly	Keep track of account billing
Communicate with seller immediately concerning billing discrepancies	Anticipate discrepancies where possible
	Handle outstanding discrepancies quickly

less overall revenue. So stations accept the fact that not all inventory, especially that in the less desirable late-night and early-morning time periods, will be sold.

From the early days of radio, resourceful station managers have sought to generate some income from this inventory. This has led to the trade deal, or barter arrangement. The station trades the time for some good or service. Since the time would not be sold otherwise, the good or service is, in essence, being acquired at no cost. The party producing the good or service receives valuable advertising time. The value of the time usually is substantially higher than the value of the good or service being provided, so the deal is attractive to this party as well. Broadcast barter can be either direct or indirect.

Direct Barter

Direct barter is the exchange of time for a product or service required by the station. These deals are made regularly by stations to acquire automobiles for news and executive use, advertising space in newspapers, airline tickets, hotel rooms for traveling executives, and restaurant meals for client entertaining. The station offers the advertiser—for example, a car dealer—time in exchange for product. Assume that the value of the car is $10,000 retail. The station offers inventory with a list price value of $15,000 for the car. The car cost the dealer only $7500, so the dealer, in effect, gets $15,000 worth of advertising for $7500. The station knew that it was not going to sell this inventory, so it, in effect, received a $10,000 car for no out-of-pocket cost.

Indirect Barter

If direct barter were the only form available, transactions would be limited to parties desiring television time that had a good or service needed by the television stations. However, the emergence of the barter house has expanded the scope of this activity through indirect barter. The barter house is an intermediary finding goods and services among many entities simultaneously. An *indirect barter* arrangement might work like this:

- Station X needs a $10,000 electronic editing component.

- XYZ Industries makes this component, but does no consumer advertising.

- XYZ is an international firm with heavy travel expenses.

- International Airways is a heavy advertiser in the station X market.

The barter house has obtained $20,000 worth of International Airways tickets from previous trade deals. It offers $10,000 worth of these tickets to XYZ Industries for the $10,000 electronic editing component. Since the cost of the component for XYZ Industries is only $5000, it accepts the trade. Then the barter house offers the component to station X for $20,000 in television time. Since station X does not expect to sell this time, it accepts the trade. Next the barter house offers the $20,000 in television time to International Airways for $30,000 in additional tickets that it can use to make future deals.

As the barter house expands its operation, it develops its own inventory of goods or services that it can use to make new deals or sell for cash. In the deal just completed, the barter house started out with $10,000 in airline tickets and ended with $30,000 in airline tickets, incurring no costs, other than administrative, along the way. Obviously, with the possibility of this kind of deal, bartering and trading for television time are a substantial industry. Today there are many barter middlemen involved in the trading of television time. Atwood-Richards claims to be the oldest barter company and to handle the largest volume, with an average inventory of $6 million to $14 million in goods and services.[1] William B. Tanner is another major barter organization active in the television time markets. In 1979, the FCC reported $100 million in television station trade and barter transactions. Most television stations engage in some barter deals; however, the level of activity varies considerably. The networks and major groups try to limit barter transactions to direct trades for station-related products and services. Smaller markets and independent stations enter into barter deals more readily and are more likely customers for the barter house.

Barter has its limitations. From the station side, the wholesale use of barter deals cheapens the market value of a station's inventory. Stations originally turned to barter as a preferable alternative to selling unsold inventory at heavily discounted rates. They felt that the pricing structure of the station would be undermined by a high-discount cash sale approach. Wholesale bartering, especially with local retailers that are cash advertisers as well as barter partners, has the same effect.

Not only does heavy barter activity eventually undermine pricing integrity, but also it reduces advertising budgets for cash customers. If the local retailers can obtain a significant amount of their required television advertising weight through barter, they might allocate existing television advertising dollars to other media or marketing sectors. A station dealing with barter houses might find itself owing the houses a substantial amount of inventory. In all barter deals the station always demands the right to approve the advertisers that eventually appear on the air as a result of a barter house trade. However, as this inventory obligation grows, pressure to accept marginal barter clients as advertisers increases. The appearance of such advertisers on the air can further cheapen the image of the station.

The advertiser receiving the television time also has some potential problems. The local car dealer might have sold the car to the station directly; the airline tickets might have been bought directly by XYZ Industries. As in the case of the station, to a certain extent the other barter partners are undermining their own markets. Also, there is the question of the quality of the time obtained through barter. Most stations limit barter to the less desirable dayparts of late-night (after 1 a.m.) and weekend daytime. Almost all barter deals are immediately preemptable, so the advertiser has little control over when and where the advertising will run. To the extent that some barter time is sold to marginal, or schlock type, advertisers, the barter advertiser's message appears in a less than desirable environment. Often barter advertisers find themselves limited to the weaker stations in a market. Market leaders take little barter advertising.

Advertisers should consider the following when approaching the question of barter for television time:

- Could the goods and/or services bring greater revenues in the normal marketplace?

- What is the real value of the time received? (Most barter time can be purchased directly at substantial discounts.)

- Is the audience delivered by the low-demand time periods the one the advertiser wants to reach?

- Will the irregular scheduling of advertising disrupt the overall advertising campaign objectives?

- How important is the advertising environment to the effectiveness of the advertiser's message?

In general, barter advertising makes sense for low-budget advertisers wishing to maximize exposure. Direct marketers have been particularly effective in their use of barter advertising. Their need for heavy message frequency makes multiple exposures in low-rated programs an ideal strategy. For the larger advertiser, barter might be an acceptable supplement to an ongoing campaign, but it should never constitute a substantial portion of that campaign.

One other form of barter advertising is prevalent in television today, barter program syndication.

Barter Program Syndication

One product every station requires is programming. Every television station runs local programming. It could cover as few as 6 to 10 hours for a network affiliate to a full schedule for an independent station. The creation of locally produced programming is expensive and, with the exception of news, difficult to do competitively. Program syndicators have filled this gap, offering off-network reruns and original programming to stations for a fee.

This syndication market has grown to become a highly competitive market. Today substantially more syndicated programming is available than local time available in a market to show it. As the cost of production goes up and as competition for off-network series escalates the prices of these programs, syndicators look for ways to defray the risk of program acquisition while improving the chance of selling their product to the local station.

Joining with an advertiser or several advertisers in a barter syndication arrangement is one popular technique. The advertiser underwrites the production of the program. Then the program is offered to stations *at no cost*. The catch is that a given percentage of the commercial time has been used to carry the sponsoring advertiser's messages. The station can sell the remaining time. For example, *The John Smith Show*, a half-hour variety program developed for the primetime access period, has been underwritten by Standard Foods. The program is formatted for 6 minutes of commercials. Standard Foods uses 2 minutes for its messages. It also receives sponsor mentions in the form of opening and closing billboards. The station may sell the remaining 4 minutes to any advertiser not competitive with Standard Foods. The station gets the program for free while the advertiser gets advertising exposure for a cost far below the collective cost of time in each market in which the program is placed.

When does barter program syndication make sense?

From the advertiser's point of view, there are two considerations: How much will it cost to underwrite the program, and what will the value of the audience delivered be? An advertiser who chooses to underwrite the development of a program for syndication is taking a big risk. If the show has less than a strong audience draw, stations will be unlikely to pick it up, even for free. After all, other free barter programs are available. Those stations that do pick it up will consign it to a less than favorable time period. A weak program consigned to a weak time period generates very low advertising value for the advertiser.

The advertiser wishing to avoid this high-risk situation has an alternative. Instead of underwriting a program, the advertiser can purchase time in a syndicated program underwritten by someone else. The

Phil Donahue Show, a popular syndicated talk show carried by stations throughout the country, sells commercial time nationally. The stations receive the program with the advertising already inserted.

Currently many such options are open to the advertiser. Syndicated programming ventures available for barter arrangements are offered by syndication companies such as Syndicast Services; major agencies such as Grey Advertising, through its Lexington Broadcast Services; major producers such as MGM and Chuck Barris; buying services such as Vitt Media International; and station consortiums such as Operation Prime Time.

From the station's point of view, accepting a barter program makes sense when the quality of the program is such that the expected revenues from the limited advertising time available for sale in that program surpass those from programs offered with full commercial availabilities, minus the cost of those programs. Also the program must fit into the station's programming mix and be consistent with the program quality that viewers expect.

Another consideration is the potential longevity of the program. If the advertiser does not achieve the market penetration and overall audience level anticipated, further episodes of the program are not likely to be produced. The last thing a station needs is a constantly changing program lineup. Stability is important. The station should evaluate the program's national potential before committing to it. Station management also should ascertain the initial commitment of the sponsor in terms of original episodes to be produced.

In summary, barter offers several options to the advertiser looking for ways to maximize advertising presence given a limited advertising budget. However, it also has many pitfalls, most of which center on the inability of the advertiser to control when or where the advertising runs. An advertiser should enter the world of barter cautiously, investigating the options carefully, and limit barter participation to a relatively small part of the overall television advertising program.

NOTE

1. "Barter: Comic Books to Big Jets," *New York Times,* May 9, 1981.

7

Cable TV:
Past, Present, and Future

Before 1975 this book would have been considered complete with the coverage of network televison and local-station television. Cable television existed, but it was regarded essentially as an alternative distribution system for television station signals. A combination of legal and technological constraints prevented cable television from utilizing its unused channels to bring new viewing options to its subscribers.

In 1975 the introduction of satellite transmission ushered in a new era for the television medium in general. This technological breakthrough was accompanied by a changing attitude in Washington, D.C. The protective climate of the 1960s was being displaced by a growing commitment to providing the most extensive array of viewing options possible to the U.S. viewing public. The most exciting period in the evolution of the television medium had begun—the cable age was here.

This chapter and the next offer some insight into cable television, the present reality and the future promise. Also covered are the other new services that are changing the television landscape. This chapter concentrates on the medium itself; Chapter 8 focuses on the advertising opportunities inherent in cable television.

WHAT IS CABLE TV?

Cable television is, essentially, television brought into the home via a cable. The traditional form of television transmission is over the air. Television signals are broadcast from powerful television station transmitters. These signals can travel up to 100 airline miles; however, the average station's effective signal radius is 50 to 75 miles. Homes within this coverage area can receive the signal by either a rooftop antenna or a built-in rabbit ears type of antenna. Of course, the rooftop antenna provides better reception.

Because of the nature of the television signal, the propagation path can be blocked by obstructions that are either natural or artificial. For this reason homes in mountainous areas or in large cities with high-rise buildings often cannot receive the signals of the television stations serving their markets. Reception is not totally intercepted, but the quality of that reception is below comfortable viewing standards. Cable television provides an alternative form of television signal reception for these homes. Master antennas pick up the over-the-air signals. Then these signals are sent out via cable to the homes much as television signals are brought into homes, except that the receiving homes get clean signals, free of obstruction and interference.

In its early years, cable television was limited to this signal enhancement and delivery service. However, even in their early stages, cable television systems could send far more signals into the home than they were picking up from the local stations. The most rudimentary cable systems had 12-channel capacities. If the market was served by only three stations, it meant that nine channels were not being utilized. Prior to 1975, cable systems had the potential for using these channels by importing television signals from outside their market via microwave transmission.

In 1975, with the launching of RCA's *Satcom I* satellite, cable systems were given the additional option of importing distant signals from satellites. In satellite transmission the program originator sends signals to the satellite through powerful transmitters. These transmitting stations are known as *uplinks*. Each satellite is equipped with 24 different *transponders*, and each transponder can receive one signal and retransmit it to earth. This *downlinking* is completed when cable system earth stations pick up the signal.

A cable system must have a separate earth station to receive signals from each satellite. The satellites revolve at the same speed as the earth. Thus they are fixed at one point on the horizon. Prime satellite space is from 95 to 130 degrees on the horizon. The earth station must be aimed at precisely that point on the horizon corresponding with the transmitting satellite's position. Therefore, if a cable system wishes to receive signals from more than one satellite, it must have more than one earth station receiver.

Figure 7-1 is a sketch of a typical cable system. Satellite signals received by the earth stations and microwave and over-the-air signals received by the antenna are fed into the *head-end* equipment. Head-end equipment processes the various signals for transmission over cable. The cable distribution system consists of a central trunk cable, a

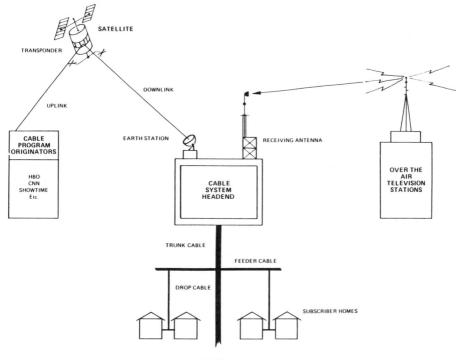

FIGURE 7-1

Typical U.S. cable television system.

series of feeder cables, and, finally, drop cables to each subscriber home. Cable systems are constructed either overhead (usually attached to existing telephone poles) or underground. Overhead, or aerial, systems are far less expensive to construct than underground systems.

At the subscriber's end, the required equipment ranges in complexity and price. A basic 12-channel system requires only a simple cable hookup. Systems consisting of more than 12 channels require more complex converters, and interactive systems that allow home-to-system reverse signals require far more expensive subscriber equipment.

Although the multichannel capacity of cable systems has existed from the earliest days of cable television, government restrictions designed to protect the interests of broadcasters prevented cable systems from employing unused channels to import television signals to the markets they served. The relaxation of these restrictions and the introduction of satellite transmission in the 1970s marked the transition of cable television from a technological to a cultural phenomenon. Today cable systems offer their subscribers a wide range of viewing options supplemental to the available over-the-air broadcaster's programming. Continued engineering breakthroughs have expanded the channel capacities from the early 12-channel limitation to up to 100 channels today. New builds—that is, new cable systems under construction today—are mostly of the 50+ channel variety, and existing 12 to 25 channel systems are gradually being updated to increase channel capacity.

Cable system franchises are rewarded on a local-market basis. Obtaining a local cable franchise today is a complex and highly competitive process. Hearings are usually lengthy, and competing systems must make significant community service commitments to obtain a franchise. Franchise awards are usually for 15 years. The franchiser pays a fee to the franchising body. All transfers of franchises must be approved by that body, and the books and records of that franchisee are always open to this franchising authority. This authority usually must approve rate increases; however, automatic rate-increase guidelines are gradually replacing direct involvement of the franchising authority in rate setting.

The 1981 average monthly subscription charge for basic cable service was $7 to $10. Pay cable services cost an additional $7 to $10 per month each. As competition for franchises rises and potential revenues from pay services increase, initial basic charges are coming down. Also cable systems are engaging more and more in a practice known as tiering, in which cable options are grouped into several tiers. Tier 1 might include only over-the-air television signals. Tier 2 would include many of the basic cable networks also. Tier 3 would introduce the pay cable options. A fixed monthly charge would be set for each tier.

With this basic outline of the structure of the cable television industry in mind, let us look at cable's past, present, and future.

FROM 1948 TO 1981

The origins of cable television date to 1948, when Community Antenna Television (CATV) introduced master antenna systems in areas in which over-the-air reception was impaired. These systems provided access only to the regular television stations serving the community. The cable television industry remained in this reception enhancement mode until the 1960s, when system operators began to wake up to the potential of their unused channels to bring additional television signals to their subscribers. Some more entrepreneurial system operators began experimenting with the importation of television signals from outside their home television station markets and with the production of their own limited local programming.

Broadcasters felt threatened by this new aspect of cable television, and they pressured the FCC for action limiting the importation of foreign television signals into their markets. From 1948 to 1962 the cable industry had grown to 800 systems serving 850,000 subscribers. By 1968, spurred on by the potential attraction of this increased viewing option capability, the number of cable systems had grown to 2000 and the total number of cable subscribers had reached 2.8 million.

However, throughout this period the FCC was becoming more receptive to the broadcasters' appeals for protection, and it took a series of actions to severely limit growth of the cable industry. The commission took its first action in 1962, in the Carter Mountain Transmission Corporation decision. The FCC refused to allow this cable system operator to provide microwave transmission of outside television signals to an area served by only one local television station.

In 1966 the FCC moved more aggressively into the cable arena after its authority to do so was upheld by the Supreme Court. The 1966 Second Report and Order extended the FCC's jurisdiction to cover all cable systems, not only those employing microwave transmission. The 1968 revision of the Second Report and Order placed onerous restrictions on the cable systems concerning the importation of distant signals. These systems were required to receive permission from the originating station, on a program-by-program basis, before they carried that station's signal to a distant market. Cable systems in major markets had to receive permission before they could import any distant signals. All cable systems had to carry the closest independent station and could not "leapfrog" over that station by bringing in an independent station from a more distant market.

These regulations virtually froze cable television development until 1972. Whereas the number of cable systems grew from 800 to 2000 between 1962 and 1968, a 16.5 percent annual rate of growth for the industry, that number increased only from 2000 to 2841 between 1962 and 1972, a low 9 percent annual rate of growth.

In 1972, the FCC presented a new, relaxed proposal for cable regulation, the 1972 Cable Television Report and Order. Cable systems were required to carry all local signals and were precluded from carrying distant stations presenting the same network programming as local stations or the same syndicated programming as local stations. The 1972 Report and Order also required systems to provide 20 channels of service and to reserve one channel for each of a variety of public uses. Technical standards were established, the FCC's role in the franchising process was spelled out, and limitations were placed on the types of programming that could be provided by pay services.

Gradually each of the major cable restrictions was knocked down.

In 1980 the FCC eliminated the syndicated exclusivity provision and the limitations on cable systems concerning the importation of distant signals. Although the broadcast industry challenged this decision in the courts, the FCC was upheld *(Malrite Broadcasting Inc. v. FCC)*. The courts also found the specification of channel capacity and the assignment of channels for various public access uses to go beyond the jurisdiction of the FCC *(Midwest Video Corp. v. FCC)*. The FCC's involvement in the franchise award process was subsequently limited to the imposition of a ceiling of 3 percent of gross revenues on the franchise fee that the local authority could charge the cable system. Finally, the restrictions on pay cable program content were eliminated as a result of *Home Box Office v. FCC* in 1977.

This effective deregulation of the cable industry stimulated substantial new interest in cable development. But even more important than the relaxation of government restrictions was the 1975 launching of RCA's *Satcom I*. In 1975 Home Box Office (HBO), a subsidiary of Time, Inc., began the satellite transmission of its pay cable service, and the cable age was upon us. By the close of 1980, more than 10 million cable subscribers were receiving some form of satellite-fed programming. The National Cable Television Association publication *A Cable Primer* listed more than 40 satellite-fed program services. *Satcom I* was joined by Western Union's *Westar III* and AT&T's *Comstar D-2*. In 1981 *Satcom I* was replaced by *Satcom III*, and in early 1982 *Satcom IV* began operation. Estimates are that three or four additional satellites can operate from 95 to 130 degrees on the horizon. Further satellite expansion will mean less separation among satellite positions and potential interference problems.

With the impetus from deregulation, satellite transmission, and a growing proliferation of cable-distributed viewing options, cable growth was dramatic from 1976 to 1981. By 1982 there were more than 4500 operating cable systems and an estimated 22 million cable subscriber homes (27 percent of U.S. television households). Table 7-1 provides a record of cable system and subscriber growth through 1982. That brings us up to the present. Now let us take a more in-depth look at the cable industry today.

CABLE TV TODAY

To get the clearest picture of the cable industry today it is necessary to divide it into its major components. First, there is the individual cable system, providing a television distribution service to a community or group of communities. Second, there are the advertising-supported basic cable programming networks providing a programming source to

TABLE 7-1
CABLE INDUSTRY GROWTH

Year	Operating systems	Total subscribers
1952	70	14,000
1955	400	150,000
1960	640	650,000
1965	1325	1,275,000
1970	2490	4,500,000
1971	2639	5,300,000
1972	2841	6,000,000
1973	2991	7,300,000
1974	3158	8,700,000
1975	3506	9,800,000
1976	3681	10,800,000
1977	3832	11,900,000
1978	3875	13,000,000
1979	4150	14,100,000
1980	4225	16,000,000
1981	4375 E*	18,300,000
1982	4825 E*	22,000,000

*E = estimates (as of January 1 of year specified). Figures for 1982 are author's estimates.

Source: *Television Factbook*, (Services volume), Television Digest, Washington, 1982.

cable subscribers for free or for a nominal charge. Third, there are the pay televison services providing commercial-free programming to cable subscribers for a fee. First, the individual cable system.

Cable System

At the close of 1981, there were an estimated 4800 cable systems in operation and a total of almost 6000 new systems either approved or in the franchise application stage. These systems represent the heart of the cable industry. The vitality of the industry is virtually guaranteed by this constant new development. The largest individual cable system in operation is Cox Cable, San Diego, with 208,000 subscribers. This is an exceptionally large cable system. Only 10 percent of all cable systems have 10,000 or more subscribers, and the median size of a cable TV system is 2500.[1]

Table 7-2 lists the 20 largest cable systems as of June 1, 1981. Many cable companies, referred to as *multiple-system operators* (*MSOs*), own more than one system. Large MSOs are a dominant force in the cable industry today; the 10 largest MSOs have a combined subscriber base of approximately 9.6 million homes, over 40 percent of all cable homes.

TABLE 7-2

20 LARGEST CABLE SYSTEMS
(As of June 1, 1981)

System	Location	Subscribers
1. Cox Cable	San Diego, CA	207,572
2. Oyster Bay, NY	Oyster Bay, NY	130,900
3. Manhattan Cable TV	New York, NY	123,000
4. East Orange, NJ	East Orange, NJ	103,000
5. Theta Cable of California	Los Angeles, CA	99,232
6. Wayne, NJ	Wayne, NJ	91,843
7. Austin, TX	Austin, TX	90,000
8. Tulsa, OK	Tulsa, OK	89,996
9. Erie County, NY	Erie County, NY	89,231
10. San Jose, CA	San Jose, CA	83,000
11. Suffolk County, NY	Suffolk County, NY	78,663
12. Audubon, NJ	Audubon, NJ	72,000
13. Teleprompter Manhattan	New York, NY	66,751
14. Orlando, FL	Orlando, FL	66,400
15. Toledo, OH	Toledo, OH	65,000
16. Wilmington, DE	Wilmington, DE	61,237
17. Teleprompter of Seattle	Seattle, WA	61,149
18. Oceanic Cablevision	Honolulu, HI	60,000
19. Flint, MI	Flint, MI	58,000
20. San Antonio, TX	San Antonio, TX	57,053

Source: *Television Factbook*, (Services volume), Television Digest, Washington, 1982.

TABLE 7-3
TOP TEN CABLE MULTIPLE-
    SYSTEM OPERATORS

Company	Subscribers
1. American Television & Communications (Time, Inc.)	1,752,000
2. Teleprompter Corp. (Westinghouse Electric)	1,570,000
3. Tele-Communications, Inc.	1,362,301
4. Cox Cable Communications (Cox Broadcasting)	1,056,863
5. Warner Amex Cable (Warner Communications and American Express)	837,00
6. Storer Cable Communications (Storer Broadcasting)	802,000
7. Times Mirror Cable (Times Mirror Co.)	650,612
8. S.I. Newhouse	557,675
9. Rogers UA Cablesystems	514,821
10. Viacom Cablevision (Viacom International)	514,720
Total	9,617,992

Source: *Broadcasting/Cablecasting Yearbook, 1982*, Broadcasting Publications, Inc., Washington, 1982.

Table 7-3 lists the top 10 cable MSOs. The power of these 10 cable systems' operators is underscored by their extensive involvement in other aspects of the cable industry and in the broadcast industry.

The average cable system has 15 channels and charges its subscribers a $16 to $20 installation fee, $7.69 on average per month for the basic cable service, and $9.13 on average per month for each pay cable service.[2] Channel capacity is increasing as older, limited channel systems are upgraded and new builds are put into operation. Approximately 10 percent of operational systems offer 30 or more channels. Major market franchises recently awarded are promising a 50- to 100-channel capacity.

The economic performance of the cable systems had been constantly on the rise until 1980. From 1975 to 1980 net income for cable systems rose from $26.9 million to $199.3 million on revenues of $1.8 billion.

Although revenues in 1980 increased to $2.2 billion, net income dropped to $168 million. Actually, operating income was up from $690 million to $799 million, but high depreciation and interest charges reduced net income. Table 7-4 provides a 6-year-trend record of cable system revenues and net income. Income tended to follow subscriber base lines. The smallest systems, with a subscriber base of 1000 or less, were most likely to have lost money in 1980, while the large, 20,000+ subscriber systems generally were the most profitable.

Although the decline in net income might cause some to question the potential of cable system investment, the revenue and operating income statistics are really more relevant. The book value of cable system assets increased 38 percent from 1976 to 1980, reaching $4.4 billion. Pay cable continued to represent a growing component of overall cable system revenues. Pay cable revenues were up 62 percent from 1979, rising to $365 million, or 26 percent of the total cable system revenues. In 1978 pay cable had accounted for only 13 percent of cable system revenues.

More than two-thirds of all cable systems provide some form of local program origination; however, over half these systems provide automatic originations only. An automatic origination is something like a time and weather service, a stock ticker, sports scores, or a community

TABLE 7-4
CABLE TELEVISION SYSTEM
EARNINGS

Year	Revenues		Net income	
	Amount*	Growth (%)	Amount*	Growth (%)
1975	$ 894.9	—	$ 26.9	—
1976	999.8	12	57.7	114
1977	1205.9	21	133.7	132
1978	1511.0	25	137.1	3
1979	1817.1	20	199.3	45
1980	2200.0	21	168.1	(16)†

*In millions.

†Operating income was up 16 percent, from $690 million in 1979 to $799 million in 1980; however, increased depreciation and interest charges resulted in a decline in net income.

Source: "FCC Cable TV Industry Financial Data," FCC, Washington, 1975–1980.

bulletin board. Only about one-quarter of all cable systems create some local programming.

Almost every cable system reports some advertising sale either in local programs or in cooperative local positions in the advertiser-supported basic cable services carried. However, few cable systems actively promote their advertising availabilities, and advertising revenues for cable systems remain negligible. As advertising entities, the cable systems have a role that will continue to be essentially one of a conduit for the advertising on national basic cable program suppliers for the next few years. Some fledgling attempts are being made to combine cable systems into viable advertising networks, but the realization of that goal is still several years away.

Advertiser-Supported Basic Cable Networks

Once the first satellite was launched, it was only a matter of time before enterprising programmers began to develop new programming services to fill the unused cable channels. The pioneer in this area was Ted Turner. In 1976 he leased space on *Satcom I* and began feeding by satellite the programming of his Atlanta-based station, WTBS, to cable systems throughout the country. Billing WTBS as the first *superstation*, Turner began charging national advertisers a higher "national" rate, reflecting his new cable distribution universe. By mid-1982 WTBS was available on cable systems that, when combined with its base Atlanta audience, comprised close to 21 million households.

Turner was the only one to promote the superstation concept actively. However, other independent stations also were being fed to cable systems. At first, these "passive" superstations resisted the efforts of third parties to provide their signals to cable systems for a fee, but they gradually recognized the value of the incremental audience they received to advertisers. WOR-TV, the New York City independent station, was received by 4 million cable homes via the *Westar V* transponder of Eastern Microwave. WGN-TV, the Chicago independent station, boasted an even greater cable audience of almost 6 million homes. WGN-TV was transmitted to these homes by the *Satcom III* transponder owned by United Video.

The superstations were joined by an array of programming networks established especially for, and limited to, satellite-fed cable transmission. Again, Ted Turner was an early entrant. In June 1980 he launched his Cable News Network (CNN), a 24-hour all-news service. By mid-1982 more than 2000 systems were carrying CNN, and its subscriber total was more than 14 million homes. But Ted Turner was not the first

TABLE 7-5
ADVERTISER-SUPPORTED BASIC CABLE PROGRAM SERVICES, 1982

Service	Owner	Description	Satellite	Systems carrying	Estimated subscribers
WTBS	Turner Broadcasting System, Atlanta	An Atlanta-based independent TV station programming a combination of general entertainment and sports; categorized as a superstation	Satcom III	4052	22 million
ESPN	ESPN, Bristol, CT (Getty Oil-financed)	A 24-hour sports network featuring live and taped sports events and sports-related programming	Satcom III	3545	16 million
CNN I	Turner Broadcasting System, Atlanta	A 24-hour news programming service	Satcom III	2142	14 million
U.S.A. Network	Jointly owned by Paramount, MCA, and Time, Inc., New York	Combination of programming services. Madison Square Garden Sports events; *Calliope* (6:30–7:30 p.m. weeknights and Saturday morning), children's programming; *The English Channel,* British programming from Granada TV; *You!;* fashion programming and *Night Flight,* rock music programming	Satcom III	1700	10 million
BET	Black Entertainment Television, Washington, D.C.	General entertainment and sports programming for a black audience	Westar V	845	NA
CBN	Christian Broadcasting Network, Virginia	Range of religious programming	Satcom III	2100	14.6 million

Service	Provider	Description	Satellite		
ABC ARTS (Alpha Repertory Television Service)	ABC Video Enterprises in conjunction with Warner Amex, New York	Cultural programming including music, drama, and dance	Satcom III	1600	6.5 million
MSN (Modern Satellite Network)	Modern Satellite Network, New York	Educational and consumer-oriented programs; features The Home Shopping Show	Satcom III	330	4.1 million
Daytime	Hearst/ABC Video Services, New York	Programming for women	Satcom III	250	4.9 million
MTV (Music Television)	Warner Amex Satellite Entertainment, New York	Taped concerts and contemporary music programming	Satcom III	600	4 million
SPN (Satellite Program Network)	SSS Corp., Tulsa	Special-interest programming, special women's features, how-to programs, some international programming	Westar V	456	4.4 million
SIN (Spanish International Network)	Spanish International Network, New York	Spanish-language entertainment and news programming	Westar V	600	2.5 million*
North American Newstime	North American Newstime, Atlanta	A slow-scan news service	Satcom III	85	870,000
WGN-TV	Chicago Tribune Company	A Chicago-based independent TV station programming a combination of general entertainment, news, and sports programming; categorized as a superstation; satellite-fed to cable systems by United Video, Tulsa	Satcom III	2520	7 million

TABLE 7-5
ADVERTISER-SUPPORTED BASIC
CABLE PROGRAM SERVICES, 1982
(*Continued*)

Service	Owner	Description	Satellite	Systems carrying	Estimated subscribers
WOR-TV	RKO Corp., New York	A New York-based independent TV station programming a combination of general entertainment, news, and sports programming; categorized as a superstation; satellite-fed to cable systems by Eastern Microwave, Syracuse, NY	Westar V	NA†	NA
ABC/Westinghouse Satellite News Channel	A joint venture of ABC and Westinghouse, New York	A 24-hour news service	Westar V	NA	2.6 million‡
Cable Health Network	A joint venture of Viacom and Reiss Development	Programming relating to health and health-related fields	Satcom III	NA	4 million‡
CNN II	Turner Broadcasting System, Atlanta	A news headline service including local news elements; companion service to CNN I	Satcom III	83	1.1 million
The Weather Channel	The Weather Channel, Atlanta	A 24-hour weather service including features and localized reports	Satcom III	172	2.5 million

*Also carried on over-the-air stations, extending total coverage to over 20 million homes.

†NA = not available.

‡Author's estimate.

to introduce an advertiser-supported cable network. Several networks predated CNN. The Entertainment and Sports Programming Network (ESPN), a 24-hour sports programming service, was introduced in September 1979. This Getty Oil venture claimed more than 16 million subscribers by mid-1982. Black Entertainment Television (BET) in March 1979, the Modern Satellite Network (MSN) in January 1979, the Spanish International Network (SIN) in September 1979, and Madison Square Garden Sports[3] in September 1977 were other significant trailblazers. By 1981 it seemed that a new network service was being announced every week. Table 7-5 lists the major advertiser-supported basic cable networks in operation in 1982.

Nielsen started measuring the audiences of WTBS in 1981, and CNN and ESPN in 1982. The WTBS 24-hour rating in households receiving this service remained at approximately a 2.5 level through June 1982, which translated to a 0.6 national rating level. The first CNN and ESPN numbers in early 1982 were running at about the 1 to 2 rating level in subscriber households, translating to a 0.2 national rating. WTBS ratings were strongest during the early evening hours. ESPN performed best on Sunday afternoons, presumably feeding off the network-generated sports audience. CNN audiences peaked between 5 and 6 p.m. on weekdays, the traditional news viewing hour.

The financial future of the advertiser-supported basic cable program services is still being debated. The superstations seem to be secure, since all are profitable over-the-air stations in their respective home markets and the bonus coverage provided by satellite distribution to cable systems allows them to charge more for their commercial time. The only possible problem facing these stations is the current copyright battle in which program producers are attempting to obtain some compensation for the presentation of their programming via a superstation to audiences beyond the boundaries of that station's home market. If the producers win, substantial copyright payments would have to be made by the receiving cable systems. These systems might choose to abandon the superstations if subscription surcharges failed to offset copyright payments.

The future of the pure basic cable programming services is more problematical. Currently most of, if not all, these services operate at a loss. Total estimated advertising revenues for all these services in 1981 were $50 million. This is approximately how much one service would require to make a profit. Unfortunately, many services were sharing these revenues.

An advertiser-supported cable programmer can go in two directions. The *narrow casting*, or *special-interest*, direction involves programming to a particular segment of the total television audience. The target

TABLE 7-6

PAY CABLE PROGRAM SERVICES
(As of January, 1982)

Service	Owner	Description	Satellite	Systems carrying	Estimated subscribers
Home Box Office (HBO)	Time, Inc., New York	A 24-hour service offering movies, specials, and some sports	Satcom III	3300	8.5 million
Showtime	Viacom, New York	A 24-hour service offering movies and specials	Satcom III	1500	3 million
The Movie Channel	Warner Amex Satellite Entertainment, New York	A 24-hour all-movie service	Satcom III	2150	2.2 million
Escapade/Playboy	Rainbow Programming Service, Woodbury, NY	Adult films and specials	Comstar D-2	115	206,000
Bravo	Rainbow Programming Service, Woodbury, NY	Film, dance, and music presentations	Comstar D-2	26	48,300
Cinemax	Time, Inc., New York	All movies	Satcom III	900	1.5 million
Home Theater Network	Home Theater Network, Portland, ME	G- and PG-rated movies	Westar V	275	155,000
Spotlight	Times Mirror Satellite Programming	Movies, specials provided to Times Mirror cable systems	Comstar D-2	50	300,000
Galavision	Galavision, New York	Movies, variety programming, and sports for Spanish-speaking audience	Satcom III	134	100,000
The Entertainment Channel	RCTV, New York	A selection of cultural and BBC programming	Satcom IV	NA*	NA

*NA = not available.

segment should be particularly attractive to advertisers, to allow the programmer to obtain a premium rate for the advertising availabilities. The programmer who chooses this approach must be able to exact a large premium, since the small absolute audience size will not generate enough advertising revenue at normal CPM levels. The second approach is to provide programming geared to a *broader audience* in the hope that the absolute size of the audience will be large enough to generate sufficient advertising revenue at normal CPM levels.

The first approach is best illustrated by ABC ARTS, a service offering cultural programming. It hopes to attract an audience with a high socioeconomic profile, an audience that will bring premium prices from advertisers. Illustrative of the broader-audience approach is CNN, an all-news service aimed at reaching a far larger audience. Neither approach has proved profitable yet. The special-interest services are programming to a small portion of an audience that is already limited by the dimensions of U.S. cable penetration and each service's penetration of that cable household universe. This translates to very small viewing levels. Although advertisers are ready to pay a premium for these audiences, they are unwilling to pay the exorbitant premiums required to cover the programming costs of these services. Indeed, CBS Cable, unable to attract a substantial enough advertising base, ceased operation at the end of 1982.

The broad-based programmers are not much better off. Currently services such as CNN and ESPN attract larger audiences than the special-interest cable services, and they have obtained a much greater penetration of the cable home universe. But the demographic profile of their audiences is not different from that of network television news and sports programming. So advertisers are reluctant to pay a CPM premium for commercial time on these cable services. At network television CPM levels, these services are not profitable now, although it is believed that ESPN is reaching a break-even level.

At present the future of the various advertiser-supported basic cable systems is in doubt. Will they survive? Which will survive? We present some possible scenarios later in this chapter.

Pay Cable

The future of advertiser-supported cable program services may be in doubt, but the future of the pay cable services seems to be ensured. Already HBO, the pioneer service, is generating handsome profits for its parent, Time, Inc., and Showtime, the second largest pay service in terms of subscribers, reported its first profit in 1981. Table 7-6 describes the pay cable services in operation during 1981.

Home Box Office is the giant in the pay cable sector. Aided by a 2-year headstart and a prime satellite position, HBO obtained channels on more than two-thirds of all the operating cable systems in the country. With this distribution base, HBO signed up almost one-third (28 percent) of all cable homes for its movie service. HBO became profitable in 1977. By 1982 its profits were estimated between $75 million and $80 million, more than one-third of the total operating profit for that year for parent Time, Inc. Showtime is the number two competitor in the pay cable race. This service, owned by Viacom, became profitable in 1981. Both pay cable programmers have expanded to 24 hours and are beginning to supplement their theatrical feature product with their own productions.

Not only were pay cable services economically viable in 1981, but also they were competitive with the networks for primetime audiences in pay cable homes. Table 7-7 shows the audience shares of the various program sources for the 1981–1982 broadcast season. Given that most cable homes receive only one pay cable service, the 20 percent share is competitive with the 20.3 percent average of the three network affiliates.

TABLE 7-7

**PAY CABLE HOUSEHOLD
AUDIENCE SHARES, 1981–1982
BROADCAST SEASON***
(Primetime, Monday–
Sunday, 8–11 p.m.)

	Pay cable households	
	Rating	**Share (%)†**
Network affiliates	42.4	61
Pay cable services	13.5	20
Basic cable services	3.8	5
Other on-air services	13.3	19
Total	69.1	

*Average of November 1981, February 1982, and May 1982 measurement periods.

†Shares are greater than 100 percent owing to simultaneous viewing.

Source: "Cable TV: A Status Report," A. C. Nielsen, Chicago, Nov. 1981; Feb., May, 1982.

The pay cable audience is not only substantial; it is better educated, more affluent, and concentrated in "A" and "B" counties (those that are most populous and in or closest to metropolitan areas). For this reason advertisers and advertising agencies have been encouraging the major pay cable services to consider carrying some form of advertising. To date, the pay services have resisted the temptation of advertising revenues, concentrating instead on the expansion of their subscriber bases.

Because of the limited number of channels available on the early cable systems, most systems would accept only one service. However, the 30 + channel systems are beginning to offer more than one pay cable service. The availability of multiple pay cable options has both increased the potential number of subscribers to each pay service and added a new level of competition among them. To the extent that subscribers sign up for more than one service, the overall pay cable universe is expanded. To the extent that a system loses its monopoly on a cable system, the subscriber recruitment process becomes more complex. This basic change in the competitive environment of the pay cable systems and their continued access to theatrical features at reasonable prices are the two unknowns facing the pay cable services.

To summarize, the state of the cable industry today is healthy and expanding. The number of cable systems is growing, and with this growth the penetration of cable television is advancing. Existing systems are being upgraded from a 12 to 20 channel capacity to a 30 + channel capacity, adding breadth to the overall cable service provided to the average subscriber. The jury is still out on the potential of advertiser-supported special-interest basic cable services; however, the broader-based services and superstations seem to be in a strong position. The pay cable networks show promise of continuing profitability and expansion.

When we deal with a phenomenon as dynamic as the cable television industry is today, it is not enough to analyze the present. Some attempt must be made to forecast the future so that decisions made today will be consistent with future conditions. In the next two sections we address the future. First, we focus on the current components of the cable television marketplace. Second, we discuss the other technological and competitive changes on the horizon for television.

CABLE TV, 1990

By 1990 it is estimated that cable television penetration will be 60 percent, with three-quarters of these cable subscriber households receiving some pay cable service. Based on a projected total of 100 million

TABLE 7-8
TELEVISION HOUSEHOLDS, 1990
VERSUS 1981

Year		TV households (000)			
		Total	Pay cable	Basic cable only	Noncable
1981	No.	81,500	10,000	12,000	59,500
	Percentage	100	12	15	73
1990	No.	100,000	45,000	15,000	40,000
	Percentage	100	45	15	40

Data for 1981 from "Cable TV: A Status Report," A. C. Nielsen, Chicago, 1981.

television households, this figure translates to 60 million cable television households, of which 45 million will receive some pay cable service.

When these 1990 totals are compared with 1981 figures, they dramatize the rapid development expected for cable television in the next decade. Table 7-8 makes this comparison. This high rate of cable television growth will have a strong impact on all three sectors of the cable television industry—the local systems, the advertiser-supported basic cable program services, and the pay cable services.

Local Cable System, 1990

By 1990 the average local cable system will have substantially greater channel capacity. This will lead to greater tiering of services. Through this tiering approach the local cable systems will be able to maximize subscription revenues, since they will be offering a program package designed for every pocketbook. It is estimated that by 1990 cable system subscription revenues will grow to more than $6 billion. Of course, there will be a far greater number of systems in 1990; nevertheless, the individual system should remain very healthy through 1990.

An area in which cable systems are expected to rise even more dramatically is advertising. Local cable system advertising revenues are small today, but as the growth of given systems stabilizes, these systems will focus more attention on their potential advertising revenues. Expanded channel capacity will allow systems to provide more local programming. This programming will draw local advertisers. In some cases channels might be devoted to advertiser-produced programs such as a fashion show sponsored by a local department store.

Another factor that will stimulate the growth of local cable advertising revenues is the combination of cable systems into mininetworks. As new systems fill in existing holes in cable coverage patterns, they can be formed into mininetworks much as suburban newspapers in major markets have been combined. This will facilitate the planning and buying process for potential advertisers, increasing the attractiveness of the cable TV alternative. Cable systems will compete more with newspapers and radio stations for local advertising revenues than with over-the-air television stations, since their coverage patterns and audience numbers will be more comparable with those for these media. Industry estimates for 1990 local cable advertising revenues vary from $500 million to $1 billion.

One aspect of the future cable universe that is much discussed today is the availability of interactive cable communication. Interactive cable communication allows the cable subscriber to send messages to the cable system head-end facility as well as to receive signals from that facility. Warner Amex has set up an experimental interactive cable system in Columbus, Ohio, known as QUBE.

The revenue-generating potential of a QUBE-type interactive system is seen to be in the *home shopping* capability it provides. Viewers can respond directly to advertising, in effect ordering the product or service over the air. The Warner Amex QUBE system represents only a rudimentary form of interactive system, but subscriber response has been discouraging to date. People do not seem to be willing to pay the premium to gain access to an interactive system.

Given the cost of developing this type of system and the lukewarm reception QUBE has received, it is unlikely that interactive cable communication will grow significantly by 1990. Nevertheless, interactive capability has become a requirement in most new-build situations, so the potential for an interactive service will increase. So, too, undoubtedly, will the entrepreneurial attempts to find some profitable application of this service. The interactive system of the future is more likely to be a telephone-based videotext system than a cable television-based system.

Advertiser-Supported Basic Cable Program Services

Three possible scenarios must be considered in forecasting the future of advertiser-supported basic cable program services:

1. The $2 billion market scenario

2. The audience/CPM-based scenario

3. The magazine-based scenario

First, let us address the $2 billion market scenario. This is simply an acceptance of the popular $2 billion projection of 1990 basic cable advertising revenues. Forecasters who hold to this $2 billion figure also talk of approximately 10 viable national basic cable services sharing these revenues. The assumption is that $200 million is the minimum revenue level at which a service could operate profitably. This scenario is included as a benchmark only.

The second scenario is built on an audience/CPM equation paralleling that of the broadcast industry. This scenario must begin with an estimate of 1990 viewing levels and shares. Table 7-9 provides 1990 share-of-viewing predictions. Unfortunately, the one area in which these predictions lack substantiation is in the case of the projected share for basic cable created options. At the conclusion of 1981, the existing basic cable services had not shown anywhere near the drawing power needed to capture such a large collective audience share. To do so, they would have to be fully competitive with existing independent television stations. Available research does not show that to be the case. Nevertheless, for the purpose of this scenario, we will give them the benefit of the doubt.

A 9 percent share of viewing during the critical viewing hours of 6 p.m. to 1 a.m. would translate into a collective average-minute audience of 675,000 adults (see Table 7-10 for the calculation). It is assumed that these program services, since they are adult-oriented, would be sold to an adult-audience as opposed to a homes-audience base.

The current network television primetime CPM ($4.46), inflated at a 10 percent compound growth rate, would yield a 1990 CPM of $9.56.

TABLE 7-9
SHARE OF VIEWING PRIMETIME
AND FRINGE, 1990

	Networks (%)	Independents/ PBS (%)	Pay cable options (%)	Basic cable-created options (%)
Pay cable households (45%)	60	6	20	14
Basic cable-only households (15%)	70	10	—	20
Noncable households (40%)	80	20	—	—
Total households	70	12	9	9

TABLE 7-10
AVERAGE AUDIENCE LEVEL OF
BASIC CABLE SERVICES, 1990

Share of viewing	9%
6 p.m.–1 a.m. households using TV	50%
Homes (000)	4,500,000*
Adult viewers per home	1.5
Adult viewers (000)	6,750,000†
Adult viewers per service (10 services)	675,000‡

*0.09 × 0.50 × 100,000,000 homes = 4,500,000 homes.
†4,500,000 × 1.5 = 6,750,000 adults.
‡6,750,000 ÷ 10 = 675,000 adult viewers per system.

Giving the basic cable services a $33^1/_3$ percent premium, because of the selective nature of their audience, would generate a $12.75 adult CPM for these services. Applying this CPM to the 675,000 average viewer base produces an $8500 cost per 30-second announcement. Eight 30-second commercials per hour (less than broadcast levels) times 7 hours per day times 7 days per week times 52 weeks equals a potential of 20,384 announcements for sale. If all these announcements were sold, they would generate $173 million per service in revenues.

It can be argued that these services could offer more than eight 30-second commercials for sale per hour. However, it can be argued that a 100 percent sellout rate is unrealistic. And, of course, some revenues can be generated before 6 p.m. and after 1 a.m. Nevertheless, $173 million seems reasonable and in line with the $200 million per system projected in the first scenario.

The third scenario is patterned after the magazine industry rather than the broadcast industry. The theory is that just as the magazine medium has changed from a mass-market-based medium to a selective market medium, so, too, the basic cable services, with their small audience bases, will evolve into a selective market medium. Given this hypothesis, it is natural to go one step further and state that the editorial product of these new cable services will conform to the most accepted forms of editorial product in the magazine industry today. Also, just as readers pay a subscription price for magazines today, they may be willing to pay a subscription price for these basic cable services in the future.

Based on the assumptions made in the previous paragraph, I have

TABLE 7-11
MAGAZINE SERVICE: SAMPLE
SUBSCRIPTION/ADVERTISING
REVENUE EQUATION, 1990
(Newsweekly*)

Household circulation	3.5 million
Monthly subscription fee	$10
Subscription revenue to system	$210 million
Adult viewers	7 million
CPM	$6.00
Page rate†	$42,000
Pages per week	48
Ad revenues per week	$2 million
Annual ad revenues	$104 million
Total revenue	$314 million

*Based on prototype of Time and Newsweek.
†Page equals three exposures per day for 1 week.

developed the following scenario: There will be eight types of cable network paralleling the eight basic top-circulation magazine formats of today. The eight types are newsweekly, cultural, adult entertainment, sports, women's services, fashion and style, shelter, and business. An additional newsweekly would bring the total network count to nine.

The magazine revenue equation is based on a combination of subscription and advertising revenues. Focusing on the newsweekly service (Table 7-11), we first estimate a total household circulation based on the current 5 percent average circulation penetration figure of Time and Newsweek. Today the price of Time and Newsweek is $1.25 per issue, or $5 per month (subscription prices are lower). Increasing this figure by a 10 percent inflation rate yields a rate of $10 per month for 1990. If we assume the cable TV newsweekly would be able to charge a monthly subscription fee of $10, the cable network probably would keep $5 out of this $10. Multiplying $5 by 3.5 million homes by 12 months gives a subscription revenue figure of $210 million.

On the advertising side, 3.5 million households times 2.0 adult viewers per household (1.4 in primetime today) yields an average adult audience of 7.0 million. The four-color-bleed full-page CPM for Time and Newsweek today is about $3. Inflating this figure by 10 percent per year brings the 1990 CPM to about \$6. Multiplying the \$6 CPM by the 7.0 million adult delivery yields a \$42,000 page rate.

Now comes the difficult part. How do you translate a magazine page to television terms? We know that not all the 7.0 million adults in subscribing households view each commercial. For our model we assumed that three spots per day over 7 days would translate to a total adult audience of 100 GRPs, or 7 million. The cable network could accommodate 48 of these page advertisers, producing \$2 million per week in advertising revenues, or \$104 million for the full year. Adding the \$210 million in subscription revenues to the \$104 million in advertising revenues yields a total of \$314 million.

We developed a similar equation for each cable network type based on its magazine counterpart. As Table 7-12 shows, the total for all nine networks is slightly over \$3 billion, or 1.5 times the estimates for the 100 percent advertiser-supported scenarios; yet advertising revenues in this scenario are only \$1 billion.

Certainly, the third scenario is the most controversial. Nevertheless, it does make a major point; that is, apparently the total revenues of a

TABLE 7-12

MAGAZINE SCENARIO:
ADVERTISER-SUPPORTED
SERVICES, 1990 REVENUES
(Millions)

	No. of networks	Circulation revenues	Advertising revenues	Total revenues
Newsweeklies	2	\$ 420.0	\$ 208.0	\$ 628.0
Cultural	1	108.0	88.4	196.4
Adult entertainment	1	480.0	161.2	641.2
Sports	1	90.0	50.0	140.0
Women's services	1	168.0	187.0	355.0
Fashion and style	1	180.0	62.0	242.0
Shelter	1	480.0	197.5	677.5
Business	1	120.0	56.0	176.0
	Grand total	\$2046.0	\$1010.1	\$3056.1

TABLE 7-13
SCENARIO SUMMARIES

	Revenue per service (000)			Ser-	Total
	Circulation	Advertising	Total	vices	revenue
Scenario 1: $2 billion market	—	$200,000	$200,000	10	$2,000,000
Scenario 2: audience/CPM projection	—	173,000	173,000	10	1,730,000
Scenario 3: magazine-based	$227,000	112,000	339,000	9	3,056,000

special-interest basic cable program service would be substantially greater if that service charged some subscription fee to supplement possible advertising revenues. If the audience does have a special interest in the programming of the service, it should be willing to pay something for it. It would be very easy to incorporate these subscription fees into a tiering approach to cable pricing. Advertising would still be carried, but in limited amounts—more to keep the subscription fees required for profitable operation low enough to prevent them from becoming too great a disincentive to potential subscribers.

Table 7-13 summarizes the three scenarios. This direct comparison illustrates the far greater revenue potential of the approach financed by the subscription fee and advertising. However, whether or not viewers will accept advertising given a subscription fee or a subscription fee given advertising remains to be tested.

Pay Cable, 1990

Pay cable revenues in 1990 will depend on the answers to two key questions:

- Will viewers subscribe to more than one service?
- Will pay services accept advertising?

It is estimated that 45 million households will subscribe to a pay cable service in 1990. Based on a $20 monthly subscription rate (roughly double today's rate) and one service per subscriber, this translates to $5.4 billion in subscription revenues (see Figure 7-2). However, the

PAY CABLE REVENUES

1990

Monthly subscription fee   = $20

System share   = $10.00

×

Subscriber homes   =   45,000,000

Monthly system revenues   = $450,000,000

Annual system revenues   = $5,400,000,000

FIGURE 7-2

Pay cable revenues, 1990.

new 30 + channel systems already offer more than one pay service, and many subscribers are purchasing multiple pay services. At 1.5 services per subscriber, this revenue figure would jump to more than $8 billion.

Obviously, the answer to the first question is critical. However, the extent to which multiple pay options become more universally available will affect the pricing of the respective pay competitors. Some degree of price competition can be expected, holding down increases in subscription fees. In all, the multiple pay subscriptions and the pressures of head-to-head competition for subscribers are likely to offset each other, resulting in total revenues in the $5 billion to $6 billion range.

Will the pay services succumb to the allure of Madison Avenue and accept some form of advertising? If they do, how much advertising revenue can they expect to generate? Working with a projected home base of 45 million, a 20 percent share of audience, and the $12.75 premium CPM results in a cost of $69,000 per 30-second spot. Given that pay services would be reluctant to interrupt their movies and so would run commercials only between features and that a maximum of 5 commercial minutes per film would be possible, the daily advertising revenues from two primetime films and one late-night film would be $1,725,000. This would add up to $620 million per year (see Figure 7-3).

This may seem like a substantial amount of money, but it must be remembered that the pay services will be competing for $5 billion to

PAY CABLE ADVERTISING REVENUES

1990

Penetration	=	45,000,000 homes
20% Share	=	12 rating
12 Rating	=	5,400,000 homes
CPM	=	$12.75
Unit Cost	=	$69,000 ($27,500 in 1980 dollars)
10 Units per movie	=	$690,000
2 Movies per night	=	$1,380,000
1 Late movie	=	$345,000
Total daily revenue	=	$1,725,000
Annual revenue	=	$620,000,000

FIGURE 7-3

Pay cable advertising revenues, 1990.

$8 billion in subscription revenues. They will be competing head to head with other pay cable services in most cases. To accept advertising unilaterally would offer the competition a distinct advantage. In this type of competitive environment, with so much subscription revenue at stake, probably the attraction of advertising revenue would remain weak.

Thus concludes the discussion of the configuration of the cable television industry, past, present, and future. Before we examine the implications of the growth of cable television for advertisers and the opportunities it offers those advertisers, we take a look at the other technological and structural changes on the video horizon.

ON THE HORIZON

In this section we discuss new developments in the video revolution other than cable TV that will impact the television industry, the advertiser, and the viewer in the coming decade. This section might have been called "Behind the Initials," for most of the new developments discussed are identified by their initials. These include DBS, LPTV, HDTV, VTR, and STV. Add to these teletext, videotext, pay per view, and video disks, and you have the subject to be discussed.

Direct-Broadcast Satellite Transmission

Direct-broadcast satellite (DBS) is a natural extension of today's satellite transmission to cable systems. Instead of the cable system receiving the satellite-fed programming and relaying it via cable to the viewing home, the home receives the satellite signal directly.

In April 1981 the FCC accepted the application of Comsat's Satellite Television Corporation for DBS transmission and invited other applications. Since then, seven other applications have been accepted, and in early 1982 as many as eight DBS systems were authorized to begin operation. These systems can distribute up to 30 channels of programming to homes throughout the country. Each receiving home must be equipped with its own rooftop satellite receiving station. Such home stations are expected to be mass-produced in sizes and at costs suitable for home use. Japanese manufacturers claim that a home satellite earth station could be mass-produced for about $250.

The introduction of DBS service raises many important questions. Broadcasters fear that this new service will allow program creators to bypass them and distribute their programming directly to the home. Broadcasters fear the potential demise of the local television station if DBS is introduced. Cable companies see DBS as preempting the natural growth of the industry. If the most affluent households gained access to a full range of programming options via DBS, they would have little interest in securing access to cable transmission. Without this important economic base, wiring communities for cable would cease to be a profitable enterprise.

DBS applicants counter that they can provide an even greater diversity of programming to broadcasters and cable companies. They argue that preemption of TV station and cable-cast audiences by direct transmission to those homes equipped with rooftop receiving stations will be more than offset by the incremental programming inventory DBS will provide to TV stations and cable companies for retransmission to homes not so equipped.

The second important DBS issue concerns the CBS application for a DBS system. CBS plans to use the DBS spectrum to transmit high-definition television (HDTV) signals. This type of DBS service would preclude offering 30 channels of programming, since HDTV transmission requires more than one channel. CBS argues that a technologically superior television service represents a valid use of the DBS spectrum, whereas competing applicants offer only access to more program options, with access already provided by the expansion of cable television. The CBS position is discussed further under "High-Definition Television."

One applicant for DBS, Hubbard Broadcasting's United States Satellite Broadcasting (USSB), is proposing to use DBS to provide a fourth television network service, combining independent stations and the new low-power television (LPTV) stations into an effective national affiliate network. Essential to this application is the speedy introduction of low-power TV stations.

Low-Power Television

In 1981 the FCC began accepting applications for low-power television stations that would operate on unused high-channel positions in areas in which such operation would be possible without interfering with existing full-service stations. There was an immediate flood of applications, and in April 1981 the FCC had to freeze applications, with more than 6000 already in hand. Now the FCC must develop some effective way of allocating the possible LPTV frequencies among these applicants. If an equitable lottery approach can be devised, the introduction of LPTV stations throughout the country might begin fairly soon. However, if some form of comparative hearings is required for each competitive application, the process could take several years.

If we assume that LPTV stations will be a reality, their impact on the overall video marketplace will be a function of the degree to which these stations can be linked into some form of network. Alone, an LPTV station with its limited coverage cannot represent a viable advertising medium for anyone other than the local marketer. However, linked to regional or program-format networks, these stations could become attractive advertising media. For example, Sears applied for LPTV station licenses in many rural communities. It proposes to provide a country music and rural programming network which would represent an effective medium for Sears catalog advertising.

The FCC has yet to resolve whether multiple-station ownership will be accepted and whether existing media owners will be allowed to own LPTV stations. It is felt that unless this form of ownership is allowed, the combination of LPTV stations into effective networks will be a long, arduous process, not completed by the end of the decade.

High-Definition Television

High-definition television (HDTV) is not a new form of television as much as it is a better quality of television. Currently color television in the United States uses the NTSC broadcast standard of 525 horizontally scanned lines encompassing a 4 to 3 aspect ratio (width-to-height image ratio). HDTV would use a 1125-line standard with a 5 to 3 aspect ratio. The NHK/Sony system developed in Japan and promoted for use in the United States by CBS also would provide better color reproduction and fidelity and stereo sound.

From the viewer's perspective, the television picture will take on the quality of film, and high-quality reception will be available on larger screens that have a shape more conducive to optimum viewing. From the programmer's perspective, HDTV represents a new creative medium combining the qualities of film and the advanced electronic editing techniques of videotape. Also it will allow for significant savings in production costs without sacrifices in quality.

No one questions the value of HDTV and its future role in television broadcasting, but there is considerable controversy about how the HDTV capacity should be introduced to the U.S. broadcasting system. CBS is proposing that DBS be used essentially as a distribution vehicle for HDTV. Since HDTV requires several channels to broadcast, use of DBS for HDTV transmission would preclude its use for the introduction of several channels of programming. Thus competing DBS applicants are challenging the CBS proposal. Even if CBS loses the battle for DBS space, HDTV transmission will still be possible via cable. The 50 + channel cable system will be able to allocate the required number of channels to HDTV. Today five channels would be needed to broadcast HDTV; however, new compression techniques should reduce this number in the near future.

CBS estimates by 1990 four HDTV channels will be available through DBS, reaching 160,000 homes. Another 640,000 HDTV sets will receive HDTV programming via cable, and 320,000 sets will use HDTV disks and cassettes. HDTV receivers initially will cost in excess of $2000; but as mass production takes place, they will drop in price to just slightly more than that of standard color console TVs.

Videotape Recorders and Video Disks

The videotape recorder (VTR) is not on the horizon; it is here. In 1982, 3 million U.S. households were equipped with VTR units, and sales were brisk. Video disk development is not so advanced. RCA, the video disk pioneer, has been disappointed by video disk unit sales to date. VTRs and video disk players are actually competitive products. It is unlikely that any but the most affluent consumers and video fanatics would buy both a VTR and a video disk unit.

The standard VTR unit offers the advantage of recording capability, whereas the video disk player is a playback unit only. Proponents of video disks point to the superior quality of video disk reception and the wide range of programming that will be available on video disk. However, videotape rental operations are opening in almost every major community, and to date videotape rental libraries are larger than video disk libraries.

VTRs and video disk players are seen as competitors for audiences with over-the-air and cable television programming. Initial research into VTR use, however, has found that its presence in the home increases viewing of over-the-air and cable television programming. Viewers are recording programs for repeat viewing and programs that air while they are out of the home or are on opposite other programs they wish to watch at some other time. This repeat viewing and delayed viewing of regular television programming is what adds to the time spent watching over-the-air and cable programming.

The future of the VTR industry has been clouded by a recent court decision stating that the off-the-air recording of television programs is a violation of the program producer's copyrights. The outcome of this legal battle, which will probably continue for several years, is certain to affect the future growth of the VTR market and the subsidiary tape rental market.

Subscription Television

Subscription television (STV) is the over-the-air broadcasting of scrambled television signals that are unscrambled by a device attached to the viewer's television set. The viewer pays a subscription fee to access the unscrambled signal.

Today, STV is used predominantly as a replacement for pay cable in areas not wired for cable television. The STV broadcaster employs an unused channel, almost always a UHF channel. STV systems usually are confined to densely populated major markets. Los Angeles' On TV and New York's Wometco Home Theater (WHT) are two large STV systems in operation today. STV broadcasters offer a program lineup dominated by movies, with some major sports attractions as well.

Many industry observers feel that STV systems are only interim participants in the video marketplace and that they will disappear as cable penetration of major markets provides HBO and other pay cable services to those markets. STV broadcasters argue that their future is ensured by their pay-per-view capability, which allows them to charge for specific programs. On TV already has successfully presented major fights on a pay-per-view basis.

Teletext

Teletext is the name given to printed and graphic material that is broadcast over the air along with regular broadcast signals and is accessible to the viewer by a special teletext decoder. Teletext information is broadcast in a page format in the vertical blanking interval of the normal TV signal. The vertical blanking interval is the black bar you see when your TV picture rolls. Broadcasters can broadcast up to 100 pages of teletext information simultaneously. The viewer can access any of these pages through a teletext control which looks like a normal remote control unit.

Teletext systems are operational in both Great Britain and France today. CBS is actively pursuing the establishment of a national teletext service in the United States. Given the successful outcome of its current Los Angeles test and the agreement by the FCC to establish one standard teletext system (the current French Antiope and British CEEFAX/Oracle systems are incompatible), CBS will launch a national teletext service in 1983. This service will contain features such as national weather reports, up-to-the-minute news headlines, the latest sports scores, and the stock market reports. The national service will be complemented by local pages provided by the affiliates. These pages might include traffic reports, theater listings, and airline arrival and departure information.

Broadcasters view teletext as essentially an advertising medium. In addition to allowing advertisers to "sponsor" the information pages, they plan to sell full pages to those advertisers. They can use the pages to list items on sale at a given time, to list places where their product can be purchased, to provide "how to order" information for direct-response ads, etc. Ads could stand on their own or be tied to regularly broadcast commercials. Figure 7-4 shows various sample teletext pages. In addition to these commercial and general information applications, teletext offers a superior captioning system for the deaf, a fact that CBS emphasizes in its promotion of the service.

If CBS introduces a national teletext system in 1983, TV set manufacturers may build teletext decoders into their high-end 1984 sets. If this is done, teletext penetration could reach as many as 25 percent of television homes by 1990. Based on this projection, analysts see a potential for $1 billion in teletext advertising by that date.

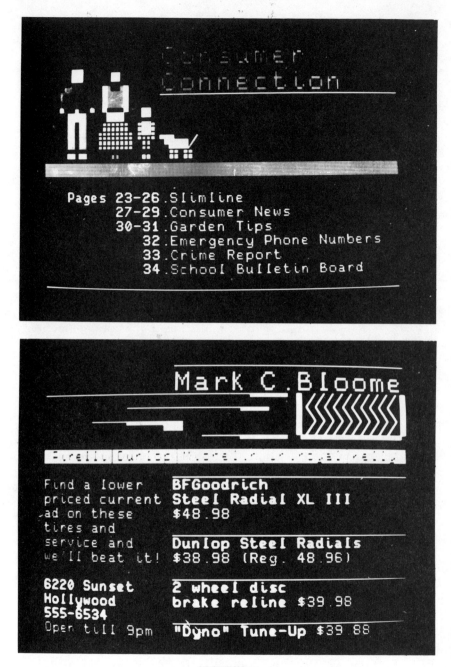

FIGURE 7-4

Sample teletext pages.

(Source: CBS Broadcast Group, New York.)

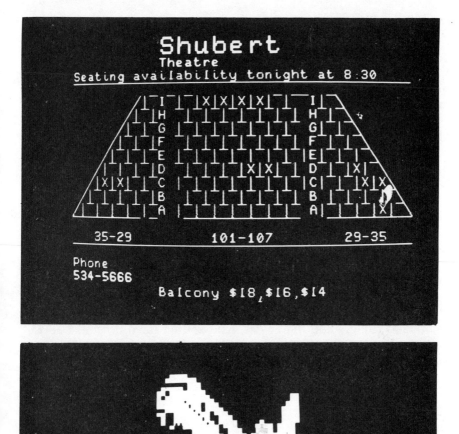

Shubert
Theatre
Seating availability tonight at 8:30

```
        I         X X X X         I
       H                         H
      G                         G
     F                         F
    E                     E
   D             X X     D     X
  C                     C       X X
 X X     B             B
      A                 A     X
```

35-29   101-107   29-35

Phone
534-5666

Balcony $18,$16,$14

LAX Traffic and Parking

until further notice due to severe fog.
Contact airlines for specific flight
information.
VSP Lot full. All other LAX parking lots
open. When at the Airport, tune to
Airport Radio 1580 for traffic and
parking updates.

Videotext or Viewdata

Videotext and *viewdata* are alternative terms that refer to information displayed in the home through a television screen. The standard videotext system calls for the accessing of information fed through telephone lines to some form of home computer console and the display of that information on a television set. All videotext systems are interactive, allowing the receiving homes to send instructions and information. Great Britain has pioneered in this field. Today the British postal system provides a videotext system called Prestel.

Development of a videotext system in the United States is just beginning. Knight-Ridder has begun experimenting with a system in Florida, and AT&T and CBS are setting up an extensive videotext experiment in Ridgewood, New Jersey. Potential applications include buy-at-home services, electronic banking, electronic Yellow Pages, and distribution of electronic newspapers and electronic mail. Also, retailers such as Sears and Montgomery Ward conceivably could provide their entire catalogs via videotext. A major breakthrough in videotext development came when the government settled its suit against AT&T, allowing this communications organization to pursue data base distribution free of antitrust restrictions.

Pay per View

Pay per view is not so much a new form of television program distribution as a new form of television revenue generation. STV currently provides pay-per-view services, and the new 50+ channel cable systems probably will offer some pay-per-view options.

The future of pay-per-view television depends on the ability of the program suppliers to distribute programming efficiently on this basis while maintaining the security required to prevent piracy. The combination of an effective pay-per-view system and HDTV might mean the end of the movie theater. Certainly it will introduce new competition to the pay TV services of today.

The television landscape is more and more crowded. The age of communications is here, and before the end of the decade the U.S. home will be transformed to an electronic nerve center. In this chapter we concentrated on the range of home entertainment options this electronics explosion will provide. However, the subject of this book is, more specifically, commercial communication through television. In Chapter 8 we focus on the implications of these dynamic changes for the television advertiser. We examine these changes in terms of both their effect on that advertiser's traditional television outlets—network and local television—and the new opportunities these represent.

NOTES

1. *The Media Cost Guide, 1982*, The Media Book, New York, p. 92.

2. "FCC Cable Television Industry Revenues Report," Federal Communications Commission, Washington, February 1982.

3. Now part of U.S.A. Network.

New Video Age from the Advertiser's Perspective

The constant discussion of the video revolution has to be disquieting to the advertiser. First, all the commentaries present the new video forms as threats to the existing commercial broadcast system, a system that is the major conduit for the delivery of the national advertiser's messages to the consuming public. Second, the new video forms represent potential commercial vehicles themselves, vehicles that must be evaluated. Investing in the right new vehicle at the right time will pay handsome future dividends, but picking the survivors from the plethora of new entrants is proving to be difficult.

Now let us address the impact of the new competition on the networks and local television stations.

IMPACT OF NEW COMPETITION ON NETWORK TELEVISION

Most articles about the impact of the new competition for viewers on the television networks focus on the diminishing audience shares for the networks. For the 1974–1975 season the three networks claimed a 93 percent share of the primetime television audience. By the 1980–1981 season this share had been reduced to 83 percent; and as Table 7-9 shows, this share is expected to decline to 70 percent by the end of the decade. Similar share declines have been experienced in other key dayparts.

Offsetting these share declines will be a growth in the number of television households and viewing levels. It is estimated that there will be 100 million television households by 1990 and that primetime viewing levels will increase 10 percent as the number of viewing options

TABLE 8-1
NETWORK PRIMETIME VIEWING
LEVELS, 1990 VERSUS 1981

	Primetime Monday–Sunday, 8–11 p.m.	
	1980–1981 season	1989–1990 season
1. Network share	83%	70%
2. HUT level	62.6	68.6
3. Homes base (000)	81,500	100,000
Network homes (1 × 2 × 3)	42,346	48,020

Data for 1981 are from A.C. Nielsen, "Nielsen Television Index," Chicago, 1981.

available to each household increases. Given these projections, the actual number of households delivered by the networks will increase despite their lower share of total viewing. Table 8-1 demonstrates this point.

These statistics should give some comfort to both the networks and their advertisers. However, a 1.4 percent annual growth in homes delivered is not going to produce the revenue growth necessary to protect profit margins in light of increased programming costs. The networks will have to increase unit costs far beyond this amount or add commercial inventory. Increased unit costs will mean higher CPMs for advertisers. Some added commercial inventory will help keep unit price increases down, but it seems certain that network television will be a less efficient advertising medium in the years ahead.

Unfortunately for the advertiser, there is no superior national advertising medium on the horizon. Compounding this problem is the fact that the network audience share loss will be incurred largely to pay cable competitors that probably will not accept advertising. As the economy grows and as increased discretionary income makes the U.S. television audience a more and more attractive target, a greater number of advertisers will compete for a relatively fixed inventory of audience impressions.

The advertiser's approach to these network market conditions must be one of careful planning. Greater use will have to be made of fringe dayparts as primetime unit costs continue to increase. Spot television in major markets will have to be used to supplement lower GRP-level network campaigns. Ad hoc networks formed by independent stations will be available to supplement network schedules. Viable advertiser-supported basic cable services will provide a means of reinforcing a national network television campaign base. Finally, teletext will offer the advertiser a means by which to expand a necessarily short network commercial message.

The overall objective of advertisers will be to maintain the proper reach/frequency formula for effective communication of their messages. Not only will network GRPs be increasingly expensive, but also more GRPs will be required to attain the same reach level. Competition from cable programmers will reduce the number of hours of network television viewed each week by the average viewer, making high reach levels a more elusive goal. While attempting to maintain reach, advertisers must be careful not to reduce frequency below an acceptable level. Smart advertisers will concentrate on reach in planning the base network schedule and then build frequency with low-cost fringe network spots, major market spot advertising, and targeted cable advertising.

This planning must start with the design of the network television schedule. To the extent that lower network shares are the result of competition from pay cable homes, the reduced network schedule reach and GRP level will be in these pay cable homes. Advertisers can compensate for this underdelivery in pay cable homes by including on their schedules programs that perform relatively well in these homes.

The Nielsen market section audiences (MSA) reports provide ratings for each network program in noncable, basic cable only, and pay cable homes. The average primetime program rating in pay cable homes in 1981 was equal to 86 percent of that program's rating in noncable homes. However, several network programs actually had higher ratings in pay cable homes than in noncable homes. In primetime, shows on Saturday evening generally shared higher pay cable home ratings. The pay services usually avoid playing their best feature on Saturday nights, because they would be competing with movie theaters for customers on that night. Other shows, such as *Hart to Hart* and *Trapper John, M.D.*, demonstrated particular strength in pay cable homes.

In addition to these primetime programs, virtually all major sports events performed at or above their noncable home levels in pay cable homes. The same was true of late-night programming and selected daytime shows. The advertiser who chooses a network schedule with the goal of balancing noncable, basic cable only, and pay cable home GRP delivery can do so effectively, using the Nielsen MSA reports as a guide.

One particular concern of network advertisers is that pay cable will outbid the networks for major sports attractions. These sports events are a major profit generator for the networks. More importantly, they are the core components of many male-oriented advertisers' marketing programs. Network television event sponsorship is supplemented by merchandising programs geared to the event. The loss of such sports attractions as the World Series, the Superbowl, and the Olympics to pay cable would leave a major gap in those advertisers' marketing programs.

Some quick arithmetic suggests that pay cable will be in a position to outbid the networks for major sports attractions by the end of the decade. Table 8-2 compares the revenue that would be generated by the annual NFL football schedule on pay cable in 1990 with the expected revenue that would be generated by the 1990 network advertising revenues from NFL telecasts. On the pay cable side, 70 million homes will have been passed by cable and, therefore, would be available for an NFL subscription.

Today 40 percent of U.S. homes watch NFL football regularly on network television. If this same 40 percent signed up for a pay cable NFL package in 1990, it would represent 28 million subscriber homes. If we estimate a $20 per month, or $60 per season, subscription fee, comparable to the expected pay movie charge, these 28 million homes would pay $1.68 billion for NFL football in 1990. The sponsoring cable programmer would keep $840 million.

On the network side, a straight projection of the 1980 network NFL advertising revenues of $280 million, by using the 12.1 percent com-

TABLE 8-2
NFL FOOTBALL: COMPARATIVE
REVENUE PROJECTIONS

Pay cable		Network TV	
Cable homes	70 million	1980 NFL advertising	$280 million
Buying NFL	40%	1980–1990 growth rate	12.1%
NFL homes	28 million	Projected 1990 advertising	$877 million
NFL subscription fee	$60	U.S. penetration	100%
Revenues	$1680 million		
To pay service	$840 million		
U.S. penetration	28%		

pound growth rate required to maintain network profit margins, would give us 1990 revenues of $877 million. Although affiliate revenues would add to this, the total would not approach the $1.68 billion pay cable figure.

So the threat of losing NFL football—not to mention the World Series and the Olympics—as an advertising medium by 1990 seems real. The major question becomes the position of the NFL and the other sports organizations vis-à-vis pay cable coverage. Both the NFL and major league baseball must guard their protected antitrust status. The withdrawal of access to the product from any portion of the U.S. public would invite government response. Also, the networks would attempt to offer some competition to the pay cable telecasts. This might take the form of more college football or possibly coverage of a rival league. Finally, limited access to any sports attraction may gradually erode its national appeal. For these reasons the various sports organizations will think long and hard before abandoning free television for pay cable. Nevertheless, the threat is real.

IMPACT OF NEW COMPETITION ON LOCAL TELEVISION STATIONS

The local television station market is shared today by network affiliates and independent stations. The impact of the new competition on local network affiliates will parallel, to a large extent, the impact of that competition on the networks themselves. Shares will decline, but absolute audiences will stay fairly constant. Actually, growth markets such as those in the sun belt probably will experience significant gains in audience while more mature market affiliates will lose some audience. These affiliates will retain their dominant position in the local advertising marketplace. The marginal local advertising opportunities presented by the national basic cable programmers should not be a significant factor. The real competition will come from the independent stations.

The impact of the new competition on independent television stations is difficult to predict. These stations have grown dramatically in the past few years. In primetime, independent stations and PBS stations together generated a 16 percent share of viewing during the 1980–1981 season, up from 14 percent for the 1979–1980 season. Most of this gain is credited to the independents. In the fringe time periods, particularly Monday to Friday from 6 to 8 p.m. (EST), often independents outperform their affiliate competition.

The long-term threat to the independents is from the basic cable pay services. Independents rely on a combination of off-network programming and major local sports franchises to form the base of their schedules. Superstations and other broad-based basic cable services could outbid independents for these events, limiting their programming options.

To counteract this threat, we expect the independents to form more ad hoc network hookups in the future. Several DBS applicants see the provision of this type of programming to a network of independents as the venture with greatest potential revenue for them. As we mentioned, these networks represent valuable advertising opportunities for national advertisers.

In summary, broadcast advertisers faced with declining audience shares for the traditional broadcast outlets will have to adjust their television planning in the future. Network and affiliate schedules will have to make greater use of fringe dayparts to protect frequency levels as the primetime base is stretched to preserve reach. Local-market spot television will help supplement national programs in key markets in which the new competitors are particularly strong. Basic cable networks

TABLE 8-3

CLASSIFICATION OF THE
ADVERTISER-SUPPORTED BASIC
CABLE SERVICES AVAILABLE IN
1982

Broad-based program services	
Station	**Service**
WTBS	Superstation
ESPN	Sports
CNN I and II	News
U.S.A. Network	Madison Square Garden sports
WGN-TV	Superstation
WOR-TV	Superstation
Satellite News Channel	News

and ad hoc networks formed by independent stations will offer another valuable supplement to network campaigns.

NEW ADVERTISING OPPORTUNITIES

Certain new advertising opportunities emanating from the new cable television universe are offered by the advertiser-supported basic cable services. These services can be divided into broad-based general-interest services and special-interest services. Table 8-3 divides the services available in 1982 into these two categories.

Broad-Based Program Services

The superstations constitute one form of broad-based basic cable programming service. They offer a combination of off-network programming, movies, and sports, with some original first-run programming. The superstations have program formats similar to those of most other

Special-interest program services	
Station	**Service**
ABC ARTS	Cultural
Daytime	Women's programming
U.S.A. Network	Caliope, the English channel
BET	Programming for blacks
CBN	Religious programming
MTV	Contemporary music
Satellite Program Network	Various special-interest programming
SIN	Spanish-language programming
Cable Health Network	Health-oriented programming

independent stations, with one exception. Major off-network program syndicators often will not sell their programs to superstations, feeling that to do so would preempt the sales of these programs to stations in markets reached by the superstations via cable. For this reason the superstations, particularly WTBS, have a more sports- and movie-dominated schedule than the typical independent.

The audiences of the superstations are also similar in profile to those of other independent television stations. Therefore an advertiser negotiating with the superstations should expect to pay prices that generate competitive CPMs vis-à-vis regular television stations. WTBS audiences are reported regularly by Nielsen in a special NTI supplement. In 1981, WTBS averaged a 2 rating between 6 p.m. and 1 a.m., reaching a high of 5. These ratings were within the WTBS universe only. Advertisers paid from $600 to $3000 for a 30-second spot on WTBS. The WTBS homes base at the end of 1981 was 20 million. At approximately $600 per rating point, the WTBS average CPM would be $3, comparable with the spot television market CPM for programs with similar ratings.

Advertisers considering the incorporation of the superstation into national advertising campaigns must keep in mind the regional concentration of these stations. Each superstation originates from one "home" market. WTBS is based in Atlanta, WGN-TV in Chicago, and WOR-TV in New York City. It is not surprising, therefore, that a disproportionate number of those stations are located in these three markets. The GRPs of an 80-spot schedule delivered by WTBS in May 1981 by region of the country were 60 nationally, 3 in the northeast, 38 on the east coast, 60 on the west coast, 156 in the south, and 12 in the Pacific area. Regional delivery ranged from virtually no effective coverage at all in the northeast and Pacific regions to 156 GRPs in the south. Obviously the 60 GRP "national" level is misleading.

This regional concentration should not be taken as a negative for the superstations. It only confirms the fact that each superstation will have its own coverage configuration, and that the superstations should be treated in the media plan as broad-coverage independent stations which can be combined with spot television to form a national television medium. They are not, in themselves, an effective national advertising medium. For example, a schedule on WTBS could be combined with spot schedules in major northeast and Pacific markets to balance national coverage.

As these stations improve their market penetration, they will offer more balanced coverage. However, the existence of strong home-market independent stations in most major markets prevents the superstations from achieving the same audience levels in these markets as they do in smaller markets not served by home-market independent stations.

The remaining broad-based general-interest cable program services rely totally on satellite-fed cable distribution. As a result, their coverage patterns follow the general pattern of cable TV penetration. These services deliver audiences similar in composition to those for the same type of programming offered by the broadcast networks. The audience for the news services parallels that for the networks' news—older, adult, and more male than the audience for entertainment programming. The viewer profile, however, is slightly more upscale than that for the networks, because the cable homes universe is more upscale than the total TV homes universe.

The sports audience also is similar to that for the corresponding type of program on the networks. In fact, ESPN viewers have been found to watch a greater than average amount of network television sports programming. The ESPN coverage pattern and the inherent upscale male appeal of sports combine to provide a superior upscale male viewer profile.

When negotiating with the superstations and the broad-based general-interest cable networks, the buyer should compare the audience profile with that for the over-the-air networks and stations. Prices should generate CPMs in line with these broadcast counterparts with perhaps a slight premium for a slightly more upscale profile. However, the broadcast media probably will offer larger ratings and greater overall reach at the same GRP level. For this reason, right now CPM parity seems justified.

If the buyer can make a long-term deal with a growing basic cable network at a CPM level comparable with the broadcast CPM for similar programming, the buyer would be wise to take advantage of this opportunity. Increased cable TV penetration and the conversion of limited 12-channel systems to the new 30+ channel capacity will result in growing coverage for the desired basic cable networks. The buyer who makes a deal on today's audience numbers will see the CPM decline as the cable network's coverage grows. Many early CNN and ESPN buyers were able to lock up multiyear deals that look like great bargains today. However, the established services are less and less willing to commit themselves to long-term deals.

Special-Interest Services

Generally special-interest services will attract smaller audiences than the broad-based general-interest services. Their programming is designed to appeal to a specific segment of the population and will have little appeal for other segments. The attraction of these services to an advertiser will depend on the degree to which the segment programmed for represents a key target market for the product or service being advertised. The arts and cultural services promote the very high socioeconomic profile of their viewers. Since the affluent are the most prized audience for most advertisers, these advertisers are willing to pay a premium to reach them. Unfortunately, at this time the combination of the low absolute audience levels of these services and their limited penetration has put the CPMs they demand to remain viable in a range that few advertisers can justify.

As cable penetration grows and the special-interest services build larger circulation bases, the CPMs they require for profitability will be reduced. However, unless several current competitors bow out of the battle, it is unlikely that any one service will be able to generate the $150 million to $200 million revenue base required for profitable 1990 operation and still charge rates that produce reasonable CPMs.

Instead, these services will have to look to some degree at subscription underwriting to make a significant contribution to their revenue base. The leverage of subscription revenues makes it possible to offset a large percentage of the required CPMs of a 100 percent advertiser-supported system with a minimal subscription charge. If a special-interest service could obtain a 25 percent penetration of the 1990 cable homes universe and could sign up 10 percent of that 25 percent for a reasonable $5.55 per month subscription, that service could generate about $100 million annually in subscription revenues.

If the service were able to maintain a 5 rating level among these 1.5 million subscriber homes versus a 1 rating among the 15 million homes receiving the service free in the 100 percent advertiser-supported situation, it could generate $100 million in advertising revenues at the same CPM level required to generate $200 million in advertising revenues previously. The advertisers would be paying the same CPM, but the unit cost would be cut in half.

The limited-budget selective market advertisers attracted to these special-interest services would be more willing to pay the premium CPMs if the total dollar outlay were reduced in this manner. The assumption would be that the 10 percent willing to pay the subscription are the 10 percent they want to reach in the first place. Therefore, the same number of impressions achieved in this selective universe is more valuable to them than the greater number of impressions derived from the broader free-service audience (Table 8-4).

Thus the advertiser interested in reaching a selective audience via cable television should encourage, not discourage, the program services designed for that audience to charge some form of subscription fee. The subscription fee would increase the selectivity of the audience while reducing the unit cost required to reach that audience.

In addition to the relationship between the selectivity of the audience

TABLE 8-4

COMPARATIVE REVENUE
STREAMS FOR A FREE VERSUS A
SUBSCRIPTION-BASED SPECIAL-
INTEREST CABLE PROGRAM
SERVICE

	Free service	Subscription service
Subscription fee	—	$5.55
Subscribers	15,000,000	1,500,000
Subscription revenues	—	$100,000,000
Subscribers	15,000,000	1,500,000
Average rating	1	5
Average audience	150,000	75,000
Unit price	$10,000	$5000
Units	20,000	20,000
Advertising revenues	$200,000,000	$100,000,000
CPM	$66.67	
Total revenues	$200,000,000	$200,000,000

and the CPM premium charged, the editorial content of the program service must be considered by the advertiser. A given special-interest program service may be focusing, in its program content, on an area particularly relevant to the advertiser's product, service, or marketplace. A business-related service will present an editorial environment favorable to the bank, stockbrokerage house, or other financial institution. A home improvement show will represent an ideal environment for a power tool manufacturer or a maker of general home improvement products. A fashion-oriented women's program will be ideal for a retailer.

To the extent that the editorial content of the program service can be considered an extension of the commercial message itself, the advertiser should be willing to pay a premium for advertising in that service's programming. Advertisers who have isolated a program service offering an editorial climate ideally suited for the presentation of their commercial messages are advised to establish some form of sponsorship identification with this programming, thereby enhancing the synergistic impact of program and commercial.

The special-interest cable program service is much like the special-interest magazine, and should be approached by the advertiser in much the same manner as the magazine. Selectivity, as opposed to absolute size, of the audience is the most important variable. For this reason a subscription based service offering smaller but more involved audiences at lower unit costs will be more attractive to the advertiser. Also, editorial content must be an important consideration, the goal being the establishment of a synergy between program and commercial.

Local Cable Advertising

Local cable systems offer the national advertiser limited advertising opportunities today. However, they offer the local advertiser a distinctive service, a very localized television advertising option. At the end of 1981 there were 4225 operating cable systems accepting advertising. Approximately another 4000 systems were being built or were in the application stage. These systems accept advertising in their locally created programming and in the programming of the various basic services that provide the systems with local availabilities.

The amount of locally created service provided by each cable system varies substantially. At this time there is very little high-quality local cable programming on cable systems. Most local programming represents a halfhearted attempt to meet the local program service requirements mandated by the local authority in the franchise agreement.

The national advertiser probably will see little interest in local system-by-system cable advertising. The planning and coordination required to combine a significant percentage of the several thousand cable systems in a national campaign render such an approach to local cable advertising impractical. One answer to this logistical constraint may be the multipoint distribution service.

A *multipoint distribution service (MDS)* is the microwave transmission of programs among groups of cable systems. Individual systems can be linked via MDS to form more substantial advertising media. These cable advertising *interconnects* are already operational. Existing interconnects are of both the microwave MDS type and the less structured tape bicycling type.

A pioneer with the interconnect concept was Gill Cable, in the San Francisco area. By the end of 1981 Gill had 30 affiliates and had generated $1 million in ad revenues through the sale of local avails on CNN and ESPN. Growth of the microwave interconnect concept will depend on whether the FCC allocates the valuable, and much desired, microwave channels to firms like the Microband Company of America that are committed to using them this way.

Although MDS systems also could be employed to develop regionalized locally created programming, the national advertisers probably will stick with the local availabilities in the national basic cable services, where audience size and profile are less unknown.

The development of any national spot marketplace will require not only the introduction of more interconnects but also the emergence of cable system representatives who, much like their counterparts in the television station marketplace, will offer advertisers and cable systems an efficient medium for negotiations, order placement, and billing. Eastman Cable Rep is already established as a cable system advertising representative. By the end of 1981 Eastman represented interconnects in 26 markets and anticipated increasing its market coverage to 50 + markets during 1982. The other major TV representative firms are also positioning themselves for entry into the cable marketplace.

There is one particularly enticing local advertising opportunity available to the national cable TV advertiser. The national advertiser can produce a program of its own for distribution to local cable systems. National advertisers have begun sponsoring the production of informational programs in health care and food preparation areas. Cable systems are willing to carry these programs if they have channels to fill.

Unfortunately, obtaining clearance for a program from a cable system does not mean that any of that system's subscribers will watch the program. If the advertiser wishes to attract a significant base of viewers, some form of advertising or promotion will be required. Advertising placed in the cable system's own program guide or the local newspapers will help build viewer awareness of the program. However, even with the most effective promotion and tune-in advertising, viewing levels will be very low.

The use of local cable advertising by the national advertiser today must be regarded as experimental. As systems mature and begin to combine into meaningful ad hoc networks, their advertiser value will grow. As existing systems of less than 20 channels are replaced and augmented by 50 + channel systems, the availability of time for the presentation of sponsored informational productions will present a more substantive advertising opportunity for the national advertiser. The national advertiser is advised to begin some experimentation in this area, probably starting with discussions with the major MSOs (see Table 7-3).

The local advertiser will probably want to move somewhat more quickly into cable advertising. To the extent that the local cable system provides access to television for the local advertiser with a concentrated market closely paralleling the cable system's coverage area in configuration, this system provides that advertiser with the first opportunity to employ television advertising efficiently.

Local retailers are likely to find that a cable system or combination of cable systems offers a coverage pattern with far less waste than that offered by the major market television stations serving their marketplaces. Neighborhood establishments such as restaurants, theaters, or services that never considered television advertising in the past may find cable TV advertising affordable.

Like their national counterparts, these local advertisers will have the choice of local system spots in national cable networks and locally created programming. The local spots in national cable networks offer a proven audience attraction. The local sporting goods store can get a lot of mileage out of an ESPN or U.S.A. Network sports buy, for example. However, that same sporting goods company may choose to sponsor the local high school sports coverage, a locally created option with some definite drawing power.

The local advertiser will find the local cable system more than willing to aid in the production of commercials. Of course, depending on the size and sophistication of the local system operator, these commercials may be quite rudimentary, probably shot with one minicam. The local advertiser should remember that the local system operator is new to the advertising game and should develop an ongoing relationship with this cable system operator. To the extent that the advertiser leads in the application of local cable resources to advertising, that advertiser will be in an excellent negotiating position regarding the rate charged for this advertising.

Pay Cable Advertising?

Today the pay cable networks—HBO, Showtime, and the Movie Channel—do not accept advertising. So why devote a section of this chapter to pay cable advertising? Madison Avenue very much wants access to the pay cable audiences. These audiences are young, affluent, and well educated. In short, these audiences are the key target market of most product and service advertisers.

Although I do not believe that the pay cable services will succumb to the allure of Madison Avenue, since to do so would be to give their competition a strong differential advantage, I do believe they might accept a particular form of advertising, the long-form "infomercial" currently seen in movie theaters. These commercials would be short (1 to 5 minutes), informative, and/or entertaining clips with minimal sponsor identification. Some examples are:

- A series of scenes from a new film promoting that film

- A performance of a cut from a new album by a group or individual performer

- A great sports moment brought to you by a beer or automobile advertiser

- A fashion report brought to you by a retailer

It is felt that this type of advertising preceding and following, but never interrupting, a film would be acceptable to pay TV subscribers. Given the profile of the pay cable audience, advertisers should be willing to switch from the hard-sell 30-second commercial approach to this softer infomercial, or sponsored entertainment, approach. If the advertiser can convince the pay cable network that these commercial segments are welcomed by the subscriber, especially if they can be credited with holding down the monthly subscription fee, then that network at least will be willing to experiment with them. I expect some such experimentation to begin in the near future. The advertiser particularly interested in the young, affluent market will be wise to encourage this development.

Advertising Opportunities from the New Technology

In addition to the advertising opportunities afforded by the growing cable television universe, the advertiser will have access to new advertising forms via the other technological advances covered in Chapter 7.

Teletext will allow the TV advertiser to complement a 30-second commercial with a page of information concerning such things as location of local distributors, the items included in a sale, or the range of product options. The advertiser who finds no need for a full page of teletext advertising might choose, instead, to sponsor the sports update or stock market report.

Teletext will present advertising opportunities for both national and local advertisers. If broadcasters are going to proceed with teletext, they will have to begin by providing a broad-based service, even though no one will be able to receive it. Only then will TV set manufacturers build the teletext decoders into the new sets. It is anticipated that during this interim period, with teletext penetration very low, advertisers will be given what amounts to a free ride. The television networks and stations will allow advertisers to experiment with teletext as they build to a reasonable penetration level. Advertisers are encouraged to get into teletext early. The experimentation will be largely, if not completely, underwritten by the broadcaster, and the experience will be valuable preparation for the optimal use of this new medium when it reaches a significant penetration level.

High-definition television (HDTV) is not so much a new medium as an enhancement of the present television medium. Although it represents no new advertising opportunities in itself, advertisers should begin thinking about the new creative potential it will allow. The HDTV commercial should be designed to take advantage of the higher color resolution, wider screen, and stereo sound elements of HDTV. As broadcasters and television program production houses are experimenting with HDTV programming, advertisers and commercial production houses should be experimenting with HDTV commercials.

Low-power television (LPTV) will represent another localized advertising opportunity, similar to that offered by the locally created programming of the local cable systems. The actual nature of that opportunity will depend on the current licensing process. Each applicant has a specific program service in mind. Only when the licenses are awarded will the nature of this medium emerge.

Applicants include commercial interests that see the potential of LPTV as an advertising force. The Hubbard Broadcasting applications have been submitted in the hope of producing another commercial television network linking independent TV stations and new low-power stations to cover the entire United States. The multiple Sears' applications are designed to form a rural network featuring country music and entertainment that will be fully sponsored by Sears.

These "network" approaches to LPTV seem the most promising to advertisers. Unfortunately, the large number of applications and the preferential treatment given to minority applications make it unlikely that the multiple-application commercial interests will prevail. Under either a lottery system or a preferential comparative hearing approach, it is unlikely that an effective commercial network of LPTV stations will emerge.

Direct-broadcast satellite (DBS) may be a more feasible "network" alternative in the near future. The winner of a DBS channel allocation could begin by distributing commercial programming to intermediary MDSs and eventually grow as home earth station penetration grows. DBS as an advertising medium would seem to be a potentiality of the 1990s but not a reality of the 1980s.

Video disks and VTR cassettes are also possible advertising media of the future. Advertisers could develop how-to tapes or disks that are instructional in their respective fields. The instructional tapes would be sponsored by the advertiser, so they could be made available to the consumer at little or no cost. Examples might include:

- "How to insulate your home," sponsored by an insulation company

- "How to tune your car," sponsored by a spark plugs manufacturer

- "The effective application of makeup," sponsored by a cosmetics firm

These tapes could be designed for in-store as well as in-home use. Given the success of the how-to books of today, the how-to tape market seems ensured.

In summary, the coming cable age will represent both challenge and opportunity for the advertiser. The challenge will come in the transition from an over-the-air network-dominated TV advertising universe to a complex multichannel system. The network television advertising campaign planner will have to make the necessary adjustments to maintain balanced national coverage and reach/frequency configuration objectives in light of this new competition. National spot television campaigns will have to include cable penetration as a variable in allocating weight by market. Local television advertisers will have to look to cable services if they wish to fortify lower rating levels in cable homes.

The opportunity afforded advertisers by the new cable television medium includes both national and localized outlets for advertising. The national advertiser can choose from broad-based general-interest and various special-interest program services. The broad-based service offers larger viewer bases, but less specific audience profiles. The planning and buying of time on these services follow the parameters of broadcast, and the advertiser desiring to advertise in the programming of these services should expect to do so for CPM levels comparable with those of network and local-market spot television.

The special-interest services provide a much narrower audience base, but one whose profile is very specific. The advertiser whose target market is similar in composition to the viewer base of a special-interest service should be willing to pay a premium to reach that specific segment, as long as the higher CPM translates to lower unit costs. Another advantage of the special-interest service centers on the editorial content of that service's programming. To the extent that editorial content is related to the product, service, or marketplace of the advertiser, a possible synergy can be established between the programming and the commercial.

The local advertiser will benefit most from the local cable system's provision of a localized television advertising medium more in line with that advertiser's narrow market than the major market television stations with their broad coverage areas. This local advertiser can select from the cooperative units available for sale locally on such networks as CNN, ESPN, and U.S.A. Network, or from locally created programming.

Finally, the other new technologies—teletext, LPTV, DBS, and video disks and cassettes—offer new advertising media. Each in its own way expands the boundaries of video advertising communications. HDTV, although not offering a new form of television medium, will so enhance the presentation aspects of that medium that it, too, will represent new advertising opportunities.

To be timely and present up-to-date information is difficult because of the speed with which new technologies are put into place. So some predictions made here may already be fact, and other possibilities may no longer be relevant. However, the essential message is valid. That is, the advertiser who gets in early and experiments with the new media options will be the best prepared to capitalize on the opportunities they hold.

Commercials

The television commercial today is an established part of U.S. culture. Some critics even go as far as to say that the television commercial *is* U.S. culture. After all, the average citizen may never even attend a symphony concert or an opera. Only a small percentage of people in the United States regularly visit art galleries. Movie attendance is also far from universal and is concentrated among those aged 18 to 34. And although television programming might be considered the U.S. art form of today, remember that during each hour of television viewing the viewers are exposed to only one or two television programs, but 10 to 20 television commercials.

It is not uncommon to find the relative merits of television commercials a source of conversation at cocktail parties, dinners, and even business luncheons. Characters such as Ronald McDonald, Tony the Tiger, and Morris the Cat are more likely to be identified correctly as the stars of their respective sponsors' television commercials than are the leading characters in the great works of fiction. Robert Morley is better known as the spokesperson for British Airways than as a distinguished actor of stage and screen. Mariette Hartley, the costar with James Garner in the award-winning Polaroid commercials, gained such recognition from these commercials that she soon became a featured actress in movies and television programs and hosted both *The Tonight Show* and *The Today Show*.

Perhaps the best example of how the television commercial can become a cultural phenomenon is in the famous Coca-Cola "Mean Joe Greene" commercial. This emotional spot featuring a touching scene between Mean Joe Greene, the Pittsburgh Steeler football star, and a young fan was probably the most talked-about television commercial of all. In fact, this commercial became so well known that the NBC television network produced a full-length motion picture for television based on it.

So, as you enter the world of television advertising, do so with some degree of trepidation and awe. Even if you are interested only in selling more cans of beer, the development of your television commercial will be, to a certain extent, a creative and artistic undertaking. You may not end up simply selling more beer; you may win a Clio, the Oscar of the television commercial industry. Unfortunately, it is possible to win a Clio and not sell more beer. This brings us to the objective of this chapter—to provide some insight into the creation of *effective* television commercials, with *effective* defined as sales-generating, first; cost-efficient, second; and creatively appealing, third.

As we move to the substance of this chapter, one caveat is in order. I do not purport to be an expert in the field of television commercial production. The following material was compiled from extensive reading, some limited experience as a client of commercial production enterprises, and a fairly substantial exposure to television program production. Interested readers should consult Busch and Landeck's *The Making of A Television Commercial* (Macmillan, New York, 1980) and S. Zeigler and H. Howard's *Broadcast Advertising: A Comprehensive Working Textbook* (Grid, Inc., Columbus, Ohio, 1978).

PREPRODUCTION DECISIONS

In Chapter 12 we present a research plan designed to provide insight into the two-part challenge of what to say and how to say it. What to say in a commercial must be based on an analysis of the purchase decision process involving the product being advertised, and it is only incidentally related to the advertising medium being used. Which advertising medium to use depends to a large degree on what is to be said. An in-depth discussion of communications theory as it relates to commercial development is beyond the scope of this text. We start after the advertiser has decided what to say. However, the decision on whether to use television as a medium for conveying the advertising message involves some consideration of communication theory.

Decision to Use Television

WORDS, SYMBOLS, AND IMAGES

Communication is essentially an encoding-decoding process. The sender of the communication uses words, symbols, and images to convey some message to the receiver. This is the encoding process. The receiver, in turn, interprets these words, symbols, and images. This is the decoding process. The effectiveness of the communication is determined by the degree to which the message received by the receiver conforms to the message the sender wished to convey. Different media deliver different combinations of words, symbols, and images with varying effectiveness. Obviously, the degree to which symbols and images—rather than words— are used in the communication influences the superiority of television over print as a communications vehicle. In addition, other variations in the manner in which these media communicate to their audiences affect their ability to effectively convey certain types of messages.

LOW INVOLVEMENT VERSUS HIGH INVOLVEMENT

Television communication is pervasive. The television audience, by its attentiveness to the television screen alone, is exposed to the communication. Its role is essentially passive. However, the magazine reader's attention must be captured as she or he leafs through the magazine. Reading the magazine ad involves an active decision on the part of the reader. Magazine advertising has little or no impact on the reader who passively flips by the ad. For this reason television is often described as a low-involvement medium and magazines as a high-involvement medium.

Purchase choices also are classified as low-involvement and high-involvement decisions. A low-involvement decision is one in which the purchaser does not differentiate a great deal among brands and is relatively indifferent to the brand choice element of the decision. Low-involvement purchase decisions usually mean relatively low-price, un-differentiated products such as soaps, paper products, or pet foods. A high-involvement purchase decision is one in which the purchaser seeks information, deliberates before making a decision, and considers many alternatives. High-involvement purchase decisions usually have to do with relatively high-priced, highly differentiated products such as automobiles, color television sets, and home computers.

Television has a distinctive advantage over magazines in the advertising of low-involvement products. Purchasers of these products are unlikely to actively seek information concerning them. Therefore, the intrusive television commercial is superior to the magazine advertisement that requires active purchaser participation to complete the communication process. Television can still be effective in communicating an advertising message for a high-involvement product, but magazine advertisements generally are able to communicate more facts to the information-seeking reader than television can to the passive viewer. For these products television commercials are designed to build awareness and arouse interest in the brand. If successful, they lead the viewer to seek further information concerning the advertised brand.

MESSAGE COMPLEXITY

Another aspect of advertising communications that affects the medium selection decision is the complexity of the message. A television commercial has only 30 to 60 seconds to communicate its message. In addition, the viewer's attention must be aroused before any complex point can be communicated. The magazine reader determines how long to spend reading the ad. Once attention is gotten and interest is aroused, the reader will probably stay with the ad until all its information has been processed. For this reason, magazines are generally considered superior to television in communicating complex commercial messages.

To the extent that the message can be conveyed most effectively through a combination of words, symbols, and images; to the extent that the message concerns a relatively low-involvement purchase decision; and to the extent that the message can be communicated simply without a great deal of processing by the receiver of the communication, television is more effective in communicating that message.

Shaping the Commercial

Once the advertiser has decided what to say and chosen television as the medium, she or he must decide how to say it. The execution of the advertising message should reflect the nature of both the message and the television medium. Developing an effective television advertising message is best done in a series of stages. Stage 1 consists of determining the intensity of the message. Stage 2 involves choosing a creative format. Stage 3 is the specification of campaign details. Stage 4 is production.

STAGE 1: INTENSITY OF THE MESSAGE

Stage 1 determines the *intensity* of the message. Should advertisers "come on strong" and state their claims in an emphatic, straightforward manner, or should they use an indirect, softer approach? Rosser Reeves of Ted Bates Advertising developed the *unique selling proposition (USP)* concept of advertising execution. This concept calls for the isolation of one unique advantage offered to the consumer by the product being advertised; the development of a hard-hitting, direct message concerning that advantage; and the repetition of that message several times within the context of the commercial. The USP approach has produced some of the most effective, if not the most aesthetically appealing, television advertising. It has been particularly effective in advertising for low-involvement products, where emphasis on the one product characteristic effectively establishes its salience and the superiority of the advertised brand regarding this characteristic at the same time.

In opposition to this approach are a variety of less direct approaches. The *borrowed-interest* technique attempts to attract the viewer's attention by adding an element to the commercial that interests the viewer. That element may have no direct relation to the product being advertised; it may be just an attention-getting device. The trick in this type of execution is to generate the interest inherent in the attention-grabbing element and then transfer that attention to the product being advertised. The danger is that the attention-getting device may overwhelm the product and product-related message.

Another subtle approach to commercial execution is what William Weilbacher, in his respected book *Advertising*, refers to as the *metaphor* approach, which he defines as follows:

> An advertising metaphor suggests the effect or experience of product use through an association of the product with a person or an atmosphere that is neither directly nor literally related to the product.[1]

Weilbacher cites the Marlboro ads as an example of a metaphoric campaign. A more recent example is the controversial Brooke Shields Calvin Klein jeans commercials. This approach works well when the product offers some intangible value to the viewer, such as style, status, or ego gratification.

Perhaps the epitome of the low-key approach to advertising execution is the heavily emotional storytelling approach employed by Coca-Cola and McDonald's. Each commercial contains a short story designed to generate an emotional reaction in the viewer. The goal is to transfer the warm feeling derived from the commercial to the sponsoring product, which is subtly interjected into the commercial. This type of execution is used most often by large-volume advertisers of well-known products.

STAGE 2: SELECTING THE CREATIVE FORMAT

During this stage the advertiser decides which creative format to utilize. Common forms of television commercial execution include the slice-of-life commercial, the comparative commercial, the testimonial, the straight product demonstration, and the celebrity spokesperson.

Slice of Life   The *slice-of-life* commercial is particularly popular with packaged goods advertisers. Two or more characters are presented in a dramatization of the product purchase or product usage situation. Often these commercials include a continuing character in a series of situations. Charmin's Mr. Whipple and Maxwell House's Cora are two of the more famous continuing characters in slice-of-life commercials. These commercials often seem contrived; however, they are not necessarily less effective. Certainly slice-of-life campaigns seem to endure longer than most.

Comparative Commercial   Among the more controversial forms of television commercial is the *comparative* commercial. Comparative commercials pit the product against one or more identified competitors. The television networks require substantial documentation to support comparative demonstrations. This adds appreciably to the development expense for this form of commercial. The question is whether it is worth the cost and effort.

First, do the viewers believe the comparison is not staged? The average television viewer does feel that the networks would not allow a staged comparative demonstration on the air. After all, the losing competitor is a client also. However, a subtler factor affects the credibility of these commercials. Viewers may believe that the sponsoring advertiser just kept running tests until it won and then presented only the winning cases. One unique comparative commerical that addressed this problem was the Schlitz beer comparative taste tests. These commercials were conducted live during the various NFL championship games, and they were well publicized in advance. Of course, the tests were conducted only among drinkers of the competing brands, a no-lose situation. With no Schlitz drinkers included, there would be no Schlitz drinkers choosing another brand. Thus, even if only one drinker of a competing brand chose Schlitz (a virtual certainty), Schlitz would still be ahead. Nevertheless, the *live* aspect added to the credibility of the comparison.

The second reservation advertisers have regarding the comparative commercial is whether the mere mentioning of the competitive brand adds to its awareness. It is generally felt that the comparative commercial is more likely to be effective for the underdog brand with less to lose than the dominant brand.

Testimonial   The *testimonial* commercial is one in which users of the product testify to its performance. Like the comparative commercial, the testimonial must be believed in order to be successful. If viewers think the testimony was rigged, they are unlikely to accept the claims made for the product being advertised. Advertisers must first convince the networks of the authenticity of their testimonial spots. The consumers used in the testimonial commercial cannot have known that their statements might be used in a future television commercial. For this reason, testimonial commercials usually are made with a hidden camera. Also, any claims made for the product by the consumer being interviewed must be true and documented. So if the interviewees say they drink Miller Lite because it only has X calories, this testimony can be used only if Miller Lite actually has X calories.

Testimonial commercials are usually expensive to set up, requiring extensive location shooting with hidden-camera setups. Because these commercials do not use professional actors and cannot be staged in terms of set, lighting, and makeup, often they sound and look amateurish. No matter how credible the testimony, a certain number of consumers will still believe that the testimony was staged or, at least, that for each endorsement used, several less complimentary testimonies were discarded. Nevertheless, this form of advertising is used widely for products of all types, from detergents to automobiles.

Product Demonstration   One of television's major advantages over other commercial media is its capacity for demonstration. A television commercial can show a product at work. It can show how well the product works or how simple its operation is. It can show one product's superiority over other products. Demonstration is often incorporated into comparative and testimonial commercials. A straight demonstration commercial must meet the same rigid standards as these forms. Demonstrations cannot be rigged or enhanced for filming. The networks require doc);umention of all performance claims. Demonstration commercials are especially suitable for products such as new appliances, tools, and innovative products that the viewer may never have seen in operation. These commercials can be used to make consumers more comfortable with products like calculators, home computers, and 35mm cameras that viewers might believe to be far more complex than they actually are.

Celebrity Spokesperson   The decision to use a celebrity spokesperson in a commercial is a critical one since, depending on the quality of the person, the added expense can be substantial. Celebrities can be used in advertisements in a borrowed-interest manner. Here, the celebrity is used only to attract interest in the commercial and thus increase the attentiveness of the commercial audience. Usually, however, advertisers expect much more from their celebrities. They expect these spokespersons either to add to the desired image of the product being advertised or to add credibility to the message. Orson Welles is considered a man of exceptional taste, so his endorsement of Paul Masson wine adds an image to that wine which it may have lacked previously. Robert Conrad's tough-guy, macho image not only appeals to the male audience, but also works beautifully with Eveready's emphasis on its tough, long-lasting battery. Beautiful actresses are used in cosmetics commercials to establish a relationship between their beauty and the product.

Celebrity spokespersons can add credibility to a commercial in two ways. First, the integrity of the celebrities can be such that their mere endorsement establishes the quality of the product and the veracity of the claims made in the ad. Second, the celebrity may be an expert in the product area or a related area. In this case the celebrity's expertise ensures the veracity of the product claims. James Stewart's ads for Firestone tires fall into the first category. Jimmy Connor's ads endorsing Wilson tennis rackets fall into the second category.

Animation   In the broadest sense, animation is the bringing to life of inanimate things. *Animation* can refer to both a creative format and an element of a creative format. It represents a creative format when the entire commercial is developed in an animated form. A commercial that uses cartoon characters in an artist-created setting is classified as animated. Animation is considered a creative element of a commercial when it is used in conjunction with other forms. Inanimate objects can be brought to life through animation. The washing machine can talk to the homemaker. The cleanser can clean the bathroom by itself. The cat and dog can talk, praising the brand of pet food they are eating. Many animated characters have made it to the big time in commercials— Charlie the Tuna, Tony the Tiger, and Speedy Alka Seltzer, to name three of the most celebrated. Although animation is not a frequently used creative format, it is a very widely used creative element.

Animation is a time-consuming and expensive process. The traditional form of animation required the creation of over 1000 separate drawings for a 1-minute commercial. Each drawing occupies a separate frame of the film and must be shot separately. Today computers are eliminating some of the labor of animation, but not the cost. Computers, in addition to speeding the process of traditional animation, have developed an animation all their own. Working in three-dimensional space, computers can produce a range of animated effects that practically cannot be duplicated by the artist. The surreal Levi's jeans commercials are an example of this type of computer-generated animation. It is still very expensive, but continuing technological advances, while expanding the range of computer animation, also lower its cost.

Humor and/or Music Two elements that can be integrated into the various creative formats are humor and music. *Humor* is, by far, the more controversial. The first problem in creating a humorous commercial is the subjectivity of humor. What is funny to me may not be the least bit humorous to you. The second problem concerns the integration of the humorous aspects of the commercial and the sales message. Many humorous commercials entertain the audience, but do not inform them.

The best humorous commercials build the humor around the product purchase or product usage situation. The Federal Express "Paper Blob" campaign is one of the most effective humorous campaigns. Recall research showed that the commercials in this series not only generated extraordinary recall scores, but also produced exceptional levels of sales point recall. A review of past Clio winners reveals a high incidence of humorous commercials, so it would seem that humor can add to the creative impact of the commercials. However, these commercials should be tested thoroughly, because the selling ability of humor in commercials is far less universally accepted.

Music can add to the entertainment value of the commercial. Original theme music can form a creative link among a variety of campaigns or creative executions of a single campaign. Today major advertisers regularly commission top songwriters and composers to develop musical themes and well-known artists to perform them. Besides adding creative continuity to television campaigns, these themes can be translated to easily recognizable elements for a radio campaign. Obviously, well-done music, especially original music, is expensive. Less expensive stock musical arrangements can be used as a background or mood-setting element.

STAGE 3: PREPARING FOR PRODUCTION

The advertiser now knows not only what to say but how to say it. The advertiser is ready to turn the creative team loose. First, a copywriter must develop the specific copy and an art director lay out the visual elements of the ad. Then a production team must be commissioned to produce the commercial. However, these people need more direction. They have to know the approximate budget for the finished commercial. And they have to know what each other is doing. The copywriter must know what the basic look of the commercial will be, the art director must have some idea of the copy platform, and the production team must have finished storyboards before it can proceed.

Budget It may be argued that budget considerations should have preceded the selection of the creative format, since different formats vary substantially in cost. Although the latter is true, it is not advisable to constrain the initial development of the creative format with tight budgetary conditions. If a given creative format is considered right for the commercial, the creative team should be allowed to work with it before it is abandoned for budgetary reasons. The team may find a way around the expensive elements.

Just what are these elements? The following add appreciably to the cost of a commercial:

- On-location shooting
- Elaborate sets
- Extensive special effects or animation
- Original music
- Large casts
- Celebrity presenters
- Extended shooting schedule
- Substantial editing
- Complicated lighting requirements

The simplest, least expensive television commercial consists of a *voice-over slide*. A single slide is shown as the visual element of the commercial while an off-camera announcer reads the copy. This type of commercial is used by small-budget advertisers and is particularly popular with direct-response advertisers. The same approach can be utilized almost as inexpensively with a series of slides.

At the other extreme are a range of very expensive commercials, such as:

- The "Be a Pepper" Dr. Pepper ads with the Broadway-show feeling and large casts, original music, and elaborate sets
- The Levi's commercials with their unique computer animation
- All the on-location automobile commercials with their difficult filming requirements and dramatic staging (for example, placing a car on top of a mountainous peak via helicopter and filming it from the air)
- Any ad using a star presenter such as Bob Hope, Frank Sinatra, James Stewart, Brooke Shields, or Cheryl Tiegs

Commercials of this type can run well into six figures. Obviously the local advertiser with a $50,000 media budget is not going to spend more than $100,000 on a commercial, and the national advertiser with a $10 million plus brand is not going to spend $1000. In between these extremes is a range of options. An attractive, well-produced commercial can be made for between $10,000 and $20,000. It may not win a Clio, but it should deliver a sales message effectively.

The advertiser and the creative team sit down and rough out creative treatments. If they are experienced professionals, they can estimate the cost of producing the ad. They also can isolate those elements that appreciably increase the cost. If they can work around those elements to reduce the cost, they will. If they cannot, the advertiser must decide whether to go over budget or abandon that particular treatment. The major national advertiser usually has great latitude in this regard. Production costs for even the most elaborate campaign are a small part of the media expenditure. Given the media investment, it always seems foolish to skimp on production. The small-budget and local advertisers have to work within a much narrower budgetary range, and so certain commercial treatments are not practical for them.

After the commercial treatment has been reviewed from the budgetary standpoint and the advertiser has estimated the production costs, the production companies are asked to bid on the job. To submit accurate bids, these companies need specific information concerning the execution of the commercial. This information is presented in the storyboard.

Storyboard   The *storyboard* is the blueprint of the commercial. It has three elements. A series of drawings, in sequential order, presents the visual element of the commercial. Under each drawing is a written description of the video element, including any special effects used in that shot. Also under each drawing is the audio to accompany that visual. This audio is divided into character dialogue and other audio elements such as music, special sound effects, and voice-over copy. Any description of an audio element other than character dialogue is usually shown in parentheses. Storyboards have 6 to 12 visual frames, or one for each 2 to 5 seconds of the commercial. A particularly high-action commercial may have more.

Once the storyboard has been developed, the advertiser is ready to submit it to top management for approval, to the legal department for review, and to the networks for preliminary clearance. Chapter 13 outlines the network commercial clearance process. We state there that commercials should be submitted for review prior to production. In so

many cases, advertisers go to the expense of producing finished commercials only to have one or more networks refuse to carry them.

With management, legal, and network approval in hand, the advertiser is ready to begin production. The first step is the selection of a
producer and production team. The selection is almost always made
through competitive bidding.

Bidding Procedure Each competing producer is presented with the
storyboards and then discusses the commercial with the advertiser.
Each prepares a detailed estimate of all production costs, including all
costs for labor, studio rental, set design, equipment rental, travel to and
expenses at location shoots, and film or tape. The final bid is presented
in one of two standard forms.

If the advertiser requests *firm* bids, the production company must
guarantee delivery of the commercial for the bid price. If, for some
reason, the commercial costs more to produce than planned, the production company must absorb the extra cost.

If the advertiser requests a *cost-plus-fee* bid, the production company
estimates the cost of the commercial and adds a fee to that figure. In
this case, overage in the cost of producing the commercial is absorbed
by the advertiser. Most cost-plus-fee bids involve a fixed fee. No matter
how much over or under budget production costs are, the production
company receives the same fee. A less common fee arrangement calls
for a percentage of the production charges to be paid to the production
company as its fee. This type of fee arrangement is not popular since,
in effect, it rewards the production company for spending more money.

It is important for the advertiser to obtain several competitive bids
for each commercial. There are hundreds of qualified commercial producers, from the very small to the big names. It is relatively easy,
therefore, to generate a list of producers capable of producing a given
commercial. However, the bids submitted by these producers will vary
substantially. Factors such as access to studios, equipment owned, and
experience with similar shooting situations affect each producer's bid.

In addition, producers all have their own perspectives concerning
the commercial. Can they fit it into their schedule? Will it involve
location shooting in an area they have always wanted to visit? Will it
offer them an entrée to a major agency? Could it win them creative
awards? All these subjective considerations influence the bids. Thus it
is not uncommon for a producer to be the low bidder on one commercial
and the high bidder on another. The advertiser who bypasses the bidding process or limits it to two or three companies is foolish. Producers
understand the bidding system and would rather bid and lose than not
get a chance to produce the commercial at all.

One final step is required before the cameras can roll—the casting of the commercial.

Casting Most major advertising agencies have their own casting departments. Smaller agencies and advertisers can turn to a number of professional talent agents. Usually local advertisers can call on the local TV and radio stations when casting their commercials.

The casting director is specifically assigned the responsibility of recruiting the cast for a commercial. She or he meets with the creative team and develops a detailed profile of each character to be cast. An initial list of actors and actresses is put together from the casting department's or agency's files and the casting director's own input. At this point the qualifiers are selected and invited to come in for a reading. Each actor and actress is given a script to read. They are all briefed concerning the overall concept of the commercial and the roles of their characters. The reading usually is videotaped. Next members of the creative team view the tapes of the finalists selected by the casting director. Often a second reading, referred to as a *callback*, takes place for the finalists. Then the creative team makes its decision for each character.

The talent in a commercial is paid in one of two ways. The actors and actresses may receive a set fee for each day of shooting and then a residual payment or royalty each time the commercial airs, or they may receive a flat fee. Two unions, the Screen Actors Guild (SAG) and the American Federation of Television and Radio Artists (AFTRA), represent the professional actresses and actors in the United States. Traditionally SAG has jurisdiction over film projects, with AFTRA having jurisdiction over videotape projects. Most actresses and actors are members of both SAG and AFTRA.

SAG and AFTRA contracts set the standard working conditions for a job and establish a minimum rate, commonly referred to as *scale* ($300 in 1982), for each day of shooting. When nonunion workers are used in a commercial, they must receive scale. Known talents usually negotiate fees substantially above scale. In the case of celebrities, these fees can run into six figures.

The second component of the actor's compensation, the residuals or royalties, also is established in accordance with SAG and AFTRA rules. These royalties are based on 13-week cycles. For network television commercials shown nationally, the actors and actresses are paid a royalty each time the commercial airs. For regional or individual market commercials, the actresses and actors are paid a certain flat rate, determined by the size of the markets in which the spot appears, for each 13-week cycle.

When the actor receives only a flat fee for the commercial, it is known as a buy-out. These buy-outs are negotiated individually and average about $10,000 for an established actress or actor in a network commercial. Celebrities generally receive substantially more.

In addition to the main on-camera performers, extras appear in many commercials. A third union, the Screen Extras Guild (SEG), represents people who regularly appear as extras in commercials. Most extras are paid on a buy-out basis. The role of an extra can range from a hand model (a person whose hands are used in a product demonstration) to members of a crowd in a crowd scene. In the latter case, usually the production company can get a waiver and use nonunion extras; however, it will probably agree to include a given number of union extras as well. SEG is really a major factor in Los Angeles only. Commercials shot elsewhere regularly use nonunion extras.

Voice-over announcers who do not appear on camera are paid according to a separate SAG and AFTRA scale. If musicians appear on camera, they must be compensated under terms dictated by the American Federation of Musicians. Testimonial commercials represent a special case. The real-life nature of these commercials precludes the use of union talent. The only union requirement is that the performers receive at least union scale. The local advertiser in a smaller market probably has no access to SAG or AFTRA talent. Compensation agreements with locally recruited talent are negotiated on an individual basis.

With the producer chosen and the casting completed, production can begin.

LIGHTS, CAMERA, ACTION: PRODUCTION OF THE COMMERCIAL

Before we discuss the various stages of the production process, it is necessary to differentiate between film and videotape production. Actually, the decision to use film or videotape would have been made prior to submission of the commercial bids, since the technical requirements and the costs involved vary considerably. The best way to compare these two forms of commercial production is to delineate their relative advantages and disadvantages.

Videotape versus Film

THE "LOOK" OF THE COMMERCIAL

The look of a videotape commercial is probably best described as realistic. It is the look of the six o'clock news—clear, sharp images in bright colors. The look of the film commercial is softer, tonal in quality.

It is the look of a motion picture. The preference for one or the other is highly subjective. Certainly, the content of the commercial itself must influence the videotape or film decision. An appliance demonstration commercial taking place in a kitchen setting probably would look best on videotape, whereas a romantic-moonlight-on-the-beach scene for a fragrance commercial would call for film.

SHOOTING THE COMMERCIAL

Videotape provides the director with instantaneous feedback. Immediately after shooting a scene, the director plays back the tape and sees exactly what was shot. Film must be processed before it can be reviewed. However, film cameras are much more portable and can be used more easily in difficult location-shooting situations. Videotape cameras are getting smaller, but they are still quite bulky.

EDITING CAPACITY

Videotape editing is done electronically. Edited sequences can be previewed before they are actually recorded. Film editing is a difficult, expensive process that must be completed before the film can be shown. However, film editing allows for more special effects. Again, in this area technological innovations are expanding the horizons of videotape regularly. The CMX system, developed to achieve frame-accurate videotape editing and special effects, has added substantially to the versatility of this medium. CMX systems with Digital Video EFX (DVE) systems create a range of special effects. Still, film offers a far greater range of special effects.

FINISHING THE COMMERCIAL

The finishing process, which we discuss later, also varies from videotape to film. Videotape finishing is much more expensive than film finishing. However, the finishing process, culminating in the production of multiple prints for distribution to the media, takes far less time with videotape.

DISTRIBUTION

Finished videotape commercials are much bulkier than film commercials. The bulk adds greatly to the cost of distributing the commercial to the networks and individual stations included on the media schedule.

Four Production Stages

The four production stages are the shooting, editing, finishing process, and distribution of the commercial.

SHOOTING THE COMMERCIAL

An advertiser attending a commercial shooting for the first time is almost certain to ask, "Who are all these people and what do they do?" This is only natural, since there are likely to be more than 20 people in the production crew, excluding talent. The advertiser is likely to find these members of the crew at the shooting:

Producer The producer is the person at the advertising agency assigned the overall responsibility for the production of the commercial. When the agency does not have its own production experts, usually the producer's responsibilities are assumed by the owner of the production company or a representative of that company.

Director The director is responsible for the physical production of the commercial and is in total charge of all the technical details of the shooting and of instructing the cast in the interpretation of their roles.

Assistant Director The assistant to the director usually is assigned responsibility for the technical aspects of the production.

Production Manager If the agency provides its own producer, the production company assigns a production manager to oversee production of the commercial. This person is responsible for making sure all the equipment and props are there for the commercial shooting, for renting studios, for recruiting and hiring crew members, for establishing the shooting schedule, and for the overall preproduction logistics. The production manager is also responsible for keeping all these aspects of production within budget.

Camera Operators Camera operators actually shoot the commercial. They follow the director's instructions, but are responsible for setting their own lighting and positioning the cameras.

Gaffers Gaffers are responsible for arranging for all the electronic aspects of production. They are basically electricians, and their major task is to light the sets according to the instructions of the camera operators.

Property Managers   Property managers are responsible for setting up all the props for the commercial.

Sound Mixers   Sound mixers are responsible for the audio elements of production. The sound mixer supervises the recording and final mixing of all the audio elements.

Script Supervisor   The script supervisor must make sure that all elements of the commercial are shot, that timing specifications are adhered to, and that the overall shooting is done with continuity. If a scene is shot over 2 days, the script supervisor must ascertain that the set is exactly the same on the second day as on the first.

Grips   Grips are responsible for all the heavy moving and set adjustments during shooting.

Set Designer   The set designer designs and oversees the construction of the set.

Production Assistant(s)   Production assistants have no specific responsibilities; they usually function as "go-fers," responding to instructions from other crew members.

   In addition to the crew members just mentioned, probably there will be a hair stylist, makeup person, and wardrobe attendant for the cast. The creative team from the agency and one or more members of the account group will be on hand, too.
   The normal commercial shooting day lasts 10 hours. Most of that time is spent setting up and running through scenes. Less than an hour of actual film or tape will be recorded. Then this footage must be reduced to 30 seconds, a formidable task.

EDITING THE COMMERCIAL

As we mentioned, the editing process varies significantly between videotape and film. The first step in editing—assembling the *dailies*—involves the initial processing of the film shot on a given day and the synchronization of this film with the audio, which has to be transferred from audio tape to 35mm film. This is done on a machine known as a *flatbed editor*. In the case of videotape productions, the dailies are ready when the day's shooting is complete; no developing or processing is required.
   From the dailies, the editor culls the individual takes selected by

the agency reviewers and integrates them into a *work print*. The work print is a full commercial in rough form without final opticals and audio mixing. The work print, referred to as a *rough cut*, is reviewed by agency management and the client. Once the required approvals are obtained, the commercial is ready for finishing.

FINISHING PROCESS

Both the visual and the audio elements must be *finished*. Finishing the audio involves mixing the various audio tracks. These tracks can include dialogue, the voice-over announcer, music, and any special sound effects. The tracks are set up on individual *dubbers* and mixed by means of a *sound console*. Then the final mixed track is equalized, or balanced, to correct for factors such as variation in the levels of the actors' voices from scene to scene.

The visual elements are finished through the use of *opticals*, which means everything from simple transition devices between scenes to complex multiple-image effects. Film opticals are created on a machine called an *optical printer*. Videotape opticals are created by a combination of CMX systems and DVE systems. These opticals include:

- *Fades:* One scene fades to black, and the other slowly appears.

- *Dissolves:* One scene fades into the other without the transitional fade to black.

- *Wipes:* One scene tends to wipe the other from the scene.

An example of a more complex optical is the simultaneous slowing of multiple scenes by placing different scenes in various sections of the screen. The optical printer allows the film editor to reduce each visual element and place it in a section of the sceen. The videotape editor can create the same effect through a DVE system device known as the *Quantel*.

Once the opticals have been completed, the optical negative is produced. It is combined with the final sound track into a *composite print*, which the client and agency review. When it is approved, release prints are produced for distribution to the networks and stations.

DISTRIBUTION

The networks and various television stations have very specific technical requirements involving the commercials received for broadcast. These specifications concern the identification of the commercials, the *leader* elements preceding the commercial itself, and the amount of safe area, free of video and audio material, at the end of the commercial.

All commercials must be identified by an eight-character industry standard commercial identification number. Before submitting commercials to the networks, an advertiser is advised to request copies of their respective commercial integration manuals. And do not forget that commercials must be cleared by the networks in finished form even if they already received preliminary approval in storyboard form.

NOTE

1. William M. Weilbacher, *Advertising*, MacMillan, New York, 1979, p. 239.

Planning the Television Campaign

Once the decision has been made to incorporate television advertising into the marketing mix, the target market has been defined, and the television commercial or commercials have been created, the media planner must design a television advertising plan to maximize the impact of the campaign. In the design the planner must address three critical issues:

1. What percentage of the target market can be reached, and how many times will each potential consumer be exposed to the commercial?

2. How should the campaign be timed, how long should it run, and should the level of advertising be constant or varied?

3. For the national product, should network television exclusively be used, or should it be combined with local spot television? If a combination of network television and local spot television is recommended, how should the optimal mix be determined?

These questions constitute the theoretical framework of the effective television advertising campaign. In this chapter we further define each separate theoretical issue and discuss the specific planning implications.

REACH/FREQUENCY CONCEPT

A television advertising campaign is composed of a series of commercial announcements. Each announcement airs on a certain date, at a

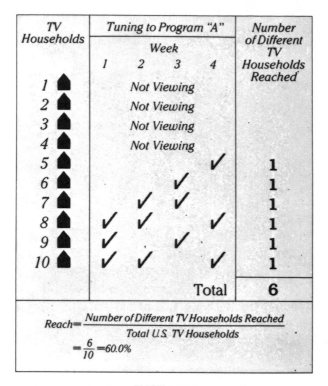

TV Households	Tuning to Program "A" Week				Number of Different TV Households Reached
	1	2	3	4	
1	*Not Viewing*				
2	*Not Viewing*				
3	*Not Viewing*				
4	*Not Viewing*				
5				✓	1
6			✓		1
7		✓	✓		1
8	✓	✓		✓	1
9	✓		✓		1
10	✓	✓		✓	1
			Total		**6**

$$Reach = \frac{Number\ of\ Different\ TV\ Households\ Reached}{Total\ U.S.\ TV\ Households}$$
$$= \frac{6}{10} = 60.0\%$$

FIGURE 10-1

Calculation of reach.

(Source: "CBS Basic Guide to Network Television," CBS Television Network, New York, 1981.)

certain time, and in a certain program context. These date, time, and program context factors determine how many viewers see each commercial announcement. The viewing of a commercial announcement by a member of the television audience is referred to as a commercial *exposure*, or *impression*.

Since members of the television audience have different viewing patterns, each member may be exposed to a different number of the commercial announcements constituting the campaign. Some may be exposed to all the announcements, others to only half of them, still others to less than half, and some to none at all. The percentage of viewers exposed to at least one announcement is called the *reach* of the campaign. The average number of times each of the television audience is exposed to an announcement is referred to as the *average frequency* of the campaign. The reach of the campaign multiplied by the average frequency of the campaign is equal to the gross rating points of the campaign. Figure 10-1 illustrates the reach concept.

Frequency Distribution: The Critical Element

Ideally, the advertiser wants to reach 100 percent of the potential purchasers of the product or service often enough to effectively communicate the sales message. In the real world, viewing patterns and budget constraints usually make the goal of 100 percent reach unattainable. In addition, the advertiser is confronted with the problem of determining how many exposures are required to effectively communicate the sales message. Before we address this central theoretical point, it is necessary to explain the concept of the frequency distribution curve. In the example in Figure 10-2, the average frequency of exposures is 2.14. Of course, no viewer is really exposed to 2.14 announcements. Each viewer is exposed to one, two, three, or four announcements; the average of each viewer's exposure yields the 2.14 figure.

Figure 10-2 depicts this exposure pattern graphically. The curve showing the number of viewers exposed to each specific number of announcements is the *frequency distribution curve*. Once an advertiser has determined the number of exposures required to effectively communicate the sales message to the viewer, the frequency distribution curve indicates what percentage of viewers each campaign alternative will reach that number of times or more. If, for example, at least three exposures were required, the advertiser would know that the campaign alternative represented by Figure 10-2 would reach 30 percent of the viewers effectively. Only three viewers, or 30 percent of all viewers, would be exposed to three or more announcements.

Armed with reach, average frequency, and frequency distribution estimates for each alternative campaign, the advertiser is prepared to

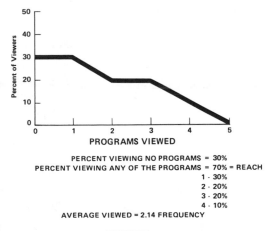

FIGURE 10-2

Frequency distribution curve.

make a selection. However, the vital theoretical question concerning how many exposures will be required to effectively communicate the sales message must be answered first.

HOW MUCH FREQUENCY IS ENOUGH?

No subject has received more attention from advertising researchers than the question of how much frequency is enough; yet no one answer has emerged as the correct answer. Such variables as the competitive "noise" in the marketplace, the complexity of the message being communicated, and the effectiveness of the creative execution complicate this problem, making it unlikely that any one exposure level will be universally optimal. However, some consensus has emerged from the research, providing the advertiser with guidelines, at least, for approaching this problem.

Although none of the research can be classified as conclusive, it does provide us with direction in establishing frequency guidelines for television campaign evaluation:

1. One exposure does seem inadequate.

2. Subsequent exposures after some point do seem to have diminishing marginal returns.

3. Rotation of visually different commercials will slow the wearout experienced with continued exposures.

APPLYING THE REACH/FREQUENCY CONCEPT

Alvin Achenbaum incorporates these findings into a theory of *effective exposure* for the evaluation of alternative advertising campaigns. He recommends that alternative campaigns be judged not on the total number of exposures they provide, but on the number of effective exposures. Using the frequency distribution curve as the source of measurement, Achenbaum discounts everyone exposed fewer than three times as ineffectively exposed. He also discounts all exposures beyond 10 as excessive. Exposures beyond 15 he considers negative exposures. Thus Achenbaum defines *effective exposures* as the third to the tenth exposure for each person.[1] Achenbaum's minimum three-exposure level is well supported. However, the maximum limit of 10 exposures and the assignment of a negative value to exposures beyond the fifteenth are not adequately supported by past research.

The 3+ exposure level would be the recommended criterion for campaign evaluation, with the maximum exposure level a function of budget constraints, dayparts used, competitive noise, and marketplace conditions. The concept of diminishing marginal returns for exposures beyond the third should be integrated into television campaign planning. Just as it is more important to reach someone who has been exposed to only one announcement a second and third time than to reach someone already exposed to three announcements a fourth or fifth time, it is more important to reach someone exposed to five announcements a sixth time than to reach someone exposed to nine announcements a tenth time. Achenbaum's hypothetically optimal television schedule would have a bell-shaped frequency distribution curve with as great a percentage of exposures falling into the 3 to 10 *effective exposure* range as possible. His assumption is that exposures 3 to 10 are of equal value and exposures beyond 10 have no value or a negative value.

An alternative schedule, following the axioms of 3+ effective exposure and diminishing marginal return beyond the third exposure, would have its modal point as close to the three-time level as possible. This schedule also would have no cutoff maximum exposure level. Figure 10-3 shows the bell-shaped curve for Achenbaum's hypothetically optimal schedule and a second curve with a lower modal exposure level and longer upper-limit tail. According to the two axioms of a three-exposure minimum and diminishing marginal returns for each subsequent exposure, the second curve would be preferred. Although this argument may seem academic, it has significant practical consequences. As Achenbaum points out in his paper, his bell-shaped curve is very difficult to achieve with a television schedule. The second curve is a more easily attainable frequency distribution curve, because of

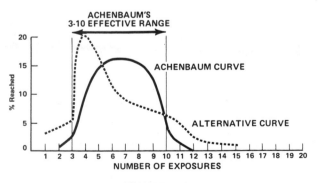

FIGURE 10-3

Alternative frequency distribution curves.

viewing differentials among various segments of the television audience.

Commercial Audience versus Program Audience

Accepting the conclusion that the goal of a television advertising campaign is to expose as large a percentage of the target audience as possible to at least three announcements, we now have to find an effective way of constructing frequency distribution curves for alternative campaigns. There are several methods for developing these curves. Both A.C. Nielsen and Arbitron provide actual frequency runs from their respective meter and diary samples. In addition, several models have been developed to provide formularized curves for hypothetical schedules.

The problem with all these approaches is that they measure *program* audience, not *commercial* audience. They tell us how many of the programs included in the schedule were viewed, not how many commercials were seen. This shortcoming is significant; research, primarily that of Burke Marketing Research, has shown commercial audiences equal to only 70 to 80 percent of program audiences. Gary Steiner's research in 1966 found this level to be approximately 84 percent.[2]

A 1963 study by Foote, Cone & Belding showed that only 72 percent of the homemakers who reported having viewed some part of the average network television program had an opportunity to see the specific commercial on the program.[3] In other words, only 70 to 80 of each 100 program viewers saw the commercials. This means that the three-exposure level is not that at all.

If we assume that the inclusion of each member of the program audience in the commercial audience is equally probable, each exposure to a program translates to a .75 probability (average of 70 to 80 percent) of commercial exposure. Thus the viewer exposed to three programs has only a .42 probability (.75 × .75 × .75) of being exposed to all three commercials. Not until the viewer is exposed to five programs is the probability of this exposure to three commercials fairly certain (.90 probability).

For this reason true *effective exposure* should be defined as the program exposure frequency discounted by the commercial audience factor. To calculate the effective, three-time commercial exposure for a television campaign, we discount the measured three-time program exposure by the .42 factor, the four-time program exposure by a .74 factor, the five-time exposure by the .90 factor, etc.

Since this method can become quite cumbersome, a shortcut is recommended in which the 3- and 4-exposure viewers are discounted and then added to the total 5 + exposure viewers:

Percentage viewing exactly X programs		Probability of viewers of X programs seeing three or more commercials		Percentage viewing three or more commercials
3 programs = 12.8	×	.42	=	5.4
4 programs = 11.5	×	.74	=	8.5
5+ programs = 39.1	×	1.00	=	<u>39.1</u>
		Effective exposure level		53.0

All subsequent references to effective reach levels in this chapter and elsewhere in the book are based on the application of this formula to program-based frequency distribution curves.

Estimating the Frequency Distribution Curve

To avoid confusion between the frequency element of the program-based frequency distribution curves and actual commercial exposure, we refer to each element in the frequency curve as an *exposure opportunity*. Five exposure opportunities translate to three probable exposures. With that understood, let us cover briefly two methods for generating frequency distribution curves for television schedules: actual and formularized.

ACTUAL CURVES

Actual frequency distribution curves are based on historical viewing patterns recorded by A.C. Nielsen and Arbitron during their ongoing television viewing surveys. Household-based curves can be derived from meter measures on a national basis by A.C. Nielsen's national television index (NTI) sample. These curves can be provided also by both Nielsen and Arbitron in metered markets (New York, Los Angeles, Chicago, San Francisco, and Philadelphia). These curves can be generated for 1 to 26 weeks, since the meter sample remains relatively constant over that period. Demographic frequency distribution curves can be provided on a national basis through the Nielsen national audience demographics (NAD) surveys. These curves cover only 4 weeks. Local demographic frequency distribution curves are available on a 1-week basis only, since both Arbitron and A.C. Nielsen local-diary households maintain these diaries for only 1 week.

The limitations of actual frequency distribution curves are both practical and theoretical. The practical limitation is cost. The generation of actual curves for several schedule variations is quite expensive. The theoretical limitation is the historical base. Future schedules are evaluated on past performance, not always a reliable measure in the rapidly changing program environment. In addition, there are the time limitations on the demographic curves in all surveys and on the household curves as well in nonmetered markets.

FORMULARIZED APPROACH

Given the limited data available to generate frequency distribution curves and the cost of regularly processing these data, researchers have been seeking a mathematical approach that would simulate actual frequency distribution patterns given the GRP level of the schedule, the number of announcements comprising the schedule, the number of vehicles (stations) used, and the dayparts included in the schedule.

Most of the pioneering work in reach and frequency measurement dealt with the print medium. Metheringham developed a technique using Monte Carlo simulation. This technique has been used widely to measure the frequency distribution of magazine schedules. However, it does not translate well to television. Attempts to find a method ideally suited for the television medium have led researchers to approaches based on the compound beta binomial distribution and the negative binomial distribution. In 1976, Headen, Klompmaker, and Teel tested both methods against 2424 one-week television schedules, covering a broad range of GRP levels, daypart mixes, and local TV markets.[4]

These researchers found the beta binomial distribution to be a superior estimator of frequency distribution patterns. The maximum error over the range of possible frequencies was 8 percent. This method's only shortcoming was in overestimating the lower-frequency classes for very heavy schedules using all available stations in a market. Even in these worst-fit cases, the estimation of 3 + exposures relative to less than 3 exposures was 4 percent at most. So the beta binomial distribution is an adequate means of measuring frequency distribution for television schedules.

This beta binomial distribution method has been incorporated into several commercially available television reach/frequency estimation programs. Interactive Market Systems (IMS) developed a beta binomial based system, Modal, for television reach/frequency estimation. This system is available to subscribers through an online computer.

LONG-TERM APPROACH

Because television viewing data are limited, reach and frequency analysis has been confined primarily to the 1-week and 4-week time frames.

However, many television campaigns extend far beyond 4 weeks. This introduces the critical question of whether frequency distribution patterns for television schedules change as a function of the time over which those schedules run.

In 1975, A.C. Nielsen published a special study on long-term reach and frequency analysis. It found that schedules of equal GRPs having the same daypart mix produced approximately the same reach/frequency configurations. Also, running the same schedules in a noncontiguous, as opposed to a continuous, weekly pattern yielded similar reach/frequency configurations.[5]

Based on this research, it seems safe to use either 4-week actual or standard formularized approaches to estimate frequency distribution curves for schedules running longer than 4 weeks. Table 10-1 shows reach, frequency, and effective reach estimates for 12 hypothetical television schedules on a 1-week to 26-week basis.

TIMING THE TELEVISION ADVERTISING CAMPAIGN

Acknowledging that the potential consumer must be exposed to at least three announcements and need not be exposed to more than 10, the planner must decide how to space those exposures. If they are too far apart, there may be some degree of forgetting on the part of the exposed person that would short-circuit the cumulative impact of multiple exposures. However, if the exposures are very close together, the overall effective time span of the campaign is lessened. The fine-tuning of a TV schedule to achieve the optimum exposure pattern must take into account a number of factors:

- The consumer's ability to recall advertising messages
- The nature of the product advertised
- The seasonality of product consumption
- The intensity of competitive advertising
- The complexity of the advertiser's message
- The purchase cycle for the product or service advertised
- The audience
- The seasonality of television rates
- The creative elements of the advertising

The first, and by far the most critical, factor is the consumer's ability to recall advertising messages. Research dating to the pioneering work

TABLE 10-1
TWELVE HYPOTHETICAL SCHEDULES

Schedule		Duration of campaign (weeks)					
		1	2	4	8	13	26
Daytime, 1-network, light	GRPs	13.9	27.5	56.7	116.3	190.8	388.6
	R*	12.7	20.7	29.6	38.6	48.2	59.8
	F†	1.1	1.3	1.9	3.0	4.0	6.5
	Eff R‡	—	—	4.6	12.8	17.0	32.9
Daytime, 3-network, moderate	GRPs	28.5	55.5	113.1	227.0	378.8	781.4
	R	23.7	35.8	50.8	62.2	72.1	81.9
	F	1.2	1.6	2.2	3.7	5.3	9.5
	Eff R	—	2.5	11.3	27.6	42.0	60.5
Daytime, 3-network, heavy	GRPs	83.8	164.2	336.7	684.7	1135.8	2324.1
	R	42.2	54.1	64.8	74.7	81.7	89.1
	F	2.0	3.0	5.2	9.2	13.9	26.1
	Eff R	6.5	19.3	37.0	53.9	64.1	77.5
Primetime, 1-network, light	GRPs	18.7	35.9	56.0	111.2	188.9	376.4
	R	18.7	29.8	37.3	58.0	73.7	88.7
	F	1.0	1.2	1.5	1.9	2.6	4.2
	Eff R	—	—	1.6	8.0	20.0	49.8
Primetime, 3-network, moderate	GRPs	36.7	72.5	109.0	227.0	360.6	704.9
	R	34.0	51.3	64.1	82.0	89.7	94.8
	F	1.1	1.4	1.7	2.8	4.0	7.4
	Eff R	—	1.6	5.5	27.2	50.6	78.7
Primetime, 3-network, heavy	GRPs	86.6	160.1	327.4	665.8	1073.2	2114.1
	R	56.7	73.4	86.6	93.0	96.0	97.7
	F	1.5	2.2	3.8	7.2	11.2	21.6
	Eff R	2.9	14.5	46.5	75.6	86.5	94.0

Daytime-primetime, 3-network	GRPs	65.2	128.0	223.0	454.0	739.3	1486.3
	R	47.4	63.1	77.4	89.7	94.2	97.7
	F	1.4	2.0	2.9	5.1	7.8	15.2
	Eff R	1.5	10.0	26.3	55.3	74.1	90.0
Primetime-late night, 3-network	GRPs	53.8	108.5	220.0	451.0	750.6	1526.6
	R	37.6	52.8	70.7	80.4	86.3	93.2
	F	1.4	2.1	3.1	5.6	8.7	16.4
	Eff R	1.6	9.8	26.5	50.5	66.4	81.6
Primetime-late night, 3-network	GRPs	61.9	125.5	217.0	451.0	732.4	1450.1
	R	45.2	62.2	76.6	87.6	92.6	96.5
	F	1.4	2.0	2.8	5.2	7.9	15.0
	Eff R	2.3	10.4	25.8	53.8	71.5	86.9
Primetime-early news, 3-network	GRPs	60.1	119.5	203.9	430.9	699.6	1393.5
	R	46.7	62.9	76.1	88.9	94.3	97.5
	F	1.3	1.9	2.7	4.8	7.4	14.3
	Eff R	0.8	8.7	23.9	54.5	72.1	89.2
Daytime-primetime-late night, 3-network	GRPs	90.5	181.0	330.0	678.0	111.2	1648.0
	R	55.0	69.6	84.2	92.6	95.4	97.9
	F	1.6	2.6	3.9	7.3	11.7	16.8
	Eff R	4.7	20.8	41.9	69.8	83.7	89.6
Daytime-primetime-early news-late night, 3-network	GRPs	113.8	228.0	424.0	881.9	1450.0	2920.1
	R	61.6	74.7	87.6	94.7	97.0	99.2
	F	1.8	3.1	4.8	9.3	14.9	29.4
	Eff R	7.9	28.3	53.4	78.6	88.2	95.0

*R = reach.

†F = frequency.

‡Eff R = effective reach (.42 × 3 exposures + .74 × 4 exposures + 1.00 × 5+ exposures).

Source: Derived from A.C. Nielsen, "Long Term Cume Analysis, October–March 1974–75," Chicago, 1975.

of Hermann Ebbinghaus in 1885 proved that people forget learned information rather quickly. Ebbinghaus found that 75 percent of all learned information was forgotten 2 weeks after it was learned, and almost all (95 percent) of this information was forgotten at the end of 4 weeks. Although these statistics are far from absolute, more recent research has supported the basic shape of the forgetting curve presented by Ebbinghaus.

If the media planner wishes to maintain awareness of a product and its advertising, exposure to at least one commercial per week is required. However, for most advertisers, such a level of advertising would be prohibitively expensive. These advertisers have to decide whether to limit the length of their advertising campaigns in order to maintain the exposure level required to minimize forgetting or to accept some level of forgetting and space their advertising throughout the year.

The first approach is referred to as *flighting*. The advertiser runs a series of 4- to 6-week campaigns interrupted by periods of no television advertising at all. These no-advertising periods are called *hiatuses*. A hiatus could last from 4 weeks to as long as 12 weeks. There are two variations of the second, full-year, approach. The advertiser could space the advertising over the entire 52-week year at one constant weekly level. This technique is called the *continuous* campaign. If the advertiser finds that a continuous approach results in too low a weekly level, she or he can select an in–out pattern. This pattern can take many specific forms, such as 1 week on, 1 week off; 2 weeks on, 1 week off; or 2 weeks on, 2 weeks off. Advertising in this type of pattern is known as *pulsing*.

Which pattern should an advertiser choose? That is determined to a certain extent by the other factors mentioned. The continuous approach distributes exposures evenly each week. If we assume that the advertiser cannot afford to reach 100 percent of all consumers weekly in this manner, the advertiser will have to settle for reaching a percentage of those consumers each week. The awareness curve builds gradually over the year, peaking at the end of the year.

The pulsing approach allows the advertiser to generate awareness more quickly, but a certain amount of forgetting lowers the awareness level during the weeks of no advertising. The awareness curve has a sawtooth pattern of peaks and valleys, with each peak slightly higher than the preceding peak. The highest peak approximately equals the final recall point of the continuous approach; however, the average weekly awareness level moves up and down as opposed to building gradually. The flighting alternative results in a series of relatively high awareness periods followed by declines to almost zero awareness during the hiatus periods.

Figure 10-4 shows three hypothetical recall curves representing each

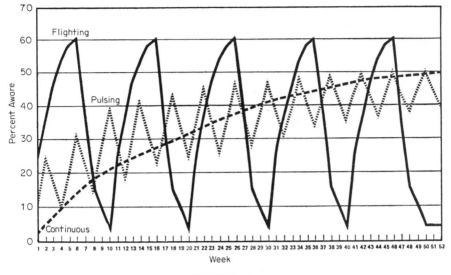

FIGURE 10-4

Hypothetical awareness curves.

alternative. Each curve represents an average weekly awareness level of approximately 33 percent; however, this is certainly one case in which averages are deceiving. The continuous curve builds gradually to a high 50 percent level. The later in the year, the higher the awareness level for this alternative. The pulsing curve also achieves a high level of 50 percent. However, its pattern is a series of peaks and valleys. The pulsing approach distributes awareness more equitably throughout the year, outperforming the continuous approach during the average first half-year week while falling below this approach during the latter half of the year. The flighting alternative achieves awareness highs of 60 percent during 5 different weeks of the year. However, it also falls to lows of 4 percent for 7 weeks.

These curves are based on the observations of Pomerance and Zielske, on the 1958 research on magazine advertising awareness conducted for Foote, Cone & Belding,[3] and on the Ebbinghaus forgetting curve. Actual curves for television could vary substantially from those shown, although the basic patterns should hold.

Which approach should an advertiser use? The answer seems to lie with the remaining factors. First, there is *competitive activity*. The smart advertiser always takes into account the competitive noise level when planning a television campaign. The timing strategy chosen will depend on the position of the brand in the marketplace.

A dominant brand most likely calls for a defensive strategy. The advertising of a dominant brand does not have to work as hard as that of a weaker or new brand, since the task is more the reinforcement of current behaviors than the changing of behavior. It is not necessary for the dominant brand to "outshout" the competition, so advertising intensity is not critical. What the planner for a dominant brand must avoid is any long period of absence from the air, because that would give the challenging brands exclusive exposure to the dominant brand's customers. Thus the dominant-brand planner should select the continuous approach or pulsing. It may not be necessary to cover the entire year if the nature of the market ensures that there will be no significant competitive advertising during certain times of the year.

The weaker brand seeking to increase its share or the new brand seeking to establish itself in the market most likely has to outshout the dominant competitors. That demands a flighting strategy or a concentrated pulsing strategy. The timing of the flights depends on whether the dominant brands choose a continuous, pulsing, or flighting strategy; the level of TV advertising employed by these competitors; and the nature of market demand.

The timing strategy chosen must reflect the *seasonality* of demand for the product. If the market is highly seasonal—such as that for skis, vacation travel, and hay fever remedies—a flighting approach is the obvious choice. Highly seasonal demand patterns favor the dominant brands, since they allow these brands to protect their franchises without committing to 52-week advertising campaigns. The weaker brands and the new brands have to either go head to head with the dominant brands during these periods or try to build a franchise through off-season advertising. The latter tactic, using counterseasonal flighting, has been effective when there is a significant amount of demand during off-season periods.

The *product purchase cycle* reflects the frequency of purchase of the product by its consumers. If a product is bought frequently, the opportunities to win a new customer (and to lose a current customer) are greater. A product such as paper towels or a soft drink that is purchased once a week on average presents 52 different purchase decisions a year, whereas the automobile purchase decision is exercised only once every few years by the average consumer.

The product category characterized by a short purchase cycle exhibits the classic pattern of dominant brands using continuous campaigns to protect their franchises, with the weaker and newer brands launching concentrated flights to try to stimulate brand switching. The long-duration purchase cycle requires careful fine-tuning of the TV advertising campaign. Since each purchase is critical to the advertiser, great efforts are made to coordinate TV advertising with the periods of greater than average sales activity. Automobile marketers concentrate advertising during the fall new-season promotion period and in the late spring.

Usually, when a period of high sales activity is isolated, all competitors, large and small, use high-level flighting. When sales activity is fairly constant throughout the year, the pattern is more likely to follow a continuous or pulsing direction. However, if the market is lucrative enough, some smaller firms will opt for the flighting approach. The determinant will be the relative profitability of low market share levels.

The *nature of the product* must be taken into account in timing the television advertising campaign. One established classification of products is by consumer involvement. A low-involvement product is one of little consequence to the consumer. The search is limited in choosing a brand in a low-involvement category. Convenience goods such as milk, bread, and paper towels are low-involvement products. Conversely, high-involvement products entail a much more deliberate search and selection process.

Advertising repetition is likely to have a greater impact in low-involvement product categories. In these categories a short flight of intensive advertising can stimulate significant brand switching and new-product trial. Advertising is a less influential component of the decision-making process for high-involvement categories. The important contribution of advertising is to maintain an adequate level of awareness to ensure some consideration of the brand. Lower-level continuous advertising or a pulsing strategy is enough to maintain this awareness level.

The *complexity of the advertising message* affects the required intensity of advertising. A more complex message is less likely to be totally comprehended after only one exposure. If too long a time passes between messages, the cumulative learning process from one exposure to the next does not take place. In such cases it is possible that most people exposed to the message never fully understand it. Intensity of advertising narrows the time between exposures and facilitates comprehension of the message.

On the opposite end of the message complexity spectrum is the reminder ad designed merely to keep the brand name in the consumer's mind. Since there is little learning from one exposure to the next, there is little concern for minimizing the time between exposures. As long as exposure occurs often enough to prevent forgetting, this type of advertising can be stretched into a longer continuous or pulsing pattern.

The *creative elements* of an advertisement affect the rate of wear-out for that advertisement. The subjectivity of this area makes it very difficult to generalize about which creative elements have what effects.

Certain unique ads with strong creative elements have a big impact after only one exposure. Excessive repetition of exposure to this type of advertising is not necessary. However, a noncreative hard-sell type of advertisement is likely to become more irritating with each successive exposure after a certain number. Then excessive frequency of exposure can have a negative effect.

The use of color, animation, humor, and music can affect the need for and value of a high frequency of exposure to an ad; however, it is virtually impossible to predict the exact effect of each. The goal is to create an ad that delivers the message in a manner requiring little frequency of exposure. If this goal is met, the advertiser can afford to stretch out the advertising over a long time in a continuous or pulsing pattern.

The predisposition of the audience also plays a role in the relative impact of various advertising exposure patterns on that audience. We stated that a dominant brand can afford a lower exposure level than a weak or new brand. This brand's advertising is seen or heard by a greater percentage of people who either are present users or are familiar with the brand at least. The predispostion of the audience need not be brand-related. Heavy users of the product category are usually more responsive to advertising in the category. Certain segments of the audience may be more attentive to a particular appeal. The diet-conscious segment may respond quickly to a low-calorie appeal; the status-conscious to a celebrity endorsement. To the extent that the audience is predisposed either to the brand or to the advertising message itself, less frequency of exposure is required.

The last factor bearing upon the timing of a television advertising schedule is the seasonal variation in TV advertising rates. Although other variables may lead the advertiser to a flighting approach, if that advertiser's key seasons are during the May–June and November–December periods, when TV rates are at their highest, the added cost of the flighting alternative may be the determining factor. The shifting of flights to periods of lower TV cost immediately prior to these high-demand months or the stretching of advertising over longer periods through a continuous or pulsing strategy may more than compensate for the loss of advertising intensity with the additional exposures that can be obtained for the same dollars. Many advertisers of products with flat demand curves take advantage of the low TV prices by running heavier-level campaigns and/or special promotions during these slower times of the year.

In summary, the decision to employ a continuous, pulsing, or flighting approach in the timing of a television advertising campaign is a complex one, involving the consideration of many factors.

Before moving on to the next theoretical issue, we must discuss one other aspect of campaign timing. So far, the three alternatives of continuity, pulsing, and flighting have been discussed in the context of equal weekly advertising weight. Actually, distributing TV advertising weight equally by week is not the most theoretically sound approach. The research conducted concerning the efficiency of repetition of advertising has shown that two to three exposures are required for advertising to complete its communication process and stimulate action.

Krugman states that three exposures are necessary, with every exposure, beginning with the third, acting as a reinforcer or reminder of the first two exposures.[6] If this is true, an advertiser would want to plan the campaign so as to reach the two- to three-exposure level as quickly as possible and would give the exposures heavier weight during the first weeks of a campaign. In fact, 2 weeks of heavy introductory advertising followed by a number of weeks of sustaining-level advertising is a common television campaign configuration.

Harold Miller of SSC&B gave a paper entitled "Flighting—It's Still the Same Old Game," which presented research demonstrating the advantage of this heavy upfront approach in terms of initially higher remembrance peaks.[7] He concluded, ". . . when it is possible to do so, advertising should be scheduled in cycles—each cycle starting with an initially heavy effort." Miller's research showed that not only did a 2-weeks-in, 1-week-out pulsing approach in 12-week cycles produce the highest initial remembrance level with no reduction in the average 12-week remembrance level, but also for each subsequent flight, it seemed to make this initial level even higher. If an advertiser can afford to boost the advertising level during the early weeks of a campaign without lowering the sustaining level for the remaining weeks below a one-exposure-per-week level, this strategy should be chosen.

TELEVISION MIX: COMBINING NETWORK TV WITH LOCAL TELEVISION OPTIONS

Allocation of television advertising dollars is a relatively simple procedure for the local advertiser. Since only one market is involved, the advertiser needs to choose only among a limited number of stations. The task of the national advertiser is much more complex, however. The national advertiser has two major options: network television and spot market television. This advertiser may choose:

- A total network television approach
- A total spot market television approach
- A combination of network television and spot market television

If we assume that a spot market or network plus spot market approach is chosen, then the advertiser must decide which markets to include in the plan and how to allocate available funds among them. In the case of network-spot combinations, the basic allocation of funds between network and spot television must be determined also.

The first consideration in this allocation procedure is for the advertiser to assign a relative value to each market. For established products in established product categories, sales by market is probably the best indicator of relative market value. For new products in established product categories, product category sales by market is a popular indicator of market value. For the new product in a new category—or one for which no data are available to the advertiser—a surrogate measure can be substituted such as retail sales, discretionary income, or sales of a similar type of product.

In practice, most sophisticated advertisers choose some weighted combination of brand sales and category sales to develop what is commonly called a brand potential index or brand development index (BDI). This system of assigning market values is based on the theory that the potential of advertising to generate sales in a market is a function of both the brand's existing franchise in that market and the as-yet-untapped potential of that market, represented by the sales of competing brands.

Once the advertiser has assigned a value to each market, the simple solution is to allocate the advertising dollars by market according to those values. For example, if a market represents 10 percent of brand sales and 15 percent of category sales and the advertiser chooses to give each equal value, that market should receive 12.5 percent of the total TV advertising budget. The problem with this approach is that it does not take into account the option of network television or consider the relative cost of television in each market.

Network television is, on a whole, much more efficient than spot television. If a buyer tried to buy all 200+ markets on a market-by-market basis instead of a network basis, that buyer would end up paying considerably more for the same advertising time. (There would be a substantial administrative cost as well.) However, if that advertiser's sales were concentrated in 10 or 20 markets, buying those markets alone would be an efficient alternative to the network buy. On a strict cost-per-point basis, the network break-even point is approximately at market 50. A buyer can purchase the whole country through network television for approximately the same cost as the top 50 markets (67 percent of the United States) purchased separately. In effect, the advertiser is getting 33 percent of the country as a bonus.

If a brand and its category have a relatively flat national distribution pattern (that is, one that follows population), network is the obvious choice. However, this is seldom the case. For most advertised brands there are several very important strong markets, and other markets have little or no value. A network-only approach allocates too little support to the key sales markets and too much to the insignificant markets. These advertisers usually establish a network television base to provide each market with some minimum level of coverage and then supplement with spot market advertising in their key markets.

When designing their television mix, the most sophisticated advertisers consider the relative efficiency of spot television in each market and the delivery of network television in each market. Market CPMs vary widely. If two markets have the same BDI and one has a relatively low CPM while the other has a much higher CPM, these advertisers will favor the first market, since they could get much greater advertising impact for their money in that market.

Spot television allocations also must reflect network delivery by market. Network program audiences vary by market. In a warm-weather market such as Los Angeles, with its seven-station competitive universe, network performance usually is below the national average. In a normal three-station market such as Omaha, network performance is above the national average. An advertiser is more likely to allocate spot television dollars to Los Angeles, given similar BDIs, since Omaha already benefits from network overdelivery.

In addition to market sales potential, spot television efficiency, and network delivery, one other component is required for an effective television advertising allocation system. The advertiser must set minimum and maximum advertising levels for individual markets. Earlier in this chapter research was cited to support the hypothesis that advertising is usually ineffective below a minimum exposure level (two to three times). If an advertiser finds that her or his TV plan has been so diluted by the attempt to maintain full national exposure that it provides marginal levels of advertising in many markets, that advertiser should concentrate all the company's advertising in key markets and eliminate all advertising in those marginally supported markets. Most likely a shift will have to be made from network to a spot market base.

An advertiser can allocate too much money to a market. If we assume that one market had the highest BDI and the lowest CPM, theoretically the most cost-effective approach is to allocate all TV advertising dollars to that market. However, the actual result of such an allocation would be an advertising level well beyond the level of diminishing, if not negative, returns in that market and no advertising in any other market. So it is necessary for the advertiser to establish a maximum advertising level for each market.

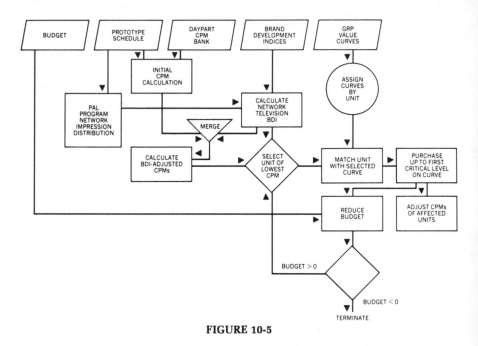

FIGURE 10-5

Flowchart of TV allocation.

(Source: "CBS Television Allocation Model," CBS Television Network, New York, 1982.)

Addressing this complex task is the CBS television allocation model (see Figure 10-5), a model I designed for CBS. This model allocates a television advertising budget between network television and individual-market spot television according to the parameters just outlined—sales potential by market, relative cost efficiency of network versus spot television and market versus market spot television, network delivery by market, and minimum and maximum advertising level constraints. Similar models have been developed by many major advertising agencies. Both IMS and Telmar, the online, computer-based media planning services, offer TV allocation models.

CABLE TV

Advertiser-supported cable television services represent a potential third element in the overall TV advertising plan. Just as spot television is used to add advertising weight in specific markets and to correct for network underdelivery in others, cable television options can add weight in key audience segments and correct for network underdelivery in specific audience segments.

Choosing the right cable services for inclusion in the television mix requires careful matching of the audience profile of the various systems and the target market profile for the brand being advertised. Unfortunately, audience research covering these services is sparse to date; however, basic profiles can be drawn. An advertiser seeking to reach affluent, educated adults should look to the various cultural services. A male-oriented advertiser should consider the sports networks, such as ESPN and Sports Channel. An advertiser seeking to reach the young adult and/or teenager should focus on Warner Amex's MTV.

These selective cable services do provide supplemental coverage in key market segments, but they deliver small, imprecisely measured audiences. At this time they should be considered after the options of network and/or spot television have been explored. They are an acceptable alternative for either of these two television advertising forms only for advertisers of specifically targeted products with limited budgets.

Cable television services can be used to correct for network underdelivery in key audience segments. For example, households receiving pay cable watch less primetime network television on average than basic cable and noncable households. Thus a primetime network TV advertising schedule is likely to underdeliver in pay cable households. The obvious solution to the imbalance is supplemental advertising on pay cable.

Unfortunately, the major pay cable services take no advertising. However, pay cable households obviously are more likely to view the advertiser-supported cable services than noncable households. So an imbalance between these two household segments can be offset by advertising on these latter cable channels.

The problem of establishing balanced audience delivery between pay cable and basic cable households by advertising on the advertiser-supported cable services is more complex. Basic cable households are likely to view more advertiser-supported cable programming than pay cable households (since they lack the option of pay cable viewing), so adding advertising weight on these channels would actually increase the imbalance between pay cable and basic cable audience delivery.

The advertiser wishing to correct for underdelivery in pay cable households also can either select network television programs with above-average ratings in pay cable households (there are several) for inclusion in the base network schedule or supplement that schedule with spot television in high-penetration pay cable markets.

NOTES

1. Alvin A. Achenbaum, " 'Effective Exposure,' A New Way of Evaluating Media," Speech delivered to the Association of National Advertisers, winter meeting, New York, February 3, 1977.

2. Gary A. Steiner, "The People Look at Commercials: A Study of Audience Behavior," *Journal of Business*, April 1966, pp. 272–304.

3. Paul E. J. Gerhold, "Television Ratings and the Audience for TV Commercials," Speech delivered to the Association of National Advertisers, spring meeting, New York, May 20–21, 1963.

4. Robert S. Headen, Jay E. Klompmaker, and Jesse E. Teel, Jr., "TV Audience Exposure," *Journal of Advertising Research*, December 1976, pp. 49–52.

5. CBS television station's analysis of the Nielsen television index, "Long-Term Cume Analysis, October–March 1974–75."

6. Herbert E. Krugman, "Why Three Exposures May Be Enough," *Journal of Advertising Research*, December 1972.

7. Harold Miller, "Flighting—It's Still the Same Old Game," Speech delivered to the Association of National Advertisers, Media Workshop, New York, March 2, 1978.

The Media Mix:
Integrating the
Television Campaign
with Advertising
in Other Media

Up to this point we discussed the television campaign in isolation. Establishing the reach/frequency mix, developing the timing of the campaign, and combining the elements of network television, spot market television, and/or cable television have been done within the context of the television campaign alone. However, most television advertisers employ other media in their overall advertising program, and the optimization of the contribution of the television component to the total advertising program must reflect those other media elements. The other media options available to the television advertiser are magazines, radio, newspapers, outdoor advertising, and direct mail. Television's role in an advertising campaign vis-à-vis these other media should be examined separately for each medium.

TELEVISION AND MAGAZINES

Media can be differentiated by the manner in which they convey the advertising message, the environment they provide for that message, and the audience they reach with that message. Comparisons between television and magazines as advertising vehicles usually center on television's "hot," visual, passive, and pervasive communications properties versus magazines' "cool," verbal, active, and selective properties.

The television commercial *environment* is relatively competition free and uncluttered, but it lacks personality. By contrast, the magazine *environment* usually is shared with many competitors, is fairly cluttered, and has a definite personality. These environmental differences stem from television's mass audience orientation and magazines' selective market orientation. Because TV networks and stations seek to reach all people with some degree of regularity, they offer a variety of mass-appeal programming. Each program may have a personality of its own, but the overall nature of the medium is eclectic.

Because television programs require a relatively long period of the viewer's time, they cannot hold an audience if they are interrupted too often or for too long. Thus the commercial element must be limited. The combination of this spacing of commercial announcements and the wide range of advertisers wishing to address the television audience allows the medium to separate competitive advertising. (This is less true in program areas such as sports, which are dominated by beer and automobile sponsors.)

Today's successful magazines, however, have distinctive personalities that offer the advertiser a more involved audience. If the advertiser's product can be identified with the "personality" of the medium, the magazine offers a more conducive advertising environment than television. One need only leaf through such publications as Playboy and Vogue to see how advertisers attempt to adapt to the personalities of specific publications.

The narrow audience base of most magazines limits their potential advertiser universe. This limited customer base forces magazines to accept a great deal of competitive advertising in each issue. Most women's magazines contain some advertising for almost every cosmetics company. Playboy and Penthouse feature a variety of stereo component competitors. Business Week and Fortune are automatic entries on the media schedules of all major business equipment manufacturers.

Magazines are not limited by any prescribed editorial-to-advertising ratio. Theoretically they can keep adding advertising pages as they sell them. Certain publications, such as the New Yorker, can claim that their advertising generates interest often equal to, if not greater than, the editorial. This high advertising-to-editorial ratio puts great pressure on each ad to stand out.

Audience Dimension

The audiences delivered by magazines and by television are also different on a composite basis. Of course, in this case within-group differentials often are more substantial than the between-group differential, but, on average, the magazine reader profile varies from that of the TV viewer.

Simmons and MRI are the primary sources of magazine readership data. These services also provide substantial data on television viewing. For Simmons, the first comparative measure of the audiences of these two media is quintile analysis. Quintile analysis divides audiences into equal fifths based on time spent with that medium. Quintile 1 consists of the 20 percent of magazine readers or television viewers who use that medium most heavily. Quintile 5 for each medium consists of the 20 percent who use that medium the least.

Table 11-1 shows the 1980 Simmons magazine readership quintiles. The adults in quintile 1, the heaviest readers, read 15 or more magazines per week. In contrast, the adults in quintile 5, the lighter readers, read no more than one magazine per week. Table 11-2 provides the same type of quintile analysis for television viewing. Here the heaviest viewing quintile, quintile 1, accounted for 50 hours of viewing per week for women and 43 hours for men, whereas the lightest viewing quintile, quintile 5, watched TV less than 6 hours per week for women and 4.5 hours for men.

Examination of the demographic composition of the heavy and light magazine reader and TV viewer quintiles reveals the differences between these media audiences. Table 11-3 makes a demographic comparison of the heavy versus light magazine reader, the heavy versus light TV viewer, and the heavy magazine reader and the heavy TV viewer. The heavy magazine reader is younger, better educated, more likely to be engaged in a professional or managerial occupation, and more affluent. The heavy television viewer is older, less educated, less affluent, and likely to be living alone.

It is obvious that the two media are complementary in terms of audience profiles and that the magazine profile is the more attractive one. However, this can be misleading. On average, the light television viewer is likely to spend as much time watching television as the heavy

TABLE 11-1

1980 SIMMONS MAGAZINE READING QUINTILES

Quintile	Average no. of magazines read, adults
1	15.4
2	7.3
3	4.4
4	2.5
5	0.4

Source: Derived from "The 1980 Study of Media and Markets," Simmons Market Research Bureau, Inc., New York, 1980.

TABLE 11-2

1980 SIMMONS TV VIEWING QUINTILES

Quintile	Average hours of viewing per week, adults*
1	47.3
2	28.8
3	20.1
4	13.3
5	5.0

*Measured over a 2-week period.

Source: Derived from "The 1980 Study of Media and Markets," Simmons Market Research Bureau, Inc., New York, 1980.

TABLE 11-3

DEMOGRAPHIC PROFILES

Selected demographics	Magazine reading quintiles, index versus total adults				TV viewing quintiles, index versus total adults				Heavy TV viewer versus heavy magazine reader, index versus total adults	
	Q1	Q2	Q3	Q4 and Q5	Q1	Q2	Q3	Q4 and Q5	Magazine quintile 1	TV quintile 1
Age:										
18–34	136	117	101	74	82	89	100	114	136	82
18–49	122	110	103	83	80	90	103	113	122	80
25–54	110	106	104	91	82	92	106	110	110	82
55–64	71	94	108	114	125	119	100	78	71	125
65+	37	66	76	156	172	118	81	65	37	172
Education: College graduate	141	135	116	57	69	83	103	122	141	69
Occupation: Professional, managerial	138	124	109	66	52	80	122	123	138	52
County size:										
A	101	103	103	97	100	105	106	94	101	100
B	115	96	86	100	99	98	98	102	113	99
C	104	105	101	95	108	93	106	96	104	108
D	67	93	116	113	83	98	83	113	67	83
Household income: $25,000+	136	122	109	69	60	97	102	120	136	60
Household size:										
1	76	75	89	128	127	100	92	91	76	127
2	94	95	100	105	118	105	100	88	94	118
3–4	108	113	102	89	83	97	103	108	108	83
5+	109	99	102	95	85	96	98	110	109	85

"1980 Study of Media and Markets," Simmons Market Research Bureau, Inc., New York, 1980.

magazine reader spends reading magazines. In fact, the heavy magazine reader may spend more time, on average, watching television than reading magazines.

If the mean level of TV viewing for each TV quintile is assigned to the heavy magazine segment, the mean average hours viewed is 21 per week. In all likelihood this represents more time than is spent each week with the 15.4 magazines they read. The younger, more affluent heavy magazine reader can be reached through television if the right television programs are selected.

When television and magazines are evaluated on a usage basis, another consideration is the number of publications included in the magazine universe. The heavy magazine reader reads several *different* magazines. Of the 125 magazines listed in Simmons, the average magazine counted only 10 percent of the heavy magazine readers in its audience. The leading magazines for an adult audience, *TV Guide* and *Readers' Digest,* did substantially better, 43.4 and 42.8 percent, respectively. However, the 41 primetime television programs included in the Simmons report on average included 11.5 percent of the heavy magazine readers in their audiences, and 38 percent of this group viewed television during the average primetime half hour.

It is not so much a question of not reaching the upscale audience with television as of reaching that audience efficiently. Magazines allow the advertiser to reach certain audience segments with little or no circulation waste. With television the selective market advertiser has to pay for a substantial number of viewers she or he may not be interested in reaching in order to reach the potential market effectively. Magazines offer to reach the advertiser's audience and only that audience. However, once the advertiser has isolated the publications that reach the target market selectively, a substantial portion of this market still may not be reached. At this point television offers an efficient alternative for achieving broad-target market coverage by filling in the gaps.

It is not our objective in this chapter to focus on the television versus magazines decision. Instead, we emphasize the effective combination of these media in the advertising campaign. From the audience perspective, in most cases this means building a broad audience base through television and adding emphasis in key target market audience segments with magazines. To aid advertisers in applying this approach, Simmons developed its *Media Imperative* audience segmentation. The Media Imperative segmentation is done for each pair of media. In the case of TV and magazines, respondents who fall into the three highest quintiles for both TV viewing and magazine readership are placed in the *dual-audience* category. Those in the three highest quintiles (1 to 3) for one medium and the two lowest quintiles (4 and 5) for the second medium are placed in the *imperative* category for the first medium. Conversely, those respondents in the lowest quintiles (4 and 5) for the first medium and the highest quintiles (1 to 3) for the second medium are placed in the *imperative* category for the second medium. The remaining respondents, those in the lowest quintiles (4 and 5) for both media, are classified as *lightly exposed*. Table 11-4 shows that 19.2 percent of all adults fall into the dual-audience category, with both television and magazines accounting for approximately another 32 percent in their imperative categories.

The objective behind the Media Imperatives concept is to provide media planners with a means of isolating the potential contribution of each medium to an overall media plan. Table 11-5 provides an example of how a planner can use these data. The domestic car advertiser focuses on domestic car buyers. Although the magazine imperative classification represents the greatest potential for this advertiser, it accounts for only about one-third of all domestic new-car buyers. The television imperative classification also represents a substantial portion of the overall target market. This type of profile calls for a TV-magazine combination plan.

The planner for an imported car employs the data on imported car buying. This planner finds that the magazine imperative group comprises almost half of all imported car buyers. Add to this the dual group, and almost two-thirds of the market is accounted for. The television imperative category represents only 22 percent of the total market. This planner should select a magazine-dominated, if not an exclusive magazine, approach.

In Combination: The Qualitative Dimension

Although the quintile analysis and Media Imperative measures provided by Simmons help the planner evaluate the potential contributions of television and magazines from an audience perspective, the planner must go beyond the numbers. The synergistic effect of using two media in combination is generally considered to be a more important consideration than the comparative audience profile of each medium. This synergistic effect is the way that exposure to advertising in one medium heightens the effects of exposure to the advertising in the other medium. The synergistic effect can be either reinforcing or complementary.

Advertising in one medium can be said to *reinforce* advertising in another medium when it repeats the same essential message. In this case the synergistic effect focuses on the heightened awareness of the message as a result of exposure in more than one context. Often a

TABLE 11-4

**DISTRIBUTION OF TOTAL ADULTS
BY MEDIA IMPERATIVE
CLASSIFICATIONS**

Media Imperative group	Total adults (%)
Magazine–television: dual	19.2
Magazine imperative	32.5
Television imperative	32.3
Lightly exposed	16.0

Source: "The 1980 Study of Media and Markets," Simmons
Market Research Bureau, Inc., New York, 1980.

TABLE 11-5

**MEDIA IMPERATIVES FOR NEW-
CAR BUYERS**

Media Imperative group	Percentage of total	Index*
	Adult decision makers bought domestic car in past 2 years	
Magazine–television: dual	20.3	106
Magazine imperative	34.0	105
Television imperative	29.9	93
Lightly exposed	15.8	99
	Adult decision makers bought imported car in past 2 years	
Magazine–television: dual	21.1	110
Magazine imperative	44.1	136
Television imperative	22.0	68
Lightly exposed	12.8	80

*Base = percentage of total adults.

Source: "The 1980 Study of Media and Markets," Simmons Market Research Bureau,
Inc., New York, 1980.

magazine ad uses a frame from the television commercial as its visual element and the theme line from that commercial as a central element in the copy. Then the print ad expands on the TV message in its body copy, providing more detail than could be given through the 30-second TV commercial. Exposure to the TV commercial provides preexposure recognition of the magazine ad, allowing the reader to "get into the ad" more quickly. The magazine ad, in turn, offers the reader more information, recall of which is triggered by subsequent exposure to the TV commercials.

The *complementary* use of television and magazines focuses more directly on the comparative communication advantages of each medium. One major advantage of TV is its visual element, which allows for effective demonstration of the product and its benefits. A contrasting advantage of magazine ads is the ability to explain complex product benefits or characteristics. The automobile industry often employs a TV-magazine mix to profit from these complementary advantages. The TV commercial might show the car in a test track situation, demonstrating its superior high-speed braking power; the magazine ad might discuss how the unique braking system makes this braking power possible.

Another advantage of television is its ability to utilize emotion for the advertiser. Nowhere is this better shown than in the award-winning AT&T "Reach Out and Touch Someone" ads. The only problem is that the successful achievement of emotional impact precludes a great deal of copy about rates. Therefore, the magazine ads complement the television ads by providing detail on when phone rates are lowest.

Often advertisers employ these two media in a more explicit complementary relationship. Dart/Kraft employs television commercials to promote the seasonal use of its products. These TV commercials direct viewers to various publications in which Kraft ads provide recipes for holiday meals. Record clubs often direct viewers of their TV commercials to magazines and newspapers carrying complete catalogs of their album selections as well as order blanks. Advertisers conducting special contests or sweepstakes promote these events with heavy TV advertising that directs viewers to magazine ads containing contest rules and entry blanks.

A final consideration in the decision of whether to employ a combined TV-magazine media strategy involves both the audience and the creative aspect of each medium. Frequently a mass market product represents something different to various consumer segments. Life-style products such as automobiles, cosmetics, stereos, wines, and clothing are perceived quite differently by various market segments. Television offers the advertiser an efficient way to communicate with these varied segments; however, the requirement of communicating with them collectively restricts the specificity of the message. With their selective audience profiles and their unique personalities or environments, magazines allow the advertiser to direct the message directly to each segment in a creative format designed to relate the product to the life-style of that segment.

The television commercial for a stereo component system might touch on the technical quality of the system, the beautiful sound of the music, and the physical attractiveness of the unit itself. This generic, all-encompassing approach could be complemented by a series of life-style magazine ads. One ad might focus on the romantic. A male-oriented version of this ad could be created for such publications as *Playboy* and *Penthouse*. A female-oriented version could be designed for *Cosmopolitan* or *Ms.* A separate approach concentrating on the technical sophistication of the product could be developed for *Esquire*, the newsweeklies, and the *New York Times Magazine*, with their older, more upscale profiles. Finally, an ad focusing on the beauty of the system in the context of an elegant home or apartment might be created for *The New Yorker*, *Apartment Life*, and *Southern Living*.

In summary, television and magazine advertising used in combination have much to offer the advertiser. Whether and when to use these media in combination can be determined to a certain extent by the numbers. The Simmons and MRI reports provide the necessary data. However, to rely on numbers alone would be shortsighted. The true value of combining TV and magazine advertising goes beyond the numbers. The planner must take into account the hot versus cool nature of TV and magazines, the personality of each medium, the reinforcing and complementary contribution of each medium to the other, and the dual-approach opportunity offered in combination. All these qualitative considerations contribute to a synergistic effect which often outweighs the relative efficiency of one medium over the other in target audience delivery.

TELEVISION AND RADIO

Radio was the precursor of television, and the two are similar in a number of ways. Both reach their respective audiences via the airwaves. Each consists of a large number of FCC-licensed stations, many of which are affiliated with national networks. Both a national and a local advertising marketplace exists for each medium.

However, although television and radio are structured similarly, radio is more similar to magazines from the advertiser's point of view. A combination of the loss of its role as the mass medium to television

TABLE 11-6
RADIO FORMATS AND THEIR AUDIENCE PROFILES

Format	Typical audience profile
Adult contemporary	M/F, younger, college, POM,* mixed income
All news	Male, older, college grad., POM, upper income
Album-oriented rock and progressive	Male, younger, HS/some college, lower income
Beautiful music	M/F, older, college, upper income
Black	Female, young, HS or less, lower income
Classical	Male, older, college grad., POM, upper income
Contemporary and disco	M/F, young, HS/some college, lower income
Country	Male, middle-aged, non-HS grad., lower income
Golden oldies	Female, younger, HS/some college, mixed income
Middle of the road	M/F, older, college, mixed income
Religious	M/F, older, non-HS grad., mixed income
Soft rock	M/F, younger, college grad., POM, middle income
Talk	M/F, older, college grad., POM, upper income

*Professional owner or manager.

Source: Derived from "The 1980 Study of Media and Markets," Simmons Market Research Bureau, Inc., New York, 1980.

and the proliferation of new stations forced the radio industry into a selective audience orientation. Radio stations today choose from various formats, each designed to reach a specific audience segment. Table 11-6 lists the major formats and briefly defines the audience profile for each.

The radio networks that once served the mass medium role which their television network counterparts serve today are becoming more specialized also. ABC, CBS, and NBC each offers more than one network. Each has a basic news-oriented network service providing affiliated stations with regular hourly national newscasts as well as special news and sports coverage. Each also has a second network aimed at the young-adult market and the radio stations catering to that market. NBC's The Source and CBS' Radioradio combine news and sports programming geared to the young adults' interests with personality features and concerts. ABC actually has four networks, each designed to provide a different mix of information and entertainment programming to the younger listener, from the teenager to the young adult.

Mutual Broadcasting and RKO also provide wired networks, those that have centrally distributed programming. In addition there are several nonwired networks, in which the programming originates from each individual station. These are groups of stations sold in combination. Usually they are created by the station representatives from their direct stations. Among these nonwired networks are those represented by Blair, Eastman, Katz, Major Market, McGavren Guild, and Torbet Radio.

Like television, radio is sold in dayparts. The standard radio dayparts are:

Morning drive time	Monday–Friday, 6–10 a.m.
Homemaker time, or midday	Monday–Friday, 10 a.m.–3 p.m.
Afternoon drive time	Monday–Friday, 3–7 p.m.
Night	Monday–Friday, 7 p.m.–midnight
Saturday morning drive time	Saturday, 6–10 a.m.
Saturday afternoon	Saturday, 3–6 p.m.
Saturday daytime	Saturday, 10 a.m.–3 p.m.
Saturday night	Saturday, 7 p.m.–midnight

By far the most important radio dayparts are morning and afternoon drive time, when large numbers of people listen to the radio in their cars. Morning drive time is the more important of the two. During these times radio audiences reach their highest levels. This is not true for all radio stations. Stations appealing to the teenage and very young adult audience often achieve higher audience levels during the nighttime daypart than during the drive-time dayparts.

Audience Dimension

A combined radio-TV campaign must start with a comparative audience analysis of the two media. Simmons reports radio listening on a Monday–Friday average daily cumulative basis as opposed to a weekly basis. Table 11-7 shows the breakdown of radio listening by quintile. The heaviest radio listeners spend more than 6 hours a day with this medium. On average, each adult spends approximately $3\frac{1}{3}$ hours each weekday listening to the radio. Weekend levels are not given; however, data from other sources suggest that the $3\frac{1}{3}$ hour figure would hold across 7 days.

Simmons reports an average of 22.8 hours of adult television viewing per week.[1] In other words, radio listening and television viewing take up equal parts of the average adult's day. Table 11-8 divides the heavy radio listener quintile by television viewing. The heavy radio listeners are overrepresented in the light TV viewer quintile; however, heavy radio listeners are distributed fairly evenly throughout each TV quintile. If we assume that the hours of TV viewing for heavy radio listeners in each TV quintile approximate those of all viewers in that quintile, then

TABLE 11-7

1980 SIMMONS RADIO QUINTILES

Quintile	Average hours of listening per day, Monday–Friday*	
	Men	**Women**
1	6+	5.75 +
2	3.25–6	3.13–5.75
3	1.75–3.25	1.63–3.13
4	0.75–1.75	0.63–1.63
5	0–0.75	0–0.63

*Measured over 2-day period.

Source: "The 1980 Study of Media and Markets," Simmons Market Research Bureau, Inc., New York, 1980.

TABLE 11-8

TV VIEWING OF HEAVY RADIO LISTENERS
(Radio quintile 1)

TV quintile	Percentage	Index*
1	18.8	96
2	16.9	84
3	19.3	96
4	23.3	118
5	21.7	107

*Base for index is period of total adults in each TV quintile.

Source: "The 1980 Study of Media and Markets," Simmons Market Research Bureau, Inc., New York, 1980.

TABLE 11-9
DEMOGRAPHIC PROFILE OF RADIO
LISTENING QUINTILES

Selected demographics	Q1	Q2	Q3	Q4 and Q5
Age:				
18–34	123	107	103	84
18–49	116	103	105	88
25–54	108	101	105	93
55–64	79	88	87	123
65 +	60	94	85	131
Education: College graduate	86	93	109	106
Occupation: Professional, managerial	111	90	105	97
County size:				
A	98	106	105	95
B	99	95	102	102
C	109	93	90	104
D	98	102	93	104
Household income: $25,000 +	106	109	105	90
Household size:				
1	96	95	86	112
2	92	98	105	103
3–4	109	100	99	96
5 +	99	108	103	95

Source: "The 1980 Study of Media and Markets," Simmons Market Research Bureau, Inc., New York, 1980.

the average hours of TV viewed by the heavy radio listener is 22. This is about half their weekly radio listening hours (40 +). Table 11-9 provides a demographic profile of each radio listening quintile. One thing is clear: Radio is primarily a young adults' medium. Although the heavy listener index for college graduates is low, the index for those who attended college is high (119), suggesting that many of these heavy listeners may still be in college.

Table 11-10 contrasts the total radio heavy listening quintile profile with those of drive-time radio only and TV viewing. Clearly, in terms of audience, radio complements television by reaching the young-adult market particularly effectively. Marketers of products appealing to teenagers or young adults find radio an effective medium for focusing on this market. By carefully selecting from the various formats available, the advertiser can concentrate on the teenager or the adults aged 25–34

TABLE 11-10
HEAVY RADIO LISTENING
QUINTILE VERSUS HEAVY DRIVE-
TIME RADIO LISTENING QUINTILE
VERSUS HEAVY TV VIEWING
QUINTILE

Selected demographics	Index versus total adults		
	Total radio listening, Q1	Drive-time radio listening, Q1	TV viewing, Q1
Age:			
18–34	123	113	82
18–49	116	112	80
25–54	108	110	82
55–64	79	82	125
65+	60	72	172
Education: College graduate	86	83	69
Occupation: Professional, managerial	111	110	52
County size:			
A	98	102	100
B	99	89	99
C	109	111	108
D	98	103	83
Household income: $25,000+	106	109	60
Household size:			
1	96	95	127
2	92	91	118
3–4	109	111	83
5+	99	96	85

Source: "The 1980 Study of Media and Markets," Simmons Market Research Bureau, Inc., New York, 1980.

end of this spectrum. Although television reaches this market, establishing an advertising campaign of substantial impact in this target market via television alone is both expensive and inefficient. A combination of television and radio allows the youth-oriented advertiser greater frequency of exposure without any substantial loss in reach.

Employing the Media Imperatives analysis for these two media (see Table 11-11) provides a profile for domestic car buyers with the imperative categories for each medium approximately equal in size and the dual category significantly smaller. For the imported car buyers, the radio-television imperative distribution is much more balanced than the TV-magazine distribution, with both imperative categories again accounting for approximately the same percentage of buyers and the dual category accounting for far less.

This Media Imperatives analysis underscores the value of radio as a frequency builder when it is combined with a television campaign. The fact that a substantial percentage of the heavy radio listeners are light TV viewers (the radio imperative category) makes radio an ideal vehicle for building frequency among adults exposed to less than the average number of the commercials in a television campaign.

A comprehensive analysis of the TV and radio audiences also should take into account when each medium attracts its audience on a daily and a seasonal basis. Since radio audience levels are greatest when television audiences are low, together these two media offer a continuum of communication with the adult population. Radio during daytime hours, particularly the drive-time hours, supplemented by prime-time television allows an advertiser to communicate to potential

TABLE 11-11
MEDIA IMPERATIVES FOR NEW-
CAR BUYERS

Media Imperative group	Percentage of total	Index*
	Adult decision makers bought domestic car in past 2 years	
Radio–television: dual	18.1	94
Radio imperative	33.6	102
Television imperative	32.9	100
Lightly exposed	15.4	103
	Adult decision makers bought imported car in past 2 years	
Radio–television: dual	16.9	114
Radio imperative	35.8	109
Television imperative	29.1	88
Lightly exposed	18.2	122

*Base = percentage of total adults.

Source: "The 1980 Study of Media and Markets," Simmons Market Research Bureau, Inc., New York, 1980.

customers from the time they get up in the morning until they retire at night. On the broader seasonal basis, radio listening remains strong during the summer months, when television viewing declines. So, for the full-year television advertiser, radio is an efficient means of correcting the seasonal imbalance in television viewing.

Radio, like magazines, can play either a reinforcing or a complementary role when combined with television.

In Combination: The Qualitative Dimension

Radio's reinforcing role vis-à-vis television is predominantly that of a frequency extender. As a rule, radio CPMs are substantially lower than those of television. The advertiser with a limited budget may not be able to reach the target market with enough frequency through television. Combining radio with television, particularly radio concentrated on a key audience segment, allows this advertiser to increase the frequency of exposure among key prospects.

Creatively, radio can reinforce television by using the same audio as the television commercial. The most common form of shared audio is a theme line, or slogan. Often this theme is presented in a musical context. Theme music is particularly adaptable to radio. Major advertisers often develop several renditions of a theme coinciding with the musical styles of the major radio formats. A more ambitious coordinated approach to a radio-TV mix calls for the audio-only presentation of the complete TV commercial including character dialogue and voice-over. This approach assumes that the listener has been exposed already to the TV commercial and will recall the video elements from that commercial. It is a high-risk approach and usually is employed only by advertisers with high-level television campaigns that have run for a long time prior to the introduction of the radio campaign.

Radio often serves as an ideal complement to television. Radio's major advantage over television is in the area of commercial production. Radio commercials are relatively inexpensive to make, and they can be made very quickly. When production costs limit the advertiser to one or two, television commercials must be designed to appeal to all potential consumers. Radio commercials, however, can be customized for each segment of the target group universe. In fact, individual radio commercials often are designed for each radio format or for different times of the week or day. The generic television commercial provides the visual element. The radio commercials trigger recall of this visual element, adding specificity to the message.

The ability to produce radio commercials quickly allows the advertiser to adapt rapidly to changing market conditions. A bank cannot afford to develop new television commercials each time interest rates change. Airlines find it very difficult to keep television commercials current regarding fares and schedules. Even when a bank or an airline does attempt to update television commercials in this fashion, its budget is often inadequate to get out the message quickly and with enough frequency of exposure to ensure effective communication. Radio allows the advertiser to make these changes overnight and provides the concentrated frequency of exposure required. When used in this manner, radio becomes the bulletin service complementing television's more stylized commercial.

Sometimes the complementary relationship of television and radio can be exploited by a nontelevision advertiser. When Anne Meara and Jerry Stiller were doing their first classic Blue Nun commercials on radio, a major study of wine advertising in New York found that most adults recalling this campaign attributed it to television. The campaign was not running on television at that time; indeed, it had not run on television at all. It seems that the visual recall of Stiller and Meara from their television appearances led respondents to think they had seen a television commercial when they had, in fact, heard a radio commercial.

TELEVISION AND NEWSPAPERS

Despite the continued growth of television advertising, newspapers remain the leading advertising medium. The majority of newspaper advertising is local; however, newspapers do obtain a significant share of the national advertisers' dollars as well. Before we address newspapers as a national and a local advertising medium used in combination with television, it is necessary to distinguish among the essential forms of newspaper advertising. First, there is the division of newspapers into their weekday and Sunday editions. Approximately two-thirds of U.S. adults read a weekday newspaper (66.9 percent). The percentage is slightly higher for a Sunday paper (67.4 percent). The Sunday paper reader is younger and has a slightly more upscale profile than the weekday reader; however, the variations are not significant. The Sunday paper itself differs from the weekday paper in size and content. The Sunday paper is much larger and contains several specialized sections. The Sunday paper also contains a great deal more advertising than its weekday counterpart.

In addition to the choice between a weekday and a Sunday paper, the advertiser has the option of advertising in the magazine section of the Sunday paper. These magazines come in two varieties. Nationally distributed newspaper supplements are carried by one of the Sunday papers in most major markets. Simmons characterized these supplements as magazines and included them in that media classification. Each of the three major national newspaper supplements boasts an adult audience equal to that of the leading magazine. They are *Sunday* (26.8 percent of all adults), *Parade* (24.4 percent), and *Family Weekly* (17.6 percent). Since these publications are essentially magazines distributed within newspapers, their use, in combination with television, would be similar to that of other mass-appeal magazines.

Local versus National Advertising

In focusing on the daily newspaper, we must address the use of this medium in combination with television from the perspective of both the local advertiser and the national advertiser.

LOCAL ADVERTISING

Most local TV-newspaper advertising campaigns fall into the retail classification. Retailers have historically placed most of, if not all, their advertising dollars in newspapers. Only recently has television found a place in the retailer's media mix. Retailers' dependence on newspapers has been partly historical and partly practical. Many major retail establishments existed before the television age began. In these pretelevision days (and, in some cases, preradio days), newspapers were the only effective means for advertising their goods.

Retail establishments moved slowly in changing from a print-based advertising approach to a broadcast-print combination. Advertising departments geared to print-ad production and staffed by print specialists were reluctant to move into broadcast. The added expense and the question of job security contributed to this reluctance. Also, in-house retail advertising departments were funded largely by cooperative advertising allowances from suppliers. There was considerable consternation over the fear that this joint funding concept could not be applied to broadcast advertising and that the venders would not go along with a broadcast approach.

From a practical point of view, most retail advertising featured a variety of products. Retailers did not see how they could translate this multiproduct advertising approach to television. Not only did it seem impossible to promote several products effectively in one 30-second commercial, but also there was the problem of changing the product mix. It might be relatively easy and inexpensive to develop a large number of newspaper ads featuring different products, but it would be very expensive to develop an equal number of television advertisements.

The transition from a newspaper-only to a newspaper-broadcast advertising strategy began with a few creative retail marketers encouraged by an increasingly aggressive retail development effort on the part of the television industry in the late 1960s and early 1970s. The success of these pioneers and the continuing development efforts by television sales executives gradually brought more and more retailers into the medium. Today virtually every major retailer uses local television as part of the basic media mix. National advertisers, far from being reluctant to convert their cooperative programs from a newspaper-only to a newspaper-broadcast basis, are actually promoting the application of cooperative dollars to television advertising.

NATIONAL ADVERTISING

Whereas the growth of the combined newspaper-television campaign on the local-market level required the introduction of local retail advertisers to television, on the national level it most often requires the selling of newspaper advertising to major television advertisers. A number of factors have mitigated against the use of newspaper advertising by national advertisers. First, newspapers cannot be purchased nationally. The national advertiser must buy newspaper space in much the same way as spot television, on a market-by-market basis.

Second, newspaper coverage by market varies considerably. The *Atlanta Journal/Constitution* offers the national advertiser almost 50 percent coverage of the Atlanta market; the *Los Angeles Times* reaches less than 25 percent of the Los Angeles market each day. For the national advertiser to bring the Los Angeles coverage up to the Atlanta level would require supplementing the *Los Angeles Times* with the *Los Angeles Herald-Examiner* and several suburban papers.

Third, there is no reliable, centralized audience measurement service for newspapers. Certainly *The New York Times* reader profile varies considerably from that of the *New York Post* and the *Chicago Sun-Times*. Without one centralized audience data bank, it is very difficult for the media planner to develop a list of newspapers for inclusion in a national newspaper buy.

Last, newspapers have suffered from the lack of a standardized advertising format. The national advertiser had to produce an advertisement in different sizes and formats for the various newspaper layouts. This was both expensive and a logistical nightmare.

The National Advertising Bureau (NAB), the marketing agent of the newspaper industry, has been working hard on the latter two problems. It is attempting to unite the major market newspapers behind one research supplier. This supplier will generate one newspaper audience measurement methodology that will be administered uniformly in every market. The result will be a compatible, centralized newspaper data bank. One important element of this data bank is the measurement of newspaper readership by television market, which will allow national advertisers to compare newspaper and television audiences on a single base. Also NAB has persuaded the major publications to accept a standardized national advertisement format. With these two hurdles removed, hopefully the first two reservations will become less significant.

With this dual-market (local and national) perspective in mind, let us examine how these two media work in combination.

Audience Dimension

Tables 11-12 through 11-15 provide the same scope of audience analysis for weekday newspapers as was provided for magazines and radio. Because of the limited number of newspapers available to the average adult each day, the adult universe cannot be divided into five different readership levels. For this reason, instead of newspaper readership quintiles, Simmons provides newspaper readership terciles. Also, because of the limited number of newspaper options, it was not possible to divide readership in the adult universe into equal thirds. As a result, the heavy reader tercile includes only 16.1 percent of all adults, while the other two terciles each represents more than 40 percent of total

TABLE 11-12

1980 SIMMONS WEEKDAY NEWSPAPER READING TERCILES

Tercile	Percentage of total adults	Newspapers read per day*
1	16.1	1.5+
2	42.6	1.0
3	41.3	<1

*Measured over 2-day period.

Source: "The 1980 Study of Media and Markets," Simmons Market Research Bureau, Inc., New York, 1980.

TABLE 11-13

TV VIEWING OF HEAVY WEEKDAY NEWSPAPER READERS
(Newspaper tercile 1)

	Adults in newspaper tercile 1	
TV quintile	Percentage	Index*
1	20.0	101
2	21.5	106
3	21.8	109
4	18.2	92
5	18.5	91

*Base for index is percentage of total adults in each TV quintile.

Source: "The 1980 Study of Media and Markets," Simmons Market Research Bureau, Inc., New York, 1980.

TABLE 11-14
DEMOGRAPHIC PROFILE OF
WEEKDAY NEWSPAPER READING
TERCILES

	Index versus total adults		
Selected demographics	Tercile 1	Tercile 2	Tercile 3
Age:			
18–34	77	91	118
18–49	89	96	109
25–54	101	100	99
55–64	138	111	74
65 +	93	105	98
Education: College graduate	169	106	67
Occupation: Professional, managerial	155	105	74
County size:			
A	129	94	95
B	105	99	99
C	75	119	91
D	47	97	124
Household income: $25,000 +	149	107	73
Household size:			
1	71	90	122
2	111	104	92
3–4	106	102	98
5 +	98	97	104

Source: "The 1980 Study of Media and Markets," Simmons Market Research Bureau, Inc., New York, 1980.

adults. As Table 11-12 shows, the heavy weekday newspaper reader is defined as someone who reads three papers or more over the 2-day Simmons measurement period, or an average of 1.5 or more newspapers per day.

Table 11-14 provides the comparative profile of the terciles. The heavy weekday newspaper reader is more likely to be older (but not over 65), a college graduate, a professional or a manager, from an upper-income household, and residing in an A or a B county. Contrasting this profile with that of the heavy television viewer in Table 11-15 reveals that both newspaper readership and television viewing are greater among older adults, but that the heavy newspaper reader generally has a much

TABLE 11-15

HEAVY NEWSPAPER READING
TERCILE VERSUS HEAVY TV
VIEWING QUINTILE

Selected demographics	Index versus total adults	
	Heavy newspaper reading tercile	Heavy TV viewing quintile
Age:		
18–34	77	82
18–49	89	80
25–54	101	82
55–64	138	125
65+	93	172
Education: College graduate	169	69
Occupation: Professional, managerial	155	52
County size:		
A	129	100
B	105	99
C	75	108
D	47	83
Household income: $25,000+	149	60
Household size:		
1	71	127
2	111	118
3–4	106	83
5+	98	85

Source: "The 1980 Study of Media and Markets," Simmons Market Research Bureau, Inc., New York, 1980.

higher socioeconomic profile than that of the heavy television viewer. Nevertheless, Table 11-13 demonstrates that the heavy weekday newspaper reader is almost equally likely to be found in each of the five TV quintiles. This would suggest that the two media would be employed more naturally to reach the same audience in two different ways than to reach different audiences.

Further insight into how the media would work together can be gained by looking at the Media Imperatives breakdown for the automobile buyer. Table 11-16 provides the Media Imperatives data for both domestic and imported car purchases. These profiles cannot be compared directly with those shown previously for the magazine-TV and radio-TV combinations, since in this case the newspaper audience is divided into terciles. The *dual* audience in a tercile-quintile combination is defined by Simmons as the highest tercile group of the one medium and the two highest quintile groups of the other.

Only 6.7 percent of all adults qualified for inclusion in the newspaper-TV dual-audience category versus 19.2 percent for both the magazine-TV and radio-TV dual categories. For this reason, the imperatives categories are very large, with the newspaper imperative category representing about 40 percent of all new-car sales for both domestic and foreign cars. This profile leads us to conclude that newspapers might be effective without television, since the television imperative percentage and index are both low.

However, the newspaper imperatives group includes adults from the three lowest viewing quintiles. One-third of these adults (35.5 percent) are from TV viewing quintile 3, for which the average weekly viewing level is 20 hours. Also included are adults who read only one newspaper a day. Almost three-quarters (72.7 percent) of the newspaper imperative group is from tercile 2, with an average newspaper readership level of

TABLE 11-16

MEDIA IMPERATIVES FOR NEW-CAR BUYERS

Media Imperatives group	Percentage of total	Index*
	Adult decision makers bought domestic car in past 2 years	
Newspaper–television: dual	8.2	122
Newspaper imperative	39.3	114
Television imperative	36.7	89
Lightly exposed	15.8	89
	Adult decision makers bought imported car in past 2 years	
Newspaper–television: dual	6.7	101
Newspaper imperative	43.6	126
Television imperative	33.0	80
Lightly exposed	16.7	94

*Base = percentage of total adults.

Source: "The 1980 Study of Media and Markets," Simmons Market Research Bureau, Inc., New York, 1980.

two newspapers over the 2-day measurement period, or one per day. If we assume that the average adult spends 1 hour or less reading the paper, more than likely the newspaper imperatives group spends more time watching television than reading newspapers. So, from the audience perspective, a combination approach is recommended.

In Combination: The Qualitative Dimension

Each medium can be used to reinforce a campaign concentrated in the other. On the local level, the newspaper-oriented retailer employs television to reinforce the ongoing newspaper advertising program. Television can be used to call attention to sales or events at a store and direct the viewer to the newspaper advertising for price-item detail. Conversely, television-oriented national advertisers can support their TV campaigns with newspaper advertising that both provides more detail and localizes the campaign by giving information on local outlets for the product or service.

The *complementary* use of the two media is similar to that of television and magazines. On the local level, retailers are turning more and more to television to create a store image. Using a combination of strong visual effects and music, these stores can create an image appealing specifically to their target market. Then they can employ their base newspaper advertising to provide their current and potential customers with specific information concerning sales and major promotions. Newspapers allow the national advertisers to localize their messages and provide the target market with detail concerning the product or service. Local television advertisers also can use newspapers this way. A local television advertiser may have outlets throughout the television market. Different newspapers will reach various parts of this market. A combination of the major market papers and the key suburban papers allows the local advertiser to promote each outlet separately.

Newspapers support television campaigns on both a national and a local level by providing an efficient means of distributing collateral promotion material to the television audience. Newspapers can carry inserts or catalogs. Television advertising directs the viewers to the newspapers in which they can find this follow-up material. Through these inserts newspapers allow the advertiser to complete the sale stimulated by the television commercials. Newspapers regularly carry coupons offering consumers discounts on certain products. Television helps build awareness of these price reductions, directing the viewers to their newspapers for the coupons. Television generates immediate awareness, starting the selling process quickly, whereas newspapers provide a means of completing the sale that is not available through television.

Magazines and newspapers reinforce and complement television in a similar fashion; however, there are differences. As a daily medium, newspapers offer a constant market presence unavailable through magazines. Magazine readership cannot be controlled as to the time of advertising exposure. Monthly and weekly magazines are read at different times. The daily newspaper may be read in the morning or evening, but most likely it will be read on the day of publication. This makes newspapers a superior medium for any type of time-sensitive campaign. Magazines, however, offer better reproduction of advertising, more options in terms of creative execution, and an editorial environment that can enhance the advertising.

TELEVISION AND OUTDOOR ADVERTISING

The outdoor advertising medium is essentially a medium for communicating with a mobile population. Since a person must be away from home to be exposed to outdoor advertising, exposure is greatest among that segment of the population that spends the greatest time away from home—the young, affluent adults. Television is almost exclusively an in-home medium, so the television viewing of this mobile population would be expected to be below average. Thus outdoor advertising could be used to build exposure to a TV-based advertising campaign among those least exposed to television commercials.

TABLE 11-17
1980 SIMMONS OUTDOOR QUINTILES

Outdoor quintile	Outdoor board exposure, 100 showing, 30 days	
	Men	Women
1	41+	30+
2	19–40	15–29
3	8–18	7–14
4	2–7	2–6
5	0–1	0–1

Source: "The 1980 Study of Media and Markets," Simmons Market Research Bureau, Inc., New York, 1980.

TABLE 11-18
TV VIEWING OF HEAVY OUTDOOR AUDIENCE
(Quintile 1)

TV quintile	Adults in outdoor quintile 1	
	Percentage	Index*
1	17.9	91
2	18.0	89
3	20.8	104
4	22.1	112
5	21.2	105

*Base for index is percentage of total adults in each TV quintile.

Source: "The 1980 Study of Media and Markets," Simmons Market Research Bureau, Inc., New York, 1980.

Audience Dimension

Table 11-17 defines the exposure-level quintiles for outdoor advertising. A *100 showing* is the number of billboards required to generate total daily exposures equal to 100 percent of the adult population. Actually, only 86.7 percent are exposed to one or more billboards during the 30-day period, with an average exposure level of 35 times, or a little over once per day.

The heavy outdoor exposure quintile would be exposed to at least one outdoor advertisement each day, or 41 + for men and 30 + for women per 30-day period. As shown in Table 11-18, members of this heavy exposure group are probably light television viewers. The seg-

TABLE 11-19
DEMOGRAPHIC PROFILE OF
OUTDOOR QUINTILES

Selected demographics	Index versus total adults			
	Q1	Q2	Q3	Q4
Age:				
18–34	133	114	94	81
18–49	118	106	98	89
25–54	110	101	100	95
55–64	70	94	99	118
65 +	62	80	110	123
Education: College graduate	112	93	92	101
Occupation: Professional, managerial	130	105	96	85
County size:				
A	99	105	100	98
B	96	94	107	101
C	111	102	91	99
D	97	96	97	105
Household income: $25,000 +	120	112	99	85
Household size:				
1	100	103	96	100
2	94	99	101	103
3–4	108	104	98	95
5 +	94	92	104	105

Source: "The 1980 Study of Media and Markets," Simmons Market Research Bureau, Inc., New York, 1980.

TABLE 11-20
HEAVY OUTDOOR QUINTILE
VERSUS HEAVY TV VIEWING
QUINTILE

	Index versus total adults	
Selected demographics	Heavy outdoor quintile	Heavy TV viewing quintile
Age:		
18–34	133	82
18–49	118	80
25–54	110	82
55–64	70	125
65+	62	172
Education: College graduate	112	69
Occupation: Professional, managerial	130	52
County size:		
A	99	100
B	96	99
C	111	108
D	97	83
Household income: $25,000+	120	60
Household size:		
1	100	127
2	94	118
3–4	108	83
5+	94	85

Source: "The 1980 Study of Media and Markets," Simmons Market Research Bureau, Inc., New York, 1980.

ment most exposed to outdoor advertising is young, college-educated, and relatively affluent. Table 11-19 provides a demographic profile of each outdoor advertising quintile. A cross-tabulation of the 18–34 age and the $25,000+ income demographics yields a high 157 index, confirming that those heavily exposed to outdoor advertising are both young and affluent. This profile is in contrast to the heavy TV viewer profile in Table 11-20. There is no question that the heavy exposure quintiles of these two media are drawn largely from different segments of the adult population.

A young, mobile adult is more likely to be a new-car purchaser. It is not surprising, therefore, that our Media Imperatives example for new-car purchasers turns out favorable to the outdoor imperative segment. The outdoor imperative segment included approximately one-third of all domestic new-car purchasers. Actually, this percentage is not as high as would be expected. The television imperative segment, although below 100 in index, represents almost as great a percentage of the domestic new-car buyers—32.2 percent. The picture is different when the imported car purchasers are analyzed. As Table 11-21 shows, 40.2 percent of new imported car buyers fall into the outdoor imperative category, and less than 25 percent fall into the television imperative category. It is not surprising that the outdoor imperative segment skews toward the imported car market, given its young, affluent composition.

Despite this qualitative audience superiority, outdoor advertising can never be considered a substitute for television advertising. Simmons' outdoor exposure estimates are based on having passed the billboards, and not on confirmed exposure to them. Even if each adult who passed

TABLE 11-21
MEDIA IMPERATIVES FOR NEW-
CAR BUYERS

Media Imperative group	Percentage of total	Index
	Adult decision makers bought domestic car in past 2 years*	
Outdoor–television: dual	18.5	101
Outdoor imperative	33.4	102
Television imperative	32.2	97
Lightly exposed	15.9	102
	Adult decision makers bought imported car in past 2 years†	
Outdoor–television: dual	18.4	100
Outdoor imperative	40.2	123
Television imperative	24.9	76
Lightly exposed	16.5	106

*Base = percentage of total adults.

†Base = percentage of total market.

Source: "The 1980 Study of Media and Markets," Simmons Market Research Bureau, Inc., New York, 1980.

a billboard actually looked at it, the time spent looking at the billboard would preclude all but minimal communication. Outdoor advertising is almost always used in combination with advertising in other media.[2]

In Combination: The Qualitative Dimension

Outdoor advertising is essentially a reminder medium. The goal is to catch the traveler's attention, with a visual image supported by a brief message. The fact that the person has been exposed already through other media to the image and the message affects not only the ability of the billboard to capture attention, but also the impact of exposure to the billboard.

Outdoor advertising can *reinforce* television advertising by recreating a visual element of the television commercial along with a theme, line, or slogan.

Outdoor advertising *complements* television advertising by moving the message out of the home. This is an important consideration for products and services purchased or used out of the home. The Budweiser billboard at the ballpark can trigger recall of the television commercial close to the place and time of purchase and/or consumption. The airline ad on the way to the airport will remind the traveler of an airline's discount rates immediately prior to traveling. In this way billboards can increase the rate of sales generation resulting from the television campaign.

One particularly creative approach involves the use of drive-time radio and billboards along major commuter routes in combination with primetime television. The audio provided by the radio advertising and the visual element provided by the billboards recreate the television commercial seen the previous evening. This second exposure not only enhances the impact of the television campaign, but also stimulates recall of the television message closer to the time and place of potential product consumption.

TELEVISION AND DIRECT MAIL

When planners analyze the various media combinations, often they overlook direct mail. One reason is that direct mail carries the sales promotion designation as opposed to the advertising designation. As sales promotion, direct mail may be the responsibility of another department or person. Although the combined value of television advertising and direct mail may be addressed in the marketing plan, the execution of these two phases of the marketing program may be done in isolation.

TABLE 11-22

VALUE OF A SECOND MEDIUM IN
COMBINATION WITH TELEVISION

Medium	Comparative audience profile
Magazines	Highly selective by magazine
	On composite, younger and more upscale
Radio	Selective by format
	Younger than TV audience
	Higher radio listening in light TV viewing hours
Newspapers	Upscale, professional owner or manager, A and B county concentration
	Strong in 25–54 and 55–64 age segments
Outdoor advertising	Younger, more affluent, the mobile population
Direct mail	Audience can be pinpointed by advertiser

Each medium's value in combination with television as:

Reinforcer	Complementer
Expands key points made in television commercial	Television commercial can stress demonstration; magazine ads give technical details
Customizes generic message to selective reader audiences	Television commercial can cover human or emotional element while magazine ads provide product information
Low unit cost allows for use as frequency builder	Low cost of commercial production allows for customization of TV ad theme for specific audience segments
Establishes continuum of communication through ad exposure during non-TV viewing hours	Ads can be created quickly and changed easily, allowing advertiser to adapt to changing market conditions
Localizes TV message	Provides detail, allowing TV advertising to be directed to image building
Provides price information	Can complete sale as distributor of catalogs, order forms, etc.
Catalogs various items	Habitual daily exposure versus irregular TV exposure
Serves as a reminder of TV ad	Takes TV message out of the home
	Stimulates recall of TV ad close to point of purchase
Customizes TV sales message for specific audiences	Closes the sale initiated by television

Direct mail as an advertising medium has no audience profile. The marketer can reach virtually every household through a mass mailing or selectively target the mailer through customized or existing mailing lists. The direct-mail audience is whomever the marketer wishes it to be. The problem is not in getting the message to the target market; it is in getting members of that market to read and respond to the message. Here is where television comes in. A television campaign can point the direct-mail recipients to the mailer, explain what the mail contains, and heighten interest in its contents.

Major national advertisers have integrated television campaigns effectively with sampling and couponing programs carried out through direct mail. *Reader's Digest* and *Publisher's Clearing House* use high-level television campaigns to increase participation in their annual sweepstakes promotions. Credit card companies combine television campaigns with direct-mail solicitations. In all these cases, television is used to initiate the selling process and direct mail to complete the sales transaction. Direct mail also can be used to complement a generic television message with information targeted to a given geographic and/ or demographic group. This capability has grown with the introduction of computerized mailings based on Zip codes.

In this chapter we discussed how television advertising can be used effectively in combination with other media. We focused on the combination of television and each of the following media: magazines, radio, newspapers, outdoor advertising, and direct mail. Comparative audience profiles were provided for each combination. We also covered how one medium complements and reinforces the other creatively when the two are used in combination. Table 11-22 summarizes the values of each medium when it is combined with television.

NOTES

1. It should be noted that TV viewing is based on a 2-week diary administered during the spring. This is a relatively low TV viewing season. Neilsen reports an average of 32 hours per week of adult TV viewing. Radio listening is also subject to seasonal variation.

2. Traveler information billboards are an exception. Hotels, gas stations, and restaurants often use billboards to attract travelers on major highways. These billboards can be effective without any other media support.

Measuring Television
Advertising Effectiveness

The sophisticated marketer calls upon the expertise of market research professionals throughout the television advertising process, from preproduction concept development to postcampaign evaluation, to help maximize the effectiveness of the television campaign. Given the considerable expense of most television advertising campaigns and the even greater revenues for which the marketer competes, an investment in market research would seem to be a required component of every television advertising plan.

Yet many marketers enter the medium with a campaign developed on intuition alone and a budget based on what was available, and they complete the campaign without even knowing whether it worked, much less what they might do to improve future campaigns. Many marketers are uncomfortable with market research. On the one hand, they see market research as too restrictive, dictating campaign specifications. On the other hand, they recognize that market research is an imprecise science at best, and that after considerable expense and delay they might find themselves no more certain of which direction to take than before the research.

As the stakes increase, top management demands more and more documentation for all marketing decisions. Therefore, despite their mixed feelings regarding its values, marketers are employing marketing research more and more in their campaign development and evaluation processes. In this chapter we discuss the various forms of market research most often used by marketers. In the first section we focus on preproduction-stage research, that is, research conducted before the television campaign is made final and aired. Then we examine the use of test markets before full implementation of a television campaign. In the next three sections we discuss the two most common forms of advertising performance evaluation, the pre/post attitude and awareness study and the audit. Finally we present two advertising effectiveness measurement programs. The first is designed to meet the particular needs of the retail advertiser. The second is the Adtel service, an advanced market research program incorporating the new technologies of cable television and supermarket scanners.

COMMERCIAL DEVELOPMENT RESEARCH

The first questions the television advertiser must answer are what to say and how to say it. If we assume that this advertiser already has accumulated data regarding who buys the product, why they buy it, how they use it, and how they choose among the brands offered, the essential content of the advertising messages should be fairly apparent. However, the creative context in which this message can be best presented is not so apparent. The advertiser must choose from among the various appeals and executions discussed in Chapter 9. The advertiser could develop several commercials incorporating different appeals and executions, produce them all, and then test them to see which yielded the best results. However, this would be prohibitively expensive. To short-circuit this process, marketers have turned to a variety of market research forms.

Focus Group

The *focus* group is a form of in-depth qualitative market research that works well for commercial concept testing. A focus group is a group of consumers or potential consumers for a product or service who are led in a discussion by a trained moderator. Group participants are recruited in accordance with demographic and product usage specifications provided by the marketer. They are invited to attend a discussion on a particular subject in return for a cash incentive. Focus group sites are located in many shopping centers and malls as well as in centrally located office buildings. The moderator leads the group in a discussion of the subject—say, airline travel—beginning with the generic and gradually moving to the specific. This is the essential focusing concept of the group session.

The testing of various commercial appeals and executions almost always is done toward the end of the session. By this time the moderator has a good idea of the general attitudes and behavior of the respondents concerning the subject and the choices available to them in that area. Advertising has been discussed, and the respondents most likely have critiqued current advertising campaigns and given their opinion of how the product or service should be advertised. At this point, the moderator introduces the alternative advertising campaign approaches. Each approach is presented in storyboard form, and the respondents tell their reactions. The moderator asks for a ranking of each campaign, often including some existing competitive campaigns among the choices, and solicits in-depth discussion of each treatment.

The value of the focus group is in the depth of evaluation it provides. The major shortcomings of using this technique are the small sample size, the lack of reliable normative data by which to measure the performance of each campaign, and the inadequacy of a storyboard in conveying a commercial involving sight, sound, and motion. The small sample size can be compensated for somewhat by using several groups. However, focus group interviewing would be too expensive and time-consuming to conduct with statistically sufficient sample sizes. The second shortcoming can be dealt with by using identical commercial evaluation questionnaires by moderators across all group interviews. However, so far no research firm has effectively demonstrated any consistent correlation between focus group commercial evaluation and subsequent commercial performance. The third shortcoming can be dealt with by using the audio recording of theme music or animative and photomatic treatments of commercials. However, if a marketer is going to incur this expense, an over-the-air test would be recommended instead of the focus group.

The real value of the focus group is highly subjective. Most focus group facilities provide a means by which the marketer can observe the group in progress—either a two-way mirror or a videotape setup. By assembling the marketing team, including the creative personnel, and having them all observe the sessions, the marketer can bring all the commercial production participants closer to the consumer. The collective insight gained by these executives through focus group observation probably will be more meaningful than the strict interpretation of the group discussion. Observation can be an enlightening—and a humbling—experience for the advertising creators.

Theater and Over-the-Air Commercial Testing

A fourth shortcoming of the focus group technique for commercial effectiveness measurement is the fact that the respondents are not exposed to the commercials in a "natural" context. The commercial exposure is not surrounded by television programming, and it does not take place in the home. Two forms of commercial testing provide the marketer with a method of avoiding these two shortcomings and the storyboard-to-finished-commercial translation shortcoming. However, at least some commercial production expense must be incurred.

Theater testing of commercials is the first method. ASI Market Research is by far the leader in this form of commercial testing. Methods vary, but they all follow the basic ASI approach. Respondents are recruited to view a new television program. This disguised motive not only aids in pre/post measurement, but also increases cooperation. The respondents are shown a television program and a series of commercials. A combination of research instruments are used to measure their reactions to the commercials.

ASI's Instantaneous Reaction Profile Recorder allows respondents to react to each element of the commercial by twisting a dial to express positive or negative response. These individual reactions are combined into a graph showing the collective reaction to each commercial segment. Respondents are asked to categorize each commercial, using contrasting adjective checklists. A third series of questions provides basic recall measurement on both a brand name and a specific sales point basis.

ASI's key measure, however, is a pre/post exposure brand preference test. On entering the theater the respondents are asked to select, from a variety of brands and product categories, the door prize or prizes they would like to receive. They are asked to make this selection again at the conclusion of the test, under the pretext that the original choice question was administered incorrectly. The change in preference for the advertised brand is used as a measure of overall commercial effectiveness. ASI samples average about 300 people. Theater testing presents commercials within a program context. However, it certainly does not replicate the normal in-home viewing environment. A second form of commercial testing, the over-the-air recall study, brings the research into the respondent's home.

The Burke day-after-recall test is the best known over-the-air form of commercial testing. The fate of many television commercials has been determined by their Burke scores. The Burke day-after-recall test is the product of Burke Marketing Research, Inc. The popularity of the Burke test is, to a large extent, the result of its longevity. In an area in which new techniques are introduced and discarded with regularity, the Burke test has endured. This has allowed Burke to develop extensive norms against which advertisers can measure a particular commercial's performance.

The Burke methodology is as follows. Commercials are run in normal program environments, identical to those of a television campaign. Advertisers either buy time in a Burke test market from a local television station or cut in on their own network television advertising, substituting the test commercial for the commercial scheduled. Respondents are contacted the day after the commercial runs. To qualify for the survey, a respondent must have been a member of the "commercial audience" during the commercial break in which the test commercial ran. Burke defines this commercial audience as follows:

> All respondents in either or both of the following categories: (a) claimed after prompting to have seen at least two of the three following program elements: the story segment immediately preceding the test commercial, the test commercial, and the story segment immediately following the test commercial;
>
> (b) were in the room with the set at the time of the test commercial, and were not asleep or changing channels.[1]

The basic Burke measurement, the Burke score, is the *related recall* measure, defined as follows:

> Recall which has either:
> (a) specific, correct audio or video details from the test commercial whether or not accompanied by any incorrect details or general, non-specific recall;
>
> (b) only correct general, non-specific recall, unaccompanied by specific incorrect details.[2]

Burke provides normative data on two bases: a standard sample base and a target sample base. A *standard sample base* refers to a general population segment, such as female heads of households, all women, or teenagers. A *target sample base* refers to a more closely defined sample, such as product users in the subject category or women aged 18–34. As expected, the norms for target sample groups are somewhat higher than those for standard samples.

In its 1981 norms publication, Burke reports an average 23 percent related recall score for commercials tested among a standard sample of women (1708 tests) versus a 24 percent average for commercials tested among a target sample of women (1147 tests). For commercials tested among men, the average scores are 21 percent for standard samples (456 tests) and 24 percent for target samples (321 tests). Burke provides norms for major product categories and for new brands versus established brands. It breaks down its samples by age, income, education, and employment status, providing norms for each demographic group. Finally, it provides norms for commercials appearing in different program-type formats—drama series, movies, comedy series, and specials. For standard samples of women, commercials for name-brand food products and housekeeping and cleaning aids score highest. Among targeted samples of women, toiletries and cosmetics and wearing apparel and clothing commercials are the top scorers. For men, automotive product commercials lead on a standard sample basis. These commercials and service commercials also score above average on a target sample basis. In general, the younger, better-educated, and more affluent respondents provide better related recall of commercials. However, the score variations are only one or two points. Commercials perform best in dramatic series and movies and poorest in comedy series.

In addition to its basic related recall score, Burke employs other qualitative measures of commercial effectiveness. Burke's *internal measurements* include recall of each sales message contained within the commercial and recall of the situation and/or visual element of the commercial. Sales messages include any benefits or attributes of or reasons to buy the product or service advertised. Situation and/or visual recall includes "recall of video details, the story line or plot of the commercial, or special audio effects."[3] Table 12-1 provides the average related recall, sales message recall, and situation and/or visual recall statistics for the Burke tests conducted from 1977 through 1979.

Gallup & Robinson is another market research firm specializing in commercial testing. The Gallup & Robinson measure comparable to the Burke related recall is the *proven commercial registration* (PCR) score. The PCR score is defined as "the percent of respondents that are able to *prove* recall of the commercial given the brand name prompt." The PCR score only counts respondents providing a specific description of the commercial. The Burke score includes those providing generic campaign recall.

In addition to providing customized commercial testing, Gallup & Robinson measures the recall of all commercials appearing in primetime during a 6-week period each year. These surveys are combined into multiyear analyses that offer insight on the effect of various en-

TABLE 12-1
BURKE NORMS, 1977–1979

30-second norms	Women (%)	Men (%)
Related recall	24	21
Sales message recall (net)	21	18
Situation and/or visual recall	21	19

Source: "Burke Day-after-Recall Norms," Burke Marketing Research, Inc., Cincinnati, Ohio, 1980.

vironmental factors on commercial recall. Among the most significant findings are the following:

- Commercial performance (PCR score) increases as the evening grows later.

- Over the years, movies have provided a good average commercial communication environment, situation comedies have consistently been above average, and sports programs have been below average.

- There is no communication weakness associated with:
  Violent programming
  Sexually oriented programming

BURKE SCORE DEBATE

No subject is likely to cause more debate within the advertising community than the validity of the Burke score as a measure of a commercial's effectiveness or potential effectiveness. In published reports of this debate, usually the quantitatively oriented MBA-trained account executive is pitted against the creative director, but the most intensive debate is likely to occur among the market research practitioners themselves. These are some reservations of market researchers concerning the Burke score:

- Is recall a valid measure of commercial effectiveness?

- Can recall be enhanced by the use of specific mnemonic devices?

- How much influence does the specific program environment have on recall?

- How much influence do the other commercials in a commercial break have on the recall of a specific commercial within that break?

- Is the one-time-only exposure to a commercial sufficient for commercial effectiveness measurement?

- Is the telephone interview, with no visual prompting, an accurate way to measure commercial recall?

The answers to these questions would require a marketing research discussion beyond the scope of this book, but evidence does support the validity of each question.

In Chapter 10, we concluded that two to three exposures are required before a commercial fully reaches its communications goal. In light of this, it would seem unfair to test commercials after only one exposure. Herbert Krugman, whose work was cited in that discussion, also explored the concept of recall as a valid measure of the effectiveness of television commercials. Krugman theorized that exposure to a television commercial was essentially a right-brain function—that is, image based—while recall of a commercial message without a visual stimulus was essentially a left-brain function. This led Krugman to conclude the following:

> I would reposition the recognition versus recall problem with this proposed addition to the theory of involvement—i.e., the nature of effective impact of communication or advertising on low-involvement topics, objects, or products consists of the building or strengthening of picture-image memory potential. Such potential is properly measured by recognition, not by recall. The use of recall obscures or hides already existing impact.[4]

Krugman and others have found recall of television commercials to be much higher when some visual stimulus is provided.

The subject of the use of mnemonic devices is a tricky one. Do these devices stimulate commercial attentiveness and recall? And if they do, does this translate to greater commercial effectiveness? My own work concerning commercial recall suggests that these devices do work quite well. High-scoring commercials tend to contain some particular element that is played back by a majority of respondents when they are asked to recall verbatim what was said or brought out in a given commercial. In particular, Merrill Lynch's bull, Lufthansa's Red Baron, the Goodyear blimp, and Xerox's Brother Dominick enhanced the recall levels for their products' commercials. However, in these cases and others, there was no evidence that the respondents' recall of the specific sales points contained in the commercials was any higher than average.

The Gallup & Robinson figures do support the conclusion that program environment can affect commercial recall. Burke's own research shows significant variation in recall by program type. In addition, there is evidence that the competitive commercials can impact on commercial recall also. On the one hand, an uninteresting commercial may turn off the audience before the test commercial appears. On the other hand, very strong commercials could overwhelm the test commercials. In many studies I have conducted, one commercial among those appearing in a specific program context dominates the unaided recall responses. In these cases, total recall, unaided and aided, for the other participating commercials tends to be lower than average.

None of these reservations can be said to invalidate the Burke score as a measure of commercial effectiveness, but they do suggest that this score should be used with some care. One approach is to run multiple Burke tests in different program contexts. Researchers also can provide Burke-type measurement after repeat exposures. Mall interviewing facilities allow for 24-hour recall surveys using visual prompts. Carefully prepared questionnaires can separate sales point recall from general recall stimulated by mnemonic devices. These can certainly be used within the basic Burke interviewing format.

In short, Burke scores are *a* measure, not *the* measure, of commercial effectiveness. Burke demonstrated that an advertiser is better off with a Burke score on a commercial than without one. But certainly more must go into the commercial evaluation equation.

TESTING THE UNFINISHED COMMERCIAL

Both theater testing and over-the-air testing require some degree of commercial production. However, both forms of commercial testing can employ less than finished commercials. In an *animatic* commercial, the storyboards are converted to videotape and presented in sequence, accompanied by the basic audio elements. This type of treatment usually can be produced for under $5000, and the commercial test results for animatic versions of commercials have been found to correlate with the results of the finished versions of these commercials.

Photomatic commercials are similar to animatic versions, except that photographs replace the drawings of each storyboard frame. These are much more expensive than animatic commercials since they often require location shooting and casting. The rough commercial is really a fully produced commercial before the final mixing. The use of rough commercials for commercial testing does not save a great deal of production expense, but it does save time.

Physiological Testing of Commercials

A final form of commercial development research is the experimental testing of commercials' physiological effects on the viewer. Usually this research is conducted in laboratory settings. Three forms of physiological research that have been conducted are pupillometric testing, galvanic skin response measurement, and brain wave research.

Pupillometric research tracks the eyeball movement of a viewer to a commercial. This type of recall tells the researcher on what particular element of the video the viewer is focusing and how long the viewer focuses on each element. This can help in the positioning of the product within the context of the ad.

Galvanic skin response measurement is the recording of the viewer's sweat gland activity during exposure to the commercial. Peaks in response, as measured by a psychogalvanometer attached to the viewer, reflect viewer involvement. Unfortunately, this response can be negative or positive. The researcher must interpret what each peak represents. Most galvanic skin response research includes written questionnaires which allow the viewer to give verbal reactions to the commercial.

Brain wave measurement is another form of determining a viewer's response to various elements of a commercial. This technique is only beginning to be used to test commercials, and the whole area of brain wave measurement is still in its infancy.

All these physiological techniques suffer from the same shortcomings:

- They require subjective interpretation.

- The viewer is in an unnatural setting in an uncomfortable, unnatural position.

- It is difficult to relate immediate physiological response with longer-term memory and behavioral response.

Once the advertiser has decided what commercial or commercials to use, the campaign can begin. But the research commitment does not end here. The smart advertiser incorporates research into the television campaign to measure its progress and to provide valuable postcampaign feedback. Even before this, the advertiser who is unsure of the best campaign strategy might decide to employ a test market approach prior to full launch.

TEST MARKET APPROACH

Given the high stakes involved in any national television campaign and the shortcomings of the commercial testing options, it is not surprising that many advertisers opt for further testing. Usually this testing involves execution of the various campaign options in selected test markets. Different creative approaches and/or media approaches can be tested through the use of test markets; the range of test market options is as broad as the range of marketing options available to the advertiser.

For our purposes, we look at only those options referring to the television advertising element of that plan. These television advertising variables might be tested:

- Variations in the TV commercial's creative elements
- Variations in the TV commercial's length

- Variations in TV advertising weight
- Variations in timing of TV campaign
- Variations in daypart mix of the TV campaign

For each variable to be tested, the advertiser must choose at least one set of matched markets, that is, markets for which all other marketing variables are fairly consistent. As those who have conducted test market experiments know, this is not always an easy task. Also, one pair of matched markets probably will not be enough, because these markets represent only one of several marketing environments in which the advertising has to perform. My recommendation is to use at least three sets of matched markets:

- Two markets with high product category sales, a strong brand share, and high competitive advertising pressure
- Two markets with high product category sales, a low brand share, and high competitive advertising pressure
- Two markets with average product category sales, average brand share, and average competitive advertising pressure

In addition to these marketing factors, several television-related variables must be considered. First, if the national plan calls for the use of network television, the translation of a network television schedule to the test market must be considered. Since network television audiences vary by market, the test market program should take these variations into account. Markets with relatively low network performance—usually markets with high cable television and/or several independent station options—should be included in the test market mix. These markets usually are large markets particularly critical to the success of the campaign. Many marketers avoid these markets in their test marketing because of the expense of testing in these areas and the difficulty in matching these large markets.

Second, network television commercials usually run in during-program positions, and local station commercial positions are concentrated in station-break positions between programs. Since commercial audiences and recall scores between in-program and station-break positions vary significantly, the test marketer must take this factor into account. One solution is to cut in on network commercials running concurrently for other company brands.

Finally, most national television advertising campaigns include spot television in key markets as well as network television. If spot television is going to be used to supplement network television in certain markets, the test program should include markets with advertising at both the higher—spot-plus-network—and the lower—network-only—levels.

An effective and increasingly available alternative to the full-test market program is a split-cable minimarket approach. This approach allows for tighter control of marketing variables, since the two alternatives—the central and the experimental treatment—are being run in the same market to people in the same geographic section or sections of that market. This approach also opens up the option of test marketing to the limited-market or single-market television advertiser. We come back to this subject later.

The measurement of test market results is basically the same as that of the performance of the full-launch campaign. Two basic forms of measuring television advertising campaign performance are available to the marketer: the pre/post attitude and awareness study and the market audit.

PRE/POST ATTITUDE AND AWARENESS STUDY

The pre/post attitude and awareness study essentially measures the communications effectiveness of the advertising campaign. Interviews are conducted among matched samples before and after the campaign. The sample size ranges from 200 + respondents per wave up. The larger the sample, the greater the number of cross-tabulations that can be employed. Following are the specific measures included in a standard attitude and awareness study.

Components

BRAND AWARENESS

Unaided

1. *Top of mind:* The one brand mentioned when the respondent is asked, "When you think of X, what brand comes to mind?"

2. *Other unaided:* Top-of-mind awareness plus those brands mentioned when the respondent is asked, "What other brands are you aware of?"

Aided　Brands for which the respondent answers affirmatively when asked, "Have you ever heard of brand X?"

ADVERTISING AWARENESS

Unaided　The brands mentioned when the respondent is asked, "For what brands do you recall seeing or hearing advertising?"

Aided   Brands for which the respondent answers affirmatively when asked, "Have you seen or heard advertising for brand X in the past month (week, day)?"

MEDIA ATTRIBUTION

Media mentioned when the respondent is asked, "Where did you see or hear this advertising for X?"

RELATED OR PROVEN RECALL

Respondents' verbatim responses to the question "What was said or brought out in the advertising for X?"

Sales Point Recall   Respondents who mention a specific sales point or sales points in response to the related recall question.

Descriptive Recall   Respondents who describe a video or audio element of the commercial in response to the related recall question.

Name-Only Recall   Respondents who can provide no further description of the commercial than the advertiser's name in response to the related recall question.

ADVERTISING EFFECTIVENESS

The brand mentioned when the respondent is asked, "Of all the advertising you saw or heard for product category X, was there one brand's advertising that you thought was particularly effective from the advertiser's point of view—that is, advertising that increased your interest in the brand?"

ATTITUDINAL BATTERIES

A variety of formats can be used to measure pre/post attitudinal change. The most common approach is to ask the respondent to rate the various brands on a series of attributes, using some scale. For example, in a survey of airlines, the format might look like this:

> I will now read to you a number of descriptions of an airline. Please indicate on a scale from 10—*very characteristic*—down to 0—*not at all characteristic*—whether this description in your view suits each airline mentioned.

Brand X—Is a major international airline
—Has friendly service on the ground
—Has friendly service on board
—Has punctual arrivals and departures
—Has convenient schedules
—Offers low fares

In addition to asking respondents to rate each brand on each attribute, most surveys also ask them to assign some value to each attribute that represents its importance in the brand choice decision.

PURCHASE INTENT

Preferred Brand   The brand mentioned when the respondent is asked, "What brand would you choose if you had to make the choice today?"

Considered Brands   The preferred brand plus the brands mentioned when the respondent is asked, "What other brand or brands would you consider?"

PURCHASE ACTIVITY

Most Recent   The brand mentioned when the respondent is asked, "What brand of X did you choose the last time you purchased X?"

Most Often   The brand mentioned when the respondent is asked, "What brand do you purchase most often?"

Ever Purchased   The brands mentioned when the respondent is asked, "What brands have you purchased at least once?"

The pre/post attitude and awareness study can provide the marketer with a wealth of valuable postcampaign feedback; however, proper interpretation of the data is critical. Following are some important considerations in reading the results of a pre/post survey.

Reading the Results

CHANGES IN BRAND AWARENESS

Depending on the brand's relative position in its category, a marketer will be more interested in the change in either the unaided or the aided aspect of brand awareness. Unaided awareness is a preemptive measure. When asked brand awareness on an unaided basis, respondents cite only a limited number of brands, no matter how many they are actually aware of. This "threshold of response" makes it very difficult for a lesser brand to obtain a significant unaided awareness score, since that requires preempting another brand.

For example, Table 12-2 shows the unaided awareness scores for airlines to Europe in a 1976 New York study of that category. The average respondent mentioned 4.3 airlines, obviously far below the actual number of airlines that could have been recalled. For a smaller airline such as Swiss Air to increase its unaided recall level, it would have to preempt the airlines ahead of it on the awareness list. Since these major airlines advertise at high levels themselves, this would be very difficult. The Swiss Air marketing executive has two choices: to focus on aided awareness instead of unaided awareness or to limit the unaided awareness competitors.

For a new brand, aided awareness dynamics would provide a good pre/post measure; however, for an established airline such as Swiss Air, aided awareness would be almost universal, providing virtually no room for pre/post growth. Instead, Swiss Air would be wise to limit the unaided awareness competitors. By excluding airlines based in the United States, it would eliminate Pan Am and TWA, the dominant airlines in unaided recall. That would not appreciably reduce the

TABLE 12-2
UNAIDED AWARENESS OF AIRLINES TO EUROPE FROM NEW YORK, 1976

	Respondents mentioning (%)*	
Airline	Wave 1	Wave 2
Pan Am	83.2	81.9
TWA	69.8	79.7
British Airways	60.9	51.9
Air France	42.9	36.1
Lufthansa	41.0	41.1
SAS	39.8	21.6
Alitalia	29.1	25.3
KLM	24.1	21.2
Swiss Air	23.7	17.7

*Average per-respondent mentions: 4.3.

Source: Study conducted by Trendex (Westport, CT) in 1976 for CBS television stations.

threshold of response for the average respondent, so Swiss Air would have a better opportunity to move into the four to five top-of-mind positions and get mentioned by each respondent.

CHANGES IN ADVERTISING AWARENESS

Pre/post change in advertising awareness is likely to be greater than the change in brand awareness on both an unaided and an aided basis. Table 12-3 shows pre/post unaided advertising awareness for the airlines in that same 1976 study. The threshold of response for unaided advertising awareness is almost always lower than the threshold of response for unaided brand awareness. In this study there were 2.5 mentions per respondent versus 4.3 for brand awareness.

Two things stand out when we compare the unaided advertising results with the unaided brand awareness. First, the changes from wave 1 to wave 2 are more dramatic. The results of a major TWA campaign and a KLM campaign are apparent. Second, Laker, a small airline that had recently been introduced in the United States, captured seventh place in unaided advertising awareness, but did not show up at all in the brand awareness question. It is also clear that the Laker campaign ended before the first wave.

TABLE 12-3

UNAIDED ADVERTISING
AWARENESS OF AIRLINES TO
EUROPE FROM NEW YORK, 1976

Airline	Respondents mentioning (%)*	
	Wave 1	Wave 2
Pan Am	53.0	49.3
British Airways	39.0	32.6
TWA	31.8	45.1
Lufthansa	26.3	27.4
SAS	25.5	9.8
Air France	12.4	14.4
Laker	10.1	3.7
KLM	6.0	9.8
Swiss Air	6.0	6.0
Alitalia	5.5	5.6

*Average per-respondent mention: 2.5.

Source: Study conducted by Trendex (Westport, CT) in 1976 for CBS television stations.

The Laker results illustrate an important phenomenon in awareness dynamics. Respondents who fail to mention a brand in response to the unaided brand awareness question often mention that brand in response to the unaided advertising awareness question. Only 9.2 percent of the respondents mentioned Laker in response to the unaided brand awareness question, whereas 10.1 percent mentioned it in response to the unaided advertising awareness question. Thus it is advisable to consider unaided awareness as the net percentage aware of either the brand or its advertising on an unaided basis. It is much easier for advertising to overcome the dominant firms' advertising than to overcome their generic brand awareness. Obviously Laker's advertising was effective in this regard.

Aided advertising awareness is a more sensitive measure than aided brand awareness. Our sample airline study was timed so that wave 1 immediately preceded, and wave 2 immediately followed, a television advertising campaign for Lufthansa airlines. Aided awareness for Lufthansa was 99.6 percent before the campaign; so obviously improvement in this regard would not be significant. However, aided advertising awareness was 70.9 percent for wave 1, which leaves some room for improvement. Aided advertising awareness for wave 2 was 76.5 percent, indicating that the new campaign did have some impact. Whether Lufthansa should be pleased with this pre/post change depends on the relative size of its advertising program prior to the first wave and between waves 1 and 2. In general, an advertising awareness level greater than 50 percent is excellent.

MEDIA ATTRIBUTION

The purpose of the media attribution question in a pre/post survey is to provide some insight into the contribution of the advertising in each medium to the overall effectiveness of the campaign. This is a particularly critical measure when a new medium such as television is added to the media mix. A two-part question format is recommended. The first part of the question follows the advertising recall question: Where did you see or hear this advertising for X? The interviewer follows this question with a second question: Where else? This second question is repeated until the respondent can supply no other media.

Responses to the first question usually are dominated by one medium. In the case of advertisers who have historically used television, television is likely to dominate. In other cases, the medium with the most advertising weight ordinarily receives the most mentions. Introducing a new medium to the media mix without reducing the absolute levels of advertising in other media will diminish the share of media attribution of the existing media. However, it might increase the absolute level of attribution for these media, since the synergistic effect of a multimedia presentation of the same advertising message usually results in greater recall of the advertising in each medium.

RELATED OR PROVEN RECALL

Having established that the public is aware of a particular advertising campaign and its sponsor, the survey focuses on just what that advertising is communicating to this public and the public's response to that message. Obviously, of the various components of related recall, sales point recall is the most important. A campaign's effectiveness is usually judged on the number of people aware of that campaign, the number of those people who can play back some aspect of that campaign, and the degree to which this playback includes the sales point or points the advertiser originally set out to communicate.

As a rule of thumb, two-thirds of those respondents claiming awareness of the advertising should be able to give a meaningful verbatim description of that advertising other than the name of the sponsor, and half or more of these proven recallers should mention some sales point detail in their responses. This varies according to the objectives of the campaign. Many campaigns are designed solely to build and maintain awareness and do not contain specific sales messages. For these campaigns an effective description of the advertising is sufficient.

Nevertheless, it is amazing how much attention is given to general advertising awareness measures and how little is paid to what is communicated by the advertising. When multimedia campaigns are used, it is advisable to ask the related recall questions by medium. Often this not only allows for the evaluation of each medium's communication effectiveness, but also reveals how the advertising in each medium interacts with that in the other media.

ADVERTISING EFFECTIVENESS

Probably the most controversial part of advertising recall research is the question or series of questions asking the respondents to evaluate the advertising. Whether these respondents are asked simply to state if they liked or disliked the advertising and why or are asked more directed questions, the meaning of their answers is the subject of much debate. Hardly anyone will admit to liking the Wisk "Ring around the Collar" or the Charmin "Please Don't Squeeze the Charmin" commercial; yet these campaigns have been found very effective by their sponsors. However, entertaining commercials such as the classic Alka-Seltzer vignettes are loved by the public, but do not seem to sell the product. Many advertising experts state that the public cannot evaluate commercials or even articulate the impact these commercials have had on them. Therefore, advertising experts conclude that these qualitative questions are meaningless.

But it is still nice to be loved. After some experimentation, I have come upon a form of commercial evaluation by the respondent that I feel has some meaning. The question, presented earlier, is simply this: Of all the advertising you saw or heard for X, was there one brand's advertising that you thought was particularly effective from the advertiser's point of view, that is, advertising that increased your interest in the brand? This question asks the respondent to evaluate the advertising from the point of view of the advertiser and specifies that the criterion is the ability of the advertising to increase interest in the brand. The inability of a campaign to register a high score for this question should not be taken as proof of its ineffectiveness, but I feel that a high score does indicate effective advertising. In other words, a high score is a sufficient, but not necessary, condition of effective advertising.

I have used this question, as shown, on a category basis, and I have used it in a different form to measure which advertiser in a particular program stood out in the minds of the viewers. This first form is the more meaningful, since the product or service being advertised will affect the score of the brands included in the study. In general, over half the respondents offer a preferred brand, and usually there are one or two clear-cut winners.

ATTITUDINAL BATTERIES

In attempting to measure attitudinal change by means of the pre/post survey, there are three major considerations:

1. The sensitivity of the measurement scale being utilized

2. The relationship between the attitudes being measured and the advertising

3. The relative importance to the respondents of the attitudes being measured

Volumes have been written on the use of various scales in attitudinal measurement. Essentially, they emphasize the need to ensure beforehand that the scale allows respondents a meaningful degree of differentiation. Otherwise, any significant change in attitude will not be measurable.

Semantic differential scales are recommended over strictly numerical scales. Although the 10-point scale used in the airline example usually provides enough range to measure pre/post attitudinal shifts, there is always some question about how different respondents interpret the scores they assign to each brand. A semantic differential scale assigns a verbal description to each possible numerical response. It can be either absolute or relative. An example of an absolute scale would read as follows:

> I am going to read a series of statements about X airline. After each statement, tell me whether you agree completely, agree somewhat, have no opinion, disagree somewhat, or disagree completely with this statement. "The meals served on X airline taste good and are well prepared."

An example of a relative scale would read as follows:

> I am going to read a series of statements concerning airlines. After each statement, tell me whether you think X airline would be rated one of the best, better than average, average, below average, or one of the poorest airlines in this regard. "Offers meals that taste good and are well prepared."

Often relative ratings are developed by asking the respondents to rank each brand on the basis of the attribute being measured.

Whether a numerical or a semantic differential scale is used, whether an absolute or a relative scale is chosen, the scale should be tested before the survey to ensure that it is sensitive enough. Sensitivity is indicated by a significant variation in responses for each brand and a significant difference among the scores of the various brands.

Once the sensitivity of the measurement scale has been established, one must ensure that the attitudinal battery contains statements that relate to the advertising. The advertising should have as part of its communications objective some specific change(s) in the brand's image. The attitudinal battery should contain statements indicative of that change. In the precampaign testing of commercial concepts, it is possible to determine what is being communicated by the advertising to the audience. The attitudinal battery should include statements incorporating the actual words provided by the respondents in the precampaign concept testing.

If the campaign is designed to improve the overall image of the brand through a generic creative approach, the advertiser has the option of using a series of attribute measurements or one "total image" type of measurement. Selection of the multiple-attribute approach implies that a positive change in brand image will translate to positive changes in all key attribute areas. Selection of the single-statement option implies that a change in brand image can be measured better by means of a single statement, since it is unlikely that the image enhancement will be reflected in all the specific attribute statements. Samples of these total-image statements are:

- Airline X is a leader among all airlines.
- Airline X is superior to other airlines in the overall service it provides to air travelers.
- On the basis of overall service, airline X would be my first choice among all airlines.
- On the basis of overall service, airline X would be one of my regular choices among all airlines.

The final consideration in the design of attitudinal batteries is the value assigned by the respondents to each attribute in the brand choice decision. If all the respondents agree that the advertising convinced them that the meals served on airline X were superior to those served on other airlines, but go on to state that the meals are totally irrelevant to them in their airline decision, then the advertising has attained a specific goal but has not contributed to the major goal of getting more people to select airline X when they travel. Hopefully, the relevance of the attributes is known before the campaign is begun. However, even in these cases, attribute evaluation by respondents can be valuable. If 30 percent of all respondents state that meal service is an important variable in airline selection, and 30 percent of the respondents who saw the commercials state that the commercials convinced them that the meal service on airline X is superior, then the advertiser still needs to know how much the two 30 percent segments overlap. Obviously, it is important that the respondents influenced by the advertising are those to whom meal service is relevant.

Methods of providing for respondent evaluation of the attributes in the brand choice decision include:

- Asking respondents to rank the attributes in order of importance
- Having the respondents distribute a set number of points among the attributes, reflecting their relative importance
- Asking the respondents to rank the attributes by a semantic differential scale of the degree of importance for each variable. The respondent would characterize a variable as very important, somewhat important, or not at all important.

PURCHASE INTENT

The purchase intent question is particularly important for advertisers of infrequently purchased products. For these products it is not easy to measure the marketplace impact of the advertising for a long period because of the relative lack of market activity. For example, if 30 percent of all airline travelers exposed to the airline X advertising were convinced that they should fly that airline the next time they went to one of its destinations, but only 2 percent of these travelers made such an airline choice during the 6 weeks of the campaign, then only 0.6 percent of all airline travelers actually would have chosen airline X, a percentage that would be virtually impossible to measure accurately at the ticket counter. The purchase intent question allows the advertiser to focus on the larger 30 percent figure.

The two-part "preferred brand plus considered brands" format is required to overcome the dominance of experience over advertising as a brand choice determinant. When asked the preferred-brand question, many respondents choose an airline they have taken in the past. However, if these respondents have been convinced to "consider" airline X, even though they prefer another airline, probably they will try airline X sometime in the near future.

PURCHASE ACTIVITY

The final questions on purchase activity can never replace its direct measurement as an indication of the successful translation of effective advertising to sales. However, these questions do provide insight into who does and who does not choose a given brand. Comparison of the "most recent" and "most often" questions also provides data telling from which brands new sales are being won. The "ever purchased" question is important, not so much for the pre/post response dynamics as for the ability to split the sample into past users and nonusers for analytical purposes.

MARKET AUDIT

The market audit can be considered a companion to or a replacement for the pre/post attitude and awareness survey as a measure of advertising campaign effectiveness. The market audit simply measures sales activity before, during, and after the campaign. The measurement is usually done on both a volume and a market share basis. Most major product categories have some statistical source they can rely on for this type of measurement. The most comprehensive auditing services are those serving the food and drug industries. The Nielsen food and drug audit, another service of the A.C. Nielsen Co., uses a national panel of supermarkets to measure sales volume and market share for almost all products regularly sold in these retail outlets. Selling Area Market Index (SAMI) is a Time, Inc., subsidiary that measures sales volume and share in terms of warehouse withdrawal of product. Both Nielsen and SAMI offer their statistics on a major market basis as well as a national basis. Both also provide custom audit services. Audits and Surveys and Market Facts are two other research companies that provide extensive auditing services.

The retail audit is preferred to the warehouse withdrawal-based audit in assessing the impact of the advertising campaign, because it measures direct consumer buying rather than retailer reaction to that consumer buying. A good retail audit includes extensive competitive information as well as brand sales data. Price promotions and in-store promotional activities of all brands are reported. Also, out-of-stock data are provided for each brand. This is particularly important in advertising evaluation. A very effective advertising campaign often takes retailers by surprise. They may be understocked and quickly run out of the brand. The lost sales caused by an out-of-stock situation must be accounted for in measuring the impact of the campaign.

In other product categories such as airlines and automobiles, government statistics assess sales volume and market share. Businesses such as cosmetics with multiple retail distributors have a more difficult time developing accurate market audits. Many firms in these categories establish their own panels of stores for auditing purposes.

PRE/POST ATTITUDE AND AWARENESS STUDY
VERSUS MARKET AUDIT AS ADVERTISING
EFFECTIVENESS MEASURE

The debate between the proponents of the pre/post attitude and awareness study and the market audit as *the* measure of advertising effectiveness goes to the heart of the larger question of the role of advertising. Those preferring the pre/post study argue that advertising is essentially communications and persuasion and that the pre/post survey, with its in-depth question format, measures communications effectiveness and persuasion best. The audit fans argue that the ultimate purpose of advertising investments is to generate incremental sales and that only a market audit can measure sales dynamics.

The pre/post study adherents claim that the audit cannot isolate the contribution of the advertising effectively, given the influence of the other marketing factors on audit results. They also point out that the promises of the advertising must be isolated from the delivery on those

Precampaign				Campaign			Postcampaign	
The Focus Group	Commercial Testing Over the Air and Theater	Pre and Post Attitude and Awareness Survey-Prewave	Market Audit Prewave	Pre and Post Attitude and Awareness Survey – Second Wave	Market Audit Second Wave	Pre and Post Attitude and Survey – Final Wave	Market Audit Third Wave	Market Audit Final Wave
Concept Development	Commercial Testing	Establish Benchmarks for Brand Awareness	Establish Benchmarks for Market share Sales volume	Optional Depending on Length of Campaign	Timed to Reflect Trial Purchase Activity	Immediately Following Completion of Campaign	Should Measure Sales and Share Immediately Following Campaign	Timed to Measure Residual Impact of Campaign During Repurchase Period
Concept Testing	Animatic	Advertising Awareness						
Commercial Testing – Storyboard Form	Photomatic	Related Recall						
	Rough	Advertising Effectiveness						
	Complete	Attitudes						
	Commercial	Purchase Intent						
		Purchase Activity						

FIGURE 12-1

Flowchart for an advertising effectiveness measurement program.

promises. No matter how effective the advertising, if the product fails to deliver, there will not be the strong repeat sales required to significantly move the market share and volume measures employed in the audit. Those supporting the audit approach respond that pre/post studies can be designed to make the advertising look good, but the advertising investment is wasted if the results do not show up at the cash register.

All these points are well taken. Together they lead to one logical conclusion: Use both techniques. An advertiser should combine the qualitative and diagnostic advantages of the pre/post survey with the economic, real-world specifics of the market audit in the evaluation of a campaign. The pre/post survey offers a quick reading of the campaign's effectiveness with full diagnostic detail. The market audit should extend beyond the campaign period, measuring sales dynamics during the campaign and market share retention afterward.

Figure 12-1 is a flowchart of the recommended advertising effectiveness measurement program from concept development to postcampaign sales dynamics. Although this type of research program is quite expensive, it is well worth the investment if it adds even 10 percent to campaign effectiveness.

We conclude this chapter with a discussion of two special advertising effectiveness measurement programs. The first addresses the unique challenge facing retailers who attempt to measure the impact of their advertising efforts. The second—the innovative Adtel program—supplies the technological advantages offered by cable television and supermarket scanners to advertising measurement.

MEASURING RETAIL ADVERTISING EFFECTIVENESS

Retailers recently shifted from a newspaper-dominated to a newspaper-television approach in their advertising programs. This shift required a refocusing of their advertising effectiveness evaluation process. Traditionally they ran newspaper ads featuring a variety of products. Then they simply measured the next day's or next week's sales for those products. Since the newspaper ads featured several products, the sales generated almost always surpassed the cost of the ad. The consistency of the advertising approach also allowed retailers to test different formats.

As these retailers contemplated adding television advertising, they searched for some way to measure the value of this incremental effort. Initially they looked to the same next-day sales measure as the comparative measure of television versus newspaper advertising payoff. Broadcasters pointed out that the true contribution of television advertising to the retailer goes beyond individual product sales, including traffic-building and overall image-building components. Broadcasters differentiated between the price-item approach to retail advertising and the image approach, recommending a combination of the two in an integrated campaign to complement the ongoing newspaper campaign.

These broadcasters were then faced with the challenge of developing a method by which to measure this multilevel impact. At the CBS television stations we developed an in-store interviewing technique that allowed us to make the required measurements. It proceeds as follows:

- Ads using a generic image theme but featuring specific sales items are run.

- Customers are interviewed upon entering the store. This brief interview consists of asking why they had come to the store that day and whether they recalled being exposed to any advertising for the store during the past few days. These customers are given a card and told that they will receive a gift if they turn it in when they leave the store.

- A second exit interview is conducted with each customer. During this interview a list is made of the items purchased by the customer and questions are asked concerning the customer's normal shopping habits.

- This in-store interviewing is supplemented by a normal pre/post attitude and awareness study.

Through this technique the retailer gets a reading on sales of the advertised items generated by the television advertising; the total sales activity generated from customers brought into the store by the advertising for these items; the total traffic-building impact of the advertising; and, through the pre/post survey, the change in store image created by television advertising. Only when they begin to appreciate these secondary traffic-building and image-building aspects do retailers accept television advertising as a required element in their advertising programs.

ADTEL PROGRAM

The Adtel program was introduced in 1968 as a result of an Advertising Research Foundation study conducted by John Adler. In 1972 Adtel merged with Booz Allen & Hamilton, and in 1979 it became part of Burke Marketing Research, Inc. The unique element of the Adtel program is its split-cable system. Adtel has isolated three markets with heavy cable penetration. It has split these cable systems in half, with each half of the cable subscribers capable of receiving a different signal. This allows Adtel to show one commercial to half the sample and another commercial to the other half. Each half of the cable system is matched to reflect the same demographic, geographic, and socioeconomic profile.

From each half of the cable system subscribers, Adtel draws a sample of approximately 1000 homes. These panel homes provide extensive marketing information to Adtel. They keep diaries of their purchases. Adtel also develops its own television ratings information from these panels.

The advantages of this unique test market facility for advertising are obvious. A test campaign can be presented to the A panel but not to the B panel. The data on purchase activity collected from the two panels allow the marketer to make a direct measure of the impact of the campaign. The television viewing data can provide specific levels of advertising exposure. The fact that both the A and B panels are located in the same market allows for a level of control over other marketing variables unattainable in traditional test market programs. Also, since the panels are confined to small samples controlled by Adtel, the test has a high degree of security. Competitors are less likely to know about the test than when full markets are used, and they can do little to upset the test even if they do discover it.

Today Adtel is adding a new dimension to its program by using supermarket scanners to provide more accurate purchase information. The cable panel members are given special cards. They shop at prescribed supermarkets where the scanners record their purchases. This allows Adtel to test advertising programs in combination with specific in-store promotional programs.

Adtel provides the best of all possible worlds for test marketing. Of course, this type of program is very expensive, but major marketers of supermarket-distributed products have found the service worth the price. Adtel has most of these marketers as clients.

NOTES

1. Burke Marketing Research, "Related Recall Norms for Day-After Recall Tests of Television Commercials, 1981," Cincinnati, 1981.

2. Ibid.

3. Ibid.

4. Herbert E. Krugman, "Memory without Recall, Exposure without Perception," *Journal of Advertising*, August 1977, p. 9.

Television Advertising Regulation and the Television Commercial Clearance Process

Advertisers who want to place their commercials on television must demonstrate that those commercials comply with all federal and local government requirements, the standards of self-regulation for both the advertising and the broadcasting industries, and the commercial clearance standards of the individual broadcast entities. In this chapter we discuss some of the requirements and standards with which the broadcaster must comply.

ADVERTISING REGULATION BY THE GOVERNMENT

The advertiser has to comply with both general advertising regulations and specific broadcast advertising regulations established by various government bodies. These regulations exist on the local, state, and federal levels. In this chapter we deal with federal regulations only. The advertiser is cautioned also to research the local and state regulations in the markets in which the advertising will run. The two federal agencies directly involved in advertising regulation are the Federal Trade Commission (FTC) and the Federal Communications Commission (FCC).

The FTC and Advertising

The FTC has the authority to monitor the advertising appearing in this country to ensure that it is not "false or misleading." The Bureau of Consumer Protection is the FTC branch charged specifically with this responsibility. The Bureau of Consumer Protection (BCP) exercises its regulatory function by means of review only. Advertisers are not required to obtain approval for their commercials prior to airing them. The bureau does not automatically review every advertisement. Instead, it responds to specific complaints from the public. If it feels that a given complaint has merit, it requests a response from the advertiser. If the complaint is severe enough, the BCP can obtain a temporary restraining order to prevent the advertiser from running the ad during the review period.

Then the ball is in the advertiser's court. The advertiser has three choices. Voluntary compliance allows the advertiser to agree in writing to withdraw the objectionable advertising without admitting any guilt or wrongdoing. If the advertiser does not choose this course or if the violation is so severe that the FTC feels the power of the law is required to ensure compliance, then the remaining options for the advertiser are to agree to an out-of-court settlement or to fight the case in the courts.

If an out-of-court settlement is ordered, it is formalized by the signing of a consent order. Although it is a voluntary compliance agreement, the consent order has the power of the law behind it. Violation of a consent decree results in a specific legal penalty. If the advertiser wishes to exhaust the legal process, the case is heard first by an FTC administrative law judge, then by the full commission, and finally by the Federal County Appeals and U.S. Supreme Court. If the advertiser ends up losing the case in this process, a cease-and-desist order is issued. Violation of this order brings much more severe legal penalties.

In addition to rendering fines and penalties, the FTC can call for *corrective advertising*. This requires the advertiser to devote some prescribed amount of its future advertising to correcting any false impressions resulting from the original advertising. In the late 1970s, the FTC became particularly aggressive in the area of advertising regulation. Investigations were begun in a number of areas, including cereal advertising, advertising to children, and over-the-counter drug advertising. However, there was a major backlash from Congress, and FTC funding was reduced. The Reagan administration quickly made it clear that it expected less, not more, regulatory activity on this front from the FTC, and all these major thrusts were abandoned.

The FCC and Advertising

The FCC's role regarding television advertising is, on balance, more that of an intimidator than a regulator. Television stations and the television networks, as owners of television stations, are licensed by the FCC. Any action by these stations that might be perceived as not in the best interests of the public can cause their licenses to be challenged and possibly lost. The comprehensive advertising self-regulation position of the broadcast industry is, to a large extent, a by-product of this constant threat of loss of lucrative licenses.

There are some specific areas of direct regulation of advertising content by the FCC. Two sections of the Communications Act pertain to advertising. Section 317 requires all commercial announcements to identify their sponsors. This section also requires the acknowledgment of promotional consideration when sponsors provide products or services that are mentioned in a show or given as prizes to people appearing on that show. Broadcasters usually comply with this regulation by using the familiar "promotional consideration provided by" credit at the end of the program.

Perhaps the most significant impact of this regulation on advertising is the limited exposure of nonbroadcast advertising on television. Broadcasters covering live sports events and other activities in public places avoid showing any advertising or promotional material on the air even though, in the absence of any payment to the program's sponsor or promotional consideration provided by the sponsor of that material, the exposure of that material on the air is not in violation of Section 317. So, when buying the billboard in the stadium, the advertiser should not count on television exposure.

Section 315 of the Communications Act contains the *fairness doctrine*. The fairness doctrine requires television stations to present both sides of controversial issues in the content of their programming. In 1967 the FCC extended the fairness doctrine to advertising when it required television stations to balance cigarette commercials with antismoking spots. Subsequent attempts by other special-interest groups to obtain air time to balance advertising claims have been denied by the FCC. However, some groups have won reversals on appeal, such as the environmentalists challenging oil company commercials and the antiwar lobbyists seeking to counter government claims. In both cases, the U.S. Supreme Court finally denied the claims of the groups and held that television stations' editorial rights included the refusal to carry editorial advertising.

The FCC also is responsible for overseeing the presentation of promotions and contests on television. Advertising that includes information concerning a contest must meet certain conditions. The contest must not be a lottery. A lottery is defined as a contest including the elements of prize, chance, and consideration. Advertisers usually comply with this regulation by allowing entry in their contests without the required purchase of the product or by the submission of a reasonable facsimile of the required proof-of-purchase element. Since these contests do not meet the three considerations required to constitute a lottery, they are acceptable. Government-run lotteries are exempt from this rule. Finally, the FCC is responsible for the exclusion of public obscenity or profanity from the airwaves.

In 1960 the FCC set up its complaints and compliance division. Complaints concerning advertising have numbered about 2500 per year since that time. More than 40 percent of these complaints concerned matters of taste. Only slightly more than 10 percent included accusations of false or misleading advertising.

Specific Laws Related to Advertising

Three laws deal specifically with the question of advertising. The first two—the Federal Food, Drug and Cosmetic Act of 1938 and the Consumer Credit Protection Act of 1968—deal with advertising claims in general. The third, the Federal Cigarette Labeling and Advertising Act of 1967, deals with television advertising in particular. The Federal Food, Drug and Cosmetic Act of 1938 is an extension of the Federal Food and Drug Act of 1906, limiting the claims that can be made for drug products in advertising. The key provision of this act relates to the differentiation between products offering relief from the symptoms of illnesses and those representing cures of the illnesses. This act is the reason why we hear the expression "for temporary relief of the symptoms of . . ." so often in drug product advertising.

The Consumer Credit Protection Act of 1968, also commonly referred to as the Truth in Lending Act, requires the full disclosure of all finance charges in advertising for credit cards, loans, or any credit purchase.

The Federal Cigarette Labeling and Advertising Act of 1967 prohibits the advertising of cigarettes on television. This is the only case in which there is a specific outlawing of advertising of a legal product, and it is the only case of advertising regulation that is limited to broadcast. At the time of its passage, cigarettes were the number one advertising category in the television medium, with the tobacco industry spending $150 million, and the impact of the loss was felt throughout broadcasting. Today, cigarette advertising on television is a distant memory, but there are still many in the tobacco industry and in the broadcast industry who feel this act is a misuse of government power.

Special Case of Cooperative Advertising

Both the FTC and the FCC have a special role in the regulation of cooperative advertising. The Robinson-Patman Act of 1936 prohibits discrimination among customers through the use of cooperative advertising allowances. These allowances must be offered to all customers, and their application to advertising programs must be documented either by tear sheets from print ads or by invoices from broadcasters.

Unscrupulous retailers, hoping to turn at least a portion of these allowances into cash, have resorted to double billing. Invoices from broadcasters are altered to reflect higher charges than those actually incurred. This is where the FCC comes in. The FCC has specific rules concerning fraudulent billing. To the extent that a broadcaster engages in fraudulent billing or even bills so as to allow others to alter the original bill, that broadcaster will be subject to severe fines and even possible license revocation.

INDUSTRY SELF-REGULATION

Both the broadcast industry and the advertising industry have established bodies to provide for the self-regulation of advertising. The broadcast body is the National Association of Broadcasters (NAB) through its NAB code. The advertiser body is the National Advertising Review Board.

NAB Code

As a result of a successful Justice Department challenge to the NAB code, stating it to be an anticompetitive pact, a consent decree between the Justice Department and the NAB was filed in 1981, and the code was suspended. However, most broadcasters have incorporated the features of the code into their own commercial clearance policies, so a review of the code provisions remains relevent.

Section IX of the NAB code dealt specifically with the presentation of advertising. The overall purpose of this part of the NAB code was expressed in the section covering the applicability of code standards:

> Commercial television broadcasters make their facilities available for the advertising of products and services and accept commercial presentations for such advertising. However, television broadcasters should, in recognition of their responsibility to the public, refuse the facilities of their stations to an advertiser where they have good reason to doubt the integrity of the advertiser, the truth of the advertising representation, or the compliance of the advertiser with the spirit and purpose of all applicable legal requirements.[1]

The NAB code explicitly prohibited advertising the following products on television:

- Hard liquor (distilled beverages)

- Ammunition, firearms, fireworks

- Astrology and similar services claiming to predict the future

- Betting or gambling (excluding government lotteries)

It also restricted advertising in other categories. Beer and wine advertising could show no actual drinking. Vocational training ads could make no promises of future employment. Certain personal products, such as male contraceptives, were banned, although tests were being conducted to ascertain the public's reaction to advertising male contraceptives on television. Advertising of all personal products was restricted by "good taste" considerations.

The NAB code covered many other important advertising areas:

> *Testimonials:* Testimonials are required to be "genuine and [to] reflect personal experience."[2] They also must be supportable. Just because an unbiased user, rather than the advertiser, claims that a product has a given property, the advertiser is not exempt from being required to document the truth of the claim.

> *Research:* Research must be both reliable and valid, and it should never be presented as absolute fact.

> *"White coat" prohibition:* No physicians, dentists, nurses, or actors purporting to be physicians, dentists, or nurses may be used in advertisements.

> *Competition:* The disparagement of competition is not acceptable. Disparagement in this case is differentiated from substantiated comparative superiority.

> *Fictitious exploitations:* The use of fictitious characters from television programs in an appeal to support the program by purchasing the advertiser's product is not permitted.

> *Multiple-product announcements:* Advertising more than one product in a commercial of less than 60 seconds is acceptable only if the message for the two or more products is integrated. A message for two products or services is considered integrated if:

> —the products or services are related and interwoven within the framework of the announcement (related products or services shall be defined as those having a common character, purpose and use); and

> —the voice(s), setting, background and continuity are used consistently throughout so as to appear to the viewer as a single message.[3]

Contests: In keeping with FCC regulations, contests cannot constitute a lottery by including the three elements of chance, prize, and consideration. Rules, details, and entry blanks must be easily accessible, and prizes must be awarded quickly after the close of the contest entries.

Premiums and other offers: Advertisers wishing to offer premiums must provide full details regarding the offer prior to airing the commercials. The final date of the offering must be specified far in advance. All premiums requiring a monetary commitment must offer money-back guarantees. The premium itself must be realistically presented, must not be harmful to persons or property, and should not "appeal to superstition on the basis of 'luckbearing' powers or otherwise."[4]

Children's guidelines: There are particularly strict limitations on advertising that appears in programs with an audience made up predominantly of children. Advertising to children and all advertising appearing in these shows must be separated from program material by some device (usually "bumpers"). No mention of any trade name is allowed in children's programming. No health claims are allowed in commercials appearing in children's programming. Finally, no use of children's program personalities or cartoon characters is allowed within or adjacent to the programs in which these characters or personalities appear.

National Advertising Review Board

The National Advertising Review Board (NARB) was established in 1971 for the purpose of self-regulation by the advertising industry. The four major advertising industry associations—the American Advertising Federation (AAF), the American Association of Advertising Agencies (AAAA), the Association of National Advertisers (ANA), and the Council of Better Business Bureaus—were the founding partners. The NARB consists of 40 advertising professionals and 10 public representatives. Of the advertising professionals 30 are advertisers, and 10 are from advertising agencies.

The NARB responds to complaints, most of which come from the national advertising division of the Council of Better Business Bureaus, a clearinghouse for consumer complaints about advertising. The NAD monitoring program accounts for nearly half of all complaints. The second greatest number of complaints to the board originates from competitors whose advertising is being challenged.

Each complaint is handled by a five-person panel conforming to the same proportion of advertiser, agency, and public representatives as the overall board (3-1-1). If the panel finds the advertising to be at fault, it asks the advertiser to withdraw or modify the advertising. If the advertiser refuses, the complaint is made public. If the complaint is severe enough, it is referred to either the proper industry regulatory body or the FTC.

The advertiser wishing to avoid a confrontation with the NARB should keep the following in mind:

- Avoid vague language; be specific about claims.

- Be able to document all research findings mentioned in ads.

- Be very careful in making comparative claims (remember, competitors represent a major source of NARB complaints).

- If you use a celebrity testimonial, make sure the celebrity actually uses the product.

TELEVISION COMMERCIAL CLEARANCE PROCESS

The thought that all these government ad industry bodies will be reviewing an advertiser's commercial is probably somewhat intimidating to that advertiser. Therefore, advertisers should take comfort in the fact that they have the commercial clearance departments of the networks and individual stations to help them stay out of trouble.

Unlike the other regulatory agents, these departments require prior approval of all commercials before they are aired. The specialists in the network commercial clearance departments are familiar with all the federal regulations concerning advertising as well as the provisions of the NAB code and the points of concern of the NARB. An advertiser dealing with these editors, as they are usually called, in a straightforward manner is unlikely to run into trouble with any of the other regulatory agents.

Unfortunately, a great deal of subjectivity is involved in the evaluation of commercials and commercial claims. Advertisers often consider the role of the various commercial clearance departments to be that of adversaries. Since each department reviews about 50,000 commercial presentations per year, they do not always have the time to engage in long, drawn-out arguments with advertisers. As a result, these departments tend to make a decision based on the original submission and stand by that decision, avoiding excessive debate with the advertiser or advertising agency representatives. The advertiser wishing to fight a commercial clearance decision is better off presenting the argument to the network's sales department and letting that department take the case to the commercial clearance department.

Commercial clearance departments review commercials first in storyboard form, then in final produced form. Each commercial must be reviewed in final form, even if it has been accepted in storyboard form. Of the 50,000 commercials submitted to a network's commercial clearance department, only about one-third make it to air. Not all the others are rejected. Some advertisers submit several variations of a commercial for approval, but follow through on only one of those accepted.

In addition to enforcing the rules of the various government agencies and the NAB code, the networks' commercial clearance editors are particularly concerned with product claim substantiation and matters of taste. All product claims must be supported by research that is reviewed for validity and reliability by the networks' research specialists. In the area of taste, the networks are particularly sensitive to any sex or violence, either implicit or explicit, in commercials. They frown on double entendre, even in its most refined form. Comparative statements also receive a great deal of scrutiny, and any disparagement of the competition is not acceptable. After all, the competition is also a client or potential client of the network.

One particular area of debate is the use of *advocacy advertising*. Advocacy advertising espouses an opinion, philosophy, or point of view opposed to that which sells a product or service. In general, the networks refuse to carry advocacy advertising, citing possible fairness doctrine implications. However, often there is a fine line between corporate advertising and advocacy advertising.

Although the networks are still more likely to turn down any ad that may be construed as advocacy advertising, most individual television stations accept such advertising today. The ABC television network began an experiment in 1981 in which it would accept advocacy advertising in its late-night programming. Initial interest in this offer was minimal because of the premium price of the time and the growing accessibility of time on television stations in major markets. Most firms and groups sponsoring advocacy advertising are interested in reaching key decision makers in major markets only.

Most individual television stations have their own commercial clearance departments. These departments review all local commercials. Usually they automatically accept any ad approved by the three networks. They also review those ads rejected by the networks and may accept some for local airing. So the advertiser determined to get a commercial on the air that has been rejected by the networks should try for spot market approval. It is possible that enough local stations will accept the commercial to put together an effective national spot market campaign. One word of warning, however. These local-station clearance personnel usually are not as well trained as their network counterparts. The advertiser who airs a commercial that has been rejected by the networks through selective station clearance may find the FTC or the NARB at the door.

In conclusion, the advertiser's message is subjected to review by a series of government bodies and industry self-regulatory agents. The best way to avoid embarrassment and possible litigation is to work honestly with the commercial clearance editors at the three networks. These professionals are trained to keep the advertisers and their own employers, the networks, out of trouble. "Getting one by" a network editor may mean bigger trouble ahead. The advertiser is advised to submit all commercials, *in storyboard form*, as soon as possible to the networks. These storyboards should be detailed. One thing to avoid always is the rejection of a finished commercial.

NOTES

1. "NAB Code," National Association of Broadcasters, Washington, 1981, p. 11.

2. Ibid., p. 15.

3. Ibid., p. 12.

4. Ibid., p. 18.

Television Advertising Budget: Alternative Approaches

HOW MUCH TO SPEND?

The simplistic answer to how much to spend is "as much as you can." This answer assumes that each television advertising impression provides a return above and beyond its cost. Of course, this is not necessarily true. Material presented elsewhere in this book has demonstrated that not all advertising impressions are created equal. In this chapter we begin with a brief review of some key conceptual considerations required of the advertising budget setter. Not included is the obvious role of the commercial itself. An effective commercial may indeed yield a positive return every time it runs, whereas an ineffective commercial may never pay.

Russell L. Ackoff and James R. Emshoff of the University of Pennsylvania, in their advertising work for Anheuser-Busch between 1963 and 1968, provided the advertising industry with the most comprehensive published account of the cumulative impact of advertising. Ackoff and Emshoff began with the hypothesis that there is a *threshold level* below which advertising has very little effect, a *saturation level* above which advertising ceases to have any incremental effect, and a *supersaturation level* above which advertising begins to have a negative effect.[1] This hypothesis is in line with Achenbaum's theory of effective reach presented in Chapter 10. Ackoff and Emshoff did find that there was a supersaturation point and that, in the Budweiser experiment, a substantial reduction in advertising actually led to an increase in sales.

However, the Budweiser findings were related to advertising dollars, not advertising exposures, so it is difficult to relate these findings specifically to an effective reach concept. The heavy advertising commitment of Budweiser would generate far more than the 15 exposures

369

established by Achenbaum as the point of negative impact. The vast majority of advertised brands would never approach the level of advertising at which Budweiser began realizing negative outcomes.

The Ackoff and Emshoff findings have little practical value concerning the required "household" level of advertising. The residual effect of post-Budweiser advertising was so high that even when all advertising support for the brand was withdrawn for one year, there was no discernible negative impact on sales performance. However, other research, mentioned in Chapter 10, has demonstrated the threshold effect effectively.

Guided by this research, we can divide the original question of how much to spend into two parts: How much is enough, and how much is too much? The television advertising budget must be large enough to penetrate the threshold level but not so large as to pass the saturation level or, worse yet, the supersaturation level. However, my opinion, expressed in Chapter 10, is that the effective manipulation of reach/ frequency dynamics together with subtle changes in the creative approach provides an effective means of avoiding the point of negative returns for all but the highest-budget brands.

With this conceptual frame of reference in mind, let us look at some classic advertising budget-setting procedures as they apply specifically to television advertising.

TRADITIONAL BUDGET-SETTING PROCEDURES

Budget-setting procedures range from the purely arbitrary or intuitive to those employing sophisticated management science techniques.

Arbitrary, or Intuitive, Approach

Not much can be said about the *arbitrary*, or *intuitive*, approach. The relative effectiveness or ineffectiveness of this approach depends on the insight of the decision maker. It is hard to believe that anyone makes a purely intuitive, or arbitrary, decision as to the size of the television advertising budget; however, it is an accepted fact that some degree of intuition or decision-maker prerogative is involved in the final budget determination. In most cases, some rule-of-thumb approaches guide the decision maker.

Rule-of-Thumb Approaches

The four *rules of thumb* widely used in advertising decision making today are percentage of sales, dollars per unit or case, objective or task, and share of market or share of voice. The *percentage-of-sales* method starts with the historical advertising-to-sales (A/S) ratio. If last year's $2 million advertising budget generated $100 million in sales, the A/S ratio would be 0.02, and this year's budget would be set at 2 percent of projected sales. The *dollars per unit or case* sold uses essentially the same type of approach, with units replacing dollars as the sales base.

Both methods have some critical weaknesses. Given that the advertising response curve follows the S-shape pattern presented by Ackoff and Emshoff, last year's advertising sales level represents a specific point on that curve. If this level is below the threshold level, an increase in advertising might generate a substantially greater increase in sales and thus a lower A/S ratio. Conversely, if last year's advertising and sales level were beyond the supersaturation point, a reduction in advertising would increase sales and produce a substantially reduced A/S ratio.

To base this year's advertising budget on last year's A/S ratio is to assume that last year's ratio represented the level of optimal advertising productivity. In practice, that is not likely. The A/S method also implies that all the other factors affecting sales will remain constant. If changes are anticipated in distribution, pricing, promotion, and/or the sales operation, the relative productivity of the advertising is likely to change also. Finally, for our purposes, these methods tell us only how much to spend for advertising, not how much to spend for television advertising.

The *objective, or task*, and the *share-of-market/share-of-voice* methods seem preferable. The objective, or task, method starts with the statement of a particular communications goal and then builds the budget required to reach this goal. A representative advertising goal might be to expose 75 percent of all U.S. adults at least 3 times to the commercial during each quarter of the year. If the advertiser wished to reach this goal via television, she or he could refer to a table similar to Table 10-1, estimate the number of GRPs required—approximately 1000 per quarter—and, using the most current cost-per-point statistics, establish a budget.

The *share-of-market/share-of-voice* (SOM/SOV) method assumes a relationship between these two measures. This relationship varies with the competitive situation. In a world of total parity in the effectiveness of the various competitors' advertising, with all other marketing variables held constant, share of market should equal share of voice. In the real world, this is hardly ever the case. New products have to spend more to attain the same market share as established products.

James Peckham, of A.C. Nielsen Company, studied 34 successful new brands over a 2-year period and found, on average, that their share of voice of share of advertising averaged approximately 1.5 times their share of market at the end of this 2-year development period.[2] However, many large, established brands can reduce their share of voice below their share of market, since their franchise position ensures them a certain share. In practice, however, many dominant brands overspend to protect their franchises and discourage new entrants.

Both approaches have the advantage of being directly applicable to the *television* budgeting process. Reach/frequency charts can be used to determine the TV budgets required to reach a specific communications goal, and BAR data allow the advertiser to plot historical SOM/SOV trends and estimate future competitive spending. Nevertheless, neither approach can be guaranteed to stand alone. The objective, or task, method is based on theoretical reach/frequency (R/F) dynamics. The purchase of television schedules that conform to these ideal R/F configurations is very difficult. The volatility of television viewing patterns, the necessity for buying new, untested programs, and the lack of reliable reach or frequency data make the precise execution of a television schedule conforming to a specific reach and frequency pattern a virtual impossibility.

The SOM/SOV approach suffers from its reliance on historical data. Chances are good that next year's competitive advertising activity will vary a great deal from this year's. New brands will enter the market, and some aging brands may withdraw. "Hot" brands probably will spend relatively more; mature brands, less. Even if the same number of dollars is spent next year as was spent in the preceding year, the likely change in the distribution of these expenditures among the brands will affect the relative productivity of competitive advertising dollars. So some combination of the two approaches would be better than either approach alone.

Model-Building Approach

Many of the most sophisticated advertisers have moved from elementary, rule-of-thumb budget-setting procedures to more complex procedures employing market research and management science techniques.

Market research is applied to the budget-setting process through the execution of market tests. The advertiser starts with one of the basic rule-of-thumb methods, but then complements that approach with a series of market tests in which advertising is set at prescribed levels below and/or above the level called for by the rule-of-thumb indicator. Through these various tests, the advertiser measures the sensitivity of sales and market share to shifts in advertising. Market tests also allow the advertiser to test variations in media mix and creative approach.

The most sophisticated advertising budget-setting method employs complex management science techniques. The method uses regression equations and linear programming to develop advertising response models. Historical patterns and the results of market tests provide the input required to develop the equations. The most complex of these models provides optimum advertising spending levels, given a specific value for each of the other relevant marketing variables.

Beginning in the 1960s, many models of this type also incorporated media planning variables and recommended the allocation of dollars by medium as well as an overall advertising expenditure level. In recent years, experimentation with advertising response and media models has declined. The vastly changing media environment has made it very difficult to model today's advertising situation on history that goes back far enough to provide the necessary statistical underpinnings. Also, the cost of developing and maintaining these computer-based models is often prohibitive.

Recommended Approach

The best approach remains a combination of the objective, or task, and SOM/SOV methods supplemented by market testing. The advertiser begins with historical SOM/SOV data. Individual market data are utilized to test the dynamics of the SOM/SOV relationship at different levels. Then BAR data are collected on a GRP, as opposed to a dollar, basis. BAR dollar estimates can be unreliable.

Next, marketplace feedback is used to ascertain any potential changes in the competitive picture—a new brand, a major change in a competitor's advertising strategy, etc. Then the SOV level, required in percentage terms to attain the target SOM, is calculated. This percentage, applied to the projected category GRP total, yields the required GRP level.

At this point, the objective, or task, approach is introduced. The required GRP level is translated into reach/frequency curves based on the various daypart mixes under consideration. The daypart mix that yields the most effective reach/frequency curve is chosen. Then the advertiser can choose between the Achenbaum effective reach strategy and the alternative effective reach concept presented in Chapter 10. If the Achenbaum strategy is chosen, all impressions below the three-times level or above the ten-times level must be discounted. If the alternative approach is chosen, only the exposures below the three-times level are discounted.

Regardless of the alternative chosen, the final selection of the best daypart mix must reflect the cost of the effective impressions delivered. First, cost-per-point projections are developed for each daypart mix.

These costs per point are multiplied by the required GRPs to produce the required budget levels. Then the effective reach provided by each daypart mix is divided into the total cost of that daypart mix. The daypart mix that yields the lowest cost per effective reach point is chosen. Table 14-1 demonstrates this procedure.

This approach may seem simplistic at first, but it is actually quite complex. The establishment of the proper SOM/SOV ratio requires a thorough analysis of the competitive variables. The determination of an effective reach level requires careful analysis of the reach/frequency dynamics of not only the daypart mixes under consideration but also the other variations discussed in Chapters 10 and 11.

Of course, going through this exercise does not ensure that the advertiser has found the ideal daypart mix and budget level. For this reason, market testing is recommended. Alternative levels above and below the national level should be tested. Also, alternative daypart mixes should be tried. In the example given, certainly the daypart 3 alternative deserves to be tested, given its close second-place finish to daypart 2 and its lower absolute cost. The local advertiser can also use

TABLE 14-1

RECOMMENDED TELEVISION ADVERTISING BUDGET-SETTING PROCEDURE, SAMPLE CALCULATIONS

1. Selected "best" historical SOM/SOV ratio	1 to 1.25
2. Projected competitive-category GRPs	10,000
3. Target share of market	10%
4. Required share of voice	12.5%
5. Required GRPs (4 × 2)	1250
6. Effective reach,* daypart mix 1	64%
Effective reach, daypart mix 2	84%
Effective reach, daypart mix 3	79%
7. Cost per point, daypart mix 1	$2200
Cost per point, daypart mix 2	$2500
Cost per point, daypart mix 3	$2400
8. Required budget, daypart mix 1 (7 × 5)	$2,750,000
Required budget, daypart mix 2	$3,125,000
Required budget, daypart mix 3	$3,000,000
9. Cost per effective reach point, daypart mix 1 (8 ÷ 6)	$42,969
Cost per effective reach point, daypart mix 2	$37,202
Cost per effective reach point, daypart mix 3	$37,975
10. Chosen daypart mix, daypart mix 2	
11. Budget	$3,125,000

*Effective reach by using approach recommended in Chapter 10.

this budget-setting procedure by substituting local market variables for the national variables.

What about the national advertiser who is also considering local-market spot television advertising? The CBS television allocation model presented in Chapter 10 deals specifically with the allocation of a television budget, between network and spot television and among the various spot television markets. The GRP value curves employed by this model can be designed to take into account both the critical effective reach factor and the relative SOM/SOV conditions in each market.

NOTES

1. Russell D. Ackoff and James R. Emshoff, "Advertising Research at Anheuser-Busch, Inc. (1963–1968)," *Sloan Management Review*, Winter 1975, pp. 1–15.

2. James Peckham, "Can We Relate Advertising Dollars to Market Share Objectives?" Speech given before 12th Advertising Research Foundation Conference, New York, Oct. 5, 1966.

Direct Marketing on Television

Direct-response advertisements complete the sale by asking the reader, listener, or viewer to place an order by mail or by phone. Most direct-response advertising is found in the print media. Direct-response ads in magazines and newspapers comprise a great deal of what is commonly referred to as *back-of-the-book* advertising material. Direct mail is the other main outlet for direct-response advertising.

Television is a relative newcomer to the game. The handicap that television must contend with as a medium for direct-response advertising is the relative difficulty in responding to an advertisement on television. The viewer must record or memorize a phone number or post office box number and address in a short time. Then the viewer must call the number or write out the response. With the print media and direct mail there is no time limitation, so the reader can store the ad and respond at any time. Also, the preprinted response card or order blank makes responding much easier. It may even allow for postage-free response.

Despite these handicaps, the use of direct-response advertising in television is growing dramatically. Advertisers are learning how to use the medium more effectively for direct-response advertising, and new developments promise to make television fully competitive with print as a direct-response medium in the future.

Direct-response advertising on television dates to the program-length Vitamix commercials of the 1950s. These commercials featured a high-pressure sales pitch from a spokesperson of almost evangelical zeal. Today, such commercials are no longer possible. The high cost of television time makes the program-length commercial prohibitively expensive, and tighter commercial standards particularly discourage the "pitchman" technique of advertising on television. However, the direct-response advertiser has learned to adapt, and today 60- and 120-second commercials effectively sell a variety of products or services directly on television.

Just how much is spent on direct-response advertising in television today is hard to measure. TVB measured more than $100 million in direct-response advertising in 1973, up from only $22 million in 1969. Today the record and tape category, largely direct response in approach, alone represents $38 million in television advertising.

The rapid growth in direct-response advertising is attributed to the consistent ability of such direct-response specialists as Al Eichoff and Sy Levy to improve on the sales action generated by the medium. Today the advertiser wishing to employ a direct-response technique on television need follow only a few basic rules.

DEVELOPING AN EFFECTIVE DIRECT-RESPONSE CAMPAIGN

The direct-response advertiser is confronted with the same two challenges as all other television advertisers: how to develop an effective commercial and where to run that commercial. Concerning the first challenge, Sy Levy of March Advertising, a direct-response specialist, provided the following five basic rules:

1. Do not set up creative restrictions because you think 60 or even 120 seconds aren't enough time to sell your story properly. First create, *then* cut.

2. Keep your message believable and uncomplicated.

3. Do not try to convey too many ideas or different images. Make as many copy points as you want or can. But be sure that viewers can easily grasp and follow and act upon them.

4. Make sure your action imperatives are clear. When you ask for the order, don't pussyfoot. Don't be afraid to be corny or repetitive. Be sure to leave enough time in your tag to repeat ordering instructions at least twice.

5. Remember that information reinforced by a video super *and* an audio mention is at least twice as effective as either alone, and that a super *without an audio* backup has relatively little value.[1]

Having decided what to say and how to say it, the direct-response advertiser must decide where to say it. In this regard, the direct-response advertiser is fortunate indeed. Research shows that the ideal environment for direct-response advertising on television is in low-rated programs appearing late at night, during weekend afternoons, and on independent television stations. These spots are a lot less expensive than the higher-rated primetime programs.

Much discussion has centered on why these low-rated spots draw so well. The differentials in response are often amazing. Cases have been cited of 1 and 2 rated spots outdrawing 7 and 9 rated spots and 4 and 7 rated spots outdrawing 13 and 20+ rated spots, respectively. Why? Eichoff and Levy both attribute this phenomenon to the low attentiveness or low involvement of audiences to these programs. The direct-response commercial requires action on the part of the viewer. A phone number must be recorded or an address written down. In the case of the tollfree 800 number, the ideal situation would be to have the viewer place the call immediately. It is unlikely that viewers of high-involvement, high-rated programs will take the time to respond to the commercial.

The low-rated spot also offers the direct-response advertiser another benefit. At a reasonable cost, the commercial can be repeated more than once on the same program. If viewers missed the phone number or address the first time, they can get it the second time. Repetition of commercials in high-rated programs would be very expensive.

Direct-response commercials work better in certain types of programs—specifically, movies, game shows, and talk shows. Again, the concept of viewer involvement comes into play. Talk shows and game shows are noted for their relatively low viewer attention levels. The same is not true of movies in general, but the low-rated movies commonly used by direct-response advertisers usually have been aired several times. The viewer seeing a movie for the second or third time is more likely to be less attentive than one seeing a movie for the first time.

The direct-response advertiser also has the advantage of seasonality. Response to the ads is at least as great in low-demand television advertising seasons as in high-demand seasons. In fact, Sy Levy points out that response is particularly strong during the January–March period, when TV sales in general are low.

The only disadvantage the direct-response advertiser faces is in commercial length. The direct-response ad requires at least 60 seconds to present and often 120 seconds. If at all possible, the advertiser should try to stick to 60 seconds, because 120-second blocks are hard to find.

In summary, the direct-response advertiser should stick to simple, believable points, be sure to ask for the order, and emphasize the critical ordering information. Spots should be concentrated in low-rated movies, game shows, and talk shows during the late night, weekend afternoon, and daytime hours. Independent stations should be included in the schedule. When possible, repetition of the message within the same program is advised. For the direct-response advertiser, frequency is more important than reach. Campaigns should be run during seasons in which demand for television time is low—specifically, January through March—if this time is compatible with the seasonality of the product or service being advertised.

Two special forms of direct-response advertising are available to the advertiser: direct-marketing support advertisement and per-inquiry advertisement.

DIRECT-MARKETING "SUPPORT" ADVERTISEMENTS

More and more, direct-response advertisers confronted with the choice of a print approach, with its advantages of high information capacity and ease of response, or television, with its advantages of demonstration and frequency, are electing to combine the two. For example, a record club places a preprinted insert containing a full catalog of its selections in the Sunday newspapers and then uses 30-second, or even 10-second, television spots to call attention to the offer. The high reach and controlled frequency of television are matched with the full information and ease of ordering provided by the newspaper insert.

In these cases, the direct-response advertiser is using television in a traditional manner. So the schedule should conform more to a normal television schedule, emphasizing the reach potential of the medium. This approach is widely used with newspapers, *TV Guide*, and direct mail. Record clubs and magazine subscription drives have found it particularly effective.

The direct-response advertiser interested in measuring the contribution of the television campaign to the results from the print or direct-mail promotion can employ a widely used research technique. The advertiser includes a special box on the order form contained in the printed material. The television commercial instructs the viewer to check that box to obtain some specified bonus. Those responses received with the box checked can be related to the television campaign. Many direct-response advertisers are using this type of keyed television campaign today.

PER-INQUIRY ADVERTISEMENTS

Per-inquiry advertising refers to advertising paid for on the basis of orders received as opposed to audience delivered. For each station agreeing to a per-inquiry (PI) deal, a separate box number or tollfree

800 number is established. Then the advertiser pays a set amount for each order received at that box number or 800 number. Per-inquiry deals can take two forms. An *open per-inquiry deal* usually involves a set payment per inquiry. Schedules are run by the station on a run-of-station basis. A *bonus-to-payout deal* involves a specific schedule and a guaranteed response. If the schedule does not generate the orders committed to, the station must run more spots until the guarantee is met.

The per-inquiry deal is a rare phenomenon today. Most television stations do not accept this type of advertising at all. Those that accept PI advertising do so in limited amounts. However, the direct-response advertiser interested in PI deals has another outlet—cable television. Many cable systems and some of the cable networks (notably CNN) accept PI deals.

In fact, cable television today represents an opportunity for the direct-response advertiser in other ways. First, many cable systems allow program-length advertisements or, at the very least, long-form commercials at reasonable costs. Many systems also accept the pitchman type of commercial. Second, cable systems have complete mailing lists, including all their subscribers, and usually mail monthly program guides to them. This allows the direct-response advertiser to combine low-cost television exposure with a targeted direct-mail campaign. The direct-response advertiser is encouraged to explore the opportunities presented by both the cable networks and the local cable systems.

If the world of cable TV represents an opportunity for the direct-response advertiser today, it represents a potential bonanza in the near future. Let us look at two technological advances that will present new opportunities to the direct-response advertiser in the near future—teletext and two-way interactive cable.

TELETEXT

Teletext offers the direct-response advertiser the ability to transfer the bulk of ordering information to a permanent display and to increase dramatically the amount of such information presented via the television set. The viewer watching the direct-response ad is told to turn to page X of the teletext magazine for complete ordering information. The teletext page presents the tollfree 800 number and/or mailing address as well as details concerning selection, color, size, etc. The direct-response advertiser has all the benefits of the television print or television direct-mail campaign with a television-only appeal.

It will be a while before teletext penetration is high enough for effective utilization by direct-response advertisers, but by 1990 teletext should be a viable direct-response medium. In the interim, broadcasters who are unwilling to accept PI advertising over the air probably will be more willing to provide teletext pages on a PI basis or perhaps even as a bonus. For this reason, the direct-response advertiser can expect to benefit quite soon from this innovation.

TWO-WAY INTERACTIVE CABLE

Two-way interactive cable, with its direct-response facility, is much farther away. More experiments like Warner Amex's QUBE system in Columbus, Ohio, can be expected, but any significant penetration of U.S. households by interactive cable will not occur until at least the 1990s. However, to the extent that direct-response advertisers can get involved in the development of this medium today, they will be better prepared to tap its potential in the years ahead. This is critical, since in more and more advertising the emergence of interactive cable will shift to some direct-response approach. Videotext represents another new opportunity for direct-response, one that is at least a decade away but that should be part of the direct marketer's experimentation and research today.

Direct-response advertising in television is a form of advertising that has grown up with the medium. From the program-length Vitamix pitches of the 1950s to today's carefully planned TV-print combination promotions, the television medium has produced the sales demanded by the advertisers. The growth of cable television is a beginning for direct-response advertising on television, a beginning that will be accelerated by such technological advances as teletext, interactive cable, and videotext.

NOTE

1. Bob Stone, "Direct Response Advertisers Have Little Concern for Nielsen Ratings," Interview with Sy Levy, *Advertising Age*, November 7, 1977, p. 64.

Index